Microsoft® Official Academic Course

Securing Windows Server 2016 Exam 70-744

WILEY

SENIOR EXECUTIVE EDITOR	Jim Minatel
MICROSOFT PRODUCT MANAGER	Microsoft Learning
SENIOR EDITORIAL ASSISTANT	Devon Lewis
TECHNICAL EDITOR	Ron Handlon
CHANNEL MARKETING MANAGER	Michele Szczesniak
CONTENT MANAGEMENT DIRECTOR	Lisa Wojcik
CONTENT MANAGER	Nichole Urban
PRODUCTION SERVICES	Box Twelve Communications
PRODUCTION COORDINATOR	Nicole Repasky
PRODUCTION EDITOR	Umamaheswari Gnanamani
COVER DESIGNER	Tom Nery

COVER PHOTO: © shutterstock/wavebreakmedia

This book was set in Garamond by SPi Global and printed by Quad/Graphics

ISBN: 9781119424604 (PBK)
ISBN: 9781119424598 (EVAL)

The inside back cover will contain printing identification and country of origin if omitted from this page. In addition, if the ISBN on the back cover differs from the ISBN on this page, the one on the back cover is correct.

Preface

Welcome to the Microsoft Official Academic Course (MOAC) program for becoming a Microsoft Certified Solutions Associate for Windows 10. MOAC represents the collaboration between Microsoft Learning and John Wiley & Sons, Inc. publishing company. Microsoft and Wiley teamed up to produce a series of textbooks that deliver compelling and innovative teaching solutions to instructors and superior learning experiences for students. Infused and informed by in-depth knowledge from the creators of Windows 10, and crafted by a publisher known worldwide for the pedagogical quality of its products, these textbooks maximize skills transfer in minimum time. Students are challenged to reach their potential by using their new technical skills as highly productive members of the workforce.

Because this knowledgebase comes directly from Microsoft, architect of the Windows operating system and creator of the Microsoft Certified Solutions Associate exams, you are sure to receive the topical coverage that is most relevant to students' personal and professional success. Microsoft's direct participation not only assures you that MOAC textbook content is accurate and current; it also means that students will receive the best instruction possible to enable their success on certification exams and in the workplace.

■ The Microsoft Official Academic Course Program

The Microsoft Official Academic Course series is a complete program for instructors and institutions to prepare and deliver great courses on Microsoft software technologies. With MOAC, we recognize that because of the rapid pace of change in the technology and curriculum developed by Microsoft, there is an ongoing set of needs beyond classroom instruction tools for an instructor to be ready to teach the course. The MOAC program endeavors to provide solutions for all these needs in a systematic manner in order to ensure a successful and rewarding course experience for both instructor and student—technical and curriculum training for instructor readiness with new software releases; the software itself for student use at home for building hands-on skills, assessment, and validation of skill development; and a great set of tools for delivering instruction in the classroom and lab. All are important to the smooth delivery of an interesting course on Microsoft software, and all are provided with the MOAC program. We think about the model below as a gauge for ensuring that we completely support you in your goal of teaching a great course. As you evaluate your instructional materials options, you may wish to use the model for comparison purposes with available products.

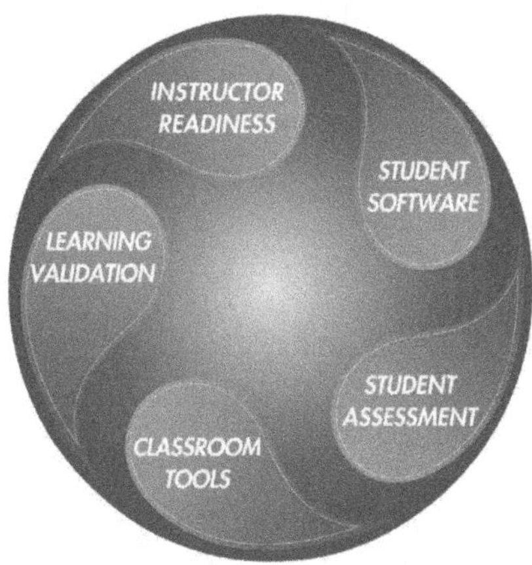

Illustrated Book Tour

■ Textbook Organization

This textbook is organized in 15 lessons, with each lesson corresponding to a particular exam objective for the 70-744 exam. This MOAC textbook covers all the learning objectives for the 70-744 MCSA certification exam. The exam objectives are highlighted throughout the textbook.

■ Pedagogical Features

Many pedagogical features have been developed specifically for Microsoft Official Academic Course programs.

Presenting the extensive procedural information and technical concepts woven throughout the textbook raises challenges for the student and instructor alike. The Illustrated Book Tour that follows provides a guide to the rich features contributing to Microsoft Official Academic Course program's pedagogical plan. Following is a list of key features in each lesson designed to prepare students for success on the certification exams and in the workplace:

- Each lesson begins with an overview of the skills covered in the lesson. More than a standard list of learning objectives, the overview correlates skills to the certification exam objective.
- Illustrations: Screen images provide visual feedback as students work through the exercises. The images reinforce key concepts, provide visual clues about the steps, and allow students to check their progress.
- Key Terms: Important technical vocabulary is listed at the beginning of the lesson. When these terms are used later in the lesson, they appear in bold italic type and are defined.
- Engaging point-of-use reader aids, located throughout the lessons, tell students why this topic is relevant (*The Bottom Line*), provide students with helpful hints (*Take Note*), or show cross-references to where content is covered in greater detail. Reader aids also provide additional relevant or background information that adds value to the lesson.
- Certification Ready features throughout the text signal students where a specific certification objective is covered. They provide students with a chance to check their understanding of that particular exam objective and, if necessary, review the section of the lesson where it is covered.
- Knowledge Assessments provide lesson-ending activities that test students' comprehension and retention of the material taught, presented using some of the question types that they'll see on the certification exam.
- An important supplement to this textbook is the accompanying lab work. Labs are available via a Lab Manual, and also by MOAC Labs Online. MOAC Labs Online provides students with the ability to work on the actual software simply by connecting through their Internet Explorer web browser. Either way, the labs use real-world scenarios to help students learn workplace skills associated with configuring a Windows infrastructure in an enterprise environment.

■ Lesson Features

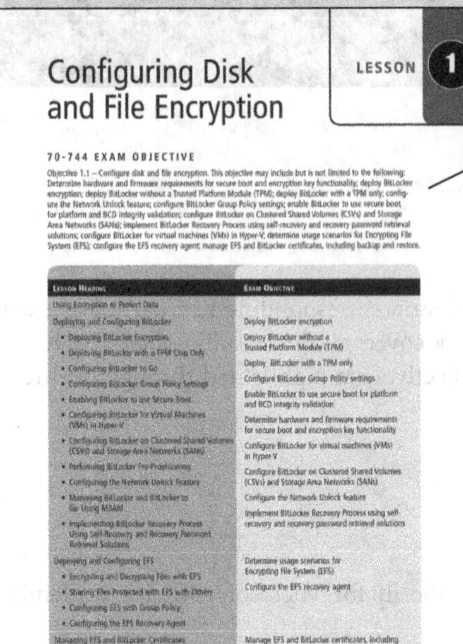

Configuring Disk and File Encryption

LESSON 1

70-744 EXAM OBJECTIVE

Exam Objective

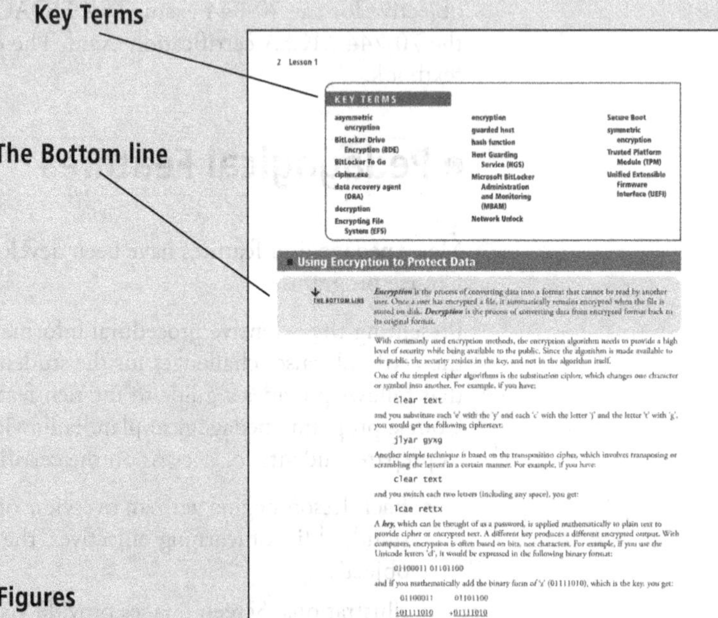

2 Lesson 1

KEY TERMS

asymmetric encryption	encryption	Secure Boot
BitLocker Drive Encryption (BDE)	guarded host	symmetric encryption
BitLocker To Go	hash function	Trusted Platform Module (TPM)
cipher.exe	Host Guarding Service (HGS)	Unified Extensible Firmware Interface (UEFI)
data recovery agent (DRA)	Microsoft BitLocker Administration and Monitoring (MBAM)	
decryption	Network Unlock	
Encrypting File System (EFS)		

■ Using Encryption to Protect Data

THE BOTTOM LINE

Key Terms

The Bottom line

46 Lesson 2

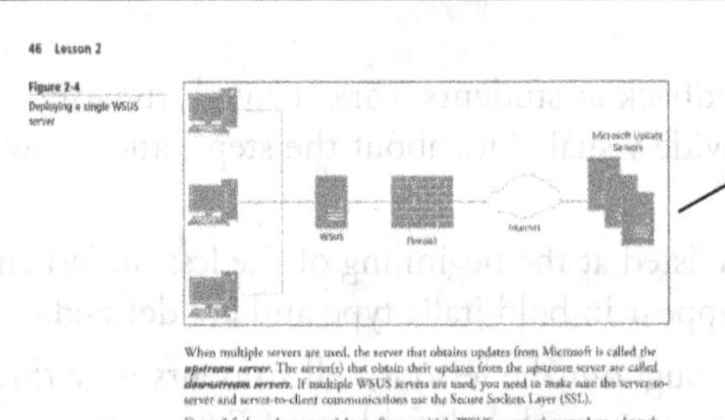

Figure 2-4
Deploying a single WSUS server

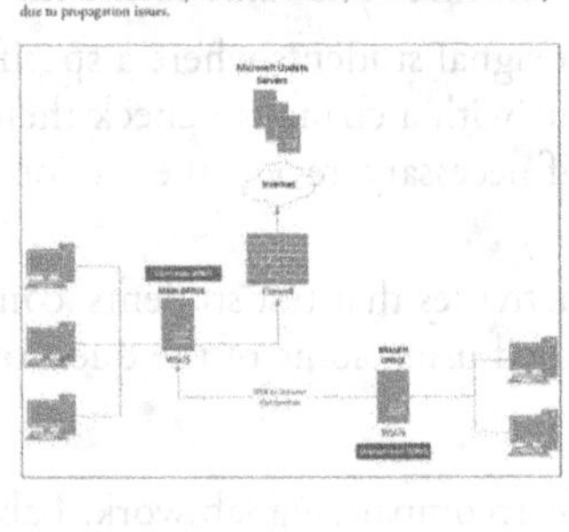

Figure 2-5
Implementing multiple WSUS servers

Figures

Step By Step Instructions

Certification Ready

Take Note

92 Lesson 3

SKILL SUMMARY

IN THIS LESSON YOU LEARNED:

- Windows Defender is designed to protect your computer against viruses, spyware, and other types of malware. It protects against these threats by providing real-time protection in which it notifies you if malware attempts to install itself on your computer or when an application tries to change critical settings.
- Because Windows Defender is a Microsoft application, it can be updated with Windows Update, WSUS, and Configuration Manager. Updates include Windows Defender and the definitions that help identify malware.
- AppLocker is a feature found in Windows Server 2012 and higher and Windows 7 and higher. It configured with GPOs, which can be used to control how users access and use programs and files and extends the functionality originally provided by the Software Restriction policy found in earlier versions of Windows operating systems.
- Code Integrity, also known as Device Guard, helps harden a computer system against malware by running only trusted applications, thereby preventing malicious code from running. Windows Server 2016 uses virtualization based security to isolate the code integrity service from the Windows kernel.
- Credential Guard isolates and hardens key system and user security information (LSA credentials).
- Device Guard can be configured to help block malware by allowing only signed software. However, many legitimate software is not digitally signed, and many applications were developed before the introduction of code signing.
- Control Flow Guard (CFG) is a highly-optimized platform security feature that is used to combat memory corruption vulnerabilities. Control Flow Guard is an option that is compiled into program which will prevent programs from executing code outside of its own memory space by extending Data Execution Prevention (DEP).
- The Enhanced Mitigation Experience Toolkit (EMET) is a free Microsoft security tool that is designed to protect software from undiscovered or zero-day exploits that may not have security fixes yet. While EMET will not protect against 100% of threats (no tool can), it is another tool that will protect against attacks.
- NTLM is a mature authentication protocol used in Windows operating system. Since NTLM authenticating protocol is less secure than the Kerberos authentication protocol, you can block the use of NTLM for authentication and force the systems use Kerberos.

Skill Summary

Knowledge Assessment

Securing Windows Server 2016 Implementing Malware Protection and Protecting Credentials 93

Knowledge Assessment

Multiple Choice

1. Which of the following features can protect a PC against malware?
   a. Windows Defender
   b. Windows Quicktime
   c. Windows File History
   d. Windows Antivirus
2. Which of the following scan options are available in Windows Defender? (Choose all that apply.)
   a. Quick
   b. Full
   c. Optional
   d. Custom
3. Which of the following tabs shows quarantined Windows Defender items?
   a. Home tab
   b. History tab
   c. Update tab
   d. Settings tab
4. In your corporation, which of the following enables you to configure Windows Defender so that the options are the same for each computer?
   a. Registry
   b. WSUS
   c. Windows Updates
   d. GPOs
5. Which Windows PowerShell cmdlet is used to start a scan?
   a. Start-DefenderScan
   b. Start-MpScan
   c. Start-Scan
   d. Begin-Scan
6. When setting up a rule using AppLocker, which of the following primary conditions should be set when you want to use the same rule again after the manufacture updates the application?
   a. Path
   b. Publisher
   c. File Hash
   d. Execute

Business Case Scenarios

96 Lesson 3

Business Case Scenarios

Scenario 3-1: Using Kerberos

You are an administrator for the Contoso Corporation, which has about 1,200 computers, mostly running Windows 10. You also administer an Active Directory domain that contains approximately 150 servers running Windows Server 2016. Your supervisor has been reading how Kerberos is much more secure than NTLM and he wants the company to discontinue its use of NTLM. Describe your recommended solution.

Scenario 3-2: Securing Your Computers

You are an administrator for the Contoso Corporation, which has about 1,200 computers, mostly running Windows 10. Over the past year, you have managed several instances of malware appearing on the computers of key personnel, leading to a compromise of some key systems. You want to ensure that this does not happen again. Describe how to make sure that users' credentials and other key parts of Windows are not compromised by rootkits or other forms of malware.

Conventions and Features Used in This Book

This book uses particular fonts, symbols, and heading conventions to highlight important information or to call your attention to special steps. For more information about the features in each lesson, refer to the Illustrated Book Tour section.

CONVENTION	MEANING
THE BOTTOM LINE	This feature provides a brief summary of the material to be covered in the section that follows.
CERTIFICATION READY	This feature signals the point in the text where a specific certification objective is covered. It provides you with a chance to check your understanding of that particular exam objective and, if necessary, review the section of the lesson where it is covered.
TAKE NOTE*	Reader aids appear in shaded boxes found in your text. *Take Note and More Information* provide helpful hints related to particular tasks or topics.
WARNING!	*Warning* points out instances when error or misuse could cause damage to the computer or network.
A ***shared printer*** can be used by many individuals on a network.	Key terms appear in bold italic.
`cd\windows\system32\ServerMigrationTools`	Commands that are to be typed are shown in a special font.
Click **Install Now**.	Any button on the screen you are supposed to click on or select will appear in bold.

Instructor Support Program

The Microsoft Official Academic Course programs are accompanied by a rich array of resources that incorporate the extensive textbook visuals to form a pedagogically cohesive package. These resources provide all the materials instructors need to deploy and deliver their courses. Instructor resources available at www.wiley.com/ include:

- **Instructor's Guide.** The Instructor's Guide contains solutions to all the textbook exercises as well as chapter summaries and lecture notes. The Instructor's Guide and Syllabi for various term lengths are available from the Instructor's Book Companion site.
- **Test Bank.** The Test Bank contains hundreds of questions organized by lesson in multiple-choice, best answer, build list, and essay formats and is available to download from the Instructor's Book Companion site. A complete answer key is provided.
- **PowerPoint Presentations.** A complete set of PowerPoint presentations is available on the Instructor's Book Companion site to enhance classroom presentations. Tailored to the text's topical coverage, these presentations are designed to convey key Windows Server 2012 concepts addressed in the text.
- **Available Textbook Figures.** All figures from the text are on the Instructor's Book Companion site. By using these visuals in class discussions, you can help focus students' attention on key elements of Windows 8 and help them understand how to use it effectively in the workplace.
- **MOAC Labs Online.** MOAC Labs Online is a cloud-based environment that enables students to conduct exercises using real Microsoft products. These are not simulations but instead are live virtual machines where faculty and students can perform any activities they would on a local virtual machine. MOAC Labs Online relieves the need for local setup, configuration, and most troubleshooting tasks. This represents an opportunity to lower costs, eliminate the hassle of lab setup, and support and improve student access and portability. MOAC Labs Online are available for students at an additional cost. Contact your Wiley rep about including MOAC Labs Online with your course offering.
- **Lab Answer Keys.** Answer keys for review questions found in the lab manuals and MOAC Labs Online are available on the Instructor's Book Companion site.
- **Lab Worksheets.** The review questions found in the lab manuals and MOAC Labs Online are gathered in Microsoft Word documents for students to use. These are available on the Instructor's Book Companion site.

Student Support Program

Book Companion Web Site (www.wiley.com)

The students' book companion site for the MOAC series includes any resources, exercise files, and Web links that will be used in conjunction with this course and any errata.

■ Microsoft Certification

Microsoft Certification has many benefits and enables you to keep your skills relevant, applicable, and competitive. In addition, Microsoft Certification is an industry standard that is recognized worldwide—which helps open doors to potential job opportunities. After you earn your Microsoft Certification, you have access to a number of benefits, which can be found on the Microsoft Certified Professional member site.

Microsoft Learning has reinvented the Microsoft Certification Program by building cloud-related skills validation into the industry's most recognized certification program. Microsoft Certified Solutions Expert (MCSE) and Microsoft Certified Solutions Developer (MCSD) are Microsoft's flagship certifications for professionals who want to lead their IT organization's journey to the cloud. These certifications recognize IT professionals with broad and deep skill sets across Microsoft solutions. The Microsoft Certified Solutions Associate (MCSA) is the certification for aspiring IT professionals and is also the prerequisite certification necessary to earn an MCSE. These new certifications integrate cloud-related and on-premise skills validation in order to support organizations and recognize individuals who have the skills required to be productive using Microsoft technologies.

On-premise or in the cloud, Microsoft training and certification empowers technology professionals to expand their skills and gain knowledge directly from the source. Securing these essential skills will allow you to grow your career and make yourself indispensable as the industry shifts to the cloud. Cloud computing ultimately enables IT to focus on more mission-critical activities, raising the bar of required expertise for IT professionals and developers. These reinvented certifications test on a deeper set of skills that map to real-world business context. Rather than testing only on a feature of a technology, Microsoft Certifications now validate more advanced skills and a deeper understanding of the platform.

Preparing to Take an Exam

Unless you are a very experienced user, you will need to use test preparation materials to prepare to complete the test correctly and within the time allowed. The Microsoft Official Academic Course series is designed to prepare you with a strong knowledge of all exam topics, and with some additional review and practice on your own, you should feel confident in your ability to pass the appropriate exam.

After you decide which exam to take, review the list of objectives for the exam. You can easily identify tasks that are included in the objective list by locating the exam objective overview at the start of each lesson and the Certification Ready sidebars in the margin of the lessons in this book.

To register for the MCSA exam, visit the Microsoft Certifications webpage for directions on how to register with Pearson VUE, the company that delivers the MCSA exams. Keep in mind these important items about the testing procedure:

- **What to expect.** Microsoft Certification testing labs typically have multiple workstations, which may or may not be occupied by other candidates. Test center administrators strive to provide a quiet and comfortable environment for all test takers.
- **Plan to arrive early.** It is recommended that you arrive at the test center at least 30 minutes before the test is scheduled to begin.
- **Bring your identification.** To take your exam, you must bring the identification (ID) that was specified when you registered for the exam. If you are unclear about which forms of ID are required, contact the exam sponsor identified in your registration information. Although requirements vary, you typically must show two valid forms of ID, one with a photo, both with your signature.
- **Leave personal items at home.** The only item allowed into the testing area is your identification, so leave any backpacks, laptops, briefcases, and other personal items at home. If you have items that cannot be left behind (such as purses), the testing center might have small lockers available for use.
- **Nondisclosure agreement.** At the testing center, Microsoft requires that you accept the terms of a nondisclosure agreement (NDA) and complete a brief demographic survey before taking your certification exam.

Acknowledgements

We thank the MOAC faculty and instructors who have assisted us in building the Microsoft Official Academic Course courseware. These elite educators have acted as our sounding board on key pedagogical and design decisions leading to the development of the MOAC courseware for future Information Technology workers. They have provided invaluable advice in the service of quality instructional materials, and we truly appreciate their dedication to technology education.

Brian Bridson, Baker College of Flint

David Chaulk, Baker College Online

Ron Handlon, Remington College – Tampa Campus

Katherine James, Seneca College of Applied Arts & Technology

Wen Liu, ITT Educational Services

Zeshan Sattar, Pearson in Practice

Jared Spencer, Westwood College Online

David Vallerga, MTI College

Bonny Willy, Ivy Tech State College

We also thank Microsoft Learning's Heidi Johnson, Larry Kaye, Rob Linsky, Colin Lyth, Paul Pardi, Merrick Van Dongen, Liberty Munson, Keith Loeber, Natasha Chornesky, Briana Roberts, Jim Clark, Anne Hamilton, Erika Cravens, and Jim Cochran, for their encouragement and support in making the Microsoft Official Academic Course programs the finest academic materials for mastering the newest Microsoft technologies for both students and instructors.

About the Author

Patrick Regan has been a PC technician, network administrator/engineer, design architect, and security analyst for the past 23 years. He has taught computer and network classes at Sacramento local colleges (Heald Colleges and MTI Colleges) and participated in and led many projects (Heald Colleges, Intel Corporation, Miles Consulting Corporation, and Pacific Coast Companies). For his teaching accomplishments, he received the Teacher of the Year award from Heald Colleges and he has received several recognition awards from Intel. As a senior system administrator, he supports approximately 120 servers and 1,500 users spread over 5 subsidiaries and 70 sites. He has authored a number of textbooks, including books on SharePoint 2010, Windows 7, Windows 8.1, Windows 10, and Windows Server 2012 and Windows Server 2016 for John Wiley & Sons.

Brief Contents

Brief Contents

Contents

Lesson 7: Securing Network Traffic 157

Lesson 8: Implementing Privilege Access Management and Administrative Forests 191

Lesson 9: Implementing Just-Enough- Administration (JEA) 211

Lesson 10: Implementing Privileged Access Workstations, Local Administrator Password Solution (LAPS), and User Rights Assignments 227

Lesson 11: Configuring Advanced Audit Policies 245

Lesson 12: Installing and Configuring Microsoft Advanced Threat Analytics (ATA) 267

Lesson 13: Determining Threat Detection Solutions Using Operations Management Suite (OMS) 281

Lesson 14: Securing Application Development and Server Workload Infrastructure 291

Lesson 15: Implementing a Secure File Services Infrastructure and Dynamic Access Control (DAC) 321

Configuring Disk and File Encryption

LESSON 1

70-744 EXAM OBJECTIVE

Objective 1.1 – Configure disk and file encryption. This objective may include but is not limited to the following: Determine hardware and firmware requirements for secure boot and encryption key functionality; deploy BitLocker encryption; deploy BitLocker without a Trusted Platform Module (TPM); deploy BitLocker with a TPM only; configure the Network Unlock feature; configure BitLocker Group Policy settings; enable BitLocker to use secure boot for platform and BCD integrity validation; configure BitLocker on Clustered Shared Volumes (CSVs) and Storage Area Networks (SANs); implement BitLocker Recovery Process using self-recovery and recovery password retrieval solutions; configure BitLocker for virtual machines (VMs) in Hyper-V; determine usage scenarios for Encrypting File System (EFS); configure the EFS recovery agent; manage EFS and BitLocker certificates, including backup and restore.

LESSON HEADING	EXAM OBJECTIVE
Using Encryption to Protect Data	
Deploying and Configuring BitLocker	Deploy BitLocker encryption
• Deploying BitLocker Encryption	Deploy BitLocker without a Trusted Platform Module (TPM)
• Deploying BitLocker with a TPM Chip Only	Deploy BitLocker with a TPM only
• Configuring BitLocker to Go	Configure BitLocker Group Policy settings
• Configuring BitLocker Group Policy Settings	Enable BitLocker to use secure boot for platform and BCD integrity validation
• Enabling BitLocker to use Secure Boot	Determine hardware and firmware requirements for secure boot and encryption key functionality
• Configuring BitLocker for Virtual Machines (VMs) in Hyper-V	Configure BitLocker for virtual machines (VMs) in Hyper-V
• Configuring BitLocker on Clustered Shared Volumes (CSVs) and Storage Area Networks (SANs)	Configure BitLocker on Clustered Shared Volumes (CSVs) and Storage Area Networks (SANs)
• Performing BitLocker Pre-Provisioning	Configure the Network Unlock feature
• Configuring the Network Unlock Feature	Implement BitLocker Recovery Process using self-recovery and recovery password retrieval solutions
• Managing BitLocker and BitLocker to Go Using MBAM	
• Implementing BitLocker Recovery Process Using Self-Recovery and Recovery Password Retrieval Solutions	
Deploying and Configuring EFS	Determine usage scenarios for Encrypting File System (EFS)
• Encrypting and Decrypting Files with EFS	Configure the EFS recovery agent
• Sharing Files Protected with EFS with Others	
• Configuring EFS with Group Policy	
• Configuring the EFS Recovery Agent	
Managing EFS and BitLocker Certificates	Manage EFS and BitLocker certificates, including backup and restore

KEY TERMS

asymmetric encryption
BitLocker Drive Encryption (BDE)
BitLocker To Go
cipher.exe
data recovery agent (DRA)
decryption
Encrypting File System (EFS)
encryption
guarded host
hash function
Host Guarding Service (HGS)
Microsoft BitLocker Administration and Monitoring (MBAM)
Network Unlock
Secure Boot
symmetric encryption
Trusted Platform Module (TPM)
Unified Extensible Firmware Interface (UEFI)

Using Encryption to Protect Data

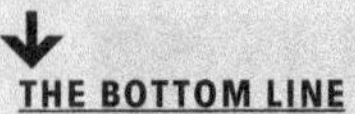

Encryption is the process of converting data into a format that cannot be read by another user. Once a user has encrypted a file, it automatically remains encrypted when the file is stored on disk. ***Decryption*** is the process of converting data from encrypted format back to its original format.

With commonly used encryption methods, the encryption algorithm needs to provide a high level of security while being available to the public. Since the algorithm is made available to the public, the security resides in the key, and not in the algorithm itself.

One of the simplest cipher algorithms is the substitution cipher, which changes one character or symbol into another. For example, if you have:

```
clear text
```

and you substitute each 'e' with the 'y' and each 'c' with the letter 'j' and the letter 't' with 'g', you would get the following ciphertext:

```
jlyar gyxg
```

Another simple technique is based on the transposition cipher, which involves transposing or scrambling the letters in a certain manner. For example, if you have:

```
clear text
```

and you switch each two letters (including any space), you get:

```
lcae rettx
```

A ***key***, which can be thought of as a password, is applied mathematically to plain text to provide cipher or encrypted text. A different key produces a different encrypted output. With computers, encryption is often based on bits, not characters. For example, if you use the Unicode letters 'cl', it would be expressed in the following binary format:

01100011 01101100

and if you mathematically add the binary form of 'z' (01111010), which is the key, you get:

01100011	01101100
+01111010	+01111010
11011101	11100110

which would show as the strange Unicode characters: Ýæ.

Similar to a password, the longer the key (usually expressed in bits), the more secure it is. For a hacker to Figure out a key, they would also have to use a brute force attack, which means the hacker would have to try every combination of bits until they Figure out the correct key. While a key could be broken given enough time and processing power, long keys are chosen so that it would take months, maybe even years, to calculate. Of course, similar to passwords, some encryption algorithms change the key frequently. Therefore, a key length of 80 bits is generally considered the minimum for strong security with symmetric encryption algorithms. Today, 128-bit keys are commonly used and considered very strong.

Encryption algorithms can be divided into three classes: Symmetric, Asymmetric, and Hash function. Symmetric and Asymmetric encryption can encrypt and decrypt data. A Hash function can only encrypt data; that data cannot be decrypted.

Symmetric encryption uses a single key to encrypt and decrypt data. Therefore, it is also referred to as secret-key, single-key, shared-key, and private-key encryption. To use symmetric key algorithms, you need to initially exchange the secret key with both the sender and receiver.

Symmetric-key ciphers can be divided into block ciphers and stream ciphers. A block cipher takes a block of plain text and a key, and outputs a block of ciphertext of the same size. Two popular block ciphers include the Data Encryption Standard (DES) and the Advanced Encryption Standard (AES), which have been designated cryptography standards by the U.S. government.

The Data Encryption Standard was selected by the National Bureau of Standards as an official Federal Information Processing Standard (FIPS) for the United States in 1976. It is based on a symmetric-key algorithm that uses a 56-bit key.

Because DES is based on a relatively small 56-bit key size, DES was subject to brute force attacks. Therefore, without designing a completely new block cipher algorithm, Triple DES (3DES) was developed, which uses three independent keys. DES and the more secure 3DES are still popular and used across a wide range of applications, including ATM encryption, email privacy, and secure remote access.

While DES and 3DES are still popular, a more secure encryption called Advanced Encryption Standard (AES) was announced in 2001 and is growing in popularity. The standard comprises three block ciphers, AES-128, AES-192, and AES-256 used on 128-bit blocks, with key sizes of 128, 192, and 256 bits, respectively. The AES ciphers have been analyzed extensively and are now used worldwide, including being used with Wi-Fi Protected Access 2 (WPA2) wireless encryption.

Stream ciphers create an arbitrarily long stream of key material, which is combined with plain text bit-by-bit or character-by-character. RC4 is a widely used stream cipher, used in Secure Sockets Layer (SSL) and Wired Equivalent Privacy (WEP). While RC4 is simple and is known for its speed, it can be vulnerable if the key stream is not discarded, nonrandom or related keys are used, or a single key stream is used twice.

Asymmetric encryption uses two keys for encryption. Asymmetric key, also known as public key cryptography, uses two mathematically-related keys. One key is used to encrypt the data, while the second key is used to decrypt the data. Unlike symmetric key algorithms, it does not require a secure initial exchange of one or more secret keys to both sender and receiver. Instead, you can make the public key known to anyone and use the other key to encrypt or decrypt the data. The public key could be sent to someone or could be published within a digital certificate via a Certificate Authority (CA). Secure Sockets Layer (SSL)/Transport Layer Security (TLS) and Pretty Good Privacy (PGP) use asymmetric keys. Two popular asymmetric encryption protocols are Diffie-Hellman and RSA.

For example, say you want a partner to send you data. First, you send the partner the public key. The partner then encrypts the data with the key and sends you the encrypted message. Then you use the private key to decrypt the message. If the public key falls into someone else's hands, they still could not decrypt the message.

The last type of encryption is the hash function. Different from the symmetric and asymmetric algorithms, a ***hash function*** is meant as a one-way encryption. This means that after data has been encrypted, it cannot be decrypted. It can be used to encrypt a password that is stored on disk and for digital signatures. Anytime a password is entered, the same hash calculation is performed on the entered password and it is compared to the hash value of the password stored on disk. If the two passwords match, the user must have typed the correct password. This avoids having to store the passwords in a readable format, where a hacker might try to access them.

■ Deploying and Configuring BitLocker

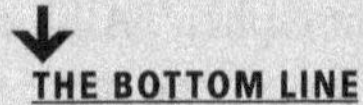

BitLocker allows you to encrypt the entire volume. Therefore, if a drive or laptop is stolen, the data is still encrypted even if the thief installs it in another system for which he is an administrator.

BitLocker Drive Encryption (BDE) is the feature in Windows Vista and higher and Windows Server 2008 and higher that will encrypt volumes using the Advanced Encryption Standard (AES) algorithm with 128-bit keys by default. You can use Group Policy to configure the use of 256-bit keys.

BitLocker can make use of the computer's ***Trusted Platform Module (TPM)***, which is a microchip that is built into a computer. It is used to store cryptographic information, such as encryption keys. Information stored on the TPM can be more secure from external software attacks and physical theft. BitLocker Drive Encryption can use a TPM to validate the integrity of a computer's boot manager and boot files at startup, and to guarantee that a computer's hard disk has not been tampered with while the operating system was offline. BitLocker Drive Encryption also stores measurements of core operating system files in the TPM.

BitLocker encrypts each volume sector individually and part of the encryption key is derived from the sector number. The encryption key is called the full-volume encryption key (FVEK), which is encrypted with a key called the volume master key (VMK). The FVEK (encrypted with the VMK) is stored on the disk as part of the volume metadata. The default key protector is the TPM, but you can configure additional protectors, such as a PIN and a USB startup key. If the system does not have a TPM, you can configure BitLocker to store a key protector on a USB drive.

TAKE NOTE* For workstations, BitLocker is a feature of Windows 7 Enterprise, Windows 7 Ultimate, Windows 8/8.1 Pro, Windows 8/8.1 Enterprise, Windows 10 Pro, and Windows 10 Enterprise. It is not supported on other editions of Windows.

The system requirements of BitLocker are:

- Because BitLocker stores its own encryption and decryption key in a hardware device that is separate from your hard disk, you must have one of the following:
  - A computer with TPM. If your computer was manufactured with TPM version 1.2 or higher, BitLocker stores its key in the TPM.
  - A removable USB memory device, such as a USB flash drive. If your computer doesn't have TPM version 1.2 or higher, BitLocker stores its key on the flash drive.

- Some motherboards provide the option to purchase and install TPM modules separately.
- Have at least two partitions: a system partition (contains the files needed to start your computer and must be at least 350 MB for computers running Windows Server 2016 or Windows 10) and an operating system partition (contains Windows). The operating system partition is encrypted, and the system partition remains unencrypted so that your computer can start. If your computer doesn't have two partitions, BitLocker creates them for you. Both partitions must be formatted with the NTFS file system.
- Your computer must have a BIOS that is compatible with TPM and supports USB devices during computer startup. If this is not the case, you need to update the BIOS before using BitLocker.

Starting with Windows 10 version 1511, and newer, BitLocker encryption uses the XTS-AES encryption algorithm. Drives that are encrypted with Windows 10 version 1511, and newer, are not backward compatible with earlier versions of Windows.

TAKE NOTE*

BitLocker is not commonly used on servers, but may become more common in the future as BitLocker has been improved to work on failover cluster volumes and SANs. Instead, most organizations use physical security for servers (such as locked server room and/or server rack that can be accessed only by a handful of people) to prevent the computer and drives from being stolen.

Instead, BitLocker is more commonly used with mobile computers and to a lesser extent, Desktop computers. However, it takes a domain infrastructure with Windows servers to get the most benefits from BitLocker and the management of systems running BitLocker.

BitLocker supports NTFS, FAT16, FAT32 and ExFAT on USB, Firewire, SATA, SAS, ATA, IDE, SCSI, iSCSI, and Fibre Channel drives. It does not support CD File System, eSATA, and Bluetooth. BitLocker also does not support dynamic volumes; it supports only basic volumes. While it can be used with hardware-based RAID arrays, it cannot be used on software-based RAID.

BitLocker has six operational modes for OS drives, which define the steps involved in the system boot process. These modes, in descending order from most to least secure, are as follows:

- **TPM + startup PIN + startup key:** The system stores the BitLocker volume encryption key on the TPM chip, but an administrator must supply a personal identification number (PIN) and insert a USB flash drive containing a startup key before the system can unlock the BitLocker volume and complete the system boot sequence.
- **TPM + startup key:** The system stores the BitLocker volume encryption key on the TPM chip, but an administrator must insert a USB flash drive containing a startup key before the system can unlock the BitLocker volume and complete the system boot sequence.
- **TPM + startup PIN:** The system stores the BitLocker volume encryption key on the TPM chip, but an administrator must supply a PIN before the system can unlock the BitLocker volume and complete the system boot sequence.
- **Startup key only:** The BitLocker configuration process stores a startup key on a USB flash drive, which the administrator must insert each time the system boots. This mode does not require the server to have a TPM chip, but it must have a system BIOS that supports access to the USB flash drive before the operating system loads.
- **TPM only:** The system stores the BitLocker volume encryption key on the TPM chip, and accesses it automatically when the chip has determined that the boot environment is unmodified. This unlocks the protected volume and the computer continues to boot. No administrative interaction is required during the system boot sequence.
- **Password only:** If your system does not have a TPM chip, you can configure BitLocker not to require TMP by using Group Policy where you will only use a password to access the encrypted drive.

When you use BitLocker on fixed and removable data drives that are not the OS volume, you can use one of the following:

- Password
- Smart card
- Automatic Unlock

When you enable BitLocker using the BitLocker Drive Encryption control panel, you can select the *TPM + startup key*, *TPM + startup PIN*, or *TPM only* option. To use the *TPM + startup PIN + startup key* option, you must first configure the *Require additional authentication at startup* Group Policy setting, found in the Computer Configuration\Policies\Administrative Templates\Windows Components\BitLocker Drive Encryption\Operating System Drives container.

Deploying BitLocker Encryption

CERTIFICATION READY
Deploy BitLocker encryption
Objective 1.1

Before you can use BitLocker on a server running Windows Server 2016, you must first install BitLocker using Server Manager. You can then determine whether you have TPM and turn on BitLocker. If your computer doesn't have TPM, you'll need a removable USB memory device to turn on BitLocker and store the BitLocker startup key on it, which you will need whenever you start your computer.

INSTALL BITLOCKER

GET READY. To install BitLocker on a computer running Windows Server 2016, perform the following steps:

1. Using Server Manager, click **Manage > Add Roles and Features.** The Add Roles and Feature Wizard opens.
2. On the Before you begin page, click **Next.**
3. Select **Role-based or feature-based installation** and then click **Next.**
4. Click **Select a server from the server pool**, click the name of the server to install BitLocker to, and then click **Next.**
5. On the Select server roles page, click **Next.**
6. On the Select features page, select **BitLocker Drive Encryption.**
7. On the Add Roles and Features Wizard page, click **Add Features.**
8. On the Select Features page, click **Next.**
9. On the Confirm installation selections page, click **Install.**
10. When BitLocker is installed, click **Close.**
11. Reboot Windows.

CERTIFICATION READY
Deploy BitLocker without a Trusted Platform Module (TPM)
Objective 1.1

Different from previous versions of Windows, Windows 10 version 1511 (November Update) and above and Windows Server 2016 includes the 256-bit XTS-AES encryption mode that provides additional integrity support. For a fixed disk or a system that only runs Windows 10 or higher, you should use the new encryption mode. If you are using BitLocker to a removable drive that can be used on older versions of Windows, you should use compatible mode.

DEPLOY BITLOCKER WITHOUT TPM

GET READY. To turn on BitLocker on a computer running Windows Server 2016, perform the following steps:

1. Right-click the **Start** button and choose **Control Panel.**
2. Click **System and Security** and click **BitLocker Drive Encryption.** The BitLocker Drive Encryption window opens.
3. Click **Turn on BitLocker** for the volume that you want to encrypt. A BitLocker Drive Encryption window opens for the selected volume.
4. On the Choose how you want to unlock this drive page (see Figure 1-1), select **Use a password to unlock the drive.** Type a password in the Enter your password and Reenter your password text boxes, and then click **Next.**

Figure 1-1

The Choose how you want to unlock this drive page

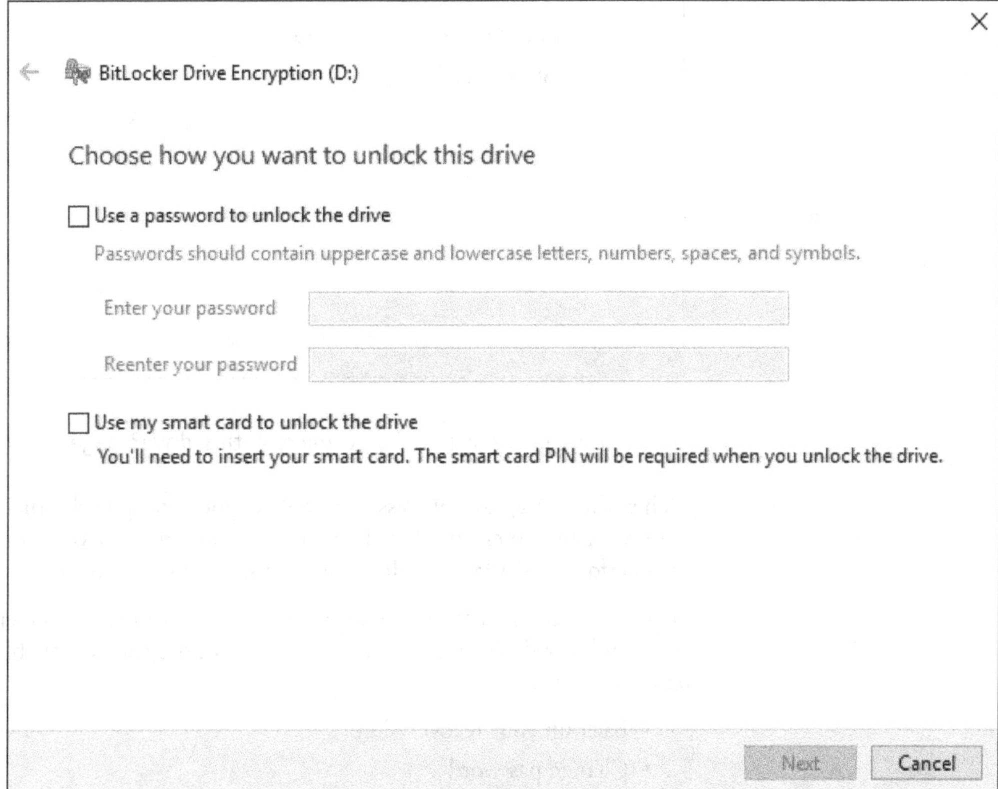

5. On the How do you want to back up your recovery key? page, click **Save to a file.**
6. In the Save BitLocker recovery key as dialog box, click **Save.**
7. After the file is saved, make sure the key is stored in a safe place. Then click **Next.**
8. On the Choose which encryption mode to use page (see Figure 1-2), click **Next.**

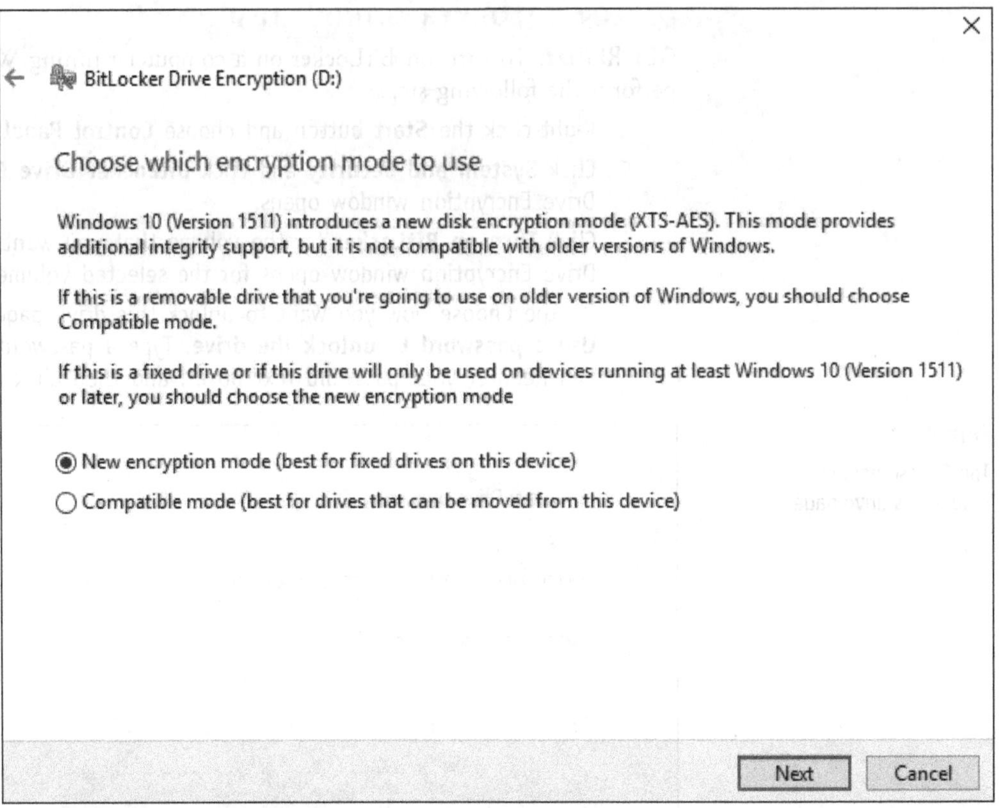
BitLocker Drive Encryption (D:)
Choose which encryption mode to use
Windows 10 (Version 1511) introduces a new disk encryption mode (XTS-AES). This mode provides additional integrity support, but it is not compatible with older versions of Windows.
If this is a removable drive that you're going to use on older version of Windows, you should choose Compatible mode.
If this is a fixed drive or if this drive will only be used on devices running at least Windows 10 (Version 1511) or later, you should choose the new encryption mode
New encryption mode (best for fixed drives on this device)
Compatible mode (best for drives that can be moved from this device)
Next
Cancel

Figure 1-2
The Choose which encryption mode to use page

9. On the Are you ready to encrypt this drive? page, click **Start encrypting**.

When the encryption process is complete, you can open the BitLocker Drive Encryption Control Panel to ensure that the volume is encrypted or you can turn off BitLocker (so you can perform a BIOS upgrade or other system maintenance).

The BitLocker Control Panel applet enables you to recover the encryption key and recovery password at will. Figure 1-3 shows the following options available after you use BitLocker to encrypt a drive:

- Back up your recovery key
- Change password
- Remove password
- Add smart card
- Turn on auto-unlock
- Turn off BitLocker

You should consider carefully how to store this information, because it allows access to the encrypted data. It is also possible to escrow this information into Active Directory.

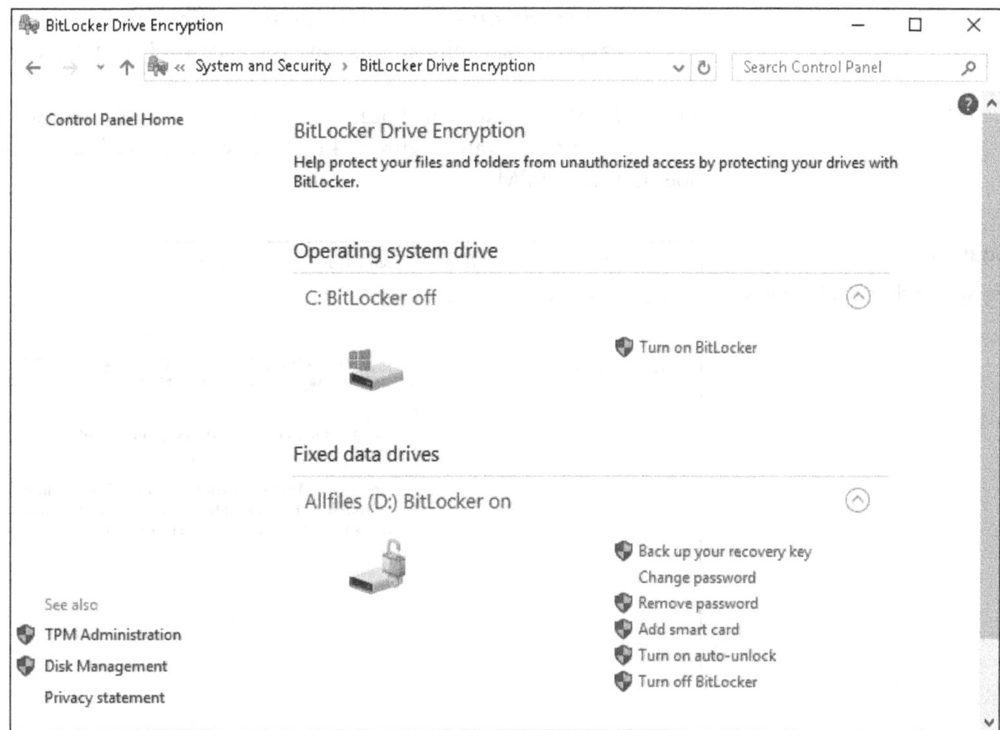

Figure 1-3

Showing the BitLocker applet options for a BitLocker-encrypted volume

Standard users can change the password or PIN if they know the current PIN or password. By default, a user has five attempts to type the current PIN or password. When this happens, the administrator must reset the volume PIN or password or the system needs to be rebooted. To make sure that password or pin is not too easy to guess, you can use a group policy to define the complexity of the password. To define the complexity, enable and configure the Configure use of passwords for fixed data drives settings found in Computer Configuration\Policies\Administrative Templates\Windows Components\BitLocker Drive Encryption\ or, if you are accessing a local policy, Computer Configuration \Administrative Templates\Windows Components\BitLocker Drive Encryption\.

Deploying BitLocker with a TPM Chip Only

CERTIFICATION READY
Deploy BitLocker with a TPM only
Objective 1.1

Some laptops, desktops, and servers have a TPM chip. Click the TPM Administration link shown in Figure 1-3 to find out whether your computer has the TPM security hardware. You can also open Device Manager and look under the Security node TPM.

If your system does have a TPM chip, you will need to initialize the TPM using the TPM Initialization Wizard. In addition, you must set the owner of the TPM. If you try to turn on BitLocker for a volume and you have TPM, you will see the Initialize TPM Security Hardware Wizard.

DETERMINE WHETHER YOU HAVE TPM

GET READY. To find out whether your computer has TPM security hardware, perform the following steps:

1. Open the **Control Panel**.
2. Click **System and Security** and click **BitLocker Drive Encryption**. The BitLocker Drive Encryption window opens.

3. In the left pane, click **TPM Administration.** If you are prompted for an administrator password or confirmation, type the password or provide confirmation.

The TPM Management on Local Computer snap-in tells you whether your computer has the TPM security hardware. Figure 1-4 displays what TPM Management shows when the system does not have TPM.

Figure 1-4

The system does not have TPM

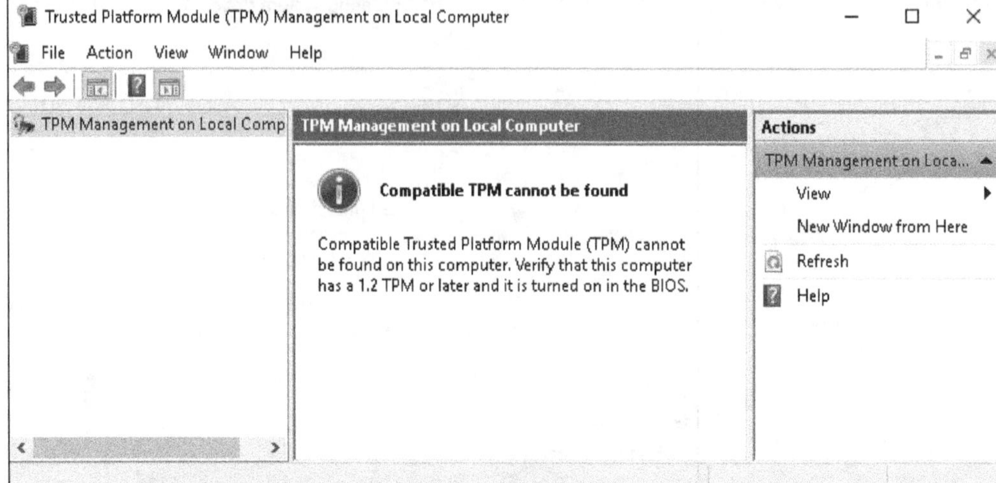

ENABLE AND CONFIGURE TPM

GET READY. To enable and configure TPM, perform the following steps:

1. Open the **Control Panel.**
2. Click **System and Security** and click **BitLocker Drive Encryption.** The BitLocker Drive Encryption window opens.
3. In the left pane, click **TPM Administration.**
4. In the Actions pane, click **Initialize TPM.** The TPM Initialization Wizard is started. If the TPM has never been turned on or is currently turned off, the TPM Initialization Wizard displays the Turn on the TPM Security Hardware page, which will give you general instructions to access the BIOS Setup program to enable TPM.
5. On the Create the TPM owner password page, click **Automatically create the password (recommended).**
6. In the Save your TPM owner password dialog box, click **Save the password.**
7. In the Save As dialog box, select a location to save the password and then click **Save.** The password file is saved as *<computer_name>*.tpm. It is commended that you save the TPM owner password to removable media.
8. Click **Initialize.**
9. Click **Close.**

DEPLOY BITLOCKER WITHOUT TPM

GET READY. To turn on BitLocker on a computer running Windows Server 2016, perform the following steps:

1. Right-click the **Start** button and choose **Control Panel.**
2. Click **System and Security** and click **BitLocker Drive Encryption.** The BitLocker Drive Encryption window displays.

3. Click **Turn on BitLocker** for the volume that you want to encrypt. A BitLocker Drive Encryption window opens for the selected volume.
4. On the How do you want to back up your recovery key? page, click **Save to a file.**
5. In the Save BitLocker recovery key as dialog box, click **Save.**
6. After the file is saved on an unencrypted drive, make sure the key is stored in a safe place. Then click **Next.**
7. On the Choose which encryption mode to use page, click **Next.**
8. On the Are you ready to encrypt this drive? page, click **Start encrypting.**

Configuring BitLocker To Go

BitLocker To Go is a feature introduced with Windows 7 and Windows Server 2008 R2 that enables users to encrypt removable USB devices, such as flash drives and external hard disks. While BitLocker has always supported the encryption of removable drives, BitLocker To Go enables you to use the encrypted device on other computers without having to perform an involved recovery process. Because the system is not using the removable drive as a boot device, a TPM chip is not required.

To use BitLocker To Go, insert the removable drive and open the BitLocker Drive Encryption Control Panel. The device appears in the interface with a Turn on BitLocker link just like that of the computer's hard disk drive.

Configuring BitLocker Group Policy Settings

CERTIFICATION READY
Configure BitLocker Group Policy settings
Objective 1.1

To control what drive encryption options are available and to configure BitLocker settings, you can use Group Policy Objects (GPOs). Local Group Policy BitLocker settings are located at Computer Configuration\Administrative Templates\Windows Components\BitLocker Drive Encryption and Group Policy Management BitLocker settings are located at Configuration\Policies\Administrative Templates\Windows Components\BitLocker Drive Encryption.

Within the BitLocker Drive Encryption node, you will find subfolders for fixed data drives, operating system drives, and removable drives (as shown in Figure 1-5). Some of the settings that you can configure with GPOs include:

- Require all removable drives to be BitLocker-protected before users can save data to them.
- Require or disallow specific methods for unlocking BitLocker-protected drives.
- Configure methods to recover data from BitLocker-protected drives if a user's unlock credentials are unavailable.
- Configure the BitLocker recovery password that is stored in AD DS.
- Require or disallow different types of recovery password storage or make them optional.
- Prevent BitLocker from activating if it is not possible to back up the keys to AD DS.
- Choose drive encryption method and cipher strength

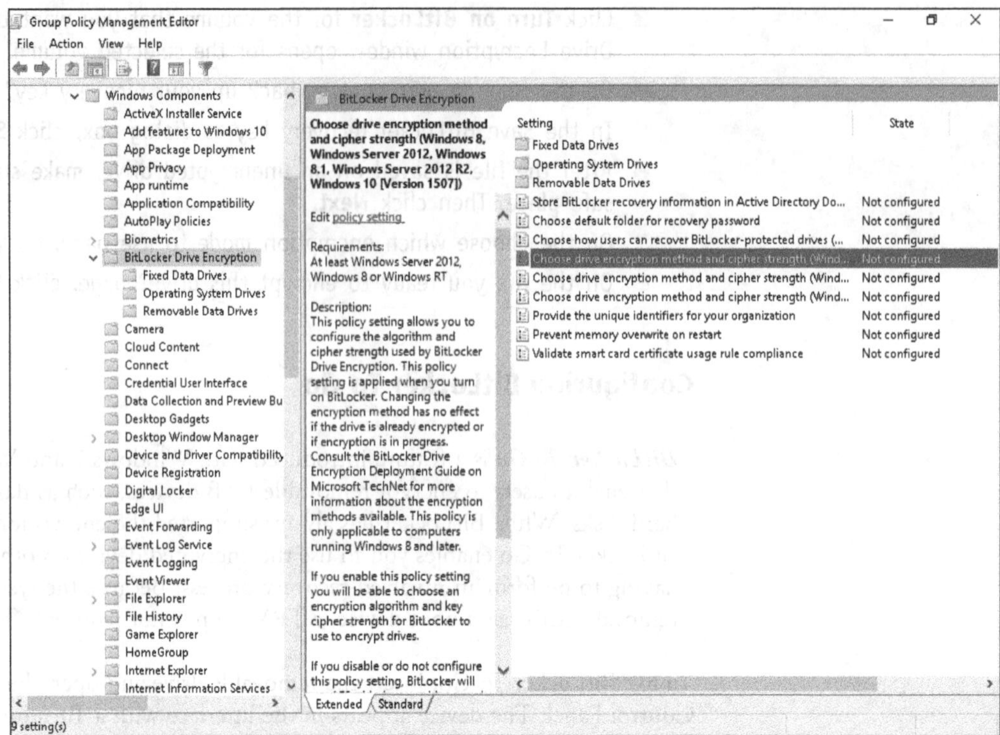

Figure 1-5

BitLocker GPO settings

In addition, you can use GPOs to configure TPM. The TPM settings are Computer Configuration\Administrative Templates\System\Trusted Platform Module Services or Computer Configuration\Policies\Administrative Templates\System\Trusted Platform Module Services. Some of the GPO settings include:

- Turn on TPM backup to Active Directory Domain Services
- Configure the list of blocked TPM commands
- Configure the level of TPM owner authorization information available to the operating system
- Configure standard user lockout duration
- Standard User Individual Lockout Threshold

Enabling BitLocker to Use Secure Boot

CERTIFICATION READY
Enable BitLocker to use secure boot for platform and BCD integrity validation
Objective 1.1

CERTIFICATION READY
Determine hardware and firmware requirements for secure boot and encryption key functionality
Objective 1.1

Secure Boot is a Unified Extensible Firmware Interface (UEFI) component that ensures that each component is loaded during the boot process is digitally signed and validated. It makes the machine boots using only software that is trusted by the PC manufacturer or the user and to help prevent malware.

When a computer boots, a boot loader are responsible for copying the operating system image into memory when the computer is started. If Secure Boot detects a boot loader that is not signed with the appropriate digital signature, it will block it.

The ***Unified Extensible Firmware Interface (UEFI)*** is a specification that defines a software interface between an operating system and platform firmware. It replaces the Basic Input/Output System (BIOS) firmware interface originally present in all IBM PC-compatible personal computers. To use Secure Boot, you must have the following hardware and firmware requirements:

- UEFI Secure Boot must be enabled when shipped or an option in the BIOS Setup program.
- You must be using UEFI version 2.31 or higher.

Secure Boot is supported by Windows 8 and higher, and Windows Server 2012 and higher. At the time of this writing, Secure Boot is supported by a number of Linux distributions including Fedora (since version 18), openSUSE (since version 12.3), RHEL (since RHEL 7), CentOS (since CentOS 7) and Ubuntu (since version 12.04.2).

To enable Secure Boot for platform and BCD integrity validation, you would either allow or not configure the "Allow Secure Boot for integrity validation" group policy item, which can be found in Computer Configuration > Administrative Templates > Windows Components > BitLocker Drive Encryption > Operating System Drives or Computer Configuration > Policies > Administrative Templates > Windows Components > BitLocker Drive Encryption > Operating System Drives.

ENABLE BITLOCKER TO USE SECURITY BOOT

GET READY. To enable BitLocker to use Security Boot, perform the following steps:

1. On a domain controller, using Server Manager, click **Tools > Group Policy Management.**
2. In the Group Policy Management console, right-click the desired GPO and choose **Edit.**
3. Navigate to **Computer Configuration > Policies > Administrative Templates > Windows Components > BitLocker Drive Encryption > Operating System Drives.**
4. Double-click the **Allow Secure Boot for integrity validation** option, as shown in Figure 1-6.

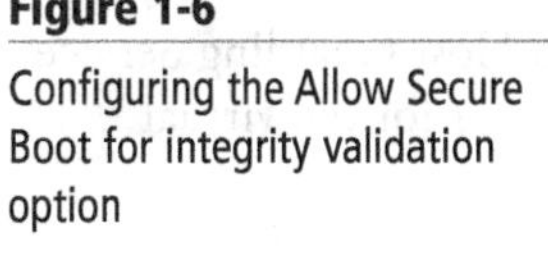

Figure 1-6

Configuring the Allow Secure Boot for integrity validation option

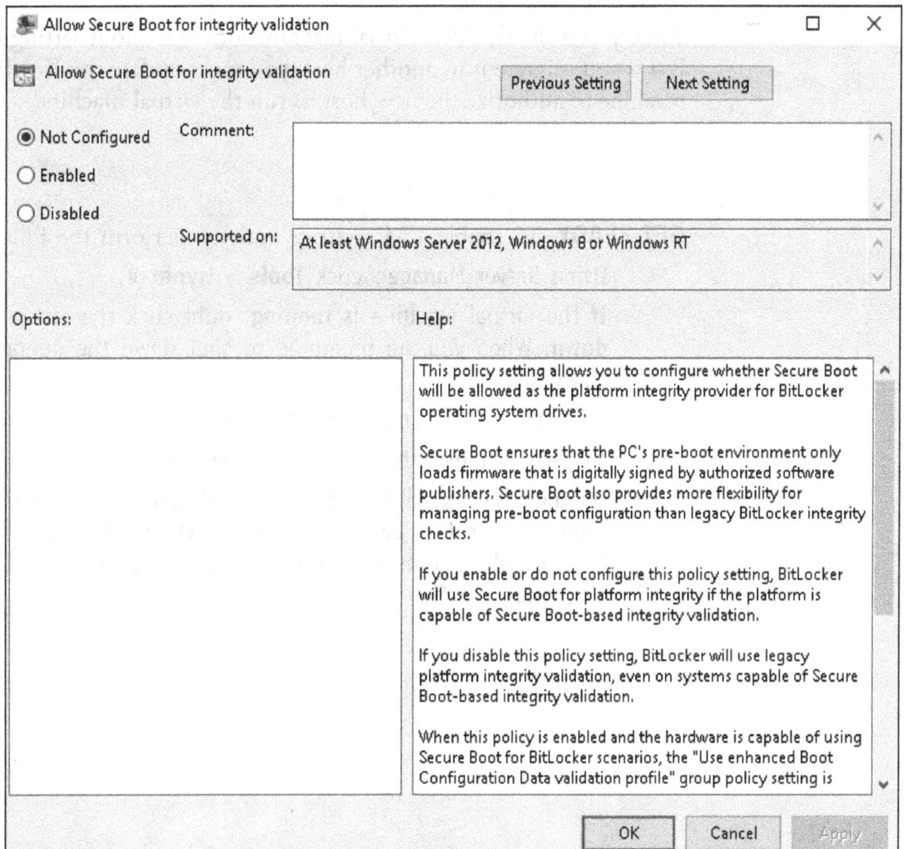

5. Click the **Enabled** option.
6. Click **OK**.

Configuring BitLocker for Virtual Machines (VMs) in Hyper-V

CERTIFICATION READY
Configure BitLocker for Virtual Machines (VMs) in Hyper-V
Objective 1.1

Windows Server 2016 includes multiple options that will help secure the virtual machines. These options include Secure Boot, Encryption Support, and Shielding.

To support Secure Boot for Windows and Linux virtual machines, the virtual machine must be generation 2. You then open the virtual machine settings, select the Security node, and make sure the Enable Secure Boot option is selected. The Enable Secure Boot option is enabled by default.

By enabling the Enable Trusted Platform Module option, you use a virtualized TPM chip available for the VM that will encrypt the virtual disk using BitLocker, even if the physical host does not have a TPM chip. By selecting the Encrypt State and VM migration traffic to encrypt the virtual machine saved state and live migration traffic.

If you select the enable Shielding option, you will disable management features like console connection, PowerShell Direct, and some integration components. In addition, the Enable Secure Boot, Enable Trusted Platform Modules, and Encrypt State and virtual machine migration traffic options will be automatically selected and enforced.

The Hyper-V host that has a shielded virtual machine is known as a ***guarded host***, which is running the ***Host Guarding Service (HGS)*** server role. The HGS will service will provide a transport key that will unlock and run a shielded VM. When you shield a virtual machine, the VM data and state is protected by using the virtual TPM, which will encrypt the VM disks. The vTPM device is encrypted with the transport key.

You can run the shielded virtual machine locally without setting up a Host Guarding Service. But if you migrate it to another host, you must update the Key Protector for the virtual machine to authorize the new host to run the virtual machine.

ENABLE VM SECURITY OPTIONS

GET READY. To enable VM security options, perform the following steps:

1. Using Server Manager, click **Tools > Hyper-V.**
2. If the virtual machine is running, right-click the virtual machine and choose **Shut down.** When you are prompted to shut down the operating system, click the **Shut Down** button.
3. Right-click a VM and choose **Settings.**
4. In the Settings window, click the **Security** node.
5. On the Security page (see Figure 1-7), Enable Secure Boot is already selected. To select TPM, select **Enable Trusted Platform Module.** If you want to encrypt state and virtual machine migration traffic, select **Encrypt state and virtual machine migration traffic.**

Figure 1-7
Selecting security options

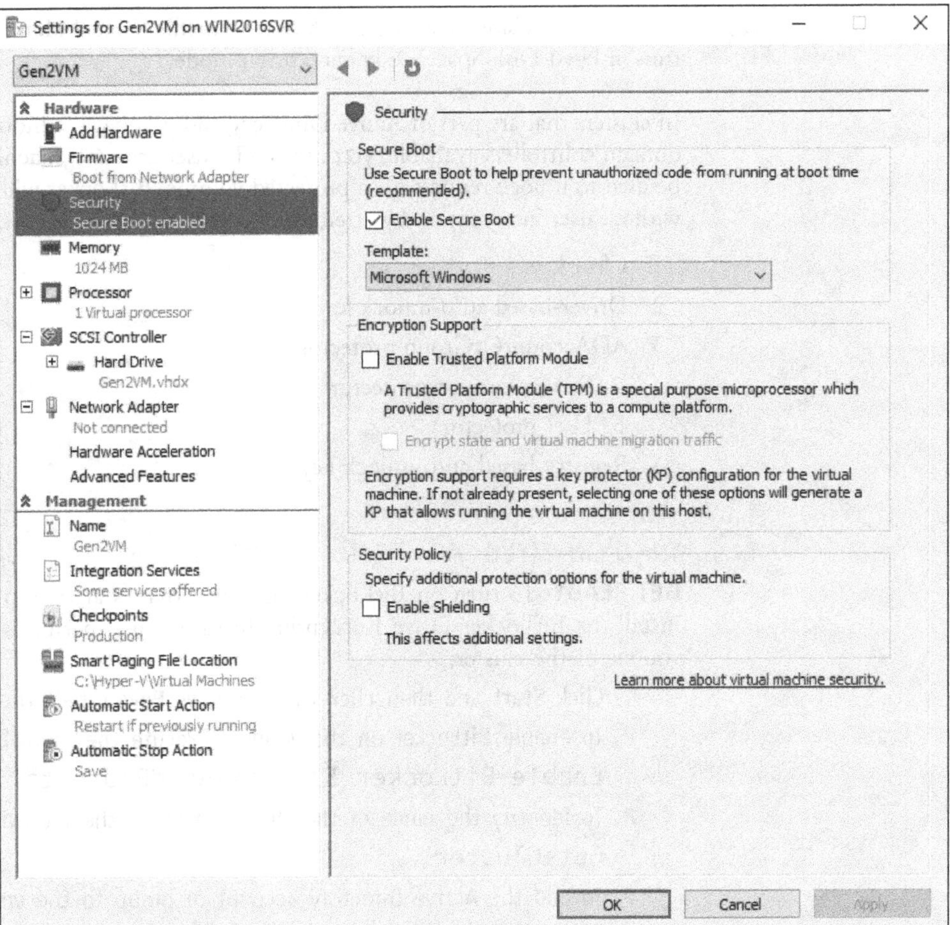

6. To shield the virtual machine, select **Enable Shielding.**
7. Click **OK.**

Configuring BitLocker on Clustered Shared Volumes (CSVs) and Storage Area Networks (SANs)

CERTIFICATION READY
Configure BitLocker on Clustered Shared Volumes (CSVs) and Storage Area Networks (SANS)
Objective 1.1

Windows Server 2016 enables you to use BitLocker-encrypted volumes on a failover cluster on physical disk resources and cluster shared volumes version 2.0 (CSV 2.0). By protecting cluster shared volumes, BitLocker can protect sensitive, highly available data. In addition, you can provide further protection by allowing only certain user accounts access to unlock the BitLocker volume.

BitLocker is applied to physical disks and cluster shared volumes based on how a cluster views the volume that needs to be protected. The volume can be a physical disk resource such as a logical unit number (LUN) on a storage area network (SAN) or network attached storage (NAS).

If you use BitLocker with cluster-shared volumes in a cluster, you should enable BitLocker on a volume prior to adding them to the storage pool within the cluster. Otherwise, you will be required to put the resource into the maintenance mode before BitLocker operations will complete. It also recommended that you use Windows PowerShell to manage BitLocker on CSV 2.0 volumes.

TAKE NOTE* For thinly provisioned storage, such as a Dynamic Virtual Hard Disk (VHD), BitLocker runs in Used Disk Space Only encryption mode.

In clusters that are part of Active Directory and you have Windows Server 2012 or higher domain controllers available, you can bind a user account, machine account or group that will be used to unlock request for a protected volume. BitLocker will unlock protected volumes without user intervention by attempting protectors in the following order:

1. Clear key
2. Driver-based auto-unlock key
3. ADAccountOrGroup protector
   a. Service context protector
   b. User protector
4. Registry-based auto-unlock key

TURN ON BITLOCKER BEFORE ADDING DISKS TO A CLUSTER

GET READY. To turn on BitLocker on a disk that is already part of a cluster, be sure to install the BitLocker Drive Encryption feature. Then perform the following steps on each volume of the cluster:

1. Click **Start** and then click the **Windows PowerShell** tile.
2. To enable BitLocker on the volume, execute the following command:
   ```
   Enable-BitLocker E: -PasswordProtector -Password $pw
   ```
3. To identify the name of the cluster, execute the following command:
   ```
   Get-Cluster
   ```
4. To add the Active Directory account or group to the volume by using the cluster name, execute the following command.
   ```
   Add-BitLockerProtected E:
   -ADAccountOrGroupProtector -ADAccountORGroup CLUSTER$
   ```

TURN ON BITLOCKER ON A CLUSTERED DISK

GET READY. To turn on BitLocker before adding disks to a cluster, install the BitLocker Drive Encryption feature, ensure the disk is formatted with the NTFS file system and a drive letter has been assigned, and then perform the following steps on each volume of the cluster:

1. Click **Start** and then click the **Windows PowerShell** tile.
2. To check the status of the cluster disk, execute the following command:
   ```
   Get-ClusterResource “Cluster Disk 1”
   ```
3. To put the physical disk into maintenance mode, execute the following command:
   ```
   Get-ClusterResource “Cluster Disk 1” |
   Suspend-ClusterResource
   ```
4. To enable BitLocker on the volume with a password protector, execute the following command:
   ```
   Enable-BitLocker E: -PasswordProtector -Password $pw
   ```
5. To identify the name of the cluster, execute the following command:
   ```
   Get-Cluster
   ```

6. To add the ADAccountorGroup protector, execute the following command:

```
Add-BitLockerProtector E:
-ADAccountOrGroupProtector -ADAccountOrGroup CLUSTER$
```

Performing BitLocker Pre-Provisioning

Starting with Windows 8, BitLocker supports pre-provisioning, which allows BitLocker to be enabled before the operating system is installed. During pre-provisioning, Windows generates a random encryption key that BitLocker uses to encrypt the volume. The random encryption key is stored on the disk, unprotected. After Windows is installed, users can fully protect the encryption key for the pre-provisioned volume by activating BitLocker on the volume and selecting the BitLocker unlock method.

To enable BitLocker pre-provisioning, use a customized Windows Preinstallation Environment (WinPE) image and execute the following command:

```
Manage-bde -on x:
```

You need to protect the drive letter (x). After Windows is installed, the BitLocker status for the volume is BitLocker Waiting for Activation.

Configuring the Network Unlock Feature

CERTIFICATION READY
Configure the Network Unlock feature
Objective 1.1

Network Unlock provides an automatic unlock of operating system volumes at system reboot when connected to a trusted wired corporate network.

The hardware and software requirements for Network Unlock include:

- Windows 10 installation on UEFI firmware with UEFI DHCP drivers.
- BitLocker Network Unlock feature using Server Manager
- Windows Server 2016 Windows Deployment Services (WDS) role
- DHCP server, separate from the WDS server and the Domain Controller
- A Network Unlock certificate
- Network Unlock Group Policy settings configured

Network Unlock works similarly to the TPM plus startup key, but instead of reading a startup key from a USB device, Network Unlock uses an unlock key. The key is composed of a key that is stored on the machine's local TPM and a key that Network Unlock receives from Windows Deployment Services. If the WDS server is unavailable such as when you are not connected directly to the organization's network, BitLocker cannot communicate with a WDS server and instead displays the startup key unlock screen.

The client requires a DHCP driver implemented in the Unified Extensible Firmware interface. As the server boots, it gets the key from the WDS server using DHCP. BitLocker Network Unlock is installed on the server with WDS server role installed. To protect the keys being transferred over the network, the WDS server needs a special X.509 certificate that must be installed on all the clients that use Network Unlock.

To deploy Network Unlock, you will need to perform the following high-level steps:

1. Install the WDS Server role.
2. Confirm the WDS Service is running.
3. Install the Network Unlock feature using Server Manager.
4. Create the Network Unlock certificate.

5. Deploy the private key and certificate to the WDS server.
6. Configure Group Policy for Network Unlock.
7. Require TPM+Pin protectors at startup.

TAKE NOTE* The WDS Server role and service was discussed in the 70-740 course.

INSTALL THE NETWORK UNLOCK FEATURE

GET READY. To install the Network Unlock feature, perform the following steps:

1. On the WDS server, using Server Manager, click **Manage > Add Roles and Features.** The Add Roles and Feature Wizard opens.
2. On the Before you begin page, click **Next.**
3. Select **Role-based or feature-based installation** and then click **Next.**
4. Click **Select a server from the server pool**, click the name of the server to install BitLocker to, and then click **Next.**
5. On the Select server roles page, click **Next.**
6. On the Select features page, select **BitLocker Network Unlock.**
7. In the Add Roles and Features Wizard dialog box, click **Add Features.**
8. On the Select Features page, click **Next.**
9. On the Confirm installation selections page, click **Install.**
10. When BitLocker is installed, click **Close.**

CREATE THE NETWORK UNLOCK CERTIFICATE

GET READY. To create the Network Unlock certificate, perform the following steps:

1. On a Certificate Authority server, to open the Certificates Template snap-in, click the **Start** button and type **certtmpl.msc.**
2. Right-click the **User** template name and choose **Duplicate Template.**
3. On the **Compatibility** tab, change the Certification Authority and Certificate recipient fields to **Windows Server 2012** and **Windows 8 / Windows Server 2012**, respectively. In the Resulting changes dialog box, click **OK.**
4. Select the **General** tab.
5. Ensure that the Template display name and Template name should clearly identify that the template will be used for Network Unlock.
6. Clear the checkbox for the **Publish certificate in Active Directory** option.
7. Select the **Request Handling** tab.
8. Click the **Purpose** drop down menu and select **Encryption.** Ensure the **Allow private key to be exported** option is selected.
9. Click the **Cryptography** tab.
10. Set the Minimum key size to **2048**, which is the default
11. Click the **Subject Name** tab.
12. Click **Supply in the request** option. If the certificate templates pop-up dialog appears, click **OK.**
13. Select the **Extensions** tab. Select **Application Policies** and choose **Edit....**
14. In the Edit Application Policies Extension options dialog box, select **Client Authentication, Encrypting File System,** and **Secure Email** and then choose **Remove.**

15. In the Edit Application Policies Extension dialog box, click **Add.**
16. In the Add Application Policy dialog box, select **New.**
17. In the New Application Policy dialog box, type the following information in the space provided and then click **OK** to create the BitLocker Network Unlock application policy (as shown in Figure 1-8):

    Name: **BitLocker Network Unlock**

    Object identifier: **1.3.6.1.4.1.311.67.1.1**

Figure 1-8

Selecting security options

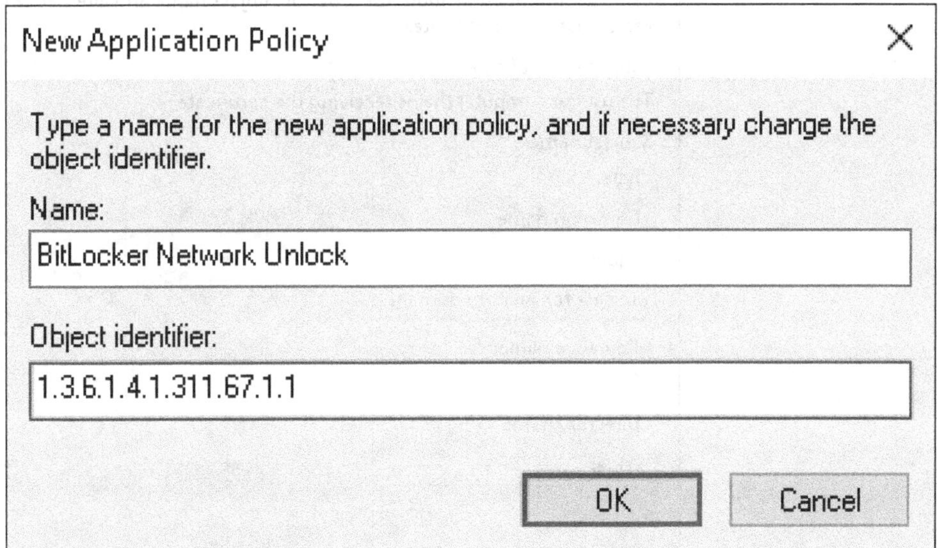

18. Select the newly created **BitLocker Network Unlock** application policy and then click **OK.**
19. Select **Key Usage** and then click **Edit.**
20. In the Edit Key Usage Extension dialog, make sure the **Allow key exchange only with key encryption (key encipherment)** and the **Make this extension critical** options are selected.
21. To close the Edit Key Usage Extension dialog box, click **OK.**
22. Click the **Security** tab.
23. Confirm that the Domain Admins group has been granted **Enroll** permission.
24. Click **OK.**
25. Right-click the Certificate Templates node and chose **New > Certificate Template to Issue.**
26. In the Enable Certificate Templates dialog box, select the Network Unlock template and then click **OK.**
27. On the WDS server, to open Certificate Manager on the WDS server, click the **Start** button, type **certmgr.msc**, and then press **Enter.**
28. Under the Certificates - Current User item, right-click **Personal** and choose **All Tasks > Request New Certificate.**
29. In the Certificate Enrollment wizard, click **Next.**
30. On the Select Certificate Enrollment Policy page, click **Next.**
31. Select the Network Unlock certificate and click **More information is required to enroll this certificate. Click here to configure settings.**

32. In the Certificate Properties dialog box, under Subject name, for the Type, select **Common Name**. Then in the Value text box, type **BitLocker Network Unlock Certificate for Adatum domain** (as shown in Figure 1-9) and then click **Add**.

Figure 1-9

Requesting a BitLocker Network Unlock certificate

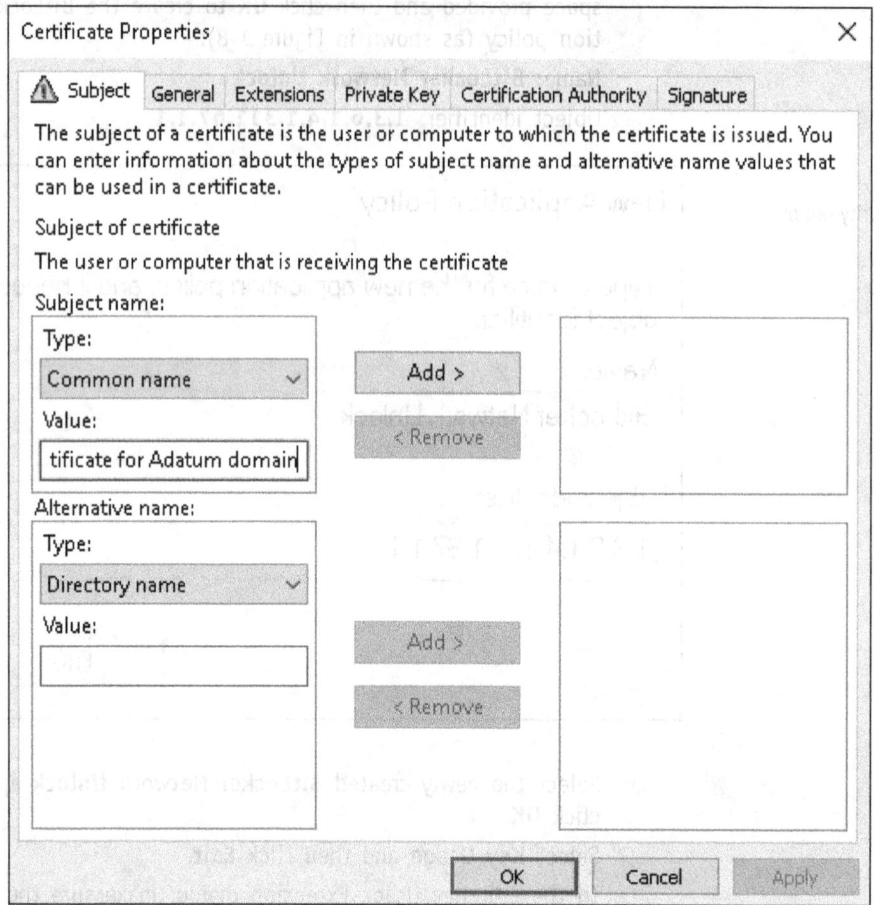

33. Click **OK**.
34. Click **Enroll**.
35. When the certificate is installed, click **Finish**.

EXPORT AND IMPORT THE CERTIFICATE TO THE WDS SERVER

GET READY. To export and import the certificate to the WDS server, perform the following steps:

1. On the Certificate Authority server, to Export the public key certificate for Network Unlock, in the certmgr console, right-click the previously created certificate and choose **All Tasks > Export**.
2. In the Certificate Export Wizard, on the Welcome to the Certificate Export Wizard page, click **Next**.
3. On the Export Private Key page, select **No, do not export the private key** and then click **Next**.
4. Select **DER encoded binary X.509 (.CER)** (as shown in Figure 1-10) and then click **Next**.

Figure 1-10

Specifying the export file format when exporting a certificate

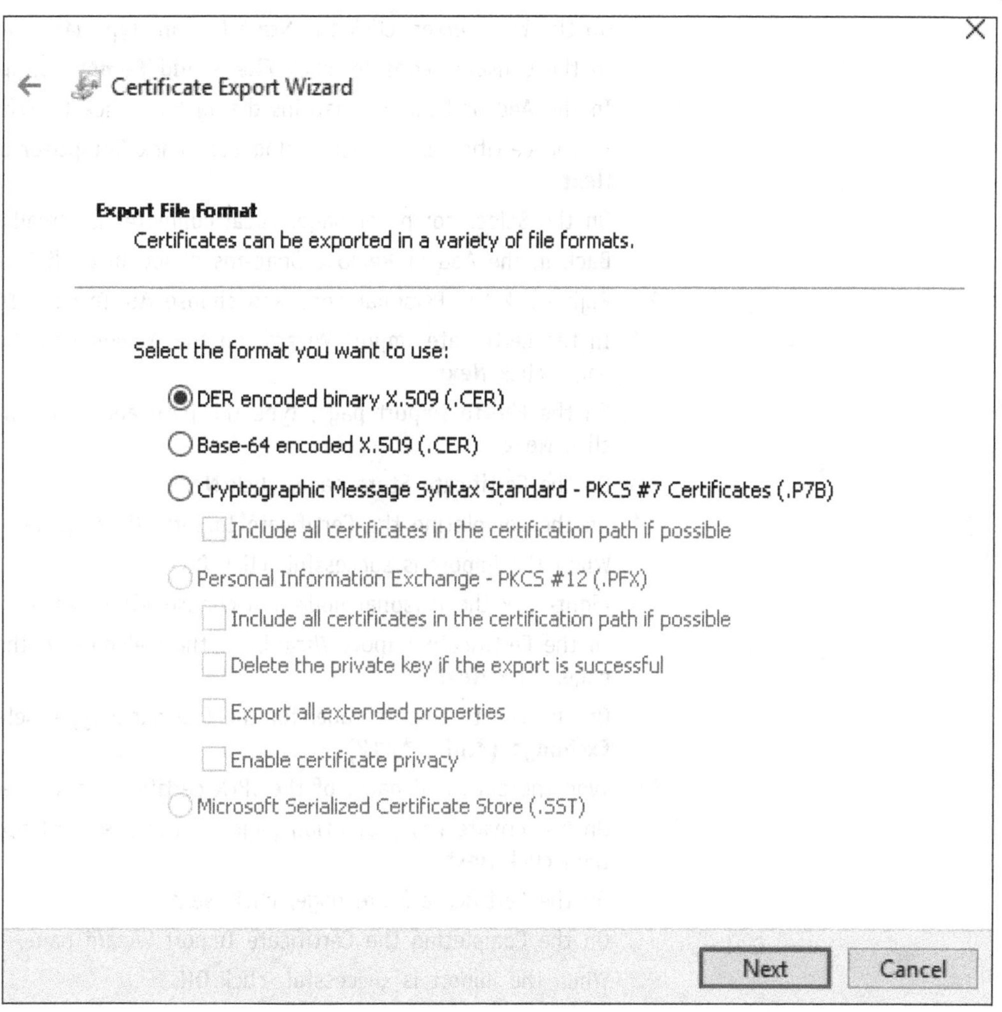

5. On the File to Export page, in the File name text box, type a name (such as **BitLocker-NetworkUnlock.cer**) and then click **Next.**
6. Click **Finish.**
7. To export the private key certificate for Network Unlock, in the certmgr console, right-click the previously created certificate and choose **All Tasks > Export.**
8. In the Certificate Export Wizard, on the Welcome to the Certificate Export Wizard page, click **Next.**
9. On the Export Private Key page, select **Yes, export the private key** and then click **Next.**
10. Select **Personal Information Exchange – PKCS #12 (.PFX)** and then click **Next.**
11. On the Security page, select **Password.** In the Password text box and the Confirm password text box, type **Pa$$w0rd.** Click **Next.**
12. On the File to Export page, in the File name text box, type a name (such as **BitLocker-NetworkUnlock.pfx**) and then click **Next.**
13. Click **Finish.**

14. On the WDS server, click the **Start** button, type **MMC**, and press **Enter**.
15. In the Console1 console, click **File > Add/Remove Snap-in**.
16. In the Add or Remove Snap-ins dialog box, click **Certificates**, and click **Add**.
17. In the Certificates snap-in dialog box, click **Computer account** and then click **Next**.
18. On the Select computer page, Local computer is already selected. Click **Finish**.
19. Back in the Add or Remove Snap-ins dialog box, click **OK**.
20. Right-click the Personal node and choose **All Tasks > Import**.
21. In the Certificate Import Wizard, on the Welcome to the Certificate Import Wizard page, click **Next**.
22. On the File to Import page, type the path and name of the .CER certificate and click **Next**.
23. On the Certificate Store page, click **Next**.
24. On the Completing the Certificate Import Wizard page, click **Finish**.
25. When the import is successful, click **OK**.
26. Right-click the Personal node and choose **All Tasks > Import**.
27. In the Certificate Import Wizard, on the Welcome to the Certificate Import Wizard page, click **Next**.
28. On the File to Import page, for the File name type, select **Personal Information Exchange (*.pfx, *p12)**.
29. Type the path and name of the .PFX certificate and then click **Next**.
30. On the Private key protection page, in the Password text box, type **Pa$$w0rd** and then click **Next**.
31. On the Certificate Store page, click **Next**.
32. On the Completing the Certificate Import Wizard page, click **Finish**.
33. When the import is successful, click **OK**.

CONFIGURE GROUP POLICY SETTINGS FOR NETWORK UNLOCK

GET READY. To configure group policy settings for Network Unlock, perform the following steps:

1. On a domain controller, using Server Manager, click **Tools > Group Policy Management**.
2. Right-click a GPO and choose **Edit**.
3. In the Group Policy Management Editor, navigate to **Computer Configuration\Policies\Administrative Templates\Windows Components\BitLocker Drive Encryption\Operating System Drives**.
4. Double-click **Require additional authentication at start (Windows Server 2008 and Windows Vista)**.
5. In the Require additional authentication at startup (Windows Server 2008 and Windows Vista) dialog box, click **Enabled**.
6. For the Configure TMP startup PIN option, select **Require startup PIN with TPM** (see Figure 1-11) and then click **OK**.

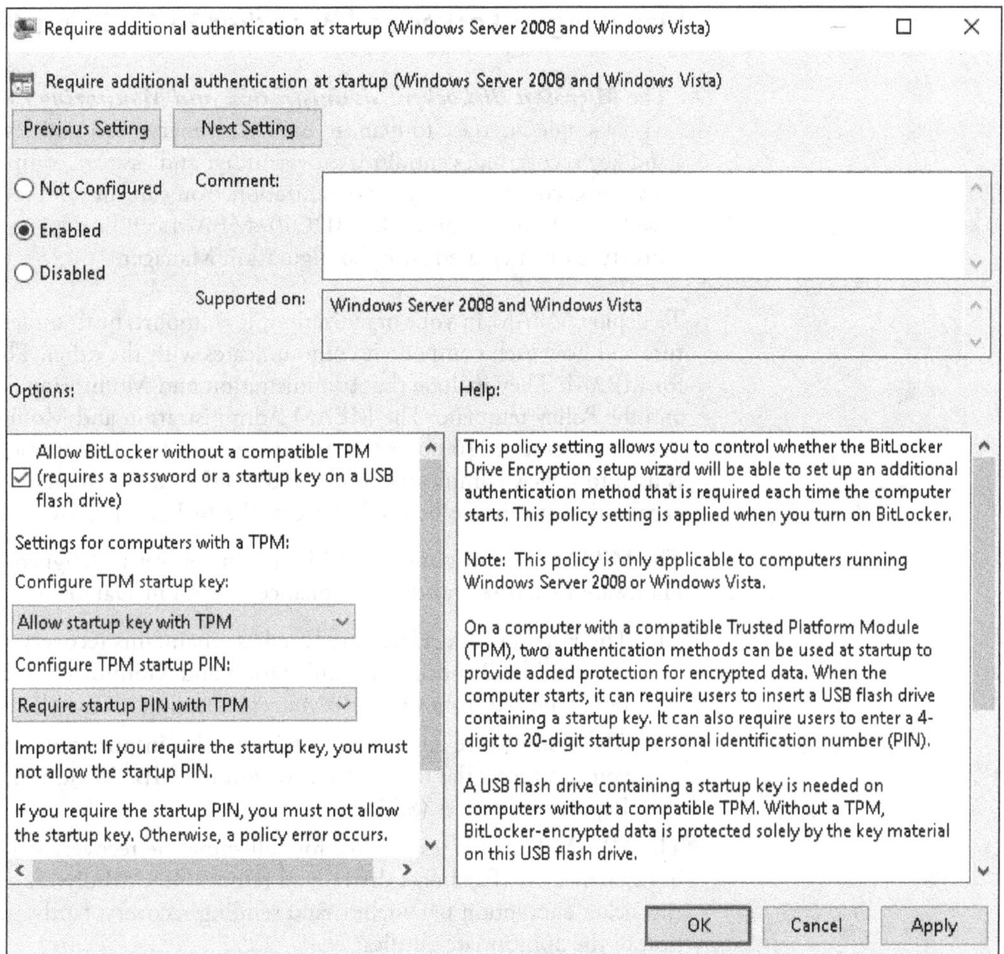

Figure 1-11

Configuring BitLocker Authentication options

7. Double-click **Allow network unlock at startup.**
8. In the Allow network unlock at startup dialog box, click **Enabled** and then click **OK.**
9. Navigate to **Computer Configuration\Policies\Windows Settings\Security Settings\Public Key Policies\BitLocker Drive Encryption Network Unlock Certificate.**
10. Right-click **BitLocker Drive Encryption Network Unlock Certificate** and choose **Add Network Unlock Certificate.**
11. In the Add Network Unlock Certificate Wizard, on the Welcome to the Network Unlock Certificate Wizard, click **Next.**
12. On the Select Network Unlock Certificate page, click the **Browse Folders** button.
13. In the Open dialog box, navigate to and double-click the **Unlock BitLocker.cer** file. Click **Next.**
14. In the Completing the Add Network Unlock Certificate Wizard, click **Finish.**

Managing BitLocker and BitLocker To Go Using MBAM

The ***Microsoft BitLocker Administration and Monitoring (MBAM)*** tool provides you with a single interface to manage BitLocker encryption policies; simplifies deployment and key recovering; centralizes provisioning; and assesses compliance and encryption status across computers in your organization. You can find the tool as part of the Microsoft Desktop Optimization Pack (MDOP). MBAM can be deployed as a stand-alone infrastructure or integrated with Configuration Manager.

To deploy MBAM in your organization, it is important to understand the MBAM architecture and how each component communicates with the other. There are three key components for MBAM: They include the Administration and Monitoring Server, the MBAM Client, and the Policy template. The MBAM Administration and Monitoring Server installed on Windows Server 2016 holds the Administration and Management web services. The website is used to review compliance status, audit BitLocker client activity, and manage hardware capabilities. It can also be used to access the BitLocker recovery keys.

The MBAM Administration and Monitoring Server is designed to use the Recovery and Hardware Database and the Compliance and Audit Database.

1. The Recovery and Hardware Database maintains recovery key data for clients that are managed by BitLocker Administration and Monitoring. It also holds hardware information collected from the MBAM agent running on the client computers.
2. The Compliance and Audit Database holds information used in compliance reporting; you can access the reports from within the MBAM Admin tool or from the SQL Server Reporting Services (SSRS).

The MBAM Client is responsible for collecting the recovery key information for the operating system drive, fixed data drives, and removable USB drives, using Group Policy to enforce BitLocker encryption parameters, and sending recovery, hardware, and compliance information to the appropriate entities.

The Policy template is used to configure the BitLocker Administration and Monitoring client policies used to determine the encryption policy options you want to apply for BitLocker drive encryption. It can be used with the Group Policy Management and Advanced Group Policy Management consoles. You can then monitor the client compliance against the policies and report status at both the enterprise and the individual computer levels.

MBAM includes a Self-Service Portal, which is a website that enables end users on client computers to independently log on to a website to get a recovery key if they lose or forget their BitLocker password.

Implementing BitLocker Recovery Process Using Self-Recovery and Recovery Password Retrieval Solutions

CERTIFICATION READY
Implement BitLocker Recovery Process using self-recovery and recovery password retrieval solutions
Objective 1.1

You can use group policy to configure BitLocker to back up the BitLocker keys and recovery keys to Active Directory. The schema extensions are available starting with Windows Server 2008 and works out of the box on Windows Server 2012 and higher. However, before this can be accomplished, there are several configuration steps that have to be done.

On the domain controller, you must install the BitLocker Drive Encryption feature, including the BitLocker Recovery Password Viewer. The BitLocker Recovery Password Viewer helps locate BitLocker Drive Encryption passwords for Windows-based computers in Active Directory Domain Services.

Next, there are several GPO settings that must be configured before you can use BitLocker Password Recovery. You must enable the Computer Configuration\Policies\Administrative

Templates\Windows Components\Bitlocker Drive Encryption\Store Bitlocker Recovery information in Active Directory Domain Services option and set the following:

1. Require BitLocker backup to AD DS selected.
2. Set BitLocker recovery information to store to Recovery passwords and key packages.

Then under the Fixed Data Drives, Operating System Drives, and Removable Data Drives nodes, enable the Choose how BitLocker-protected fixed drives can be recovered option and set the following:

1. Allow data recovery agent.
2. Save BitLocker recovery information to AD DS for <drive type> drives.
3. Set Configure storage of BitLocker recovery information to AD DS to Backup recovery passwords and key packages.

RECOVER A BITLOCKER-ENCRYPTED OPERATING SYSTEM DRIVE

GET READY. To recover a BitLocker-encrypted operating system drive, perform the following steps on each volume of the cluster:

1. On a domain controller with the BitLocker tools installed, in Server Manager, click **Tools > Active Directory Users and Computers.**
2. In the Active Directory Users and Computers window, navigate to the computer with BitLocker. Then right-click the computer and choose **Properties.**
3. Click the **BitLocker Recovery** tab. You should see an entry for each drive encrypted with BitLocker, as shown in Figure 1-12. Click **OK.**

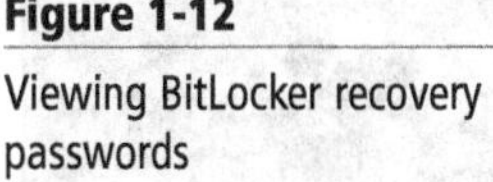

Figure 1-12

Viewing BitLocker recovery passwords

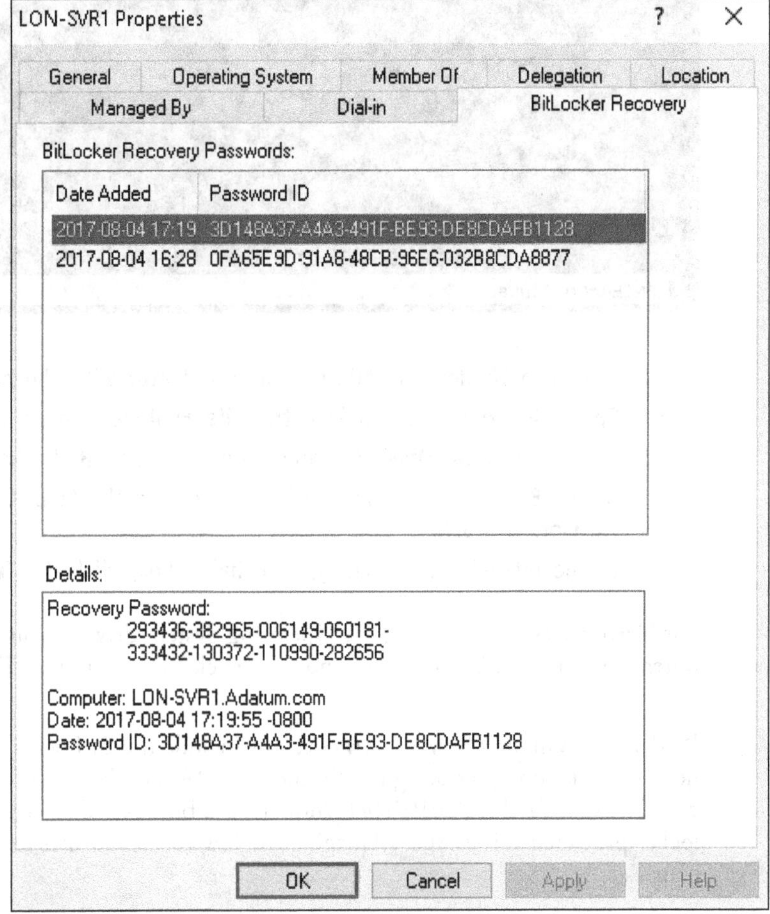

4. On the computer with the BitLocker encrypted drives, right-click the **Start** button, choose **Shut down**, and then click **Restart**.
5. When the computer restarts, on the BitLocker page, in the Enter the password to unlock this drive text box, press **Esc** for BitLocker recovery.
6. In the Enter the recovery key for this drive text box, type the 48-digit recovery password shown on the Active Directory BitLocker Recovery tab and then press **Enter**. To see the characters (see Figure 1-13), press the **Insert** key. If you press the Insert key before typing the numbers, the dashes will be added. You do not type the dashes.

Figure 1-13

Typing the BitLocker recovery password in the BitLocker recovery screen

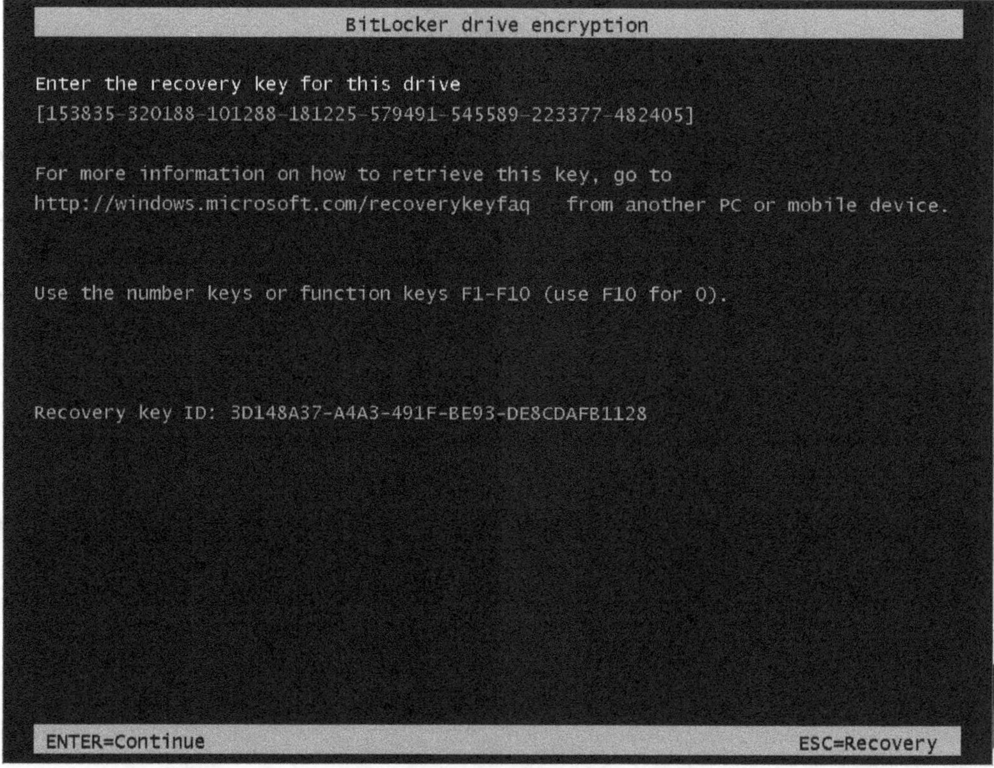

7. Log in to Windows as **Adatum\Administrator** with the password of **Pa$$w0rd**.
8. Open File Explorer by clicking the **File Explorer** tile on the taskbar.
9. Right-click **Local Disk (C:)** and choose **Manage BitLocker**.
10. In the BitLocker Drive Encryption window, in the C: BitLocker on section, click **Turn off BitLocker**.
11. In the BitLocker Drive Encryption dialog box, click the **Turn off BitLocker** button.

For Fixed drives not including the Operating System drive, if you are logged in to the computer, you can click Unlock drive and then click More options > Enter recovery key.

TAKE NOTE*

By default, Windows Server 2016 does not include the BitLocker DRA template. If you need information on creating the BitLocker DRA template, visit http://blogs.technet.com/b/askcore/archive/2010/10/11/how-to-use-bitlocker-data-recovery-agent-to-unlock-bitlocker-protected-drives.aspx. Managing the CA and certificates are discussed in the 70-742 course.

A ***data recovery agent (DRA)*** is a user account that is an administrator who is authorized to recover BitLocker fixed drives for an entire organization with a digital certificate on a smart card. In most cases, administrators of Active Directory Domain Services (AD DS) networks use DRAs to ensure access to their BitLocker-protected systems while avoiding maintaining a large number of individual keys and PINs.

To create a DRA for BitLocker, you must do the following:

1. Add the user account you want to designate to the Computer Configuration\Policies\Windows Settings\Security Settings\Public Key Policies\BitLocker Drive Encryption\Provide the unique identifies for your organization.
2. Enable DRA recovery for each type of BitLocker resource you want to recover:
    - Choose how BitLocker-protected operating system drives can be recovered.
    - Choose how BitLocker-protected fixed drives can be recovered.
    - Choose how BitLocker-protected removable drives can be recovered.

■ Deploying and Configuring EFS

THE BOTTOM LINE

Encrypting File System (EFS) can encrypt files on an NTFS volume that cannot be used unless the user has access to the keys required to decrypt the information. By default, when you encrypt a file with EFS, the file or folder icon has a gold lock to show that the file is encrypted. While BitLocker will encrypt an entire disk or volume, EFS will only encrypt specified files and folders that are on an NTFS disk or volume.

CERTIFICATION READY
Determine usage scenarios for Encrypting File System (EFS)
Objective 1.1

After a file has been encrypted, you do not have to manually decrypt an encrypted file before you can use it. Instead, you work with the file or folder just like any other file that is not encrypted. When you open a file that is encrypted with EFS, the file is automatically decrypted as needed. When you save the file, it is automatically decrypted. However, if another user tries to access the same file, he cannot open it because he does not have the proper key to open the file.

EFS uses an encryption key to encrypt your data, which is stored in a digital certificate. The first time a user encrypts a file or folder, an encryption certificate and key are created and bound to the user account. The user who creates the file is the only person who can read it. As the user works, EFS encrypts the files using a key generated from the user's public key. Data encrypted with this key can be decrypted only by the user's personal encryption certificate, which is generated using a private key.

Encrypting and Decrypting Files with EFS

To encrypt or decrypt a folder or file, enable or disable the encryption attribute just as you set any other attribute, such as read-only, compressed, or hidden. If you encrypt a folder, all files and subfolders created in the encrypted folder are automatically encrypted. The file icon of an EFS encrypted file will show a small gold padlock.

Microsoft recommends that you encrypt at the folder level. You can also encrypt or decrypt a file or folder using the `Cipher` command.

ENCRYPT A FOLDER OR FILE USING EFS

GET READY. To encrypt a folder or file, perform the following steps:

1. Right-click the folder or file you want to encrypt and choose **Properties.** The Properties dialog box opens.
2. On the General tab, click the **Advanced** button. The Advanced Attributes dialog box appears (see Figure 1-14).

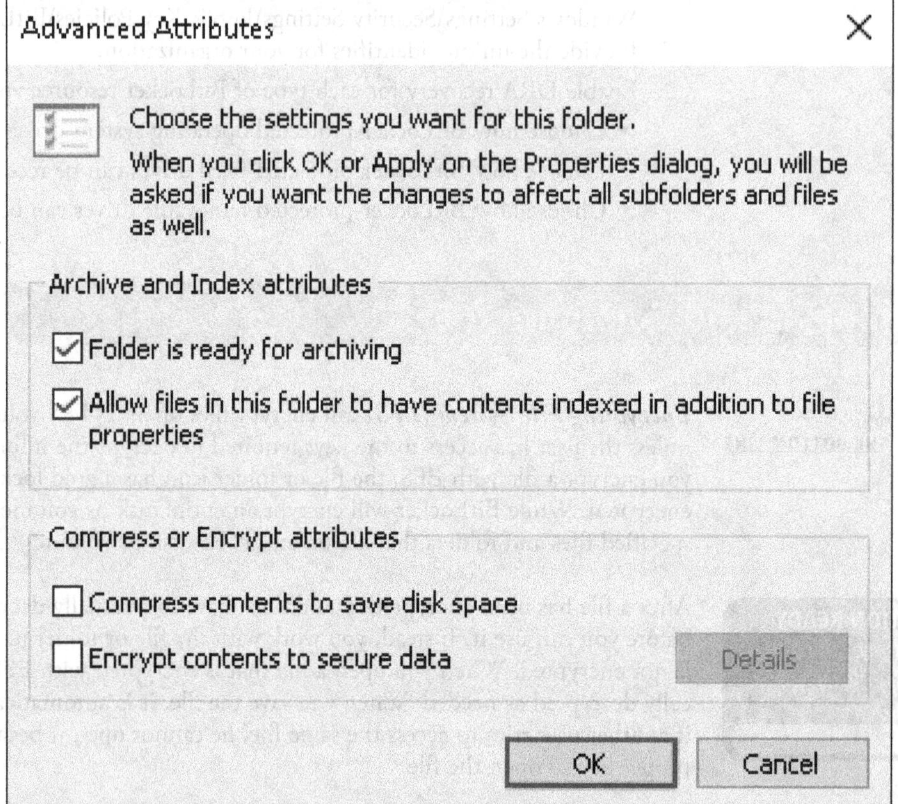

Figure 1-14

The Advanced Attributes dialog box

3. Select the **Encrypt contents to secure data** checkbox and then click **OK.**
4. Click **OK** to close the Properties dialog box.
5. If you encrypt a file in an unencrypted folder, it displays a warning. Select either **Apply changes to this folder only** or **Apply changes to this folder, subfolders and files.** Click **OK.** If you want to encrypt the folder and all content in the folder, select **Encrypt the file and its parent folder (recommended).** Click **OK.**
6. If you encrypt a folder, you are prompted to confirm the changes. If you want to encrypt only the folder, select **Apply changes to this folder only.** If you want to apply to all folders, select the **Apply changes to this folder, subfolders and files** option. Click **OK.**

DECRYPT A FOLDER OR FILE

GET READY. To decrypt a folder or file, perform the following steps:

1. Right-click the folder or file you want to decrypt and choose **Properties.** The Properties dialog box opens.
2. Click the **General** tab and then click **Advanced.** The Advanced Attributes dialog box opens.
3. Clear the **Encrypt contents to secure data** checkbox and then click **OK.**
4. Click **OK** to close the Properties dialog box.
5. You are prompted to confirm the changes. If you want to decrypt only the folders, select **Apply changes to this folder only.** If you want to apply to all folders, select the **Apply changes to this folder, subfolders and files** option. Click **OK.**

When working with EFS, keep the following in mind:

1. You can encrypt or compress NTFS files only, not both. If the user marks a file or folder for encryption, that file or folder is uncompressed.
2. If you encrypt a file, it is automatically decrypted if you copy or move the file to a volume that is not an NTFS volume.
3. Moving unencrypted files into an encrypted folder automatically causes those files to be encrypted in the new folder.
4. Moving an encrypted file from an EFS-encrypted folder does not automatically decrypt files. Instead, you must explicitly decrypt the file.
5. Files marked with the System attribute or that are in the root directory cannot be encrypted.
6. An encrypted folder or file does not protect against the deletion of the file or the listing of files or directories. To prevent deletion or listing of files, use NTFS permissions.
7. Although you can use EFS on remote systems, data that is transmitted over the network is not encrypted. If encryption is needed over the network, use SSL/TLS (Secure Sockets Layer/Transport Layer Security) or IPsec.

The ***cipher.exe*** command displays or alters the encryption of folders and files on NTFS volumes. If you use the `cipher` command without parameters, `cipher` displays the encryption state of the current folder and any files it contains.

The syntax of the `cipher` command includes the following:

```
CIPHER /options [pathname [...]]
```

- /C displays information on the encrypted file.
- /D decrypts the specified files or directories.
- /E encrypts the specified files or directories. Directories are marked so that files added afterward will be encrypted. The encrypted file can become decrypted when it is modified if the parent directory is not encrypted. It is recommended that you encrypt the file and the parent directory.
- /H displays files with the hidden or system attributes. These files are omitted by default.
- /K creates a new certificate and key for use with EFS. If this option is chosen, all the other options are ignored.
- /N works only with /U. This prevents keys from being updated. It is used to find the encrypted files on the local drives.

- /R generates an EFS recovery key and certificate and then writes them to a .PFX file (containing certificate and private key) and a .CER file (containing only the certificate).
- /S performs the specified operation on the given directory and all files and subdirectories in it.
- /U tries to touch all the encrypted files on local drives. This updates the user's file encryption key or recovery keys to the current ones if they are changed. This option does not work with other options except /N.
- /W removes data from available unused disk space on the entire volume. If this option is chosen, all other options are ignored. The directory specified can be anywhere in a local volume. If it is a mount point or points to a directory in another volume, the data on that volume is removed.
- /X backs up the EFS certificate and keys to the specified filename that follows the /X:. If EFS file is provided, the current user's certificate(s) used to encrypt the file is backed up. Otherwise, the user's current EFS certificate and keys are backed up.
- /ADDUSER adds a user to the specified encrypted file(s).
- /REKEY updates the specified encrypted file(s) to use the configured EFS current key.
- /REMOVEUSER /certhash:<Hash> removes a user from the specified file(s). CERTHASH must be the SHA1 hash of the certificate to remove.

For example, to use cipher to encrypt a subfolder named c:\Data\Reports, execute the following command:

```
cipher /e c:\Data\Reports
```

To decrypt the folder, execute the following command:

```
cipher /d c:\Data\Reports
```

Sharing Files Protected with EFS

When EFS was originally created, an EFS file could be accessed by only the user who encrypted the file. In later versions of NTFS, if you need to share an EFS-protected file with other users, you add an encryption certificate to the file.

If the user that you want to add cannot be found because the user does not have an encryption certificate, the user has not encrypted a file with EFS and therefore, he does not have an EFS certificate. However, EFS certificates can be generated with group policies and a Microsoft Certificate Authority (CA).

SHARE A FILE PROTECTED WITH EFS

GET READY. To share a file protected with EFS with others, perform the following steps:

1. Right-click the encrypted file and choose **Properties.**
2. On the General tab, click **Advanced.**
3. Click **Details.** The User Access dialog box opens.
4. In the User Access dialog box (as shown in Figure 1-15), click the **Add** button.
5. Select the user you want to grant access to and then click **OK.**
6. Click **OK** to close the User Access dialog box.

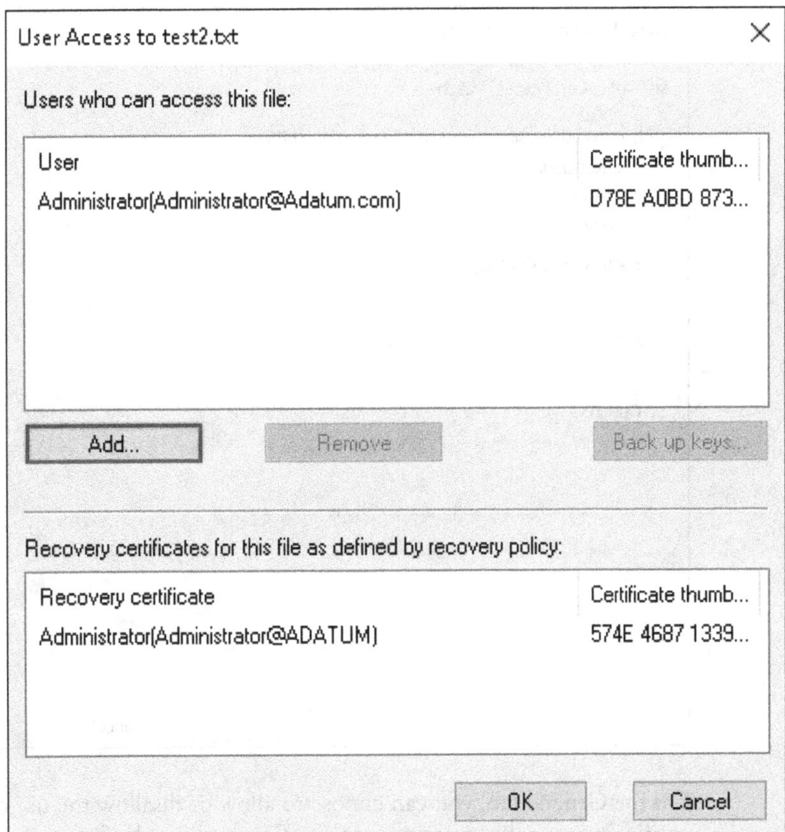

Figure 1-15

Opening the User Access dialog box

7. Click **OK** to close the Advanced Attributes dialog box.
8. Click **OK** to close the Properties dialog box.

Configuring EFS with Group Policy

To help you manage the use of EFS, you can use group policies to meet your organization's security needs. To establish an EFS policy, right-click Computer Configuration\Policies\Windows Settings\Security Settings\Public Key Policies\Encrypting File System and choose Properties. The properties dialog box is shown in Figure 1-16.

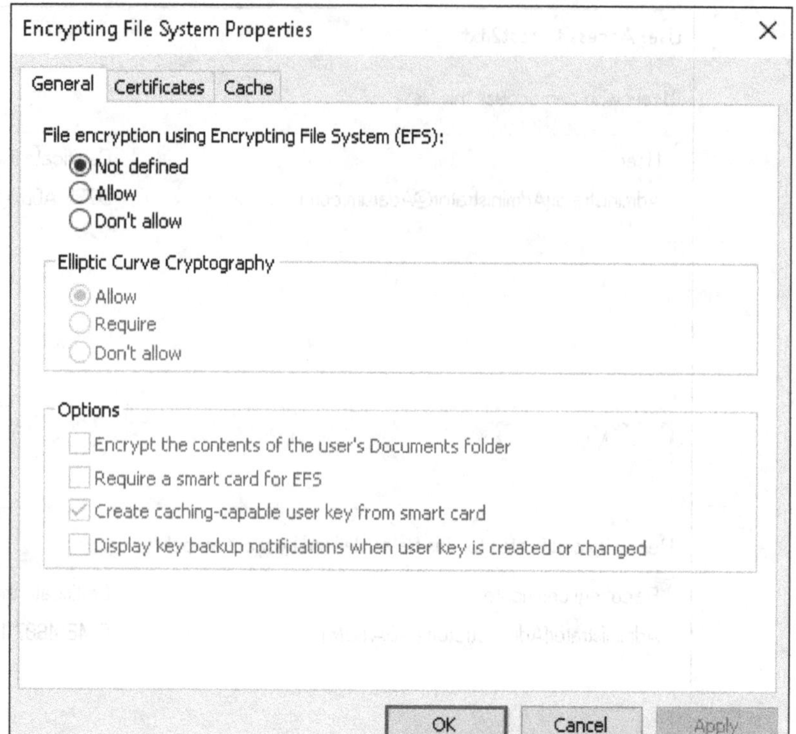

Figure 1-16
Selecting Encrypting File System properties

On the General tab, you can choose to allow or disallow the use of EFS. If you do not configure any policy settings for EFS, EFS is allowed. If you choose to use EFS, you can automatically encrypt a user's Documents folder, require a smart card for use with EFS, or notify users to make backup copies of their encryption keys. In addition, you can require strong encryption and you can use Elliptic Curve Cryptography (ECC) encryption.

On the Certificates tab, you can specify the key size for the certificates and allow EFS to generate self-signed certificates when a CA is not available.

Configuring the EFS Recovery Agent

CERTIFICATION READY
Configure the EFS recovery agent
Objective 1.1

If a user leaves the company or loses the original key and the encrypted files cannot be read, you can set up a data recovery agent that can recover EFS encrypted files for a domain.

To define DRAs, you can use Active Directory group policies to configure one or more user accounts as DRAs for your entire organization. However, to accomplish this, you need to have an enterprise CA.

ADD RECOVERY AGENTS FOR EFS

GET READY. To add new users as recovery agents, assign the EFS recovery certificates issued by the enterprise CA to the user account and then perform the following steps:

1. Log in as the DRA account.
2. Open the **Group Policy Management** console.
3. Expand **Forest**, **Domains**, and then the **name of your domain.**
4. Right-click the **Default Domain Policy** and choose **Edit.**
5. Expand **Computer Configuration\Policies\Windows Settings\Security Settings\Public Key Policies\.**

6. Right-click **Encrypting File System** and choose **Create Data Recovery Agent.**
7. Click **Encrypting File System** and notice the certificates that are displayed (see Figure 1-17).

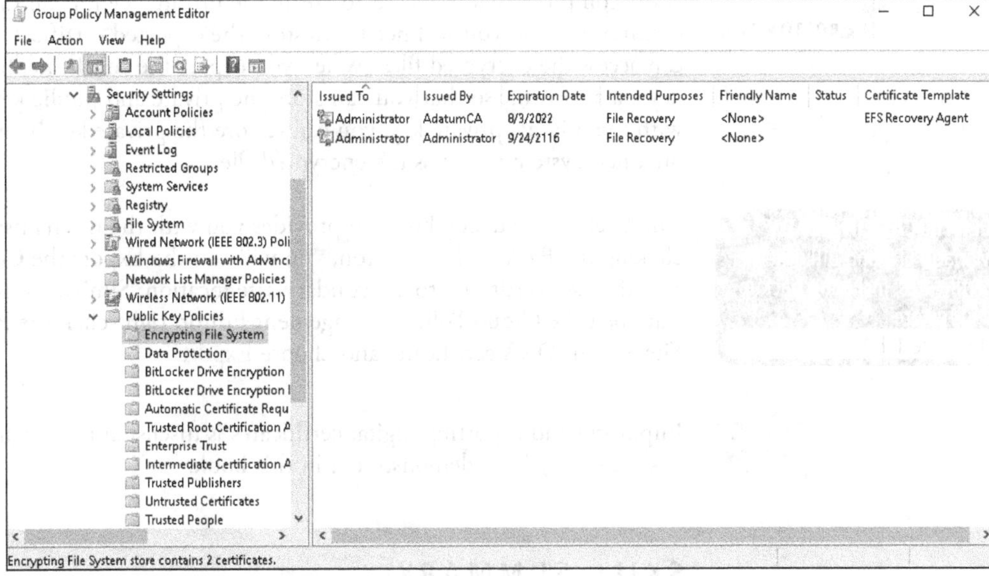

Figure 1-17
Viewing the Encrypting File System certificates

8. Close the **Group Policy Management Editor.**
9. Close **Group Policy Management** console.

After the DRAs are defined in a GPO, when you encrypt a file with EFS, the recovery certificate will be listed in the Recovery certificates for this file as defined by recovery policy, as shown in Figure 1-18.

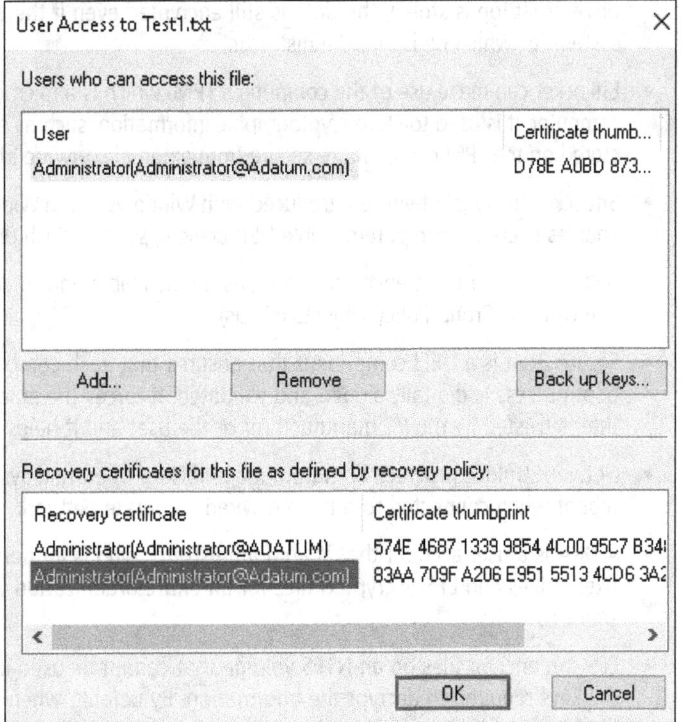

Figure 1-18
Viewing the Recovery certificate in an EFS encrypted file

Managing EFS and BitLocker Certificates

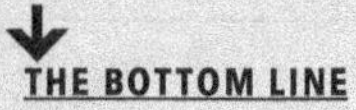

THE BOTTOM LINE

If the computer that was used to create the private key for the EFS encryption or recovery certificate is lost, you will need to restore the exported certificate from backup before you can access the encrypted files. When you export the certificate, be sure to export the private key via a PFX file so that you can store the private and public key. If you lose the computer with the original private key, you can restore the private key by importing the private key on a new system to access the encrypted file.

CERTIFICATION READY
Manage EFS and BitLocker certificates, including backup and restore
Objective 1.1

The User Access dialog box also provides you with the mechanism to back up EFS keys. By clicking the Back up keys button, you will run the Export the Certificate Export Wizard to save the user certificate to a secondary safe location. Similar to user EFS user certificates, you can open the Group Policy Management Editor, right-click the Public Key Policies\Encrypted File System DRA certificate, and choose Export.

TAKE NOTE*

Importing and exporting digital certificates is discussed thoroughly in the 70-742 book and has previously been demonstrated in this book.

SKILL SUMMARY

IN THIS LESSON YOU LEARNED:

- Encryption is the process of converting data into a format that cannot be read by another user. Once a user has encrypted a file, it automatically remains encrypted when the file is stored on disk. Decryption is the process of converting data from encrypted format back to its original format.
- BitLocker Drive Encryption (BDE) allows you to encrypt the entire volume. Therefore, if a drive or laptop is stolen, the data is still encrypted even if the thief installs it in another system for which he is an administrator.
- BitLocker can make use of the computer's TPM, which is a microchip that is built into a computer. It is used to store cryptographic information, such as encryption keys. Information stored on the TPM can be more secure from external software attacks and physical theft.
- BitLocker To Go is a feature introduced with Windows 7 and Windows Server 2008 R2 that enables users to encrypt removable USB devices, such as flash drives and external hard disks.
- To control what drive encryption options are available and to configure BitLocker settings, you can use Group Policy Objects (GPOs).
- Secure Boot is a UEFI component that ensures that each component is loaded during the boot process is digitally signed and validated. It forces the machine to boot only software that is trusted by the PC manufacturer or the user and it helps prevent malware.
- Network Unlock provides an automatic unlock of operating system volumes at system reboot when connected to a trusted wired corporate network.
- A DRA is a user account that is an administrator who is authorized to recover BitLocker fixed drives and EFS encrypted files for an entire organization with a digital certificate on a smart card.
- EFS can encrypt files on an NTFS volume that cannot be used unless the user has access to the keys required to decrypt the information. By default, when you encrypt a file with EFS, the file or folder icon has a gold lock to show that the file is encrypted. While BitLocker will encrypt an entire disk or volume, EFS will only encrypt specified files and folders that are on an NTFS disk or volume.

Knowledge Assessment

Multiple Choice

Select the correct answer for each of the following questions.

1. Which encryption technology protects individual files on a computer running Windows Server 2016?
   a. EFS
   b. BitLocker
   c. IPSec
   d. SSL
2. When using EFS, the encryption key is stored in which of the following?
   a. Text file
   b. Passkey
   c. Digital certificate
   d. Token
3. Which of the following statements best describes what occurs when you move an EFS encrypted file to a FAT32 volume?
   a. It remains encrypted.
   b. It is re-encrypted.
   c. It is decrypted.
   d. You have the option to decrypt or encrypt.
4. Which encryption algorithm uses a single key to encrypt and decrypt data?
   a. Symmetric
   b. Asymmetric
   c. Hash function
   d. Antimetric
5. How are DRAs defined?
   a. By using the Registry
   b. By using Active Directory Users and Computers
   c. By using GPOs
   d. By using Active Directory Sites and Services
6. Which of the following statements best describes how to decrypt an EFS-encrypted file for a user who has left an organization?
   a. By creating the master certificate to encrypt the certificate, and then decrypt the certificate
   b. By using a USB with the username and username password in a text file
   c. By removing the computer with the files from the domain
   d. By using a DRA

7. If you don't have a TPM on your computer, what can be used to store the key to use BitLocker?
   a. A text file on a CD or DVD
   b. A second hard drive
   c. The BIOS Setup program
   d. USB memory device
8. Which Windows technology is used to encrypt a USB disk device?
   a. BitLocker
   b. BitLocker To Go
   c. EFS
   d. SSL
9. Which command encrypts a folder with EFS?
   a. The EFS command.
   b. The Cipher command.
   c. The Encrypt command
   d. The EFSConfig command
10. How do you configure Windows to automatically encrypt a user's Documents folder?
   a. By using the Control Panel
   b. By using the Cipher command
   c. By using the group policies
   d. By using the Security tab in Windows Explorer
11. Which of the following ensures that each component loaded during the boot process is digitally signed and validated?
   a. Secure Boot
   b. Host Guarding Service
   c. Network Unlock
   d. data recovery agent.

Best Answer

Choose the letter that corresponds to the best answer. More than one answer choice may achieve the goal. Select the BEST answer.

1. Which of the following should be used to protect a drive and all its files if it is stolen?
   - **a.** EFS
   - **b.** BitLocker
   - **c.** IPSec
   - **d.** SSL
2. How can you control the key size used in BitLocker?
   - **a.** By using the cipher command
   - **b.** By using a GPO
   - **c.** By using a certificate
   - **d.** By using a DRA
3. To automatically unlock a drive protected by BitLocker, which of the following servers would the client get a key from?
   - **a.** WDS server
   - **b.** DHCP server
   - **c.** BitLocker Web server
   - **d.** Any server with a BitLocker encrypted drive
4. Which of the following occurs when you have an EFS encrypted file and you copy the file to a folder that is not encrypted and on an NTFS volume?
   - **a.** The file automatically becomes decrypted.
   - **b.** The file remains encrypted.
   - **c.** The file remains encrypted if it is locked.
   - **d.** The file becomes decrypted if it has the System attribute turned on.
5. Which server is the BitLocker Network Unlock feature installed on?
   - **a.** WDS Server
   - **b.** DHCP server
   - **c.** BitLocker Web server
   - **d.** DNS Server

Matching and Identification

1. Identify the requirements to use Network Unlock.

_____ You need a DHCP Server, separate from WDS and DC.

_____ The BitLocker Network Unlock feature must be installed.

_____ You must have a DNS Server with Unlock Service resource record.

_____ You must have Network Unlock certificates.

_____ You must have a Windows Server 2016 WDS role.

_____ You must have a Windows 10 Network Unlock Agent.

Build List

List the correct order of steps necessary to protect a drive with BitLocker. (Not all steps will be used)

_____ Save the recovery key to a USB device.

_____ Click System and Security.

_____ Click Turn on BitLocker.

_____ Click Encryption.

_____ Specify a password.

_____ Open Control Panel.

_____ Encrypt the drive.

_____ Test the drive.

_____ Click BitLocker Drive Encryption.

■ Business Case Scenarios

Scenario 1-1: Protecting a Laptop

You have just purchased 75 new laptops that will be given to the sales team and 50 new laptops that will be given to the engineering team. Last year, a user from the marketing department lost a laptop with proprietary information and this information was leaked to competitors via the Internet. Describe how you can ensure that if this happens again, the information will remain protected?

Scenario 1-2: Accessing EFS Encrypted Files

A user encrypts several of his data files with EFS. When his manager tries to open the files, he cannot read the files because the manager does not have the correct key. Describe how to unlock these files.

Implementing Server Patching and Updating Solutions

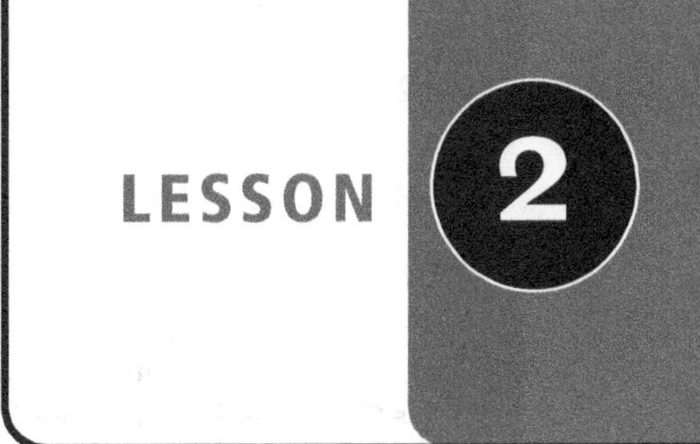

70-744 EXAM OBJECTIVE

This content of this lesson does not correlate to a 70-744 exam objective. It is provided as supplementary information that covers material that is beneficial to administering Windows Server 2016 systems, particularly as it relates to ensuring systems are updated and secure. The following concepts are *not* covered on the exam.

LESSON HEADING	EXAM OBJECTIVE
Managing Updates Using WSUS • Configuring Update Settings • Managing Windows Update Settings with Group Policy	(None)
Implementing Windows Server Update Services (WSUS) Solutions • Installing and Configuring WSUS • Understanding the WSUS Infrastructure • Configuring Automatic Updates • Creating WSUS Computer Groups • Configuring Update Approvals and Deployments • Configuring WSUS Reporting • Administrating WSUS with Commands • Troubleshooting Problems with Installing Updates	(None)

KEY TERMS

autonomous (distribution) mode
client-side targeting
critical update
cumulative patch
downstream server
hotfix
out-of-band patches
Patch Tuesday
replica mode
security update
server-side targeting
service pack
synchronization
upstream server
Windows Server Update Services (WSUS)
Windows Update

■ Managing Updates Using WSUS

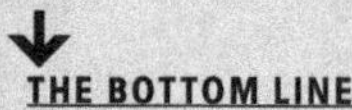

Intruders and some viruses, worms, rootkits, spyware, and adware gain access to a system by exploiting security holes in Windows, Internet Explorer, Microsoft Office, or other software applications. Therefore, the first step you should take to protect yourself against malware is to keep your system up to date with the latest service packs, security patches, and other critical fixes.

Microsoft routinely releases security updates on the second Tuesday of each month, commonly known as ***Patch Tuesday***. Although most updates are released on Patch Tuesday, there might be occasional patches (known as ***out-of-band patches***) released at other times when the patches are deemed critical or time-sensitive.

Because computers are often used as production systems, you should test any updates to make sure they do not cause problems for you. Although Microsoft performs intensive testing, occasionally problems do occur, either as a bug or as a compatibility issue with third-party software. Therefore, always be sure you have a good backup of your system and data files before you install patches so that you have a back-out plan, if necessary.

Microsoft classifies updates as Important, Recommended, or Optional:

- **Important updates:** These updates offer significant benefits, such as improved security, privacy, and reliability. They should be installed as they become available and can be installed automatically with Windows Update.
- **Recommended updates:** These updates address noncritical problems or help enhance your computing experience. Although these updates do not address fundamental issues with your computer or Windows software, they can offer meaningful improvements.
- **Optional updates:** These include updates, drivers, or new software from Microsoft to enhance your computing experience. You need to install these manually.

Depending on the type of update, Windows Update can deliver the following:

- **Security updates:** A ***security update*** is a broadly released fix for a product-specific, security-related vulnerability. Security vulnerabilities are rated based on their severity, which is indicated in the Microsoft security bulletin as critical, important, moderate, or low.
- **Critical updates:** A ***critical update*** is a broadly released fix for a specific problem addressing a critical, non-security-related bug.
- **Service packs:** A ***service pack*** is a tested, cumulative set of hotfixes, security updates, critical updates, and updates, as well as additional fixes for problems found internally since the release of the product. Service packs might also contain a limited number of customer-requested design changes or features. After an operating system is released, many corporations consider the first service pack as the time when the operating system has matured enough to be used throughout the organization. Typically by installing a cumulative patch will update the build number of the operating system or application.
- **Cumulative patch:** A cumulative patch combines multiple patches and hotfixes into a single package. Some cumulative patches will contain changes to design and features. Typically, installing a cumulative patch will update the build number of the operating system or application. Newer operating systems and applications use cumulative patches instead of service packs.

Not all updates can be retrieved through Windows Update. Sometimes, Microsoft might offer the fix for a specific problem in the form of a hotfix or cumulative patch that you can install. A ***hotfix*** is a single package that includes one or more files that are used to address a problem in a software product, such as a software bug. Typically, hotfixes are made to address a specific customer situation, and they often have not gone through the same extensive testing as patches retrieved through Windows Update.

Configuring Update Settings

Windows Update provides your Windows 10 and Windows Server 2016 users with a way to keep their computers current by checking a designated server. The server provides software that patches security issues, installs updates that make Windows and your applications more stable, fixes issues with existing Windows programs, and provides new features. The server can be hosted by Microsoft or it can be set up and managed in your organization by running the Windows Server Update Services (WSUS) or System Center 2016 Configuration Manager.

When you first perform a clean install of Windows Server 2016, you can choose how you want Windows Update to function. On a Windows Server 2016 computer, open Settings and click Update & security to open the Windows Update page (see Figure 2-1).

Figure 2-1

The Windows Update page

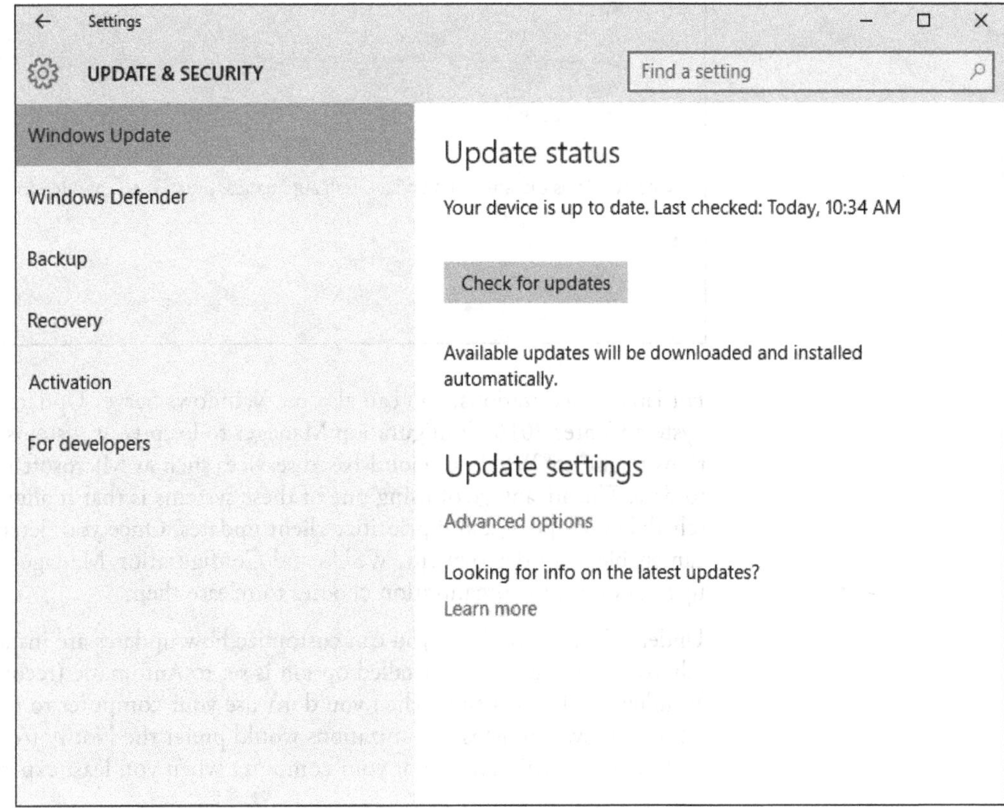

By clicking Advanced options, you can configure for Automatic Updates, give updates for other Microsoft products when Windows is updated, defer upgrades, and view update history (as shown in Figure 2-2).

Figure 2-2

The Windows Update Advanced Options page

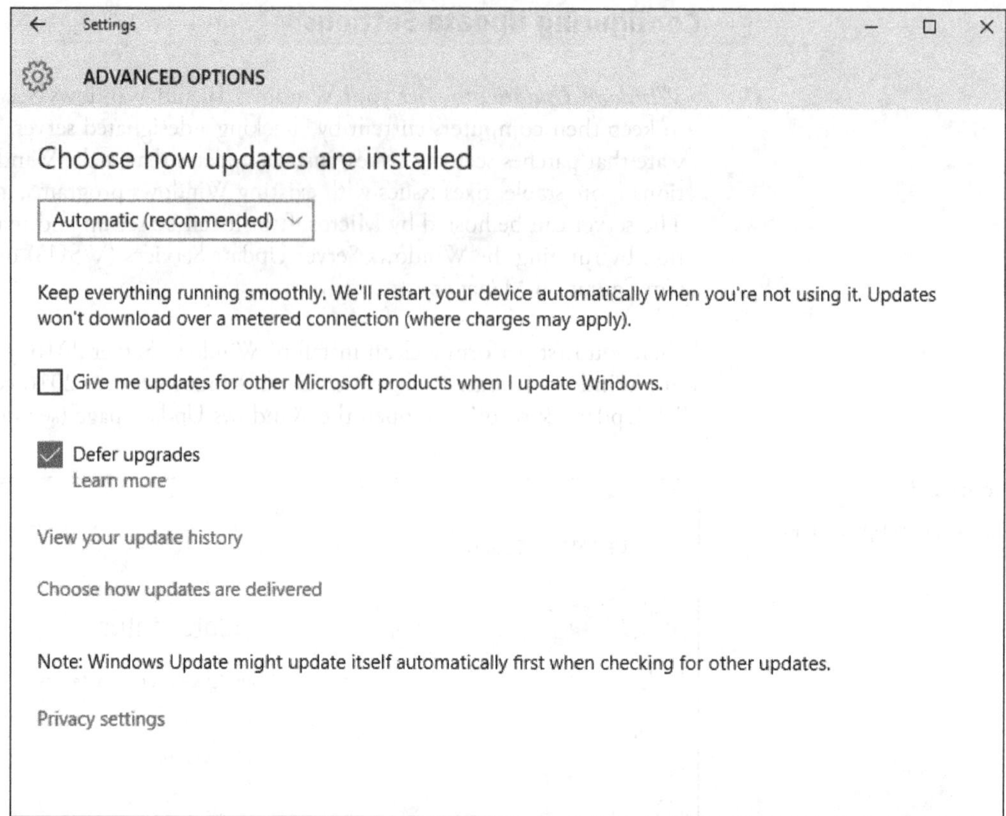

For larger organizations, you can also use Windows Server Update Services (WSUS) or System Center 2016 Configuration Manager to keep your systems updated. Smaller organizations might use WSUS or cloud-based services such as Microsoft Intune to keep systems up to date. The advantage of using one of these systems is that it allows you to test the patch, schedule the updates, and prioritize client updates. Once you determine a patch is safe, you can enable it for deployment. WSUS and Configuration Manager allow you to defer new upgrades until the organization chooses to release them.

Under Advanced options, you can customize how updates are installed. By default, the Choose how updates are installed option is set to Automatic (recommended), which means Windows will pick a time when you don't use your computer to install the updates and reboot the system. Most organizations would prefer the Notify to schedule restart option so that Windows will not reboot your computer when you least expect it.

Windows Server 2016 lets you defer upgrades to your PC. By selecting the Defer upgrades option, new Windows features won't be downloaded or installed for several months. This option is typically used to help avoid problems with an update that might cause problems within your organization.

WARNING! Deferring upgrades does not affect security updates, but it does prevent you from getting the latest Windows features as soon as they are available.

If Windows Update fails to retrieve any updates, you should check your proxy settings in Internet Explorer to see whether the program can get through your proxy server (if any) or firewall. You should also make sure you can access the Internet, such as by going to the Microsoft website.

You can view your update history by opening the Advanced Options and selecting View your update history. On the Update History page, each update, including the KB article number, the version, and the date installed, is shown. If you click *Successfully installed on <date>* for a specific update, it will give a brief description of the update.

At the top of the View Your Update History page, you can click *Uninstall updates* to open the Installed Updates page, as shown in Figure 2-3. To uninstall or roll back an update, right-click the desired update and choose Uninstall. You are then prompted to uninstall the update. When you click Yes, the update will be uninstalled.

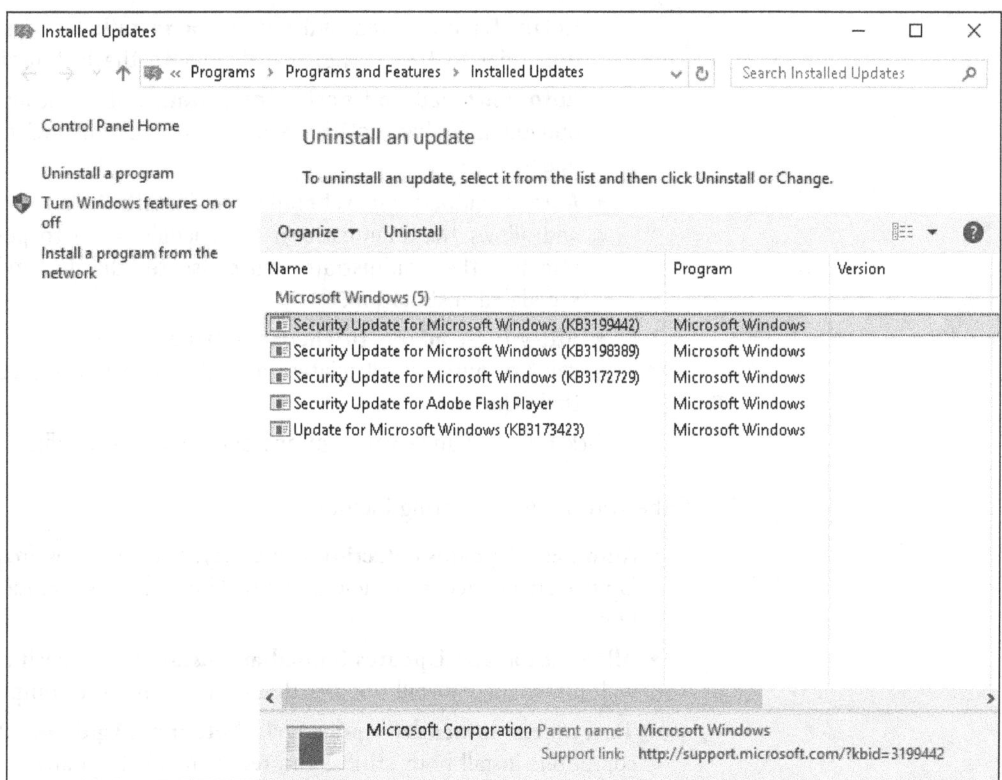

Figure 2-3

The Control Panel Installed Updates page

Managing Windows Update Settings with Group Policy

Group Policy can automatically configure Windows Update settings so that you have better control of when the system gets updates and when a reboot is performed after updates are installed. These same settings can also be used with other Windows Update platforms, such as WSUS and System Center 2016 Configuration Manager.

As with most Windows components, you can also use group policies to automatically configure how Automatic Updates behaves. For example, you can configure for updates to be automatically downloaded and installed or you can configure the user to be notified when updates are available.

CONFIGURE AUTOMATIC UPDATES USING GROUP POLICIES

GET READY. To configure Automatic Updates using group policies, perform the following steps on a domain controller or any computer that has the Group Policy Management Console installed.

1. Open Server Manager.
2. Click **Tools > Group Policy Management.**

3. Using the Group Policy Management Console, open the Group Policy Object Editor for a group policy.
4. In the Group Policy Object Editor, expand **Computer Configuration > Policies > Administrative Templates > Windows Components > Windows Update.**
5. In the details pane, double-click **Configure Automatic Updates.** The Configure Automatic Updates page appears.
6. Click **Enabled** and then select one of the following options:
   - **Notify for download and notify for install:** Notifies a logged-on administrative user prior to the download and prior to the installation of the updates.
   - **Auto download and notify for install:** Automatically begins downloading updates and then notifies a logged-on administrative user prior to installing the updates.
   - **Auto download and schedule the install:** Automatically downloads the updates and allows the administrator to schedule when to perform the installation. If selected, the administrator must also set the day and time for the recurring scheduled installation.
   - **Allow local admin to choose setting:** Specifies that local administrators who can use Automatic Updates in Control Panel to select a configuration option of their choice.
7. Click **OK** to change your options and close the Configure Automatic Updates page.

Other settings worth noting include:

- **Automatic Updates detection frequency**: Specifies how frequently the Windows Update client checks for new updates. The default is a random time between 17 and 22 hours.
- **Allow Automatic Updates immediate installation**: Specifies whether Windows Update will immediately install updates that don't require the computer to be restarted.
- **Turn on recommended updates via Automatic Updates**: Determines whether client computers install both critical and recommended updates.
- **No auto-restart with logged on users for scheduled automatic updates installations**: Specifies that if a computer needs a restart, it will wait for a user to perform the restart.
- **Re-prompt for restart with scheduled installations**: Specifies how often the Windows Update client prompts the user to restart the computer.
- **Delay Restart for scheduled installations**: Specifies how long the Windows Update client waits before automatically restarting.
- **Reschedule Automatic Updates scheduled installations:** Specifies how long Windows Update waits after a reboot before continuing with a scheduled installation that was missed previously.
- **Enable client-side targeting**: Specifies which group the computer is a member of.
- **Enabling Windows Update Power Management to automatically wake up the system to install scheduled updates**: If a computer supports Wake On LAN, automatically starts up and installs an update at the scheduled time.
- **Allow signed updates from an intranet Microsoft update service location**: Specifies whether Windows will install an update that is signed even if the certificate is not from Microsoft.

Implementing Windows Server Update Services (WSUS) Solutions

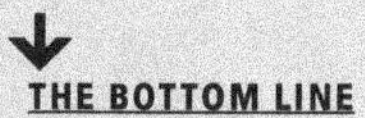

WSUS provides a centralized server that can be used to manage the deployment of updates from Microsoft. Instead of having each of your Windows computers connect to Microsoft to check for updates, consider using ***Windows Server Update Services (WSUS)***. WSUS enables you to centrally manage the deployment of updates released through Microsoft, track compliance, and provide basic reporting functions.

The main components of WSUS are:

- **Windows Server Update Services (WSUS):** This is installed on a Windows server behind your perimeter firewall. This service enables you to manage and distribute updates to WSUS clients. It can also update sources for other WSUS servers.
- **Microsoft Update:** This is the Microsoft website WSUS connects to for updates.
- **Update Services console:** This is the console that can be accessed to manage WSUS.

Setting up WSUS involves the following:

1. Determining a deployment strategy
2. Installing the WSUS server role
3. Specifying an update source for the WSUS server
4. Synchronizing updates to the WSUS server
5. Setting up client computers
6. Approving and installing updates on the client computers

Installing and Configuring WSUS

Determining the appropriate deployment strategy for WSUS ensures that you have the correct servers installed in the appropriate locations based on how your organization is geographically dispersed. It also helps you recognize when and where to place WSUS to reduce needless traffic across your WAN links.

You can deploy a single WSUS server to connect to the Microsoft Update servers and download updates. Figure 2-4 shows an example of a single WSUS deployment in which the clients are connecting to a single server running WSUS. The server connects and downloads updates directly from the Microsoft Update servers. The process of connecting and downloading updates is called ***synchronization***. Although a single server option works well in a small office environment, it does not scale very well for companies that have their employees located across branch offices.

In situations where you need to service many clients or where your computers are dispersed geographically, you should consider implementing more than one WSUS server. The additional WSUS servers can be configured to obtain their updates from the first WSUS server or they can get them directly from the Microsoft Update servers.

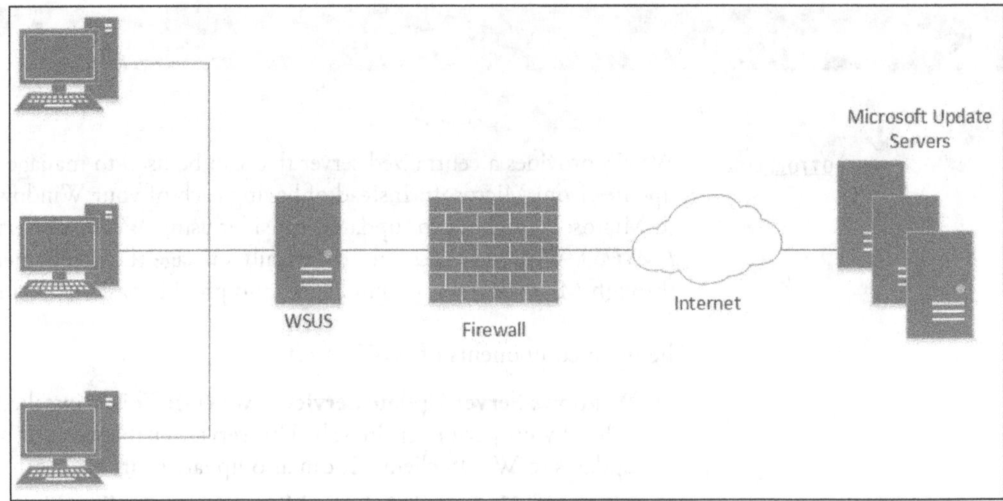

Figure 2-4
Deploying a single WSUS server

When multiple servers are used, the server that obtains updates from Microsoft is called the ***upstream server***. The server(s) that obtain their updates from the upstream server are called ***downstream servers***. If multiple WSUS servers are used, you need to make sure the server-to-server and server-to-client communications use the Secure Sockets Layer (SSL).

Figure 2-5 shows how you might configure multiple WSUS servers when you have a branch office. In this example, the WSUS server at the branch office functions as the downstream server obtaining its updates from the WSUS server (upstream) at the main office either over a VPN or over an intranet connection. The WSUS server at the main office will download the updates from the Microsoft Update servers and distribute them to the downstream WSUS servers. Both the main office and branch office servers can then make the updates available to their clients on their own local network. This utilizes bandwidth more efficiently. In general, Microsoft recommends that you do not create a hierarchy that is more than three levels deep due to propagation issues.

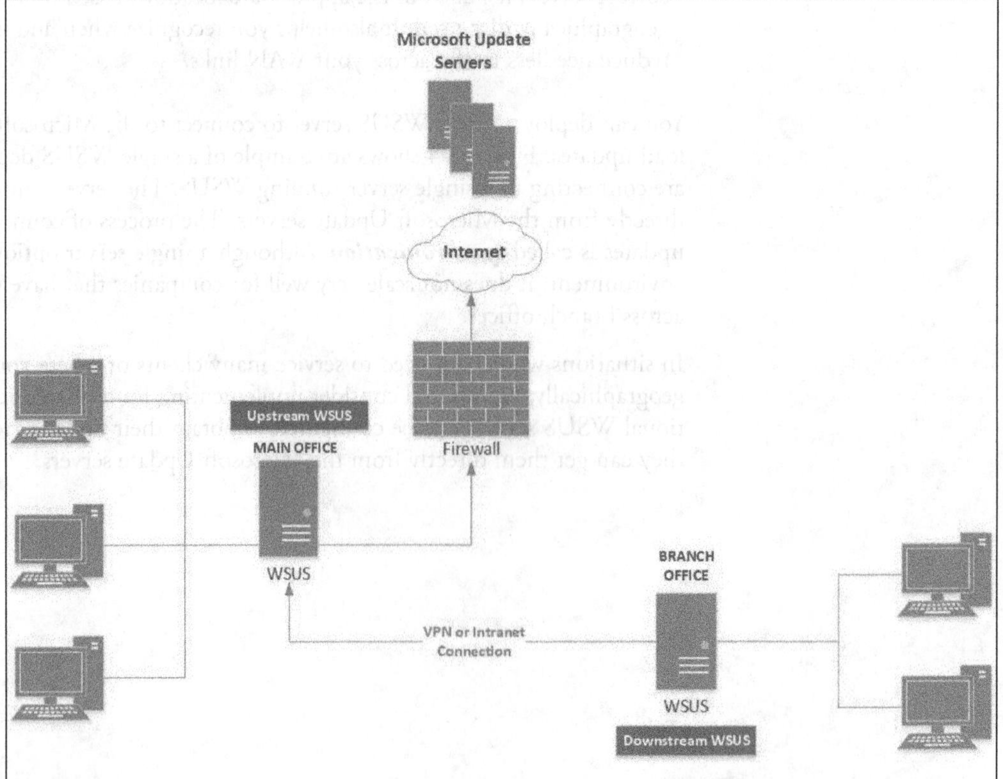

Figure 2-5
Implementing multiple WSUS servers

WSUS uses port 8530 for the HTTP protocol and port 8531 for HTTPS to obtain updates from the Microsoft Update servers. In order to communicate with the Microsoft Update servers, make sure you do not block them at your perimeter firewall.

INSTALL AN UPSTREAM WSUS SERVER

GET READY. To install an upstream WSUS server on a computer running Windows Server 2016, log on with administrative privileges and then perform the following steps.

1. Open Server Manager. Click **Manage > Add Roles and Features** and then click **Next.**
2. Select **Role-based or Feature-based installation** and then click **Next.**
3. On the Select Destination Server page, make sure your domain controller is highlighted and then click **Next.**
4. On the Select Server Roles page, click **Windows Server Update Services.**
5. When you are prompted to install additional features required for WSUS, click **Add Features** and then click **Next.**
6. Click **Next** to continue.
7. On the Select Features page, click **Next** to continue.
8. Read the information about WSUS and then click **Next.**
9. Under Role services, confirm **WID Database** and **WSUS Services** are checked and then click **Next.** The SQL Server Connectivity option is used for the WID database to be hosted on a dedicated SQL server.
10. On the Content Location Selection page, make sure **Store updates in the following location** is checked, type **C:\WSUSupdates**, and then click **Next.**

    This drive location, which must have at least 6 GB of free disk space, can be used to store updates for client computers to download quickly.
11. Read the information about the Web Server Role (IIS) and then click **Next.**
12. On the Select Role Services page, click **Next** to accept the defaults.
13. Click **Install.**
14. On the Installation Progress page, click **Close** and then wait for the installation to complete.
15. In the Server Manager console, click the **yellow triangle** and then click **Launch Post-Installation tasks.**

    When you see the message *Configuration completed for Windows Server Update Services at <servername>*, you can continue to the next step.
16. Click **Tools > Windows Server Update Services.** In the Windows Server Update Services Configuration Wizard, click **Next.**

    You might need to minimize Server Manager to see the Windows Server Update Services Configuration Wizard.
17. On the Join the Microsoft Update Improvement Program page, deselect the option **Yes, I would like to join the Microsoft Update Improvement Program** and then click **Next.**
18. On the Choose Upstream Server page, click **Next** to choose to synchronize this server with Microsoft Update.
19. On the Specify Proxy Server page, click **Next.**
20. On the Connect to Upstream Server page, click **Start Connecting.**
21. After the server connects, click **Next** to proceed.

22. Click **Download updates only in these languages** and then choose **English**. Click **Next**.
23. Scroll down and deselect **Office**. Continue to scroll until you see *Windows*. Deselect everything except **Windows 10**, **Windows Server 2016**, and **Windows Defender**. Click **Next** to continue.

    This reduces the space and time needed to download updates. If this were a real production server, you would download the application and operating system updates to match your needs.
24. On the Choose Classifications page, Critical Updates, Definition Updates, Security updates, and Upgrades are already selected. Select **Service Packs** and click **Next**.
25. On the Set Sync Schedule page, click **Next** to accept the default setting.
26. Click **Begin initial synchronization** and then click **Next**.
27. Click **Finish**.

    Your system synchronizes with the Microsoft Update servers in the background.
28. On the Update Services page, you can expand your server name and then click **Synchronizations** to view the progress (see Figure 2-6).

Figure 2-6

Monitoring the progress of the WSUS synchronization

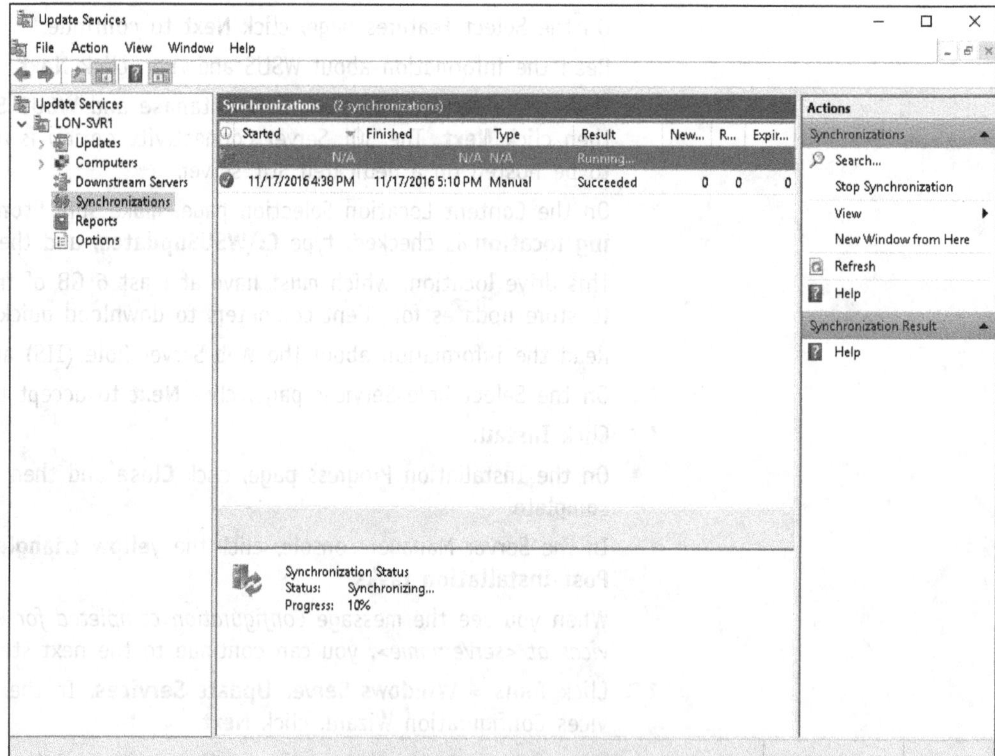

Now that you have your upstream server configured, you can set up a downstream WSUS server on another computer in your domain. In the following exercise, you use a non–domain controller (for example, the member server).

INSTALL A DOWNSTREAM WSUS SERVER

GET READY. To install a downstream WSUS server on a Windows member server, log on with administrative privileges and perform the following steps.

1. Click **Manage > Add Roles and Features** and then click **Next**.
2. Click **Role-based or Feature-based installation** and then click **Next**.

3. On the Select Destination Server page, make sure your member server is highlighted and then click **Next.**
4. On the Select Server Roles page, select **Windows Server Update Services.**
5. When you are prompted to install additional features required for WSUS, click **Add Features** and then click **Next.**
6. Click **Next** to continue.
7. On the Select Features page, click **Next** to continue.
8. Read information about WSUS and then click **Next.**
9. Under Role services, confirm **WID Database** and **WSUS Services** are checked and then click **Next.**
10. On the Content Location Selection page, make sure **Store updates in the following location** is checked, type **c:\WSUSupdates**, and then click **Next.**

    This drive location, which must have at least 6 GB of free disk space, can be used to store updates for client computers to download quickly.
11. Read the information about the Web Server Role (IIS) and then click **Next.**
12. On the Select Role Services page, click **Next** to accept the defaults.
13. Click **Install.**
14. On the Installation Progress page, click **Close** and then wait for the installation to complete.
15. In the Server Manager console, click the **yellow triangle** and then click **Launch Post-Installation tasks.** When you see the message *Configuration completed for Windows Server Update Services at <servername>*, you can continue to the next step.
16. Click **Tools > Windows Server Update Services.** In the Windows Server Update Services Configuration Wizard, click **Next.**

    You might need to minimize the Server Manager to see the Windows Server Update Services Configuration Wizard.
17. On the Choose Upstream Server page, click **Synchronize from another Windows Server Update Services server.** In the Server name field, type the name of the server that you configured in the previous exercise and then click **Next.**
18. On the Specify Proxy Server page, click **Next.**
19. On the Connect to Upstream Server page, click **Start Connecting.** This might take a few minutes.
20. After the server connects, click **Next** to proceed.
21. On the Choose Languages page, to accept the default settings of Download updates only in these languages and English, click **Next.**
22. On the Choose Products page, click **Next.**
23. On the Set Sync Schedule page, click **Next** to accept the default setting.
24. Select **Begin initial synchronization** and then click **Next.**
25. Click **Finish.** Your system synchronizes with the upstream server in the background.
26. On the Update Services page, you can expand your server name and then click **Synchronizations** to view the progress.

When the downstream WSUS server synchronizes with the upstream WSUS server, it downloads updates in the form of metadata and files. The update metadata can be found in the WSUS database. The update files are stored on either the WSUS server or on the Microsoft Update servers. The location is determined when you set up WSUS. In the earlier examples, we configured the WSUS server to store the updates in the *c:\WSUSUpdates* folder.

If the server is a downstream server, the products (Office, Developer Tools, Exchange, Skype, System Center, Windows, and so on) and classifications (critical updates, definition updates, drivers, security updates, and so on) included with the synchronization are set up on the upstream server.

The first time the downstream server synchronizes, it downloads all of the updates you specified. After the first synchronization has completed, the server downloads only updates made since the last synchronization.

Now that you have installed an upstream and a downstream WSUS server, you might wonder which components are installed with WSUS:

- **.NET Framework 4.5:** A software framework that provides core support for running ASP.NET 4.5 stand-alone applications and applications that are integrated with IIS.
- **Remote Server Administration Tools:** A set of tools that includes snap-ins and command-line tools for remotely managing roles and features.
- **Web Server (IIS):** An ASP.NET web service application that requires IIS to deliver access to the services it provides.
- **Windows Internal Database (WID) used by WSUS:** A relational data store used only by Windows roles and features.
- **Windows Process Activation Service:** A software component that generalizes the IIS process model and removes the dependency on HTTP.

After completing the installation, you can access the Update Services console. In Server Manager, choose Tools > Windows Server Update Services. Figure 2-7 shows the Options node.

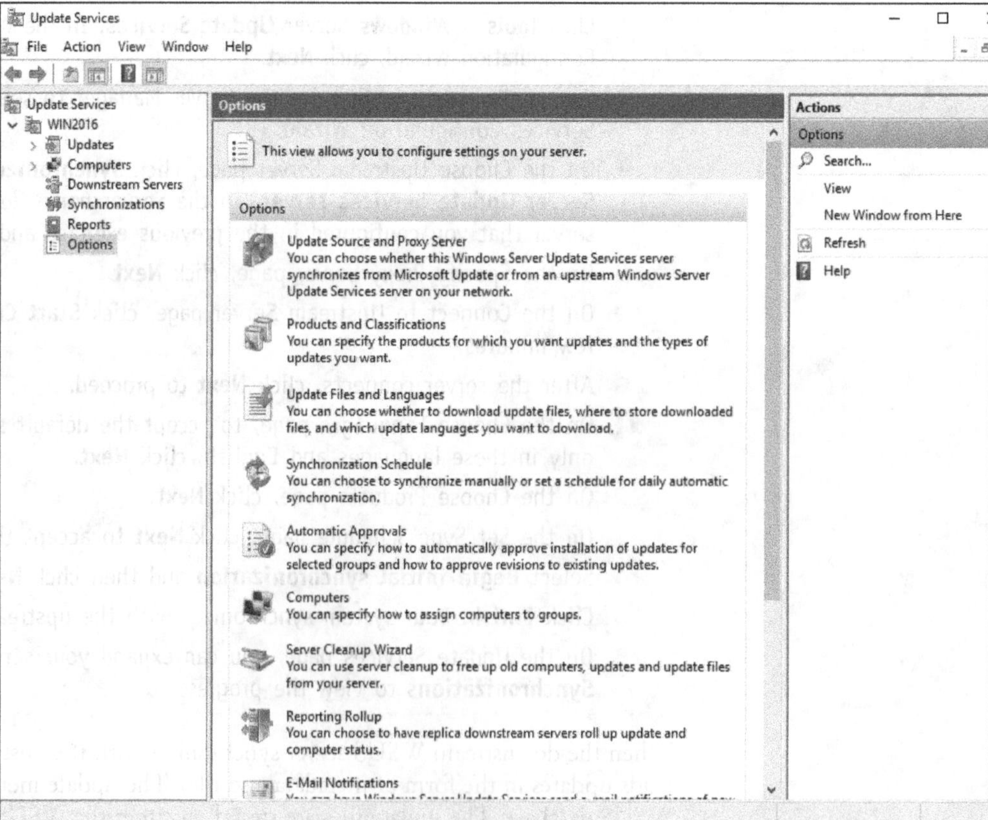

Figure 2-7
Reviewing the folders in the Update Services console

The Update Services console includes the following features:

- **Updates:** Updates, used to repair and/or replace software, consist of metadata (properties of the actual updated data) that allows you to determine its uses and the update files that are required to install the update on a computer. These updates are categorized under the following nodes: All Updates, Critical Updates, Security Updates, and WSUS Updates.
- **Computers:** These groups are created by default during the WSUS installation. Groups enable you to target your updates to specific computers and to stagger your rollout of updates. You do not see any computers in the console until you have configured the clients to use WSUS.
  - **All Computers:** This includes all computers.
  - **Unassigned Computers:** If a computer is not assigned to a group, it is added to this node the first time it contacts the WSUS server.
- **Downstream servers:** This lists the downstream servers that obtain their update files, metadata, and approvals from this WSUS server instead of from Microsoft Update or Windows Update.
- **Synchronizations:** During synchronization, the WSUS server downloads updates in the form of metadata and files from an update source. This can be another WSUS server or from the Microsoft servers and Windows Update servers.
- **Reports:** These reports allow you to monitor updates, computers, and synchronization results. You can also roll up data from downstream servers.
- **Options:** This folder provides access to tools you can use to modify settings on the WSUS server. Using the tools provided, you can specify how you want to approve the installation of updates, change your synchronization schedule, clean up old computers, update files from the server, and choose how data is displayed in the Update Services console.

Understanding the WSUS Infrastructure

When you have both upstream and downstream WSUS servers running on your network, you might want to control how update approvals, settings, computers, and groups are managed. To do this, you must first understand the two modes WSUS can run in: replica and autonomous.

As you learned from setting up the upstream and downstream WSUS servers earlier, you have two options about where you obtained your updates. You can synchronize directly from the Microsoft Update servers or from another WSUS server on your network. The choice you did not have to make at the time was whether or not your downstream WSUS server was going to run in replica or autonomous mode. By default, your downstream WSUS server was automatically set to run in in autonomous (distribution) mode.

In ***replica mode***, a WSUS server mirrors update approvals, settings, computers, and groups from the upstream server. In other words, the downstream server cannot be used to approve updates; they must be performed on the upstream server.

If you are operating the WSUS server in ***autonomous (distribution) mode***, it enables you to configure separate update approval settings while still retrieving updates from the upstream WSUS server.

Now that you understand the difference between the two, there might come a time when you decide that you want to manage the approval of all updates from the upstream server. This is common in situations where you have a downstream WSUS server at a branch office that has no IT support staff. If that happens, you need to understand how to configure your downstream WSUS server to run in replica mode.

CONFIGURE A DOWNSTREAM WSUS SERVER TO RUN IN REPLICA MODE

GET READY. To assign your downstream WSUS server to run in replica mode, log on to your member server with administrative privileges and then perform the following steps.

1. The Server Manager console should open automatically. If it does not open, on the taskbar, click the **Server Manager** icon.
2. Click **Tools > Windows Server Update Services.**
3. From the pane on the left, click **Options** and then choose **Update Source and Proxy Server.**
4. Click **This server is a replica of the upstream server** and then click **OK.**
5. From the left pane, expand **Updates** and then click the **All Updates** folder.
6. In the middle pane, change the status to **Any** and then click **Refresh** (see Figure 2-8).

Figure 2-8

Reviewing All Updates

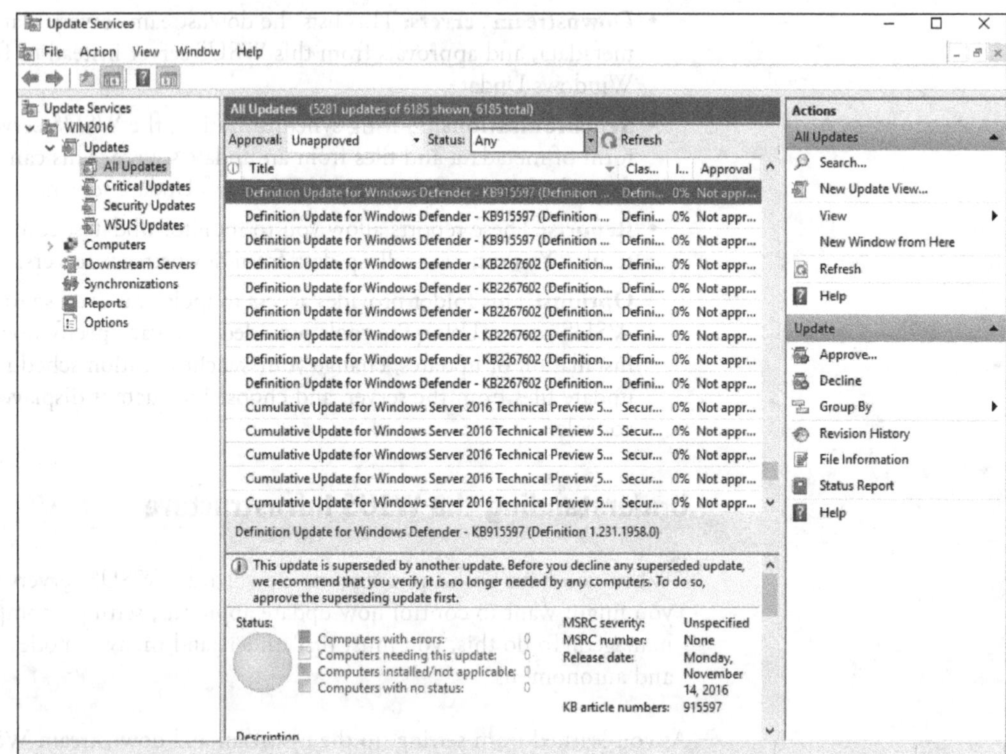

7. Right-click the first update in the list. In the menu that appears, notice that the options to Approve or Decline the update are disabled. The downstream server has been configured in replica mode earlier. Updates can be approved only on the upstream server.
8. Close the Update Services console.

Configuring Automatic Updates

For clients to obtain their information from your WSUS servers, you need to first configure them. By default, your computers are configured to communicate directly with the Microsoft Update servers. With an Active Directory domain present, you can create a Group Policy Object to configure your clients.

CREATE A GPO TO ENABLE AUTOUPDATE FOR CLIENT COMPUTERS

GET READY. To create a GPO to enable AutoUpdate for client computers in an Active Directory domain, log on with administrative credentials, and then on your domain controller, perform the following steps.

TAKE NOTE* This can be performed on a Windows 10 client with Administrative Tools or at the domain controller for the domain using the Group Policy Management Console.

1. The Server Manager console opens automatically. If it does not open, on the taskbar, click the **Server Manager** icon.
2. Click **Tools > Group Policy Management.**
3. Right-click the **Group Policy Objects** folder and choose **New.**
4. In the Name field, type **WSUS AutoUpdate** and then click **OK.**
5. Expand the **Group Policy Objects** folder, right-click **WSUS AutoUpdate**, and then choose **Edit.**
6. Expand **Computer Configuration > Policies > Administrative Templates > Windows Components > Windows Update.**
7. In the details pane, double-click **Configure Automatic Updates.**
8. Under Configure Automatic Updates, click **Enabled** and under Configure automatic updating, review the options.
9. Under Configure automatic updating, make sure **3-Auto download and notify for install** is visible. Read the information in the help panel to understand how this setting works. Click **OK** when finished.
10. Double-click **Specify intranet Microsoft update service location.**
11. Under Specify intranet Microsoft update service location, click **Enabled** and then type the URL of the upstream WSUS server you set up earlier. For example, if your domain controller's name is LON-SVR1, type **http://LON-SVR1:8530**. (8530 is the default port used by WSUS.)
12. For the intranet statistics server, type the same information.
13. Click **OK.**
14. Close the Group Policy Management Editor.
15. Right-click the domain container (contoso.com) and choose **Link an existing GPO.**
16. Choose **WSUS AutoUpdate** and then click **OK.**
17. Close the Group Policy Management Console.
18. Restart your Windows 10 or Windows Server 2016 computer and then log on with administrative credentials to the domain.

TAKE NOTE* Perform these steps on a Windows 10 or Windows Server 2016 computer that is a member of the Active Directory domain.

19. Click **Start**, type **cmd**, and then press **Enter**.
20. From the Command Prompt window, type **gpresult /r** and then press **Enter**.

    The WSUS AutoUpdate GPO should appear under the Computer Settings > Applied Group Policy Objects section of the report. If it does not, type **gpupdate /force** and then try **gpresult /r** again.
21. Type **wuauclt /detectnow** and then press **Enter**. This forces the Windows computer to contact the WSUS server immediately.
22. Open the Update Services console on the domain controller running WSUS (**Server Manager > Tools > Windows Server Update Services**).
23. Expand the **Computers > All Computers** group. You can see the computer under the Unassigned Computers group.

Creating WSUS Computer Groups

After configuring your clients to use WSUS, you should organize them into computer groups. This enables you to target specific systems for updates. WSUS comes with two built-in groups: All Computers and Unassigned Computers. If you don't have a need to configure and manage your computers separately, you can stay with these groups. If you want to test the impact the updates will have on your computers and any line-of-business applications before rolling them out to your entire organization, then new groups should be created.

Here are a few things to note about computer groups:

- When a computer is not assigned to a specific group, it appears in the Unassigned Computers group in the console.
- A computer can be a member of more than one group and groups can be built in a hierarchical structure.
- When you create a group hierarchy, an update rolled out to a parent group is also distributed to child groups.

CREATE A GROUP IN WSUS

GET READY. To create a group on your domain controller running WSUS, log on with administrative privileges and then perform the following steps.

1. Open the Update Services console if you closed it earlier (**Server Manager > Tools > Windows Server Update Services**).
2. Expand the **Computers** node, right-click **All Computers**, and then choose **Add Computer Group**.
3. In the Name field, type **IT Staff** and then click **Add**.
4. Confirm the group appears under the All Computers node. Keep the Update Services console open to use in the next exercise.

Computers can be assigned to groups using either server-side targeting or client-side targeting. ***Server-side targeting*** involves moving clients to computer groups using the Update Services console. ***Client-side targeting*** involves using Group Policy for domain computers or Local Group Policy Editor for non–domain computers. When using client-side targeting, you configure the computers to add themselves automatically to the computer groups by specifying the group in the *Computer Configuration Policies\Administrative Tools\Windows Components\Windows Update\Enable client-side targeting* policy. Client-side targeting works well when you organize your computers into organizational units based on their configuration or function.

These settings are configured on the WSUS Server via Update Services > Options > Computers.

Selecting the Use the Update Services console option uses server-side targeting; computers are automatically added to the Unassigned Computers group. The other option, Use Group Policy or registry settings on computers, configures the WSUS server to support client-side targeting.

USE SERVER-SIDE TARGETING TO MOVE A COMPUTER TO A GROUP

GET READY. To use server-side targeting on your domain controller running WSUS, log on with administrative privileges and then perform the following steps.

1. In the Update Services console, expand **Computers.**
2. In the Unassigned Computers group, right-click the **Windows 10 computer** and choose **Change Membership.**
3. Select **IT Staff** and then click **OK** to add the computer to the group.
4. Click the **IT Staff** group, and in the middle pane, confirm the computer appears. Keep the Update Services console open to use in the next exercise.

Configuring Update Approvals and Deployments

Most companies have mixed environments, which consist of multiple versions of client operating systems (such as Windows 7, 8.1, and 10) and multiple versions of server operating system (Windows Servers 2012 R2 and Windows Server 2016). When you determine which updates you need to deploy, you need to review updates for all of the Microsoft client, server, and application versions that you have.

Updates downloaded to the upstream server will not be distributed to WSUS clients automatically. As the WSUS administrator, you have to approve them first. If you look under Options > Automatic Approval, you can see the following default WSUS settings:

- **Update Rules:** Under this tab, you can specify rules for automatically approving latest updates when they are synchronized. The default rule approves security and critical updates for all computers.
- **Advanced tab:** The following options are configured by default under this tab: Automatically approve updates to the WSUS product, Automatically approve new revisions of updates that are already approved, and Automatically decline updates when a new revision causes them to expire.

As the administrator, you can change which updates are automatically detected, which ones are automatically approved, and which groups of computers are targeted to receive the updates.

APPROVE AND DEPLOY WSUS UPDATES

GET READY. To approve and deploy WSUS updates, on your domain controller running WSUS, log on with administrative privileges and then perform the following steps.

1. In the Update Services console, expand **Updates** and then click **All Updates.**
2. Right-click one of the updates and choose **Approve.**
3. In the Approve Updates box, click **IT Staff > Approved for Install.** You should see a green circle with white checkmark check box for IT Staff, as shown in Figure 2-9.

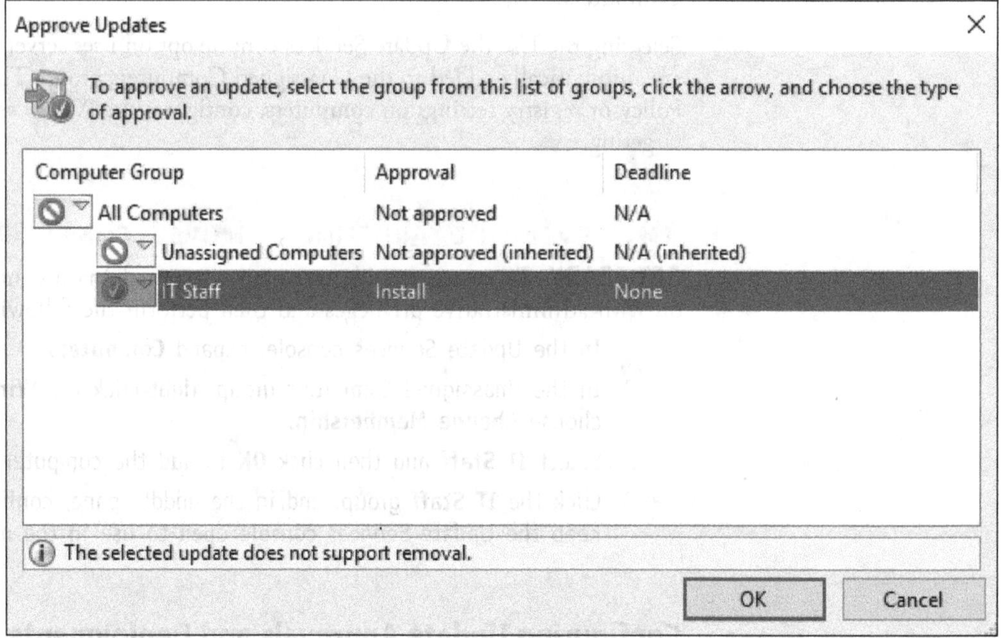

Figure 2-9
Approving an update

4. Click **OK.**
5. When the approval process completes, click **Close.**
6. On the Windows Server 2016 system, perform the following steps:
   a. Log on to a Windows Server 2016 system that is a member of the domain.
   b. Click **Start**, type **cmd**, and then press **Enter.**
   c. From the Command Prompt window, type **wuauclt /detectnow** and then press **Enter.** Close the Command Prompt window.
   This causes the client to detect available updates, automatically queue them for download via Background Intelligent Transfer Service (BITS), and then present a notification to install the updates on the client.
   d. Right-click the notification icon and choose **Open Windows Update.**
   e. Click **Install Updates.**
7. If you are prompted after the updates are completed, click **Restart now** to complete the installation of the update.

Configuring WSUS Reporting

To see detailed information about updates, computers, and synchronization, you can run the WSUS built-in reports.

WSUS includes the following reports (see Figure 2-10):

- **Update Status Summary:** Shows detailed information about every update that you choose to report on, the computer groups that an update has been approved for, and the number of computers the update was installed on.
- **Update Detailed Status:** Shows detailed information about every update that you choose to report on, the computer groups that an update has been approved for, and the number of computers the update was installed on. It also shows the update status for all computers.
- **Update Tabular Status:** Similar to the Update Status Summary report and the Update Detailed Status report, but uses a table format that can be exported.
- **Update Tabular Status for Approved Updates:** Shows a summary of the update status in a tabular view for approved updates, which can be exported to a spreadsheet.
- **Computer Status Summary:** Displays update information for every computer within the organization.
- **Computer Detailed Status:** Displays each update installed on each computer.
- **Computer Tabular Status:** Displays information similar to the Computer Status Summary and Computer Detailed Status, but uses a table format that can be exported.
- **Computer Tabular Status for Approved Updates:** Shows all approved updates in a table format that can be exported.
- **Synchronization Results:** Displays the results of the last synchronization.

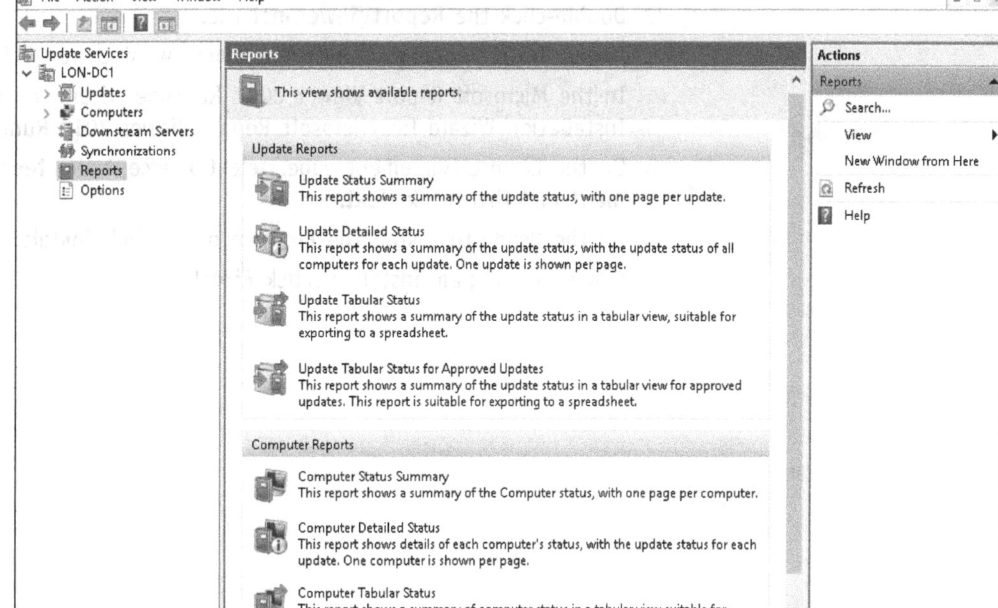

Figure 2-10

Viewing Update Services reports

To view the reports, you must download and install Microsoft System CLR Types for SQL Server 2012 and Microsoft Report Viewer 2012 Redistributable from the Microsoft website.

TAKE NOTE* If a message appears, alerting you to the fact that "Your current security settings do not allow this file to be downloaded," click Tools > Internet Options. Click the Security tab and then click Internet Zone > Custom Level. In the Downloads section, select Enable for File Download and then click OK.

INSTALL MICROSOFT SYSTEM SLR TYPES FOR SQL SERVER 2012 AND MICROSOFT REPORT VIEWER 2012 REDISTRIBUTABLE

GET READY. To install Microsoft System SLR Types for SQL Server 2012 and Microsoft Report Viewer 2012 Redistributable, perform the following steps.

1. On the WSUS server, open File Explorer by clicking the **File Explorer** tile on the taskbar.
2. Using File Explorer, open the **\\LON-DC1\Software** folder or the folder in which you downloaded the Microsoft System SLR Types for SWL Server 2012 and Microsoft Report Viewer 2012 Redistributable installation packages.
3. Double-click the **SQLSysClrTypes.msi** file.
4. If you are prompted to confirm that you want to run this file, click **Run.**
5. In the Microsoft System CLR Types for SQL Server 2012 Setup wizard, on the Welcome to the Installation Wizard for Microsoft System CLR Types for SQL Server 2012 page, click **Next.**
6. On the License Agreement page, select **I accept the terms in the license agreement** and click **Next.**
7. On the Ready to Install the Program page, click **Install.**
8. When the program installed, click **Finish.**
9. Double-click the **ReportViewer.msi** file.
10. If you are prompted to confirm that you want to run this file, click **Run.**
11. In the Microsoft Report Viewer 2012 Runtime wizard, on the Welcome to the Installation Wizard for Microsoft Report Viewer 2012 Runtime page, click **Next.**
12. On the License Agreement page, select **I accept the terms in the license agreement** and then click **Next.**
13. On the Ready to Install the Program page, click **Install.**
14. When the program installed, click **Finish.**

Administrating WSUS with Commands

While commands can be incorporated into scripts, often commands can perform functions that you could not do otherwise. With WSUS with Windows Server 2016, you can use WSUSutil.exe and PowerShell.

WSUSutil.exe (located in the %drive%\Program Files\Update Services\Tools folder on your WSUS server) allows you to manage the WSUS from the command line. Some of the options include:

- `export`: Exports the update metadata to an export package file.
- `import`: Imports the update metadata from an export package file.
- `movecontent`: Changes the file system location where the WSUS server stores update files and optionally copies any update files from the old location to the new location.
- `reset`: Checks that every update metadata row in the database has corresponding update files stored in the file system.
- `deleteunneededrevisions`: Purges the update metadata for unnecessary update revisions from the database.

Since PowerShell was introduced with Windows 2008, the use of PowerShell has been expanded with each new version of Windows Server. Starting with Windows Server 2012, Windows includes PowerShell commands to manage the WSUS server. The following commands are available in Windows Server 2012 PowerShell:

- `Add-WsusComputer`: Adds an already registered specified client computer to a specified target group.
- `Approve-WsusUpdate`: Approves an update to be applied to clients.
- `Deny-WsusUpdate`: Declines the update for deployment.
- `Get-WsusClassification`: Gets the list of all WSUS classifications currently available in the system.
- `Get-WsusComputer`: Gets the WSUS computer object that represents the client computer.
- `Get-WsusProduct`: Gets the list of all products currently available on WSUS by category.
- `Get-WsusServer`: Gets the value of the WSUS update server object.
- `Get-WsusUpdate`: Gets the WSUS update object with details about the update.
- `Invoke-WsusServerCleanup`: Performs the process of cleanup on a specified WSUS server.
- `Set-WsusClassification`: Sets whether the classifications of updates that WSUS synchronizes are enabled or disabled.
- `Set-WsusProduct`: Sets whether the product representing the category of updates to synchronize is enabled or disabled.
- `Set-WsusServerSynchronization`: Sets whether the WSUS server synchronizes from Microsoft Update or from an upstream server and uses the upstream server properties.

To list all the cmdlets that are available, use the `Get-Command *-Wsus*` cmdlet. To find more about the syntax, use the `Get-Help <cmdletname>` or search for the command on the TechNet website.

Troubleshooting Problems with Installing Updates

If you have problems with updates being installed with WSUS, there are several tools that can be used to troubleshoot the problem, including using the Event Viewer, viewing logs files, and using the Wuauclt command.

WSUS uses the following logs:

- **Application event log:** By opening the Application logs in the Event Viewer on the WSUS system, you can find errors related to synchronization, Update Services console errors, and WSUS database errors.
- **C:\Program Files\Update Services\LogFiles\Change.txt**: This log stores the record of every update installation, synchronization, and WSUS configuration change.
- **C:\Program Files\Update Services\LogFiles\softwareDistribution.txt**: This is a detailed log file usually used by Microsoft Support to debug a problem.

If WSUS is having problems synchronizing with Windows Update, open Windows Update on the server and see if you can download and install updates.

If you have a particular client having problems, verify that that client is connecting to the correct WSUS server. In Windows 10 and Windows Server 2016, Windows Update Agent uses Event Tracing for Windows (ETW) to generate diagnostic logs, much like what you will find in the Event Viewer. You can use the Windows PowerShell Get-WindowsUpdateLog cmdlet to merge and convert the .etl files into a single readable WindowsUpdate.log file.

You can review the group policy results for the computer and you can review the C:\Windows\WindowsUpdate.log file. You can verify that a client can connect to the WSUS server by opening the following WSUS URL with Internet Explorer:

http://*WSUSServerName*/iuident.cab

If you are prompted to download the file, you are connecting the WSUS server, which would rule out connectivity problems and name-resolution problems. Lastly, look at the System logs and the Application logs in the client's event viewer.

If you make changes and you want to the changes to take effect immediately, you need to restart the Windows Update service. To restart this service, you can use the Services console, or you can use the following two commands:

```
Net stop wuauserv
Net start wuauserv
```

To make the Windows Update service query the WSUS server, you can run the following command:

```
Wuauclt /detectnow
```

Of course, after you start the services or start a query, you should then look at the client logs.

If you are using client-side targeting and change group membership, use the following command to check for updates and to update the WSUS update computer group membership:

```
Wuauclt /resetauthorization /detectnow
```

Lastly, to look at the installed updates that have been installed, you can use the Control Panel. Similarly, if an update is problematic, you can also use the Control Panel to remove the update.

SKILL SUMMARY

IN THIS LESSON YOU LEARNED:

- The first step you should take to protect yourself against malware is to keep your system up to date with the latest service packs, security patches, and other critical fixes.
- Windows Update provides your Windows 10 and Windows 2016 users with a way to keep their computers current by checking a designated server. The server provides software that patches security issues, installs updates that make Windows and your applications more stable, fixes issues with existing Windows programs, and provides new features.
- Windows Server Update Services (WSUS) enables you to centrally manage the deployment of updates released through Microsoft, track compliance, and provide basic reporting functions.\
- When you have both upstream and downstream WSUS servers running on your network, you might want to control how update approvals, settings, computers, and groups are managed. To do this, you must first understand the two modes WSUS can run in replica and autonomous.
- For clients to obtain their information from your WSUS servers, you need to first configure them. By default, your computers are configured to communicate directly with the Microsoft Update servers. With an Active Directory domain present, you can create a Group Policy Object to configure your clients.
- After configuring your clients to use WSUS, organize them into computer groups. This enables you to target specific systems for updates. WSUS comes with two built-in groups: All Computers and Unassigned Computers.
- To see detailed information about updates, computers, and synchronization, you can run the WSUS built-in reports.
- If you have problems with updates being installed with WSUS, there are several tools that can be used to troubleshoot the problem, including using the Event Viewer, viewing logs files, and using the Wuauclt command.

■ Knowledge Assessment

Multiple Choice

1. You have just added a new update to the WSUS server and you want to test the update to your test group. Which of the following commands is used so that you don't have to wait for the update to be deployed?
   a. `gpupdate /force`
   b. `wuauclt.exe /detectnow`
   c. `update /now`
   d. `wsusserver /startupdate`
2. Which type of update is a tested, cumulative set of hotfixes, security updates, critical updates, and updates, as well as additional fixes for problems found internally.
   a. Security update
   b. Critical update
   c. Service pack
   d. Cumulative patch
3. Which tool is used to remove a Windows update?
   a. Windows Settings
   b. Windows Control Panel
   c. Windows GPO
   d. Windows WSUS
4. Which of the following statements is true of a replica mode WSUS server? (Choose all that apply)
   a. It mirrors update approvals, settings, computers, and groups from the upstream server.
   b. It mirrors update approvals, settings, computers, and groups from the downstream server.
   c. It can be used to approve updates.
   d. It cannot be used to approve updates.
5. Which of the following statements best describes server-side targeting? (Choose all that apply)
   a. Server-side targeting uses the Update Services console to move computers into computer groups.
   b. Server-side targeting uses Local Group Policy editor to create a group policy designating the computer group to add the computer to.
   c. Server-side targeting uses Group Policy Management console to create a group policy designating the computer group to add the computer to.
   d. Server-side targeting results in computers initially being added to the Unassigned Computers group.

6. Which of the following commands, when run on a Windows 10 client, detects available updates from the WSUS server, queues them, and then presents a notification to install the updates.
   - a. `wuauclt /detect`
   - b. `wuauclt /detectnow`
   - c. `wuauclt /force`
   - d. `wuauclt /renew`
7. Which of the following is required in order to view reports in WSUS?
   - a. .Net Framework Viewer
   - b. SQL Server Table Displayer
   - c. Microsoft Report Viewer 2012 Redistributable
   - d. Text Converter
8. Which of the following is the default database used by WSUS?
   - a. PID
   - b. FIX
   - c. WID
   - d. SID
9. Which of the following is the best strategy for getting all clients within an organization to use a WSUS server?
   - a. Modify the registry of the client computers.
   - b. Use a router that redirects to WSUS.
   - c. Change the WSUS.TXT file in the C:\Windows folder.
   - d. Use group policies.
10. If a client is not part of a domain, client-side targeting can be accomplished by doing which of the following?
    - a. By using group policies
    - b. By modifying the registry
    - c. Modify the NTFS permissions
    - d. Add the WSUS client role

Best Answer

Choose the letter that corresponds to the best answer. More than one answer choice may achieve the goal. Select the BEST answer.

1. Which of the following provides the easiest way to ensure all of your computers include the newest Windows updates while still ensuring that those updates do not cause any problems for the users?
   - a. Task Scheduler
   - b. WSUS
   - c. Windows updates
   - d. GPOs

2. To ensure computers in three branch offices (with no IT support onsite) receive Windows Updates on a regular basis along with those in a main office, which WSUS configuration provides the best solution with the least amount of administrative for the approval and distribution of updates and the least amount of traffic over the WAN link?
   a. Single WSUS server at main office. Branch office PCs configured to use this server.
   b. WSUS server at main office and downstream WSUS servers at each branch office running in autonomous mode. PCs configured to use the local WSUS server.
   c. WSUS server at main office and downstream WSUS servers at each branch office running in replica mode. PCs configured to use the local WSUS server.
   d. WSUS server at main office and downstream WSUS servers at two branch offices running in replica mode and one running in autonomous mode.
3. Which Windows Update option ensures your system receives and uses the most current updates?
   a. Install updates but let me choose whether to install them.
   b. Download updates but let me choose whether to install them.
   c. Check for updates but let me choose whether to download and install them.
   d. Centrally approve and deploy updates using WSUS.
4. You administer a server (Server1) with WSUS and you discover that certain updates listed in the WSUS administrative console are unavailable on Server1. Which of the following options ensures that all of the updates listed in the WSUS administrative console are available on the server?
   a. Running wsusutil.exe with the `/verify` option
   b. Running wuauclt.exe with the `/detectnow` option
   c. Running wuauclt.exe with the `/resetauthorization` option
   d. Running wsusutil.exe with the `reset` option
5. You administer a server (Server1) with WSUS and you use a group policy to configure all WSUS client computers to detect every update and install updates weekly. You just downloaded a critical update; which of the following actions should be taken to install the critical update during the next detection interval?
   a. Run the wuauclt.exe `/force` command.
   b. Configure the deadline settings for the update.
   c. Configure the Synchronization Schedule.
   d. Run the `gpupdate /force` command.

Build List

1. Specify the correct order of the steps necessary to set up a WSUS Server.
   ______ Specify an update source for the WSUS server.
   ______ Synchronize updates to the WSU server.
   ______ Determine a deployment strategy.
   ______ Install the WSUS server role.
   ______ Set up client computers.
   ______ Approve and install updates on client computers.
2. Specify the correct order of the steps necessary to create a computer group in WSUS from the Update Services console.
   ______ Expand the Computers node, right-click All Computers, and choose Add Computer Group.
   ______ Confirm the group appears under the All Computers node.
   ______ Open the Update services console.
   ______ Type a name and then click Add.
   ______ Log on with Administrative privileges.

■ Business Case Scenarios

Scenario 2-1: Distributing Windows Update Across a Network

You support Richman Investments, a brokerage firm that employs 20 brokers. Each broker has his own client computer, and the firm has a server running Windows Server. All the client computers are configured identically.

Over the past six months, some Windows updates have caused the computers to hang, leaving the brokers without computers to conduct business. How can you ensure that the Windows updates that install on client computers will not cause usability issues?

Scenario 2-2: Deploying WSUS

WSUS server is set up at a branch office that gets its updates from a WSUS server at the main office. The option to approve updates is not available on the branch office server, yet it receives updates from the WSUS server at the main office on a regular basis. What is the problem?

Scenario 2-3: Creating Computer Groups in WSUS

You have the following departments within your organization:

Sales	150 computers
Marketing	75 computers
Management	50 computers
Manufacturing	200 computers
Information Technology	50 computers

How many groups should you create in WSUS? Why?

Implementing Malware Protection and Protecting Credentials

LESSON 3

70-744 EXAM OBJECTIVE

Objective 1.2 – Implement malware protection. This objective may include but is not limited to: Implement antimalware solution with Windows Defender; integrate Windows Defender with WSUS and Windows Update; configure Windows Defender using Group Policy; configure Windows Defender scans using Windows PowerShell; implement AppLocker rules; implement AppLocker rules using Windows PowerShell; implement Control Flow Guard; implement Code Integrity (Device Guard) Policies; create Code Integrity policy rules; create Code Integrity file rules.

Objective 1.2 – Protect credentials. This objective may include but is not limited to: Determine requirements for implementing Credential Guard; configure Credential Guard using Group Policy, WMI, command prompt, and Windows PowerShell; implement NTLM blocking.

Lesson Heading	Exam Objective
Implementing an Antimalware Solution with Windows Defender • Using Windows Defender • Integrating Windows Defender with WSUS and Windows Update • Configuring Windows Defender Using Group Policy • Configuring Windows Defender Scans Using Windows PowerShell	Implement antimalware solution with Windows Defender Integrate Windows Defender with WSUS and Windows Update Configure Windows Defender using Group Policy Configure Windows Defender scans using Windows PowerShell
Using AppLocker to Manage Applications • Implementing AppLocker Rules • Implementing AppLocker Rules Using Windows PowerShell	Implement AppLocker rules Implement AppLocker rules using Windows PowerShell
Implementing Windows Security Features • Implementing Device Guard • Creating Code Integrity Policy Rules • Implementing Credential Guard • Implementing Control Flow Guard • Using Enhanced Mitigation Experience Toolkit (EMET)	Implement Code Integrity (Device Guard) Policies Create Code Integrity policy rules Create Code Integrity file rules Determine requirements for implementing Credential Guard Configure Credential Guard using Group Policy, WMI, command prompt, and Windows PowerShell Implement Control Flow Guard
Implementing NT LAN Manager (NTLM) Blocking	Implement NTLM blocking

KEY TERMS

AppLocker
buffers
Code Integrity
Control Flow Guard (CFG)
Credential Guard
Data Execution Prevention
Device Guard
Enhanced Mitigation Experience Toolkit (EMET)
NT LAN Manager (NTLM)
virtual secure mode (VSM)
Windows Defender

Implementing an Antimalware Solution with Windows Defender

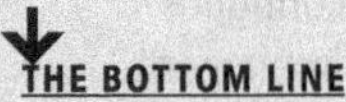

THE BOTTOM LINE

Windows Defender is designed to protect your computer against viruses, spyware, and other types of malware. It protects against these threats by providing real-time protection in which it notifies you if malware attempts to install itself on your computer or when an application tries to change critical settings.

It can also be configured to scan your computer on a regular basis and remove or quarantine malware it finds.

TAKE NOTE* Windows Defender automatically disables itself when you install another antivirus product.

CERTIFICATION READY
Implement antimalware solution with Windows Defender
Objective 1.2

At the heart of Windows Defender are its definition files, which are downloaded from Windows Update. The definition files, which contain information about potential threats, are used by Windows Defender to notify you of potential threats to your system.

Using Windows Defender

To access Windows Defender, click Start, type Windows Defender, and choose it from the Results. Figure 3-1 shows the Windows Defender Home tab.

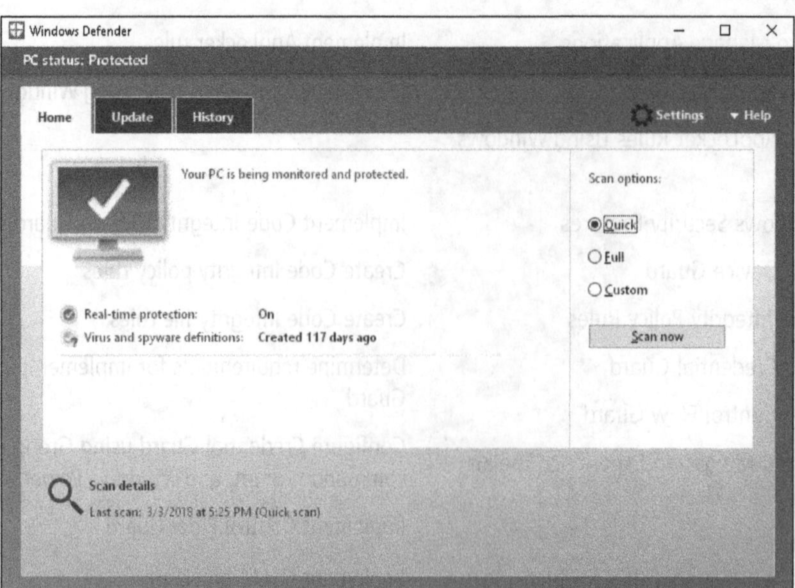

Figure 3-1
Viewing the Windows Defender Home tab

The Home tab allows you to check the status of Windows Defender, including whether Windows Defender is up to date and whether Windows Defender is protecting your system. It also gives you the option to initiate a scan.

When looking at the Home tab, you should always look for a green message indicating *Your PC is being monitored and protected* and you should also make sure your system is up to date. Other components include:

- **Real-time protection:** Real-time protection uses signature detection methodology and heuristics to monitor and catch malware behavior. Signature detection uses a vendor's definition files to detect malicious programs. If the program contains code that matches the signature, the program most likely contains the virus. This works well when the threat has already been identified, but what happens in between the time the virus is released and the definition file is made available? That's where heuristics can help. It is used to monitor for suspicious activity by a program. Suspicious activity includes a program trying to copy itself into another program, a program trying to write to the disk directly, or a program trying to manipulate critical system files required by the operating system. These are indicators of possible malware activity that heuristics can detect.
- **Virus and spyware definitions:** When a new virus is discovered, Microsoft creates a new virus signature/definition update. Each definition file contains a piece of the actual virus code that is used to detect a specific virus or malware. During scans, the content on the computer is compared with information in the definition files. Because new viruses are created every day and existing viruses are modified regularly, it's important to keep your definitions updated.
- **Scan options (Quick, Full, and Custom):** A Quick scan checks the areas that malicious software, including viruses, spyware, and unwanted software, are most likely to infect. A Full scan checks all the files on your disk, including running programs. A Custom scan is designed to check only locations and files you specify.
- **Scan Details:** This area of the Home tab provides information on when the last scan was performed on the computer.

The Update tab provides you with information about your virus and spyware definitions. It is important to keep these current to ensure your computer is protected at all times.

The Update tab provides information about when the definition files were created, the last time you updated them, and the current version numbers for the virus and spyware definitions. Windows Defender updates the definition files automatically, but you can manually check for updates by clicking Update definitions on this tab.

The History tab provides information about items that have been detected in the past and the actions that were taken with them.

The categories of items are as follows:

- **Quarantined items:** These items were not allowed to run but were not removed from your computer.
- **Allowed items:** These items were allowed to run on your computer.
- **All detected items:** These items provide a list of all items detected on your computer.

REMOVE A QUARANTINED ITEM

GET READY. To remove an item that has been quarantined, perform the following steps.

1. Open Windows Defender.
2. Click the **History** tab.
3. Click **Quarantined Items.**
4. Click **View Details.**
5. Select the detected item and then read the description.
6. Click **Remove.**

The Settings option is where you can fine-tune how Windows Defender works. In Settings (as shown in Figure 3-2), you can:

- Enable or disable real-time protection.
- Enable or disable cloud-based protection, which will send potential security problems to Microsoft.
- Enable or disable automatic sample submission.
- Select the files and folders, file types, and processes to exclude from the scan.

Figure 3-2

Configuring Windows Defender settings

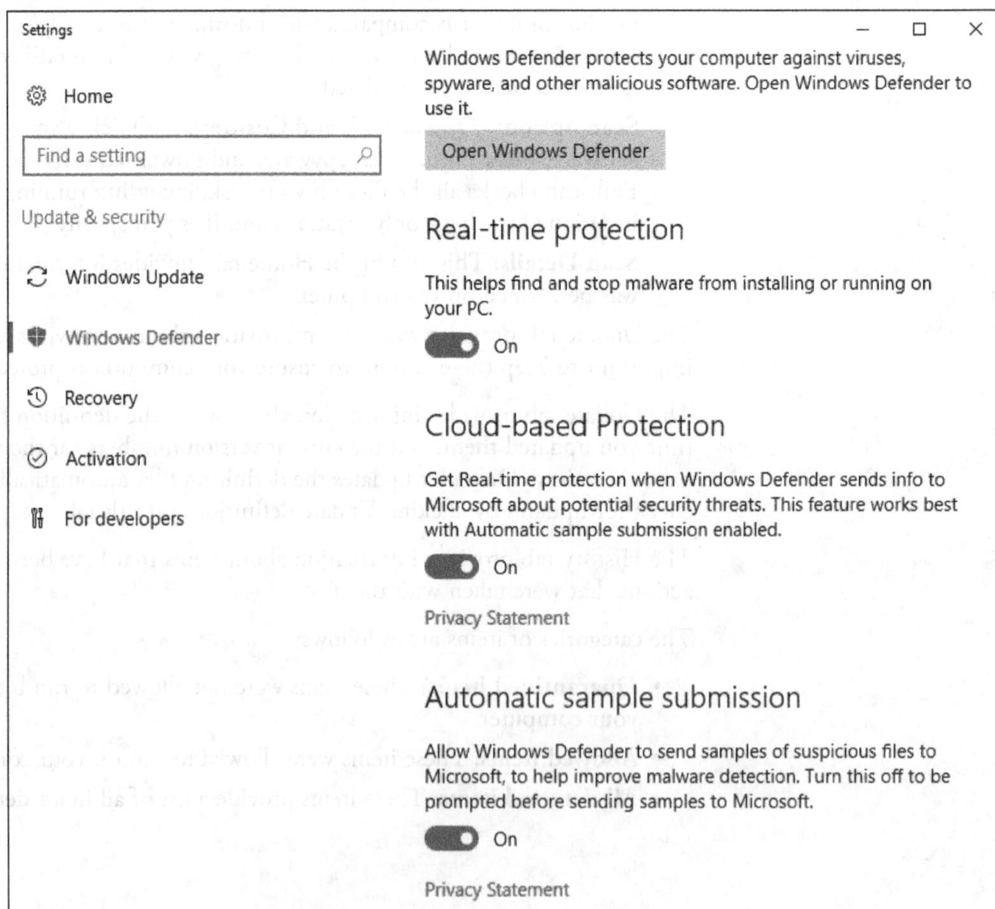

To keep a machine updated, you not only should keep Windows Defender and definitions up to date, you should periodically run a full scan on your system. You can use Task Manager to automatically initiate a full scan.

SCHEDULE A WINDOWS DEFENDER SCAN

GET READY. To schedule a Windows Defender scan, log on with administrative privileges and then perform the following steps.

1. Click **Start**, type **taskschd.msc**, and then press **Enter**.
2. In the left pane, expand **Task Scheduler Library > Microsoft > Windows > Windows Defender.**
3. Double-click **Windows Defender Scheduled Scan.**
4. Click the **Triggers** tab and then click **New.**
5. In the Begin the Task field, choose **On a schedule.**
6. Under Settings, select **One time** and in the Start field, change the time to 5 minutes from your current time.
7. Make sure the **Enabled** check box is checked and then click **OK.**
8. To close the Windows Defender Scheduled Scan Properties dialog box, click **OK.**
9. Open Windows Defender to see the status of the scan on the Home tab. Click **Cancel scan.**

Integrating Windows Defender with WSUS and Windows Update

Because Windows Defender is a Microsoft application, it can be updated with Windows Update, WSUS, and Configuration Manager. Updates include Windows Defender and the definitions that help identify malware.

CERTIFICATION READY
Integrate Windows Defender with WSUS and Windows Update
Objective 1.2

When updates are installed using Windows Update, the Windows Update program also updates Windows Defender. However, to update Windows Defender, you must select Windows Defender, so that it will update the program and definitions.

Configuring Windows Defender Using Group Policy

Like most Windows components, you can use group policy to configure and manage Windows Defender Antivirus for your endpoints. Group policy allows you to avoid configuring each machine one at a time.

CERTIFICATION READY
Configure Windows Defender Using Group Policy
Objective 1.2

The GPO settings for Windows Defender for GPOs are located at Computer Configuration\Policies\Administrative Templates\Windows Components\Windows Defender Antivirus or Computer Configuration \Administrative Templates\Windows Components\Windows Defender, as shown in Figure 3-3.

Figure 3-3

Configuring Windows Defender settings

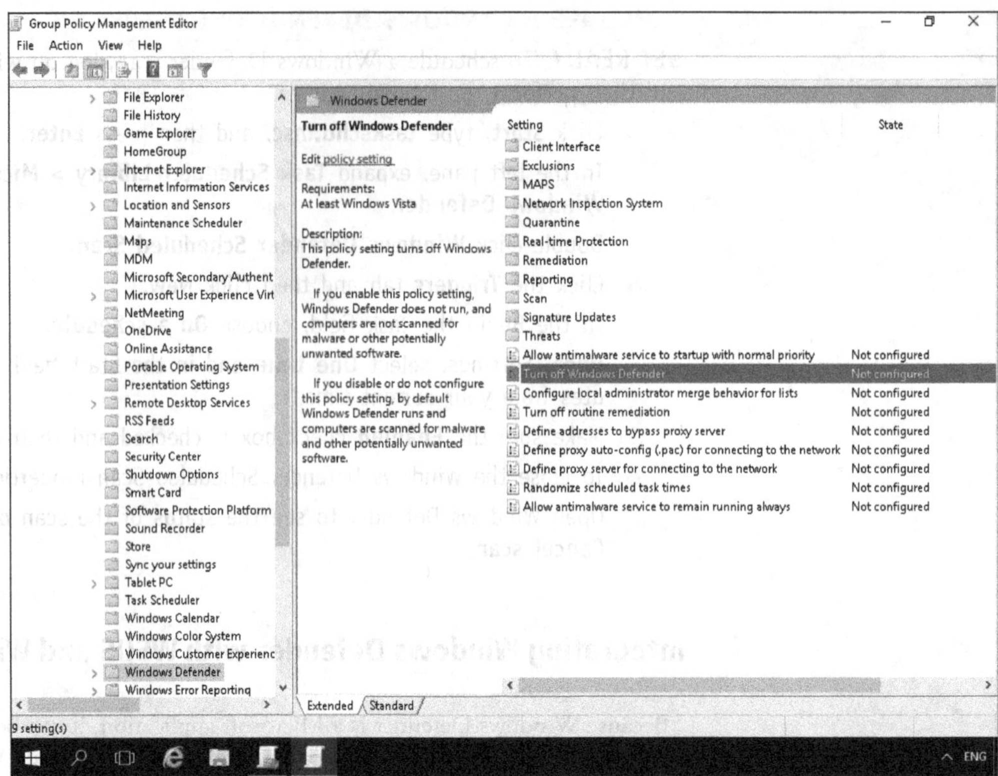

Some of the popular settings include the following:

- **Client Interface\Enable headless UI mode:** Prevent users from seeing or interacting with the Windows Defender AV user interface
- **Client interface\Display additional text to clients when they need to perform an action:** Configure the notifications that appear on endpoints
- **Client interface\Suppress all notifications:** Configure the notifications that appear on endpoints
- **Client interface\Suppresses reboot notifications:** Configure the notifications that appear on endpoints
- **Exclusions\Extension Exclusions:** Configure and validate exclusions in Windows Defender AV scans
- **Exclusions\Path Exclusions:** Configure and validate exclusions in Windows Defender AV scans
- **Exclusions\Process Exclusions:** Configure and validate exclusions in Windows Defender AV scans
- **Quarantine\Configure local setting override for the removal of items from Quarantine folder:** Prevent or allow users to locally modify policy settings
- **Quarantine\Configure removal of items from Quarantine folder:** Configure remediation for Windows Defender AV scans
- **Real-time protection\Configure local setting override for monitoring file and program activity on your computer:** Prevent or allow users to locally modify policy settings

- **Real-time protection\Configure local setting override for monitoring for incoming and outgoing file activity:** Prevent or allow users to locally modify policy settings
- **Real-time protection\Configure local setting override for scanning all downloaded files and attachments:** Prevent or allow users to locally modify policy settings
- **Real-time protection\Scan all downloaded files and attachments:** Enable and configure Windows Defender AV always-on protection and monitoring
- **Real-time protection\Turn off real-time protection:** Enable and configure Windows Defender AV always-on protection and monitoring
- **Remediation\Configure local setting override for the time of day to run a scheduled full scan to complete remediation:** Prevent or allow users to locally modify policy settings
- **Remediation\Specify the day of the week to run a scheduled full scan to complete remediation:** Configure scheduled scans for Windows Defender AV
- **Remediation\Specify the time of day to run a scheduled full scan to complete remediation:** Configure scheduled scans for Windows Defender AV
- **Scan\Check for the latest virus and spyware definitions before running a scheduled scan:** Manage event-based forced updates
- **Scan\Run full scan on mapped network drives:** Configure scanning options in Windows Defender AV
- **Scan\Scan network files:** Configure scanning options in Windows Defender AV
- **Scan\Scan packed executables:** Configure scanning options in Windows Defender AV
- **Scan\Scan removable drives:** Configure scanning options in Windows Defender AV
- **Scan\Specify the maximum depth to scan archive files:** Configure scanning options in Windows Defender AV
- **Turn off Windows Defender:** Disables Windows Defender.

CONFIGURE WINDOWS DEFENDER WITH GPOS

GET READY. To configure Windows Defender with GPOs, perform the following steps.

1. On a domain controller, using Server Manager, click **Tools Group Policy Management.**
2. In the Group Policy Management console, right-click the desired GPO and choose **Edit.**
3. Navigate to the **Computer Configuration > Policies > Administrative Templates > Windows Components > Windows Defender** node.
4. Click **the Exclusions** tab.
5. Double-click the **Path Exclusions** option.
6. In the Path Exclusions dialog box, click the **Enabled** option.
7. Click the **Show** button.
8. In the Show Contents dialog box, as shown in Figure 3-4. under Value name, type **c:\folder1**. Under Value, type **0**.

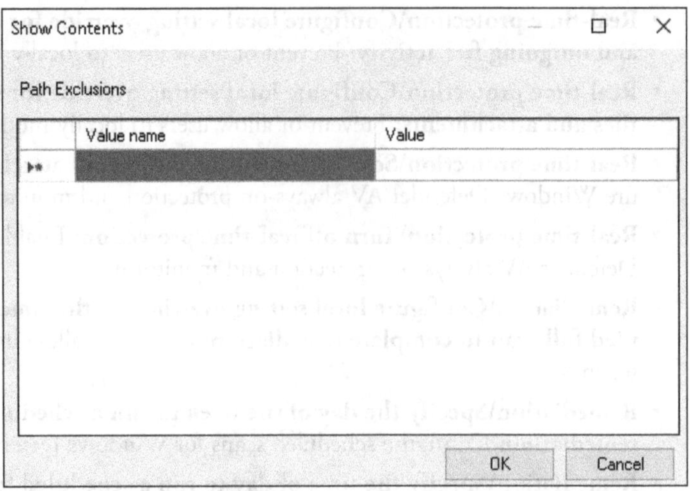

Figure 3-4
Configuring path exclusions

9. Close the Show Contents dialog box by clicking **OK**.
10. Close the Path Exclusions dialog box by clicking **OK**.
11. Click the Scan node.
12. Double-click the **Turn on e-mail scanning** option.
13. In the Turn on-email scanning dialog box, click **Enabled**.
14. Close the Turn on e-mail scanning dialog box by clicking **OK**.
15. Close the Group Policy Management Editor.

Configuring Windows Defender Scans Using Windows PowerShell

To create scripts, or to quickly perform a scan, use Windows PowerShell commands.

CERTIFICATION READY
Configure Windows Defender scans using Windows PowerShell
Objective 1.2

The 12 cmdlets for Windows Defender include:

- **Add-MpPreference:** Modifies settings for Windows Defender
- **Get-MpComputerStatus:** Gets the status of anti-malware software on the computer
- **Get-MpPreference:** Gets preferences for the Windows Defender scans and updates
- **Get-MpThreat:** Gets the history of threats detected on the computer
- **Get-MpThreatCatalog:** Gets known threats from the definitions catalog
- **Get-MpThreatDetection:** Gets active and past malware threats that Windows Defender detected
- **Remove-MpPreference:** Removes exclusions or default actions
- **Remove-MpThreat:** Removes active threats from the computer
- **Set-MpPreference:** Configures preferences for Windows Defender scans and updates
- **Start-MpScan:** Starts a scan on the computer
- **Start-MpWDOScan:** Starts a Windows Defender offline scan
- **Update-MpSignature:** Updates the anti-malware definitions on the computer

To start an offline scan, which will cause the machine to reboot before starting the scan, execute the following command:

```
Start-MpWDOScan
```

To start a quick scan, execute the following command:

Start-MpScan –ScanType QuickScan

To start a full scan, execute the following command:

```
Start-MpScan -ScanType FullScan
```

To get the current status of anti-malware software on your computer, execute the following command:

```
Get-MpComputerStatus
```

To check for update the virus signature updates and update Windows Defender, execute the following command:

```
Update-MpSignature
```

To disable Defender real-time protection, execute the following command:

```
Set-MpPreference -DisableRealtimeMonitoring $true
```

Using AppLocker to Manage Applications

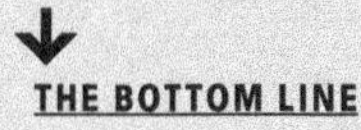

Removing users from the administrative role on computers can reduce the number of applications they can install, but it does not prevent them from loading apps that do not require administrative privilege to run. Using AppLocker, you can fine-tune what programs your users are allowed to run by establishing rules.

AppLocker is a feature available in Windows Server 2012 and higher and Windows 7 and higher. It is configured with GPOs, which can be used to control how users access and use programs and files and extends the functionality originally provided by the Software Restriction policy found in earlier versions of Windows operating systems.

Implementing AppLocker Rules

AppLocker uses rules and file properties to determine the programs and files that are allowed to run on the computer.

CERTIFICATION READY
Implement AppLocker rules
Objective 1.2

To use AppLocker, you will need to start the Application Identity Service, which is used to determine and verify the identity of applications. If the Application Identity Services is stopped will prevent AppLocker policies from being enforced.

You can access AppLocker using the Local Group Policy editor (gpedit.msc) by performing the steps in the following exercise.

ACCESS APPLOCKER

GET READY. You can access AppLocker by using the Local Group Policy editor (gpedit.msc) or by using Group Policy Management. To use Group Policy Management, perform the following steps.

1. On a domain controller, using Server Manager, click **Tools > Group Policy Management.**
2. In the Group Policy Management console, right-click the desired GPO and choose **Edit.**
3. Navigate to the **Computer Configuration > Policies > Windows Settings > Security Settings > Application Control Policies.** Expand the **AppLocker** node.

As shown in Figure 3-5, AppLocker includes four rule collections:

- Executable Rules
- Windows Installer Rules
- Script Rules
- Packaged app Rules

Figure 3-5

The AppLocker rule collections

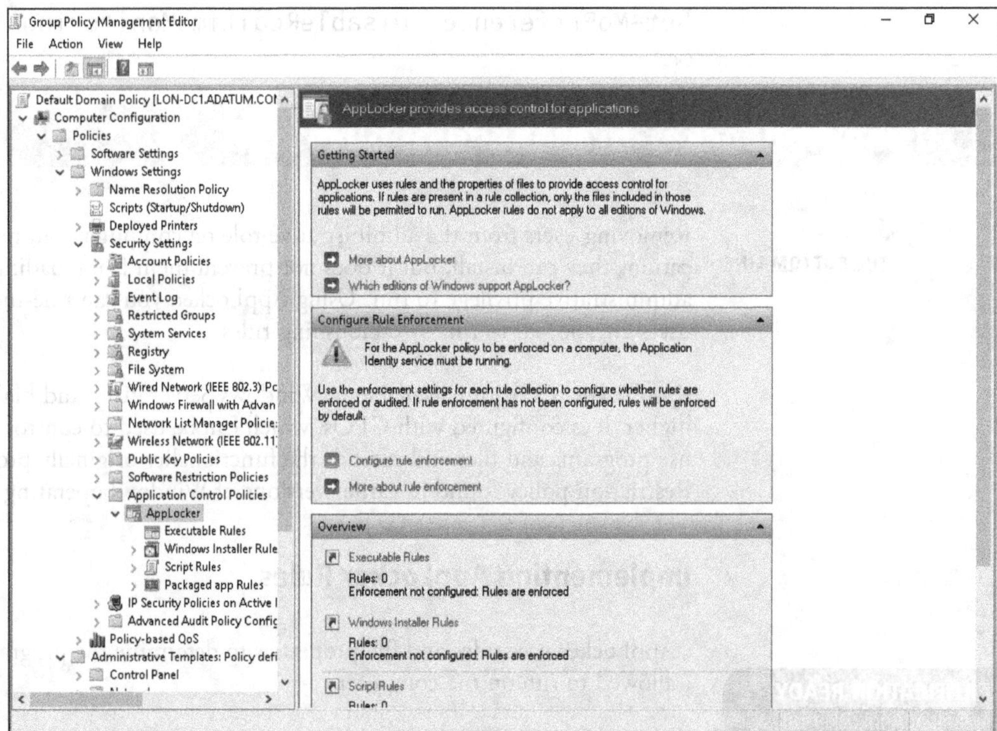

These rule collections allow you to differentiate the rules for different types of applications. AppLocker uses rules and a file's properties to determine whether applications are allowed to run.

A traditional app consists of several components (exe, DDLs, scripts, and so on). These components may not share the same publisher, product, or product version attribute. In order to manage the traditional app, AppLocker needs to control them using different rule collections. On the other hand, a Windows app (packaged app) shares the same attributes; therefore, you can create a single rule to control the entire application.

Rule collections include:

- Executable files (.exe, .com)
- Scripts (.ps2, .bat, .js, .cmd, vbs)
- Windows Installer files (.msi, .mst, .msp)
- Appx (Packaged apps and Packaged app installers) (.appx): This includes Windows Apps and side-loaded LOB apps.

By default, there are no rules in any of the rule collections; therefore, AppLocker will allow every file covered in each collection to run.

When creating rules with AppLocker, the following options are available:

- **Create New Rule:** This wizard walks you through the process of creating one AppLocker rule at a time—setting permissions, publishers, exceptions, and providing a name for the rule.
- **Automatically Generate Rules:** This wizard creates rules for multiple packaged apps in a single step. You can select a folder and let the Wizard create the applicable rules for the files in the folder or for packaged apps create rules for all Windows apps on your computer.
- **Create Default Rules:** This wizard creates rules that are meant to ensure that some key Windows paths are allowed for execution (c:\Windows files or c:\Program files). If you do not have the default rules in place, when creating a new rule, AppLocker will prompt you to create them.

Prior to configuring a rule, you must install the application for which you want to create the rule. After it is installed, perform the following steps to configure the rule:

1. Set permissions. AppLocker uses three rule types:
   - **Allow:** Programs on the list are allowed to run; all other programs are blocked.
   - **Deny:** Programs on the list are not allowed to run; all other programs are allowed.
   - **Exceptions:** Used for both allow and deny rules to provide exceptions to the rule.
2. Set the primary condition (publisher, path or file hash):
   - **Publisher:** This option identifies an application based on the manufacturer's digital signature. The digital signature contains information about the company that created the program (publisher). If you use this option, the rule can survive an update of the application as well as a change in the location of its files. This allows you to push out the updated version of the application without having to build another rule.
   - **Path:** This option identifies an application based on its location in the file system. For example, if the application is installed in the Windows directory, the AppLocker path would be %WINDIR%.
   - **File hash:** This option causes the system to compute a hash on the file. Each time the file is updated (upgrade, patch), you need to update the hash.
3. Add an exception (optional). In this step, you can add an exception to the rule (if applicable). For example, you might have enabled access for a suite (Microsoft Office) but you do not want selected users to be able to use Microsoft Access because you have a limited number of licenses.
4. Type a name for the rule. In this step, you give the rule a name and add an optional description.

TAKE NOTE* Rules created for a packaged app can use only the Publisher condition. Windows does not support unsigned packaged apps or installers.

CREATE AND TEST AN APPLOCKER RULE

GET READY. To create and test an AppLocker rule that blocks the use of the Microsoft Paint program (mspaint.exe), log on to a Windows Server 2016 computer as an administrator and then perform the following steps:

1. On a domain controller, in Server Manager, click **Tools .> Group Policy Management.**
2. In the Group Policy Management console, right-click the desired GPO and choose **Edit.**
3. Navigate to the **Computer Configuration > Policies > Windows Settings > Security Settings > Application Control Policies > AppLocker** node.
4. Click, then right-click **Executable Rules** and choose **Create New Rule.**
5. Read the Before You Begin screen and then click **Next.**
6. On the Permissions page, click **Deny.**
7. Click **Select** and in the Enter the object name to select box, type **Users.** Click **OK.**
8. Click **Next.**
9. On the Publisher's page, click **Publisher** and then click **Next.**
10. Click **Browse** and then navigate to the **\\Lon-DC1\Software\LGPO\LGPO.exe** directory. Click the **mspaint.exe** file and then click **Open.**
11. Drag the slider to **File name** (see Figure 3-6) and then click **Next.** This setting ensures the rule will block all instances of the Microsoft Paint program (mspaint.exe) regardless of the version.
12. On the Exception page, click **Next.** You do not set an exception to this rule.

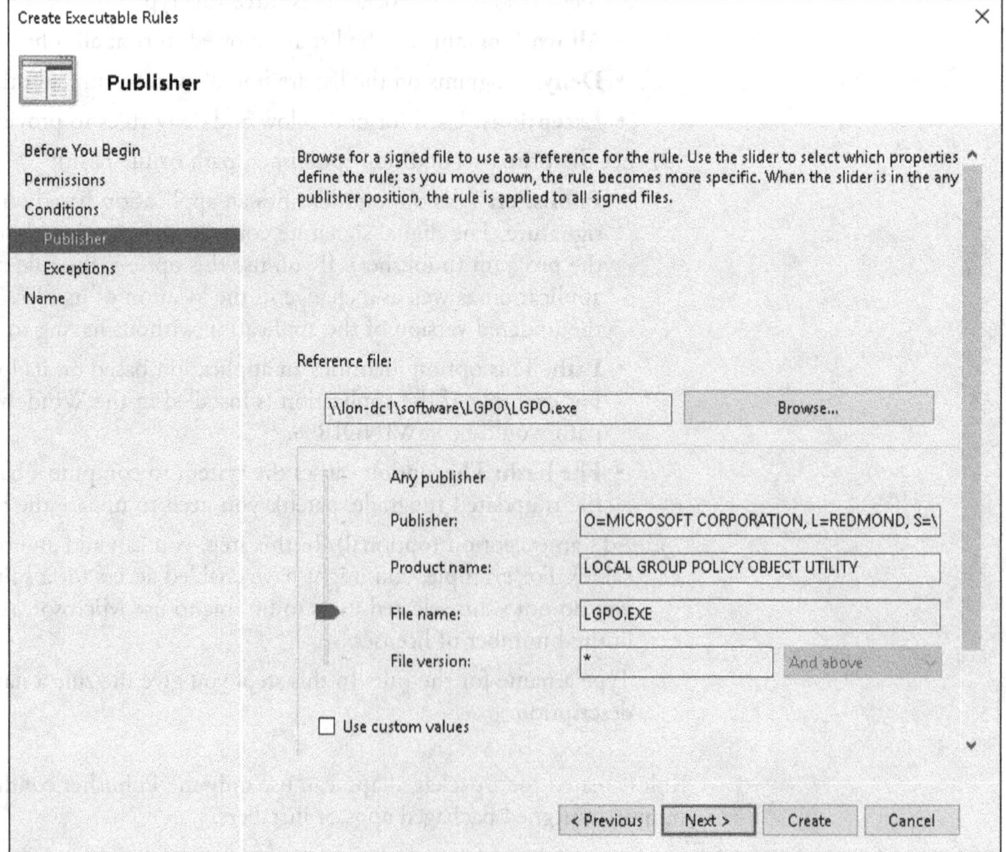

Figure 3-6

Viewing the Executable Rules/Publisher Information for the AppLocker rule

13. Type a name for the rule and a description (optional). For example, you might type Disallow Microsoft Paint Program.
14. Click **Create.**
15. When prompted to create the default rules, click **Yes.** This ensures that the created rule is allowed to run.
16. Close the Group Policy Editor.
17. To force Group Policy to update, press the **Windows logo key + r** and in the Run box, type `Gpupdate /force`. Click **OK.**
18. After a GPO is linked to an OU and is applied to a computer, log on with any user account and test the policy
19. Press the **Windows logo key + r** and in the Run box, type **mspaint.exe.** Click **OK.** The user will see a message indicating Your system administrator has blocked this program.

When you create the default rules, the default rules include:

- Allow Everyone to run files found in the C:\Program Files folder.
- Allow Everyone to run files found in the C:\Windows folder
- Allow BUILTIN\Administrators to run all files.

Therefore, if you want to block Windows built-in applications, you will need to put exceptions in the default rule, and then define rules to application the application.

If you create a policy using the Local Group policy editor, you are applying the policy to the local computer and the users who log into it. If you decide later that you want to use the same policy but apply it to multiple computers across your Active Directory domain, you can simply export the policy and then import it into a Group Policy Object linked to a container in the Active Directory hierarchy (site, domain, or organizational unit). This eliminates the need to recreate the policy settings.

EXPORT THE LOCAL POLICY

GET READY. To export the local policy, log on to the Windows 10 client computer as an administrator and then perform the following steps.

1. Press the **Windows logo key + r** and in the Run box, type **gpedit.msc.** Click **OK.** The Local Group Policy Editor displays.
2. Click **Computer Configuration > Windows Settings > Security Settings > Application Control Policies.**
3. Right-click **AppLocker** and choose **Export Policy.**
4. In the File name field, type a name for the policy and then click **Save.**

   For example, you might type Remote Desktop Connection client on Company Systems. Make a note of the location you are saving the policy to. This location must be accessible from your domain controller.
5. When a message indicates the four rules have been exported from the policy, click **OK.**

IMPORT THE LOCAL POLICY

GET READY. To import the local policy settings into a Group Policy Object in Active Directory and apply it to all computers in your domain, perform the following steps.

1. Log on to a domain controller or a Windows 10 client computer that is a member of a domain with an administrative account that has access to the Group Policy Management console.
2. Press the **Windows logo key + r** and in the Run box, type **gpmc.msc**. Click **OK**. The Group Policy Management Editor displays.
3. Right-click the **Group Policy Objects** folder and choose **New**.
4. Type a name for the new GPO and then click **OK**.

   For example, you might type Disallow Remote Desktop Connection client on Company Systems.
5. 5Right-click the GPO and choose **Edit**.
6. Click **Computer Configuration > Policies > Windows Settings > Security Settings > Application Control Policies.**
7. Right-click **AppLocker** and choose **Import Policy**.
8. Browse to the local policy file you exported earlier, select the policy file, and then click **Open**.
9. When prompted to import the policy now, click **Yes**.
10. When a message indicates the four rules have been exported from the policy, click **OK**.
11. Close the Group Policy Management Editor.
12. In the Group Policy Management console, right-click the domain name **(adatum)** and choose **Link an Existing GPO**.
13. In the Group Policy objects section, click **Disallow Remote Desktop Connection client on Company Systems** and then click **OK**.

    Now, no computer in your domain will be allowed to use the Remote Desktop Connection program.

Implementing AppLocker Rules Using Windows PowerShell

The AppLocker Windows PowerShell cmdlets are designed to streamlined the administration of AppLocker policy. It can be used to create, test, and troubleshooting AppLocker policy.

CERTIFICATION READY
Implement AppLocker rules using Windows PowerShell
Objective 1.2

The AppLocker Windows PowerShell cmdlets are:

- **`Get-AppLockerFileInformation`:** Gets the required information needed to create AppLocker rules from a list of files or the event log. For example, to see the path, publisher, and hash for the .exe file at the specified location, execute the following command:

```
Get-AppLockerFileInformation -Path C:\Folder1\*.exe
|Format-List
```

If the folder names include spaces, you will need to include quotes (“) around the path.

- **`Get-AppLockerPolicy`:** Used to retrieve local (`-Local`), effective (`-Effective`), or a domain (**`-Domain`**) AppLocker policy. You can also specify `-Xml` to output the results as an XML value. For example, to retrieve the domain AppLocker policy, execute the following command:

```
Get-AppLockerPolicy -Domain
```

- **New-AppLockerPolicy:** Creates a new AppLocker policy from a list of specified information.
- New-AppLocker Policy -RuleType Publisher, Hash
- -User Everyone -RuleNamePrefix DesktopEXE
- **Set-AppLockerPolicy:** Sets the AppLocker policy for a specified group policy object. We noted how to create an XML file using Get-AppLockerPolicy cmdlet previously, this is the sort of file that can be sent into **Set-AppLockerPolicy**. For example, to set the GPO specified in the LDAP path to contain the AppLocker policy that is specified in C:\Policy.xml, execute the following command:

```
Set-AppLockerPolicy -XMLPolicy C:\Policy.xml -LDAP "LDAP://
DC13.Contoso.com/CN={31B2F340-016D-11D2-945F-00C04FB984F9},CN=P
olicies,CN=System,DC=Contoso,DC=com"
```

- **Test-AppLockerPolicy:** Used to determine whether or not a specific user or group of users will be able to perform an action based on the policy specified in the AppLocker policy. For example, if you pull the effective policy with the Get-AppLockerPolicy, you can the test access to a specified folder by executing the following command:

```
Get-AppLockerPolicy -Effective | test-AppLockerPolicy -Path C:\
Folder1\*.exe -User Everyone
```

If the folder names include spaces, you will need to include quotes (") around the path.

Implementing Windows Security Features

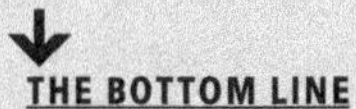

Over the years, malware has changed dramatically and has become quite sophisticated. Microsoft developed several technologies to help restrict what software and applications can access and protect your computer from malware. This technology is based on the Unified Extensible Firmware Interface (UEFI) and the trusted platform module (TPM), which help isolate security areas.

Windows Server 2016 has multiple layers of protection that help address emerging threats. This includes.

- Code Integrity (Device Guard)
- Credential Guard
- Control Flow Guard

Implementing Device Guard

CERTIFICATION READY
Implement Code Integrity (Device Guard) Policies
Objective 1.2

Code Integrity, also known as ***Device Guard***, helps harden a computer system against malware by running only trusted applications, thereby preventing malicious code from running. Windows Server 2016 uses virtualization based security to isolate the code integrity service from the Windows kernel. ***Credential Guard*** isolates and hardens key system and user security information (LSA credentials).

Code Integrity uses Windows Server 2016 ***virtual secure mode (VSM)***, which, in turn, uses the processor's virtualization to protect the PC, including data and credential tokens on the system's disks. By using hardware virtualization, Windows Server 2016 is organized into multiple containers. Windows runs one container; the Active Directory security tokens that allow access to your organization's resources run in another container. Each container is isolated from the other. Therefore, if Windows is compromised by malware, the tokens are protected because they are isolated in their own encrypted container.

The requirements for using VSM are as follows:

- UEFI running in Native Mode (not Compatibility/CSM/Legacy mode)
- 64-bit version of Windows 10 Enterprise or Windows Server 2016
- 64-bit processor that supports Second Layer Address Translation (SLAT) and Virtualization Extensions (such as Intel VT or AMD V)
- If running directly on a computer, computer hardware must be Windows 10 Enterprise Ready or Windows Server 2016 Ready.
- If running on a Hyper-V virtual machine, the Hyper-V virtual machine must be Generation 2 with secure boot enabled and virtual TPM enabled.

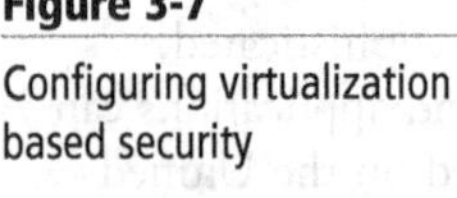

Device Guard and nested virtualization cannot be enabled at the same time.

ENABLE A VIRTUAL MACHINE SECURE BOOT AND TPM

GET READY. To install enable a virtual machine secure boot and TPM, perform the following steps.

1. In Server Manager, click **Tools > Hyper-V Manager.**
2. In the Hyper-V Manager, right-click a generation 2 machine that is turned off and choose **Settings.**
3. In the Settings dialog box, click the **Security** vertical tab.
4. Select the **Enable Secure Boot** and **Enable Trusted Platform Module** options, as shown in Figure 3-7.

Figure 3-7

Configuring virtualization based security

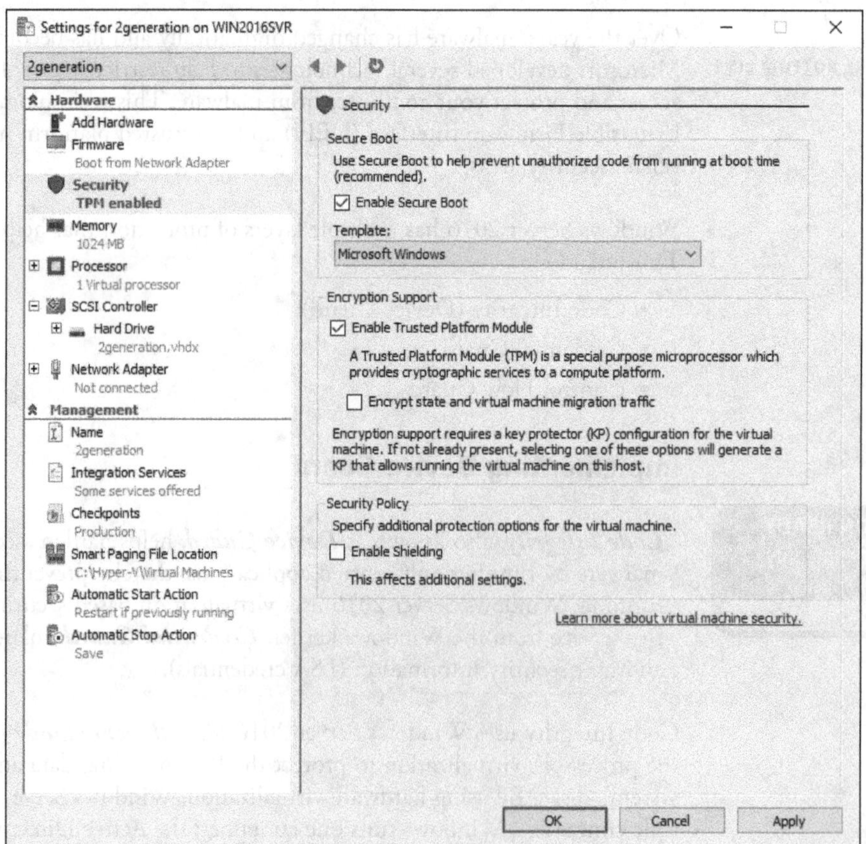

5. Close the Settings dialog box by clicking **OK.**

ENABLE DEVICE GUARD

GET READY. To enable Device Guard, perform the following steps.

1. On a domain controller, in Server Manager, click **Tools > Group Policy Management.**
2. In the Group Policy Management console, right-click a GPO and choose **Edit.**
3. Navigate to **Computer Configuration\Policies\Administrative Templates\System\Device Guard\Turn On Virtualization Based Security** (as shown in Figure 3-8).

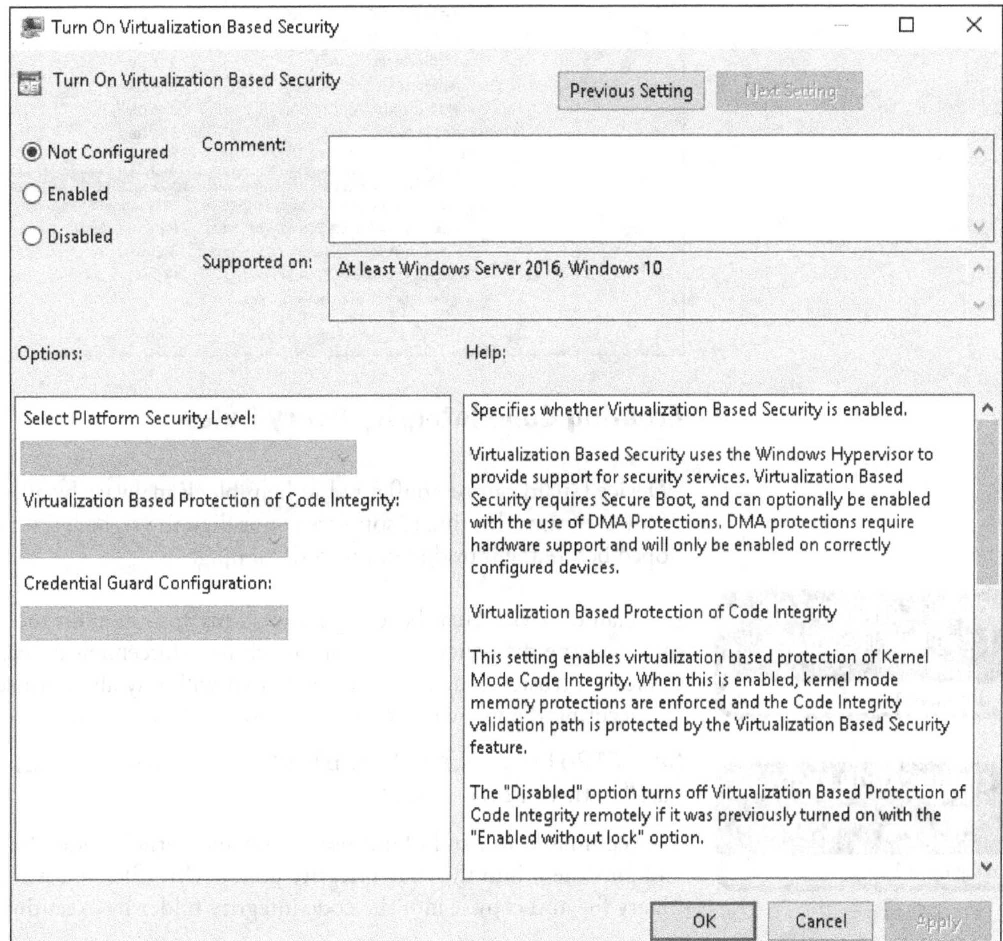

Figure 3-8

Turning on virtualization based security

4. Click **Enabled.**
5. To enable Device Guard, for the **Virtualization Based Protection of Code Integrity** option, select **Enable with UEFI lock.**
6. Close the Turn On Virtualization Based Security window by clicking **OK.**

After the GPO is received by the computer, and the computer is running, you can open System Information to verify that the Device Guard Virtualization based security is running. See Figure 3-9.

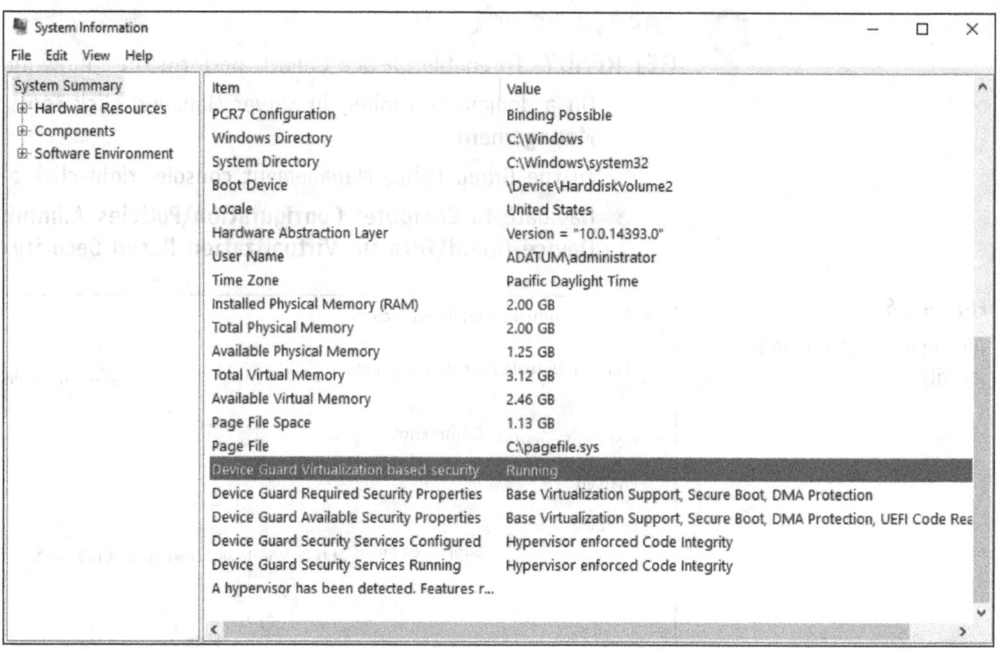

Figure 3-9

Verifying Device Guard is enabled and running

Creating Code Integrity Policy Rules

Device Guard can be configured to help block malware by allowing only signed software. However, most legitimate software is not digitally signed; several applications were developed before the introduction of code signing.

CERTIFICATION READY
Create Code Integrity policy rules
Objective 1.2

CERTIFICATION READY
Create Code Integrity file rules
Objective 1.2

By default, Device Guard's configuration runs apps in audit mode. By using audit mode, you can fine-tune the policy before you switch to enforcement mode. A common configuration is to create a trusted code integrity policy that will only allow trusted publisher-signed software by executing the following Windows PowerShell command:

```
New-CIPolicy -Level Publisher -FilePath "C:\CI\audit-publisher.
xml" -UserPEs -audit
```

This command will audit both user mode and kernel mode files, and then finds all the signers and puts them into the code integrity policy XML file. You will then convert the file into a binary file and copy it into the code integrity folder by executing the following command:

```
ConvertFrom-CIPolicy .\auditpublisher.xml .\auditpublisher.bin
```

You then copy the .bin file to the C:\Windows\System32\CodeIntegrity by executing the following command:

```
Copy-Item .\auditpublisher.bin C:\Windows\System32\
CodeIntegrity\sipolicy.p7b
```

When you restart the system, the policy will be applied and Device Guard will be put into audit mode. In audit mode, every time you execute a program that does not have a signature, the program will start and an event will be written to the Code Event Viewer Integrity folder node. You can capture policies from several servers and combine them with the `Merge-CIPolicy` cmdlet.

You can use the Windows PowerShell `Set-Rule` option to configure Device Guard configuration:

- **0 Enabled: UMCI**: By default, only kernel-mode binaries are restricted. By using this option, it will restrict both kernel-mode and user-mode binaries, which includes executables and scripts.

- **2 Required: WHQL**: By default, legacy drivers that are not Windows Hardware Quality Labs (WHQL) signed are allowed to execute. Enabling this option requires that every executed driver is WHQL signed and removes legacy driver support. However, starting with Windows 10, every new Windows 10-compatible driver must be WHQL certified.
- **3 Enabled: Audit Mode**: Enables the execution of binaries outside of the code integrity policy but logs each occurrence in the CodeIntegrity event log. To begin enforcing a code integrity policy, delete this option.
- **4 Disabled: Flight Signing**: If enabled, code integrity policies will not trust flightroot-signed binaries. This would be used in the scenario in which organizations only want to run released binaries, not flighted builds.
- **6 Enabled: Unsigned System Integrity Policy**: Allows the policy to remain unsigned. When this option is removed, the policy must be signed and have UpdatePolicySigners added to the policy to enable future policy modifications.
- **8 Required: EV Signers**: In addition to being WHQL signed, this rule requires that drivers must have been submitted by a partner that has an Extended Verification (EV) certificate. All Windows 10 and later drivers will meet this requirement.
- **9 Enabled: Advanced Boot Options Menu**: The F8 preboot menu is disabled by default for all code integrity policies. Setting this rule option allows the F8 menu to appear to physically present users.
- **10 Enabled: Boot Audit On Failure**: Used when the code integrity policy is in enforcement mode. When a driver fails during startup, the code integrity policy will be placed in audit mode so that Windows will load. Administrators can validate the reason for the failure in the CodeIntegrity event log.

The other options are not currently supported.

After you configure your audit policy and it is running successfully, you can convert it to the enforcement mode by specifying `Option 3` by executing the following command:

```
Set-RuleOption -Option 3 -FilePath [file location] -Delete
```

Then when you execute the following command and reboot the computer, Device Guard will be placed in enforcement mode:

```
ConvertFrom-CIPolicy C:\CI\MergedPolicy.xml c:\CI\auditpub-
lisher.bin
```

Implementing Credential Guard

> Credentials are associated with an account and provide a user with access to resources. Attackers often attempt to harvest the credentials to compromise security and the related services. ***Credential Guard*** isolates and hardens key system and user security information (LSA credentials) by using the same virtual secure mode that was discussed with Device Guard to store domain credentials in a virtualized environment.

CERTIFICATION READY
Determine requirements for implementing Credential Guard
Objective 1.3

CERTIFICATION READY
Configure Credential Guard using Group Policy, WMI, command prompt, and Windows PowerShell
Objective 1.3

Credential Guard protects the stored credentials for the following:

- Unconstrained Kerberos delegation
- NT LAN Manager version 1 (NTLMv1)
- Microsoft Challenge Handshake Authentication Protocol (MS-CHAPv2)
- Digest authentication
- Credential Security Support Provider (CredSSP)
- Kerberos DES encryption

Credential Guard can be enabled with one of the following methods:

- Group Policy
- Registry
- Device Guard and Credential Guard hardware readiness tool

Similar to the Device Guard, you can use System Information to review the status of Credential Guard.

ENABLE CREDENTIAL GUARD USING A GPO

GET READY. After you have turned on Virtual Machine Secure Boot and TPM, you can enable Credential Guard using a GPO by performing the following steps.

1. On a domain controller, in Server Manager, click **Tools > Group Policy Management.**
2. In the Group Policy Management console, right-click a GPO and choose **Edit.**
3. Navigate to **Computer Configuration\Policies\Administrative Templates\System\Device Guard\Turn On Virtualization Based Security.**
4. Click **Enabled.**
5. Open a GPO and then navigate to **Computer Configuration\Administrative Templates\System\Device Guard\Turn On Virtualization Based Security.**
6. To enable Credential Guard, for the Credential Guard Configuration option, select **Enable with UEFI lock.**
7. Close the Turn On Virtualization Based Security window by clicking **OK.**

ENABLE CREDENTIAL GUARD USING REGEDIT

GET READY. To enable Credential Guard using RegEdit, perform the following steps.

1. Open Registry Editor by clicking the **Start** button, typing **regedit**, and pressing **Enter.**
2. Enable virtualization-based security by navigating to and clicking the **HKEY_LOCAL_MACHINE\System\CurrentControlSet\Control\DeviceGuard** node.
3. Right-click the **DeviceGuard** node and choose **New > DWORD (32-bit) Value.** Type **EnableVirtualizationBasedSecurity** and press **Enter.**
4. In the Edit DWORD (32-bit) Value dialog box, double-click the **EnableVirtualizationBasedSecurity** value, and then set the Value data to **1** (as shown in Figure 3-10).

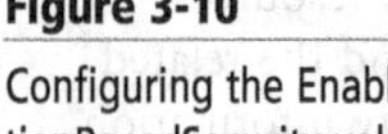

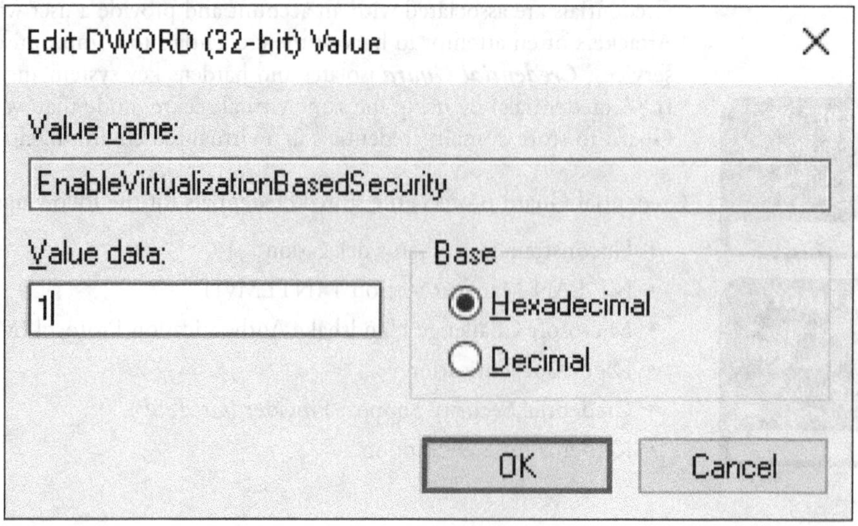

Figure 3-10
Configuring the EnableVirtualizationBasedSecurity value in the registry

5. Click **OK** to close the Edit DWORD (32-bit) Value dialog box.
6. Right-click the **DeviceGuard** node and choose **New > DWORD (32-bit) Value.** Type **RequirePlatformSecurityFeatures** and press **Enter.**
7. In the Edit DWORD (32-bit) Value dialog box, double-click the **RequirePlatformSecurityFeatures** value, set the Value data to **1** to use Secure Boot only or to **2** to use Secure Boot and DMA protection.
8. Click **OK** to close the Edit DWORD (32-bit) Value dialog box.
9. Navigate to and click the **HKEY_LOCAL_MACHINE\System\CurrentControlSet\Control\LSA** node.
10. Right-click the **LSA** node and choose **New > DWORD (32-bit) Value.** Type **LsaCfgFlags**, and then press **Enter.**
11. In the Edit DWORD (32-bit) Value dialog box, double-click the **LsaCfgFlags** value,
12. Set the Value data to **1** to enable Credential Guard with UEFI lock or **2** to enable Credential Guard without lock.
13. Click **OK** to close the Edit DWORD (32-bit) Value dialog box.
14. Close Registry Editor.

The registry settings can be changed from the command prompt or a batch file. To enable VBS and require Secure boot only, execute the following commands:

```
reg add "HKLM\SYSTEM\CurrentControlSet\Control\DeviceGuard" /v
"EnableVirtualizationBasedSecurity" /t REG_DWORD /d 1 /f
```

```
reg add "HKLM\SYSTEM\CurrentControlSet\Control\DeviceGuard" /v
"RequirePlatformSecurityFeatures" /t REG_DWORD /d 1 /f
```

Then, to enable Credential Guard with UEFI lock, execute the following command:

```
reg add "HKEY_LOCAL_MACHINE\System\CurrentControlSet\Control\
LSA" /v "LsaCfgFlags" /t REG_DWORD /d 1 /f
```

The Device Guard and Credential Guard hardware readiness tool can be searched for and downloaded from the Microsoft website. After you download the zip file, to enable Credential Guard, execute the PowerShell script by using the following command:

```
DG_Readiness_Tool_v3.2.ps1 -Enable -AutoReboot
```

Implementing Control Flow Guard

Control Flow Guard (CFG) is a highly-optimized platform security feature that is used to combat memory corruption vulnerabilities. The security options discussed in this lesson that run on the server limit what can run on the system and what cannot run on the system. Control Flow Guard is an option that is compiled into a program, which will prevent programs from executing code outside of its own memory space by extending ***Data Execution Prevention (DEP).***

CERTIFICATION READY
Implement Control Flow Guard
Objective 1.2

Buffers are areas of memory that are set aside to hold data. A buffer overrun occurs when a program or process tries to write more data than the buffer can hold. DEP is a system-level memory protection that enables the system to mark one or more pages of memory as non-executable. Marking memory regions as non-executable means that code cannot be run from that region of memory, which makes it harder for the exploitation of buffer overruns.

If an application compiled with CFG reduces the attack surface of the application. If it is running on a non-aware system, it will continue to run.

Using Enhanced Mitigation Experience Toolkit (EMET)

The ***Enhanced Mitigation Experience Toolkit (EMET)*** is a free Microsoft security tool that is designed to protect software from undiscovered or zero-day exploits that may not have security fixes yet. While EMET will not protect against 100% of threats (no tool can), it is another tool that will protect against attacks.

EMET runs on Windows Vista SP2 and higher and Windows Server 2008 SP2 and higher. However, Windows 10 and Windows Server 2016 support the mitigations for untrusted fonts. EMET requires Microsoft .NET Framework 4.

EMET includes the following:

- **Attack Surface Reduction (ASR) Mitigation:** Blocks the usage of specific modules and plugins in target applications.
- **Data Execution Prevention (DEP) Security Mitigation:** Prevents an attacker from placing executable code in certain areas of memory. Using EMET, you can force applications compiled without Control Flow Control support/DEP flag to also use DEP.
- **Structured Execution Handling Overwrite Protection (SEHOP) Security Mitigation:** Protects against one of the most common attack vectors for exploiting stack overflows in Windows.
- **Heapspray Allocation Security Mitigation:** Prevents shellcode from being placed into commonly used memory pages.
- **NullPage Security Mitigation:** Prevents potential null deference issues in user mode.
- **Export Address Table Filtering (EAF) Security Mitigation:** Filters access to the Export Address Table based on the calling code origination.
- **Mandatory Address Space Layout Randomization (ASLR) Security Mitigation:** Randomizes the addresses where modules are loaded to prevent an attacker from using predictable memory locations.
- **Bottom Up ASLR Security Mitigation:** Randomizes the base address of bottom-up allocations.
- **Load Library Check [Return-Oriented Programming (ROP) Security Mitigation]:** Prevents .dll files from being loaded from UNC paths.
- **Memory Protection Check [Return-Oriented Programming (ROP) Security Mitigation]:** Disallows making the stack area executable.
- **Caller Checks – [Return-Oriented Programming (ROP) Security Mitigation – 32-bit processes only]:** Ensures critical functions are reached via a CALL instruction rather than RET.
- **Simulate Execution Flow – [Return-Oriented Programming (ROP) Security Mitigation – 32-bit processes only]:** Following a call to a critical function, tries to detect ROP gadgets.
- **Stack Pivot [Return-Oriented Programming (ROP) Security Mitigation]:** If the stack is pivoted, the stack register present in certain APIs is validated.
- **Windows 10 untrusted fonts:** Protects systems from untrusted fonts that are installed outside of the C:\Windows\Fonts directory.
- **Certificate Trust:** Adds additional checks to certificate trust validation to protect systems from man-in-the-middle attacks.

Implementing NT Lan Manager (NTLM) Blocking

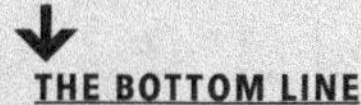

NTLM is a mature authentication protocol used in Windows operating system. Because NTLM authenticating protocol is less secure than the Kerberos authentication protocol, you can block the use of NTLM for authentication and force the systems use Kerberos.

CERTIFICATION READY
Implement NTLM blocking
Objective 1.3

NT LAN Manager (NTLM) is a suite of Microsoft security protocols that provides authentication, integrity, and confidentiality to users. NTLM is an integrated Single Sign-On mechanism, which is probably best recognized as part of Integrated Windows Authentication for HTTP authentication. It provides maximum compatibility with different versions of Windows and compared with Kerberos, it is the easiest to implement.

NTLM uses a challenge-response mechanism for authentication in which clients are able to prove their identities without sending a password to the server. After a random 8-byte challenge message is sent to the client from the server, the client uses the user's password as a key to generate a response back to the server using an MD4/MD5 hashing algorithm (one-way mathematical calculation) and DES encryption (a commonly used encryption algorithm that encrypts and decrypts data with the same key).

Although Kerberos v5 is the preferred authentication protocol for Active Directory–based environments, NTLM is used for systems running Windows NT 4.0 and earlier and for computers that are a member of a workgroup. It is also used when authenticating to a server that belongs to a different Active Directory forest.

Therefore, before you decide to block NTLM, you need to make sure that existing applications are no longer using NTML. To audit NTLM traffic, you can enable the following GPO security options, which are found in the Computer Configuration\Policies\Windows Settings\Security Settings\Local Policies\Security Options node:

- **Network security:** Restrict NTLM: Outgoing NTLM Traffic to remote servers. Configure this policy with the Audit All setting.
- **Network security:** Restrict NTLM: Audit Incoming NTLM Traffic. Configure this policy with the Enable auditing for all accounts setting (as shown in Figure 3-11.
- **Network security:** Restrict NTLM: Audit NTLM authentication in this domain. Configure this policy with the Enable all setting on domain controllers only setting. You should not configure this policy on all computers.

Figure 3-11

Enabling auditing of NTLM

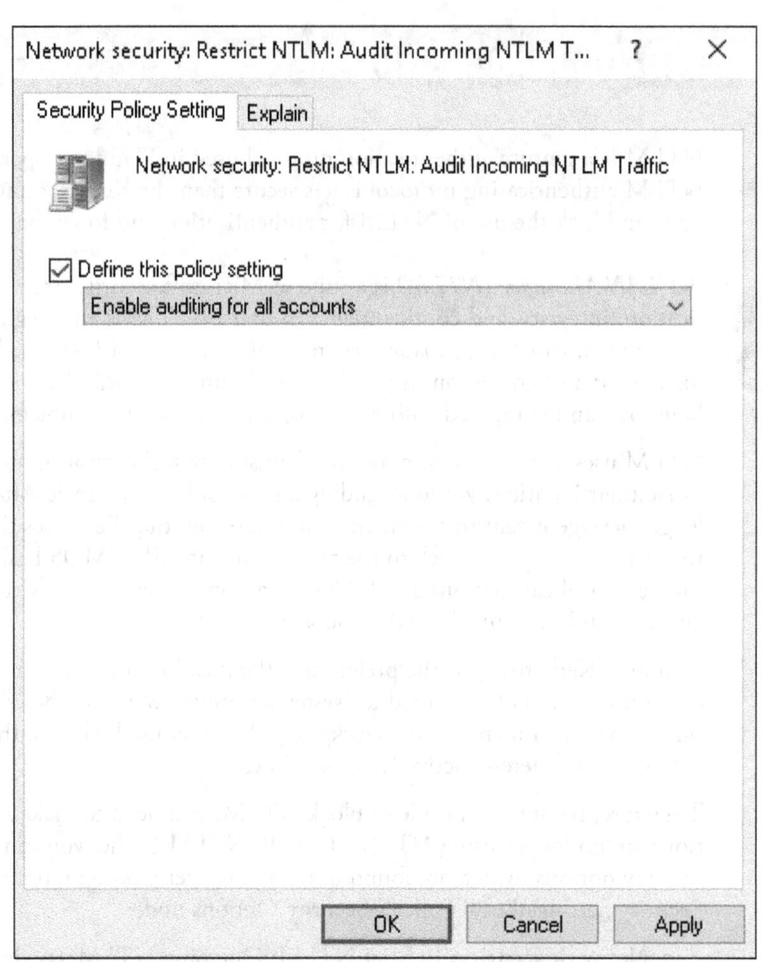

Audit events are recorded in the Event Viewer Applications and Services Log/Microsoft/Windows/NTLM/Operations, as shown in Figure 3-12.

Figure 3-12

Viewing NTLM events

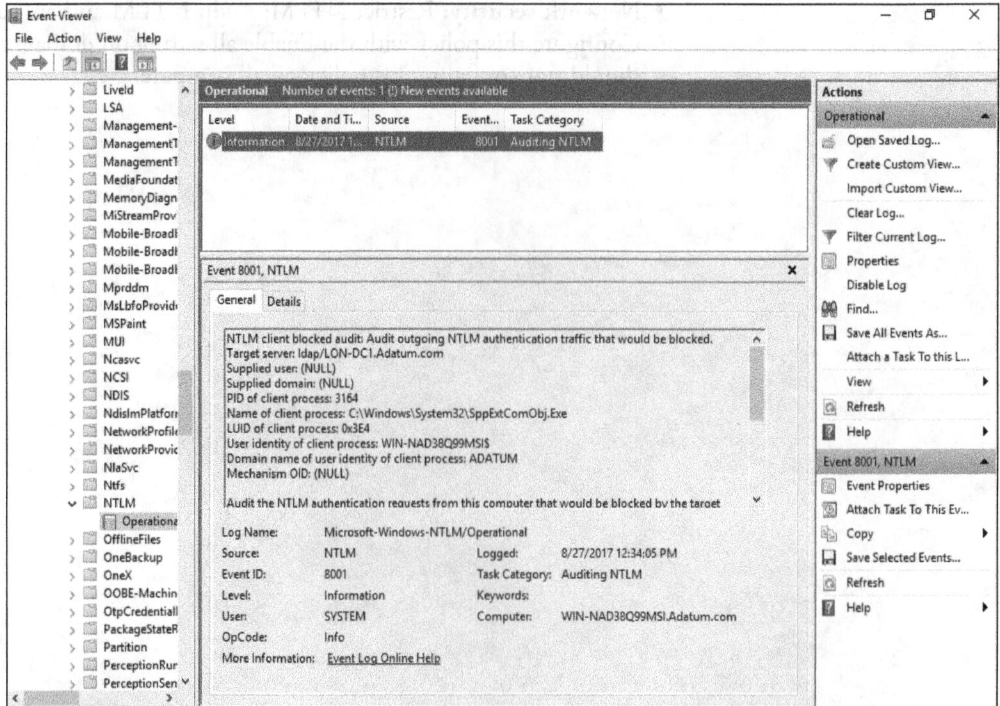

When you have eliminated use of NTLM and you want to restrict NTLM, enable the following options in the GPO Computer Configuration\Policies\Windows Settings\Security Settings\Local Policies\Security Options node.

- **Allow domain logon-related NTLM and NTLM traffic to servers in this domain:** The domain controller will allow all NTLM pass-through authentication requests within the domain.
- **Allow domain logon-related NTLM traffic or NTLM traffic to servers in this domain:** The domain controller will deny all NTLM authentication logon attempts to all servers in the domain that are using domain accounts and display an NTLM blocked error unless the server name is on the exception list in the Network Security: Restrict NTLM: Add server exceptions for NTLM authentication in this domain policy setting.
- **Deny domain logon-related NTLM traffic in this domain:** The domain controller will deny all NTLM authentication logon attempts from domain accounts and display an NTLM blocked error unless the server name is on the exception list in the Network Security: Restrict NTLM: Add server exceptions for NTLM authentication in this domain policy setting.
- **Deny NTLM traffic to servers in this domain:** The domain controller will deny NTLM authentication requests to all servers in the domain and display an NTLM blocked error unless the server name is on the exception list in the Network Security: Restrict NTLM: Add server exceptions for NTLM authentication in this domain policy setting.
- **Deny NTLM traffic in this domain:** The domain controller will deny all NTLM pass-through authentication requests from its servers and for its accounts and display an NTLM blocked error unless the server name is on the exception list in the Network Security: Restrict NTLM: Add server exceptions for NTLM authentication in this domain policy setting.

SKILL SUMMARY

IN THIS LESSON YOU LEARNED:

- Windows Defender is designed to protect your computer against viruses, spyware, and other types of malware. It protects against these threats by providing real-time protection in which it notifies you if malware attempts to install itself on your computer or when an application tries to change critical settings.
- Because Windows Defender is a Microsoft application, it can be updated with Windows Update, WSUS, and Configuration Manager. Updates include Windows Defender and the definitions that help identify malware.
- AppLocker is a feature found in Windows Server 2012 and higher and Windows 7 and higher. It configured with GPOs, which can be used to control how users access and use programs and files and extends the functionality originally provided by the Software Restriction policy found in earlier versions of Windows operating systems.
- Code Integrity, also known as Device Guard, helps harden a computer system against malware by running only trusted applications, thereby preventing malicious code from running. Windows Server 2016 uses virtualization based security to isolate the code integrity service from the Windows kernel.
- Credential Guard isolates and hardens key system and user security information (LSA credentials).
- Device Guard can be configured to help block malware by allowing only signed software. However, many legitimate software is not digitally signed, and many applications were developed before the introduction of code signing.
- Control Flow Guard (CFG) is a highly-optimized platform security feature that is used to combat memory corruption vulnerabilities. Control Flow Guard is an option that is compiled into program, which will prevent programs from executing code outside of its own memory space by extending Data Execution Prevention (DEP).
- The Enhanced Mitigation Experience Toolkit (EMET) is a free Microsoft security tool that is designed to protect software from undiscovered or zero-day exploits that may not have security fixes yet. While EMET will not protect against 100% of threats (no tool can), it is another tool that will protect against attacks.
- NTLM is a mature authentication protocol used in Windows operating system. Since NTLM authenticating protocol is less secure than the Kerberos authentication protocol, you can block the use of NTLM for authentication and force the systems use Kerberos.

Knowledge Assessment

Multiple Choice

1. Which of the following features can protect a PC against malware?
   a. Windows Defender
   b. Windows Quicktime
   c. Windows File History
   d. Windows Antivirus
2. Which of the following scan options are available in Windows Defender? (Choose all that apply.)
   a. Quick
   b. Full
   c. Optional
   d. Custom
3. Which of the following tabs shows quarantined Windows Defender items?
   a. Home tab
   b. History tab
   c. Update tab
   d. Settings tab
4. In your corporation, which of the following enables you to configure Windows Defender so that the options are the same for each computer?
   a. Registry
   b. WSUS
   c. Windows Updates
   d. GPOs
5. Which Windows PowerShell cmdlet is used to start a scan?
   a. Start-DefenderScan
   b. Start-MpScan
   c. Start-Scan
   d. Begin-Scan
6. When setting up a rule using AppLocker, which of the following primary conditions should be set when you want to use the same rule again after the manufacture updates the application?
   a. Path
   b. Publisher
   c. File Hash
   d. Execute

7. Which of the following options cause the system to compute a hash on the file when using AppLocker—and each time the app is updated or patched, you must update the hash again?
   a. EFS
   b. Path hash
   c. Folder hash
   d. File Hash
8. Which of the following rule collections are used in AppLocker? (Choose all that apply)
   a. Executable files
   b. Scripts
   c. Windows Image files
   d. Appx
9. Which security feature is used by Code Integrity and Credential Guard?
   a. AppLocker
   b. Windows Defender
   c. WSUS
   d. virtual secure mode (VSM)
10. Which of the following is the default mode for Code Integrity?
   a. Audit
   b. Enforcement
   c. Logging
   d. Published

Best Answer

Choose the letter that corresponds to the best answer. More than one answer choice may achieve the goal. Select the BEST answer.

1. In an organization, which of the following provides the best way to keep Windows Defender up to date?
   a. Windows Update
   b. WSUS
   c. SCOM
   d. Update Manager
2. Which security technology is used to isolate and harden key system and user security information/LSA credentials?
   a. Code Integrity
   b. Device Guard
   c. Credential Guard
   d. virtual secure mode (VSM)

3. Which of the following is the best method to ensure that only signed applications run on systems running Windows 10 and Windows Server 2016?
   a. AppLocker
   b. Code Integrity
   c. SCOM
   d. Update Manager
4. Which feature must be enabled when compiling a program that will combat memory corruption vulnerabilities?
   a. Credential Guard
   b. Device Guard
   c. Control Flow Guard
   d. Data Execution Prevention
5. Which free Microsoft security suite can help protect against software from undiscovered or zero-day exploits?
   a. Credential Guard
   b. Device Guard
   c. EMET
   d. Control Flow Guard

Build List

1. Specify the correct order of steps necessary to remove a quarantined item in Windows Defender.
   _____ Click Quarantined Items.
   _____ Open Windows Defender.
   _____ Select the detected item and read the description.
   _____ Click View Details.
   _____ Click the History tab.
   _____ Click Remove.
2. Specify the correct order of steps necessary to enable Device Guard.
   _____ Create a trusted code integrity policy.
   _____ Turn on virtualization based security.
   _____ Copy the bin file to the C:\Windows\System32\CodeIntegrity.
   _____ Make sure Secure Boot and Trusted Platform Module is enabled.
   _____ Convert the .xml file to a .bin file.

■ Business Case Scenarios

Scenario 3-1: Using Kerberos

You are an administrator for the Contoso Corporation, which has about 1,200 computers, mostly running Windows 10. You also administer an Active Directory domain that contains approximately 150 servers running Windows Server 2016. Your supervisor has been reading how Kerberos is much more secure than NTLM and he wants the company to discontinue its use of NTLM. Describe your recommended solution.

Scenario 3-2: Securing Your Computers

You are an administrator for the Contoso Corporation, which has about 1,200 computers, mostly running Windows 10. Over the past year, you have managed several instances of malware appearing on the computers of key personnel, leading to a compromise of some key systems. You want to ensure that this does not happen again. Describe how to make sure that users' credentials and other key parts of Windows are not compromised by rootkits or other forms of malware.

Creating Security Baselines

LESSON 4

70-744 EXAM OBJECTIVE

Objective 1.4 – Create security baselines. This objective may include but is not limited to: Install and configure Microsoft Security Compliance Toolkit; create, view, and import security baselines; deploy configurations to domain and non-domain joined servers.

Lesson Heading	Exam Objective
Creating Security Baselines with Microsoft Security Compliance Toolkit	
• Installing and Configuring Microsoft Security Compliance Toolkit	Install and configure Microsoft Security Compliance Toolkit
• Creating, Viewing, Importing, and Deploying Security Baselines	Create, view, and import security baselines Deploy configurations to domain and non-domain joined servers

KEY TERMS

LGPO (LGPO.exe)
Microsoft Security Compliance Toolkit
Policy Analyzer (PolicyAnalyzer.exe)
security baseline

■ Creating Security Baselines with Microsoft Security Compliance Toolkit

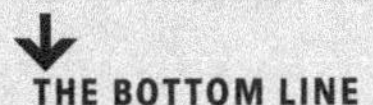

Microsoft Security Compliance Toolkit is a free set of tools that allow enterprise security administrators to download, analyze, test, and store Microsoft-recommended security baselines for Windows and other Microsoft products while comparing them against other security configurations. It replaces the Security Compliance Manager (SCM).

A ***security baseline*** is a collection of configurations items for a Microsoft product that provides prescribed values to help maintain security of a system or to solve a specific use case or scenario. To help you establish and deploy security baselines, you can use a toolkit to provide ready to deploy policies and configuration packages that are based on Microsoft Security guide recommendations and industry best practices. When deployed as a Group Policy Object (GPO), you can manage configuration drift, address compliance requirements, and reduce security threats.

The ***Microsoft Security Configuration Toolkit*** can compare current GPOs with Microsoft-recommended GPO baselines or other baselines, edit the GPOs, store the GPO settings in a GPO backup file format, and apply them via a Domain Controller.

The Security Configuration Toolkit consists of:

- ***Policy Analyzer (PolicyAnalyzer.exe):*** A utility for analyzing and comparing sets of GPOs, showing the redundant settings and highlighting differences between versions or sets of Group Policies. It can also compare current local policy settings, local registry settings, and then export results to a Microsoft Excel spreadsheet.
- ***LGPO (LGPO.exe):*** A tool for transferring Group Policy directly between a host's registry and a GPO backup file, which gives you a simple method to test the effects of Group Policy settings directly without deploying through domain controllers.

Installing and Configuring Microsoft Security Compliance Toolkit

The Microsoft Security Compliance Toolkit can be downloaded from the Microsoft website. The toolkit is supported by Windows 10, Windows Server 2012 R2, and Windows Server 2016. To use the toolkit, you need .NET Framework 4.6 or later. The toolkit consists of multiple executable files; there is no real installation. Instead, you download the files from the Microsoft website and unzip the files.

CERTIFICATION READY
Install and configure Microsoft Security Compliance Toolkit
Objective 1.4

The high-level steps to use the Security Compliance Toolkit are as follows:

1. Search for and download the toolkit (PolicyAnalyzer.zip and LGPO.zip) with the necessary baselines of the desired Windows versions.
2. Back up your GPOs.
3. Load an existing Group Policy Backup and a downloaded baseline into Policy Analyzer.
4. Make edits to the existing Group Policy Backup within Policy Analyzer, and save the revised version.
5. Use LGPO to load the revised Backup into a host for testing.
6. Restore the revised backup as the new GPO for deployment.

Creating, Viewing, Importing, and Deploying Security Baselines

CERTIFICATION READY
Create, view, and import security baselines
Objective 1.4

CERTIFICATION READY
Deploy configurations to domain and non-domain joined servers
Objective 1.4

When you download the toolkit, Microsoft provides a set of downloadable security baselines, published both as spreadsheets and as GPO backups, for Windows releases Windows 10 version 1507, 1511 and 1607 and Windows Server 2012 R2 and 2016. Additional baselines will be added as time goes on. You can use these baselines to see if you follow recommended security settings.

With the Group Policy Management Console, you can back up all GPOs or individual GPOs. Every time a backup is performed, a new backup version of the GPO is created.

BACK UP GPOS

GET READY. To back up GPOs, perform the following steps.

1. Log on to a domain controller such as **LON-DC1** as **adatum\administrator** with the password of **Pa$$w0rd.**
2. Open **Server Manager.**
3. In Server Manager, click **Tools > Group Policy Management.**

4. In the Group Policy Management Console, navigate to and click the **Group Policy Objects** container.
5. To back up all GPOs, right-click the **Group Policy Objects** container and choose **Back Up All.** The Back Up Group Policy Object dialog box opens (see Figure 4-1).

Figure 4-1

Opening the Back Up Group Policy Object dialog box

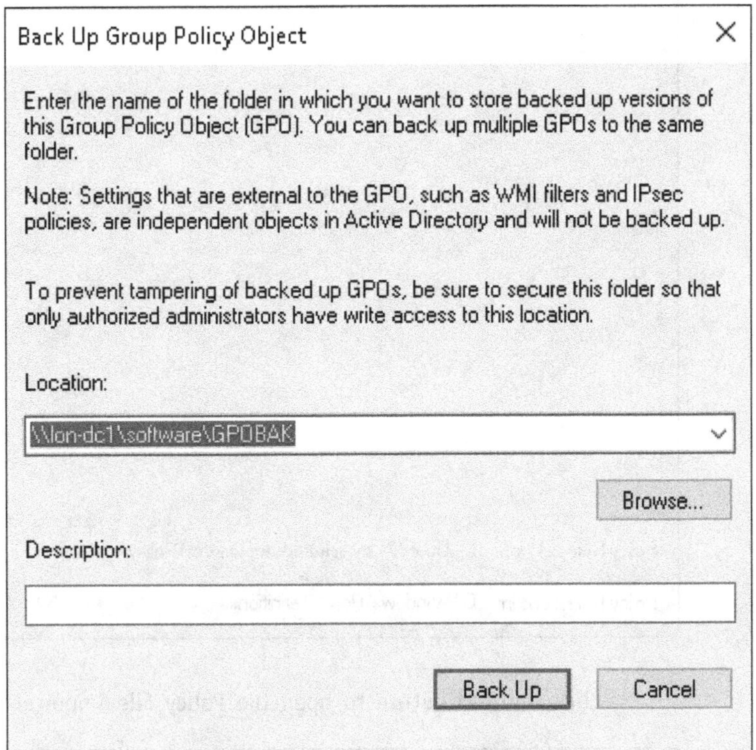

6. In the Location text box, type the location where you want to store the backups and click **Back Up.**
7. When the backup is complete, click **OK.**
8. Close the Group Policy Management Console.

LOAD AND COMPARE GPO SETTINGS

GET READY. To load and compare GPO settings, perform the following steps.

1. Log on to a domain controller such as **LON-DC1** as **adatum\administrator** with the password of **Pa$$w0rd.**
2. Double-click the **PolicyAnalyzer.exe** file. If you are prompted to confirm that you want to run this file, click **Run.** The Policy Analyzer opens, as shown in Figure 4-2.

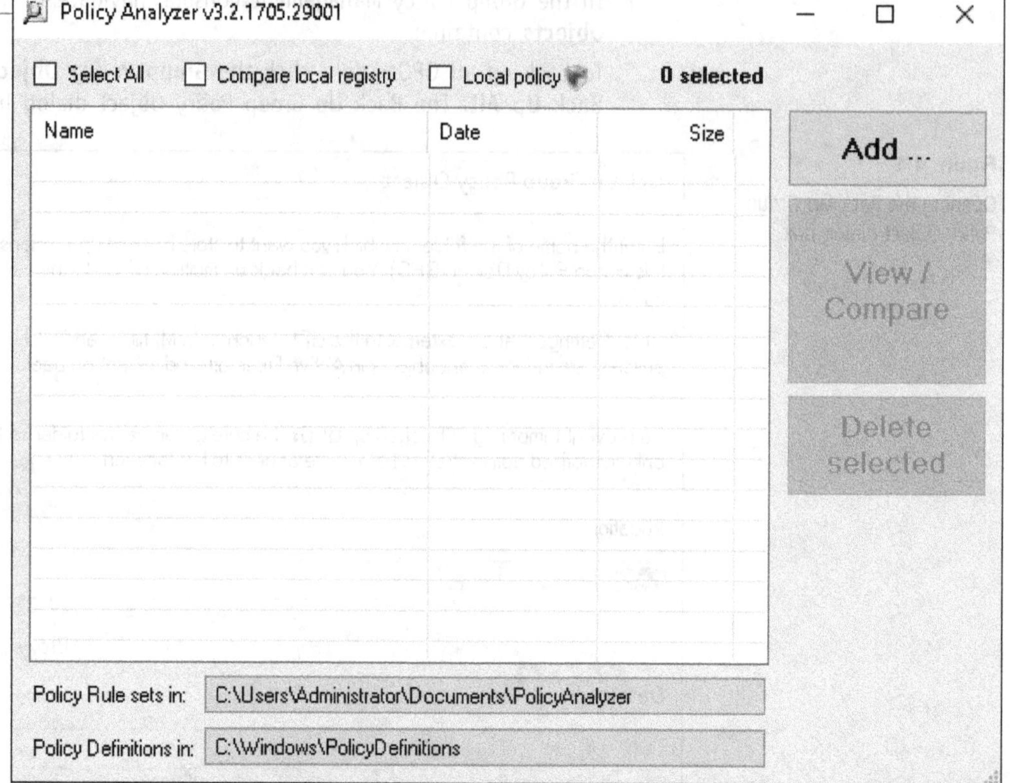

Figure 4-2

Opening the Policy Analyzer

3. Click the **Add** button to open the Policy File Importer.

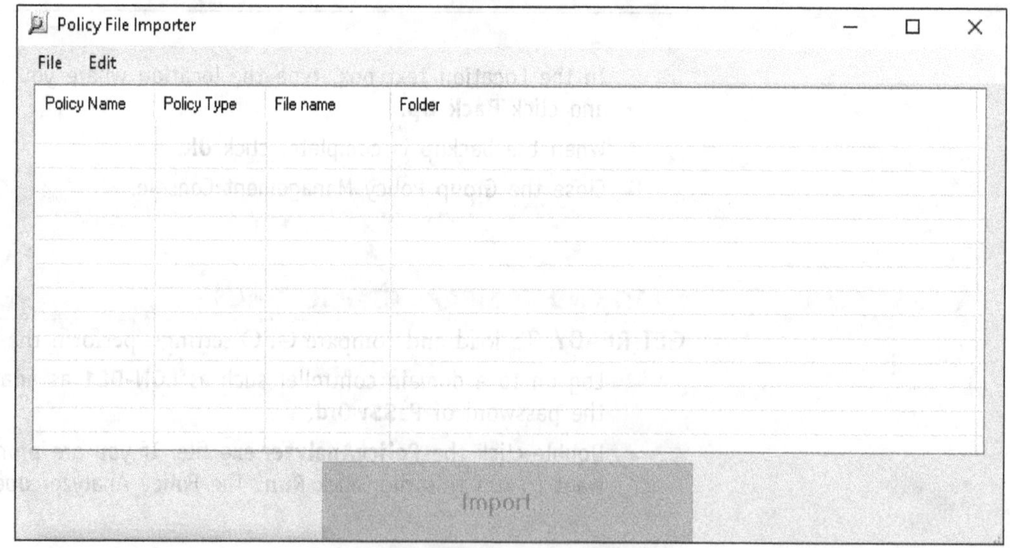

Figure 4-3

Opening the Policy File Importer

4. Click **File > Add files from GPO(s).**
5. Navigate to the folder that contains the GPO backups and click **Select Folder.**
6. Back in the Policy File Importer dialog box, click **Import.**
7. In the Import Policy Rules dialog box, in the File name text box, type **PolRule1** and click **Save.** If you are prompted to confirm that you want to run the file, click **Run.**
8. Click the **Add** button to open the Policy File Importer.

9. Click **File > Add files from GPO(s)**.
10. Navigate to the folder that contains the GPO Templates/Baselines and click **Select Folder**.
11. Back on the Policy File Importer dialog box, click **Import**. If you are prompted to confirm you want to run PolicyRulesFileBilder.exe, click **Run**.
12. Back on the Policy Analyzer window, click **View/Compare**.
13. Scroll down and look through the various settings, as shown in Figure 4-4.

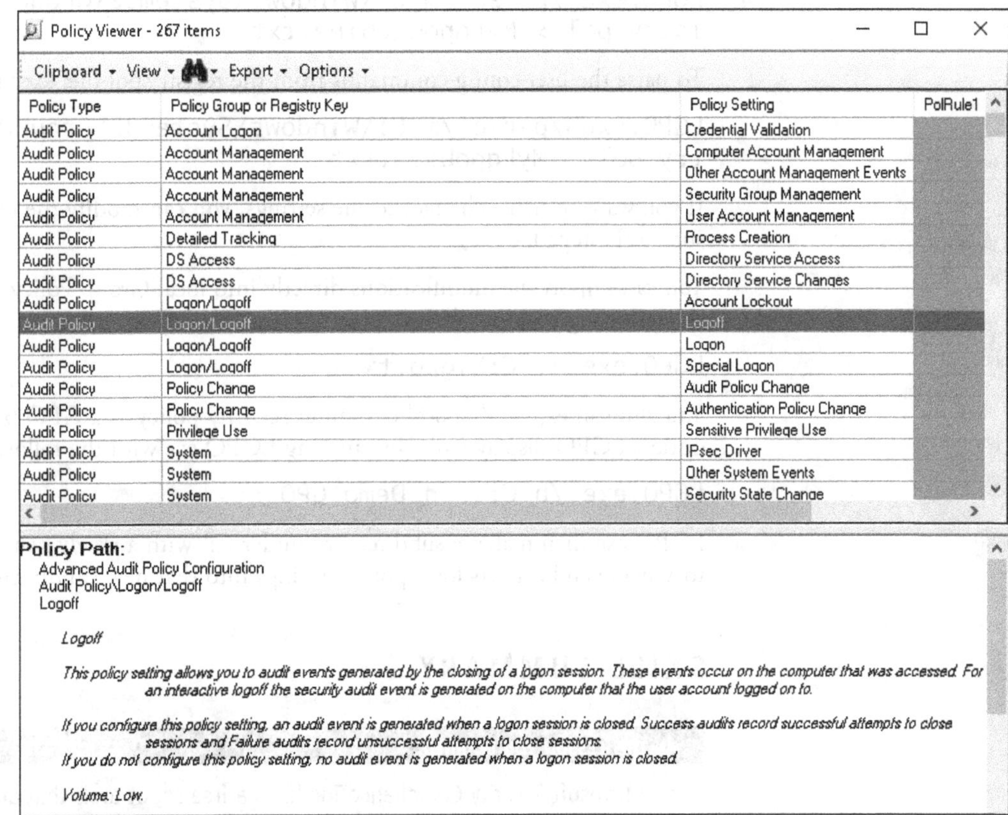

Figure 4-4

Viewing policies with the Policy Viewer

14. Click **View > Show only Differences**.

Policy Analyzer can import three types of GPO files:

- Registry policy files
- Security templates
- Audit policy backup files

The registry policy files are binary file format that contains information for the Computer Configuration (HKLM) or User Configuration (HKCU), which is created by Group Policy editors such as GpEdit.msc. Security template files are text files in the old Windows 3.x ".ini" file format. The Security template files typically contain settings from the Account Policies and Local Policies sections under Computer Configuration\Windows Settings\Security Settings in the GPO editor. These settings include password policy, account lockout policy, legacy audit policy, user rights assignments, and security options. Audit policy backup files (usually "audit.csv") are comma-separated values (CSV) text files that contain data representing the settings in the Advanced Audit Policy Configuration folder under Security Settings.

In Policy Viewer, you can search for specific settings by clicking File > Find or Find again. By opening the Export menu, you can export the table to Excel or export all data to Excel.

To deploy baseline settings to a local Group Policy management console, the toolkit provides LGPO.exe. Therefore, when a client or server is not part of an AD DS domain environment, you can save the baseline as a GPO, then use the LGPO.exe to import the GPOs directly into the computer's configuration.

If you are using Group Policy, the registry.pol files can be found in the User and Machine subfolders located C:\Windows\System32\GroupPolicy folder. To parse the machine config commands from the registry.pol file, execute the following command:

```
LGPO.exe /parse /m C:\Windows\System32\GroupPolicy\Machine\registry.pol > MyLgpoMachine.txt
```

To parse the user config commands from the registry.pol file, execute the following command:

```
LGPO.exe /parse /m C:\Windows\System32\GroupPolicy\User\registry.pol > MyLgpoUser.txt
```

If you want to make changes to the settings, you can modify the text files with a text editor such as Notepad.

You can import the modifications directly into local Group Policy using the `/t` option, which the following example shows:

```
LGPO.exe /t C:\lgpo.txt
```

You also can export the local computer security policy as a GPO backup and include an optional GPO display name by running LGPO.exe with the following command:

```
LGPO.exe /b C:\ /n Demo_GPO
```

LGPO.exe then makes a subdirectory under C:\ with a newly generated GUID for the directory name and exports local policy settings into that new subdirectory.

SKILL SUMMARY

IN THIS LESSON YOU LEARNED:

- Microsoft Security Compliance Toolkit is a free set of tools that allows enterprise security administrators to download, analyze, test, and store Microsoft-recommended security baselines for Windows and other Microsoft products while comparing them against other security configurations. It replaces the Security Compliance Manager.
- A security baseline is a collection of configurations items for a Microsoft product that provides prescribed values to help maintain security of a system or to solve a specific use case or scenario.
- To help you establish and deploy security baselines, you can use toolkit to provide ready-to-deploy policies and configuration packages that are based on Microsoft Security guide recommendations and industry best practices.
- The Policy Analyzer is a utility for analyzing and comparing sets of GPOs, showing the redundant settings and highlighting differences between versions or sets of Group Policies. It can also compare current local policy settings, local registry settings, and then export results to a Microsoft Excel spreadsheet.
- To deploy baseline settings to a local Group Policy management console, the toolkit provides LGPO.exe.

Knowledge Assessment

Multiple Choice

1. Which of the following is a collection of configuration items for a Microsoft baseline that provides values to help maintain security of a system or to solve a specific user case or scenario?
   a. security baseline
   b. security policy
   c. security collection
   d. security tree

2. Which free Microsoft software enables you to quickly view and compare GPO security settings with Microsoft best practices for computers running Windows using Group Policy?
   a. SCM
   b. SCCM
   c. SCOM
   d. Microsoft Security Compliance Toolkit

3. Which of the following best describes how to deploy security settings defined with Microsoft Security Compliance Toolkit to your domain computers?
   a. Running an executable file on the domain computer that was generated by the toolkit
   b. Loading the toolkit client on the domain computer
   c. Creating a spreadsheet of recommended settings and then importing the settings into a GPO with Policy Analyzer
   d. Using Policy Analyzer to import policies into a domain controller.

4. Which tool is used to deploy security settings to local GPOs generated by the Microsoft Security Compliance Toolkit to systems running Windows Server 2016 that are not part of your domain?
   a. LocalGPO.exe
   b. LGPO.exe
   c. LGPOPush.exe
   d. DeployGPO.exe

Best Answer

Choose the letter that corresponds to the best answer. More than one answer choice may achieve the goal. Select the BEST answer.

1. Which of the following is the easiest way to define and deploy security settings to all of your domain computers so that they comply with Microsoft's best practices?
   a. Using SCCM
   b. Using Microsoft Security Compliance Toolkit
   c. Using SCOM
   d. Using Security Manager

Build List

1. List the correct order of steps necessary to use Microsoft Security Compliance Toolkit to defined security settings.
   _____ Back up your GPOs.
   _____ Restore the revised backup as the new GPO for deployment.
   _____ Download the Security Compliance Toolkit and related baselines.
   _____ Load an existing Group Policy backup and a download baseline into Policy Analyzer.
   _____ Use LGP to load the revised Backup into a host for testing.
   _____ Make edits to the existing Group Policy Backup within Policy Analyze and save the revised versions.

■ Business Case Scenarios

Scenario 4-1: Deploying Security Settings

You are an administrator at the Contoso Corporation, which uses more than 500 servers running Windows Server 2012 R2 and Windows Server 2016. You need to ensure that each server has the appropriate security settings. How can you select the appropriate security settings and deploy them to the servers?

LESSON 5

Securing Virtual Machines with Guarded Fabric and Shielding VMs

70-744 EXAM OBJECTIVE

Objective 2.1 – Implement a Guarded Fabric solution. This objective may include but is not limited to the following: Install and configure the Host Guardian Service (HGS); configure Admin-trusted attestation; configure TPM-trusted attestation; configure the Key Protection Service using HGS; migrate Shielded VMs to other guarded hosts; and troubleshoot guarded hosts.

Objective 2.2 – Implement Shielded and encryption-supported VMs. This objective may include but is not limited to the following: Determine requirements and scenarios for implementing Shielded VMs; create a Shielded VM using only a Hyper-V environment; enable and configure vTPM to allow an operating system and data disk encryption within a VM; determine requirements and scenarios for implementing encryption-supported VMs; and troubleshoot Shielded and encryption-supported VMs.

Lesson Heading	Exam Objective
Implementing a Guarded Fabric Solution • Installing and Configuring the Host Guardian Service (HGS) • Configuring Attestation • Configuring the Key Protection Service (KPS) Using HGS • Migrating Shielded VMs to Other Guarded Hosts • Configuring Nano Server as a TPM-Attested Guarded Host • Troubleshooting Guarded Hosts	Install and configure the Host Guardian Service (HGS) Configure Admin-trusted attestation Configure TPM-trusted attestation Configure the Key Protection Service using HGS Migrate Shielded VMs to other guarded hosts Troubleshoot guarded hosts
Implementing Shielded and Encrypted-Supported VMs • Determining Requirements and Scenarios for Implementing Encrypted and Shielded VMs • Creating a Shielded VM and Configuring vTPM for Data Disk Encryption • Troubleshooting Shielded and Encryption-Supported VMs	Determine requirements and scenarios for implementing Shielded VMs Determine requirements and scenarios for implementing encryption-supported VMs Create a Shielded VM using only a Hyper-V environment Enable and configure vTPM to allow an operating system and data disk encryption within a VM Troubleshoot Shielded and encryption-supported VMs

KEY TERMS

Attestation services
baseline policy
code-integrity (CI) policy
fabric
guarded fabric
Host Guardian Service (HGS)
Key Protection Service (KPS)
shielded VM

■ Implementing a Guarded Fabric Solution

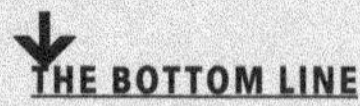

Today, most corporations are running a virtualized environment, which consists of one or more hosts running multiple virtual machines. A virtual machine consists of files that define the characteristics of the virtual machine and runs in its own partitions (memory, processing disk, and networking). While locked doors and cages, cameras, and guards will protect the physical server, you will need to take additional steps to protect virtual machines from a compromised physical host. A ***guarded fabric*** is a Windows Server 2016 Hyper-V fabric capable of protecting workloads against inspection, theft, and tampering. You can think of a ***fabric*** as a platform or framework.

A guarded fabric in Windows Server 2016 consists of the following.

- One Host Guardian Service (HGS), which typically includes a cluster of three nodes
- One or more guarded Hyper-V hosts
- A set of shielded VMs

A ***shielded VM*** is a Generation 2 VM that has a virtual TPM, is encrypted by using BitLocker Drive Encryption. By using a guarded fabric and shielded VMs, you can provide a more secure environment for tenant VMs where you have different clients running on your virtual environment.

Installing and Configuring the Host Guardian Service (HGS)

The ***Host Guardian Service (HGS)*** is a server role introduced in Windows Server 2016 for configuring guarded hosts and running shielded VMs (virtual machines) in Windows Server and System Center Virtual Machine Manager. It provides Attestation and Key Protections services that are needed to enable Hyper-V on healthy hosts to run Shielded VMs. ***Attestation services*** validate a Hyper-V host as a "guarded host," which then enables the ***Key Protection Service (KPS)*** to provide the transport key required to unlock and subsequently run Shielded VMs.

CERTIFICATION READY
Install and configure the Host Guardian Service (HGS).
Objective 2.1

You can install the HGS role by using Server Manager or Windows PowerShell. It is recommended to use a dedicated physical computer running the Server Core installation option for HGS. After installing the HGS role, HGS is configured and managed by using Windows PowerShell.

The hardware requirements for an HGS server are:

- Use TPM so that you can enable BitLocker
- Enable Secure Boot

The software requirements for an HGS server are:

- Enable BitLocker to help ensure the data is secure while at rest (not in transit).
- Enable Windows Firewall.
- Install HGS role on Windows Server 2016.
- Ensure that the HGS server has at least one static IP address for each HGS node.
- Use HTTPS for the representational state transfer (REST) API so that Secure Sockets Layer (SSL) can be enabled for the REST API calls.
- Provision a valid SSL certificate, which needs to be issued in the name of the HGS Service fully qualified domain name (FQDN).
- The host should not be part of a domain.

To install the HGS server role, you must be a member of the local Administrators group on the server. To help ensure that shielded VMs can run on guarded hosts in the event of a server outage, you should have three instances of the HGS server role.

After you install and initialize the HGS server role, the AD DS server role is automatically installed on the server, and promoted to a domain controller on the private AD DS. Additional HGS servers will be configured as domain controllers in the same domain. In addition, the server automatically becomes a failover cluster member. Lastly, the server is automatically configured with a Just Enough Administration profile and registered with predefined Active Directory user groups. Just Enough Administration is discussed in Lesson 9.

INSTALL THE HGS ROLE

GET READY. To install and configure the GHS role on a server that is running Windows Server 2016 and not part of the domain, perform the following steps:

1. Click the **Start** button and then click **Windows PowerShell**.
2. Install the Host Guardian Service role by executing the following command:
```
Install-WindowsFeature HostGuardianServiceRole
-IncludeManagementTools -Restart
```
3. If the server reboots, log on to the server and open the Windows PowerShell window.
4. Install the HGS server:
```
$safepass = ConvertTo-SecureString -String "Pa$$w0rd"
-AsPlainText -Force
Install-HgsServer -HgsDomainName "contoso.com"
-SafeModeAdministratorPassword $safepass -Restart
```
5. Create two self-signed certificates (one for signing and one for encryption) and export them to a PFX file:
```
$signCert = New-SelfSignedCertificate -Subject "CN=HGS
Signing Certificate"
Export-PfxCertificate -FilePath c:\signCert.pfx
-Password $safepass -Cert $signCert
Remove-Item $signCert.PSPath
$encCert = New-SelfSignedCertificate -Subject "CN=HGS
Encryption Certificate"
Export-PfxCertificate -FilePath c:\encCert.pfx -Password
$certificatePassword -Cert $encCert
Remove-Item $encCert.PSPath
```

6. Initialize the HGS server, which will configure the HGS cluster and web services for key protection and attestation:

```
Initialize-HgsServer -LogDirectory C:\HGS
-HgsServiceName HGS -Http -TrustActiveDirectory
     -SigningCertificatePath 'C:\signCert.pfx'
     -SigningCertificatePassword $safepass
     -EncryptionCertificatePath 'C:\encCert.pfx'
     -EncryptionCertificatePassword $safepass
```

7. Validate the HGS server configuration by running the HGS diagnostics to ensure that the server is correctly configured:

```
Get-HgsTrace -RunDiagnostics
```

Configuring Attestation

When you start a specific shielded VM from a guarded host, the VM needs to be unlocked. Therefore, the guarded host sends a key request to the HGS. The attestation process will measure specific health characteristics to determine whether the host is authorized and healthy to run Shielded VMs.

There are two types of attestation modes you can use with the host guardian service:

- Admin-trusted attestation (also known as AD-based attestation or Windows Server Active Directory based attestation)
- TPM-trusted attestation

CONFIGURING ADMIN-TRUSTED ATTESTATION

CERTIFICATION READY
Configure Admin-trusted attestation
Objective 2.1

Admin-trusted attestation is designed to protect data while both at rest and in transit. The Admin-trusted attestation has a simplified deployment and configuration that will most likely work with existing hardware. While the Admin-trusted attestation will be the most common, it is considered the weaker of the two attestation modes because the fabric admin is trusted, no hardware-rooted trust, Measured Boot, or enforced CI policy exists.

The minimum requirements for Admin-trusted attestation are:

- One HGS server running Windows Server 2016
- One guarded Hyper-V host running Windows Server 2016

Although the HGS can be joined to an existing domain, it is best practice that it runs on its own forest.

When using Admin-trusted attestation, the guarded host sends a request to the HGS node via an encrypted REST API. The steps in the process are:

1. Start a shielded VM.
2. The attestation client initiates the attestation protocol.
3. The host presents a Kerberos service ticket.
4. The HGS validates group membership to the Active Directory attestation host group.
5. The HGS issues a signed attestation certificate encrypted to the host.

With admin-trusted attestation, HGS uses the global security group membership of the Hyper-V host for attestation, which is based on the computer accounts membership, not a user's membership. A trust relationship must be set up between the fabric AD and the HGS forest.

To ensure that your virtual machines running on a host can function within the corporate domain, you will need to configure the fabric domain server. This includes:

- Configuring a DNS Conditional Forwarder zone
- Creating a HGSHosts group

CONFIGURE THE FABRIC DOMAIN SERVER

GET READY. To configure the fabric domain server, perform the following steps.

1. On **LON-DC1**, click the **Start** button and then click **Windows PowerShell.**
2. Create a DNS Conditional Forwarder zone by executing the following command:
   ```
   Add-DnsServerConditionalForwarderZone -Name 'contoso.com'
   -ReplicationScope "Forest"
   -MasterServers 172.16.0.11
   ```
3. Create a one-way forest trust:
   ```
   netdom trust contoso.com /domain:adatum.com /userD:adatum.
   com\Administrator /passwordD:Pa$$w0rd /ad
   ```
4. On **LON-DC1**, in Server Manager, click **Tools > Active Directory Users and Computers.**
5. In the Active Directory Users and Computers console, click, then right-click **Users** and choose **New > Group.**
6. In the Group name text box, type **HGSHosts**, and then click **OK.**
7. In the Users container, double-click **HGSHosts** and then click the **Members** tab.
8. On the Members tab, click **Add.**
9. Click **Object Types.**
10. Click **Computers** and then click **OK.**
11. In the Enter the object names to select text box, type the name of the HGS server, such as **LON-HOST1**, and then click **OK** twice.
12. At a Windows PowerShell command prompt, execute the following command:
    ```
    Get-ADGroup HGSHosts
    ```
13. Review the output from the cmdlet. Find the SID row and then copy the SID to the clipboard.
14. On the desktop, click the **Start** button and then type **Notepad.** Press **Enter.**
15. Paste the SID into Notepad and then save it as **C:\SID.txt.**
16. Authorize the Active Directory group's security ID (SID) with the Attestation Service:
    ```
    Add-HgsAttestationHostGroup -Name HGSHosts
        -Identifier <SID_recorded_in_SID.txt>
    ```

CERTIFICATION READY
Configure TPM-trusted attestation
Objective 2.1

CONFIGURING TPM-TRUSTED ATTESTATION

TPM-trusted attestation is the recommended mode because it secures the system at the hardware level. However, the setup and configuration requires registering each Hyper-V host's TPM with the HGS service. TPM-trusted attestation is likely to be used by hosting providers. Host hardware and firmware must include TPM 2.0 and UEFI 2.3.1 with secure boot enabled. This mode is more complicated to set up, but it's more secure. TPM-trusted attestation is likely to be used by hosting providers.

TPM-trusted attestation allows hosts that you've designated as guarded hosts and that are running code that you've identified as trusted to start shielded VMs. Each TPM uses a unique

Endorsement Key (EK) that cannot be removed or changed. It is an asymmetric key that is injected inside the TPM at manufacturing time. The EK uses a set of keys: the public key that is referred to as EKpub and the private key that is referred to as EKPriv. The TPM manufacturer might issue a certificate for the EKpub that is called an EKCert.

HGS will determine the health of the Hyper-V host using a baseline policy and a code-integrity (CI) policy. The ***baseline policy*** describes the binaries loaded by the operating system during the boot process. The ***Code Integrity (CI) policy*** contains a whitelist of binaries (drives, tools, and so on) that are allowed to run on the Hyper-V host.

When a shielded VM is started, the guarded host will send a key request to the HGS. Therefore, the attestation client initiates the attestation protocol that sends boot and CI measurements, which are stored in the Trusted Computing Group (TCG) log file. The HCG compares the TCG log file to TPM. If the GHS Attestation Service determines that the two are the same, the guarded host sends its CI policy to ensure that the code is deemed healthy.

The guarded host sends its CI policy to ensure it can only run the code that's deemed healthy. If the host passes the validation by the Attestation Service, the Attestation Service sends an attestation certificate to the guarded host indicating that the host is healthy and approved. The host resends the key request to the HGS with a current health certificate. If the HGS determines that the health certificate is valid, the host decrypts a portion of the VM, re-encrypts it to the Virtual Secure Mode of the guarded host, and then sends the key to the guarded host's Virtual Secure Mode. If the VM is moved to a different host or the VM is started by a user that is not authorized, the VM will not be decrypted and it will not start.

To initialize HGS using TPM-trusted attestation, follow these high-level steps:

1. Initialize the HGS cluster in a new forest (default) or initialize the HGS cluster in an existing bastion forest.
2. Install trusted TPM root certificates.
3. Configure the fabric DNS.

To deploy and configure the guarded hosts using TPM-trusted attestation, you must generate files on the guarded host:

1. Retrieve the TPM identifier (guarded host's TPM 2.0 EK), which will be used to register the specific host with the HGS server.
2. Create the CI policy that will be used to ensure the software running on the host is trusted.
3. Capture the TPM baseline, which will be used to measure the pre-OS UEFI firmware loaded on the host to ensure only those that are trusted and authorized can be loaded on each guarded host.
4. Configure the Hyper-V guarded host's HGS server.

To retrieve the TPM identifier, execute the following PowerShell commands:

```
$out = Get-PlatformIdentifier -Name "HGSHost"
$out.InnerXML > C:\HGS\HGSHost_EKub.xml
```

Next, copy the newly created file and use the `Add-HgsAttestationTpmHost` cmdlet:

```
Add-HgsAttestationTpmHost -Name "HGSHost" -Path C:\HGS\HGSHost_
EKub.xml
```

TAKE NOTE* For more information on CIPolicy, see Lesson 3.

To add a CI policy, execute the following command:

```
Add-HgsAttestationCIPolicy -Name "CIPolicy" -Path C:\SIPolicy.p7b
```

To capture the TPM baseline policy, execute the following command:

```
Get-HgsAttestationBaselinePolicy -Path C:\tcglog.bin
```

To copy the .bin file to your HGS server, execute the following command:

```
Add-HgsAttestationTmpPolicy -Name "TpmPolicy1" -Path C:\tcglog.bin
```

Then, to configure the HGS client, execute the `Get-HgsServer` cmdlet on the HGS server and use the two URLs it provides to run the `Set-HgsClientConfiguration` cmdlet on each guarded host:

```
Set-HgsClientConfiguration -KeyProtectionServerURL $url1
-AttestationServerUrl $url2
```

Configuring the Key Protection Service (KPS) Using HGS

Key Protection Service (KPS) is one of the two services that run as part of the HGS Windows Service role that provides the Transport Keys that are required to unlock and run shielded VMs on a healthy Hyper-V host. It is best practice to use HSM-backed keys.

CERTIFICATION READY
Configure the Key Protection Service using HGS
Objective 2.1

To initialize the HGS server using signing and encryption keys that are backed by an HSM, execute the following Windows PowerShell syntax:

```
$Certs = Get-ChildItem Cert:\LocalMachine\My\
-dnsname HGS*
$Certs
$signing = $Certs[0].Thumbprint
$encryption = $Certs[1].Thumbprint
Initialize-HgsServer -HgsServiceName tpmHGS
-SigningCertificateThumbprint $signing
-EncryptCertificateThumbprint $encryption -TrustTpm
```

The signing and encryption keys used to initialize HGS will be the default keys used for protecting shielded VMs. If you initialized HGS using keys other than those in an HSM, or you simply want to replace the default keys that HGS uses, you can add the new encryption and signing keys using `Add-HgsKeyProtectionCertificate`. To view HGS's current certificates, use `Get-HgsKeyProtectionCertificate`. You can set newly added HSM-backed keys as the primary set of encryption and signing keys by using `Set-HgsKeyProtectionCertificate`.

When importing a new set of signing and encryption keys, ensure that you add them to the Certificate Store under Local Computer. Ensure that the user account under which the KPS service executes (KeyProtection app pool) has Read access rights to the private keys of the HSM-backed keys. To do this, complete the following high-level steps:

1. Launch IIS Manager.
2. Select the Application Pools node.
3. Note the account under which the KeyProtection app pool is running.

4. Open the Local Machine Certificate Management Console by running certlm.msc.
5. Locate the encryption and signing certificates under the Personal folder.
6. Right-click each of the certificates and choose All Tasks > Manage Private Keys to verify (or add the permission if necessary to) the user account from the first step to the list of Groups and Users permitted to manage the private keys. The Read permission is the only one needed.

The signing and encryption keys must be available on every node in the HGS cluster. Therefore, on each host, you must install the same encryption and signing certificates. After the certificates are installed, grant the KPS App Pool identity Read access to the private keys, as before.

Migrating Shielded VMs to Other Guarded Hosts

CERTIFICATION READY
Migrate Shielded VMs to other guarded hosts
Objective 2.1

If you want to move a shielded VM to other hosts, the other hosts must be deemed healthy by the HGS Attestation Service. If the host is considered not healthy, the shielded VM cannot be powered on or live-migrated. Therefore, you should make sure that you have installed the necessary certificates, add Host Guardian Hyper-V Support feature and configure the host's key protection and attestation URLs.

If you are using System Center Virtual Machine Manager (VMM), you must first configure VMM globally with the URLs of the fabric's HGS cluster. VMM will then configure all guarded hosts to connect to the same HGS server to ensure that a shielded VM running on any one guarded host.

To check whether a guarded host has successfully attested with HGS, perform the following high-level actions:

1. Open the fabric workspace and find the host group containing your guarded hosts.
2. Find the host that you wish to inspect. Right-click that host and choose View Status. You will see various health measurements on this screen. The ones related to HGS and shielded VMs are all contained under HGS Client Overall.
3. If you see one or more items with status as Warning, review the error details.

Configuring Nano Server as a TPM-Attested Guarded Host

To manage Nano Server, you will use Remote PowerShell. To prepare a Nano Server for the Guarded Fabric, Microsoft provides a set of scripts. However, there are some files that you will need in order to copy a server running Windows Server 2016 with a Desktop Experience installation to the Nano Server image.

The files include:

- C:\Windows\System32\wbem\platid.dll
- C:\Windows\System32\wbem\en-us\platid.dll.mui
- C:\Windows\System32\WindowsPowerShell\v1.0\Modules\PlatformIdentifier\MSFT_PlatformIdentifier.cdxml
- C:\Windows\System32\WindowsPowerShell\v1.0\Modules\PlatformIdentifier\PlatformIdentifier.psd1

In addition, you will have to search for Prepare Nano Server Script for Guarded Fabric from the technet.microsoft.com website to download the PrepareNanoTP5.ps1. At this time of writing, a newer script is not available.

To create an image, you will need to perform the following steps:

1. Copy the NanoServerImageGenerator folder from the \NanoServer folder in the Windows Server 2016 Installation ISO, to the C:\NanoServer\ folder.
2. Click the Start button and then click Windows PowerShell.
3. Change the directory to the folder where you have placed the C:\NanoServer\NanoServerImageGenerator folder.
4. Execute the following command:

   ```
   Import-Module .\NanoServerImageGenerator -Verbose
   ```
5. Create the Nano server image by executing the following command:

   ```
   $mediapath = < location of the mounted TP5 ISO image, e.g.
   E:\>
   ```
6. The next command assumes that you are running the Nano Server Image cmdlets on a machine running Windows Server 2016. If you are not, update the paths to the location where you copied the missing files.

   ```
   $FilesToBeCopied = "C:\Windows\System32\wbem\platid.
   dll","C:\Windows\System32\wbem\en-us\platid.dll.mui",
   "C:\Windows\System32\WindowsPowerShell\v1.0\ Modules\
   PlatformIdentifier\MSFT_PlatformIdentifier.cdxml","C:\
   Windows\System32\WindowsPowerShell \v1.0\Modules\
   PlatformIdentifier\ PlatformIdentifier.psd1","c:\
   PrepareNanoTP5.ps1"
   ```

To create a Nano server .vhdx file with the necessary packages and files to support shielded VMs, execute the following command:

```
New-NanoServerImage -MediaPath $mediapath

-TargetPath <nanovhd path> -ComputerName "<nanoserver name>"
-OEMDrivers -Compute -DeploymentType Host

-Edition Datacenter -Packages Microsoft-NanoServer-
SecureStartup-Package, Microsoft-NanoServer-ShieldedVM-Package
-EnableRemoteManagementPort

-CopyFiles $FilesToBeCopied -SetupCompleteCommands @("power-
shell.exe -NonInteractive -ExecutionPolicy Bypass -File C:\pre-
pareNanoTP5.ps1") -DomainName <Domain Name>
```

If this is the first Nano server you are building and you're using TPM-trusted attestation, you will need to create a CI policy based on this image. You will then mount the Nano server .vhdx and execute the following command:

```
New-CIPolicy -FilePath .\NanoCI.xml -Level FilePublisher
-Fallback Hash -ScanPath G:\

-PathToCatroot G:\Windows\System32\CatRoot\
```

After the Nano server image creation completes, you will need to set it as the default boot operating system. You can do this by copying the Nano server .vhdx file to the physical computer and then configure it to boot from the physical server by using the following steps:

1. Mount the generated .vhd file by right-clicking the file in File Explorer and choosing Mount.
2. Run bcdboot D:\windows.
3. Unmount the VHD by right-clicking the VHD file in the File Explorer and choosing Eject.
4. Restart the computer to boot into Nano Server.

The prepareNanoTP5 script will run once, and the machine will restart again.

After you determine the Nano Server IP address, you need to connect to the Nano Server remotely to manage it by executing the following commands:

```
Set-item WSMan:\localhost\Client\TrustedHosts <nano server ip
or name>
```

```
Enter-PSSession -ComputerName <nano server name or ip> -creden-
tial <nano server name or ip>\administrator
```

If you see an "Access denied" error message, you may need to reset the Windows Remote Management (WinRM) settings and firewall rules on the Nano Server by signing in to the Nano Server recovery console and selecting the WinRM option.

Troubleshooting Guarded Hosts

To determine if a host is guarded, you need to make sure the HGS and cluster nodes are running. You will then need to review the settings for a guarded host.

To verify that the Host Guardian Hyper-V Support feature is enabled, execute the following command:

```
Get-WindowsFeature HostGuardian
```

To determine whether the host is guarded, execute the following command:

```
Get-HgsClientConfiguration
```

If the host is not guarded, the following information is returned:

```
IsHostGuarded                 : False
Mode                          : Local
KeyProtectionServerUrl        :
AttestationServerUrl          :
AttestationOperationMode : Unknown
AttestationStatus             : NotConfigured
AttestationSubstatus          : NoInformation
```

If the host is guarded, the following information is returned:

```
IsHostGuarded                 : True
Mode                          : HostGuardianService
KeyProtectionServerUrl        : http://contoso.com/
           KeyProtection
AttestationServerUrl          : http://contoso.com/
           Attestation
AttestationOperationMode : ActiveDirectory
AttestationStatus             : Passed
AttestationSubstatus          : NoInformation
```

To determine whether the HGS server is responding, you can test whether the Key Protection Service is responding correctly by opening the following URL on an HGS server:

```
http://localhost/KeyProtection/service/metadata/2014-07/meta-
data.xml
```

If you manage multiple HGS servers, you will need to test each GHS server. You can then verify that the guarded hosts can resolve the FQDN and retrieve the metadata.xml file. If this does not work, and the metadata.xml was opened on the local host, it is most likely a name resolution problem or a network connectivity problem.

Implementing Shielded and Encrypted-Supported VMs

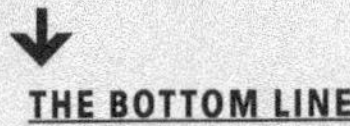

THE BOTTOM LINE Locked doors, logged cages, guards, and cameras can prevent someone from stealing a physical server, but when dealing with virtual machines, it is easy for someone who has administrative access to the virtual machines to copy multiple VMs or virtual disks to a USB removable drive and walk out the front door with the confidential data without being detected. In addition, a user can grab a domain controller so that they can perform a brute force attack on the virtual machine to crack passwords, giving them access to everything within the domain. However, by using encryption, you can protect these virtual machines or virtual disk.

As previously mentioned, a shielded VM is a Generation 2 VM that has a virtual TPM and is encrypted by using BitLocker Drive Encryption. A guarded fabric can run three types of virtual machines:

1. A normal VM that offers no protections.
2. An encryption-supported VM whose protections can be configured by a fabric admin.
3. A shielded VM whose protections are switched on and cannot be disabled by a fabric admin.

Both encrypted and shielded VMs require vTPM to enable BitLocker, leverage a key protect, and use VMWP to harden VM work process that encrypts state information and live migration.

Determining Requirements and Scenarios for Implementing Encrypted and Shielded VMs

If a VM is encrypted or shielded, the VM cannot be started if it cannot be decrypted. And the VM will not be decrypted until it is running on a healthy Hyper-V host and the HGS provides the keys to a Hyper-V host.

CERTIFICATION READY
Determine requirements and scenarios for implementing Shielded VMs
Objective 2.1

CERTIFICATION READY
Determine requirements and scenarios for implementing encryption-supported VMs
Objective 2.1

The encrypted and shielded VM requires the following:

- It must have a GUID partition Table (GPT) disk, which is needed for Generation 2 virtual machines to support UEFI.
- It must use basic disks logical disk type, since BitLocker does not support dynamic disks.
- It must have a disk with at least two partitions: One drive on which the Windows operating system is installed that BitLocker will encrypt. The second disk contains the bootloader and remains unencrypted so that the computer can be started.
- The file system must be NTFS.
- It must use a guest operating system that supports Generation 2 virtual machines and Microsoft Secure Boot, including Windows Server 2012, Windows Server 2012 R2, Windows Server 2016, Windows 8, Windows 8.1, or Windows 10.
- The operating system must be generalized with sysprep.exe.
- The virtual machines must be running Windows Server 2016 Enterprise Edition.

Encryption-supported VMs are intended for use in fabrics where fabric administrators are fully trusted and where compliance is necessary. Shielded VMs can be used to protect against inspection, theft, and tampering, whether by administrators or by malware.

The following operations are required for Generation 2 encrypted support and enforce for Generation 2 shielded virtual machines:

1. Secure Boot
2. vTPM
3. Encrypt VM state and live migration traffic
4. Integration components

With Generation 2 encrypted supported machines, Virtual Machine Connection (console) is on but disabled.

Lastly, COM/serial ports and the ability to attach a debugger to a VM process is supported. However, with Generation 2 shielded virtual machines, the Virtual Machine Connection, COM/serial ports, and the ability to attach a debugger to the VM process is disabled and cannot be enabled.

Creating a Shielded VM and Configure vTPM for Data Disk Encryption

Generation 2 virtual machines have additional Hyper-V security options that are not available with Generation 1 virtual machines. These options include Secure Boot, vTPM (labeled simply as Trusted Platform Module), and Security Policy, as shown in Figure 5-1.

Figure 5-1

Security settings for a Generation 2 virtual machine

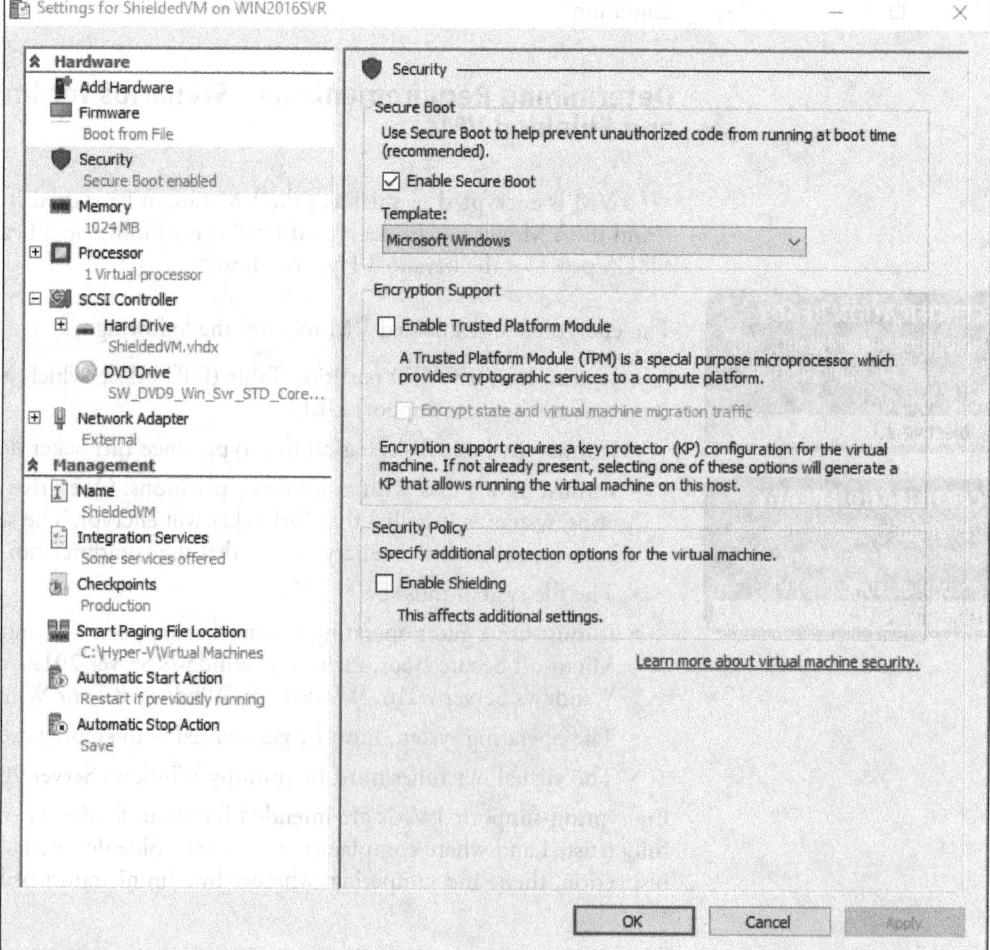

CERTIFICATION READY
Create a Shielded VM using only a Hyper-V environment
Objective 2.1

CERTIFICATION READY
Enable and configure vTPM to allow an operating system and data disk encryption within a VM
Objective 2.1

By default, Secure Boot is enabled for Generation 2 virtual machines. It helps prevent unauthorized firmware, operating systems, or Unified Extensible Firmware Interface (UEFI) drivers (also known as option ROMs) from running at boot time.

If you select the Enable Trusted Platform Module option and you select the Encrypt State and VM migration traffic option, you will encrypt the virtual machine saved state and live migration traffic. By selecting the Enable Shielding option, you will disable management features like console connection, PowerShell Direct, and some integration components. If you select this option, Secure Boot, Enable Trusted Platform Module, and Encrypt State and VM migration traffic options are selected and enforced.

CREATE A GENERATION 2 VIRTUAL MACHINE

GET READY. To create a virtual machine, perform the following steps.

1. On a host running Hyper-V, in Server Manager, click **Tools > Hyper-V Manager.**
2. In Microsoft Hyper-V Manager, click **New > Virtual Machine.**
3. On the Before You Begin page, click **Next.**
4. In the Name text box, type **ShieldedVM** and then select the **Store the virtual machine in a different location** check box.
5. Click **Browse** and then browse to **Local Disk (C:).**
6. In the Local Disk (C:) drive, right-click and choose **New.** Click Folder, name the folder **ShieldedVMs**, and then click **Select Folder.** Click **Next.**
7. In the Specify Generation dialog box, select the **Generation 2** option and then click **Next.**
8. Accept the default Startup memory of 1024 MB by clicking **Next.**
9. In the Configure Networking dialog box, for the Connection, click **External** and then click **Next.**
10. On the Connect Virtual Hard Disk page, change the Size to **20** GB and then click **Next.**
11. On the Installation Options pave, select the **Image file (.iso)** option and then click **Browse.**
12. In the Open dialog box, navigate to and double-click a Windows Server 2016 ISO file and then click **Next.**
13. Click **Finish.**
14. Right-click **ShieldedVM** and choose **Connect.**
15. Click the green **Start** button for the virtual machine and when prompted with Press Any Key to Boot from CD, click a key on the keyboard.
16. Click **Next** and then click **Install now.**
17. Select **Windows Server 2016 Datacenter Evaluation (Desktop Experience)** and then click **Next.**
18. Select the check box next to **I accept the license terms** and then click **Next.**
19. Click **Custom: Install Windows only (advanced).**
20. On the Where do you want to install Windows page, click **Next.**
21. When the installation is completed, on the Customize settings page, in the Password fields, type **Pa$$w0rd** and then click **Finish.**

In the next exercise, you will prepare the VM for shielding. However, since a shielded VM will not have access to Virtual Machine Connection (console), you must make sure that you have access to the machine via Remote Desktop.

PREPARE THE VM FOR SHIELDING

GET READY. To prepare the VM for shielding, perform the following steps.

1. Log on to the ShieldedVM as **administrator** with the password of **Pa$$w0rd.** If the Networks pane displays, click **Yes.**
2. In Server Manager click **Local Server.**
3. Click the **Remote Desktop Disabled** link.
4. In System Properties, select **Allow remote connections to this computer.**
5. Clear the **Allow connections only from computers running Remote Desktop with Network Level Authentication (recommended)** check box. Click **OK.**
6. Click **Start**, type **cmd**, and then press **Enter.**
7. In the Command window, type **IPConfig.** Record the IPv4 address.
8. On **LON-HOST1**, click **Start** and then click **Remote Desktop.**
9. In the Remote Desktop dialog box, type the IPv4 address of ShieldedVM. Click **Connect.**
10. At the Windows Security dialog box, type **Pa$$w0rd** and then click **OK.** Click **Yes** at the certificate prompt.
11. Verify that you can remote into ShieldedVM and close the Remote Desktop window and then click **OK.**
12. On **LON-HOST1**, click **Start** and then click **Windows PowerShell.**
13. Call the key protection web service and save the configuration locally by executing the following command:
```
md C:\HGS
Invoke-WebRequest http://LON-SVR1.contoso.com/
Keyprotection/service/metadata/2014-07/metadata.xml
-OutFile 'C:\HGS\HGSGuardian.xml'
```
14. Stop the VM to be converted to a Shielded VM by typing the following commands and pressing **Enter** at the end of each line:
```
$VMName = 'ShieldedVM'
Stop-VM -VMName $VMName
```
15. To create a new key protector, execute the following commands:
```
$KP = New-HgsKeyProtector -Owner $Owner -Guardian
$Guardian -AllowUntrustedRoot
Set-VMKeyProtector -VMName $VMName -KeyProtector $KP.
RawData
Set-VMSecurityPolicy -VMName $VMName -Shielded $true
```
16. Enable the vTPM by executing the following command:
```
Enable-VMTPM -VMName $VMName
```
You will no longer be able to access the shielded VM through the Virtual Machine connection.

Troubleshooting Shielded and Encryption-Supported VMs

When you have problems with a shielded or encrypted supported VM, you need to ensure that the HGS is available and the virtual machines are running on a healthy Hyper-V host. You should make sure that the VMs are Generation 2 virtual machines.

CERTIFICATION READY
Troubleshoot Shielded and Encryption-Supported VMs
Objective 2.1

If you cannot connect to a VM and the shielded VM is blocked, you can choose between two options:

1. You can disable the shielding data security profile.
2. You can copy a VM .vhdx file to a secure host, create a new Generation 2 VM based on the .vhdx of the shielded VM, and when prompted for a BitLocker key, press the Esc key to enter a recovery key. Of course, you will need to keep a backup of all of your TPM keys in a safe place.

To disable the shielding data security profile, perform the following steps:

1. Export the VM from the guarded host and import it into a host with the owner's guardian key.
2. After you import the VM into Hyper-V, you can perform any of the following steps:
   1. Open a Windows PowerShell command prompt and execute the following command: `Set-VMSecurityProfile -vmname $vmname -ShieldingRequested $false`
   2. In the Hyper-V console, open the VM settings. Click Security, and then under the Security Profile section, change the Shielding setting to No additional protection.

To determine whether a VM is shielded, you can verify that TPM is enabled and you can use the following Windows PowerShell command to determine whether the virtual machine is shielded (ShieldedRequested should be True):

```
get-vmsecurity -vmname $vmName
The returned data should be similar to:
TpmEnabled                 : True
ShieldingRequested         : True
Shielded                   :
DataProtectionRequested : False
DataProtected              :
CimSession                 : CimSession
ComputerName               : VM1
IsDeleted                  : False
```

If the VM being started is a shielded VM that has been moved from its Host Guardian, you will see one of the following errors:

```
An error occurred while attempting to start the selected virtual machine(s).
```

```
<vm-name> could not initialize
```

```
The virtual machine <vm-name> cannot start because Isolated User Mode is off.
```

In addition, VMM will generate the following error message:

```
Error (12700)
```

```
VMM cannot complete the host operation on the
'HyperVHost.contoso.com' server because of the error:
'<vm-name>' failed to start. (Virtual machine ID
682B5B89-6B65-4645-80C7-05128E1A024F)
```

```
'<vm-name>' could not initialize. (Virtual machine ID
682B5B89-6B65-4645-80C7-05128E1A024F)
Unknown error (0x8007)
Recommended Action
Resolve the host issue and then try the operation again.
```

Move the VM on a host with the Host Guardian Hyper-V Support feature enabled and the HGSClientConfiguration configured with the proper AttestationServer and KeyProtectionServer URLs.

If you see the following error message, the Hyper-V host is not completely configured:

```
An error occurred while attempting to start the selected
virtual machine(s).
<vm name> failed to start.
<vm name> could not initialize.
```

A shielded VM can only be started on a host with the Host Guardian Hyper-V Support feature enabled and the HGSClientConfiguration configured with the proper AttestationServer and KeyProtectionServer URLs. Therefore, you will need to complete the configuration or migrate the VM to a guarded host.

If you try to generate a new HGS key using the Windows PowerShell New-HGSKeyProtector cmdlet and you see the following message, you are using self-signed certificates for the guardian keys.

```
New-HgsKeyProtector: A certificate chain processed, but terminated
in a root certificate which is not trusted by the trust provider.
```

To solve this problem, you will have to add the –AllowUntrustedRoot parameter to the New-HgsKeyProtector cmdlet when testing with self-signed certificates.

SKILL SUMMARY

IN THIS LESSON YOU LEARNED:

- A guarded fabric is a Windows Server 2016 Hyper-V fabric capable of protecting workloads against inspection, theft, and tampering. You can think of a fabric as a platform or framework.
- A guarded fabric in Windows Server 2016 consists of one Host Guardian Service (HGS), which typically includes a cluster of three nodes, one or more guarded Hyper-V hosts, and a set of shielded VMs.
- A shielded VM is a Generation 2 VM that has a virtual TPM and is encrypted by using BitLocker Drive Encryption. By using a guarded fabric and shielded VMs, you can provide a more secure environment for tenant VMs when you have different clients run on your virtual environment.
- The Host Guardian Service (HGS) is a server role introduced in Windows Server 2016 for configuring guarded hosts and running shielded VMs (shielded virtual machines) in Windows Server and System Center Virtual Machine Manager. It provides Attestation and Key Protections services that are needed to enable Hyper-V on healthy hosts to run Shielded VMs.
- The Attestation services validate a Hyper-V host as a "guarded host," which then enables the Key Protection service (KPS) to provide the transport key required to unlock and subsequently run Shielded VMs.
- There are two types of attestation modes you can use with the host guardian service: Admin-trusted attestation (also known as AD-based attestation or Windows Server Active Directory based attestation) and TPM-trusted attestation
- To determine whether a host is guarded, you need to make sure the HGS and cluster nodes are running. You will then need to review the settings for a guarded host.
- If a VM is encrypted or shielded, the VM cannot be started if it cannot be decrypted. And the VM will not be decrypted until it is running on a healthy Hyper-V host and the HGS provides the keys to a Hyper-V host.
- Generation 2 virtual machines have additional Hyper-V security options that are not available with Generation 1 virtual machines. These options include Secure Boot, vTPM (labeled simply as Trusted Platform Module), and Security Policy.

■ Knowledge Assessment

Multiple Choice

1. Which of the following statements are true of a shielded VM? (Choose two answers)
   a. A shielded VM must be a Generation 2 VM.
   b. A shielded VM must be a Generation 1 VM.
   c. You must use SSL to protect network traffic
   d. A shielded VM must have a virtual TPM
2. Which of the following is used to measure the health of a host, including making sure that the host is also authorized and healthy to run shielded VMs?
   a. Guarded host
   b. Attestation
   c. Key Protection Service
   d. TPM
3. Which attestation method is considered the most secure?
   a. Admin-trusted attestation
   b. TPM-trusted attestation
   c. Guarded attestation
   d. Secure Boot attestation
4. With TPM attestation, which policies are used to determine the health of the Hyper-V host? (Choose two answers)
   a. Fabric permission policy
   b. Authorization policy
   c. Code-integrity (CI) policy
   d. Baseline policy
5. Which of the following statements are true of encrypted and shielded VMs? (Choose all that apply)
   a. An encrypted VM cannot be accessed by a fabric admin using the virtual machine connection.
   b. Will only operate on the host that the virtual machine was created.
   c. A shielded VM cannot be disabled.
   d. An encrypted VM cannot be disabled.
6. You are trying to start a shielded VM and you see a the following error message:

```
An error occurred while attempting to start the selected
virtual machine(s).
VM1 could not initialize
The virtual machine VM1 cannot start because Isolated User
Mode is off.
```

7. Which of the following best describes how to solve this problem?
   - **a.** Change the self-signed certificate to a trusted certificate.
   - **b.** Move the VM to a host with the Host Guardian Hyper-V Support feature is enabled and configured with the proper AttestationServer and KeyProtectionServer URLs.
   - **c.** Make sure the Hyper-V services is running with the proper credentials.
   - **d.** Make sure the Hyper-V services account has proper access to the virtual machine files.
8. Which of the following is found in the baseline policy?
   - **a.** A description of the binaries loaded by the operating system during the boot process
   - **b.** A whitelist of binaries that are allowed to run on the Hyper-V host
   - **c.** A list of the valid certificates
   - **d.** A list of the valid hosts that the VM can run on
9. How do you prepare a nanoserver to be a TPM attested guarded host?
   - **a.** Copy additional files from a server running Windows Server 2016 with a Desktop Installation.
   - **b.** Create a .xml configuration file.
   - **c.** Download and execute the Prepare Nano Server script from Microsoft.
   - **d.** Enable Remote Desktop services.
10. Which of the following is required for TPM-trusted attestation? (Choose all that apply)
    - **a.** **a**Windows Server 2017 Enterprise Edition
    - **b.** TPM 2.0
    - **c.** UEFI 2.3.1
    - **d.** REFS file system
11. Which Windows PowerShell command is used to validate the GHS server configuration?
    - **a.** Get-HgsTrace -RunDiagnostics
    - **b.** Run-HGSDiagnostics
    - **c.** Start-HGSDiag
    - **d.** RunDiagnosticHGS

Best Answer

Choose the letter that corresponds to the best answer. More than one answer choice may achieve the goal. Select the BEST answer.

1. Which of the following is used to protect workloads against inspection, theft, and tampering in a Hyper-V environment?
   - **a.** Shielded VM
   - **b.** Software Defined Network
   - **c.** attestation services
   - **d.** Guarded fabric

2. Which attestation method would you recommend if you were hosting multiple customers in your Hyper-V environment?
   a. Admin-trusted attestation
   b. TPM-trusted attestation
   c. Guarded attestation
   d. Secure Boot attestation

Build List

1. Specify the correct order of steps necessary to configure TPM-trusted attestation. Not all answers will be used.

_____ Capture the TPM baseline.

_____ Install trusted TPM root certificates.

_____ Initialize the HGS cluster in a new forest.

_____ Run the bcdboot command.

_____ Configure the fabric DNS.

2. Specify the correct order of steps necessary to install and configure the GHS role.

_____ Install the Host Guardian Service role.

_____ Create two self-signed certificates.

_____ Validate the HGS server configuration.

_____ Initialize the GHS server.

_____ Install the HGS Server.

■ Business Case Scenarios

Scenario 5-1: Protecting Your Virtual Machines

You are an administrator for the Adatum Corporation. Your manager wants to make the virtual machines more secure to make sure that someone copies the virtual machine files to removable disks. Describe your recommended solution.

Scenario 5-2: Selecting an Attestation Method

Your manager wants a better understanding of the attestation method. Therefore, she wants you to explain the differences between the two and describe when you should use the two methods. Describe your answer.

LESSON 6

Configuring Windows Firewall and a Software-Defined Datacenter Firewall

70-744 EXAM OBJECTIVE

Objective 3.1 – Configure Windows Firewall. This objective may include but is not limited to: Configure Windows Firewall with Advanced Security; configure network location profiles; configure and deploy profile rules; configure firewall rules for multiple profiles using Group Policy; configure connection security rules using Group Policy, the GUI management console, or Windows PowerShell; configure Windows Firewall to allow or deny applications, scopes, ports, and users using Group Policy, the GUI management console, or Windows PowerShell; configure authenticated firewall exceptions; import and export settings.

Objective 3.2 – Implement a software-defined Datacenter Firewall. This objective may include but is not limited to: Determine requirements and scenarios for Datacenter Firewall implementation with software-defined networking; determine usage scenarios for Datacenter Firewall policies and network security groups; Configure Datacenter Firewall Access Control Lists.

Objective 3.3 – Secure network traffic. This objective may include but is not limited to: Configure connection security rules. All other Objective 3.3 topics are covered in Lesson 7.

Lesson Heading	Exam Objective
Configuring Windows Firewall • Configuring Advanced Sharing Settings and Network Locations • Configuring Windows Firewall with Advanced Security • Configuring Windows Firewall to Allow or Deny Applications, Scopes, Ports, and Users • Importing and Exporting Settings • Configuring Firewall Rules for Multiple Profiles Using Group Policy • Configuring Connection Security Rules • Configuring Authenticated Firewall Exceptions	Configure network location profiles Configure Windows Firewall with Advanced Security Configure and deploy profile rules Configure Windows Firewall to allow or deny applications, scopes, ports, and users using Group Policy, the GUI management console, or Windows PowerShell Import and export settings Configure firewall rules for multiple profiles using Group Policy Configure connection security rules using Group Policy, the GUI management console, or Windows PowerShell Configure connection security rules Configure authenticated firewall exceptions
Implementing a Software-Defined Datacenter Firewall • Implementing Network Controller • Determining Scenarios for Implementation of Software Load Balancer (SLB) for North-South and East-West Load Balancing • Determining Requirements and Scenarios for Datacenter Firewall Implementation with Software-Defined Networking • Determining Usage Scenarios for Datacenter Firewall Policies and Network Security Groups	Determine requirements and scenarios for Datacenter Firewall implementation with Software-Defined Networking Determine usage scenarios for Datacenter Firewall policies and network security groups

KEY TERMS

Authentication Header (AH)
connection security rules
Datacenter Firewall
Distributed Firewall Manager
domain network
domain profile
dynamic IP addresses (DIPs)
East-West traffic
Encapsulating Security Payload (ESP)
firewall
home network
host-based firewalls
inbound rules
IP security (IPsec)
Network Controller
network perimeter firewalls
Network security groups (NSGs)
Northbound API
North-South traffic
outbound rules
private profile
public network
public profile
router
SLB Multiplexer (MUX)
Software Load Balancing (SLB)
Software-Defined Networking (SDN)
Southbound API
transport mode
tunnel mode
virtual IP addresses (VIPs)
Windows Firewall
Windows Firewall with Advanced Security (WFAS)
work network

■ Configuring Windows Firewall

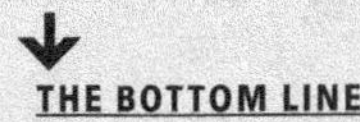

Designing a strategy for protecting your network involves implementing multiple levels of defense. Although most companies have a firewall to protect their perimeter, they don't normally do a good job of protecting the individual hosts behind the firewall.

After you determine your IP addressing schemes and how you want to configure your network from a logical/physical layout, it's time to determine how to secure it. This starts with looking at your network perimeter(s), which are the locations in your network in which your trusted network connects to another, probably untrusted, network. These gateways between networks enable you to implement security, control the types of traffic allowed to enter and exit your network, and reduce your overall network traffic. The most obvious perimeter is where your company's network connects to the Internet, but other perimeters might exist.

It's common for administrators to build network subnets to isolate and control traffic within their own private network so they can restrict traffic to a certain subnet and improve overall performance. It can also help isolate certain areas of the network that contain sensitive information. For example, you might create a subnet that contains just the finance department's systems due to the confidential nature of the information they work with.

The device used to segment a network is a ***router***. Although routers can provide basic traffic management (inbound/outbound), their primary role is to forward traffic between networks. Companies that are serious about their network security add a commercial-level firewall at the perimeter that leads to the Internet. In most cases, that should be sufficient enough to protect your network, but what happens when something is compromised on that firewall or when misconfiguration allows it to be bypassed? What if mobile users connect behind the firewall and attempt to gain access to a server or computer they are not authorized to use? This is where a host-based firewall can help.

A ***firewall*** is a software program or piece of hardware that protects networks or individual computers by screening and controlling incoming and outgoing network traffic based on a set of rules. There are two basic types of firewalls (see Figure 6-1):

Figure 6-1

Reviewing a network firewall and host-based firewall deployment

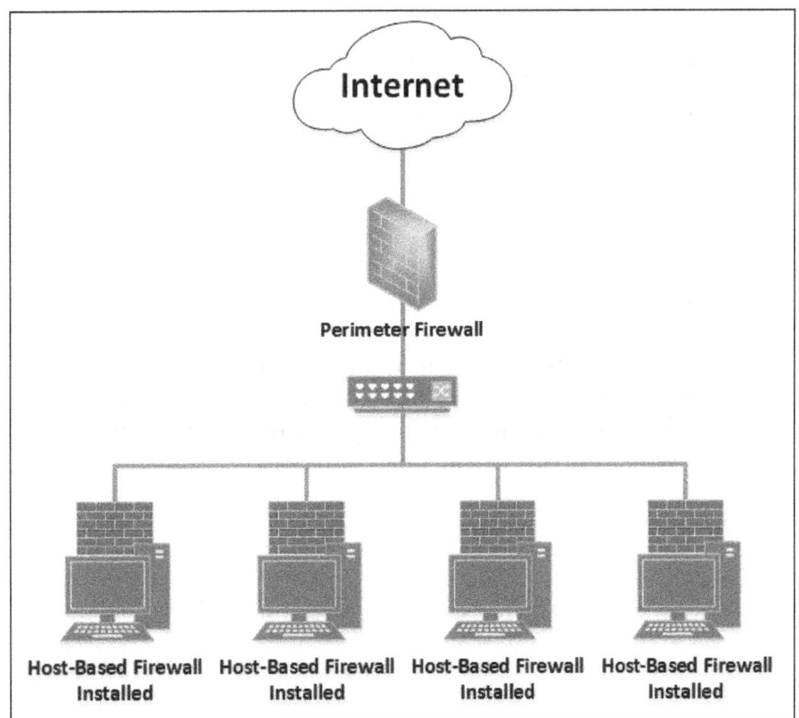

- ***Network perimeter firewalls:*** These firewalls are found on the boundary between an internal and external network. They can be hardware- or software-based and provide several types of functionality, including managing and monitoring traffic through stateful connection analysis, providing Internet Protocol security (IPsec) authentication and encryption, and providing NAT.
- ***Host-based firewalls:*** These firewalls run on individual computers (hosts) within the local network. They are designed to provide a second layer of defense, protect the computer from attacks and unauthorized access, and block specific types of traffic.

Because a network perimeter firewall monitors only traffic coming in and out of the network, it represents a single point of failure and does very little to protect against attacks that occur from within the private network. Without an additional layer of defense, using only a network perimeter firewall can put your entire network at risk. To create an additional level of protection, consider using a host-based firewall such as the Windows Firewall with Advanced Security (WFAS).

Windows Firewall is a host-based firewall that is included with Windows Server 2016. Basic Windows Firewall operations are controlled from the Windows Server 2016 Control Panel, as shown in Figure 6-2. You can view the firewall status, and enable or disable the Windows Firewall based on network locations.

Figure 6-2

The Windows Firewall Control Panel

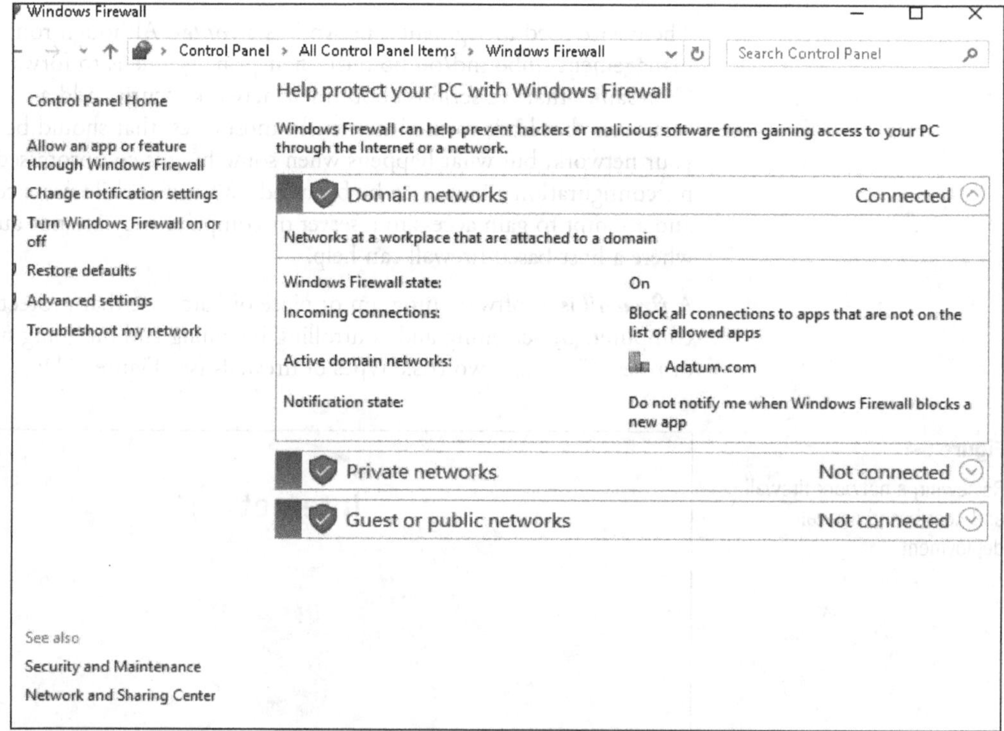

In Control Panel, you can click the Allow apps to communicate through Windows Firewall option to easily control what applications can communicate through the firewall. Limiting what programs can access through the firewall stops unknown programs from communicating over the Internet or with other suspicious systems.

Configuring Advanced Sharing Settings and Network Locations

CERTIFICATION READY
Configure network location profiles
Objective 3.1

Windows Server 2016 includes Advanced Sharing settings, a feature that allows you to configure network sharing settings based on your network location. To access the advanced sharing settings, open the Network and Sharing Center and click Change advanced sharing. The Advanced sharing settings are shown in Figure 6-3.

Figure 6-3

Configuring advanced sharing settings

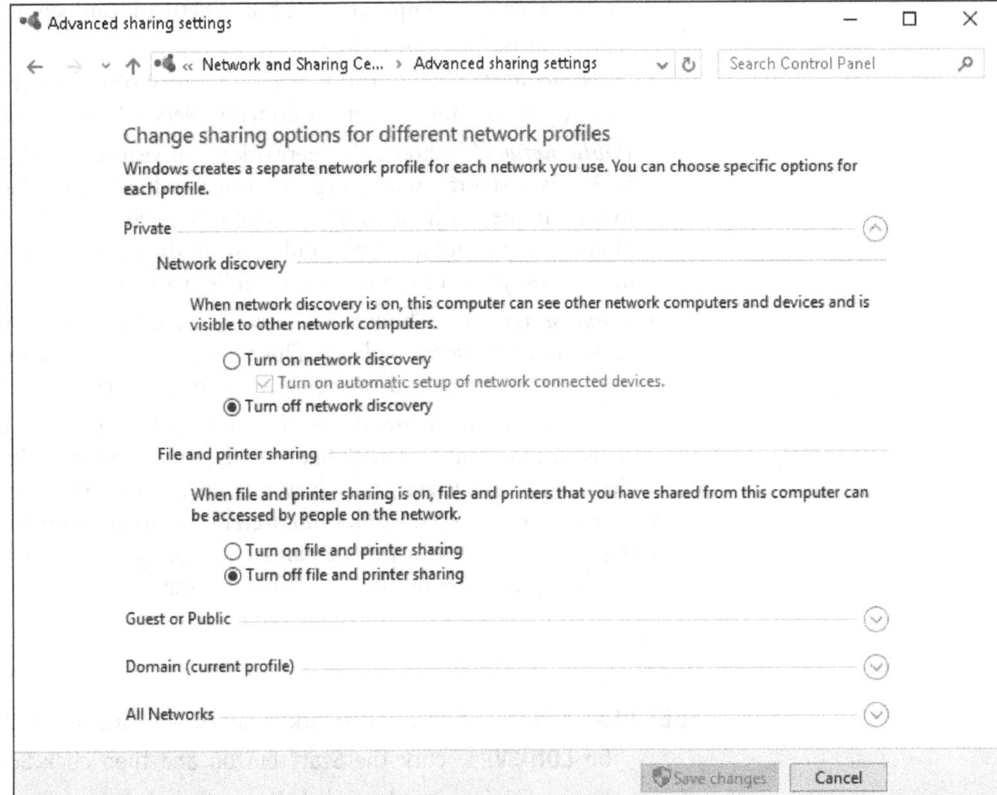

Windows Server 2016 is organized into three sections: Private, Guest or Public, and All Networks. Each network profile features its own default, which is applied when connecting to and selecting a network connection.

- **Turn on or off network discovery**: When enabled, this setting will search for other devices on the network and allow other computers and devices on the same network find your Windows-based computer of device.
- **Turn on or off file and printer sharing**: When enabled, you can share files and printers with other computers and devices on your network.
- **Turn on or off HomeGroup Connections**: For Private connections, when enabled, you can use and manage HomeGroups.
- **Turn on or off public folder sharing**: When enabled, Homegroup users can access files from the computer's Public Folder, which is located at C:\Users\Public\.
- **Turn on or off media streaming**: When enabled, you can stream multimedia files using Windows Media Player and other programs.
- **Encryption for file sharing connections**: When enabled, it allows users to access your shared files and folders only if you have a user account and password set on the computer.

When you first connect to a network, you must choose a network location, which will be assigned specific network sharing settings. For example, you can define your network connection as Work network or Domain network location. Your home network is typically defined as the Home network. When you visit a client or you connect the Internet from your local coffee shop, you would select the Public network.

There are four network locations:

- ***Home network:*** Choose this network when you know and trust the people and devices on the network. Computers on a home network can belong to a homegroup and network discovery will be enabled.
- ***Work network:*** Choose this network for small office or other workplace networks that are not part of your computer's domain. Network discovery will be enabled.
- ***Public network:*** Choose this network when visiting public places such as hotels, coffee shops, restaurants, and airports. You should also use this option if you're connected to the Internet without using a router, or by using a mobile broadband connection. HomeGroup is not available, and network discovery is turned off, which prevent other users to see your computer on the public network.
- ***Domain network:*** Choose this network when you're accessing domain networks, such as those at enterprise workplaces. This type of network location is controlled by your network administrator and can't be selected or changed.

When you connect to a network for the first time in Windows Server 2016, the network location is automatically set to Public, which prevents other Windows computers and devices from detecting your system. In such situations, you may want to change the network location to Private to make your computer discoverable to other computers. If the network connection is configured for a home or private connection and your computer is not part of a domain, you can change the network location from Settings.

CONFIGURE A NETWORK LOCATION

GET READY. To configure a network location, perform the following steps.

1. On **LON-SVR1**, click the **Start** button and then click **Settings**.
2. In the Settings window, click **Network & Internet**.
3. On the Network & Internet page, click **Ethernet**.
4. On the Ethernet page, click the network connection that you want to change.
5. On the Network page, you can enable or disable the Make this PC discoverable option, as shown in Figure 6-4.

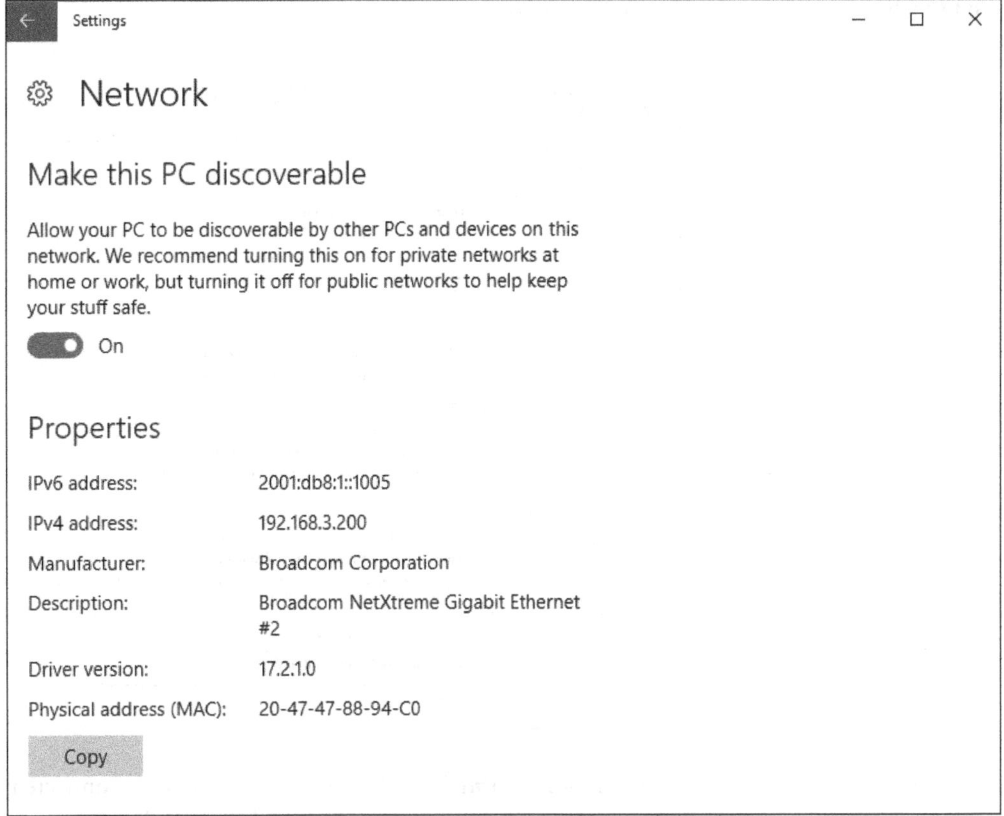

Figure 6-4

Configuring advanced sharing settings

6. Close the **Settings** window.

Configuring Windows Firewall with Advanced Security

Windows Firewall with Advanced Security (WFAS) combines a stateful host-based firewall with IPsec. It is designed to protect against attacks that originate from within your network or those that might bypass the network perimeter firewall(s). WFAS inspects both IPv4 and IPv6 packets that enter and leave your computer and then compares them against the criteria contained in the firewall's rules. If the packet matches a rule, the action configured in the rule is applied. If the packet does not match a rule, the firewall discards it and records an entry in its log files.

CERTIFICATION READY
Configure Windows Firewall with Advanced Security
Objective 3.1

WFAS is network location-aware, so it can determine the type of network you are connecting to. After it identifies the type of network, it applies the appropriate profile to provide protection against attacks that can originate from inside and outside of your network. The following WFAS profiles (see Figure 6-5) can be used to apply settings to your computer:

- A ***domain profile*** is used when your computer is connected to its corporate domain and can authenticate to the domain controller through one of its connections.
- A ***private profile*** is used when your computer is connected to a private network location (home or small office network) and is located behind a firewall and/or a device that performs NAT. If you are using this profile with a wireless network, you should implement encryption (WPA v2).

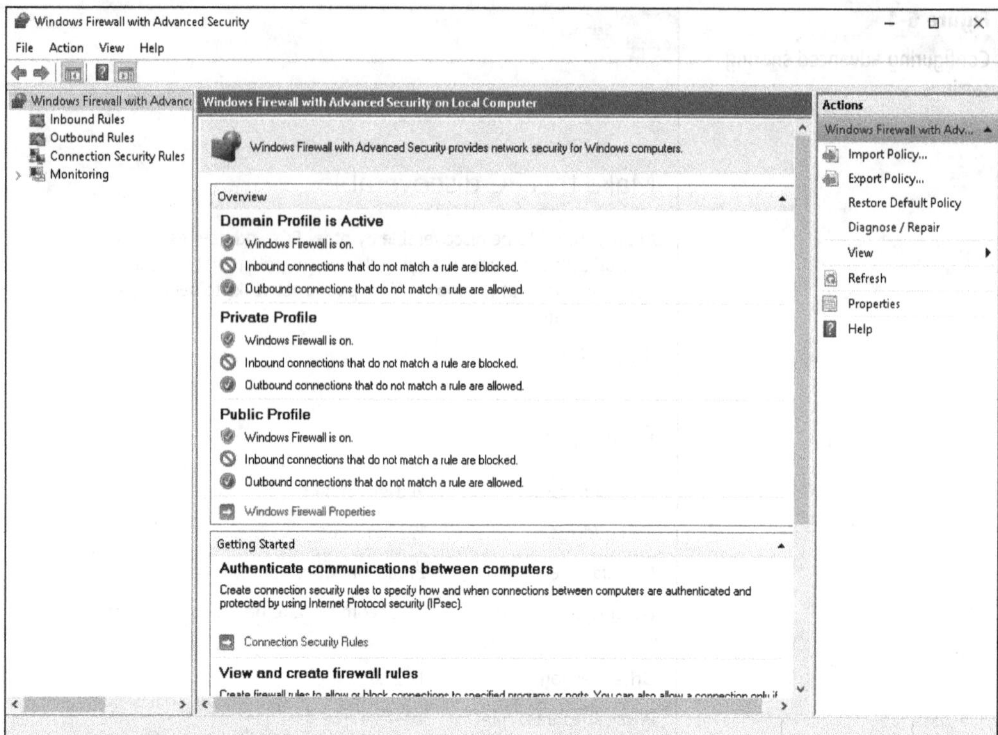

Figure 6-5
WFAS profiles

- A ***public profile*** is used when your computer is connected to a public network (for example, directly connected to the Internet). It is assigned to the computer when it is first connected to a new network; rules associated with this profile are the most restrictive.

You can click the Windows Firewall Properties link to see the range of settings available within each of the three profiles (see Figure 6-6).

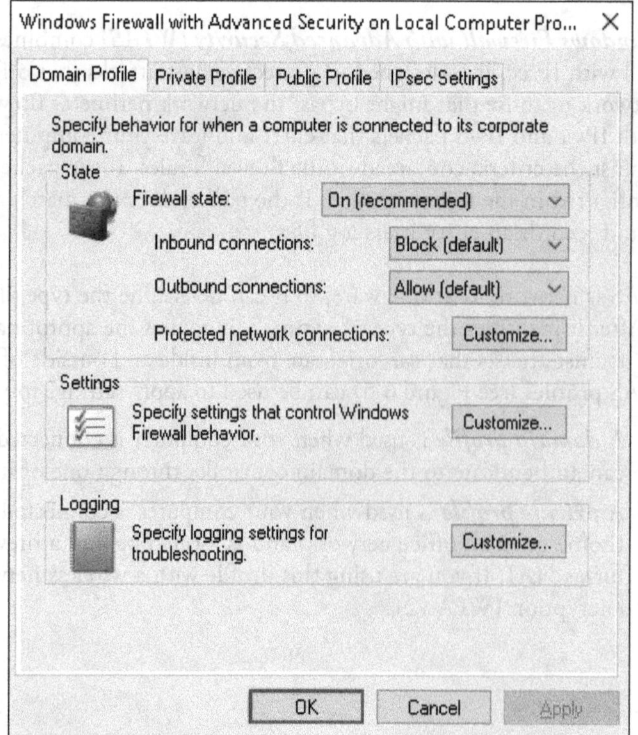

Figure 6-6
Understanding WFAS profile property settings

These settings include the following:

- **Firewall state:** Set to On or Off.
    - **Inbound connections:** Set to Block, Block all connections, or Allow.
    - **Outbound connections:** Set to Allow or Block.
    - **Protected network connections:** Select the connections/interfaces you want Windows Firewall to help protect.
- **Settings:** Display notifications when a program is blocked from receiving inbound connections; allow unicast response to multicast or broadcast network traffic; rule merging (allow rules created by local administrators to be merged with rules distributed via Group Policy).
- **Logging:** Set the location for storing firewall logs along with the size limit for the log file; log dropped packets; log successful connections.

The IPsec Settings tab can be accessed when you want to control how keys are exchanged, how your data is protected, and the authentication methods you want to use:

- **IPsec defaults:** These settings determine how your computer will establish a secure connection by identifying how the keys will be exchanged, how data will be protected, and the authentication method to use.
- **IPsec exemptions:** These settings enable you to exempt Internet Control Message Protocol (ICMP) to simplify the troubleshooting process; ICMP is designed to detect and report error conditions.
- **IPsec tunnel authorization:** These settings enable you to specify the users and computers that are authorized to establish IPsec tunnel connections with your computer.

Configuring Windows Firewall to Allow or Deny Applications, Scopes, Ports, and Users

WFAS enables you to configure three types of firewall rules (inbound, outbound, and connection security) that can be applied to one or more of the profiles (domain, private, public). These rules govern how the computer sends and/or receives traffic from users, computers, applications, and services. When a packet matches the rule's criteria, it allows the connection, explicitly blocks the connection, or allows it only when the connection is using IPsec to secure it.

CERTIFICATION READY
Configure and deploy profile rules
Objective 3.1

CERTIFICATION READY
Configure Windows Firewall to allow or deny applications, scopes, ports, and users using Group Policy, the GUI management console, or Windows PowerShell
Objective 3.1

When configuring inbound/outbound rules, you have the option of selecting criteria that include a program name, TCP/UDP port number, system service name, local and remote interfaces, interface types, users/groups, computers/computer groups, and protocols:

- ***Inbound rules:*** These rules explicitly allow or block inbound traffic that matches the criteria set in the rule. To set up an inbound rule, select the type (program, port, predefined, or custom), select the entity to which the rule applies (for example, program [all or path to specific .exe], port name/number), determine the action (allow, block, or allow if it is secure), select the profile it applies to (domain, private, public), and provide a name for the rule. When your system is set up, it is automatically configured to not allow unsolicited inbound traffic. If you decide to set up a service on your computer (a test website) and want others to connect to it, configure an inbound rule that allows traffic to the web service (typically running on TCP port 80).
- ***Outbound rules:*** These rules explicitly allow or deny outbound traffic that originates from the computer when it matches the criteria set in the rule. The setup for an outbound rule is identical to the options discussed in the inbound rule. Because outbound traffic is allowed by default, you create an outbound rule to block traffic that you do not want to send.

- ***Connection security rules:*** These rules secure the connection with both authentication (Kerberos, digital certificates, pre-shared keys) and encryption protocols. Connection security rules are used to determine how the traffic between the computer and others is secured. The process for creating a connection security rule involves setting the type of connection security you want to create (isolation, authentication exception, server-to-server, tunnel), selecting when you want authentication to occur on inbound/outbound connections (request but don't require it, require it for inbound but request for outbound, require for both), selecting the authentication method to use, selecting which profile to apply the rule to (domain, private, public), and then providing a name for the rule.

TAKE NOTE* Connection security rules specify how and when authentication occurs but they do not allow connections. You need to create an inbound or outbound rule to allow the connection.

When firewall rules conflict, they are applied in the following order (as soon as an incoming packet matches a rule, that rule is applied and processing stops):

1. **Authenticated bypass rules**: These are rules that allow a connection even when the existing firewall rules would block it. For example, you might be blocking a specific type of traffic but then want to allow a certain group of users and computers to bypass the block. These types of rules require that the authenticated computers utilize IPsec to prove their identity.
2. **Block connection**: These rules block matching inbound traffic.
3. **Allow connection**: These rules allow matching inbound traffic.
4. **Default profile behavior**: These rules block unsolicited inbound traffic; allow all outbound traffic.

CREATE AN OUTBOUND RULE

GET READY. To create an outbound rule, perform the following steps.

TAKE NOTE* Before performing the following steps, close Internet Explorer.

1. On **LON-SVR2**, click the **Start** button, type **Windows Firewall**, and then choose **Windows Firewall with Advanced Security.**
2. Right-click **Outbound Rules** and choose **New Rule.**
3. Select **Program** and then click **Next.**
4. Click **Browse** and then navigate to the location of your installation of Internet Explorer. This can usually be found at c:\%ProgramFiles%\Internet Explorer\iexplore.exe.
5. Click **iexplore.exe** and then click **Open.**
6. In the New Outbound Rule Wizard dialog box, click **Next.**
7. Select **Block the connection** and then click **Next.**
8. Select **Domain, Private,** and **Public,** and then click **Next.**
9. For the name of the profile, type **IE Restriction**; for the description, type **Restricts IE from connecting to the Internet.**
10. Click **Finish.**
    Do not close the Windows Firewall with Advanced Security dialog box.
11. Attempt to access the Internet using Internet Explorer. You should see a message indicating This page can't be displayed.
12. Close the Internet Explorer window.

13. Disable the rule by right-clicking the **IE Restriction** rule and choosing **Disable Rule.** Attempt to access the Internet using Internet Explorer. You should be successful.

CREATE AN INBOUND RULE

GET READY. To create an inbound rule based on ports, perform the following steps.

1. On **LON-SVR2**, click the **Start** button, type **Windows Advanced** and then choose **Windows Firewall with Advanced Security.**
2. Right-click **Inbound Rules** and choose **New Rule.**
3. On the Rule Type page, select the **Port** option and then click **Next.**
4. On the Protocol and Ports page, with TCP selected, select **Specific local ports.** Then type the following ports and click **Next:**

   22, 80, 443
5. On the Action page, with the Allow the connection option already selected, click **Next.**
6. On the Profile page, click **Next.**
7. On the Name page, in the Name text box, type **Allow SSH, HTTP, and HTTPS** and then click **Finish.**

USING POWERSHELL

You can manage services using Windows PowerShell by using the following cmdlets:

- **`Enable-NetFirewallRule:`** Enables a previously disabled firewall rule.
- **`Disable-NetFirewallRule:`** Disables a firewall rule.
- **`Get-NetFirewallRule:`** Retrieves firewall rules from the target computer.
- **`New-NetFirewallRule:`** Creates a new inbound or outbound firewall rule and adds the rule to the target computer.
- **`Set-NetFirewallRule:`** Modifies existing firewall rules.
- **`Remove-NetFirewallRule:`** Deles one or more firewall rules that match the specified criteria.
- **`Copy-NetFirewallRule:`** Copies an entire firewall rule, and associated filters, to the same or to a different policy store.

For example, to enable the firewall, at the Windows PowerShell command prompt, execute the following command:

```
Set-NetFirewallProfile -Profile Domain,Public,Private -Enabled
True
```

To retrieve all of the firewall rules in the active store, execute the following command:

```
Get-NetFirewallRule -PolicyStore ActiveStore
```

To create a firewall rule that allows inbound telnet for the tlntsvr.exe program, execute the following command:

```
New-NetFirewallRule -DisplayName "Allow Inbound Telnet"
-Direction Inbound -Program %SystemRoot%\System32\tlntsvr.exe
-RemoteAddress LocalSubnet -Action Allow
```

To modify an existing rule, that changes the remote address, execute the following command:

```
Set-NetFirewallRule -DisplayName "Allow Web 80" -RemoteAddress
192.168.0.2
```

To create an outbound rule that blocks all of the traffic from the local computer that originates on TCP port 80, execute the following command:

```
New-NetFirewallRule -DisplayName "Block Outbound Port 80"
-Direction Outbound -LocalPort 80 -Protocol TCP -Action Block
```

To delete an existing rule, execute the following command:

```
Remove-NetFirewallRule -DisplayName "Block Outbound Port 80"
```

To create an inbound firewall rule that allows traffic for the Windows Messenger program only from computers on the same subnet as the local computer, execute the following command:

```
New-NetFirewallRule -DisplayName "Allow Messenger" -Direction
Inbound -Program "C:\Program Files (x86)\Messenger\msmsgs.exe"
-RemoteAddress LocalSubnet -Action Allow
```

Importing and Exporting Settings

CERTIFICATION READY
Import and export settings
Objective 3.1

After you export the current firewall configuration, you can import it on another standalone system or copy it to a folder to use as a backup in case you make changes to the policy and need to return it to a known state. Policy files are exported as (*.wfw) files.

When you perform the import and export policy, the entire firewall configuration is imported and exported. When you import a configuration, custom rules that are on the target system are overwritten.

EXPORT AND IMPORT A FIREWALL POLICY

GET READY. To export and import a firewall policy, perform the following steps.

1. In the Windows Firewall with Advanced Security window, click the **Windows Firewall with Advanced Security** option in the left pane, click **Action**, and then choose **Export Policy.**
2. Navigate to a folder that you can access from your Windows Server 2016 computer. In the File name field, type **IE Restriction** and then click **Save.**
   Make a note of where you stored this policy; you will use it in the next exercise.
3. When the Policy successfully exported message is displayed, click **OK.**
4. Return to the Windows Firewall with Advanced Security dialog box and click **Outbound Rules.**
5. Locate the Internet Explorer restriction rule you created earlier, right-click it, and then choose **Delete.** Click **Yes** to confirm you want to delete the rule.
6. To import the policy, right-click Windows Firewall with Advanced Security and choose Import Policy.
7. When you are prompted to confirm that you want to import a policy now, click **Yes.**
8. Navigate to and click **IE Restriction.wfw** and then click **Open.**
9. When the policy has been successfully imported, click **OK.**

In addition, you can restore the Default policy by right-clicking the Windows Firewall with Advanced Security and choosing Restore Default Policy. When you are prompted to confirm that you want to continue, click Yes.

Configuring Firewall Rules for Multiple Profiles Using Group Policy

CERTIFICATION READY
Configure firewall rules for multiple profiles using Group Policy
Objective 3.1

When you create several firewall rules and you want to deploy those rules to multiple computers, the simplest and quickest way to deploy those rules is to use Group Policy Object (GPO). You then need only to export the firewall policy and import the firewall settings into the policy.

Since the exporting and importing of firewall policies include all rules, you should start with a fresh computer that has a set of clean rules before you do the export. You can then link the GPO to any container that you desire.

IMPORT A WINDOW FIREWALL RULE INTO A GROUP POLICY OBJECT

GET READY. To import the firewall policy you created earlier into a GPO and restrict the use of Internet Explorer for your domain, log on with administrative privileges to your domain controller and then perform the following steps.

1. On **LON-DC1**, in Server Manager, click **Tools > Group Policy Management.**
2. Expand the **adatum.com** domain folder, right-click **Group Policy Objects** and choose **New.**
3. For the name, type **IE Restriction** and then click **OK.**
4. Double-click the **Group Policy Objects** folder and click **IE Restriction.**
5. Right-click **IE Restriction** and choose **Edit.**
6. Expand **Computer Configuration > Policies > Windows Settings > Security Settings > Windows Firewall with Advanced Security.**
7. Right-click the **Windows Firewall with Advanced Security** policy (which is in the Windows Firewall with Advanced Security node, as shown in Figure 6-7) and choose **Import Policy.**

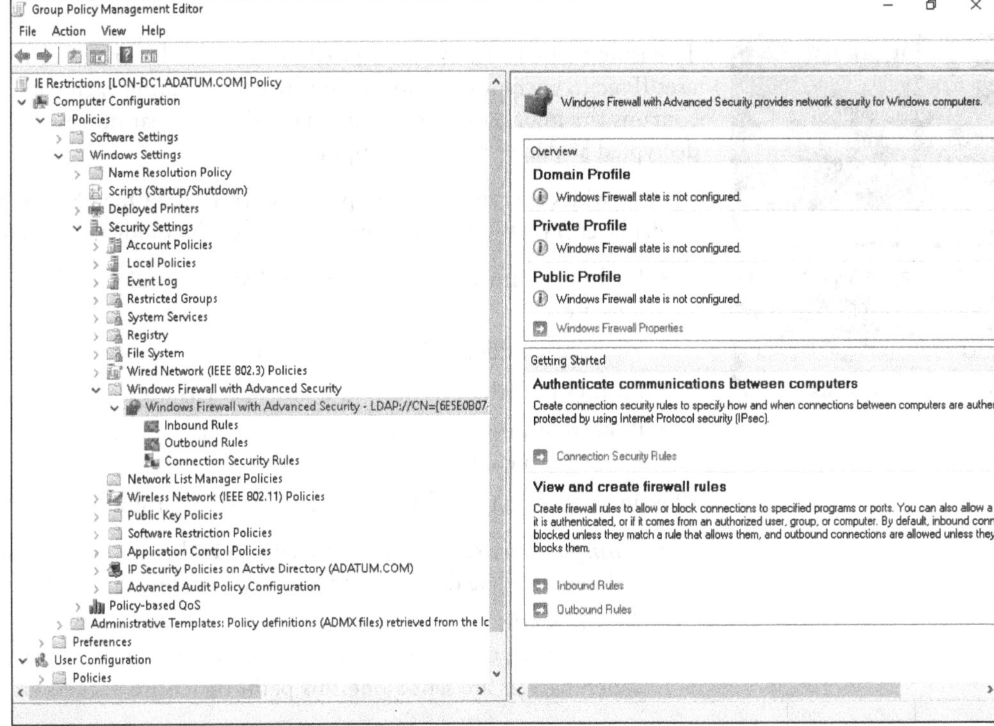

Figure 6-7

Importing a Windows Firewall policy into a GPO

8. When you are prompted to confirm that you want to import a policy now, click **Yes.**
9. Browse to the folder where you saved the IE Restriction policy in the previous exercise. Click the **IE Restriction** policy and then click **Open.**
10. When a message indicates Policy successfully imported, read the warning and then click **OK.**
11. Click the **Outbound Rules** folder. The IE Restriction policy is now listed in the GPO.
12. Close the Group Policy Management Editor window.
13. In the Group Policy Management Console, right-click the **adatum.com** domain and choose **Link an Existing GPO.**
14. Click **IE Restriction** and then click **OK.**
15. Close the Group Policy Management Console window. The GPO is now applied to your domain.

Similar to using the Windows Firewall with Advanced Security console, you can create, delete, and modify rules by accessing the GPO Inbound Rules, Outbound Rules, and Connection Security Rules nodes. In addition, you can right-click the Windows Firewall with Advanced Security node and choose Properties. You can also configure the settings in the Domain Profile tab, the Private Profile tab, the Public Profile tab, and the IPsec Settings tab.

Configuring Connection Security Rules

IP security (IPsec) is a suite of protocols that provides a mechanism for data integrity, authentication, and privacy for the Internet Protocol by providing message authentication and/or encryption. It can be used to protect data sent between hosts on a network by creating a secure electronic tunnel between two hosts. It can also be used for remote access/ VPN connections.

CERTIFICATION READY
Configure connection security rules using Group Policy, the GUI management console, or Windows PowerShell
Objective 3.1

CERTIFICATION READY
Configure connection security rules
Objective 3.3

To ensure that data cannot be viewed or modified by unauthorized users, the source computer uses IPsec to encrypt the information by encapsulating each data packet in a new packet that contains the information to set up, maintain, and tear down a virtual tunnel. The data is then decrypted at the destination computer.

IPsec provides encryption for all protocols from the Open Systems Interconnection (OSI) model layer 3 (network layer) and it can offer the following benefits:

- Performs mutual authentication so that the sending and receiving systems prove who they are
- Provides confidentiality by ensuring that no unauthorized parties can access the data
- Ensures integrity by rejecting traffic that has been modified
- Protects against replay attacks to ensure that no one can resend previous sent packets to jump into a conversation

IPsec includes a couple of modes and a couple of protocols. The two modes:

- ***Transport mode:*** Used to secure end-to-end communications such as between a client and a server. The data payload is encrypted, but the header data remains unchanged.
- ***Tunnel mode:*** Used for server-to-server or server-to-gateway configurations by creating a virtual path that a packet takes from the source computer to the destination computer. When packets are sent along this path, the entire packets are encrypted.

The two IPsec protocols:

- ***Encapsulating Security Payload (ESP)*:** Provides confidentiality (encryption), authentication (proves identity), integrity (verifies the packet has not been changed), and anti-replay (prevents packets from being reused to bypass security) for the IP payload only, not the entire packet. ESP operates directly on top of IP, using IP protocol number 50.
- ***Authentication Header*** (AH): Provides authentication, integrity, and anti-replay for the entire packet (both the IP header and the data payload carried in the packet). Because the payload is not encrypted, it does not provide confidentiality. The data is readable but protected from modification. AH operates directly on top of IP, using IP protocol number 51.

ESP and AH can be combined to provide authentication, integrity, and anti-replay for the entire packet, and confidentiality for the payload.

The AH protocol is not compatible with Network Address Translation (NAT) because NAT devices need to change information in the packet headers. To allow IPsec-based traffic to pass through a NAT device, you must ensure that IPsec NAT-T is supported on your IPsec peer computers.

A connection security rule forces authentication between two peer computers before they can establish a connection and transmit security-enhanced information. Windows Firewall with Advanced Security uses IPsec to enforce these rules.

The configurable connection security rules are:

- **Isolation:** Isolates computers by restricting connections based on credentials such as domain membership or health status. Use isolation rules to implement an isolation strategy for servers or domains.
- **Authentication exemption:** Designates connections that do not require authentication based on specific IP address, an IP address range, a subnet, or a predefined group such as a gateway.
- **Server to Server:** Helps protect connections between specific computers.
- **Tunnel:** Helps protect connections between gateway computers.
- **Custom:** Uses a custom rule to authenticate connections between two endpoints when you cannot set up the authentication rules that you need by using the other rules available in the New Connection Security Rule Wizard.

When you enable and configure a connection security rule, you must define the following properties:

- **Requirements:** Select whether the rule requests authentication, requires inbound authentication, or requires both inbound and outbound authentication.
- **Authentication methods:** Select among several authentication methods:
  - **Default:** Uses the authentication method specified in the IPsec settings.
  - **Computer and User (Kerberos V5):** Restricts communications to connections from domain-joined users and computers.
  - **Computer (Kerberos V5):** Restricts communications from domain-joined computers.
  - **Advanced:** Specifies custom authentication methods as the first and second authentication methods. Options for first authentication method include computer (Kerberos V5), computer (NTLMv2), computer certificate from the certificate authority (CA), and Preshared key. Options for second authentication method include computer (Kerberos V5), computer (NTLMv2), user certificate from the certificate authority (CA), and computer health certificate from the certificate authority (CA).
- **Profile:** Associate the rule with the appropriate network profile, such as Domain, Private, or Public.

- **Exempt computers:** Define the exempt computers by specifying their IP addresses, the IP address range, or the IP subnet.
- **Endpoints:** For server-to-server rules, you can define the IP addresses affected by the rule.
- **Tunnel endpoints:** For tunnel rules only, you can define the tunnel endpoints affected by the rule.

To configure IPsec between two hosts, you will configure connection security rules using the Windows Firewall with Advanced Security. The rules that you will create include:

1. Enable the protocol that you want to secure.
2. Create a Connection Security rule on the first host.
3. Create a Connection Security rule on the second host.
4. Test the rules and monitor the results.

ENABLE THE ICMP TRAFFIC ON THE SENDING HOST

GET READY. To enable ICMP traffic on a computer running Windows Server 2016, perform the following steps.

1. On **LON-SVR2**, using Windows Firewall with Advanced Security, click, then right-click **Inbound Rules** and choose **New Rule.**
2. In the New Inbound Rule Wizard dialog box, on the Rule Type page, click **Custom** (as shown in Figure 6-8) and then click **Next.**
3. On the Program page, click **Next.**

Figure 6-8

Defining a rule type in the Inbound Rule Wizard

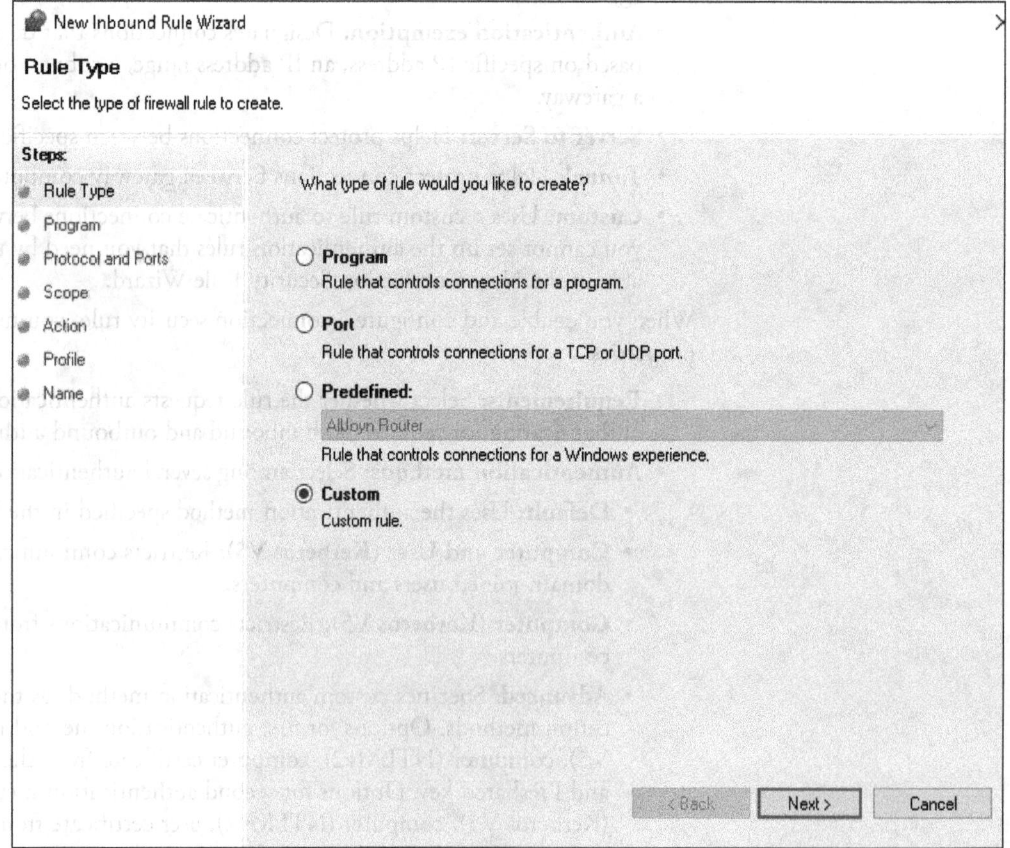

4. On the Protocols and Ports page, in the Protocol type list, select **ICMPv4** and then click **Next.**
5. On the Scope page, click **Next.**
6. On the Action page, click **Allow the connection if it is secure** and then click **Next.**
7. On the Users page, click **Next.**
8. On the Computers page, click **Next.**
9. On the Profile page, click **Next.**
10. On the Name page, in the Name box, type **ICMPv4 Allowed** and then click **Finish.**

CREATE A CONNECTION SECURITY RULE

GET READY. To create a connection security rule, perform the following steps.

1. On **LON-SVR1**, using the Windows Firewall with Advanced Security, click, then right-click **Connection Security Rules** (the main node under Windows Firewall with Advanced Security) and choose **New Rule.**
2. In the New Connection Security Rule Wizard (as shown in Figure 6-9), on the Rule Type page, click **Server-to-server** and then click **Next.**

Figure 6-9

Defining a new connection security rule

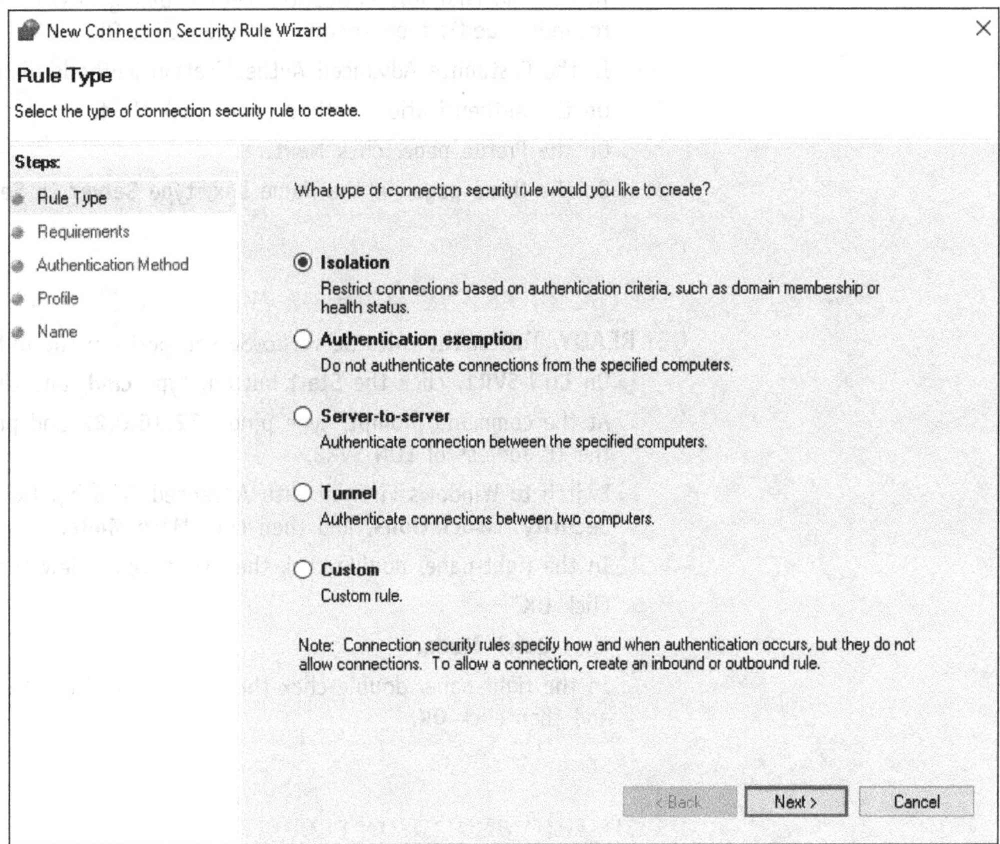

3. On the Endpoints page, click **Next.**
4. On the Requirements page, click **Require authentication for inbound and outbound connections** and then click **Next.**
5. On the Authentication Method page, click **Advanced** and then click **Customize.**

6. In the Customize Advanced Authentication Methods dialog box, under First authentication, click **Add**.
7. In the Add First Authentication Method dialog box, click **Preshared Key (not recommended)**, type **secret**, and then click **OK.**
8. In the Customize Advanced Authentication Methods dialog box, click **OK**.
9. On the Authentication Method page, click **Next**.
10. On the Profile page, click **Next**.
11. On the Name page, in the Name box, type **Server to Server** and then click **Finish**.
12. On **LON-SVR2**, using Windows Firewall with Advanced Security, click, then right-click **Connection Security Rules** and choose **New Rule**.
13. In the New Connection Security Rule Wizard, on the Rule Type page, click **Server-to-Server** and then click **Next**.
14. On the Endpoints page, click **Next**.
15. On the Requirements page, click **Require authentication for inbound and outbound connections** and then click **Next**.
16. On the Authentication Method page, click **Advanced** and then click **Customize**.
17. In the Customize Advanced Authentication Methods dialog box, under First authentication, click **Add**.
18. In the Add First Authentication Method dialog box, click **Preshared Key (not recommended)**, type **secret**, and then click **OK**.
19. In the Customize Advanced Authentication Methods dialog box, click **OK**.
20. On the Authentication Method page, click **Next**.
21. On the Profile page, click **Next**.
22. On the Name page, in the Name box, type **Server to Server** and then click **Finish**.

TEST THE RULES AND MONITOR THE RESULTS

GET READY. To test the rules Server-to-Server, perform the following steps.

1. On **LON-SVR1**, click the **Start** button, type **cmd**, and then press **Enter**.
2. At the command prompt, type ping **172.16.0.22** and press **Enter**. 172.16.0.22 is the IP address of LON-SVR2.
3. Switch to Windows Firewall with Advanced Security. Expand **Monitoring**, expand **Security Associations**, and then click **Main Mode**.
4. In the right-pane, double-click the listed item. View the information in Main Mode.
5. Click **OK**.
6. Click **Quick Mode**.
7. In the right-pane, double-click the listed item. View the information in Quick Mode and then click **OK**.

DELETE THE CONNECTION SECURITY RULES

GET READY. To delete the Connection Security Rules, perform the following steps.

1. On **LON-SVR1**, click the **Connection Security Rules** node under Windows Firewall with Advanced Security. Do not click the Connection Security Rules under Monitoring.
2. Right-click the **Server to Server** security rule and choose **Delete**. When you are prompted to confirm that you want to delete this rule, click **Yes**.

3. On **LON-SVR2**, click **Connection Security Rules** node under Windows Firewall with Advanced Security. Do not click the Connection Security Rules under Monitoring.
4. Right-click the **Server to Server** security rule and choose **Delete.** When you are prompted to confirm that you want to delete this rule, click **Yes.**
5. Click the **Inbound Rules** node.
6. Right-click the **ICMPv4 Allowed** rule and choose **Delete.** When you are prompted to confirm that you want to delete this rule, click **Yes.**

As discussed in the section entitled "Configuring Windows Firewall to Allow or Deny Applications, Scopes, Ports, and Users," you can use Windows PowerShell to manage your firewall rules. For example, to allow inbound Telnet traffic only if the traffic is authenticated, execute the following command:

```
New-NetFirewallRule -DisplayName "Allow Authenticated Telnet"
-Direction Inbound -Program %SystemRoot%\System32\tlntsvr.exe
-Authentication Required -Action Allow
```

Lastly, as discussed in the section entitled "Configuring Firewall Rules for Multiple Profiles Using Group Policy," you can configure connection security rules using Group Policy. From the Connection Security Rules node, you can create, delete, and edit your Connection Security rules.

Configuring Authenticated Firewall Exceptions

CERTIFICATION READY
Configure authenticated firewall exceptions
Objective 3.1

Inbound firewall rules specify computers and users that are authorized to access the local computer over the network. However, with the Windows Firewall with Advanced Security, you can create an authentication exemption that designates computers that do not require authentication, such as those computers that are in an isolated domain.

In isolated server/domain scenarios, there are some computers or devices that cannot communicate by using IPsec. To overcome this problem, you can create rules that exempt those computers from the authentication requirements of your isolation policies. Unfortunately, when adding computers to the exemption list, security is reduced for the zone because it permits computers in the zone to send network traffic that is unprotected by IPsec to the computers on the list.

CREATE AN AUTHENTICATION EXCEPTION RULE

GET READY. To create an authentication exception rule, perform the following steps.

1. On **LON-SVR2**, in the Windows Firewall with Advanced Security console, click **Connection Security Rules** (the main node under Windows Firewall with Advanced Security), right-click it, and then choose **New Rule.**
2. In the New Connection Security Rule Wizard, on the Rule Type page, click **Authentication exemption** and then click **Next.**
3. On the Exempt Computers page, to create a new exemption, click **Add.** To modify an existing exemption, click it and then click **Edit.**
4. In the IP Address dialog box, do one of the following:
   - To add a single IP address, click **This IP address or subnet**, type the IP address of the host in the text box, and then click **OK.**
   - To add an entire subnet by address, click **This IP address range** and then type the IP address of the subnet, followed by a forward slash (/) and the number of bits in the corresponding subnet mask. For example, you could type **10.50.0.0/16.** Click **OK** when you are finished.

- To add the local computer's subnet, click **Predefined set of computers**, select **Local subnet** from the list, and then click **OK**.

5. When you have all of the necessary IP addresses, click **Next**.
6. On the Profile page, check the profile for each network location type (Domain, Private, and/or Public) to which this set of exemptions applies and then click **Next**.
7. On the Name page, type the name of the exemption rule, such as **Authentication Exemption**, and then click **Finish**.

Implementing a Software-Defined Distributed Firewall

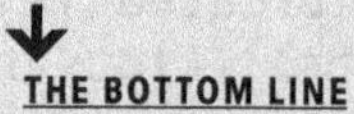

Software-Defined Networking (SDN) allows you to centrally configure and manage physical and virtual network devices, including routers, switches, and gateways in your data center. When creating a virtual infrastructure, you will configure Hyper-V virtual switches, Hyper-V Network Virtualization, and Windows Server Gateway. However, you also need to use and manage physical switches, routers, and other hardware devices and integrate the virtual devices and physical devices together.

By using SDN, you can merge the physical and virtual components that make up a virtual infrastructure. The applications and virtual servers will run on the physical network and you can virtualize network management by creating virtual IP addresses, ports, and switches. You can also define policies that will manage traffic flow across both physical and virtual networks.

Microsoft has implemented Software-Defined Networking in Windows Server 2012, Windows Server 2012 R2, and Windows Server 2016 Hyper-V by providing the following components:

- **Network Controller:** New to Windows Server 2016, Network Controller provides centralized management, configuration, monitoring, and troubleshooting of both your virtual and physical network infrastructure.
- **Hyper-V Network Virtualization (HNV):** HNV helps you abstract or separate your applications and workloads from the underlying physical network by using virtual networks.
- **Hyper-V Virtual Switch:** Hyper-V virtual switches give you the ability to connect virtual machines to both virtual networks and your physical network. Similar to a physical switch, Hyper-V virtual switches provide security, isolation, and service-level policy enforcement.
- **RRAS Multi-tenant Gateway:** RRAS Multi-tenant Gateway gives you the ability to extend your network boundaries to Microsoft Azure or another provider to deliver on-demand hybrid infrastructure.
- **NIC Teaming:** NIC Teaming allows you to configure multiple network adapters as a team for bandwidth aggregation and traffic failover to guard against network component failure.

In addition, System Center provides SDN technologies in System Center Operations Manager, System Center Virtual Machine Manager, and Windows Server Gateway.

Datacenter Firewall, which is a new service in Windows Server 2016, is one component in an SDN deployment. It is a distributed firewall solution well suited for helping to protect virtual environments. Derived from Microsoft Azure, it provides a stateful, multitenant firewall that is operating-system agnostic.

Implementing Network Controller

The ***Network Controller*** is a Windows Server 2016 server role that provides two application programming interfaces (APIs): the Southbound API and the Northbound API. The ***Southbound API*** is used to communicate with the network, whereas the ***Northbound API*** gives you the ability to communicate with the Network Controller. For example, using the Network Controller, you can manage the Hyper-V virtual machines and virtual switches, Datacenter Firewall, RAS Multi-tenant Gateways, virtual gateways, gateway pools, and load balancers.

The Southbound API is used to communicate with network devices, services, and components. With it, you can discover network devices, detect service configuration, and gather information about the network.

The Northbound API allows you to gather network information from the Network Controller, which can be used to monitor and configure the network. It uses Windows PowerShell, Representational State Transfer (REST) API, and management applications to configure, monitor, troubleshoot, and deploy new devices on the network.

When you deploy a Network Controller in an AD DS domain, the Network Controller authenticates users and devices with Kerberos. When you deploy a Network Controller in a non-domain environment, you must deploy digital certificates to provide authentication.

You can deploy Network Controller on a server running Windows Server 2016 Datacenter edition. The management client must be installed on a computer running Windows 8/8.1 or Windows 10. You must configure dynamic DNS registration to enable registration of required DNS records for Network Controller.

If the computers or virtual machines running Network Controller or the management client for Network Controller are joined to a domain, you must create the following security groups:

- A security group that holds all the users who have permission to configure Network Controller
- A security group that holds all the users who have permission to configure and manage the network by using Network Controller

In addition, users added to these groups must also belong to the Domain Users group.

CREATE THE REQUIRED AD DS SECURITY GROUPS

GET READY. To create the required AD DS security groups, perform the following steps.

1. Log on to LON-DC1 as **adatum\administrator** with the password of **Pa$$w0rd.**
2. Click **Start** and then click **Server Manager.**
3. In Server Manager, click **Tools > Active Directory Users and Computers.**
4. In Active Directory Users and Computers, expand **Adatum.com** and then click **IT.**
5. Right-click **IT** and choose **New > Group.**
6. In the New Object - Group dialog box, in the Group name text box, type **Network Controller Admins** and then click **OK.**
7. In the details pane, double-click **Network Controller Admins**, and in the Network Controller Admins Properties dialog box, on the Members tab, click **Add.**
8. In the Select Users, Contacts, Computers, Service Accounts, or Groups dialog box, in the Enter the object names to select (examples) text box, type **administrator** and then click **OK** twice.
9. Right-click **IT** and choose **New > Group.**

10. In the New Object – Group dialog box, in the Group name text box, type **Network Controller Ops** and then click **OK**.
11. In the details pane, double-click **Network Controller Ops**, and in the Network Controller Ops Properties dialog box, on the Members tab, click **Add**.
12. In the Select Users, Contacts, Computers, Service Accounts, or Groups dialog box, in the Enter the object names to select (examples) text box, type **administrator** and then click **OK** twice.
13. Close Active Directory Users and Computers.

If the system running Network Controller or the management client for Network Controller is not joined to a domain, you must configure certificate-based authentication:

- You must create a certificate for use on the management client that is trusted by the Network Controller.
- The certificate subject name must match the DNS name of the computer or virtual machine holding the Network Controller role, the server authentication purpose is present in enhanced key usage (EKU) extensions, and the certificate subject name should resolve to the IP address of the Network Controller, if Network Controller is deployed on a single computer or virtual machine, or the REST IP address, if Network Controller is deployed on multiple computers, multiple virtual machines, or both.
- The certificate must be trusted by all the REST clients, the SLB MUX, and the southbound host computers that Network Controller manages.

REQUEST A CERTIFICATE FOR AUTHENTICATING NETWORK CONTROLLER

GET READY. To request a certificate for authenticating Network Controller, perform the following steps.

1. Log on to LON-SVR2 as **adatum\administrator** with the password of **Pa$$w0rd.**
2. Right-click **Start** and choose **Run.**
3. In the Run dialog box, type **mmc.exe** and press **Enter.**
4. In the Console1 – [Console Root] window, click **File > Add/Remove Snap-in.**
5. In the Add or Remove Snap-ins dialog box, in the Snap-in list, double-click **Certificates.**
6. Click **Computer** account, click **Next** and then click **Finish.**
7. Click **OK.**
8. In the navigation pane, expand **Certificates** and then expand **Personal.**
9. Right-click **Personal** and choose **All Tasks > Request New Certificate.**
10. In the Certificate Enrollment dialog box, on the Before You Begin page, click **Next.**
11. On the Select Certificate Enrollment Policy page, click **Next.**
12. Select the **Computer** check box and then click **Enroll.**
13. Click **Finish.**
14. Close the management console and do not save changes.

You can deploy the Network Controller role by following these high-level steps:

1. Install the Network Controller server role.
2. Configure the Network Controller cluster.
3. Configure the Network Controller application.
4. Validate the Network Controller deployment.

Do not deploy the Network Controller server role on physical hosts. Instead deploy Network Controller on a Hyper-V virtual machine (VM) that is installed on a Hyper-V host.

DEPLOY NETWORK CONTROLLER

GET READY. To deploy Network Controller, perform the following steps.

1. Log on to LON-SVR2 as **adatum\administrator** with the password of **Pa$$w0rd.**
2. Click **Start** and then click **Server Manager.**
3. In Server Manager, in the details pane, click **Add roles and features.**
4. In the Add Roles and Features Wizard, on the Before You Begin page, click **Next.**
5. On the Select Installation Type page, click **Next.**
6. On the Select Destination Server page, click **Next.**
7. On the Select Server Roles page, in the Roles list, select the **Network Controller** check box.
8. Click **Add Features** and then click **Next.**
9. On the Select Features page, click **Next.**
10. On the Network Controller page, click **Next.**
11. On the Confirm Installation Selections page, click **Install.**
12. When the role is installed, click **Close.**
13. Right-click **Start** and choose **Shut down or sign out > Restart.**
14. In the Choose a reason that best describes why you want to shut down this computer dialog box, click **Continue.**
15. After LON-SVR2 has restarted, log on as **Adatum\administrator** with the password of **Pa$$w0rd.**

Alternatively, you can install the Network Controller server role by executing the following Windows PowerShell command:

```
Install-WindowsFeature -Name NetworkController
-IncludeManagementTools
```

After performing this task, restart your computer or virtual machine.

To configure the cluster, complete the following steps:

1. You must create a node object for each computer or virtual machine that is a member of the Network Controller cluster executing `New-NetworkControllerNodeObject`. For example, to create a Network Controller node object named Node1 on NodeNC. Adatum.com, with Ethernet as the name of the interface on the computer listening to REST requests, execute the following command:

   ```
   New-NetworkControllerNodeObject -Name "Node1"
   -Server "NodeNC.Adatum.com" -FaultDomain "fd:/rack1/host1"
   -RestInterface "Ethernet"
   ```

2. To configure the cluster, execute the following commands:

   ```
   Install-NetworkControllerCluster cmdlets:
   $NodeObject = New-NetworkControllerNodeObject
   -Name "Node1" -Server "NCNode1.Adatum.com"
   -FaultDomain "fd:/rack1/host1" -RestInterface "Ethernet"
   Install-NetworkControllerCluster -Node $NodeObject
   -ClusterAuthentication Kerberos
   ```

To configure the Network Controller application, execute `Install-NetworkController`. For example, to create a Network Controller node object, and then store it in the `$NodeObject` variable, execute the following command:

```
$NodeObject = New-NetworkControllerNodeObject -Name
"Node01" -Server "NCNode11" -FaultDomain "fd:/rack1/host1"
-RestInterface Ethernet
```

Then, to get a certificate named NCEncryption, and store it in the `$Certificate` variable, execute the following command:

```
$Certificate = Get-Item Cert:\LocalMachine\My | Get-ChildItem |
where {$_.Subject -imatch "NCEncryption" }
```

To create the Network Controller cluster, execute the following command:

```
Install-NetworkControllerCluster -Node $NodeObject

-ClusterAuthentication None
```

In a test environment with a single node, there is no high-availability support; the Network Controller employs no authentication between the cluster nodes, between the REST clients and Network Controller. The following command specifies the `$Certificate` to encrypt the traffic between the REST clients and Network Controller:

```
Install-NetworkController -Node $NodeObject

-ClientAuthentication None -RestIpAddress "10.0.0.1/24"
-ServerCertificate $Certificate
```

After you have deployed the Network Controller, you can validate the deployment by adding a credential to the Network Controller and then retrieving the credential.

Complete this task by performing the following steps:

1. Open Windows PowerShell (Admin) and then execute the following commands:

```
$cred=New-Object Microsoft.Windows.Networkcontroller.
credentialproperties

$cred.type="usernamepassword"

$cred.username="admin"

$cred.value="abcd"

New-NetworkControllerCredential -ConnectionUri https://network-
controller -Properties $cred
-ResourceId cred1
```

2. Retrieve the credential that you added to Network Controller by executing the following command:

```
Get-NetworkControllerCredential -ConnectionUri https://network-
controller -ResourceId cred1
```

Determining Scenarios for Implementation of Software Load Balancer (SLB) for North-South and East-West Load Balancing

When you have large workloads, you can try to manage the workload by distributing network traffic among virtual network resources. Windows ***Software Load Balancing (SLB)*** evenly distributes tenant and tenant customer network traffic among the virtual network resources. Like Network Load Balancing (NLB), Windows Server SLB enables multiple servers to host the same workload, providing high availability and scalability.

When looking at network traffic patterns within a data center, you can organize traffic into two types. The ***North-South traffic*** is traffic between servers and clients. The ***East-West traffic*** is traffic between servers. SLB can be used in both types of traffic.

To provide load balancing, SLB maps ***virtual IP addresses (VIPs)*** to ***dynamic IP addresses (DIPs)***, which are part of a cloud service set of resources in the data center. VIPs are single IP addresses that give public access to a pool of load-balanced VMs. DIPs are the IP addresses of the member VMs of the load-balanced pool. Clients connect to a server via the VIP, which then translates to the appropriate DIP. The VIPs are in the ***SLB Multiplexer (MUX)***, which uses Border Gateway Protocol (BGP) to advertise each VIP on routers.

Network Controller hosts the SLB Manager and performs the following actions for SLB:

- Processes SLB commands that come in through the Northbound API
- Calculates policy for distribution to Hyper-V hosts and SLB MUXs
- Provides the health status of the SLB infrastructure

The Network Controller role can be used with SLB to distribute traffic based on the policies defined in the load balancer:

- Layer 4 load balancing for North-South and East-West network traffic
- Internal and external network traffic
- Dynamic IP addresses
- Health probes

Determining Requirements and Scenarios for Datacenter Firewall Implementation with Software-Defined Networking

CERTIFICATION READY
Determine requirements and scenarios for Datacenter Firewall implementation with Software-Defined Networking
Objective 3.2

The Network Controller's ***Datacenter Firewall*** allows you to configure and manage firewall access control rules for both East-West and North-South network traffic in your data center. The Datacenter Firewall is a network layer, stateful, multi-tenant firewall. When deployed, tenant administrators can install and configure firewall policies to help protect their virtual networks from unwanted traffic from Internet and intranet networks, and between tenants. A stateful firewall looks at the state of current connections and allows inbound connections based on the outbound response for a connection.

The firewall is enforced at the VMSwitch as traffic attempts to ingress into or egress from a connected vNIC. Like other firewalls, the firewall uses a set of policies that define Access Control Lists (ACLs), which are distributed from a component called the ***Distributed Firewall Manager***. The Distributed Firewall Manager is part of the Network Controller. The ACLs are applied to a virtual subnet or a network interface.

The firewall policies created for Datacenter Firewall are deployed through Network Controller and enforced at the vSwitch for each virtual machine in the Hyper-V environment. The service provider can offer Datacenter Firewall as a service, allowing tenant administrators to create their own firewall policies to help protect their virtual networks from malicious traffic. Datacenter Firewall policies are managed via the Northbound APIs of Network Controller.

Determining Usage Scenarios for Datacenter Firewall Policies and Network Security Groups

Network security groups (NSGs) allow you to define rules to segment your virtual environment into virtual subnets, which support multitiered environments. An NSG contains Access Control List rules that either allow or deny traffic to or from a virtual subnet or virtual machine.

CERTIFICATION READY
Determine usage scenarios for Datacenter Firewall policies and network security groups
Objective 3.2

The Datacenter Firewall provides a highly scalable and manageable solution that can be offered to multiple tenants. It also allows you to move tenant virtual machines to different hosts while keeping the firewall configuration for the tenant. Because the firewall policies are applied to a subnet or network interface, the protection is applied regardless of the tenant guest operating system.

For tenants, the Datacenter Firewall provides the ability to:

- Define firewall rules that can help protect Internet-facing workloads on their virtual networks.
- Define firewall rules that can help protect traffic between virtual machines on the same L2 virtual subnet and also between virtual machines on different L2 virtual subnets.
- Define firewall rules that can help protect and isolate network traffic between tenant on-premises networks and their virtual networks at the service provider.

Configuring Datacenter Firewall Access Control Lists

You can enable and configure Datacenter Firewall by creating ACLs that are applied to a virtual subnet or a network interface. Just as you would with any other firewall, you define rules that specify which traffic is allowed based on IP addresses, protocol, and inbound versus outbound.

CERTIFICATION READY
Configure Datacenter Firewall Access Control Lists
Objective 3.2

Each rule will have the following:

- A name
- Five-tuple set (destination port range, destination IP range using CIDR notation, source port range, source IP range using CIDR, and protocol, such as TCP, UDP, or *)
- Type (inbound or outbound)
- Priority (101–65,000 for user ranges)
- Action (allow or deny)

The default rules have lower priorities (high number).

The following commands configure various properties that lead to ACLrule1 and ACLrule2, which allow all inbound traffic and allow all outbound traffic. Before each rule, you define protocol, port ranges, action, and addresses.

```
$ruleproperties = new-object Microsoft.Windows.
NetworkController.AclRuleProperties
$ruleproperties.Protocol = "All"
$ruleproperties.SourcePortRange = "0-65535"
$ruleproperties.DestinationPortRange = "0-65535"
$ruleproperties.Action = "Allow"
$ruleproperties.SourceAddressPrefix = "*"
$ruleproperties.DestinationAddressPrefix = "*"
$ruleproperties.Priority = "100"
$ruleproperties.Type = "Inbound"
$ruleproperties.Logging = "Enabled"
```

```
$aclrule1 = new-object Microsoft.Windows.NetworkController.
AclRule
$aclrule1.Properties = $ruleproperties
$aclrule1.ResourceId = "AllowAll_Inbound"

$ruleproperties = new-object Microsoft.Windows.
NetworkController.AclRuleProperties
$ruleproperties.Protocol = "All"
$ruleproperties.SourcePortRange = "0-65535"
$ruleproperties.DestinationPortRange = "0-65535"
$ruleproperties.Action = "Allow"
$ruleproperties.SourceAddressPrefix = "*"
$ruleproperties.DestinationAddressPrefix = "*"
$ruleproperties.Priority = "110"
$ruleproperties.Type = "Outbound"
$ruleproperties.Logging = "Enabled"
$aclrule2 = new-object Microsoft.Windows.NetworkController.
AclRule
$aclrule2.Properties = $ruleproperties
$aclrule2.ResourceId = "AllowAll_Outbound"

$acllistproperties = new-object Microsoft.Windows.
NetworkController.AccessControlListProperties
$acllistproperties.AclRules = @($aclrule1, $aclrule2)
New-NetworkControllerAccessControlList -ResourceId "AllowAll"
-Properties $acllistproperties
-ConnectionUri <NC REST FQDN>
```

With the Windows Server 2016 Datacenter Firewall, you can apply specific ACLs to network interfaces. If ACLs are set on the virtual subnet to which the network interface is connected, both ACLs are applied, but the network interface ACLs are prioritized above the virtual subnet ACLs.

If you want to override the default ACL on the virtual subnet with a specific ACL for an individual network interface, follow these steps:

1. Get or create the NIC to which you will add the ACL.
2. Get or create the ACL you will add to the NIC.
3. Add the ACL to the AccessControlList property of the NIC.

This consists of the following commands:

```
$nic = get-networkcontrollernetworkinterface
-ConnectionUri $uri -ResourceId "MyVM_Ethernet1"
$acl = get-networkcontrolleraccesscontrollist
-ConnectionUri $uri -resourceid "AllowAllACL"
$nic.properties.ipconfigurations[0].properties.
AccessControlList = $acl
```

SKILL SUMMARY

IN THIS LESSON YOU LEARNED:

- A firewall is a software program or piece of hardware that protects networks or individual computers by screening and controlling incoming and outgoing network traffic based on a set of rules.
- Host-based firewalls are firewalls run on individual computers (hosts) within the local network. They are designed to provide a second layer of defense, protect the computer from attacks and unauthorized access, and block specific types of traffic. Windows Firewall is a host-based firewall that is included with Windows Server 2016.
- Windows Firewall with Advanced Security (WFAS) combines a stateful host-based firewall with IPsec. It is designed to protect against attacks that originate from within your network or those that might bypass the network perimeter firewall(s). WFAS inspects both IPv4 and IPv6 packets that enter and leave your computer and then compares them against the criteria contained in the firewall's rules. If the packet matches a rule, the action configured in the rule is applied. If the packet does not match a rule, the firewall discards it and records an entry in its log files.
- WFAS enables you to configure three types of firewall rules (inbound, outbound, and connection security) that can be applied to one or more of the profiles (domain, private, public). These rules govern how the computer sends and/or receives traffic from users, computers, applications, and services. When a packet matches the rule's criteria, it allows the connection, explicitly blocks the connection, or allows it only if the connection is using IPsec to secure it.
- When you create several firewall rules and you want to deploy those rules to multiple computers, the simplest and quickest way to deploy those rules is to use Group Policy Object (GPO). You just need to export the firewall policy and import the firewall settings into the policy.
- IP security (IPsec) is a suite of protocols that provides a mechanism for data integrity, authentication, and privacy for the Internet Protocol by providing message authentication and/or encryption. It can be used to protect data sent between hosts on a network by creating a secure electronic tunnel between two hosts. It can also be used for remote access/VPN connections.
- Connection security rules are rules secure the connection with both authentication (Kerberos, digital certificates, pre-shared keys) and encryption protocols. Connection security rules are used to determine how the traffic between the computer and others is secured.
- Connection security rules: These rules secure the connection with both authentication (Kerberos, digital certificates, pre-shared keys) and encryption protocols. Connection security rules are used to determine how the traffic between the computer and others is secured.
- Software-Defined Networking (SDN) allows you to centrally configure and manage physical and virtual network devices, including routers, switches, and gateways in your data center. When creating a virtual infrastructure, you will configure Hyper-V virtual switches, Hyper-V Network Virtualization, and Windows Server Gateway.
- The Network Controller's Datacenter Firewall allows you to configure and manage firewall access control rules for both East-West and North-South network traffic in your data center. The Datacenter Firewall is a network layer, stateful, multi-tenant firewall.

Knowledge Assessment

Multiple Choice

1. Which of the following WFAS profiles is assigned to a computer when it is first connected to a new network?
   a. Public profile
   b. Domain profile
   c. Private profile
   d. WFAS new profile

2. Which of the following rules specifies how and when authentication occurs?
   a. Public rule
   b. Inbound rule
   c. Connection security rule
   d. Outbound rule

3. Which of the following is true regarding WFAS rules? (Choose all that apply)
   a. Outbound traffic is allowed by default.
   b. Unsolicited inbound traffic is not allowed.
   c. Solicited inbound traffic is allowed.
   d. Connection security rules require inbound/outbound rules to allow connections.

4. Which of the following tools is used to manage secure connections based on IPsec in Windows 10?
   a. Windows Firewall
   b. Windows Firewall with Advanced Security
   c. IPsec manager
   d. Server Manager

5. Which of the following mechanisms is most often used in firewall rules to allow traffic onto the network?
   a. Protocol numbers
   b. IP addresses
   c. Port numbers
   d. Hardware addresses

6. Which of the following actions cannot be performed from the Control Panel Windows Firewall?
   a. Turning Windows Firewall off for all three profiles
   b. Managing firewall exceptions for the domain profile
   c. Allowing a program through the firewall in all three profiles
   d. Creating firewall exceptions based on port numbers

7. Windows Firewall uses three profiles to represent the type of network to which the server is connected. Which of the following correctly lists the three profiles?
   a. Private, Temporary, and Authenticated
   b. Domain, Private, and Public
   c. Internet, Secure, and Private
   d. Private, Public, DMZ
8. Exporting the Windows Firewall policy creates a file with a .wfw extension that contains which of the following?
   a. All of its rules, including the preconfigured rules and the ones you have created or modified.
   b. All of the rules you have created or modified.
   c. Preconfigured rules to be applied to another firewall.
   d. Firewall settings as specified by the Group Policy settings.
9. With Windows Firewall with Advanced Security, which of the following statements is true of authentication exception rules?
   a. Authenticated exceptions weaken security.
   b. Authentication exceptions strengthen security.
   c. Authentication exceptions can only be implemented on outgoing packets.
   d. It is required to have a master authentication exception rule.
10. Which of the following Windows Firewall profiles should be configured by a user when she is at the airport?
   a. Domain
   b. Private
   c. Public
   d. Protected

Best Answer

Choose the letter that corresponds to the best answer. More than one answer choice may achieve the goal. Select the BEST answer.

1. Which network location should be used when you use a personal computer at your workplace?
   a. Home
   b. Work
   c. Public
   d. Domain
2. Which of the following is the primary objective of a firewall?
   a. To permit traffic in and out for legitimate users, and to block the rest
   b. To authenticate and authorize users past the network perimeter
   c. To compare traffic information against a list of known valid traffic
   d. To protect a network by allowing certain types of network traffic in and out of the system
3. When creating a firewall exception, which of the following best describes the difference between opening a port and allowing an application?
   a. Opening a port is permanent, and thus is less risky than allowing an application.
   b. Allowing an application opens the specified port only while the program is running, and thus is less risky.
   c. Both options are available in the Windows Firewall with Advanced Security console.
   d. There is no functional difference between opening a port and allowing an application.
4. Windows Firewall allows users to create inbound, outbound, and connection security rules for individual servers or systems. Which of the following statements best describes how this can be done for multiple systems?
   a. Delegate to administrators the task of performing the same configuration to their local servers.
   b. Create a new Group Policy Object (GPO) and create matching rules to match the desired configuration. Then deploy the GPO to other systems on the network.
   c. Visit individual systems and configure them as you the same as the initial system.
   d. Create a new GPO and import settings from an exported policy file created earlier. Then deploy the GPO to other systems on the network.

Build List

1. Specify the correct order of the steps necessary to create an outbound rule that blocks a program.

_____ Browse to the program's install location, select the program's executable, and then click Open.

_____ Open the Windows Firewall with Advanced Security console.

_____ Select the program to block and then click Next.

_____ Right-click Outbound Rules and choose New Rules.

_____ Select Block the connection.

_____ Type a name and description for the rule and then click Finish.

_____ Select Domain, Private, and/or Public profile.

2. Specify the correct order of the steps to applying WFAS rules.

_____ Allow connections

_____ Default profile behavior

_____ Block connections

_____ Authenticated bypass rules

■ Business Case Scenarios

Scenario 6-1: Configuring Windows Firewall

You are an administrator at the Contoso Corporation and several users are reporting that their computers have been hacked while traveling and then used without their knowledge. Describe how to secure the computers and how to limit users' access while out of the office while allowing for full access when they are at work.

Scenario 6-2: Maximizing Security for Confidential Mobile Computer

You are an administrator at the Contoso Corporation and you administer a computer that includes confidential information that is used by a demonstration team. You want to ensure that all of the information accessed from the computer is encrypted when that computer is used outside of the office. Describe your recommended solution.

Securing Network Traffic

LESSON 7

70-744 EXAM OBJECTIVE

Objective 3.3 – Secure network traffic. This objective may include but is not limited to: Configure IPsec transport and tunnel modes; configure IPsec authentication options; configure connection security rules*; implement isolation zones, implement domain isolation; implement server isolation zones; determine SMB 3.1.1 protocol security scenarios and implementations; enable SMB encryption on SMB Shares; configure SMB signing via Group Policy; disable SMB 1.0; secure DNS traffic using DNSSEC and DNS policies; install and configure Microsoft Message Analyzer (MMA) to analyze network traffic.

**Covered in Lesson 6*

Lesson Heading	Exam Objective
Configuring IPsec Policies	Configure IPsec transport and tunnel modes
• Understanding IPsec	Configure IPsec authentication options
• Understanding the Security Negotiation Process	Implement isolation zones
• Configuring IPsec Using GPOs	Implement domain isolation
• Implementing Isolation Zones	Implement server isolation zones
Securing SMB Protocol	Determine SMB 3.1.1 protocol security scenarios and implementations
• Implementing SMB 3.1.1 Encryption	Enable SMB encryption on SMB Shares
• Configuring SMB Signing via Group Policy	Configure SMB signing via Group Policy
• Disabling SMB 1.0	Disable SMB 1.0
Configuring Security for DNS	Secure DNS traffic using DNSSEC and DNS policies
• Implementing DNS Policies	
• Configuring DNSSEC	
• Configuring DNS Socket Pool	
• Configuring DNS Cache Locking	
• Enabling Response Rate Limiting (RRL)	
• Configuring DNS-based Authentication of named Entities (DANE)	
Installing and Configuring Microsoft Message Analyzer (MMA) to Analyze Network Traffic	Install and configure Microsoft Message Analyzer (MMA) to analyze network traffic

KEY TERMS

automated key rollover
Common Internet File System (CIFS)
digital signature
DNS-based Authentication of Named Entities (DANE)
DNS Cache Locking
DNS policies
DNS Security (DNSSEC)
DNS socket pool
DNSSEC Resource records
domain isolation
Internet Key Exchange (IKE)
Internet Security Association and Key Management Protocol (ISAKMP)
IPsec driver
ISAKMP SA
isolation zones
Key Signing Key (KSK)
main mode SA
Microsoft Message Analyzer (MMA)
Name Resolution Policy Table (NRPT)
Response Rate Limiting (RRL)
security association (SA)
Security Parameters Index (SPI)
server isolation
Server Message Block (SMB)
signing the zone
SMB encryption
SMB signing
trust anchor
universal naming convention (UNC)
Zone Signing Key (ZSK)
Zone Signing Parameters

Configuring IPSec Policies

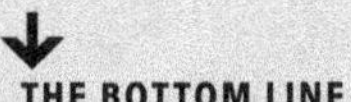

IP security (IPsec) was introduced in the previous chapter, as it relates to configuring connection security rules. Besides configuring IPsec with the firewall, you can also configure using a Group Policy Object (GPO).

IPsec can be used in the following scenarios:

- Securing host-to-host traffic on specific paths, which can be between servers, static IP addresses, or subnets.
- Securing traffic to servers, including restricting to which computers can connect to a server.
- Use with L2TP for secure VPN connection.
- Site-to-site (gateway-to-gateway) tunneling.
- Enforcing logical networks (server/domain isolation), which can logically isolate server and domain resources in a Windows-based network, and can be used to limit access to authenticated and authorized computers.

However, it is not recommended to use IPsec for the following:

- **Providing security between domain members and domain controllers:** Encrypting this traffic will reduce overall network performance, but will enable authentication to occur with the domain control when trying to establish an IPsec session.
- **Securing all network traffic:** The constant encryption and decryption of all traffic can severely reduce network performance. IPsec does not negotiate security for multicast and broadcast traffic, and some applications that use Internet Control Message Protocol (ICMP) or peer-to-peer applications may be incompatible with IPsec. Lastly, network management functionality may be degraded or not work at all.

Understanding IPsec

A ***security association (SA)*** is the combination of security services, protection mechanisms, and cryptographic keys mutually agreed to by communicating peers. The SA contains the information needed to determine how the traffic is to be secured (the security services and protection mechanisms) and with which secret keys (cryptographic keys). Two types of SAs are created when IPsec peers communicate securely: the ISAKMP SA and the IPsec SA.

Internet Security Association and Key Management Protocol (ISAKMP) is used for establishing Security Associations (SA) and cryptographic keys in an Internet environment. The ***ISAKMP SA***, also known as the ***main mode SA***, is used to protect IPsec security negotiations. The ISAKMP SA is created by negotiating the cipher suite (a collection of cryptographic algorithms used to encrypt data) used for protecting future ISAKMP traffic, exchanging key generation material, and then identifying and authenticating each IPsec peer. When the ISAKMP SA is complete, all future SA negotiations for both types of SAs are protected. This is an aspect of secure communications known as protected cipher suite negotiation. Not only is the data protected, but the determination of the protection algorithms negotiated by the IPsec peers is also protected. To break IPsec protection, a malicious user must first determine the cipher suite protecting the data, which represents another barrier. For IPsec, the only exception to complete protected cipher suite negotiation is the negotiation of the cipher suite of the initial ISAKMP SA, which is sent as plaintext.

The IPsec SA, also known as the quick mode SA, is used to protect data sent between the IPsec peers. The IPsec SA cipher suite negotiation is protected by the ISAKMP SA so that no information about the type of traffic or the protection mechanisms is sent as plaintext. For a pair of IPsec peers, two IPsec SAs always exist for each protocol in use: one that is negotiated for inbound traffic and one that is negotiated for outbound traffic. The inbound SA for one IPsec peer is the outbound SA for the other.

For each IPsec session that is established between two hosts, the IPsec peers must track the usage of three SAs:

- The ISAKMP SA
- The inbound IPsec SA
- The outbound IPsec SA

To identify a specific SA for tracking purposes, a 32-bit number known as the ***Security Parameters Index (SPI)*** is used. The SPI, which is stored as a field in the IPsec headers, indicates which SA the destination should use and is sent with every packet. The responder is responsible for providing a unique SPI for each protocol.

The ***Internet Key Exchange (IKE)*** is a standard that defines a mechanism to establish SAs. IKE combines ISAKMP and the Oakley Key Determination Protocol, a protocol that is based on the Diffie-Hellman key exchange algorithm, to generate secret key material. The Diffie-Hellman key exchange algorithm allows two peers to determine a secret key by exchanging unencrypted values over a public network. In order to perform this task, the Diffie-Hellman key exchange process derives a secret key known only to the two peers by exchanging two numbers over a public network. A malicious user who intercepts the key exchange packets can view the numbers, but cannot perform the same calculation as the negotiating peers in order to derive the shared secret key.

The Diffie-Hellman key exchange process does not prevent a man-in-the-middle attack, in which a malicious user between the negotiating peers performs two Diffie-Hellman exchanges, one with each peer. When both exchanges are complete, the malicious user has the secret keys to communicate with both peers. To prevent such an attack, Windows Server IPsec performs an immediate authentication after the Diffie-Hellman key exchange is complete. If the IPsec peer cannot perform a valid authentication, the security negotiation is abandoned before any data is sent. Windows Server IPsec also supports dynamic rekeying, which is the determination of new keying material through a new Diffie-Hellman exchange on a regular basis. Dynamic rekeying is based on an elapsed time, 480 minutes or 8 hours by default, or the number of data sessions created with the same set of keying material (by default, this number is unlimited).

The ***IPsec driver*** receives the active IP filter list from the IPsec Policy Agent. The Policy Agent then checks for a match of every inbound and outbound packet against the filters in the list. The IPsec driver stores all current quick mode SAs in a database. The IPsec driver uses the Security Parameter Index (SPI) field to match the correct SA with the correct packet. When an outbound IP packet matches the IP filter list with an action to negotiate security, the IPsec driver queues the packet, and then the IKE process begins negotiating security with the destination IP address of that packet.

Understanding the Security Negotiation Process

IPsec processing can be organized according to two types of negotiation: main mode negotiation and quick mode negotiation. In this section, you will learn about both negotiation processes.

Let's look at a high-level overview of the overall security negotiation process between two computers, COMPUTERA and COMPUTERB:

1. COMPUTERA requests secured communications with COMPUTERB.
2. Main mode negotiations begin and are completed for the master key and the IKE SA—see the remainder of this section for further detail.
3. Quick mode negotiation of an SA pair (inbound and outbound) for each host is completed.
4. The application packets from COMPUTERA are passed by the TCP/IP driver to the IPsec driver.
5. The IPsec driver formats and cryptographically processes the packets and then sends them to COMPUTERB using the outbound SA.
6. Secure packets cross the network.
7. The IPsec driver on COMPUTERB cryptographically processes the packets arriving on the inbound SA, formats them as normal IP packets, and then passes them to the TCP/IP driver.
8. The TCP/IP driver passes the packets to the application on COMPUTERB.

Now let's look at each negotiation process in more detail.

Oakley main mode negotiation is used to determine encryption key material and security protection for use in protecting subsequent main mode or quick mode communications, as follows:

1. A communication packet is sent from COMPUTERA to COMPUTERB.
2. The IPsec driver on COMPUTERA checks its outbound IP filter lists and concludes that the packets match a filter, and that the filter action is "Negotiate Security," meaning that the packets must be secured.
3. The IPsec driver begins the IKE negotiation process.
4. COMPUTERA checks its policy for the main mode settings (authentication, Diffie-Hellman group, encryption, and integrity) to propose to COMPUTERB.
5. COMPUTERA sends the first IKE message using UDP source port 500 and destination port 500.

6. COMPUTERB receives the IKE main mode message that requests secure negotiation and then uses the source IP address and destination IP address of the packet to look up its own IKE filter. The IKE filter provides the security requirements for communications from Host A.
7. If the security settings proposed by COMPUTERA are acceptable to COMPUTERB, negotiation of the main mode or IKE SA begins.
8. Both computers negotiate options, exchange identities and authenticate them, and generate a master key. The IKE SA is established.

In summary, main mode negotiation creates the ISAKMP SA. The initiator and responder exchange a series of ISAKMP messages to negotiate the cipher suite for the ISAKMP SA (in plaintext), exchange key determination material (in plaintext), and finally identify and authenticate each other (in encrypted text).

When main mode negotiation is complete, each IPSec peer has selected a specific set of cryptographic algorithms for securing main mode and quick mode messages, has exchanged key information to derive a shared secret key, and has performed authentication. Before secure data is sent, a quick mode negotiation must occur to determine the type of traffic to be secured and how it will be secured. A quick mode negotiation is also done when a quick mode SA expires.

Quick mode messages are ISAKMP messages that are encrypted using the ISAKMP SA. As noted previously, the result of a quick mode negotiation is two IPsec SAs: one for inbound traffic and one for outbound traffic. The process is as follows:

1. COMPUTERA performs an IKE mode policy lookup to determine the full policy.
2. COMPUTERA proposes its options (cryptographic, as well as frequency of key changes, and so on) and filters to Host B.
3. COMPUTERB does its own IKE mode policy lookup. If it finds a match with the one proposed by COMPUTERA, it completes the quick mode negotiation to create a pair of IPsec SAs.
4. One SA is outbound and the other one is inbound. Each SA is identified by an SPI, and the SPI is part of the header of each packet sent. COMPUTERA's IPsec driver uses the outbound SA and signs and, if specified, encrypts the packets. If hardware offload of IPsec cryptographic functions is supported by the network card, the IPsec driver just formats the packets; otherwise, it formats and cryptographically processes the packets.
5. The IPsec driver passes the packets to the network adapter driver.
6. The network adapter driver puts the network traffic onto the physical network media.
7. The network adapter at COMPUTERB receives the (encrypted) packets from the network.
8. The SPI is used to find the corresponding SA. (This SA has the associated cryptographic key necessary to decrypt and process the packets.)
9. If the network adapter is specifically designed to perform encryption and therefore can decrypt the packets, it will do so. It passes the packets to the IPsec driver.
10. COMPUTERB's IPsec driver uses the inbound SA to retrieve the keys and processes the packets if necessary.
11. The IPsec driver converts the packets back to normal IP packet format and passes them to the TCP/IP driver, which in turn passes them to the receiving application.
12. IPsec SAs continue processing packets. SAs are refreshed by IKE quick mode negotiation for as long as the application sends and receives data. When the SAs become idle, they are deleted.

Unlike quick mode negotiations, IKE main mode negotiations are not deleted when traffic is idle. IKE main mode has a default lifetime of 8 hours, but this number is configurable from 5 minutes to a maximum of 48 hours. Within the configured time frame, any new network communications between COMPUTERA and COMPUTERB will trigger only a new quick mode negotiation. If IKE main mode expires, a new IKE mode is negotiated as described above.

Configuring IPsec Using GPOs

Group Policy Objects can be used to implement and configure IPsec policies. The IPsec settings are located at Computer Configuration\Policies\Windows Settings\Security Settings\IP Security Policies on Active Directory (as shown in Figure 7-1). Although three IPsec policies are available, you can assign only one IPsec rule to a GPO and each client can have only one IPsec policy applied to it at a time.

Figure 7-1

Configuring IPsec with GPOs

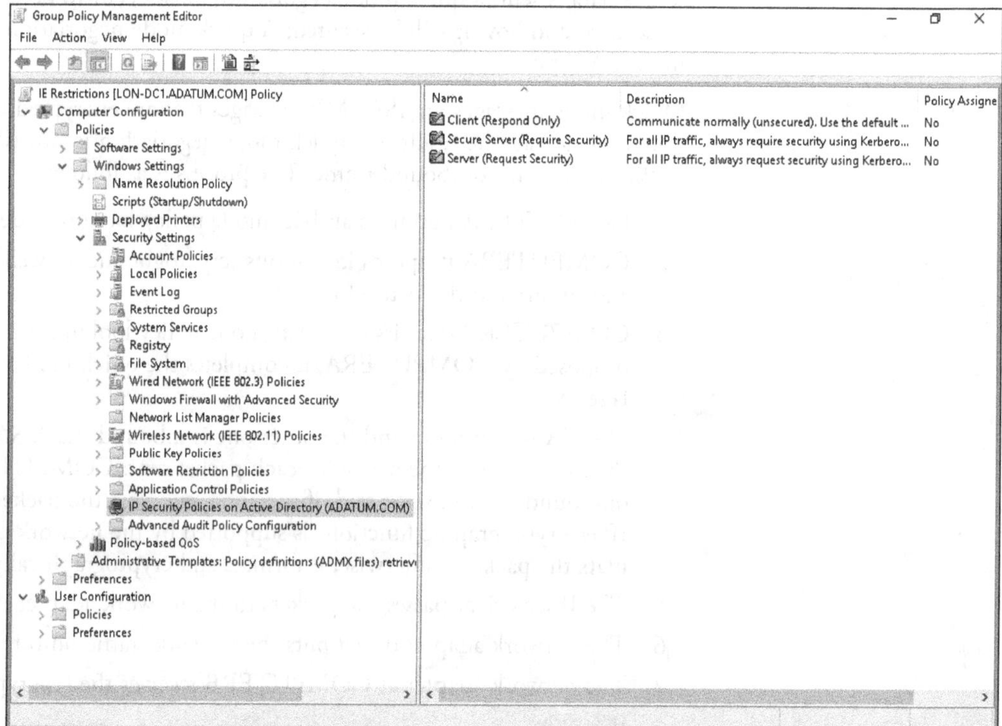

CERTIFICATION READY
Configure IPsec transport and tunnel modes
Objective 3.3

CERTIFICATION READY
Configure IPsec authentication options
Objective 3.3

The three predefined policies are:

- **Client (Respond Only):** Configures computers to negotiate security and authentication methods when requested.
- **Server (Request Security):** Configures a computer to always request security by using the Kerberos V5 authentication protocol for all IP traffic, and it allows unsecured communications.
- **Secure Server (Require Security):** Configures a computer to always require a secure connection for all IP traffic and to block untrusted computers. By default, this rule uses only the Kerberos V5 authentication protocol.

Upon opening an IPsec policy, you will find IP security rules (as shown in Figure 7-2) that specify which traffic will be affected. You can then click Add to add a new rule or click Edit to modify a rule. You can then define the following:

- **IP Filter List:** Allows you to define IP traffic source, IP traffic destination, IP protocol type (such as ICMP, TCP, UDP, or other), and IP Protocol Port
- **Filter Action:** Specifies to permit, block, or negotiate security.
- **Authentication Methods:** Specifies allowed authentication method including Active Directory (Kerberos V5 protocol), certificate from this certification authority (CA), and use this string (preshared key)
- **Tunnel Settings:** Specifies either This rule does not specify an IPsec tunnel or Tunnel endpoints as specified by these IP addresses. By default, no tunnel is used.
- **Connection Type:** Specifies the connection type to which the rule applies (All network connections, Local area network [LAN], or Remote access)

Figure 7-2

Viewing GPO IP Security rules

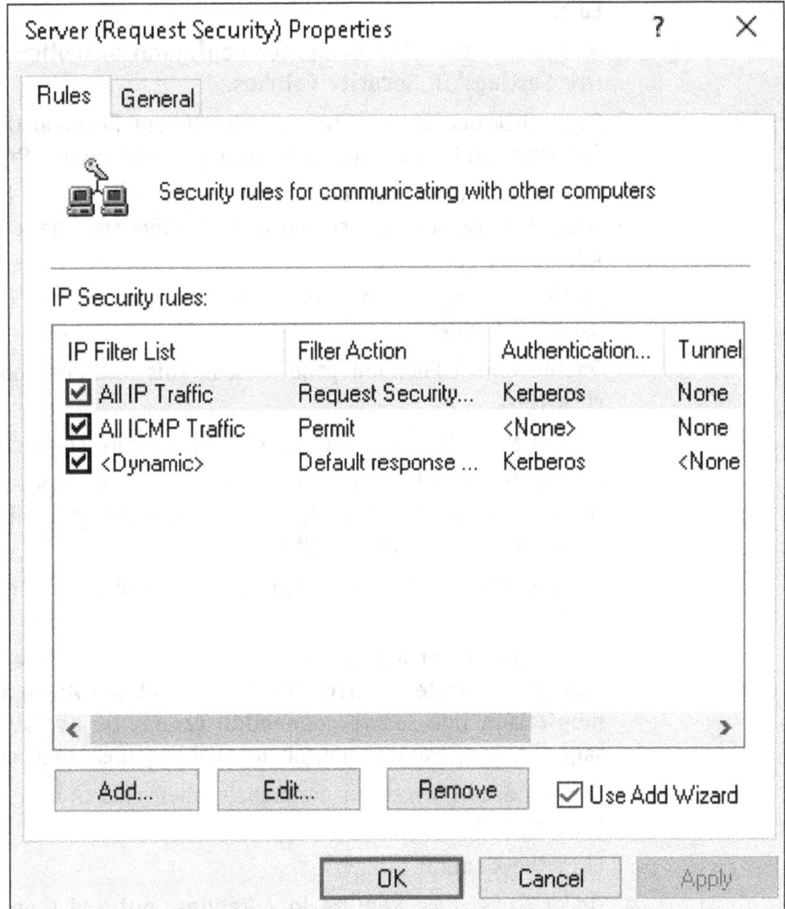

While it is quite easy to create a policy on one computer and its IPsec peers, you will most likely need to create a set of IPsec policies if you want to use those policies throughout your organization. To accomplish this:

1. Create IP filter lists that match the computers, subnets, and conditions in your environment.
2. Create filter actions that correspond to how you want connections to be authenticated, data integrity to be applied, and data to be encrypted.
3. Create a set of policies that match the filtering and filter action (security) requirements you need.
4. Deploy policies that use Permit and Block filter actions
5. Monitor your IPsec environment, and adjust previous configured policies.

6. Deploy the policies using the Negotiate Security filter action with the option to fall back to clear text communications.
7. After refinements have been made, remove the fall back to clear text communications actions.
8. Monitor the environment including the Main Mode Negotiation Failures statistic.

ADD AN IPSEC POLICY RULE

GET READY. To add an IPsec policy rule, perform the following steps.

1. In Server Manager, click **Tools > Group Policy Management.**
2. In the Right Policy Management console, right-click a created GPO and choose **Edit.**
3. Navigate to and click **Computer Configuration\Policies\Windows Settings\Security Settings\IP Security Policies.**
4. Right-click one of the IPsec policies (Client Respond Only), Secure Server (Required Security), and Server (Request Security) and choose **Properties.**
5. If you want to create the rule in the property dialog box, clear the **Use Add Wizard** check box. To use the wizard, leave the check box selected and then click **Add.**
6. In the Security Rule Wizard, on the Welcome to the Create IP Security Rule Wizard page, click **Next.**
7. On the Tunnel Endpoint page, choose This rule does not specify a tunnel and then click **Next.**
8. On the Network Type page, choose All network connections and then click **Next.**
9. On the IP Filter List page, under IP filter lists, select **All IP Traffic** and then click **Next.** If the desired filter list is not available, you will first have to click **Add** and then create additional IP filter lists.
10. On the Filter Action page, clear the **Use Add Wizard** check box and then click **Add.**
11. In the New Filter Action Properties dialog box, on the Security Methods tab, choose **Negotiate security** and then select the **Allow fallback to unsecured communication if a secure connection cannot be established** check box. If a message displays, warning you about enabling unsecured communication, click **Yes.**
12. Next to Security method preference order, click **Add**, choose **Integrity only**, and then click **OK.**
13. Click the **General** tab.
14. Under Name, type **Require in / Request out** and then click **OK.**
15. Select the new filter action you just created and then click **Next.**
16. On the Authentication Method page, choose **Use a certificate from this certification authority (CA)** and then click **Browse.** If a message displays, warning that Active Directory does not contain a shared certificate store, click **Yes.**
17. Click the name of the root CA in your CA hierarchy and then click **OK.**
18. Click **Next** and then click **Finish.**
19. Verify that All IP Traffic is selected under IP Filter List, that Filter Action is Require in / Request out, and that Authentication Method is Certificate, and then click **OK.**
20. In the Group Policy Management Editor, right-click the new IPsec rule and choose **Assign.**

Implementing Isolation Zones

CERTIFICATION READY
Implement isolation zones
Objective 3.3

Isolation zones logically separate your network into computers that can authenticate with one another and those that cannot authenticate. To create an isolation zone, you will create a subnet with the various types of computers. Computers in an isolated network will ignore all requests to initiate communication from computers that are not in the isolated network.

Computers in the isolated network will be configured to initiate communications with any computer, regardless of whether they are isolated. You will then configure computers that are not in the isolated network so that they can initiate computers with other computers that are not in the isolated network and they cannot initiate communications with computers in the isolated network. Windows Server 2016 supports two types of isolation:

- Domain isolation
- Server isolation

IMPLEMENTING DOMAIN ISOLATION

CERTIFICATION READY
Implement domain isolation
Objective 3.3

Domain isolation isolates computers within a domain so that they can only communicate with other computers within the same domain. Domain isolation can be accomplished using IPsec, which is accomplished by accepting only connections from computers that are authenticated as member of the same isolated domain.

By performing domain isolation, you provide an additional layer of protection, including:

- Restricting incoming connections to domain member computers
- Supplementing other security mechanisms that prevent unwanted communications
- Encouraging domain membership
- Helps to protect traffic between domain member computers.

To enforce domain isolation with connection security rules, follow these high-level steps:

1. Create a connection security rule that requests authentication.
2. Deploy and test your connection security rules.
3. Change the isolation rule to require authentication.
4. Test isolation with a computer that does not have the domain isolation rule.
5. Create exemption rules for computers that are not domain members.

CREATE A NEW GPO FOR DOMAIN ISOLATION

GET READY. To create a new GPO for Domain Isolation, perform the following steps.

1. In Server Manager, click **Tools > Group Policy Management.**
2. In the Right Policy Management console, right-click a created GPO and choose **Edit.**
3. Navigate to and click **Computer Configuration\ Policies\Windows Settings\Security Settings\Windows Firewall with Advanced Security\Windows Firewall with Advanced Security - LDAP://cn={GUID},cn=policies,cn=system,DC=contoso,DC=com.**
4. Right-click **Connection Security Rules** and choose **New rule.**
5. On the Rule Type page, click **Isolation** and then click **Next.**
6. On the Requirements page, confirm that Request authentication for inbound and outbound connections selected and then click **Next.**

7. On the Authentication Method page, click **Computer and user (Kerberos V5)** and then click **Next.**
8. On the Profile page, clear the **Private** and **Public** check boxes and then click **Next.**
9. On the Name page, type **Request Inbound Request Outbound** and then click **Finish.**

CHANGE THE POLICY FROM REQUESTING AUTHENTICATION TO REQUIRING AUTHENTICATION

GET READY. To change the policy from requesting authentication to requiring authentication, perform the following steps.

1. In Server Manager, click **Tools > Group Policy Management.**
2. In the Right Policy Management console, right-click a created GPO and choose **Edit.**
3. Navigate to and click **Computer Configuration\ Policies\Windows Settings\Security Settings\Windows Firewall with Advanced Security\Windows Firewall with Advanced Security - LDAP://cn={GUID},cn=policies,cn=system,DC=contoso,DC=com.**
4. Right-click **Request Inbound Request Outbound** and choose **Properties.**
5. In the Name text box, change the name to **Require Inbound Request Outbound** to accurately reflect its new behavior.
6. Click the **Authentication** tab.
7. Under Requirements, change Authentication mode to **Require inbound and request outbound** (as shown in Figure 7-3) and then click **OK.**

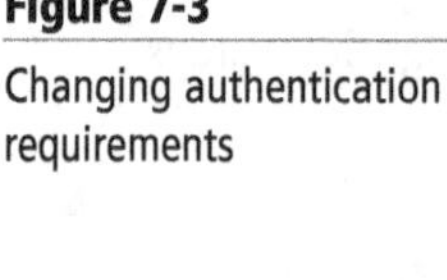

Figure 7-3

Changing authentication requirements

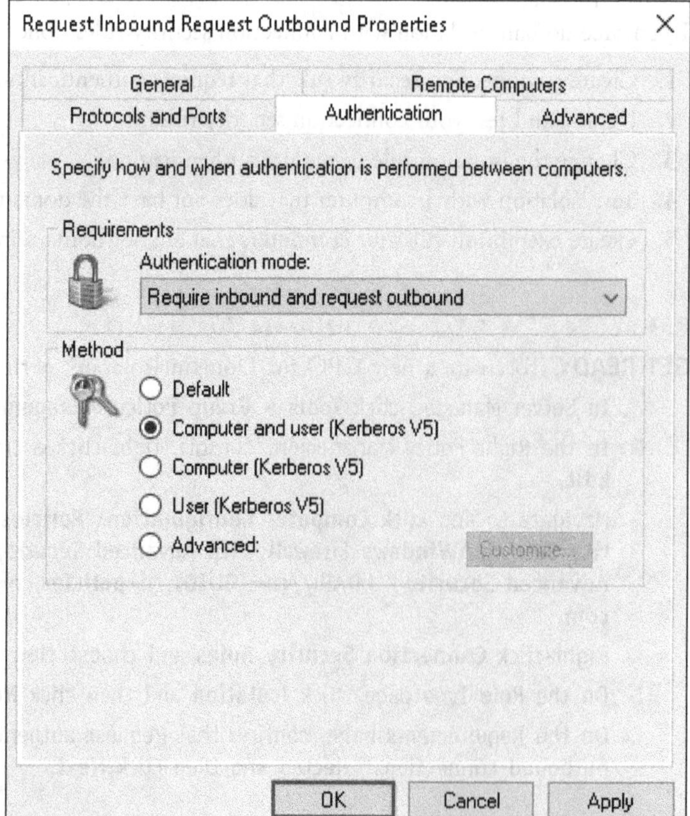

IMPLEMENTING SERVER ISOLATION ZONES

CERTIFICATION READY
Implement server isolation zones
Objective 3.3

Server isolation enforces a network policy that requires specific domain member servers or computers to accept only authenticated traffic from other domain member computers. To make it even more secure, you can optionally specify that data must be encrypted.

To enforce server isolation with connection security rules, follow these high-level steps:

1. Create the security group (Authorized to access LON-SVR2) that will be used to specify who is authorized to communicate with server.
2. Modify a firewall rule to require group membership and encryption.
3. Create a firewall rule for the client to support Encryption.
4. Test the rule when user not member of the group.
5. Add user to group and testing again.

CREATE A FIREWALL RULE THAT ALLOWS INBOUND TRAFFIC FOR A PROGRAM

GET READY. To create a firewall rule that allows inbound traffic for a program (which will be modified in next exercise), perform the following steps.

1. In Server Manager, click **Tools > Group Policy Management.**
2. In the Right Policy Management console, right-click a created GPO and choose **Edit.**
3. Navigate to and click **Computer Configuration\ Policies\Windows Settings\Security Settings\Windows Firewall with Advanced Security\Windows Firewall with Advanced Security - LDAP://cn={GUID},cn=policies,cn=system,DC=contoso,DC=com**, and then click **Inbound Rules.**
4. Right-click **Inbound Rules** and choose **New rule.**
5. On the Rule Type page, click **Custom** and then click **Next.**
6. Select This program path. In the text box for This program path, type **%systemroot%\system32\mstsc.exe.**
7. Under Services, click **Customize.**
8. In the Customize Service settings dialog box, select **Apply to this service**, select **Remote Desktop Services**, click **OK**, and then click **Next.**
9. On the Protocols and Ports page, click **Next.**
10. On the Scope page, click **Next.**
11. On the Action page, select **Allow the Connection** and then click **Next.**
12. On the Profile page, clear the **Private** check box and the **Public** check box. Confirm that Domain is selected and then click **Next.**
13. On the Name page, type **Allow Inbound Remote Desktop** and then click **Finish.**

MODIFY A FIREWALL RULE TO REQUIRE GROUP MEMBERSHIP AND ENCRYPTION

GET READY. To modify a firewall rule to require group membership and encryption, perform the following steps.

1. In Server Manager, click **Tools > Group Policy Management.**
2. In the Right Policy Management console, right-click a created GPO and choose **Edit.**

3. Navigate to and click **Computer Configuration\ Policies\Windows Settings\Security Settings\Windows Firewall with Advanced Security\Windows Firewall with Advanced Security - LDAP://cn={GUID},cn=policies,cn=system,DC=contoso,DC=com.** Then click **Inbound Rules.**
4. In the results pane, right-click a rule and choose **Properties.**
5. Change the name to an appropriate name, such as **Allow Encrypted Inbound Remote Desktop to Group Members Only.**
6. Select **Allow the connection if it is secure**, click **Customize**, select **Require the connections to be encrypted** (as shown in Figure 7-4), and then click **OK.**

Figure 7-4

Requiring the connection to be encrypted

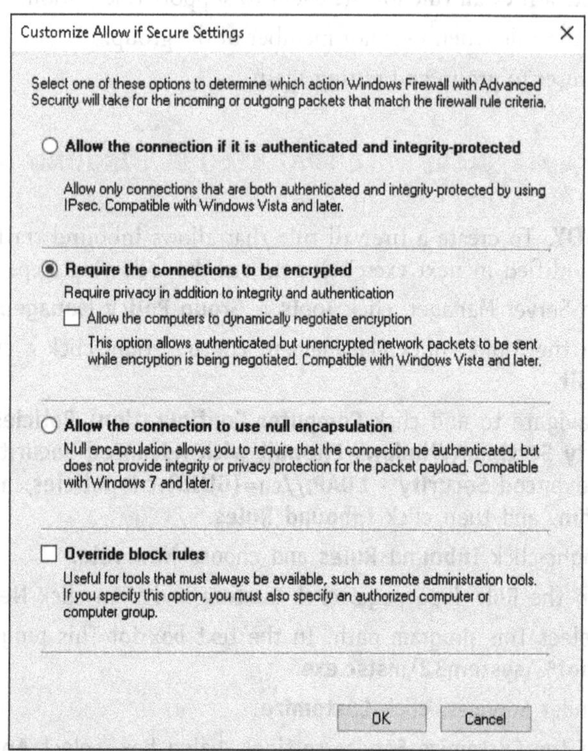

7. Click the **Remote Users** tab.
8. Under Authorized users, select **Only allow connections from these users** and then click **Add.**
9. In the Select User or Groups dialog box, type **Authorized to access LON-SVR2**, click **Check Names** to make sure that it resolves, and then click **OK.**
10. Click **OK** to close the Allow Inbound Remote Desktop Properties page.
11. Close the Group Policy Management Editor.

Securing SMB Protocol

When you share a folder in Windows, you are usually using ***Server Message Block (SMB)***, also known as ***Common Internet File System (CIFS)***. SMB has been around for years to provide shared access to files and printers. While SMB is usually associated with computers running Windows, it has become the de facto standard, which may be accessed by most other operating systems including Linux, UNIX and Macintosh systems. To access a shared folder, you use the ***universal naming convention (UNC)***, which is syntax used to access a Windows shared folder based on the \\servername\sharename format.

SMB is a client/server file-sharing protocol that was created in 1984 by Microsoft. Through the years, there have been different versions, as shown in Table 7-1.

Table 7-1

SMB Versions

SMB Version	Operating System
SMB 3.1.1	Windows 10 and Windows Server 2016
SMB 3.0.2	Windows 8.1 and Windows Server 2012 R2
SMB 3.0	Windows 8 and Windows Server 2012
SMB 2.1	Windows 7 and Windows Server 2008 R2
SMB 1.x	Windows Vista and Windows Server 2008

CERTIFICATION READY
Determine SMB 3.1.1 protocol security scenarios and implementations
Objective 3.3

Server Message Block (SMB) 3.0 was introduced with Windows 8 and Windows Server 2012. It brought significant changes, adding functionality and improving performance, particularly in virtualized data centers.

SMB 3.0 includes the following features:

- **SMB Transparent Failover:** Provides continually available properties that allow SMB 3.0 clients to not lose an SMB session when failover occurs. Both the SMB client and SMB server must support SMB 3.0 to take advantage of the SMB Transparent Failover functionality.
- **SMB Scale Out:** Allows users to scale shared bandwidth by adding cluster nodes. Both the SMB client and SMB server must support SMB 3.0 to take advantage of the SMB Scale Out feature. SMB 1.0 clients do not contain the required client functionality to access SMB scale-out file shares and receive an "Access Denied" error message when they try to connect to a scale-out file share. SMB 2.x clients can connect to SMB scale-out file shares but do not benefit from the SMB Transparent Failover functionality.
- **SMB Multichannel:** Uses multiple network interfaces to provide both high performance through bandwidth aggregation and network fault tolerance through the use of multiple network paths to data on an SMB share. SMB 1.0 and SMB 2.x clients use a single SMB connection.
- **SMB Direct (SMB over Remote Direct Memory Access [RDMA]):** Enables direct memory-to-memory data transfers between servers, with minimal CPU utilization and low latency, using standard RDMA-capable network adapters (iWARP, InfiniBand, and RoCE). It also minimizes the processor utilization when performing large file I/O operations. SMB Direct functionality requires that the SMB client and SMB server support SMB 3.0.

- **SMB Encryption:** Performs encryption by selecting a check box. Both the SMB client and SMB server must support SMB 3.0 to take advantage of the SMB Encryption functionality.
- **VSS for SMB file shares:** Extends the Windows Volume Shadow Copy Service infrastructure to enable application-consistent shadow copies of server application data stored on SMB file shares, for backup and restore purposes. Both the SMB client and SMB server must support SMB 3.0 to take advantage of the Volume Shadow Copy Service (VSS) for SMB file shares functionality.
- **SMB Directory Leasing:** Reduces the latency when accessing files over slow WAN links by caching directory and file metadata for longer periods, which reduces the associated round-trips to fetch the metadata from the server. Both the SMB client and SMB server must support SMB 3.0 to take advantage of the SMB Directory Leasing functionality.
- **SMB PowerShell:** Introduces SMB PowerShell management cmdlets in Windows Server 2012 and in Windows 8.

Implementing SMB 3.1.1 Encryption

CERTIFICATION READY
Enable SMB encryption on SMB Shares
Objective 3.3

SMB 3.1.1 was introduced with Windows Server 2016 and Windows 10. While it has all of the features and abilities of SMB 3.0, it also offers pre-authentication integrity, SMB encryption improvements, and cluster dialog fencing. ***SMB encryption*** is the encryption of SMB packets as they traverse over the network.

SMB 3.1.1 has the following new features:

- **Pre-authentication integrity:** Protects from man-in-the-middle attacks by using a Secure Hash Algorithm 512 (SHA-512) hash to verify packet contents during session setup
- **SMB encryption improvements:** Improves SMB encryption so that it now defaults to AES-128-GCM encryption algorithm, which has better performance than AES-128-CCM, which was used in SMB 3.0.2
- **Cluster dialect fencing:** Supports rolling upgrades of Scale-Out File Server clusters

SMB encryption is available to Windows 8 and higher and Windows Server 2012 and higher. Similar to IPsec encryption, SMB 3.0.x encryption provides data packet confidentiality and helps prevent tampering with or eavesdropping of data packets. The disadvantage of SMB encryption is that it adds some overhead to network communication. Therefore, it is not enabled by default.

Pre-authentication integrity improves protection from a man-in-the-middle attack that tampers with, hijacks, or jumps into a connection. Pre-authentication also enables the client and server to trust the connection and session properties mutually.

TAKE NOTE*

SMB encryption does not encrypt data on the disk like Encrypting File System (EFS) or BitLocker. Instead, it encrypts SMB traffic sent over the network.

To use SMB encryption, you can configure it on a per-share basis or for an entire file server. However, when you enable SMB encryption, you restrict the file share or file server to only SMB 3.x clients. Therefore, older clients will not be able to access those shared folders. To encrypt a folder, you can use Windows PowerShell or Server Manager.

To use Windows PowerShell to enable SMB encryption on an existing file share, open a Windows PowerShell command prompt and execute the following command:

```
Set-SmbShare -Name <sharename> -EncryptData $true
```

To encrypt all shares on a file server, execute the following command:

```
Set-SmbServerConfiguration -EncryptData $true
```

To create a new SMB file share and enable SMB encryption simultaneously, execute the following command:

```
New-SmbShare -Name <sharename> -Path <pathname>
-EncryptData $true
```

To enable SMB encryption,

In Server Manager, using File and Storage Services, you can enable encryption on a share through the Shares management page:

1. Right-click the appropriate share and choose Properties.
2. On the Settings page, click Encrypt data access.

To allow connections that do not use SMB 3 encryption, such as when older servers and clients are still in your network, open a Windows PowerShell command prompt and execute the following command:

```
Set-SmbServerConfiguration -RejectUnencryptedAccess $false
```

ENABLE SMB ENCRYPTION

GET READY. To enable SMB encryption for a shared folder, perform the following steps.

1. In Server Manager, click **File and Storage Services.**
2. Click **Shares.**
3. Right-click a shared folder and choose **Properties.**
4. Under Settings, select the **Encrypt data access** option, as shown in Figure 7-5.

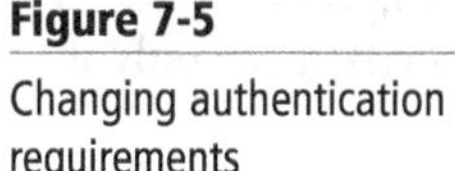

Figure 7-5

Changing authentication requirements

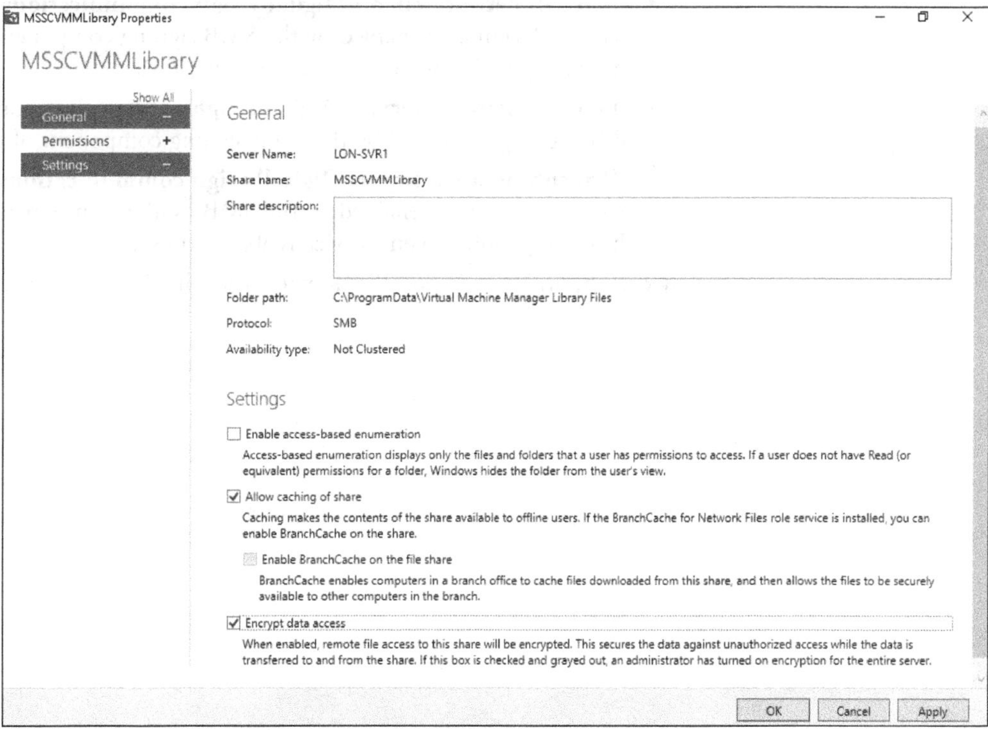

5. Close the Properties dialog box by clicking **OK.**

Configuring SMB Signing via Group Policy

SMB signing is a feature whereby SMB communication is digitally signed at the packet level. Digitally signing the packets enables the recipient of the packets to confirm their point of origination and their authenticity. This security mechanism in the SMB protocol helps avoid issues like tampering of packets and man-in-the-middle attacks. It does not provide confidentiality, which would be provided by SMB encryption.

CERTIFICATION READY
Configure SMB signing via Group Policy
Objective 3.3

A ***digital signature*** is a mathematical scheme that is used to demonstrate the authenticity of a digital message or document. It is also used to ensure that the message or document has not been modified. The sender uses the receiver's public key to create a hash of the message, which is stored in the message digest. The message is then sent to the receiver. The receiver will then use his or her private key to decrypt the hash value, perform the same hash function on the message, and compare the two hash values. If the message has not been changed, the hash values will match.

To prove that a message comes from a particular person, you can perform the hashing function with your private key and attach the hash value to the document to be sent. When the document is sent and received by the receiving party, the same hash function is completed. You then use the sender's public key to decrypt the hash value included in the document. If the two hash values match, the user who sent the document must have known the sender's private key, proving who sent the document. It will also prove that the document has not been changed.

To enable SMB signing, go to Computer Configuration\Policies\Windows Settings\Security Settings\Local Policies\Security Options and configure the following (as shown in Figure 7-6):

- **Microsoft network client: Digitally sign communications (always)** indicates that Server Message Block (SMB) signing is enabled by the SMB signing component of the SMB client at all times.
- **Microsoft network client: Digitally sign communications (if server agrees)** indicates that SMB signing is enabled by the SMB signing component of the SMB client only if the corresponding server service is able to do so.
- **Microsoft network server: Digitally sign communications (always)** indicates that SMB signing is enabled by the SMB signing component of the SMB server at all times.
- **Microsoft network server: Digitally sign communications (if server agrees)** indicates that SMB signing is enabled by the SMB signing component of the SMB server only if the corresponding client service is able to do so.

By default, SMB signing on the domain controller is already enabled.

Figure 7-6

Enabling SMB signing - Digitally sign communications (Always)

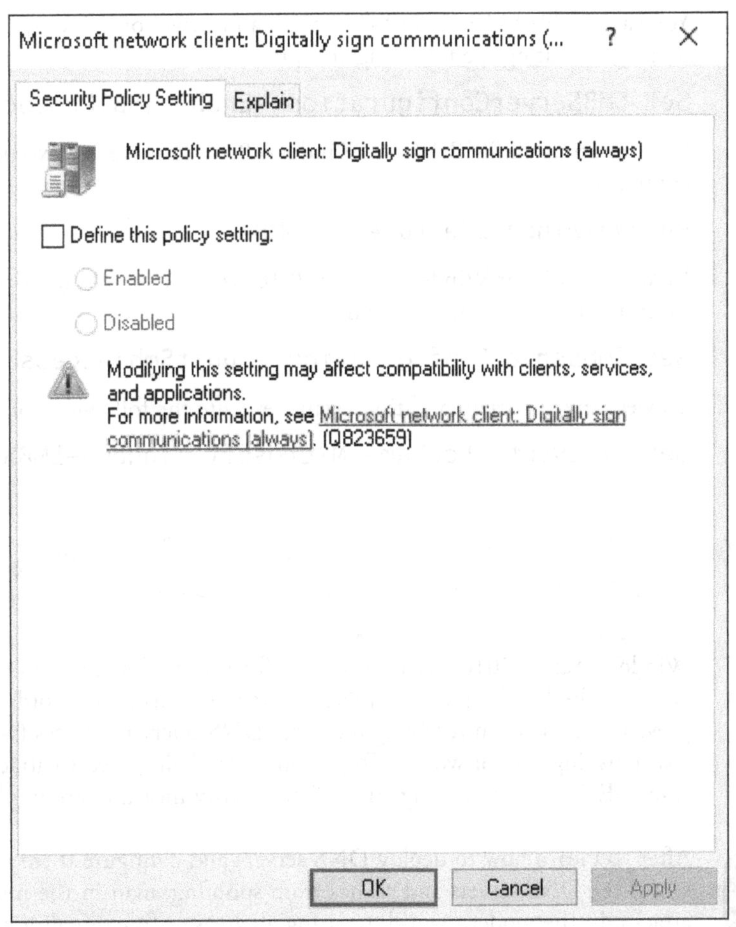

To enable SMB client configuration for SMB signing using Windows PowerShell, execute the following command:

```
Set-SmbClientConfiguration -RequireSecuritySignature $true
```

To enable SMB server configuration setting for SMB signing, execute the following command:

```
Set-SmbServerConfiguration -RequireSecuritySignature $true
```

Disabling SMB 1.0

CERTIFICATION READY
Disable SMB 1.0
Objective 3.3

For years, SMB 1.0 has been considered unsafe, particularly when compared with later versions of SMB. It does not provide pre-authentication integrity, secure dialog negotiation, SMB encryption, and message signing. Therefore, Microsoft recommends disabling this version of SMB, especially if you do not have Windows XP, Windows Server 2013 or earlier, and you have no applications that require SMB 1.0.

You can disable SMB 1.x on Windows 7, Windows Server 2008 R2, Windows Vista, and Windows Server 2008 systems by editing the registry or by executing the following Windows PowerShell command:

```
Set-ItemProperty -Path "HKLM:\SYSTEM\CurrentControlSet\
Services\LanmanServer\Parameters" SMB1 -Type DWORD -Value 0
-Force
```

You can disable SMB 1.x in Windows 8 and newer or Windows Server 2012 and newer systems by executing the following command:

```
Set-SMBServerConfiguration -EnableSMB1Protocol $false
```

You can uninstall SMB 1 from Windows 8.1 and newer by executing the following command:

```
Remove-WindowsFeature FS-SMB1
```

In Windows 10 or Windows Server 2016, you can enable auditing of SMB 1.x traffic by executing the following command:

```
Set-SmbServerConfiguration -AuditSmb1Access $true
```

To view any generated auditing events, execute the following command:

```
Get-WinEvent -LogName Microsoft-Windows-SMBServer/Audit
```

■ Configuring Security for DNS

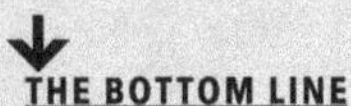

Windows Server 2016 has a number of features to domain naming services (DNS) security. Securing the DNS server and DNS records prevents false records from being added and prevents clients from receiving incorrect DNS query responses (which might lead them to visit phishing sites or worse). To prevent DNS being used to attack systems, DNS Security (DNSSEC), Cache Locking, and other security measures are implemented.

CERTIFICATION READY
Secure DNS traffic using DNSSEC and DNS policies
Objective 3.3

After you learn how to deploy DNS servers and configure them successfully, the need arises to secure the DNS servers and caches from spoofing, man-in-the-middle, and cache-poisoning attacks. In the modern world, securing all areas of functionality is a necessity. DNS is a common area for attacks via interception and tampering.

Implementing DNS Policies

DNS Policy is a new feature introduced in Windows Server 2016. ***DNS policies*** are used to manipulate how a DNS server handles queries based on different parameters. For example, you can redirect users to a specific server based on application high availability, traffic management, the time of day, or if they are internal or external. You can also filter or block DNS queries and you can redirect DNS clients to a sinkhole instead of the computer they are trying to reach.

When you configure DNS policies, you must identify groups of records in a zone, groups of clients on a network, or other elements that tie the DNS clients together.

- **Client subnet:** Represents the IPv4 or IPv6 subnet from which queries are sent to a DNS server.
- **Recursion scope:** Represents unique instances of a group of settings that control whether the system will use recursion or not for a given set of queries.
- **Zone scopes:** Specifies the same resource records across multiple scopes, with different IP addresses depending on the scope. You can also specify zone-transfer policies, which will define zone transfers.

You can apply both DNSSEC and DNS policy types at the server or zone level. As you define policies, policies will be assigned different values that will be used to determine processing order.

DNS policies are created and managed by executing the following Windows PowerShell commands:

- **Add-DnsServerClientSubnet:** Adds a client subnet to a DNS server.
- **Add-DnsServerQueryResolutionPolicy:** Adds a policy for query resolution to a DNS server.
- **Add-DnsServerRecursionScope:** Adds a recursion scope on a DNS server.
- **Add-DnsServerResourceRecord:** Adds a resource record of a specified type to a specified DNS zone.
- **Add-DnsServerZoneScope:** Adds a zone scope to an existing zone.
- **Remove-DnsServerClientSubnet:** Deletes a client subnet to a DNS server.
- **Remove-DnsServerQueryResolutionPolicy:** Deletes a policy for query resolution to a DNS server.
- **Remove-DnsServerRecursionScope:** Deletes a recursion scope on a DNS server.
- **Remove-DnsServerZoneScope:** Adds a zone scope to an existing zone.
- **Set-DnsServerClientSubnet:** Updates the IP addresses in a client subnet.
- **Set-DnsServerQueryResolutionPolicy:** Updates settings of a query resolution policy on a DNS server.
- **Set-DnsServerRecursionScope:** Updates a recursion scope on a DNS server.
- **Set-DnsServerResourceRecord:** Changes a resource record in a DNS zone.

Windows PowerShell version 5.0 or higher is used to create and manage DNS policies. In the following example, traffic management policies are created to direct the client name resolution requests from a certain subnet in the New York datacenter and from another subnet to a San Francisco datacenter. This will be done by first defining the client subnets and zone scopes. You will then define the resource records in the zone and configure DNS server query resolution policies.

```
Add-DnsServerClientSubnet -Name "NewYorkSubnet" -IPv4Subnet
"172.21.33.0/24"

Add-DnsServerClientSubnet -Name "SanFranciscoSubnet"
-IPv4Subnet "172.10.44.0/24"

Add-DnsServerZoneScope -ZoneName "Contoso.com" -Name
"NewYorkZoneScope"

Add-DnsServerZoneScope -ZoneName "Contoso.com" -Name
"SanFranciscoZoneScope"

Add-DnsServerResourceRecord -ZoneName "Contoso.com"
-A -Name "www" -IPv4Address "172.10.97.97" -ZoneScope
"SanFranciscoZoneScope"

Add-DnsServerResourceRecord -ZoneName "Contoso.com" -A -Name
"www" -IPv4Address "172.21.21.21" -ZoneScope "NewYorkZoneScope"

Add-DnsServerQueryResolutionPolicy -Name "NewYorkPolicy"
-Action ALLOW -ClientSubnet "eq,NewYorkSubnet" -ZoneScope
"NewYorkZoneScope,1" -ZoneName "Contoso.com"

Add-DnsServerQueryResolutionPolicy -Name "SanFranciscoPolicy"
-Action ALLOW -ClientSubnet "eq, SanFranciscoSubnet" -ZoneScope
"SanFranciscoZoneScope,1" -ZoneName "contoso.com"
```

Configuring DNSSEC

DNS Security (DNSSEC) is a suite of protocols defined by the Internet Engineering Task Force (IETF) for use on IP networks. DNSSEC provides DNS clients, or resolvers, with proof of identity of DNS records and verified denial of existence. DNSSEC does *not* provide availability or confidentiality information.

A client that uses DNS to connect is always vulnerable to redirection to an attacker's servers unless the zone has been secured using DNSSEC. The process for securing a zone using DNSSEC is called ***signing the zone***. Once signed, any queries on the signed zone will return digital signatures along with the normal DNS resource records. The digital signatures are verified using the public key of the server or zone from the ***trust anchor***, which defines the top of the chain of trust by using public keys. The trust anchor verifies that a digital signature and associated data is valid.

Once this public key has been obtained, the resolver or client is able to validate the responses it receives. The trust anchor is the most important link in this chain. The server, resolver, or zone must be configured with this trust anchor. Once this is achieved, the client will be able to confirm that the DNS information it receives came from a valid server, was unchanged, and does or does not actually exist.

DNSSEC can be enabled on an Active-Directory Integrated zone (ADI) or on a primary zone. As with all security measures and particularly advanced implementations, planning is important. Which zones do you want to secure? Who has access to the zone? Who has access to the server and the administration of the server security? The answers to these and other questions depend on the security requirements of your organization. By the time you are ready to implement DNSSEC on your DNS server, the security documentation should have already been created and approved.

DNSSEC is installed as part of the DNS Server role. To enable DNSSEC, Windows Server 2016 provides a DNSSEC Zone Signing Wizard. This wizard is run from the DNS console and configures the ***Zone Signing Parameters,*** which are settings that ensure the zone is signed correctly and securely. Follow the instructions to configure DNSSEC for the given ADI zone.

Once a zone is signed, there are several new ***DNSSEC Resource records*** available; these records provide the proof of the identity of DNS records and are in addition to the standard A, NS, and SRV records in an unsigned zone. These DNSSEC Resource records include DNSKEY, RRSIG, and NSEC. DNSKEY records are used to sign the records. The RRSIG record is returned to the client in response to a successful query along with the A record. The NSEC record is returned to positively deny that the requested A record exists in the zone.

DNSSEC uses a series of keys to secure the server and the zones. These include the ***Key Signing Key (KSK)*** and the ***Zone Signing Key (ZSK)***. The KSK is an authentication key that signs all the DNSKEY records at the root of the zone, and it is part of the chain of trust. The ZSK is used to sign zone data.

Automated key rollover is the process by which a DNSSEC key management strategy for key management is made easier with automated key regeneration.

CONFIGURE DNSSEC ON AN ACTIVE DIRECTORY INTEGRATED ZONE

GET READY. Using administrative privileges, log on to the computer where you installed the DNS Server role and the Adatum.com ADI zone. To configure DNSSEC on an Active Directory integrated zone, perform the following steps:

1. Open **Server Manager** and click **Tools > DNS**. This loads the DNS Manager console.
2. Expand DNS Server by clicking the **arrow** to the left of the server name.
3. Expand the Forward Lookup Zones by clicking the **arrow** to the left of Forward Lookup Zones.
4. Click and then right-click the **Adatum.com** zone. Choose **DNSSEC > Sign the Zone.**
5. In the DNSSEC Zone Signing Wizard, click **Next.**
6. On the Signing Options page, as shown in Figure 7-7, there are three options to define the parameters used to sign the zone. Select **Customize zone signing parameters** and then click **Next.**

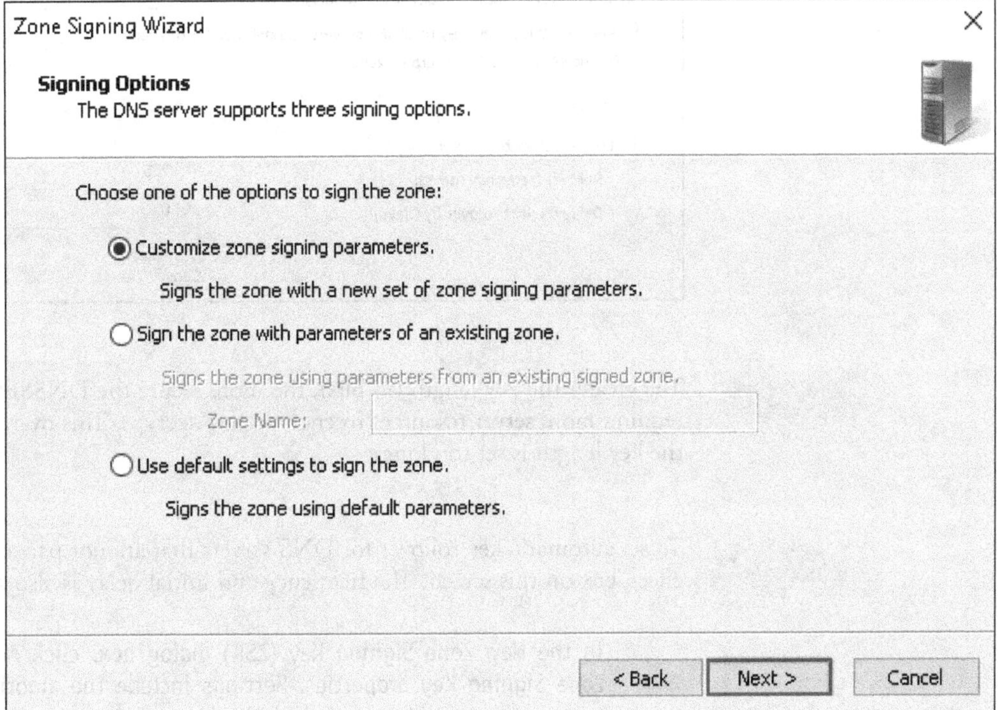

Figure 7-7
Selecting the signing options

7. On the Key Master page, the default is the current server. Click **Next.**
8. On the Key Signing Key (KSK) page, click **Next.**
9. In the Key Signing Key (KSK) dialog box, click **Add.** The New Key Signing Key (KSK) dialog box opens, as shown in Figure 7-8.

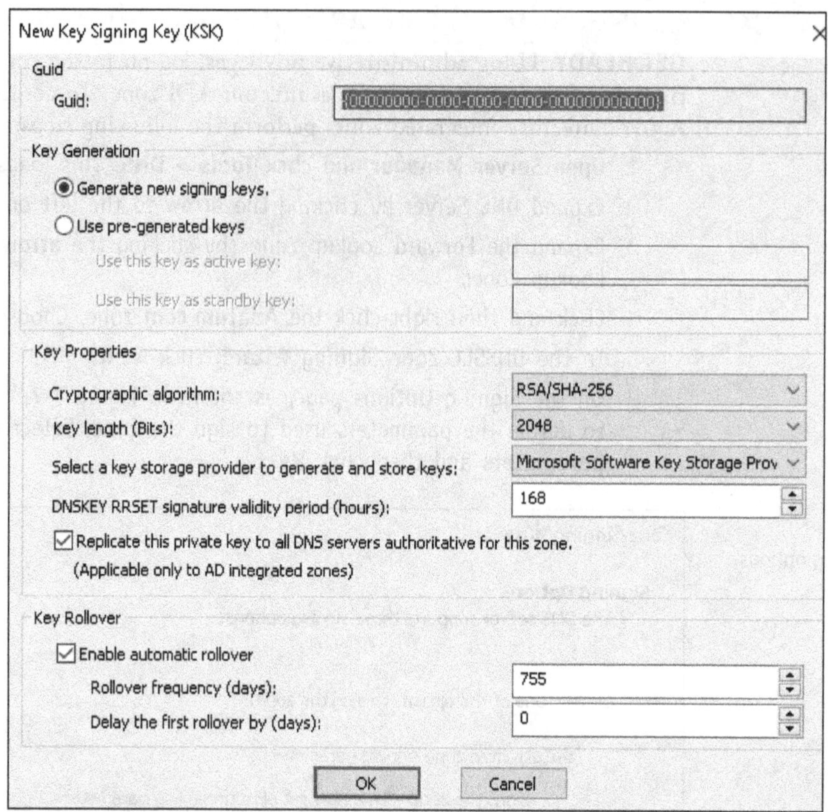

Figure 7-8

Creating a new Key Signing Key (KSK)

TAKE NOTE* The greater the key length (in bits), the more secure the DNSSEC keys will be. A long key requires more server resources to encrypt and decrypt. This overhead can be noticeable if the key length is set too long.

TAKE NOTE* To set automatic key rollover for DNS servers that are not part of a domain, select the check box on this screen. The frequency and initial delay is also set here.

10. In the New Zone Signing Key (ZSK) dialog box, click **Add** and then configure your Zone Signing Key properties. Settings include the algorithm, key length, key storage provider, validity period of the keys, and auto rollover. Click **OK** and then click **Next.**
11. An NSEC record provides authenticated denial of existence. (If a DNS client requests a record that does not exist, the server provides an authoritative denial and the NSEC or NSEC3 record verifies this as genuine. On the Next Secure (NSEC) page, the options are for NSEC or NSEC3. NSEC3 is the default. Click **Next.**
12. On the Trust Anchors (TAs) page, configure the distribution of trust anchors and rollover keys. If the DNS server is also a domain controller, when the Enable the distribution of trust anchors for this zone option is enabled, every other DNS server that is also a domain controller in the forest will receive the trust anchors for the zone. This speeds up the key retrieval. For the Enable automatic update of trust anchors on key rollover (RFC 5011) option, automated key rollover should be set if trust anchors are required on nondomain-joined computers. Click **Next.**
13. On the Signing and Polling Parameters page (see Figure 7-9), Signing and Polling Parameters allows for the configuration of the delegation key record algorithm (DS record) and the polling intervals for the delegated zones. Accept the defaults by clicking **Next**, then click **Next**, again. The wizard signs the zone.

Figure 7-9

Selecting the Signing and Polling Parameters

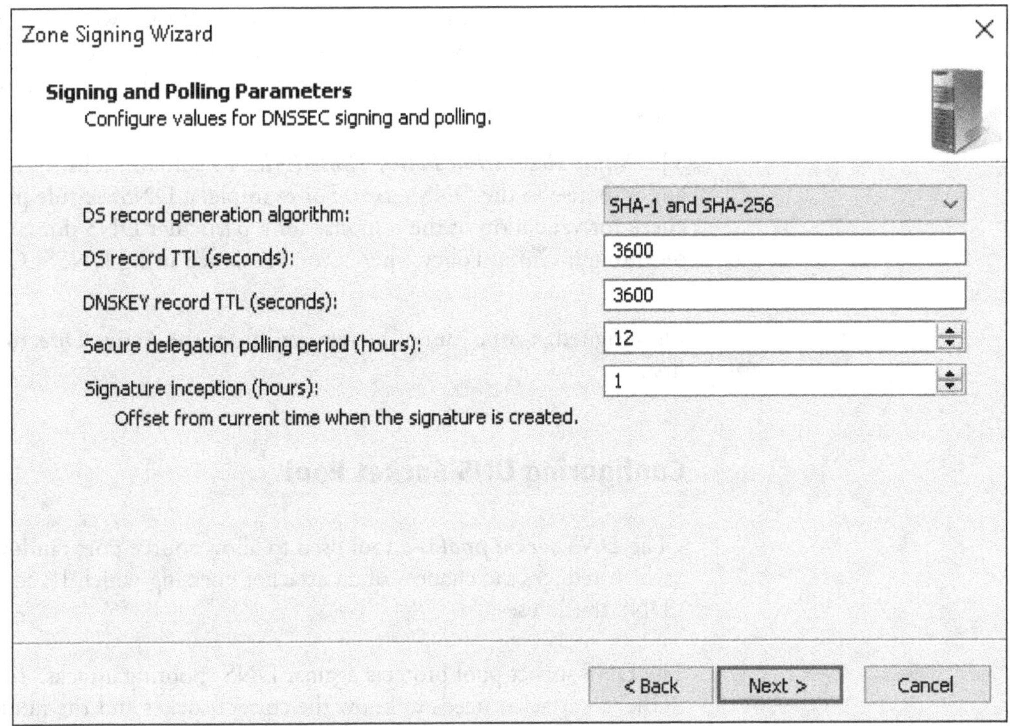

14. When the zone is signed, click **Finish**. The new DNSSEC records can now be seen in the DNS Manager. If they do not show immediately, press the F5 key to refresh the list.

Note that the padlock at the root of the Adatum.com zone (see Figure 7-10) shows the zone is signed. Also note the additional records visible in the zone DNSKEY (Public Key for the zone), RRSIG, and NSEC3. As shown in the figure, each original entry now has four records: the A, RRSIG for the A, NSEC3, and the RRSIG for the NSEC3 record.

Figure 7-10

Displaying the signed zone

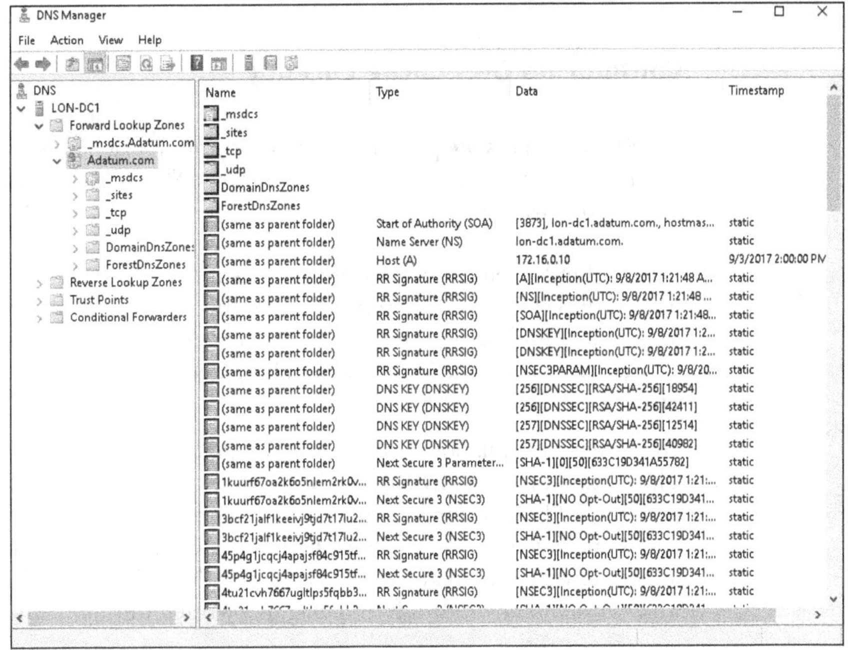

When you right-click the zone and choose DNSSec, two more options are available on the zone DNSSEC context menu: Properties and Unsign the Zone. The Properties dialog contains the settings you made in the wizard. Unsign the Zone removes all the records and disables DNSSEC for this zone.

The ***Name Resolution Policy Table (NRPT)*** contains a list of rules for DNS client access and response to the DNS server. For example, a DNSSec rule prompts the client computer to check for validation of the response for a particular DNS domain suffix. NRPT is normally set through Group Policy when a zone is signed using DNSSEC.

TAKE NOTE* Once signed, a zone cannot be removed from the Active Directory unless it is unsigned first.

Configuring DNS Socket Pool

The ***DNS socket pool*** is a tool used to allow source port randomization for DNS queries, which reduces the chances of an attacker guessing which IP address and port (socket) the DNS traffic uses.

The DNS socket pool protects against DNS spoofing attacks. To be able to tamper with DNS traffic, an attacker needs to know the correct socket and the randomly generated transaction ID. DNS socket pooling is enabled by default in Windows Server 2016. The default size of the DNS socket pool is 2500 and the available settings range from 0 to 10,000. The larger the number of ports available to the pool, the more secure the communication.

Windows Server 2016 also allows for an exclusion list to be created. The preferred method to set the socket pool size is by using the **dnscmd** command-line tool, as shown here:

1. Launch an elevated command prompt.
2. Execute the following command:

```
dnscmd /Config /SocketPoolSize <value>
```

The value must be between 0 and 10,000.

Configuring DNS Cache Locking

DNS Cache Locking prevents an attacker from replacing records in the resolver cache while the Time to Live (TTL) is still in force. When cache locking is enabled, records cannot be overwritten.

When a DNS client or server (resolver) has received the DNS record of a requested resource, that entry is stored in the resolver cache until the TTL for that record expires. (The TTL is set on the record itself at the zone level.) It is possible for this information to be altered by an attacker while it sits in the cache. This allows an attacker to divert the client to a different (unsafe) resource.

To prevent this situation, Windows Server 2016 provides the DNS Cache Locking feature. This feature prevents any changes being made to the contents of a record in the resolver cache until the TTL has expired. DNS Cache Locking uses a percentage of the TTL to set the lock. For example, when the cache locking value is set to 75, the record would not be available to be overwritten until at least 75 percent of the TTL expires. The optimum setting is 100, which prevents any record from being overwritten during the time its TTL is valid.

The preferred method to set the DNS cache locking value is by using the **dnscmd** command-line tool, as shown here:

1. Launch an elevated command prompt.
2. Execute the following command:

   ```
   dnscmd /Config /CacheLockingPercent <percent>
   ```

3. Restart the DNS Service to apply the new settings. From the command prompt, execute `net stop DNS`, wait for the service to stop, and then execute `net start DNS`

USING POWERSHELL

To change the cache locking value using PowerShell, execute `Set-DnsServerCache -LockingPercent 100`

Enabling Response Rate Limiting (RRL)

A DNS amplification attack is when attackers forge the IP address of the victim network and send a lot of queries to the DNS servers. As a result, the network and server become congested, causing a denial of service attack (DoS). To prevent this type of attack, DNS servers starting in Windows Server 2016 provide an option to enable ***Response Rate Limiting (RRL)***, which helps identify the potentially malicious queries. If a lot of queries originate from a single source asking for similar names within a specified time window, it will cause the DNS server to not respond to those queries or to respond with a truncation, which reverts back to TCP, which uses a three-way handshake for validation. Overall, with RRL enabled, the Windows DNS server will put an upper limit to the number of similar responses that it will send to clients from the same subnet.

To enable RRL on a DNS server, use the Windows PowerShell `Set-DnsServerResponseRateLimited` cmdlet. For example, execute the following command:

```
Set-DnsServerResponseRateLimiting -WindowInSec 7 -LeakRate 4
-TruncateRate 3 -ErrorsPerSec 8 -ResponsesPerSec 8
```

- The `-WindowInSec 7` option specifies the period (in seconds) over which rates are measured and averaged for RRL.
- The `-LeakRate 4` option specifies the rate at which the server responds to dropped queries. In this example, if LeakRate is 4, the server responds to one in every 4 queries. The allowed range for LeakRate is 2 to 10. If LeakRate is set to zero, no responses are leaked by RRL. The default value for LeakRate is 3.
- The `-TruncateRate 3` option specifies the rate at which the server responds with truncated responses. For queries that meet the criteria to be dropped due to RRL, the DNS server still responds with truncated responses once per TruncateRate queries. For example, if TruncateRate is 3, one in every 2 queries receives a truncated response. The allowed range for TruncateRate is 2 to 10. If it is set to 0, this behavior is disabled. The default value is 2.
- The `-ErrorsPerSec 8` option specifies the maximum number of times that the server can send an error response to a client within a one-second interval. The error responses include: REFUSED, FORMERR and SERVFAIL.
- The `-ResponsesPerSec 8` option specifies the maximum number of times that the server sends a client the same response within a one-second interval.

To reset the RRL parameters on the DNS server to the default values, execute the following command:

```
Set-DnsServerResponseRateLimiting -ResetToDefault
```

Configuring DNS-based Authentication of Named Entities (DANE)

DNS-based Authentication of Named Entities (DANE) is a protocol that uses X.509 digital certificates to be bound to the DNS name using DNSSEC. It can be used to authenticate Transport Layer Security (TLS) client and server entities without a certificate authority (CA). DANE is used to prevent man-in-the-middle attacks whereby a user may be directed to fake web site. It specifically prevents corruption of a DNS cache that points to a website and prevents the use of a fake certificate that is issued from a different CA.

DANE informs a DNS client which CA should have provided a certificate for a specified domain. DANE is implemented by adding a resource record using the Windows PowerShell `Add-DnsServerResourceRecord -TLSA` cmdlet. For example, to create a DNS resource record TLSA for the ms1.dnslab.adatum.com, execute the following command:

```
add-dnsserverresourcerecord -TLSA -CertificateAssociationData
"25d645a7bd304ae552c629ca5e7061a70f921afc4d-
d49c1ea0c8f22de6595be7" -CertificateUsage
DomainIssuedCertificate -MatchingType Sha256Hash -Selector
FullCertificate -ZoneName ms1.dnslab.adatum.com -Name 25._tcp.
ev1-exch.ms1.dnslab.adatum.com.
```

Installing and Configuring MMA to Analyze Network Traffic

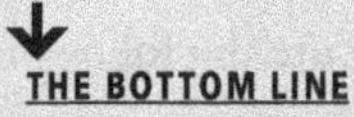

Microsoft Message Analyzer (MMA) is a free Microsoft packet/protocol analyzer tool that can be used to capture network traffic, which then can be displayed and analyzed. You can use MMA to monitor live network traffic or to import, aggregate, and analyze data from log and trace files.

CERTIFICATION READY
Install and configure Microsoft Message Analyzer (MMA) to analyze network traffic
Objective 3.3

You can use MMA to perform the following network analysis tasks:

- Capturing message data
- Saving message data
- Importing message data
- Viewing message data
- Filtering message data

MMA can be searched for and downloaded from the Microsoft web site.

INSTALL MICROSOFT MESSAGE ANALYZER

GET READY. To install MMA, perform the following steps.

1. On a computer running Windows Server 2016, double-click the **MessageAnalyzer64.msi** file. If you are prompted to confirm that you want to run this file, click **Run.**
2. On the Welcome to the Microsoft Message Analyzer Setup Wizard page, click **Next.**
3. On the End-User License Agreement page, select **I accept the terms in the License Agreement** and click **Next.**
4. On the Microsoft Message Analyzer Optimization page, click **Next.**
5. On the Ready to install Microsoft Message Analyzer page, click **Install.**
6. When the installation is complete, click **Finish.**

A protocol analyzer grabs every packet on a network interface, puts a timestamp on the packet, and stores the packets. You can then use a filter to specify the packets that will be displayed and then you can open each packet to look at the various TCP/IP layers to see what is happening. The packets can be saved to a file so that they can be analyzed later.

When you first capture packets on an interface, you will notice that there are hundreds of packets. Usually, most of these packets can be ignored because they are not associated with the problem you are trying to analyze. In these cases, you need use a filter to show only the packets that you are concerned with.

When you open the MMA console (as shown in Figure 7-11), you can start capturing packets by clicking the Start Local Trace button. To stop capturing packets, click the Stop button. MMC offers an intelligent view when looking at the packets. For example, as shown in Figure 7-12, MessageNumber 77 shows that a computer with an address of 192.168.3.118 is trying to perform a DNS query with a system at 208.84.0.53. When you expand the packet, it shows the response was MessageNumber 80.

Figure 7-11

Opening Microsoft Message Analyzer

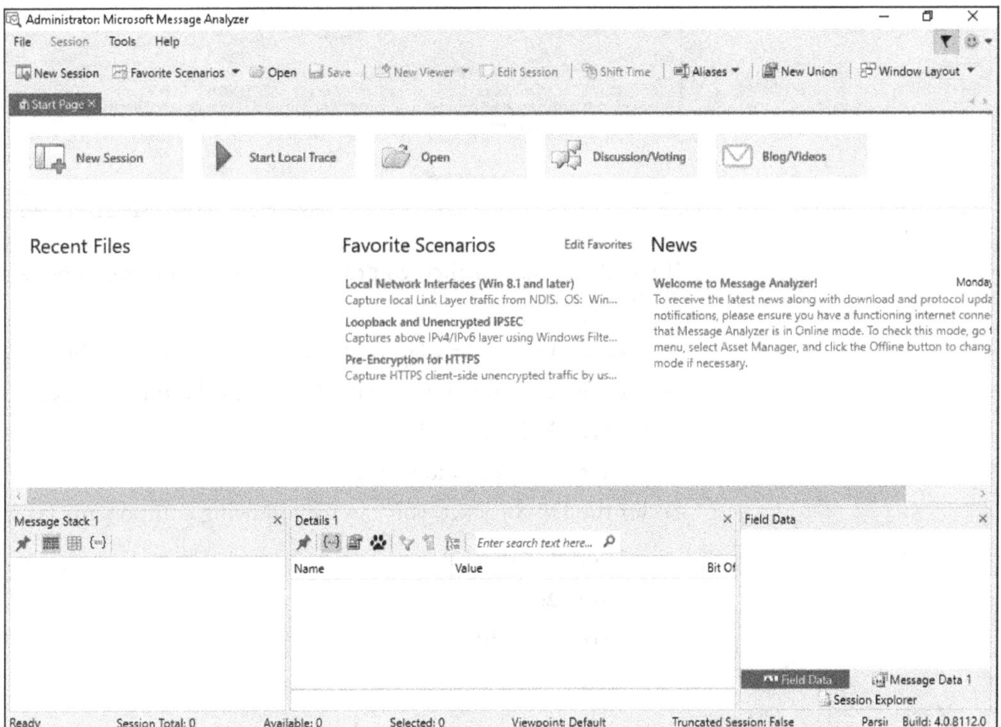

Figure 7-12

Looking at a DNS query

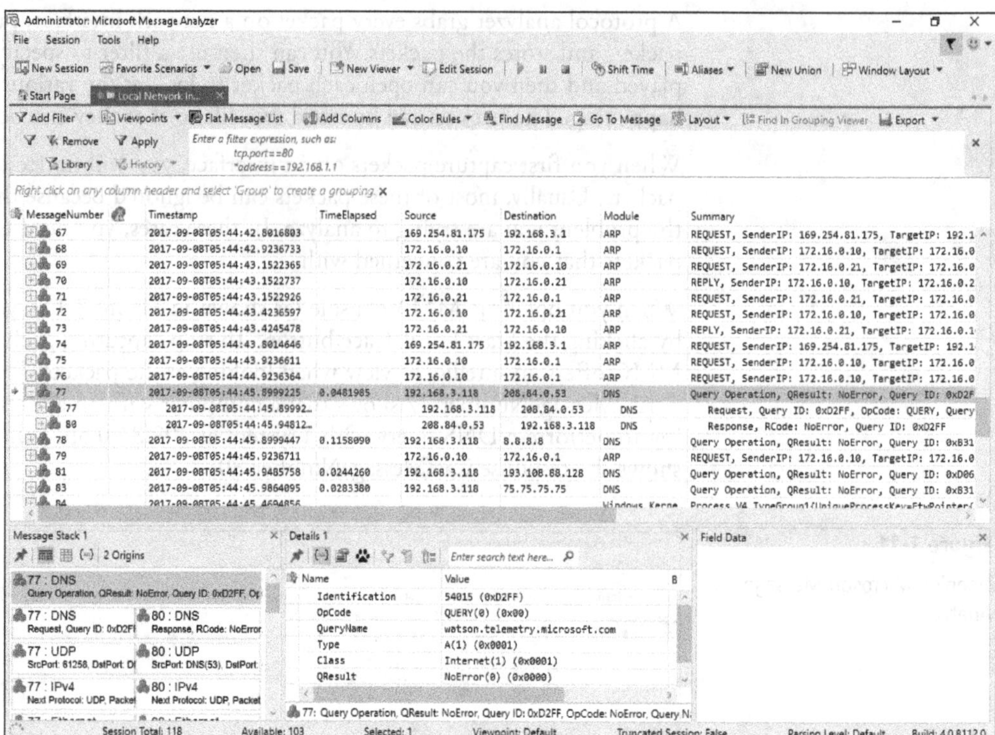

If you drill down further, you can look at the various components of the packet based on the TCP/IPI model:

- **Layer 1:** Data link layer (also simply known as the link layer)
- **Layer 2:** Network layer (also known as the Internet layer)
- **Layer 3:** Transport layer
- **Layer 4:** Application layer

So for the DNS packet, you can see following components (as shown in Figure 7-13):

- **Layer 1:** Ethernet
- **Layer 2:** IPv4
- **Layer 3:** UDP
- **Layer 4:** DNS

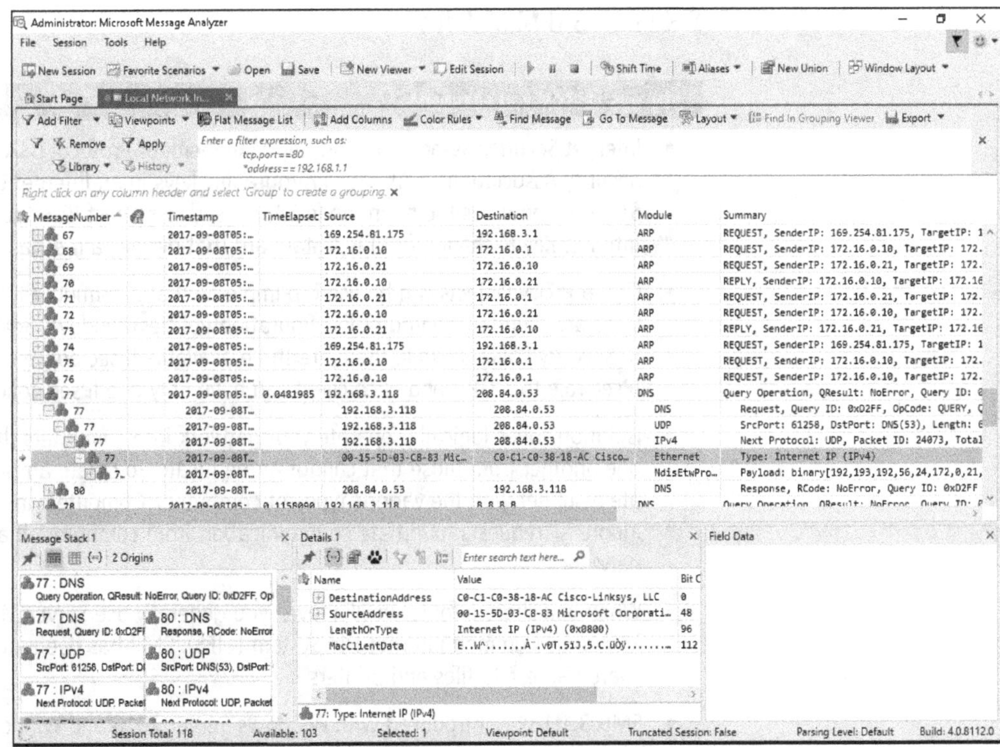

Figure 7-13

Looking at the components of a packet

Using viewpoints and filters, you can capture or display only those frames that meet the criteria you specify. MMA also offers viewpoints, which also able to focus on messages of interests and to display data from a specific protocol or module.

You can filter on any protocol, protocol element, or property. For example, you can only capture frames that originate from a particular IP address or port. To focus on only the packets that are relevant, you can use the filter. For example, to show DNS packets, you can use udp.port==53. Don't forget to click Apply for the filter to take in effect.

If you want to show packets to and from an address (such as 192.168.1.1), type:

```
*address==192.168.1.1
```

To combine, the two, use &&:

```
*address==192.168.1.1 && udp.port==53
```

MMA is capable of loading data from native MMA files, event tracing log (.etl) files, Network Monitor capture files (.cap), comma-separated values (.csv) files, and several other formats.

SKILL SUMMARY

IN THIS LESSON YOU LEARNED:

- Internet Security Association and Key Management Protocol (ISAKMP) is used to establish Security Associations (SA) and cryptographic keys in an Internet environment. The ISAKMP SA, also known as the main mode SA, is used to protect IPsec security negotiations. The Internet Key Exchange (IKE) is a standard that defines a mechanism to establish SAs.
- Group Policy Objects can be used to implement and configure IPsec policies. The IPsec settings are found at Computer Configuration\Policies\Windows Settings\Security Settings\IP Security Policies. While there are three available IPsec policies, you can only assign one IPsec rule to a GPO and each client can have only one IPsec policy applied to it at a time.
- Isolation zones logically separate your network into computers that can authenticate with one another from those that cannot authenticate. To create an isolation zone, you will create a subnet with the various types of computers. Computers in an isolated network will ignore all requests to initiate communication from computers that are not in the isolated network.
- When you share a folder in Windows, you generally use Server Message Block (SMB), also known as Common Internet File System (CIFS). SMB has been around for years to provide shared access to files and printers.
- SMB 3.1.1 was introduced with Windows Server 2016 and Windows 10. While it has all of the features and abilities of SMB 3.0, it also offers pre-authentication integrity, SMB encryption improvements and cluster dialog fencing.
- SMB signing is a feature whereby SMB communication is digitally signed at the packet level. Digitally signing the packets enables the recipient of the packets to confirm their point of origination and their authenticity.
- Windows Server 2016 adds a number of features to domain naming services (DNS) security. Securing the DNS server and DNS records prevents false records from being added and prevents clients from receiving incorrect DNS query responses, which could lead them to visit phishing sites or worse. To prevent DNS being used to attack systems, DNS Security (DNSSEC), Cache Locking, and other security measures are implemented.
- Microsoft Message Analyzer (MMA) is a free Microsoft packet/protocol analyzer tool that you use to capture network traffic, which can be displayed and analyzed. . You can use MMA to monitor live network traffic or to import, aggregate, and analyze data from log and trace files.

Knowledge Assessment

Multiple Choice

1. Which type of keys are used in DNSSEC?
   - a. KSK
   - b. PLK
   - c. ZSK
   - d. VFK
2. Which of the following can be used to limit how many DNS queries a DNS server will respond to so that it will reduce the effect of a Denial of Service attack?
   - a. Netmask ordering
   - b. DANE
   - c. Response Rate Limiting
   - d. Round robin
3. Which of the following uses a digital certificate to ensure that a user is not being directed to a fake website because the DNS cache was corrupted?
   - a. Netmask ordering
   - b. DANE
   - c. DNSSEC
   - d. Round robin
4. Which of the following methods enable you to apply IPsec on a server running Windows Server 2016? (Choose two answers)
   - a. Using Server Manager
   - b. Using a GPO
   - c. Using the IPsec Manager
   - d. Using Windows Firewall with Advanced Security
5. Which of the following is a combination of security services, protection mechanisms, and cryptographic keys mutually agreed to by communicating peers?
   - a. Trust anchor
   - b. SMB
   - c. SA
   - d. Socket pool
6. Which of the following specifies that packets will be encrypted between two endpoints?
   - a. A tunnel
   - b. A transport
   - c. A cache
   - d. A zone

7. Which of the following can be used to protect SMB packets being sent over a network from being read by unauthorized people?
   a. SMB encrypting
   b. SMB signing
   c. SMB caching
   d. Trust anchor
8. Which of the following should normally be disabled in current networks? (Choose all that apply)
   a. SMB 1.0
   b. SMB 2.0
   c. SMB 3.0
   d. SMB 3.1
9. Which of the following enables SMB signing for multiple computers?
   a. Server Manager
   b. a Firewall
   c. A GPO
   d. Operations Manager
10. Which of the following versions of Windows support SMB 3.1.1. (Choose all that apply)
   a. Windows Server 2012 R2
   b. Windows Server 2016
   c. Windows 8
   d. Windows 10
   e. Windows 7

Best Answer

Choose the letter that corresponds to the best answer. More than one answer choice may achieve the goal. Select the BEST answer.

1. Which of the following DNS Cache locking settings should be used?
   a. 30 percent
   b. 0 percent
   c. 100 percent
   d. 50 percent
2. Which mechanism establishes a security association in IPsec?
   a. Internet Key Exchange
   b. IPsec driver
   c. Name Resolution Policy Table
   d. Trust anchor

3. Which of the following is used to ensure that only domain systems can talk to a server?
   - **a.** Domain isolation
   - **b.** Server isolation
   - **c.** Zone isolation
   - **d.** Connection isolation
4. An application will not connect to a server and you have confirmed that the server is accessible. Which of the following is the best tool to use to examine why the application is not connecting?
   - **a.** Server Manager
   - **b.** Ping and Ipconfig commands
   - **c.** nslookup command
   - **d.** Microsoft Message Analyzer

Build List

1. Specify the correct order of steps necessary to create and deploy an IPsec policy to your users and computers.

_____ Deploy policies that use Permit and Block filter actions.

_____ Deploy the policies using the Negotiate Security filter action with the option to fall back to clear text communications.

_____ Create filter actions that correspond to how you want connections to be authenticated, data integrity to be applied, and data to be encrypted.

_____ Monitor your IPsec environment, and adjust previous configured policies.

_____ Monitor the environment, including the Main Mode Negotiation Failures statistic.

_____ After refinements have been made, remove the fall back to clear text communications actions.

_____ Create IP filter lists that match the computers, subnets, and conditions in your environment.

_____ Create a set of policies that match the filtering and filter action (security) requirements you need.

2. Specify the correct order of the steps necessary to perform domain isolation.

_____ Test isolation with a computer that does not have the domain isolation rule.

_____ Create a connection security rule that requests authentication.

_____ Create exemption rules for computers that are not domain members.

_____ Change the isolation rule to require authentication.

_____ Deploy and test your connection security rules.

Business Case Scenarios

Scenario 7-1: Protecting Your Servers

You administer several servers running Windows Server 2016 that contain confidential information. You want to encrypt data using BitLocker on the disk and you want to encrypt the data being transmitted over the network using IPsec. You just completed enabling and configuring BitLocker. Describe how to implement IPsec to protect the servers.

Scenario 7-2: Protecting Your Shared Data

You administer several servers running Windows Server 2016 that have shared folders and these folders contain highly confidential information. You need to ensure that when the shared files are accessed, they are as secure as possible. In addition, you want to prevent older operating systems (like Windows XP, Windows Vista, or Windows 7) from accessing these shares. Describe your recommended solution.

LESSON 8

Implementing Privilege Access Management and Administrative Forests

70-744 EXAM OBJECTIVE

Objective 4.1 – Implement Just-in-Time (JIT) Administration. This objective may include but is not limited to: Create a new administrative (bastion) forest in an existing Active Directory environment using Microsoft Identity Manager (MIM); configure trusts between production and bastion forests; create shadow principals in a bastion forest; configure the MIM web portal; request privileged access using the MIM web portal; determine requirements and usage scenarios for Privileged Access Management (PAM) solutions; create and implement MIM policies; implement Just-in-Time administration principals using time-based policies; request privileged access using Windows PowerShell.

Objective 4.3 – Implement Privileged Access Workstations (PAWS) and User Rights Assignments. This objective may include but is not limited to: Determine usage scenarios and requirements for implementing ESAE forest design architecture to create a dedicated administrative forest. Other Objective 4.3 objectiv es are covered in Lesson 10.

LESSON HEADING	EXAM OBJECTIVE
Implementing Enhanced Security Administrative Environment (ESAE)	Determine usage scenarios and requirements for implementing ESAE forest design architecture to create a dedicated administrative forest
Implementing Just-In-Time (JIT) Administration	Configure the MIM web portal
• Installing and Configuring the Microsoft Identity Manager (MIM) Service and Web Portal	Create a new administrative (bastion) forest in an existing Active Directory environment using Microsoft Identity Manager (MIM)
• Creating a New Administrative Forest and Configuring Trust Between Production and Bastion Forests	Configure trusts between production and bastion forests
• Creating Shadow Principals in a Bastion Forest	Create shadow principals in a bastion forest
• Requesting Privileged Access and Managing PAM Roles	Request privileged access using the MIM web portal
	Determine requirements and usage scenarios for Privileged Access Management (PAM) solutions
	Create and implement MIM policies
	Implement Just-in-Time administration principals using time-based policies
	Request privileged access using Windows PowerShell

KEY TERMS

clean source principal
Enhanced Security Administrative Environment (ESAE)
ESAE forest
Identity Manager Client Add-ins and Extensions
Just-in-time (JIT) administration
Microsoft Identity Manager (MIM)
Privileged Access Management (PAM)
role-based access control (RBAC)
shadow principal

Implementing Enhanced Security Administrative Environment (ESAE)

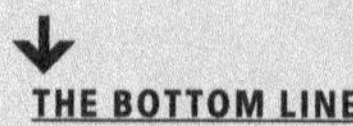

Enhanced Security Administrative Environment (ESAE) uses administrative forests combined with recommended practices to provide an administrative environment and workstations with enhanced security protection that will minimize exposure of administrative credentials. ESAE uses an Active Directory administrative tier model design that uses buffer zones between full administrative control of the Environment (Tier 0) and the high-risk workstation assets that attackers frequently compromise.

CERTIFICATION READY
Determine usage scenarios and requirements for implementing ESAE forest design architecture to create a dedicated administrative forest
Objective 4.3

An ***ESAE forest*** is a special Active Directory forest/bastion forest that is separate from the production Active Directory Domain Services forest that hosts privileged accounts. Since the ESAE is a separate forest, you can apply stronger security policies to reduce the possibility of an account being compromised.

The ESAE forest provides the following benefits:

- **Locked-down accounts:** Administrator accounts on one domain do not have access to systems in other domains unless privilege is given. Therefore, when an account is compromised, it is restricted to his or her domain and still not have access to resources in the other domain.
- **Selective authentication:** You can specify which ESAE forest accounts can access the production forest and which specific systems the ESAE account can access. You can even grant access to privileged access workstations or jump servers to access the remote resources so that they can complete day-to-day tasks, but not have administrative control over everything.
- **Simple way to improve security:** You can provide security improvements without completely rebuilding your environment. Also, the ESAE forest doesn't require a large hardware/software footprint; the forest affects only the IT Operations team users.

When designing, implementing, and maintaining security, you need to use the ***clean source principal***, which specifies that all security dependencies are as trustworthy as the items being secured. Every software component, every update, and every account created must be checked to see if it is trustworthy. Therefore, when working with ESAE forests, the forests should have the following properties:

- The ESAE forest should be a single-domain Active Directory forest.
- The ESAE forest should have strict security policies, including authentication requirements.
- The ESAE forest is limited to the hosting accounts of administrative users for the production forest.
- You should not deploy applications or additional resources in the ESAE forest unless it is to increase security when implementing Privileged Access Management (PAM).
- A one-way trust must be configured in which the production forests trust the ESAE forest

so that users from the ESAE forest can access resources in the production forest.

- Accounts used for administrative tasks in the production forest should be standard user accounts in the ESAE forest. If an account is compromised in the production forest, it cannot be used to elevate privileges in the ESAE forest.
- Installation media used in the ESAE forest should be validated and tightly controlled.
- Servers in the ESAE forest should be running the most recent versions of Windows Server operating system and should be updated regularly. Since the ESAE forest is not used to run applications, there should be little, if any, problems with updates.
- Servers in the ESEA forest should be part of the secure virtual environment, which include secure boot, BitLocker volume encryption, credential guard, device guide, and shielded virtual machines.
- Servers should be configured to block USB storage.
- Servers should be on isolated networks. Inbound and outbound Internet connections should be blocked.
- Software downloaded from the Internet should be checked against vendor-provided file hashes to ensure that it has not been tampered with by unauthorized third parties.

ESAE can be accomplished with two forests: a production forest with the necessary managed resources and an admin/ESAE forest. You would then configure a one-way trust relationship with the production forest, which means accounts from the ESAE forest can access servers and resources in the production forest, but accounts in the production forest cannot access resources in the ESAE forest.

This ESAE forest is configured with a one-way trust relationship with a production forest (as shown in Figure 8-1). A one-way trust relationship means that accounts from the ESAE forest can be used in the production forest, but accounts in the production forest cannot be used in the ESAE forest. A production forest is a forest in which administrators perform an organization's day-to-day activities. The production forest is then configured so that administrative tasks in the production forest can be performed only by using accounts that the ESAE forest hosts.

Figure 8-1

ESAE Forests

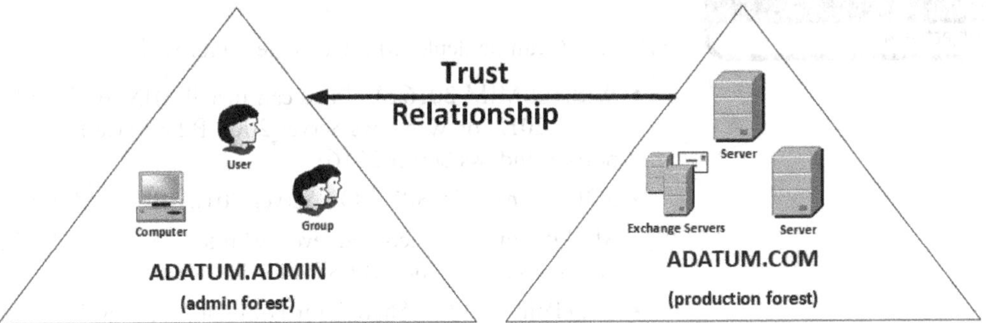

When securing the ESAE forest, ensure that ESAE domain controllers are running on a secure virtualization fabric and that security technologies such as device guard, credential guard, and BitLocker are in use. The clean-source principle also applies to installation media. If installation media is infected, then all software and operating systems that are deployed from that installation media are untrustworthy and at risk for control by attackers. Software obtained from vendors through physical media needs to be validated. Software downloaded from the Internet should be checked against vendor-provided file hashes to ensure that it has not been tampered with by unauthorized third parties. You can use the certutil.exe command, built into the Windows operating system, to compare a downloaded file with the hash file that the vendor provided.

■ Implementing Just-In-Time (JIT) Administration

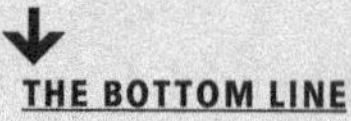

Active Directory provides multiple tools to create, modify, and delete user accounts. However, AD does not provide many tools that automate the lifecycle management tasks such as password reset, group management, and certificate management. ***Microsoft Identity Manager (MIM)*** is an on-premise identity and access management solution that allows you to manage users, credentials, policies, access, certificates, and privileged identities.

MIM offers self-service password reset and account lockout remediation, self-service user attribute management, role management and assignments, password synchronization across directories, and analytics and compliance reporting. It can also provide tools to manage, create, modify and delete groups and users, including automation tools. Lastly, MIM allows assignment of privileges on a temporary basis.

A component of MIM is ***Privileged Access Management (PAM)***, which is a solution that helps organizations restrict privilege access within an existing Active Directory environment. PAM uses a separate bastion environment/administrative forest to manage the production Active Directory forest. By using a separate bastion environment the effect of malicious attacks will be greatly reduced and will reduce the risk of the administrative credentials being stolen.

PAM allows ***just-in-time (JIT) administration***, which automates the provisioning of temporary admin access using a shadow high-security admin forest. As a user needs administrative access, you just assign the appropriate role to the user.

Installing and Configuring the Microsoft Identity Manager (MIM) Service and Web Portal

CERTIFICATION READY
Configure the MIM web portal
Objective 4.1

The newest version of MIM is MIM 2016 with SP1, which you will need to load on a Windows Server and will provide access to a SQL server.

MIM 2016 can be deployed on a single server with the following requirements:

- Without MIM 2016 SP1, you can install MIM on Windows Server 2012 R2, Windows Server 2012, or Windows Server 2008 R2 Service Pack 1 (SP1). MIM 2016 SP1 supports Windows Server 2016.
- SQL Server 2014 SP1, SQL Server 2012 SP2, or SQL Server 2008 R2 SP3.
- AD DS domain functional level: Windows Server 2012 R2, Windows Server 2012, or Windows Server 2008 R2 SP1.
- SharePoint 2013 or SharePoint Foundation 2013. MIM 2016 SP1 supports SharePoint 2016.
- If used for Privileged Access Management, MIM must be installed in a separate Active Directory forest configured by using a one-way trust relationship with the production forest.
- MIM service reporting requires System Center 2012 Service Manager SP1.

To install MIM, you must have several service accounts:

- **MIM Service account:** Used as the main MIM service account, which will process requests and approvals, and it needs to be associated with an email address in a production environment. You cannot use a GMSA for this account.
- **Management Agent service account:** Used to synchronize MIM with the portal.

- **PAM Monitoring Service:** Used as the PAM Monitoring service, which will monitor changes in the production forest.
- **PAM Component Service:** Used by the PAM component service.
- **Synchronization Service:** Used to synchronize data with other identity directories.

You will also need the credentials of the following accounts when deploying MIM:

- SharePoint server
- SQL Server

The MIM Service, PAM Monitoring Service, and PAM Component Service require the following user rights:

- Log on as a service
- Deny access to this computer from the network
- Deny sign-in locally
- Deny sign-in as a batch job
- Deny sign-in through Remote Desktop Services (RDS)

INSTALL AND CONFIGURE THE MIM SERVICE AND WEB PORTAL

GET READY. To install and configure the MIM Service and Web Portal, perform the following steps.

1. On **SYD-MIM**, log on as **adatumadmin\MIMAdmin** with the password of **Pa$$w0rd.**
2. Navigate to and Double-click the MIM2016SP1 ISO file.
3. Double-click **FIMSplash.htm.** Click **Yes** to run active content. The Microsoft Identity Manager installation page opens, as shown in Figure 8-2.

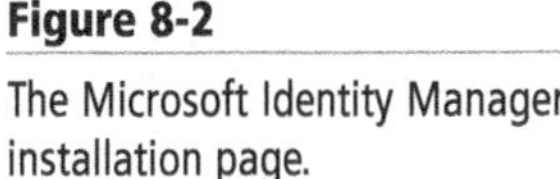

Figure 8-2

The Microsoft Identity Manager installation page.

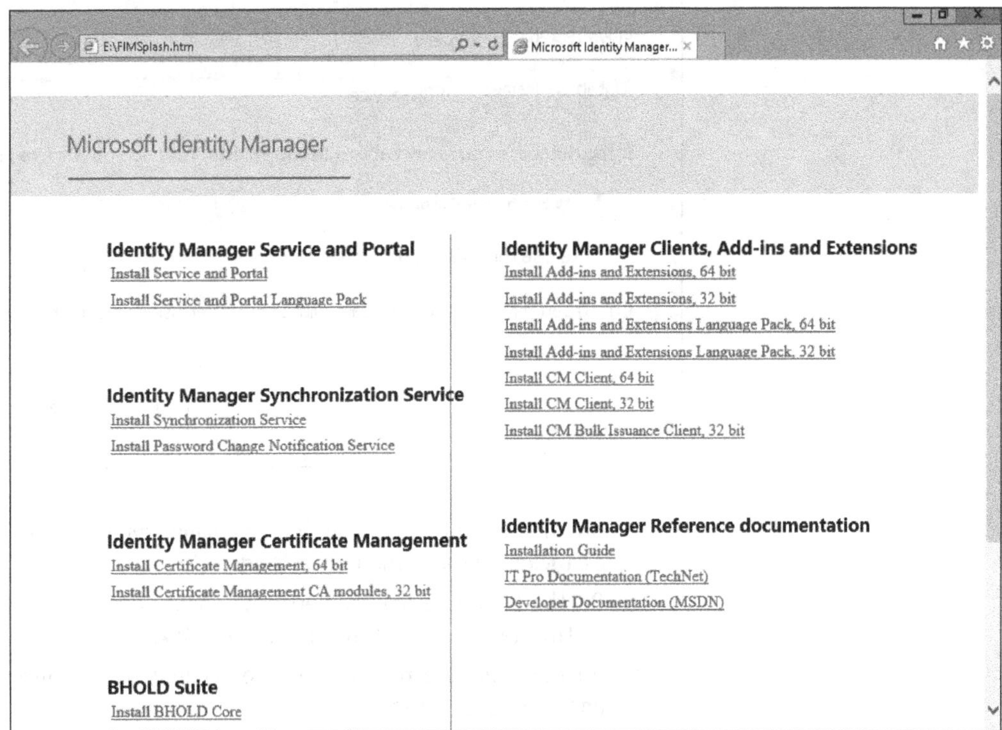

4. Click the **Install Service and Portal** link. When you are prompted to confirm that you want to run or save setup.exe, click **Run.** If you are prompted to confirm that you want to allow the program to make changes to the computer, click **Yes.**

5. In the Welcome to the Microsoft Identity Manager 2016 –Service and Portal wizard, click **Next.**
6. In the End-User License Agreement page, select **I accept the terms in the License Agreement** and then click **Next.**
7. On the MIM Customer Experience Improvement Program page, click **Next.**
8. On the Custom Setup page, MIM portal is already selected. Click **Privileged Access** and then click **Entire feature will be installed on local hard drive.**
9. Click **MIM Password Registration Portal** and then click **Entire Feature will be unavailable.**
10. Click **MIM Password Reset Portal**, click **Entire Feature will be unavailable**, and then click **Next.**
11. On the MIM Customer Experience Improvement Program page, click **I don't want to join the program at this time** and then click **Next.**
12. Click **Next.**
13. On the Configure Common Services page, specify the database server and database name, as shown in Figure 8-3, click **Next.**

Figure 8-3

Specifying database settings

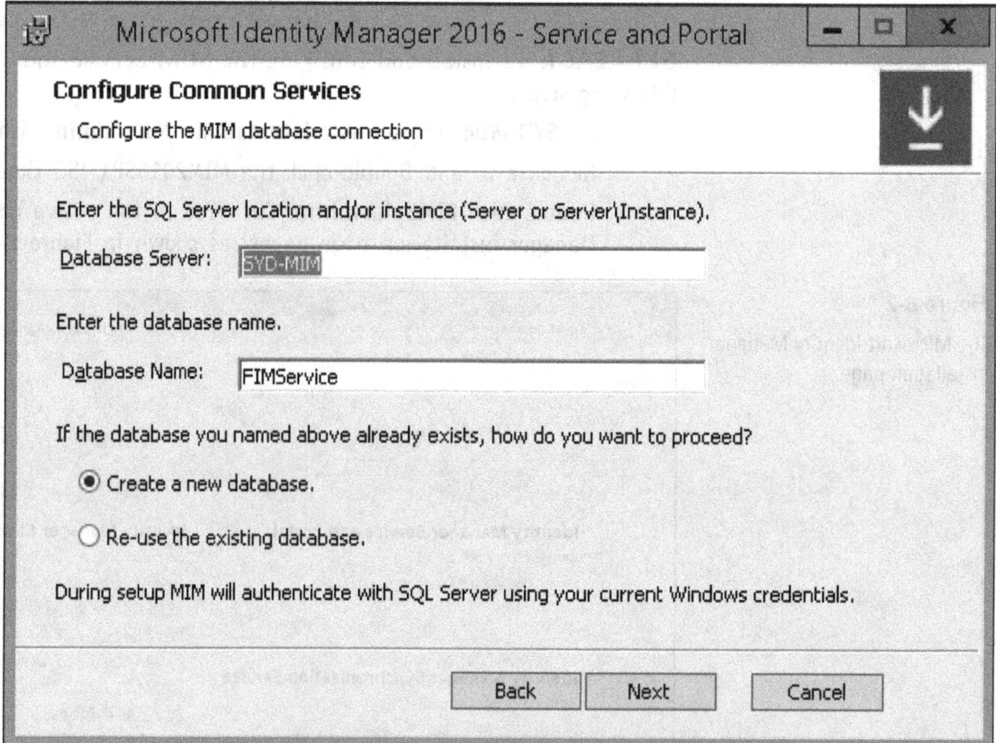

14. On the Configure Common Services page, type the name of your mail server (such as **localhost**) and then click **Next.**
15. On the Configure Service Certificate page, ensure that Generate a new self-issued certificate is selected and then click **Next.**
16. On the Configure the MIM service account page, configure the following settings and then click **Next:**
    - Service Account Name: **mimservice**
    - Service Account Password: **Pa$$w0rd**
    - Service Account Domain: **adatumadmin**
    - Service Email Account: **mimservice@adatumadmin.com**

17. On the Enter information about the MIM synchronization server page, type the following information and then click **Next**.
    - Synchronization Server: **SYD-MIM**
    - MIM Management Agent Account: **adatumadmin\Mimma**
18. On the Configure Common Services page, a warning indicates that the synchronization server does not exist. Click **Next.**
19. On the Configure MIM Service and Portal, to enter the server address for the MIM Portal, type the MIM Service Server address as **syd-mim.adatumadmin.com.** Click **Next.**
20. On the page to enter the URL to the SharePoint Site Collection, type the following SharePoint Site Collection URL: **http://syd-mim.adatumadmin.com:82**. Click **Next.**
21. On the Configure MIM Service and Portal page, leave the Registration Portal URL field blank and then click **Next.**
22. On the page that indicates clients cannot connect to the MIM service unless ports are opened in the firewall, enable the following options and then click **Next:**
    - **Open ports 5725 and 5726 in firewall**
    - **Grant authenticated users access to the MIM Portal site**
23. On the Configure MIM Password Registration Portal page that requests binding information for the Privileged Access Management REST API, provide the following information and then click **Next:**
    - Host Name: **syd-mim.adatumadmin.com**
    - Port: **8086**
24. On the Password Registration Portal Warning page, click **Next.**
25. On the Configure Privileged Access Management REST API page that requests the credentials for the application pool, provide the following information and then click **Next:**
    - Application Pool Account Name: **SharePoint**
    - Application Pool Account Password: **Pa$$w0rd**
    - Application Pool Account Domain: **adatumadmin**
26. On the Configure the PAM Component Service page that addresses entering the credentials for the PAM Component Service, type the following information and then click **Next:**
    - Service Account Name: **mimcomponent**
    - Service Account Password: **Pa$$w0rd**
    - Service Account Domain: **adatumadmin**
27. On the Configure the Privileged Access Management Monitoring Service page that requests the credentials of the account under which the Privilege Access Management Monitoring Service runs, type the following information and then click **Next:**
    - Service Account Name: **mimmonitor**
    - Service Account Password: **Pa$$w0rd**
    - Service Account Domain: **adatumadmin**
28. On the Enter Information for MIM Password Portals page that describes optional passwords for portal configuration, click **Next.**
29. On the Install Microsoft Identity Manager Service and Portal page, click **Install.**
30. When the installation completes, click **Finish.** When you are prompted to restart the computer, click **Yes.**

Creating a New Administrative Forest and Configuring Trust Between Production and Bastion Forests

CERTIFICATION READY
Create a new administrative (bastion) forest in an existing Active Directory environment using Microsoft Identity Manager (MIM)
Objective 4.1

In previous courses, particularly the 70-742 course, you learned how to create new forests and how to configure trust relationships between two forests. In the section entitled "Implementing Enhanced Security Administrative Environment (ESAE)," the ESAE or administrative forest was introduced. In this section, you will create a trust using the Privileged Access Management component of MIM to establish a trust between the administrative forests and the production forest.

The Windows PowerShell New-PAMTrust cmdlet creates a trust relationship of the PAM domain from a domain in an existing forest. The New-PAMDomainConfiguration cmdlet updates a domain in an existing forest to add configuration data required by PAM.

CONFIGURE A TRUST RELATIONSHIP

CERTIFICATION READY
Configure trusts between production and bastion forests
Objective 4.1

CERTIFICATION READY
Implement an Enhanced Security Administrative Environment (ESAE) administrative forest design approach.
Objective 4.3

GET READY. To configure a trust relationship, perform the following steps.

1. On **SYD-MIM**, log on as **adatumadmin\MIMAdmin** with the password of **Pa$$w0rd**.
2. Click the **Start** button and then click **Windows PowerShell (Admin)**.
3. In the Windows PowerShell window, execute the following command:
```
$ca = get-credential  -UserName Adatum\Administrator -
Message "Adatum forest domain admin credentials"
```
4. When you are prompted to log on to the Adatum forest/domain, in the Password text box, type **Pa$$w0rd** and then click **OK**.
5. In the Windows PowerShell window, type the following commands, pressing Enter after each command (some commands may take several minutes to execute, depending on the speed of your virtual machines):
```
New-PAMTrust -SourceForest "adatum.com"
-Credentials $ca
New-PAMDomainConfiguration -SourceDomain "adatum"
-Credentials $ca
Test-PAMTrust -SourceForest "adatum.com"
-CorpCredentials $ca
Test-PAMDomainConfiguration -SourceDomain "adatum"
-Credentials $ca
```
6. On **MEL-DC1**, log on as **adatum\administrator** with the password of **Pa$$w0rd**.
7. On **MEL-DC1**, from the Server Manager console, click **Tools > Active Directory Users and Computers.**
8. In the Active Directory Users and Computers console, right-click **Adatum.com** and choose **Delegate Control.**
9. On the Welcome to the Delegation of Control Wizard page of the Delegation of Control Wizard, click **Next.**
10. On the Users or Groups page, click **Add.**
11. On the Select Users, Computers, or Groups page, click **Locations.**
12. In the Locations dialog box, click **ADATUMADMIN.COM** and then click **OK.**
13. In the Select Users, Computers, or Groups dialog box, type **Domain Admins** and then click **OK.**
14. In the Enter Network Credentials dialog box, provide the following credentials and then click **OK:**

- Username: **adatumadmin\administrator**
- Password: **Pa$$w0rd**

15. In the Select Users, Computers, or Groups dialog box, after Domain Admins, type **Mimmonitor**, click **Check Names**, and then click **OK**.
16. On the Users or Groups page, click **Next**.
17. On the Tasks to Delegate page, select **Read All User Information**, click **Next**, and then click **Finish**.

Creating Shadow Principals in a Bastion Forest

A ***shadow principal*** is a copy of an account or group that exists in the production or source forest. By using SID History mirroring, the shadow security group in the administrative forest will have the same security identifier in the production forest.

CERTIFICATION READY
Create shadow principals in a bastion forest
Objective 4.1

When a user is added to a PAM role, MIM adds the user's shadow account to the shadow group in the administrative forest. When the user logs on, the Kerberos token includes a security identifier that matches the security identifier of the original group from the production forest.

To create a new shadow user, you will use the New-PAMUser cmdlet, where you will specify the source domain and account name. To create a shadow group, you will use the New-PAMGroup cmdlet.

CONFIGURE ACCOUNTS AND SHADOW PRINCIPALS

GET READY. To configure accounts and shadow principals, perform the following steps.

1. On **MEL-DC1**, log on as **adatumadmin\MIMAdmin** with the password of **Pa$$w0rd.**
2. In the Windows PowerShell window, create a new group named CorpAdmins by executing the following command:
```
New-ADGroup -Name CorpAdmins -GroupCategory Security
-GroupScope Global -SamAccountName CorpAdmins
```
3. In the Windows PowerShell window, create a new user named Wayne by executing the following command:
```
New-ADUser -SamAccountName Wayne -Name Wayne
$jp = ConvertTo-SecureString 'Pa$$w0rd'
-AsPlainText -Force
Set-ADAccountPassword -Identity Wayne
-NewPassword $jp
Set-ADUser -Identity Wayne -Enabled 1
-DisplayName "Wayne"
```
4. On **SYD-MIM**, execute the following commands, pressing **Enter** after each command:
```
$sj = New-PAMUser -SourceDomain adatum.com
-SourceAccountName Wayne
$jp = ConvertTo-SecureString 'Pa$$w0rd'
-asplaintext -force
Set-ADAccountPassword -identity priv.Wayne
-NewPassword $jp
Set-ADUser -identity priv.Wayne -Enabled 1
$ca = get-credential -UserName Adatum\Administrator -
Message "Adatum forest domain admin credentials"
```
5. In the dialog box, sign in by using the **Pa$$w0rd** password and then click **OK**.

6. In the Windows PowerShell window, execute the following commands:

```
$pg = New-PAMGroup -SourceGroupName "CorpAdmins" -
SourceDomain adatum.com -SourceDC mel-dc1.adatum.com -
Credentials $ca
$pr = New-PAMRole -DisplayName "CorpAdmins"
-Privileges $pg -Candidates $sj
```

7. On **SYD-DC1**, in Server Manager, click **Tools > Active Directory Users and Computers.**

8. Open the PAM Objects container and verify that the ADATUM.CorpAdmins group and PRIV.Wayne user are present, as shown in Figure 8-4.

Figure 8-4

Viewing Active Directory Users and Computers PAM objects

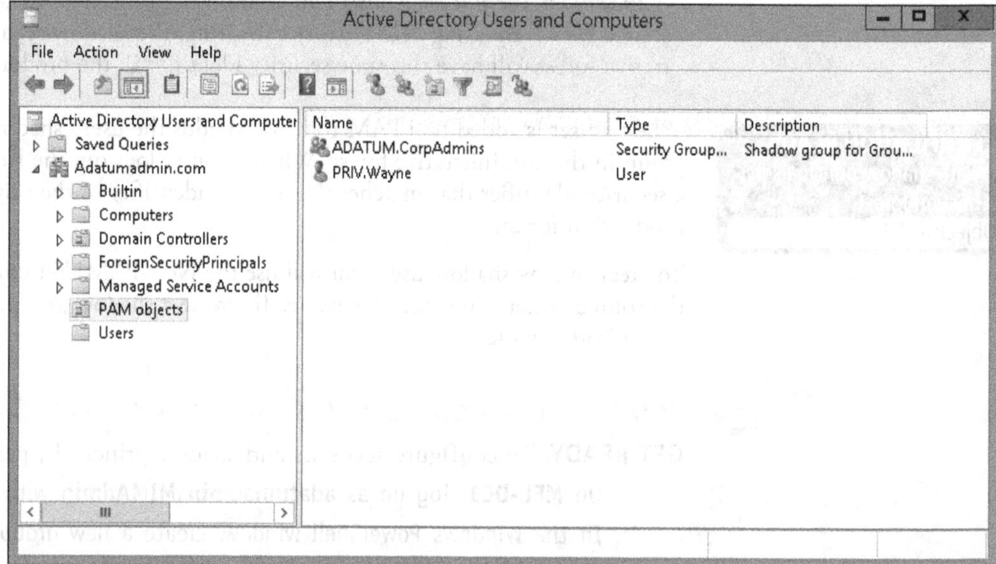

9. Return to the Windows PowerShell window and then execute the following commands:

```
Get-ADGroup -identity Adatum.corpadmins -properties
SIDHistory
Get-ADGroup -server mel-dc1.adatum.com -identity
corpadmins
```

Requesting Privileged Access and Managing PAM Roles

CERTIFICATION READY
Determine requirements and usage scenarios for Privileged Access Management (PAM) solutions
Objective 4.1

PAM allows you to manage access via ***role-based access control (RBAC)***, whereby access is based on the role a user plays in the organization. With PAM, you can assign users to privileged roles so that they can be activated as needed for just-in-time access. These roles are defined manually and established in the administrative/bastion forest, as needed by your organization.

There are many usage scenarios in which PAM can be used to control security. For example, a server might fail in the middle of the night yet the usual help desk personal might not have administrative access to the server. You could use PAM to grant access for a limited time to access the server. You can also use a password manager to store passwords for network firewalls or highly privileged servers. You can use PAM to provide limited access to the servers so that administrators can retrieve passwords.

For client users to access PAM, they will need to install the ***Identity Manager Client Add-ins and Extensions***. After the client add-in and extension is loaded, clients will be able to import the Windows PowerShell MIMPAM module, which will then allow users to make PAM requests.

CERTIFICATION READY
Request privileged access using the MIM web portal
Objective 4.1

CERTIFICATION READY
Create and implement MIM policies
Objective 4.1

CERTIFICATION READY
Implement Just-in-Time administration principals using time-based policies
Objective 4.1

CERTIFICATION READY
Request privileged access using Windows PowerShell
Objective 4.1

The PAM system requirements are:

- The management forest has to be Windows Server 2012 R2 with forest functional level set to 2012 R2
- The PAM client is supported under Windows 7, Windows 8, Windows 8.1, and Windows 10.
- PowerShell version 2.0 or higher is needed if the PowerShell cmdlets will b***e used.***

Each role contains the following parameters:

- **Display name:** The name of the PAM role.
- **PAM privileges:** A list of security groups that a user who has been granted access to the role is temporarily added to.
- **PAM role TTL (sec):** The maximum amount of time that the member can be granted this role. The default is 3600 seconds (1 hour). It is recommended that you configure the maximum lifetime for a Kerberos user ticket in line with the Time to Live (TTL) value to ensure that a user's ticket is updated to reflect the change in group membership after the PAM Role TTL expires.
- **MFA enabled:** MFA is short for Multi-Factor Authentication (which requires two more forms of authentication). MIM's PAM functionality can be integrated with Azure MFA.
- **Approval required:** Specifies that PAM roles can be configured only if a PAM administrator approves the request.
- **Availability window enabled:** Specifies the hours in which the role is available.
- **Description:** Provides a description of the PAM role.

INSTALL PAM COMPONENTS

GET READY. To install PAM components, perform the following steps.

1. On **MEL-SVR1**, log on as **adatumadmin\MIMAdmin** with the password of **Pa$$w0rd.**
2. Navigate to and double-click the **MIM2016SP1** ISO file.
3. Double-click **FIMSPlash.htm.** The Microsoft Identity Manager installation web page opens. If you are prompted to confirm that you want to run active content, click **Yes.**

4. On the Microsoft Identity Manager page, under Identity Manager Clients, Add-ins, and Extensions, click **Install Add-ins and Extensions, 64-bit.** When you are prompted to run or save the setup.exe dialog box, click **Run.**
5. On the Welcome to the Microsoft Identity Manager Add-ins and Extensions Setup Wizard page, click **Next.**
6. On the End-User License Agreement page, click **I accept the terms in the License Agreement** and then click **Next.**
7. On the MIM Customer Experience Improvement Program page, click **I don't want to join the program at this time** and then click **Next.**
8. On the Custom Setup page, click **MIM Add-in for Outlook** and then **click Entire feature will be unavailable.**
9. On the Custom Setup page, click **MIM Password and Authentication** and then click **Entire feature will be unavailable.**
10. On the Custom Setup page, click **PAM Client**, click **Entire feature will be installed on local hard drive**, and then click **Next.**
11. On the Configure MIM PAM Service Address page, configure the following settings and then click **Next:**
    - PAM Server Address: **syd-mim.adatumadmin.com**
    - Port: **5725**
12. Click **Install.** When the installation finishes, click **Finish.**
13. Right-click the **Start** button and choose **Computer Management.**
14. In the Computer Management console, expand **Local Users and Groups**, click **Groups**, and then double-click the **Administrators** group.
15. In the Administrators Properties dialog box, click **Add.**
16. In the Select Users, Computers, Service Accounts, or Groups dialog box, type **adatumadmin\adatum.corpadmins** (as shown in Figure 8-5) and then click **Check Names.**

Figure 8-5

Specifying a remote domain group

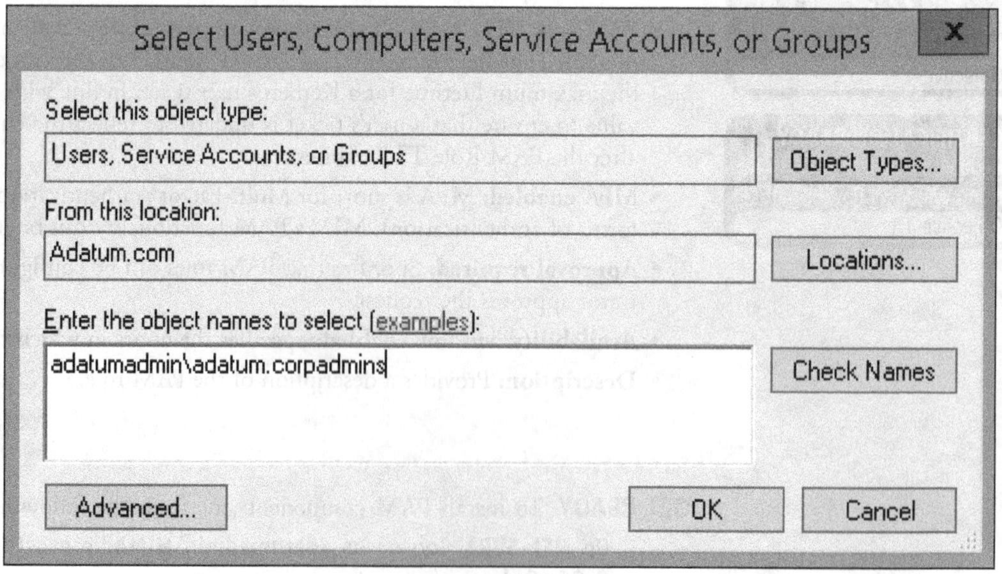

17. Type the credentials **adatumadmin\administrator** and the password **Pa$$w0rd** and click **OK** three times.
18. Right-click **Start**, choose **Shut Down or Sign Out**, click **Restart**, and then click **Continue.**

REQUEST AND VERIFY PRIVILEGED ACCESS

GET READY. To request and verify privileged access, perform the following steps.

1. Log on to **MEL-SVR1** as **adatum\Wayne** with the **Pa$$w0rd** password.
2. On **MEL-SVR1**, on the Taskbar, click **Windows PowerShell**. In the Windows PowerShell window, execute the following command:
   ```
   Whoami /groups
   ```
3. Verify that the Wayne account is not a member of the CorpAdmins group.
4. On the Taskbar, click **Server Manager**.
5. Click **Manage > Add Roles and Features**.
6. On the Before you begin page, click **Next** four times.
7. On the Select Features page, click **WINS Server**. When you are prompted to confirm that you want to add features, click the **Add Features** button.
8. Click **Next** and then click **Install**.
9. Review the message that informs you that you do not have adequate user rights to make changes to the target computer and then click **Close**.
10. Right-click the **Start** button, choose **Shut down or sign out**, and then click **Sign out**.
11. Log on to **MEL-SVR1** as **adatumadmin\priv.Wayne** with the **Pa$$w0rd** password.
12. On the Taskbar, click **Windows PowerShell**.
13. In the Windows PowerShell window, execute the following command:
    ```
    Whoami /groups
    ```
14. Verify that the account is not a member of the CorpAdmins group.
15. On the Taskbar, click **Server Manager**.
16. Click **Manage > Add Roles and Features**.
17. On the Before you begin page, click **Next** four times.
18. On the Select Features page, click **WINS Server**. When you are prompted to confirm that you want to add features, click the **Add Features** button.
19. Click **Next** and then click **Install**.
20. Review the message that informs you that you do not have adequate user rights to make changes to the target computer and then click **Close**.
21. To list the roles for which the priv.Wayne account can apply and the TTL for the role listed, execute the following commands:
    ```
    Import-Module MIMPAM
    Get-PAMRoleForRequest
    ```
22. In the Windows PowerShell window, execute the following command:
    ```
    New-PamRequest -RoleDisplayName CorpAdmins
    ```

TAKE NOTE* The Request Status is set to Processing, as shown in Figure 8-6.

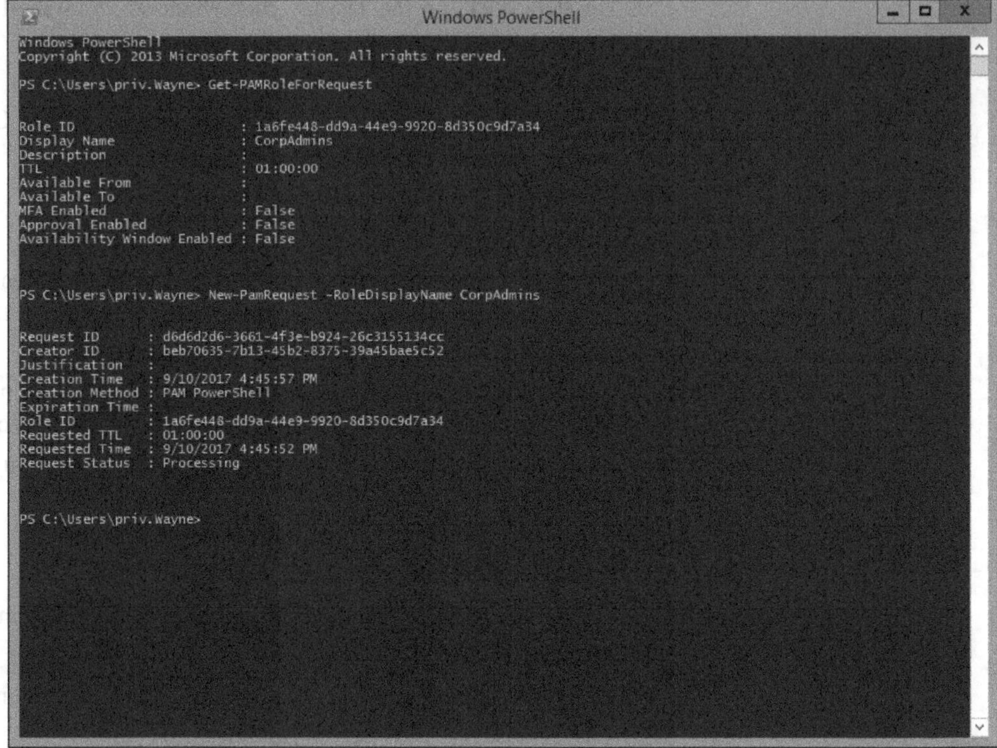

Figure 8-6
Performing a PAM request

23. Right-click the **Start** button, choose **Shut down or sign out**, and then click **Sign out.**
24. Log on to **MEL-SVR1** as **adatumadmin\priv.Wayne** with the **Pa$$w0rd** password.
25. On the Taskbar, click **Windows PowerShell.** In the Windows PowerShell window, execute the following command:

    ```
    Whoami /groups
    ```
26. Verify that the account is a member of the CorpAdmins group.
27. On the Taskbar, click **Server Manager.**
28. Click **Manager > Add Roles and Features.**
29. On the Before you begin page, click **Next** four times.
30. On the Select Features page, click **WINS Server.** When you are prompted to confirm that you want to add features, click the **Add Features** button.
31. Click **Next** and then click **Install.**
32. When the feature installs, click **Close.**

You can use the web portal to modify the PAM Role TTL and add users to a PAM role. Under the Requests & Approval section, you can view and approve requests.

MANAGE PAM

GET READY. To manage PAM, perform the following steps.

1. On **MEL-DC1**, make sure you are logged on as **adatum\administrator**.
2. To create a new user named Gavin that you will enable for PAM, in the Windows PowerShell window, type the following commands, pressing **Enter** after each command:

```
New-ADUser -SamAccountName Gavin -Name Gavin
$jp = ConvertTo-SecureString 'Pa$$w0rd'
-AsPlainText -Force
Set-ADAccountPassword -Identity Gavin
-NewPassword $jp
Set-ADUser -Identity Gavin -Enabled 1
-DisplayName "Gavin"
```

3. On **SYD-MIM**, ensure that you are signed in as **adatumadmin\MIMAdmin.**
4. In the Windows PowerShell window, type the following commands, pressing **Enter** after each command:

```
$sj = New-PAMUser -SourceDomain adatum.com
-SourceAccountName Gavin
$jp = ConvertTo-SecureString 'Pa$$w0rd'
-AsPlainText -force
Set-ADAccountPassword -Identity priv.Gavin
-NewPassword $jp
Set-ADUser -Identity priv.Gavin -Enabled 1
```

5. Launch **Internet Explorer** and go to **http://syd-mim.adatumadmin.com:82/IdentityManagement/default.aspx.** After a few minutes, the web page opens, as shown in Figure 8-7. If prompted, sign in as **adatumadmin\Mimadmin** with the **Pa$$w0rd** password.

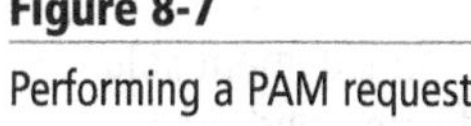

Figure 8-7

Performing a PAM request

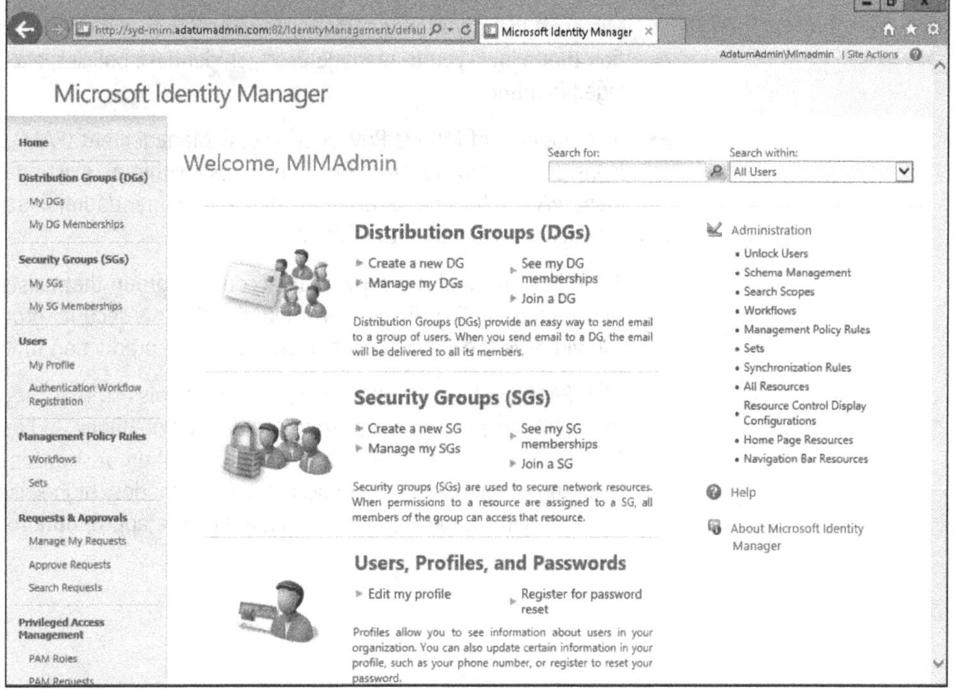

6. In the Microsoft Identity Manager console, under Privileged Access Management, click **PAM Roles.**
7. In the list of Privileged Access Management roles, click **CorpAdmins**.
8. In the General tab of the Corpadmins dialog box, change the PAM Role TTL(sec) from 3600 to **600**, click **OK**, and then click **Submit.**
9. In the list of Privileged Access Management roles, click **Corpadmins**.
10. On the Candidates tab of the Corpadmins dialog box, click **Browse.**
11. In the Select Users dialog box, click the magnifying glass next to Search. Wayne and Adatum.Wayne should already be selected. Select **ADATUM.Gavin** and **Gavin** and then click **OK.**
12. Click **OK** and then click **Submit** to close the CorpAdmins dialog box.
13. In Internet Explorer, on the Microsoft Identity Manager web page, under Privileged Access Management, click **PAM Requests.**
14. Review PAM Requests.
15. Click **PRIV.Wayne** and review the details of when the request was made, when the request expires, and the role requested.

SKILL SUMMARY

IN THIS LESSON YOU LEARNED:

- Enhanced Security Administrative Environment (ESAE) uses administrative forests combined with recommended practices to provide an administrative environment and workstations with enhanced security protection that will minimize exposure of administrative credentials.
- An ESAE forest is a special Active Directory forest/bastion forest that is separate from the production Active Directory Domain Services forest that hosts privileged accounts. Since the ESAE is a separate forest, you can apply stronger security policies to reduce the possibility of an account being compromised.
- Microsoft Identity Manager (MIM) is an on-premise identity and access management solution that allows you to manage users, credentials, policies, access, certificates, and privileged identities.
- A component of MIM is Privileged Access Management (PAM), which is a solution that helps organizations restrict privilege access within an existing Active Directory environment. PAM will use a separate bastion environment/administrative forest to manage the production Active Directory forest.
- A shadow principal is a copy of an account or group that exists in the production or source forest. By using SID History mirroring, the shadow security group in the administrative forest will have the same security identifier in the production forest.
- With PAM, you can assign users to privileged roles so that they can be activated as needed for just-in-time access. These roles are defined manually and established in the administrative/bastion forest, as needed by your organization. Just-in-time (JIT) automates the provisioning of temporary admin access using a shadow high security admin forest. As a user needs administrative access, you just assign the appropriate role to the user.

■ Knowledge Assessment

Multiple Choice

1. Which of the following are advantages offered by an ESAE forest? (Choose all answers that apply)
   a. Simple way to improve security
   b. Locked-down accounts
   c. Selective authentication
   d. Firewalled forest
2. Which of the following specifies that all security dependencies are as trustworthy as the items being secured?
   a. Selective principal
   b. Shadow principal
   c. Target principal
   d. Source principal
3. How many domains should an ESAE forest have?
   a. one domain
   b. two or more domains
   c. One domain for each global group
   d. One domain for each PAM server
4. Which of the following tools helps organizations restrict privilege access within an existing Active Directory environment?
   a. SharePoint
   b. ESAE
   c. IPAM
   d. MIM
5. Which MIM component helps organizations restrict privilege access within an existing Active Directory environment?
   a. BHOLD Suite
   b. Privilege Access Management
   c. Password Change Portal
   d. Synchronization Service
6. To use PAM, you must create a trust between a production forest and which of the following?
   a. A shadow forest
   b. A bastion forest
   c. A backward compatibility forest
   d. An authoritative forest

7. Which cmdlet is used to create a trust relationship of the PAM forest and the production forest?
   a. New-PAMTrust
   b. New-PAMDomainConfiguration
   c. New-Forest-Trust
   d. New-ADTrust
8. Which of the following is a copy of an account or group that exists in the production or source forest?
   a. PAM role
   b. Replicated principal
   c. Shadow principal
   d. Secure principal
9. Which of the following is used for the client to make PAM role requests? (Choose two answers)
   a. MFA
   b. MIM Service web site
   c. Active Directory Domains and Trusts console
   d. PowerShell modules from Identity Manager Client Add-ins and Extensions
10. Which Windows PowerShell cmdlet is used to list the current role requests?
   a. Get-PAMDomainConfiguration
   b. Test-PAMTrust
   c. Get-PamRoleForRequest
   d. Get-RoleRequests
   e.

Best Answer

Choose the letter that corresponds to the best answer. More than one answer choice may achieve the goal. Select the BEST answer.

1. Which of the following is a special Active Directory forest that is separate from the production Active Directory Domain Services forest that hosts privileged accounts?
   a. ESAE forest
   b. A firewalled forest
   c. RBAC forest
   d. Shadow forest

Build List

1. Specify the correct order of steps necessary to install and configure the Microsoft Identity Manager Service and Web Portal.

_____ Double-click the FIMSplash.htm.

_____ Select the desired features including the Privileged Access.

_____ Specify database settings.

_____ Accept the license agreement.

_____ Configure the certificates.

_____ Specify URL to SharePoint site collection.

_____ Select Install Service and Portal link.

_____ Specify MIM synchronization service accounts.

_____ Specify the Privilege Access Management Monitoring Service accounts.

_____ Specify the PAM Component service accounts.

2. Specify the correct order of steps necessary to install the Identity Manager Client Add-ins and Extension.

_____ Double-click the FIMSplash.htm.

_____ Accept the license agreements.

_____ Specify the MIM PAM Service Address settings.

_____ Click Install Add-ins and Extensions, 64-bit.

_____ Click Install.

_____ Make sure the PAM client is selected and then click Next.

Business Case Scenarios

Scenario 8-1: Granting Temporary Access

You are an administrator for the Adatum Corporation. On occasion, help desk personnel need temporary access to several key servers. You want to provide the temporary access as needed yet have it automatically revoked after one hour. Describe your recommended solution.

Scenario 8-2: Managing Your Domain Securely

You are developing new security procedures that will help secure your domain. You want to minimize the effect of a domain account being compromised as well as the impact of malware being executed on the domain. Describe your recommended solution.

LESSON 9

Implementing Just-Enough-Administration (JEA)

70-744 EXAM OBJECTIVE

Objective 4.2 – Implement Just-Enough-Administration (JEA). This objective may include but is not limited to: Enable a JEA solution on Windows Server 2016; create and configure session configuration files; create and configure role capability files; create a JEA endpoint; connect to a JEA endpoint on a server for administration; view logs; download WMF 5.1 to a Windows Server 2008 R2; configure a JEA endpoint on a server using Desired State Configuration (DSC).

LESSON HEADING	EXAM OBJECTIVE
Implementing Just-Enough-Administration (JEA)	Enable a JEA solution on Windows Server 2016
• Creating and Configuring Role Capability Files	Create and configure role capability files
• Creating and Configuring Session-Configuration Files	Create and configure session-configuration files
• Creating and Connecting to a JEA Endpoint	Create a JEA endpoint
• Configuring a JEA Endpoint on a Server Using Designed State Configuration (DSC)	Connect to a JEA endpoint on a server for administration
• Viewing JEA Logs	Configure a JEA endpoint on a server using Desired State Configuration (DSC)
• Downloading and Installing WMF 5.1 to Windows Server 2008 R2	View logs
	Download WMF 5.1 to a Windows Server 2008 R2

KEY TERMS

JEA endpoint
Just-Enough-Administration (JEA)
role-capability files
session-configuration file
virtual account
Windows Management Framework (WFM)
Windows PowerShell Desired State Configuration (DSC)

■ Implementing Just-Enough-Administration (JEA)

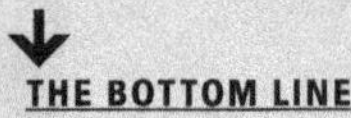

Just-Enough-Administration (JEA) provides role-based access control (RBAC) functionality built on Windows PowerShell remoting, which allows one computer to perform activities on another computer. Rather than giving someone full access to a system, you can specify who is authorized to connect to the system and which Windows PowerShell cmdlets, parameters, and values they can use. You can also specify which scripts and commands they can execute.

CERTIFICATION READY
Enable a JEA solution on Windows Server 2016
Objective 4.2

Virtual accounts—which were discussed in the 70-742 course—are accounts that emulate a Network Service account that has the name NT Service\servicename. The virtual account can simplify service administration, including automatic password management and basic SPN management.

When connecting to an endpoint, JEA allows tasks to be performed by using a special, privileged virtual account rather than the user's account. By using virtual accounts:

- The user's credentials are not stored on the remote system. Therefore, if the remote system is compromised, the user's credentials cannot be stolen from the system and cannot be used to access other resources.
- The user account does not need to be a privileged account. Instead, the endpoint system only needs to be configured to allow connections from specified user accounts.
- The virtual account is limited to the system on which it is hosted, which means that if the account is compromised, it cannot be used to access other protected servers.
- While the virtual account has local administrator privileges, it is still limited by performing the activities defined by JEA.

TAKE NOTE* JEA only works with Windows PowerShell sessions. Therefore, JEA requires that administrative tasks be performed from the command line.

JEA works on Windows Server 2016 and Windows 10, version 1511 or later. If the Windows Management Framework (WFM) 5.0 or 5.1 is installed on the system, JEA will also work with Windows 8, Windows 8.1, Windows Server 2012, and Windows Server 2012 R2. Since Windows Server 2008 R2 and Windows 7 does not support virtual accounts, all activity is performed by using an account that might need to be added to the appropriate security group.

When you configure JEA, you configure JEA role with precise cmdlets, parameters, aliases, and values that are needed to perform administrative tasks, which makes it ideal for routine administrative or configuration tasks, such as restarting a computer or service. Unfortunately, JEA is less suitable for tasks where the problem, solution, or set of tasks are not clearly defined.

Creating and Configuring Role Capability Files

CERTIFICATION READY
Create and configure role capability files
Objective 4.2

Role-capability files allow you to define JEA roles, including what the role can do in a Windows PowerShell session. The JEA role is based on the name of the role capability file, which has a .psrc filename extension. For example, if the file is named DNSOps.psrc, you are defining what the JEA DNSOps role can do in the session. After you define the JEA roles (one role for each role-capability file), you will reference roles in the session-configuration file. If it is not specified in the role-capability or session-configuration file, the action is not allowed.

To create a new, blank role-capability file, use the Windows PowerShell New-PSRoleCapabilityFile cmdlet. After the file is created, you then edit the file by adding cmdlets, functions, and external commands as necessary. You can allow entire Windows PowerShell cmdlets or functions or you can list which parameters and parameter values can be used.

File-capability files allow you to add the following capabilities:

- **ModulesToImport:** Allows you to specify custom modules to import. JEA should auto-load any standard modules already present on the computer, although you can manually add them here if necessary.
- **VisibleAliases:** Lists which aliases to make available in the JEA session.
- **VisibleCmdlets:** Lists which Windows PowerShell cmdlets are available in the session. You can choose to list cmdlets, allowing all parameters and parameter values to be used, or you can limit cmdlets to specific parameters and parameter values.
- **VisibleFunctions:** Lists which Windows PowerShell functions are available in the session. You can choose to list functions, allowing all parameters and parameter values to be used, or you can limit functions to specific parameters and parameter values.
- **VisibleExternalCommands:** Allows users who are connected to the session to run external commands, such as c:\windows\system32\whoami or c:\windows\system32\ipconfig.
- **VisibleProviders:** Lists Windows PowerShell providers that are visible to the session.
- **ScriptsToProcess:** Allows you to configure Windows PowerShell scripts to run automatically when the session is started.
- **AliasDefinitions:** Allows you to define Windows PowerShell aliases for the JEA session.
- **FunctionDefinitions:** Allows you to define Windows PowerShell functions for the JEA session.
- **VariableDefinitions:** Allows you to define Windows PowerShell variables for the JEA session.
- **EnvironmentVariables:** Allows you to specify environment variables for the JEA session.
- **TypesToProcess:** Allows you to configure Windows PowerShell-type files to load for the JEA session.
- **FormatsToProcess:** Allows you to configure Windows PowerShell formats to load for the JEA session.
- **AssembliesToLoad:** Allows you to specify which assemblies to load for the JEA session.

For example, to use the Restart-Service cmdlet, add the following line in the role-capability file:

```
VisibleCmdlets = 'Restart-Service'
```

If you want to limit the Restart-Service cmdlet to be used only to restart the DNS service, add the following line:

```
VisibleCmdlets = @{ Name = 'Restart-Service'; Parameters = @{
Name='Name'; ValidateSet = 'DNS'}}
```

If you want to allow the whoami.exe command to be used, configure the VisibleExternalCommands options by adding the following line:

```
VisibleExternalCommands = 'C:\Windows\System32\whoami.exe'
```

CREATE AND CONFIGURE A ROLE CAPABILITY FILE

GET READY. To create and configure a role capability file, perform the following steps.

1. Log on to **LON-SVR1** as **adatum\administrator** with the password of **Pa$$w0rd**.
2. On **LON-SVR1**, click the **Start** button and then click **Windows PowerShell ISE**.
3. In the Windows PowerShell pane, execute the following commands:

```
Cd 'c:\Program Files\WindowsPowerShell\Modules'
Mkdir DNSOps
Cd DNSOps
New-ModuleManifest .\DNSOps.psd1
Mkdir RoleCapabilities
Cd RoleCapabilities
    New-PSRoleCapabilityFile -Path .\DNSOps.psrc
Ise DNSOps.psrc
```

4. In the DNSOps.psrc script pane of the Windows PowerShell ISE (as shown in Figure 9-1), navigate to and place the cursor under the line that starts with # VisibleCmdlets = and then type the following:

```
VisibleCmdlets = @{ Name = 'Restart-Service'; Parameters
= @{ Name='Name'; ValidateSet = 'DNS'}}
```

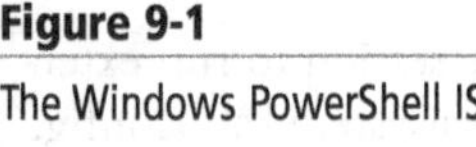

Figure 9-1

The Windows PowerShell ISE

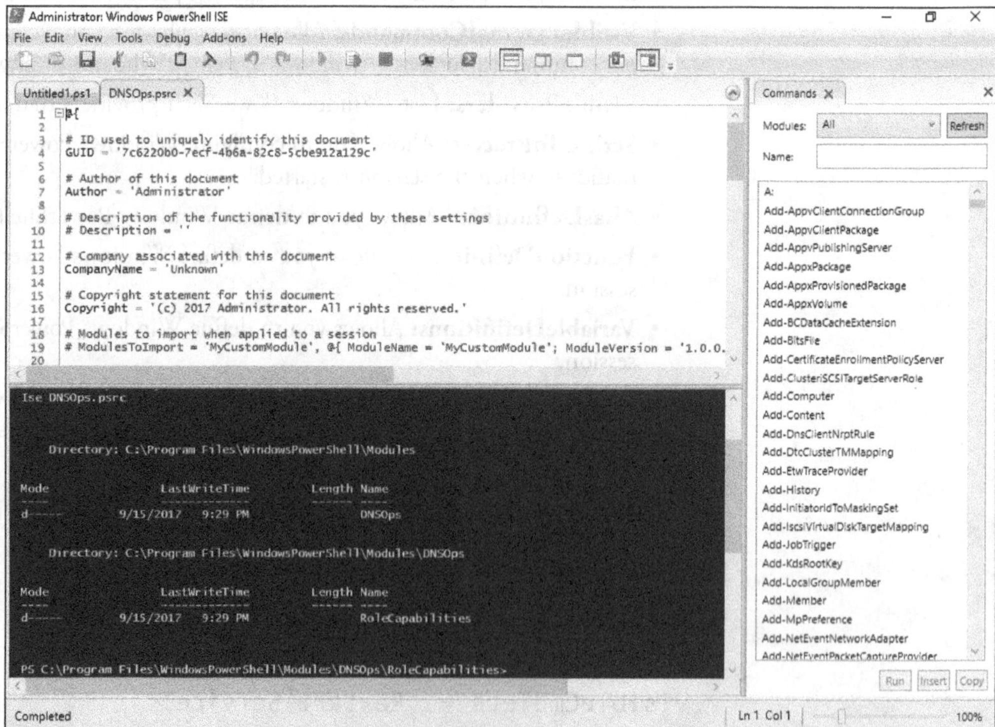

5. Navigate to and place the cursor under the line that starts with # VisibleFunctions = and then type the following:

```
VisibleFunctions = 'Add-DNSServerResourceRecord',
'Clear-DNSServerCache', 'Get-DNSServerCache', 'Get-
DNSServerResourceRecord','Remove-DNSServerResourceRecord'
```

6. Navigate to and place the cursor under the line that starts with # VisibleExternal-Commands = and then type the following:

```
VisibleExternalCommands = 'C:\Windows\System32\whoami.exe'
```

7. Click **File > Save As.** In the File name text box, type **\\LON-DC1\Software\DNSOps.psd1** and then press **Enter.** Click **Save.**

Creating and Configuring Session-Configuration Files

A ***session-configuration file is*** a special type of file that specifies what can be done in a JEA session. It will map the JEA roles to users or a group. If a cmdlet, parameter, parameter value, alias, external script, or executable is not listed in a session-configuration file, it cannot be used in a JEA session with that session-configuration file.

CERTIFICATION READY
Create and configure session-configuration files
Objective 4.2

To create a new session-configuration file, use the New-PSSessionConfigurationFile cmdlet. The session-configuration file will have a .pscc file name extension.

- **SessionType:** Configures the session's default settings. If it's SessionType= RestrictedRemoteServer, you can use the Get-Command, Get-FormatData, Select-Object, Get-Help, Measure-Object, Exit-PSSession, Clear-Host, and Out-Default cmdlets. No PowerShell providers are available, nor are any external programs (executables, scripts, and so on.). The session-execution policy will be set to RemoteSigned, which means that all downloaded scripts must be signed by a trusted publisher before they can be run, assuming you can run scripts.
- **RoleDefinitions:** Maps users (users or groups) to roles. For example, you can assign the adatum\DNSOps to the JEA DNSOps role by using:

```
RoleDefinitions =@{'Adatum\DNSOps' = @
{RoleCapabilities='DNSOps'}}
```

- **RunAsVirtualAccount:** Allows JEA to use a privileged virtual account created just for the JEA session.
- **TranscriptDirectory:** Specifies the location where JEA activity transcripts are stored.
- **RunAsVirtualAccountGroups:** Specifies the groups of which the virtual account is a member if you do not want the virtual account to be a member of the local Administrators group (or Domain Admins on a domain controller).

CREATE AND CONFIGURE A SESSION-CONFIGURATION FILE

GET READY. To create and configure a session-configuration file, perform the following steps.

1. On **LON-SVR1**, click the **Start** button and then click **Windows PowerShell ISE.**
2. In the Windows PowerShell pane of the Windows PowerShell ISE, execute the following commands:

```
New-PSSessionConfigurationFile -Path .\DNSOps.pssc -Full
Ise DNSOps.pssc
```

3. In the DNSOps.pssc script pane of the Windows PowerShell ISE, navigate to SessionType = 'Default' and change it to:

```
SessionType = 'RestrictedRemoteServer'
```

4. Navigate to #RunAsVirtualAccount = $true and remove the # so that the line is RunAsVirtualAccount = $true.
5. Navigate to # RoleDefinitions, place the cursor under this line, and then type the following:
```
RoleDefinitions = @{ 'ADATUM\DNSOps' = @{ RoleCapabilities = 'DNSOps' };}
```
6. Click **Save.**

Creating and Connecting to a JEA Endpoint

CERTIFICATION READY
Create a JEA endpoint
Objective 4.2

CERTIFICATION READY
Connect to a JEA endpoint on a server for administration
Objective 4.2

A ***JEA endpoint*** is a Windows PowerShell endpoint that is configured so that only specified authenticated users can connect to the endpoint and execute the allowed Windows PowerShell cmdlets, parameters, and values. You can create multiple JEA endpoints based on the tasks that need to be done. For example, you can create a DNSOps endpoint to perform DNS administrative tasks and a DHCPOps endpoint to perform DHCP administrative tasks without being a member of the local administrators or domain administrators group.

To create a JEA endpoint, you will use the Register-PSSessionConfiguration cmdlet, in which you specify an endpoint name and a session-configuration file hosted on the local machine. For example, to create the endpoint DNSOps using the DNSOps.pssc session-configuration file, execute the following command:

```
Register-PSSessionConfiguration -Name DNSOps -Path DNSOps.pssc
```

CREATE AND CONNECT TO A JEA ENDPOINT

GET READY. To create and connect to a JEA endpoint, perform the following steps.

1. On **LON-SVR1**, click the **Start** button and then click **Windows PowerShell ISE.**
2. In the Windows PowerShell pane of the Windows PowerShell ISE, execute the following commands:
```
Register-PSSessionConfiguration -Name DNSOps -Path \\LON-DC1\Software\DNSOps.pssc
Restart-Service WinRM
Get-PSSessionConfiguration
```
3. Verify that DNSOps is listed as a Windows PowerShell endpoint, as shown in Figure 9-2.

Figure 9-2

The JEA endpoint

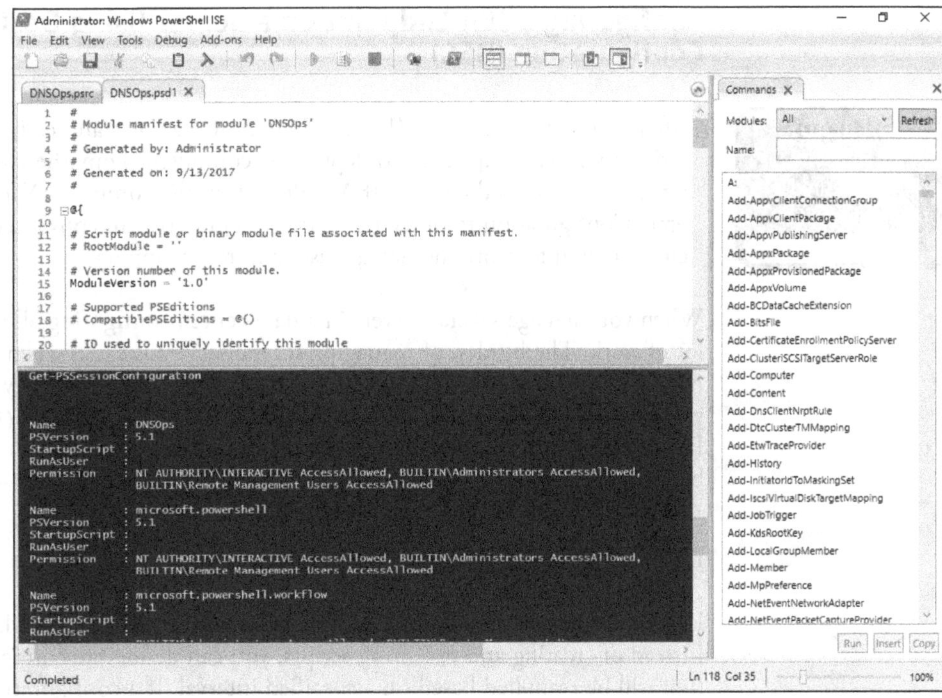

4. Click **Start** and then click **Windows PowerShell**.
5. In the Windows PowerShell window, execute the following commands:

```
Enter-PSSession -ComputerName LON-DC1
(get-command).count
Whoami
Exit-PSSession
```

6. Log off **LON-SVR1**.
7. Log on to **LON-SVR1** as **adatum\beth** with the password of **Pa55w.rd**.
8. Click **Start** and then click **Windows PowerShell**.
9. In the Windows PowerShell window, execute the following commands. Press **Y** to confirm when necessary:

```
Enter-PSSession -ComputerName LON-DC1
-ConfigurationName DNSOps
(Get-Command).count
Whoami
Get-DNSServerResourceRecord -ZoneName Adatum.com
Add-DNSServerResourceRecord -ZoneName "Adatum.com" -A
-Name "MEL-SVR1" -IPv4Address "172.16.0.101"
Add-DNSServerResourceRecord -ZoneName "Adatum.com" -A
-Name "MEL-SVR2" -IPv4Address "172.16.0.102"
Get-DNSServerResourceRecord -ZoneName Adatum.com
Remove-DNSServerResourceRecord -ZoneName "Adatum.com"
-RRTYPE "A" -Name "MEL-SVR2" -Confirm
Get-DNSServerResourceRecord -ZoneName Adatum.com
Get-DNSServerCache
Clear-DNSServerCache
Get-DNSServerCache
Get-Service
Restart-Service DNS
Restart-Service WinRM
```

Configuring a JEA Endpoint on a Server Using Desired State Configuration (DSC)

CERTIFICATION READY
Configure a JEA endpoint on a server using Desired State Configuration (DSC)
Objective 4.2

After you have tested your JEA configuration files, you are ready to deploy the configuration to other computers. To deploy the computers, copy the configuration files to the target computer and create a JEA endpoint on the computer. You can use the JEA Desired State Configuration resource to centrally deploy JEA to computers in your organization, enabling you to centrally manage user and role mapping.

When you manage several servers in a data center, configuring all of those servers requires a lot of work. The burden of managing several servers is eased when those servers share a common configuration. To reduce the time necessary to configure all your data center servers, you can use ***Windows PowerShell Desired State Configuration (DSC)***, which is a Windows PowerShell management platform that is used to configure system, role, and feature settings based on your declared configuration.

TAKE NOTE* DSC was discussed in the 70-740 course.

DSC is an extension of Windows PowerShell and the Windows Management Framework. Instead of creating and executing scripts, you can define the configuration and the configuration will be reapplied based on a specified interval. If a configuration on a system has drifted, it will correct the configuration drift. DSC can be deployed in centralized and decentralized environments and the systems do not have to belong to an Active Directory domain. It can also be used to manage any operating system with an OMI-compliant Common Information Model (CIM) server, such as CentOS, or other varieties of Linux.

Although you can deploy the same JEA configuration to different computers in your organization, it is likely that each computer serves a different purpose and therefore might need a unique JEA configuration. It might also be that you will need to configure separate session-configuration files even if you use the same role-capability file. For example, you might create a role-capability file that allows management of DNS but configure separate session-configuration files for each DNS server because you want to allow different user groups to perform DNS administration tasks.

TAKE NOTE* Although DSC takes some time and effort to establish, its benefits can be realized when you administer hundreds of systems (virtual or physical) for which you need to maintain the system configuration.

The following syntax shows a sample DSC configuration, which uses JEA configuration files stored in the \\LON_DC1\Software folder:

```
Configuration JEAMaintenance
{
Import-DscResource -Module JustEnoughAdministration,
PSDesiredStateConfiguration

    File MaintenanceModule
    {
        SourcePath = "\\LON-DC1\Software"
        DestinationPath = "C:\Program Files\WindowsPowerShell\
Modules\AdatumMaintenance"
        Checksum = "SHA-256"
        Ensure = "Present"
        Type = "Directory"
        Recurse = $true
    }

    JeaEndpoint JEAMaintenanceEndpoint
    {
        EndpointName = "JEAMaintenance"
RoleDefinitions = "@{ 'ADATUM\DNSOps' = @{ RoleCapabilities =
DNSOps' }; }"
        TranscriptDirectory = 'C:\ProgramData\
JEAConfiguration\Transcripts'
        DependsOn = '[File]MaintenanceModule'
    }
}
```

Viewing JEA Logs

CERTIFICATION READY
View logs
Objective 4.2

The JEA logs can be found in Event Viewer, specifically in Applications and Services Logs\Microsoft\Windows\PowerShell\Operational. However, to see these log events, you have to turn on the Windows PowerShell\Operational logging.

To turn on the necessary Windows PowerShell logging, you must enable the following settings:

- **Turn on Module Logging:** Turns on logging for Windows PowerShell modules.
- **Turn on PowerShell Script Block Logging:** Enables logging of all PowerShell script input.
- **Turn on PowerShell Transcription:** Captures the input and output of Windows PowerShell commands into text-based transcripts.

ENABLE POWERSHELL MODULE AND SCRIPT BLOCK LOGGING

GET READY. To enable PowerShell Module and Script Block Logging, perform the following steps.

1. On **LON-DC1**, log on as **adatum\administrator** with the password of **Pa$$w0rd.**
2. In Server Manager, click **Tools > Group Policy Management.**
3. Navigate to and right-click the **Default Domain Policy** and choose **Edit.**
4. Navigate to **Computer Configuration\Policies\Administrative Templates\Windows Components\Windows PowerShell**, as shown in Figure 9-3.

Figure 9-3

Viewing the Windows PowerShell GPO settings

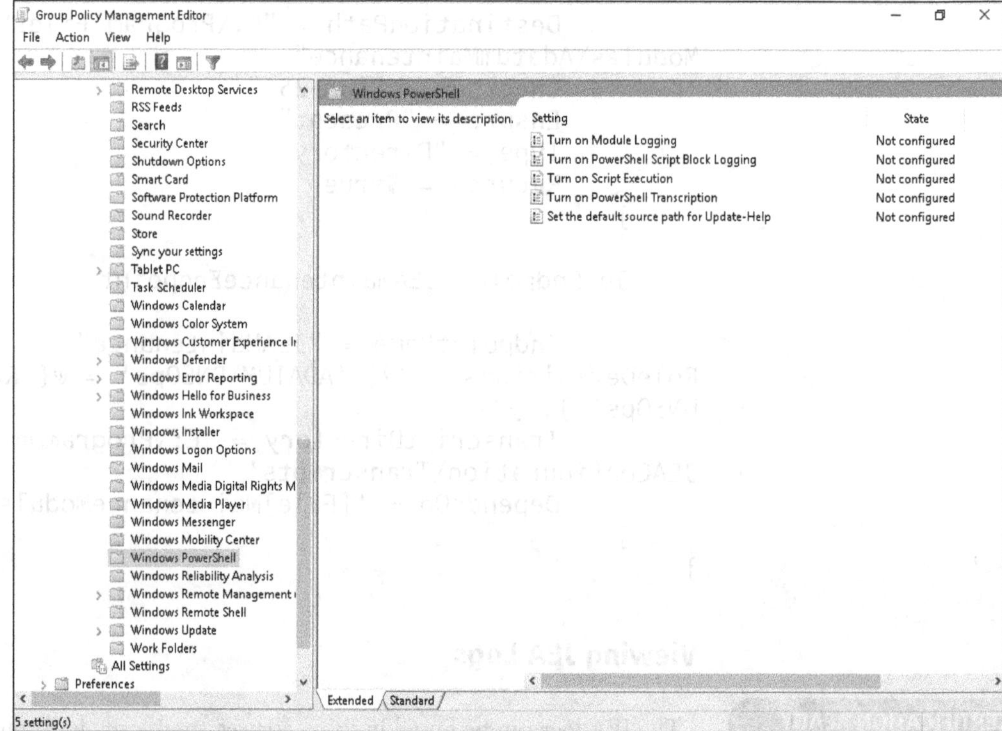

5. Double click **Turn on Module Logging.**
6. Click **Enabled.**
7. In the Turn on Module Logging dialog box, in the Options section, next to Module Names, click **Show.**
8. To log commands for all modules, type * in the pop up window and then press **Enter.**
9. Click **OK** to close the Show Contents dialog box.
10. Click **OK** to set the policy and to close the Turn on Module Logging dialog box.
11. Double click **Turn on PowerShell Script Block Logging.**
12. In the Turn on PowerShell Script Block Logging dialog box, click **Enabled.**
13. Click **OK** to close the Turn on PowerShell Script Block Logging dialog box.
14. Double-click **Turn on PowerShell Transcription.**
15. In the Turn on PowerShell Transcription dialog box, select the **Enabled** option.
16. In the Transcript output directory text box, type a path to a folder, such as **C:\Temp.**

17. Click **OK** to close the Turn on PowerShell Transcription dialog box.
18. Close the Group Policy Management Editor and Group Policy Management console.

After logging has been turned on, the 4103 event shows the events being shown (see Figure 9-4). The parameters include:

- **CommandInvocation:** The command the user ran.
- **ParameterBinding:** Any options that were included with that command.
- **User:** The temporary identity (virtual account) used by JEA during that session.
- **ConnectedUser:** The non-privileged account that connected to the JEA endpoint and ran the command.

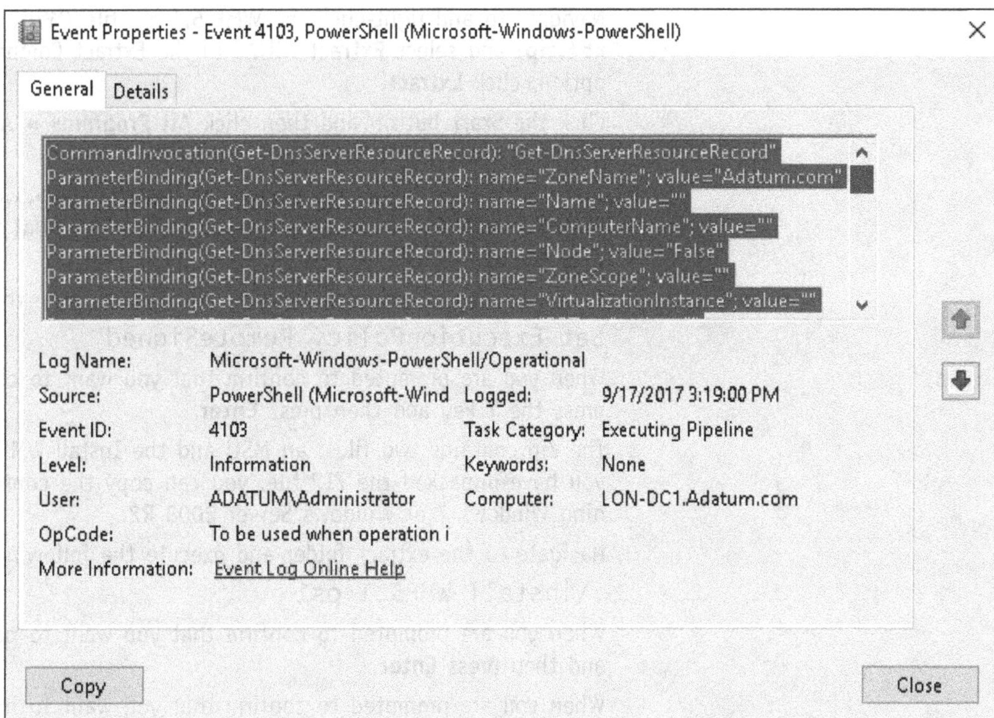

Figure 9-4
Logging remote PowerShell commands in Event Viewer

Downloading and Installing WMF 5.1 to Windows Server 2008 R2

CERTIFICATION READY
Download WMF 5.1 to a Windows Server 2008 R2
Objective 4.2

Windows Management Framework (WFM) is the delivery mechanism that provides a consistent management interface across Windows. Earlier versions of Windows did not include WMF. If you want to use JEA, you must search for and download WMF 5.1 from the Microsoft website. WMF 5.1 requires .NET Framework 4.5.2 or higher, which also has to be downloaded and installed.

WMF 5.1 includes the PowerShell, WMI, WinRM, and Software Inventory Logging (SIL) components that were released with Windows Server 2016. It also includes installing the JEA modules.

INSTALL WMF 5.1 ON WINDOWS SERVER 2008 R2 WITH SP1

GET READY. To install WMF 5.1 on a system running Windows Server 2008 R2 with SP1 or higher, perform the following steps.

1. On a server running Windows Server 2008 R2 with SP1 (or higher), log on as **adatum\administrator** with the password of **Pa$$w0rd.**
2. Navigate to and double-click the .NET Framework 4.5.2 (**NDP452-KB2901907-x886-x64-AllOS-ENU**) file. If you are prompted to confirm that you want to run this file, click **Run.**
3. After the files are extracted, on the .NET Framework 4.5.2 Setup page, select **I have read and accept the license terms** and then click **Install.**
4. After the installation is complete, click **Finish.**
5. Navigate to and right-click the WMF 5.1 zip file (**Win7AndW2K8R2-KB3191566-x64.zip**) and select **Extract All....** In the Extract Compressed (Zipped) Folders option, click **Extract.**
6. Click the **Start** button and then click **All Programs > Administrative Tools > Windows PowerShell Modules.**
7. In the extracted folder, right-click the **Install-WMF5.1.PS1** file and choose **Run with PowerShell.** If you are prompted to confirm that you want to open this file, click **Open.**
8. In the Windows PowerShell Modules window, execute the following command:

   ```
   Set-ExecutionPolicy RemoteSigned
   ```

   When you are prompted to confirm that you want to change the execution policy, press the **Y** key and then press **Enter.**
9. The Zip contains two files: an MSU and the Install-WMF5.1.PS1 script file. Once you have unpacked the ZIP file, you can copy the contents to any machine running Windows 7 or Windows Server 2008 R2.
10. Navigate to the extract folder and execute the following command:

    ```
    .\install-WMF5.1.ps1
    ```

    When you are prompted to confirm that you want to run this software, press **R** and then press **Enter.**
11. When you are prompted to confirm that you want to install the update, click **Yes.**
12. On the Read these license terms page, click **I Accept.**
13. When the installation is complete, click **Restart Now.**

SKILL SUMMARY

IN THIS LESSON YOU LEARNED:

- Just-Enough-Administration (JEA) provides RBAC functionality built on Windows PowerShell remoting, which allows one computer to perform activities on another computer. Rather than giving someone full access to a system, you can specify who is authorized to connect to the system and which Windows PowerShell cmdlets, parameters, and values can be used.
- Role-capability files allow you to define JEA roles, including what the role can do in a Windows PowerShell session. The JEA role is based on the name of the role capability file, which features a .psrc filename extension.
- A session-configuration file is a special type of file that specifies what can be done in a JEA session. It will map the JEA roles to users or group. If a cmdlet, parameter, parameter value, alias, external script, or executable is not listed in a session-configuration file, it cannot be used in a JEA session with that session-configuration file.
- A JEA endpoint is a Windows PowerShell endpoint that is configured so that only specified authenticated users can connect to the endpoint and execute the allowed Windows PowerShell cmdlets, parameters, and values.
- To reduce the time necessary to configure all your data center servers, you can use Windows PowerShell Desired State Configuration (DSC) to manage and maintain systems based on your declared configuration.
- The JEA logs can be found in Event Viewer, specifically at Applications and Services Logs\Microsoft\Windows\PowerShell\Operational. However, to see these log events, you have to turn on Windows PowerShell\Operational logging..

Knowledge Assessment

Multiple Choice

1. Which account emulates a Network Service account that has the name NT Service\ servicename, which is used for simplified service administration?
   a. Virtual account
   b. JEA
   c. DSC
   d. WFM
2. Which of the following statements best describe why JEA is important in your efforts to keep a system secure? (Choose all that apply)
   a. With JEA, a privilege account is not needed to run the remote commands.
   b. JEA protects a system if an account is compromised.
   c. JEA is used to encrypt credentials when sent over the network.
   d. With JEA, user credentials are not stored on the remote server.
3. Which of the following are the minimum requirements for JEA? (Choose all that apply)
   a. Windows 10, version 1511 or later
   b. Windows Server 2012 R2
   c. Windows Server 2012
   d. Windows server 2016
4. Which of the following must be created to use JEA? (Choose two answers)
   a. AllowAction files
   b. AllowHost files
   c. Role-capability files
   d. Session-configuration files.
5. Which of the following is used to define JEA roles?
   a. AllowAction files
   b. AllowHost files
   c. Role-capability files
   d. Session-configuration files.
6. Which of the following can a user connect to in order to execute Windows PowerShell commands remotely using a virtual account?
   a. JEA endpoint
   b. DSC endpoint
   c. RDC endpoint
   d. port endpoint

7. Which files are used to specify what can be done in a JEA session?
   a. AllowAction files
   b. AllowHost files
   c. Role-capability files
   d. Session-configuration files.
8. If you are running Windows Server 2012, which of the following must be downloaded and installed?
   a. .NET Framework 4.5
   b. WMF
   c. JEA installation package
   d. DSC
9. In which of the following locations can the JEA logs be viewed?
   a. C:\Windows\System32\Logs folder
   b. Event Viewer System
   c. Event Viewer Security
   d. Event Viewer Applications and Services Logs\Microsoft\Windows\PowerShell\Operational
10. In JEA, which of the following is used to tie an Active Directory group to JEA role?
   a. AllowAction files
   b. AllowHost files
   c. Role-capability files
   d. Session-configuration files.

Best Answer

Choose the letter that corresponds to the best answer. More than one answer choice may achieve the goal. Select the BEST answer.

1. Which of the following provides role-based access control functionality built on Windows RemoteShell remoting, allowing one computer to perform activities on another computer?
   a. Virtual account
   b. JEA
   c. DSC
   d. WFM
2. Which of the following allows you to centrally deploy JEA to multiple computers?
   a. RDC
   b. DSC
   c. CIM
   d. Telnet

Build List

1. Specify the correct order of steps necessary to create and connect to a JEA endpoint.

_____ Restart WinRM.

_____ Open PowerShell ISE.

_____ Execute the Enter-PSSession command.

_____ Execute the Register-PSSessionConfiguration command.

_____ Execute the allowed PowerShell commands.

2. Specify the correct order of steps necessary to install WMF 5.1 on Windows Server 2008 R2 with SP1.

_____ Accept the license and complete the installation.

_____ Execute the install-WMF5.1.ps1 file.

_____ Download and double-click the 4.5.2 installation file. If prompted, click run.

_____ Open Windows PowerShell Modules.

_____ After the installation, restart the computer.

_____ Set the PowerShell execution policy to remotesigned.

_____ Download the WFM file. Double-click the WFM zip file and extract the files.

■ Business Case Scenarios

Scenario 9-1: Configuring the Help Desk to Create DHCP Reservations

You would like help desk personnel to be able to make DHCP reservations. Describe how to provide them with the ability to create DHCP reservations on the DHCP server without providing them administrative access to the DHCP server.

Scenario 9-2: Configuring JEA Endpoints

You administer nearly 100 servers and IT personnel need to perform specific tasks via Windows PowerShell commands. Describe your solution for configuring these machines efficiently with JEA endpoints.

Implementing Privileged Access Workstations, Local Administrator Password Solution (LAPS), and User Rights Assignments

LESSON 10

70-744 EXAM OBJECTIVE

Objective 4.3 – Implement Privileged Access Workstations (PAWs) and User Rights Assignments. This objective may include but is not limited to: Implement a PAWS solution; configure User Rights Assignment group policies; configure security options settings in Group Policy; enable and configure Remote Credential Guard for remote desktop access. The following objectives are covered in Lesson 8: Implement an Enhanced Security Administrative Environment (ESAE) administrative forest design approach; determine usage scenarios and requirements for implementing ESAE forest design architecture to create a dedicated administrative forest.

Objective 4.4 – Implement Local Administrator Password Solution (LAPS). This objective may include but is not limited to: Install and configure the LAPS tool; secure local administrator passwords using LAPS; manage password parameters and properties using LAPS.

Lesson Heading	Exam Objective
Understanding the Principle of Least Privilege	(None)
Running Programs as an Administrator	(None)
Implementing Privileged Access Workstations (PAWS)	Implement a PAWS solution
Implementing User Rights Assignments	Configure User Rights Assignment group policies
Configuring Security Options Settings in Group Policy	Configure security options settings in Group Policy
Enabling and Configuring Remote Credential Guard for Remote Desktop Access	Enable and configure Remote Credential Guard for remote desktop access
Implementing Local Administrator Password Solutions (LAPS)	Install and configure the LAPS tool Secure local administrator passwords using LAPS Manage password parameters and properties using LAPS

KEY TERMS

Local Administrator Password Solutions (LAPS)
permission
Principle of Least Privilege
Privileged Access Workstations (PAWs)
user right
Windows Defender Credential Guard

■ Understanding the Principle of Least Privilege

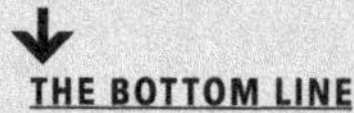

THE BOTTOM LINE

The ***Principle of Least Privilege*** is a security discipline that requires that a user, system, or application be given no more privilege than necessary to perform its function or job. On its face, this sounds like a commonsense approach to assigning permissions; when seen on paper, it is. However, when applying this principle in a complex production environment, it becomes significantly more challenging.

The Principle of Least Privilege has been a staple in the security arena for a number of years, but many organizations struggle to implement it successfully. However, with an increased focus on security from both a business as well as a regulatory perspective, organizations are working harder to build their models around this principle. The regulatory requirements of Sarbanes-Oxley, HIPAA, HITECH, PCI, and the large number of state data/privacy breach regulations—coupled with an increased focus by businesses into the security practices of their business partners, it is more important for organizations to invest in tools, processes, and other resources in order to ensure this principle is followed.

But why is a principle that sounds so simple on paper so difficult to implement in reality? The challenge is largely related to the complexity of a typical environment. It is very easy to visualize how to handle this for a single employee. On a physical level, they would need access to the building they work in, to the common areas, and to their office.

Logically, the employee needs to be able to log on to his computer, have user access to some centralized applications, a file server, a printer, and an internal website. Now, imagine that user multiplied by a thousand. And imagine those thousand employees working in six office locations. Some employees need access to all the locations while others need only to access their own locations. Still others need access to subsets of the six locations; for example, they might need access to the two offices in their region. Some will need access to the data center so they can provide IT support.

Logically, instead of a single set of access requirements, there are multiple departments with varying application requirements. The different user types vary from a normal user to a power user to an administrator. You need to determine not only which employee is which type of user but you need to manage their access across all the internal applications. Add to this mix new hires, employees being transferred or promoted, and employees who leave the company. Now you have a better understanding of why the process of ensuring each employee has only the minimum amount of access required to do her job can be a time-intensive activity.

But wait, we're not done. In addition to the physical and logical user permissions, in many IT environments, applications also need to access data and other applications. In order to follow the Principle of Least Privilege, it is important to ensure the applications have only minimum access in order to function properly. This can be extremely difficult when working in an Active Directory environment because of the extremely detailed permissions permitted in Active Directory. Determining which permissions an application requires to function properly with Active Directory can be extremely challenging.

To further complicate matters, in industries which are heavily regulated (like the finance or medical industries) or when regulations like Sarbanes-Oxley are in effect, there are additional requirements that are audited regularly to ensure the successful implementation and validation of privileges across the enterprise.

Getting into a detailed discussion of how to implement and maintain the Principle of Least Privilege is beyond the scope of this book, but there are some high-level tools and strategies to be aware of:

- **Groups:** Groups can be used to logically group users and applications so that permissions need not be applied on a user-by-user basis or on an application-by-application basis.
- **Multiple user accounts for administrators:** One of the major challenges to consider when implementing the Principle of Least Privilege relates to administrators. Administrators are typically also normal users, so it is seldom a promising idea for administrators to perform their daily user tasks as an administrator. To address this issue, many companies issue their administrators two accounts—one for their role as a standard user of the company's applications and systems and the other for their role as an administrator.
- **Account standardization:** The best way to simplify a complex environment is to standardize on a limited number of account types. Each account type permitted in an environment adds an order of magnitude to the permissions management strategy. Standardizing on a limited set of account types simplifies the managing of the environment.
- **Third-party applications:** There are a variety of third-party tools designed to simplify the management of permissions. These can range from account lifecycle management applications to auditing applications and application firewalls.
- **Processes and procedures:** One of the easiest ways to manage permissions in an environment is to develop a solid framework of processes and procedures for managing accounts. With this framework to rely on, the support organization doesn't have to address each account as a unique circumstance. They can rely on the defined process to determine how an account is created, classified, permissioned, and maintained.

TAKE NOTE* A perfect implementation of the Principle of Least Privilege is very rare. A best effort is typically all that can be expected and achieved.

Running Programs as an Administrator

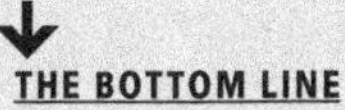

Because administrators have full access to a computer or the network, it is recommended that a standard non-administrator user should perform most tasks (such as reading reports and sending email). Then, to perform administrative tasks, use the `runas` command or the built-in options that are included with the Windows operating system.

To perform many management tasks, you need to have administrative access. Unfortunately, when you are using administrative tasks, you have access to sensitive systems and information. Therefore, you need to make sure that you take extra steps so that administrative access is not accessed by unauthorized users.

Before Windows Vista, an administrator account was needed to do certain things, such as changing system settings or installing software. When logged on as a limited user, the `runas` command eliminated the need to log off and then log back on as an administrator. For example, to run the widget.exe as the admin account, you would execute the following command:

```
runas /user:admin /widget.exe
```

In newer versions of Windows, including Windows 10 and Windows Server 2016, the `runas` command has been changed to Run as administrator. With User Account Control (UAC), the Run as administrator command is rarely used because Windows automatically prompts for an administrator password when needed.

RUN A PROGRAM AS AN ADMINISTRATOR

GET READY. To run a program as an administrator, perform the following steps.

1. Right-click the program icon or file that you want to open and choose **Run as administrator.** See Figure 10-1. If you want to right-click an item in the Start menu, right-click the program's icon, choose **More**, and then click **Run as administrator.**

Figure 10-1

Running a program as an administrator

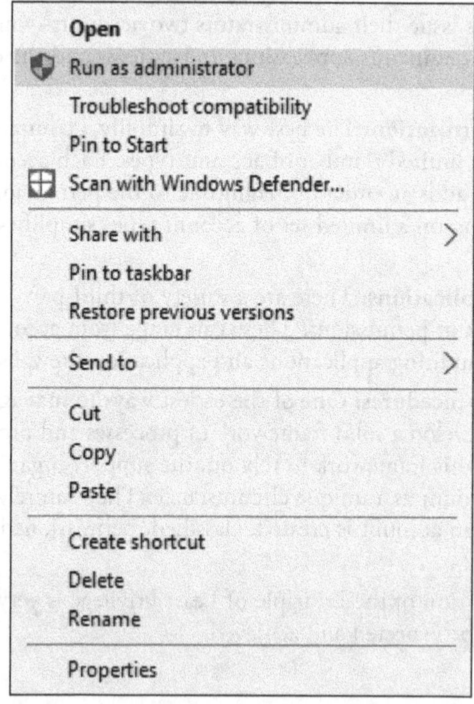

2. Select the administrator account that you want to use, type the password, and then click **Yes.**

■ Implementing Privileged Access Workstations (PAWs)

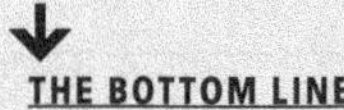

Privileged Access Workstations (PAWs) provides a system that is locked down and protected from various attacks and threats. By using a separate system for sensitive administrative tasks, you help protect the organization against a wide range of attacks, including phishing attacks, application and OS vulnerabilities, various impersonation attacks, and credential theft attacks.

CERTIFICATION READY
Implement a PAWS solution
Objective 4.3

IT operations personnel are high-value targets for attackers. Attackers might infect a computer with malware that includes keylogger functionality, which captures credentials as you type them. When you type credentials for administrators in standard credential boxes, those credentials can be used by a hacker to access confidential data and to perform their own administrative tasks.

TAKE NOTE*

By using other forms of authentication, such as the biometrics used with Windows Hello, you can avoid typing credentials that can be captured by hackers.

As previously mentioned, you should use non-administrative accounts to perform daily tasks (such as checking email, browsing the Internet, and opening files). You should use administrative accounts to perform administrative tasks. Similarly, you can go a step further by not using the same system to perform daily tasks and administrative tasks. By using separate systems, you reduce the impact should your non-administrative machine become compromised.

A Privileged Access Workstation is a secure administrative host that is used to perform only privileged administrative tasks. It isn't used to read emails, browse the Internet, or open files. A PAWs should:

- Ensure that only authorized administrative users can sign in to the Privileged Access Workstations.
- Use Device Guard and AppLocker policies to allow only authorized trusted applications needed to perform administrative tasks.
- Enable Credential Guard to help protect against credential theft.
- Enable BitLocker to help protect the boot environment and disks.
- Ensure that Privileged Access Workstations can access external sites by the perimeter network firewall.

To keep the entire environment secure, you need to also ensure that only Privileged Access Workstations can connect to servers. You should block Remote Desktop Protocol (RDP), Windows PowerShell, and management console connections from any computer that is not a Privileged Access Workstation.

Implementing User Rights Assignments

CERTIFICATION READY
Configure User Rights Assignment group policies
Objective 4.3

Specifying what a user can do on a system or to a resource is determined by two things: permissions and rights. User rights, which specify the actions that can be performed on a system, are managed using GPOs (including the local GPO).

A ***permission*** defines the type of access that is granted to an object (an object can be identified with a security identifier) or object attribute. The most common objects assigned permissions are NTFS files and folders, printers, and Active Directory objects. To keep track of all this, information such as which user can access an object and what the user can do is recorded in the access control list (ACL), which lists all users and groups that have access to the object.

A ***user right*** authorizes a user to perform certain actions on a computer, such as logging on to a system interactively or backing up files and directories on a system. User rights are assigned through local policies or Active Directory group policies. See Figure 10-2.

Figure 10-2

A User Rights Assignment

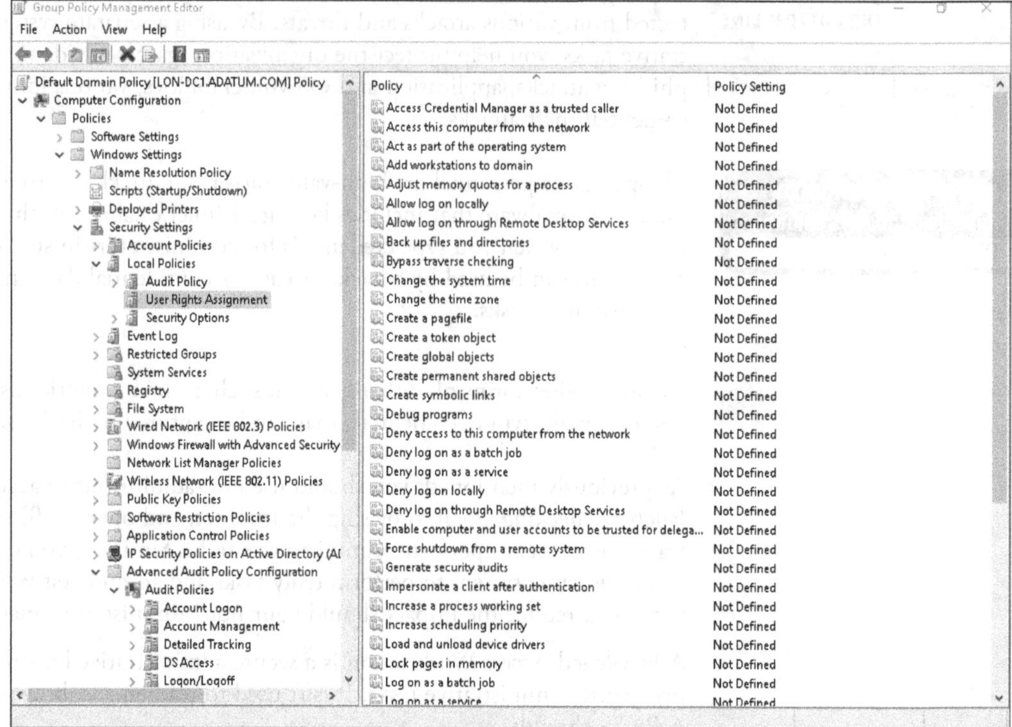

Some of the user rights include:

- **Access this computer from the network:** Determines which users and groups can connect to the computer from the network. Does not affect Remote Desktop Services.
- **Add workstations to domain:** This policy setting determines which users can add a computer to a specific domain.
- **Allow log on locally:** This policy setting determines which users can start an interactive session on the computer. The error message the users will see without this permission is "The local policy of this system does not permit you to logon interactively." Users who do not have this right are still able to start a remote interactive session on the computer if they have the Allow logon through Remote Desktop Services right.
- **Allow log on through Remote Desktop Services:** This policy setting determines which users can log on to the computer through a Remote Desktop connection. You should not assign this user right to additional users or groups. Instead, it is a best practice to add users to or remove users from the Remote Desktop Users group to control who can open a Remote Desktop connection to the computer.
- **Back up files and directories:** This policy setting determines which users can circumvent file and directory permissions to back up the computer.
- **Change the system time:** This policy setting determines which users can adjust the time on the computer's internal clock.
- **Create a token object:** This policy setting determines which user accounts can be used by processes to create tokens that allow accesses to local resources. You should not assign this right to any user who you do not want to give complete control of the system to because it can be used to leverage local Administrator privileges.

- **Deny access to this computer from the network:** This policy setting blocks specified users and groups from accessing the computer from the network. This setting overrides the policy that allows access from the network.
- **Deny log on as a batch job:** This policy setting blocks specified users and groups from signing in as a batch job. Overrides the Log on as a batch job policy.
- **Deny log on as a service:** This policy setting blocks service accounts from registering a process as a service. It also overrides the Log on as a service policy. It does not apply to Local System, Local Service, or Network Service accounts.
- **Deny log on locally:** This policy setting blocks accounts from signing on locally. This policy also overrides the allow log on locally policy.
- **Deny log on through Remote Desktop Services:** This policy setting blocks accounts from signing in by using Remote Desktop Services. It also overrides the allow sign on through Remote Desktop Services policy.
- **Force shutdown from a remote system:** Users assigned this right are allowed to shut down computers from remote locations on the network.
- **Impersonate a client after authentication:** This policy setting allows apps running on behalf of a user to impersonate a client. This right can be a security risk and You should assign it to trusted users.
- **Load and unload device drivers:** This policy setting determines which users can dynamically load and unload device drivers. This user right is not required if a signed driver for the new hardware already exists in the Driver.cab file on the computer.
- **Lock pages in memory:** Accounts assigned this right can use a process to keep data stored in physical memory, blocking that data from being paged to virtual memory.
- **Log on as a batch job:** Accounts assigned this right can be signed in to the computer by means of a batch-queue facility. This right is relevant only to older versions of the Windows operating system and you should not use it with newer versions, such as Windows 10 and Windows Server 2016.
- **Log on as a service:** This policy setting determines which service accounts can register a process as a service. In Windows Server 2016 and Windows 10, only the Network Service account has this right by default. Any service that runs under a separate user account must be assigned this user right.
- **Manage auditing and security log:** Users assigned this right can configure object access auditing options for resources such as files and AD DS objects. Users assigned this right can also view events in the security log and clear the security log. Because attackers are likely to clear the security log as a way of hiding their tracks, you should not assign this right to user accounts that would not normally be assigned local Administrator permissions on a computer.
- **Replace a process level token:** With this policy setting, the user account can call the CreateProcessAsUser API so that one service can trigger another.
- **Restore files and directories:** This security setting determines which users can bypass file, directory, registry, and other persistent objects permissions when restoring backed up files and directories, and determines which users can set any valid security principal as the owner of an object.
- **Shut down the system:** This policy setting determines which users can shut down the local computer.
- **Synchronize directory service data:** This policy setting assigns the ability to synchronize AD DS data.
- **Take ownership of files or other objects:** This policy setting determines which users can take ownership of any securable object in the computer, including Active Directory objects, NTFS files and folders, printers, registry keys, services, processes, and threads.

Configuring Security Options Settings in Group Policy

CERTIFICATION READY
Configure security options settings in Group Policy
Objective 4.3

Besides configuring usernames and passwords, you need to configure additional security options to help keep an account secure—including limiting how and when users can access their accounts.

You can configure the following user account security options (as shown in Figure 10-3) for an account, by opening Active Directory Users and Computers, double-clicking a user account, and then clicking the Account tab:

- By default, accounts are configured so that users can sign in at all times. To prevent a user from logging on during a specific time, click the Account tab and click the Logon Hours button. You can then specify the logon hours.. For example, you can specify that a user can log on only during business hours (from 7 AM to 6 PM Monday through Friday).
- By default, any account can log on to any computer. However, you can limit which systems a user account can use by clicking the Log On To button. You can use this setting to ensure that users can use privileged accounts only on specific, specially configured administrative workstations or certain servers.
- You should never use the Password Never Expires option because it will bypass the domain password policy. Using non-expiring passwords can be compromised with brute force. Given enough time, any password can be determined. You can use products such as Microsoft Identity Manager to assist with password management for privileged accounts.
- To ensure strong security, you should use multi-factor authentication. For example, you can scroll down and use the Smart card is required option for interactive logon, which will ensure that a smart card must be present for the account sign-in to occur.
- By scrolling down and using the Account is sensitive and cannot be delegated option, you ensure that trusted applications cannot forward the account credentials to other services or computers on the network. You should enable this setting for highly privileged accounts.
- Scrolling down and using the Use only Kerberos DES encryption types for this account option configures an account to use only Data Encryption Standard (DES) encryption, which is weaker than Advanced Encryption Standard (AES). Therefore, you should not use this option for on a secure network. You should consider using the GPO Network Security: Configure Encryption types allowed for Kerberos policy to disable DES.
- Scrolling down and using This account supports Kerberos AES 128 bit encryption option and the This account supports Kerberos AES 256 bit encryption option allows users to use Kerberos AES 128-bit encryption and Kerberos AES 256 bit encryption option. You should enable This option allows Kerberos AES 256-bit encryption on any privileged accounts.
- Scrolling down and using the Do not require Kerberos preauthentication option reduces the risk of replay attacks. Therefore, you should enable the Do not require Kerberos preauthentication option.
- In the Account expires section, you should choose the End of option on any privileged account with expiration dates so you can ensure that privileged accounts do not remain in AD DS after they are no longer in use.

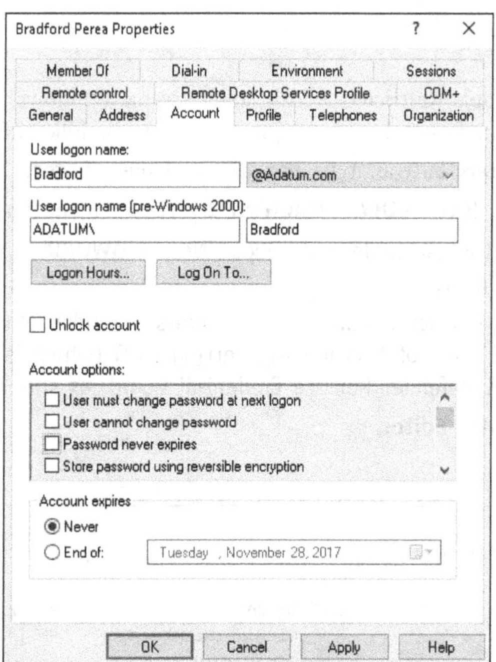

Figure 10-3

Configuring user settings

Enabling and Configuring Remote Credential Guard for Remote Desktop Access

CERTIFICATION READY
Enable and configure Remote Credential Guard for remote desktop access
Objective 4.3

Starting with Windows 10 and Windows Server 2016, Windows offers ***Windows Defender Credential Guard***, which helps protect your credentials over a Remote Desktop connection by redirecting Kerberos requests back to the device that is requesting the connection. As a result, if the target device is compromised, your credentials are not exposed because the credential and credential derivatives are never passed over the network to the target device. Therefore, you should use Windows Defender Remote Credential Guard to connect during Remote Desktop sessions. It also provides single sign-on experiences for Remote Desktop sessions.

An alternative to Windows Defender Remote Credential Guard is Restricted Admin Mode, which can use either Kerberos or NTLM but cannot be used to access services from a server.

To use Windows Defender Remote Credential Guard, the Remote Desktop client:

- Must be running at least Windows 10, version 1703 or higher to be able to supply credentials
- Must use Kerberos authentication to connect to the remote host, which requires connecting to a domain controller

The Remote Desktop remote host:

- Must be running at least Windows 10, version 1607 or Windows Server 2016
- Must allow Restricted Admin connections
- Must allow the client's domain user to access Remote Desktop connections
- Must allow delegation of non-exportable credentials

Windows Defender Remote Credential Guard does not support compound authentication, such as when you are accessing a file server from a remote host that requires a device claim. Windows Defender Remote Credential Guard cannot be used to connect to a device that is not domain-joined to Active Directory, including hosts that are joined to Azure Active Directory.

ENABLE RESTRICTED ADMIN AND WINDOWS DEFENDER REMOTE CREDENTIAL GUARD USING REGISTRY EDITOR

GET READY. To enable Restricted Admin and turn on Windows Defender Remote Credential Guard on the remote host using the registry, perform the following steps.

1. Click the **Start** button, type **regedit**, and press **Enter.**
2. Navigate to **HKEY_LOCAL_MACHINE\System\ CurrentControlSet\Control\Lsa.**
3. Right-click the Lsa node and choose **New > DWORD**. Type **DisableRestrictedAdmin** and press **Enter.**
4. To turn on Restricted Admin and Windows Defender Remote Credential Guard, change the value of this registry setting to **0** (which is the default value) to turn on Windows Defender Remote Credential Guard, as shown in Figure 10-4.
5. Close **Registry Editor.**

Figure 10-4

Enabling Restricted Admin and turning on Windows Defender Remote Credential Guard

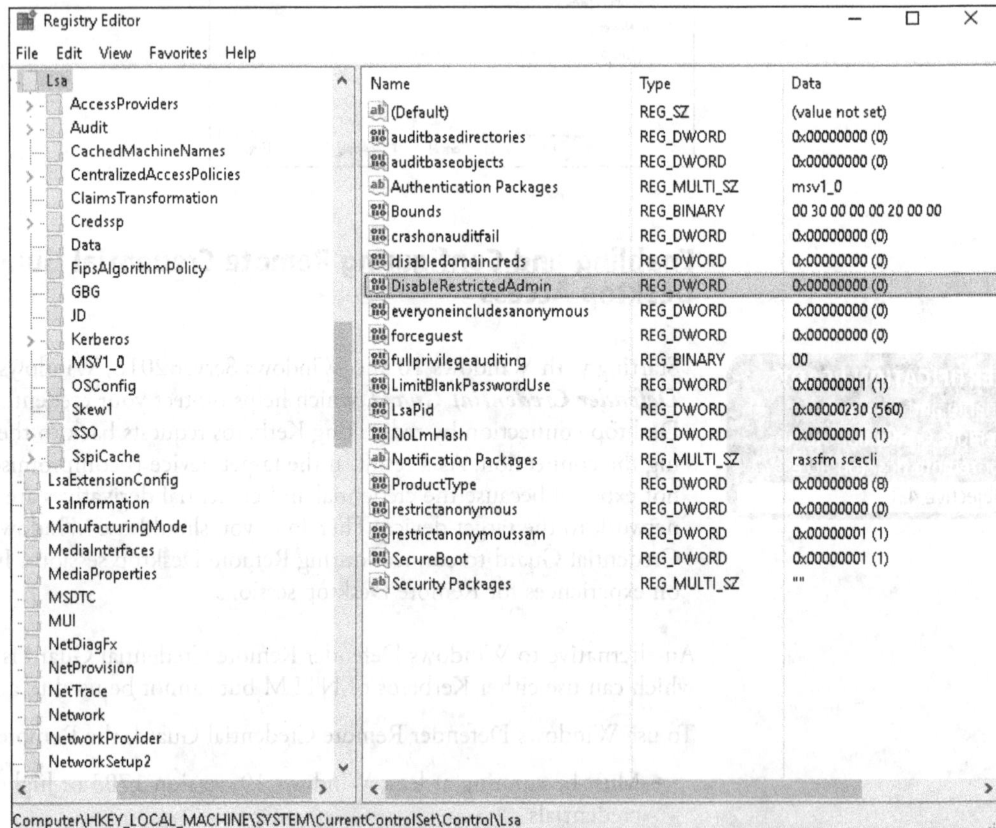

Beginning with Windows 10 version 1703, you can enable Windows Defender Remote Credential Guard on the client device either by using Group Policy or by using a parameter with the Remote Desktop Connection.

TURN ON WINDOWS DEFENDER REMOTE CREDENTIAL GUARD BY USING GROUP POLICY

GET READY. Turn on Windows Defender Remote Credential Guard by Using Group Policy, perform the following steps.

1. On a domain controller, in Server Manager, click **Tools > Group Policy Management.**
2. In the Group Policy Management console, right-click the desired GPO and choose **Edit.**
3. Navigate to **Computer Configuration\Administrative Templates\System\Credentials Delegation.**
4. Double-click **Restrict delegation of credentials to remote servers.** Select **Enabled.**
5. Under Use the following restricted mode:
   - If you want to require either Restricted Admin mode or Windows Defender Remote Credential Guard, choose **Prefer Windows Defender Remote Credential Guard.**
   - If you want to require Windows Defender Remote Credential Guard, choose **Require Windows Defender Remote Credential Guard.**
   - If you want to require Restricted Admin mode, choose **Require Restricted Admin.**
6. Click **OK.**
7. Close the Group Policy Management Console.

Implementing Local Administrator Password Solutions (LAPS)

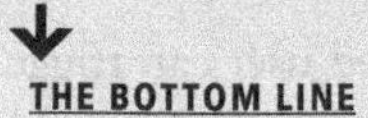

THE BOTTOM LINE

Each computer has a local Administrator account, which can be used to gain full access to the computer without establishing connectivity to the domain. To maintain security, you need to update the Administrator password on a regular basis. ***Local Administrator Password Solutions (LAPS)*** provides a central repository for local administrator passwords for domain-member machines.

CERTIFICATION READY
Install and configure the LAPS tool
Objective 4.4

CERTIFICATION READY
Secure local administrator passwords using LAPS
Objective 4.4

CERTIFICATION READY
Manage password parameters and properties using LAPS
Objective 4.4

When using LAPS, local administrator passwords will be unique on each computer that LAPS uses. It will randomize and change local administrator passwords regularly and store the passwords securely within AD DS. You can then configure who has access to the passwords. Passwords that LAPS retrieves are transmitted to the client in a secure encrypted manner.

LAPS can work with any Windows computer that is a member of an Active Directory domain. LAPS requires an Active Directory domain functional level of Windows Server 2003 or newer. LAPS requires that .NET Framework 4.0 and Windows PowerShell 2.0 or newer are installed on the computers for which it will manage the local administrator passwords.

To use LAPS, you must update the Active Directory schema by executing the Windows PowerShell `Update-AdmPwdADSchema` cmdlet. The `Update-AdmPwdADSchema` cmdlet is available when you download and install LAPS on a computer. The cmdlet should be executed by a member of the Schema Admins group and you should run this cmdlet on a computer that is in the same Active Directory site as the computer that holds the Schema Master role for the forest.

PREPARE ACTIVE DIRECTORY FOR LAPS

GET READY. To prepare Active Directory for LAPS, perform the following steps.

1. On a domain controller, double-click the **LAPS.x64.msi** file. When you are prompted to confirm that you want to run this file, click **Run**.
2. In the Local Administrator Password Solution Setup wizard, click **Next.**
3. On the End-User License Agreement page, select **I accept the terms in the License Agreement** and click **Next.**
4. On the Custom Setup page, select the down arrow for Management Tools and click **Entire feature will be installed on local hard drive.** Click **Next.**
5. On the Ready to install Local Administrator Password Solution page, click **Install.**
6. When the installation is complete, click **Finish.**
7. Click the **Start** button and then click **Windows PowerShell.**
8. Execute the following command:

```
Update-AdmPwdADSchema
```

Each client must have the LAPS agent installed. The easiest way to deploy the LAPS agent is by using Group Policy client-side extension or by using System Center Configuration Manager.

When the Group Policy refreshes, LAPS determines whether the password of the local Administrator account has expired. If the password hasn't expired, LAPS does nothing. If the password has expired, LAPS performs the following steps:

- Changes the local Administrator password to a new random value based on the configured parameters for local Administrator passwords
- Transmits the new password to AD DS, which is stored in the computer account
- Transmits the new password-expiration date to AD DS

Authorized users can read passwords from AD DS and an authorized user can trigger a local Administrator password change on a specific computer.

To specify an organizational unit (OU) that has computers that will be managed by LAPS, execute the following command:

```
Set-AdmPwdComputerSelfPermission -Identity "<Organizational Unit>"
```

For example, to configure the Sales OU, execute the following command:

```
Set-AdmPwdComputerSelfPermission -Identity "Sales"
```

By default, accounts that are members of the Domain Admins and Enterprise Admins groups can access and view stored passwords. To add additional groups, use the `Set-AdmPwdReadPasswordPermission` cmdlet. For example, to assign the IT group the ability to view the local administrator password on computers in the Sales OU, use the following command:

```
Set-AdmPwdReadPasswordPermission -Identity "Sales"
-AllowedPrincipals "IT"
```

Using the LAPS GPO templates (as shown in Figure 10-5), you can configure the following:

- **Name of administrator account to manage:** Allows you to identify custom local Administrator accounts.
- **Password settings:** Allows you to configure the complexity, length, and maximum age of the local Administrator password. The default is that you can use uppercase and lowercase letters, numbers, and special characters. The default password length is 14 characters and the default password maximum age is 30 days.
- **Do not allow password expiration time longer than required:** When enabled, password updates are determined by the domain password expiration policy.
- **Enable local admin password management:** By enabling this option, you enable LAPS, allowing you to manage the local Administrator account password centrally.

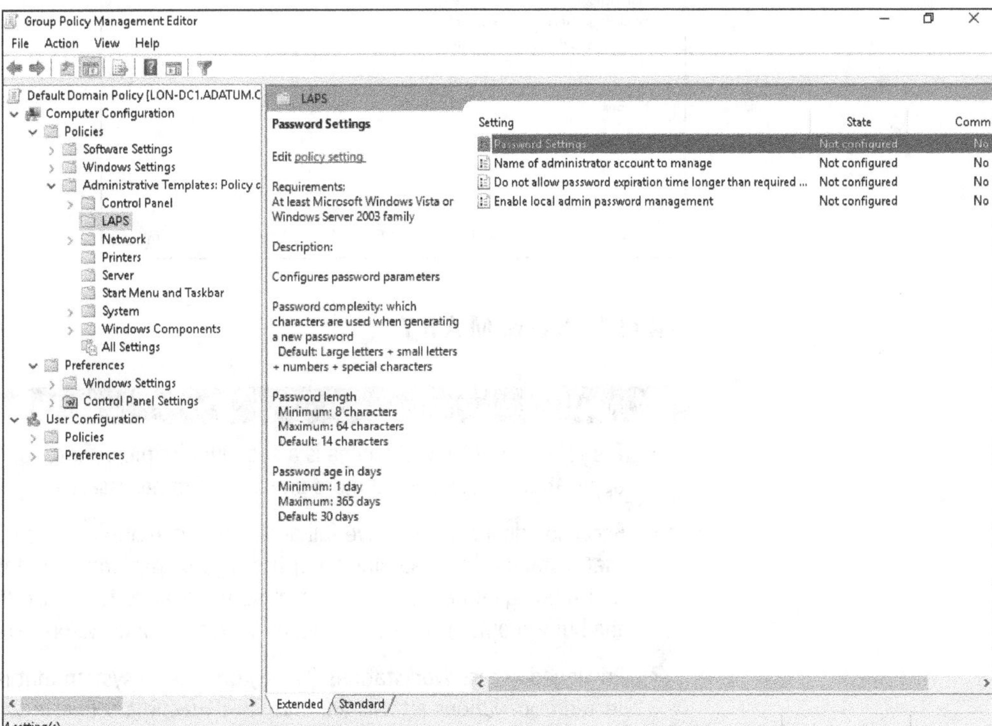

Figure 10-5

Viewing the LAPS settings

You can view passwords assigned to a computer as follows:

- You can examine the ms-Mcs-AdmPwd attribute by viewing the properties of the computer account with Advanced Features enabled in Active Directory Users and Computers, as shown in Figure 10-6.
- You can use the LAPS user interface (UI) app.
- You can use the `Get-AdmPwdPassword` Windows PowerShell cmdlet, which is available when you install LAPS.

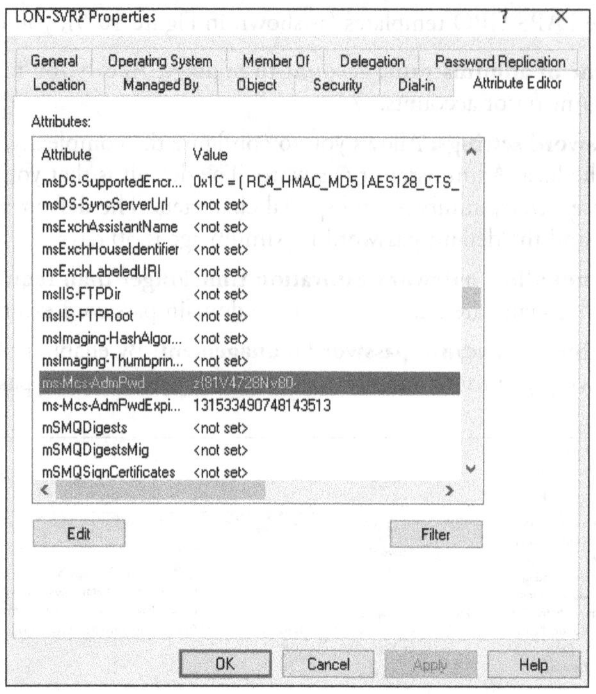

Figure 10-6

Viewing the local administrator password

SKILL SUMMARY

IN THIS LESSON YOU LEARNED:

- The Principle of Least Privilege is a security discipline that requires that a user, system, or application is provided no more privilege than necessary to perform its function or job.
- Because administrators have full access to a computer or the network, it is recommended that a standard non-administrator user should perform most tasks, such as reading reports and sending email. Then, to perform administrative tasks, use the `runas` command or the built-in options that are included with the Windows operating system.
- Privileged Access Workstations (PAWs) provides a system that is locked down and protected from various attacks and threats. By using a separate system for sensitive administrative tasks, you help protect the organization against a wide range of attacks, including phishing attacks, application and OS vulnerabilities, various impersonation attacks, and credential theft attacks.
- A user right authorizes a user to perform certain actions on a computer, such as logging on to a system interactively or backing up files and directories on a system. User rights are assigned through local policies or Active Directory group policies.
- Besides using username and passwords, you need to configure additional security options, such as limiting how and when users can access their accounts.
- Starting with Windows 10 and Windows Server 2016, Windows offers Windows Defender Credential Guard, which helps protect your credentials over a Remote Desktop connection by redirecting Kerberos requests back to the device that is requesting the connection. As a result, if the target device is compromised, your credentials are not exposed because the credential and credential derivatives are never passed over the network to the target device.
- Each computer has a local Administrator account, which can be used to gain full access to the computer without establishing connectivity to the domain. To maintain security, you need to update the Administrator password on a regular basis.
- Local Administrator Password Solutions (LAPS) provides a central repository for local administrator passwords for domain-member machines.

Knowledge Assessment

Multiple Choice

1. Which of the following requires that a user, system, or application is provided with no more privilege than necessary to perform its function or tasks?
   a. Separation of duties
   b. DREAD
   c. Defense in depth
   d. Principle of Least Privilege
2. Which of the following provides a system that is locked down, protected from various attacks and threats, and is used to specifically run sensitive administrative attacks.
   a. JEA
   b. PAWS
   c. LAPS
   d. PLP
3. Which of the following statements best describe PAWS? (Choose all that apply)
   a. With PAWS, only authorized administrators are able to log on to the administrative workstation.
   b. To use PAWS, you need to enable Credential Guard.
   c. To use PAWS, you need to install administrative tools and production software, such as Microsoft Office
   d. To use PAWS, you need to enable BitLocker.
4. Which of the following defines the type of access that is granted to an object or object attribute?
   a. Permissions
   b. User rights
   c. Administration access
   d. Role access
5. Which of the following authorizes a user to perform certain actions on a computer?
   a. Permissions
   b. User rights
   c. Administration access
   d. Role access
6. You have been assigned an Allow log on locally user right. However, when you log directly on to the computer, a message displays, indicating "The local policy of this system does not permit you to login interactively." Which of the following best describes the cause of this problem?
   a. You do not have the Allow log on through Remote Desktop Services right.
   b. The workstation is not added to the domain.
   c. The token object is not created when you log on.
   d. You have been assigned the Deny log on locally right.

7. Which of the following options is recommended for authentication?
   a. Kerberos AES 128 bit encryption
   b. Kerberos AES 256 bit encryption
   c. Kerberos DES
   d. NTLM
8. Which of the following technology allows you to protect your credentials over a Remote Desktop connection by not exposing the credentials?
   a. PAWS
   b. LAPS
   c. NTLM
   d. Windows Defender Remote Credential Guard
9. Which of the following allows you to automatically change local administrative passwords on a system?
   a. LAPS
   b. PAWS
   c. NTLM
   d. JEA
10. Which of the following are requirements for LAPS? (Choose all that apply)
   a. Windows PowerShell 2.0 or newer
   b. .NET Framework 3.5
   c. .NET Framework 4.0
   d. WINRM

Best Answer

Choose the letter that corresponds to the best answer. More than one answer choice may achieve the goal. Select the BEST answer.

1. Which of the following is recommended when performing administrative tasks on a user workstation?
   a. You should log on as a domain administrator on your personal workstation.
   b. You should use a non-administrative account and use the `runas` option to perform administrative tasks.
   c. You should add your standard user account to the Administrator group.
   d. You should turn on all auditing options.

Build List

1. Specify the correct order of steps necessary to implement LAPS on a workstation.

_____ Install the LAPS agent on the individual computers that you want to manage.

_____ Accept the license.

_____ Update the schema.

_____ Download the LAPS installation files.

_____ Double-click the LAPS.x64.msi file.

_____ Choose the Entire feature will be installed on local hard drive option.

_____ Open a Windows PowerShell window.

_____ Execute the `Set-AdmPwdComputerSelfPermission` command.

Business Case Scenarios

Scenario 10-1: Identifying User Rights

Open the local security policy on a Windows Server 2016 computer and then open the User Rights Assignment, which is located in the local policies under Computer Configuration. Which user rights are assigned to the Administrator or Administrator's group?

Scenario 10-2: Administrating Your Network

Several administrators need to administer sensitive applications. You need to ensure that their systems are free any malware that could compromise the network and applications. Describe your recommended solution.

Scenario 10-3: Managing Local Administrator Passwords

You administer several sensitive application servers and you need to ensure that the local administrator passwords are changed on a frequent basis and with strong passwords. In addition, you want to enforce the use of a unique password for each workstation. Describe your recommended solution.

LESSON 11

Configuring Advanced Audit Policies

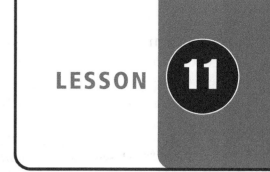

70-744 EXAM OBJECTIVE

Objective 5.1 – Configure advanced audit policies. This objective may include but is not limited to the following: Determine the differences and usage scenarios for using local audit policies and advanced auditing policies; implement auditing using Group Policy and AuditPol.exe; implement auditing using Windows PowerShell; create expression-based audit policies; configure the Audit PNP Activity policy; configure the Audit Group Membership policy; enable and configure Module, Script Block, and Transcription logging in Windows PowerShell.

Objective 6.2 – Implement a secure file services infrastructure and Dynamic Access Control (DAC). This objective may include but is not limited to the following: Configure file access auditing. Other Objective 6.2 topics are covered in Lesson 15.

LESSON HEADING	EXAM OBJECTIVE
Configuring Advanced Audit Policies	Determine the differences and usage scenarios for using local audit policies and advanced auditing policies
• Implementing Auditing Using Group Policy	Implement auditing using Group Policy and AuditPol.exe
• Implementing Advanced Audit Policy Settings	Configure File Access Auditing
• Implementing Auditing Using AuditPol.exe	Create expression-based audit policies
• Implementing Auditing Using Windows PowerShell	Configure the Audit PNP Activity policy
• Viewing Audit Events	Configure the Audit Group Membership policy
• Creating Expression-Based Audit Policies	Enable and configure Module, Script Block, and Transcription logging in Windows PowerShell
• Configuring the Audit PNP and Removable Storage Devices Activity Policy	
• Configuring the Audit Group Membership Policy	
• Enabling and Configuring Module, Script Block, and Transcription Logging in Windows PowerShell	

KEY TERMS

advanced audit policy settings
auditing
AuditPol.exe
Dynamic Access Control
Global Object Access Auditing
module logging
nonrepudiation
plug-and-play (PnP)
script block
transcription logging

Configuring Advanced Audit Policies

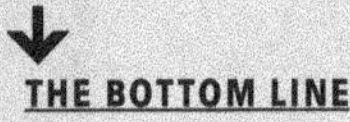
THE BOTTOM LINE

Security can be divided into three areas. Authentication is used to prove the identity of a user. Authorization gives access to the user who was authenticated. To complete the security picture, you need to enable ***auditing***, which is the monitoring and recording of user and system actions, so that you can have a record of the users who have logged on, what those users accessed or tried to access, and which actions the users performed (such as rebooting, shutting down a computer, or accessing a file). By using auditing, an organization can implement ***nonrepudiation***, which is the assurance that someone cannot deny something that he or she did.

CERTIFICATION READY
Determine the differences and usage scenarios for using local audit policies and advanced auditing policies
Objective 5.1

It is important that you protect your information and service resources from people who should not have access to them; at the same time, it's important you make those resources available to authorized users. Along with authentication and authorization, you need to enable auditing so that you can have a record of:

- Who has successfully logged on
- Who has attempted to log on but failed
- Who has made changes to accounts in Active Directory
- Who has accessed or changed certain files
- Who has used a certain printer
- Who has restarted a system
- Who has made system changes

Using auditing logs enables you to determine whether any security breaches have occurred and to what extent.

Implementing Auditing Using Group Policy

CERTIFICATION READY
Implement auditing using Group Policy and AuditPol.exe
Objective 5.1

To enable auditing, use Group Policy or the local security policy (Computer Settings\Policies\Security Settings\Local Policies\Audit Policy) to specify which system events to audit.

Table 11-1 shows the basic events to audit that are available in Windows 10 and Windows Server 2016. After you enable logging, you can then open the Event Viewer Security logs to view the security events. As you can see, most major Active Directory events are already audited, although there is not a group policy that includes these settings.

Event	Explanation	Default Settings Defined for Domain Controllers
Account logon	Determines whether the operating system (OS) audits each time the computer validates an account's credentials, such as account logon. Account logon events are generated when a domain user account is authenticated on a domain controller.	Successful account logons
Account management	Determines whether to audit each event of account management on a computer, including changing passwords and creating or deleting user accounts.	Successful account management activities
Directory service access	Determines whether the OS audits user attempts to access Active Directory objects, the previous change value, and the new assigned value.	
Logon	Determines whether the OS audits each instance of a user attempting to log on to or log off his computer. Logon events are generated when a domain user interactively logs on to a domain controller or a network logon to a domain controller is performed to retrieve logon scripts and policies.	Successful logons
Object access	Determines whether the OS audits user attempts to access non–Active Directory objects, including NT File System (NTFS) files, folders, and printers.	
Policy change	Determines whether the OS audits each instance of an attempt to change user rights assignments, auditing policies, account policies, or trust policies.	Successful policy changes
Privilege use	Determines whether to audit each instance of a user exercising a user right.	
Process tracking	Determines whether the OS audits process-related events, such as process creation, process termination, handle duplication, and indirect object access. This is usually used for troubleshooting because enabling the auditing of process tracking can affect performance.	
System	Determines whether the OS audits if the system time is changed, if the system is started or shut down, if there is an attempt to load extensible authentication components, if there is a loss of auditing events due to auditing system failure, and if the Security log exceeds a configurable warning threshold level.	Successful system events

Table 11-1

Audit Events

Although it is easy to enable auditing for everything, it is usually not a good idea. Any time that you enable auditing, you need to select only what you need for the following reasons:

- High levels of auditing can affect the performance of the computer that you audit.
- When you search through the Security logs, you will find far too many events, which can make it more difficult to find the potential problems you need to find.
- The logs quickly fill up, replacing older events with newer events.

Most audit settings require you to enable only specific audit settings. However, object auditing is a little bit more complex. After you enable object access auditing, you have to enable auditing on the specific object that you want to enable. These objects include registry objects, files, folders, and printers.

When you enable object auditing, you generate many other events that also get recorded, including Audit Filtering Platform Connection and Audit Filtering Platform Packet Drop, which shows packets that get connected or dropped at the Transmission Control Protocol (TCP) and User Datagram Protocol (UDP) level. To cut these packets, you can use the advanced audit policy Configuration for Object Access or the AuditPol.exe command to not record these events. Advanced audit policy configuration and AuditPol are discussed in the following section.

IMPLEMENT AN AUDIT POLICY

GET READY. To audit account logon successes and failures, perform the following steps.

1. Log on to **LON-DC1** as **adatum\administrator** with the password of **Pa$$w0rd.** Server Manager opens.
2. In Server Manager, click **Tools > Group Policy Management** to open the Group Policy Management Console.
3. Expand **Domain Controllers** to show the Default Domain Controllers Policy. Then right-click the **Default Domain Control Default Policy** and choose **Edit**. Group Policy Management Editor appears.
4. Expand **Computer Configuration**, **Policies**, **Windows Settings**, **Security Settings**, **Local Policies**, and select **Audit Policy** (see Figure 11-1).

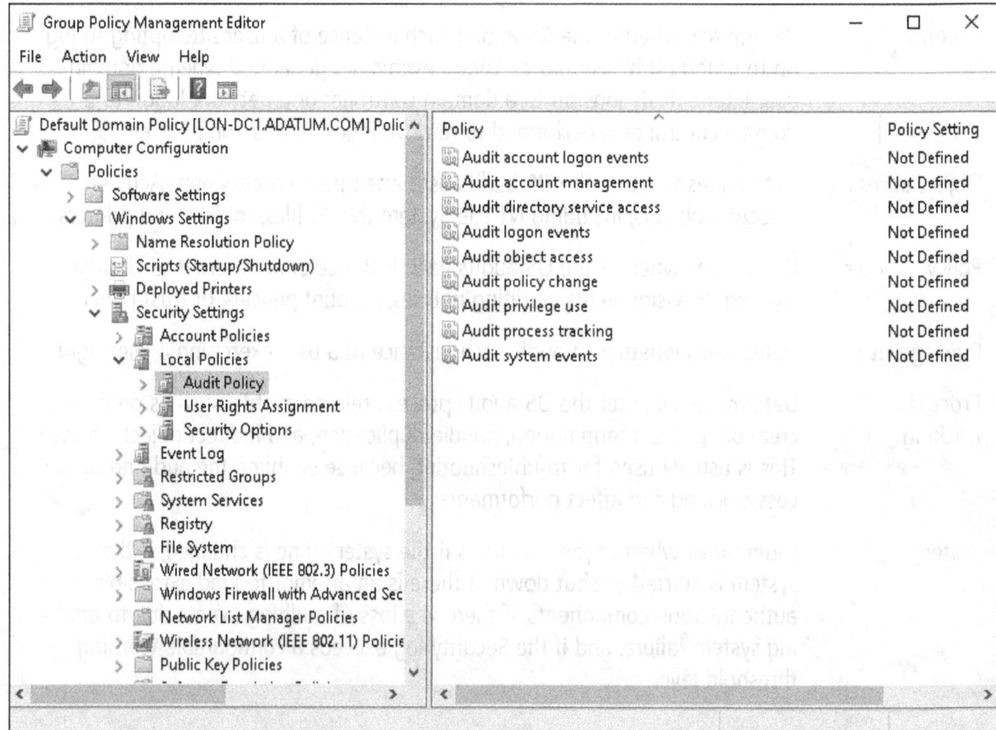

Figure 11-1

Enabling auditing using group policies

CERTIFICATION READY
Configure File Access Auditing
Objective 6.2

5. Double-click **Audit account logon events.** The Audit account logon events Properties dialog box opens.
6. Select **Define these policy settings** and select both **Success** and **Failure.**
7. Click **OK** to close the Audit account logon events Properties dialog box.

Auditing NTFS files, NTFS folders, and printers is a two-step process. You must first enable object access using Group Policy. Then you must specify which objects you want to audit.

TAKE NOTE* You should not audit every file and folder on a computer. Auditing every file and folder can dramatically affect the performance of the computer.

AUDIT FILES AND FOLDERS

GET READY. To audit files and folders, perform the following steps.

1. Log on to **LON-DC1** as **adatum\administrator** with the password of **Pa$$w0rd.** Server Manager automatically opens.
2. In Server Manager, click **Tools > Group Policy Management** to open the Group Policy Management Console.
3. Right-click a group policy and choose **Edit.** The Group Policy Management Editor opens.
4. Expand **Computer Configuration**, **Policies**, **Windows Settings**, **Security Settings**, **Local Policies** and select **Audit Policy.**
5. Double-click **Audit object access.** The Audit object access Properties dialog box displays.
6. Select **Define these policy settings** and select both **Success** and **Failure.**
7. Click **OK** to close the Audit account logon events Properties dialog box.
8. Close the Group Policy Management Editor and the Group Policy Management console.
9. Right-click the **Start** button and choose **File Explorer.**
10. Right-click the file or folder (such as a C:\Data folder) that you want to audit and choose **Properties.** Click the **Security** tab.
11. Click the **Advanced** button.
12. When the Advanced Security Settings dialog box opens, click the **Auditing** tab, as shown in Figure 11-2.

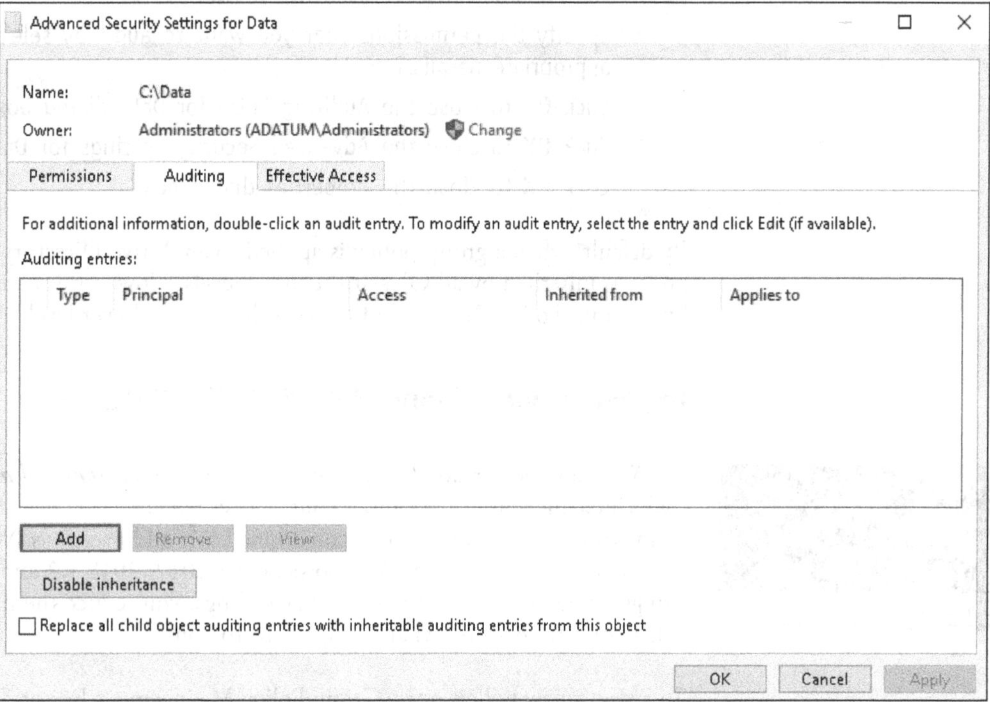

Figure 11-2

Managing auditing settings of a folder

13. To add an auditing entry, click **Add.** The Auditing Entry for Data dialog box opens (see Figure 11-3).

Figure 11-3

Opening the Auditing Entry for Data dialog box

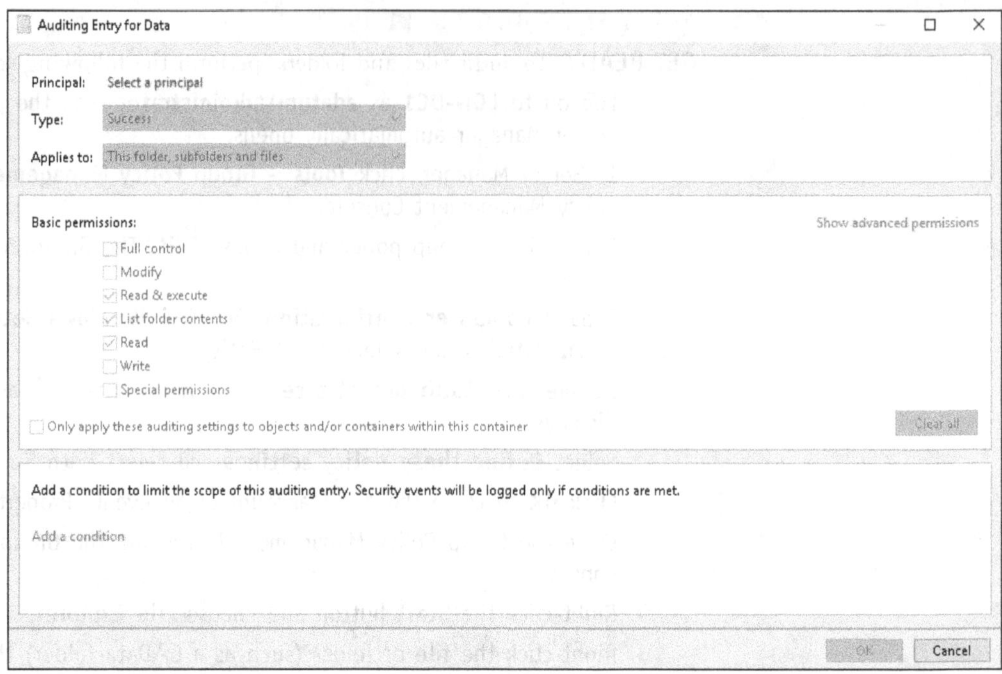

14. To specify a user or group, click **Select a principal**. In the Select User, Computer, Service Account, or Group dialog box, type a name for a user name or group and then click **OK**.
15. For Type, select **Success**, **Fail**, or **All**.
16. Specify the permissions that you want to audit by selecting or deselecting the appropriate permission.
17. Click **OK** to close the Auditing Entry for Data dialog box.
18. Click **OK** to close the Advanced Security Settings for Data dialog box.
19. Click **OK** to close the Properties dialog box.

By default, when a group policy is applied to an Active Directory domain or OU, the group policy is inherited by all OUs at the lower levels. However, inherited policy can be overridden by a Group Policy Object (GPO) that is linked at a lower level.

Implementing Advanced Audit Policy Settings

CERTIFICATION READY
Implement auditing using Group Policy and AuditPol.exe
Objective 5.1

In Windows Server 2008 R2, Windows introduced ***advanced audit policy settings***, which enable you to have more control over which events get recorded by using multiple subsettings instead of the traditional nine basic audit settings. Windows Server 2008 R2 introduced 53 subsettings. Windows Server 2012, 2012 R2 and 2016 feature 56 subsettings. By using advanced audit policy settings, you reduce the number of log entries so that you can focus on what is important to you.

To access a new policy, open Group Policy Management Editor for a group policy and go to Computer Configuration\Policies\Windows Settings\Security Settings\Advanced Audit Policy Configuration\Audit Policies\. Figure 11-4 shows the Account Logon settings.

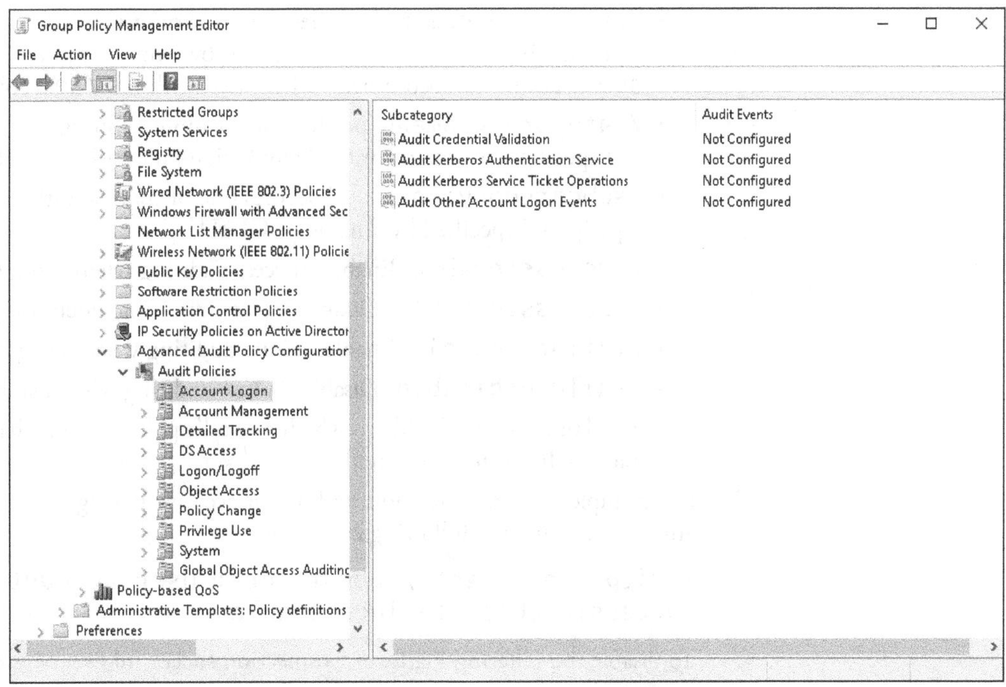

Figure 11-4

Accessing advanced audit policy settings

It is not recommended to use both basic audit policy settings and advanced audit policy settings because they might cause conflicts or erratic behavior. By default, when you apply Advanced Audit Policy Configuration, the basic audit policies are ignored.

If you need to go back to the basic audit settings after enabling Advanced Audit Policy Configuration, you need to perform the following steps:

1. Set all Advanced Audit Policy subcategories to Not configured.
2. Delete the %systemroot%\security\audit\audit.csv on the domain controllers for group policies and on the local computer for local policies.
3. Reconfigure and apply the basic audit policy settings.

Implementing Auditing Using AuditPol.exe

CERTIFICATION READY
Implement auditing using Group Policy and AuditPol.exe
Objective 5.1

To manage auditing at the command prompt or by creating scripts, use the ***AuditPol.exe*** command, which displays information about and performs functions to manipulate audit policies.

The syntax for `AuditPol.exe` includes the following commands:

- `/get`**:** Displays the current audit policy
- `/set`**:** Sets the audit policy
- `/list`**:** Displays selectable policy elements
- `/backup`**:** Saves the audit policy to a file
- `/restore`**:** Restores the audit policy from a file that was previously created by using `auditpol /backup`
- `/clear`**:** Clears the audit policy
- `/remove`**:** Removes all per-user audit policy settings and disables all system audit policy settings
- `/resourceSACL`**:** Configures global resource SACLs
- `/?`**:** Displays help at the command prompt

`Auditpol.exe` also includes the following subcommands:

- /user:<username>: Specifies the security principal for a per-user audit. Specify the username by security identifier (SID) or by name. Requires either the /category or /subcategory subcommand when used with the /set command.
- /category:<name>: Specifies one or more auditing categories separated by a pipe (|) and specified by a name or Globally Unique Identifier (GUID).
- /subcategory:<name>: Specifies one or more auditing subcategories separated by a pipe (|) and specified by a name or GUID
- /success:enable: Enables success auditing when using the /set command
- /success:disable: Disables success auditing when using the /set command
- /failure:enable: Enables failure auditing when using the /set command
- /failure:disable: Disables failure auditing when using the /set command
- /file: Specifies the file to which an audit policy is to be backed up or from which an audit policy is to be restored

For example, to configure auditing for user account management for success and failed attempts, execute the following command:

```
auditpol.exe /set /subcategory:"user account management" /
success:enable /failure:enable
```

To disable the Filtering Platform Connection successful events, execute the following command:

```
auditpol.exe /set /subcategory:"Filtering
Platform  Connection" /success:disable
```

To delete the per-user audit policy for all users, reset, or disable the system audit policy for all subcategories, and you want to set the audit policies settings to disable, execute the following command:

```
auditpol.exe /clear
```

If you want to delete the per-user audit policy for all users, reset, or disable the system audit policy for all subcategories, and you want to set all the audit policies settings to disable without a confirmation prompt, execute the following command:

```
auditpol.exe /clear /y
```

To remove the per-user audit policy for the jsmith account, execute the following command:

```
auditpol.exe /remove /user:jsmith
```

To remove the per-user audit policy for all users, execute the following command:

```
auditpol.exe /remove /allusers
```

To see all possible categories and subcategories, execute the following command:

```
auditpol.exe /list /subcategory:*
```

If you want to get an authoritative report on what audit settings are being applied, execute the following command:

```
auditpol.exe /get /category:*
```

To back up the audit policy for all users into a .CSV text file called auditpolicy.csv, execute the following command:

```
auditpol.exe /backup /file:C\auditpolicy.csv
```

To restore system audit policy settings from the auditpolicy.csv file, execute the following command:

```
auditpol.exe /restore /file:c:\auditpolicy.csv
```

Implementing Auditing Using Windows PowerShell

CERTIFICATION READY
Implement auditing using Windows PowerShell and AuditPol.exe
Objective 5.1

Windows PowerShell allows you to manage audit policies and review the events that occurred by using various number of Windows PowerShell cmdlets.

The following Windows PowerShell cmdlets are available.

- `Clear-EventLog`: Deletes all entries from specified event logs on a local or remote computer
- `Get-Event`: Gets the events in the event queue
- `New-Event`: Creates a new event
- `New-EventLog`: Creates a new event log and a new event source on a local or remote computer
- `Remove-Event`: Deletes events from the event queue
- `Remove-EventLog`: Deletes an event log or unregisters an event source
- `Show-EventLog`: Displays the event logs of the local or remote computer in Event Viewer
- `Write-EventLog`: Writes an event to an event log
- `Limit-EventLog`: Sets the event log properties that limit the size of the event log and the age of its entries

For example to retrieve all of the logs in the security log, you would execute the following command:

```
Get-EventLog
```

To show Failures, you will use a filter for the `EntryType`. For example, to show the newest 20 failure events, execute the following command:

```
$events = Get-EventLog Security -newest 20 | Where-Object {$_.
EntryType -eq 'FailureAudit'}
```

Viewing Audit Events

When an event happens that matches an audit policy, the event is recorded in the Event Viewer Security logs. Therefore, to view all audit events, you need to open the Event viewer and click Security, as shown in Figure 11-5.

Figure 11-5

Opening Security logs in Event Viewer

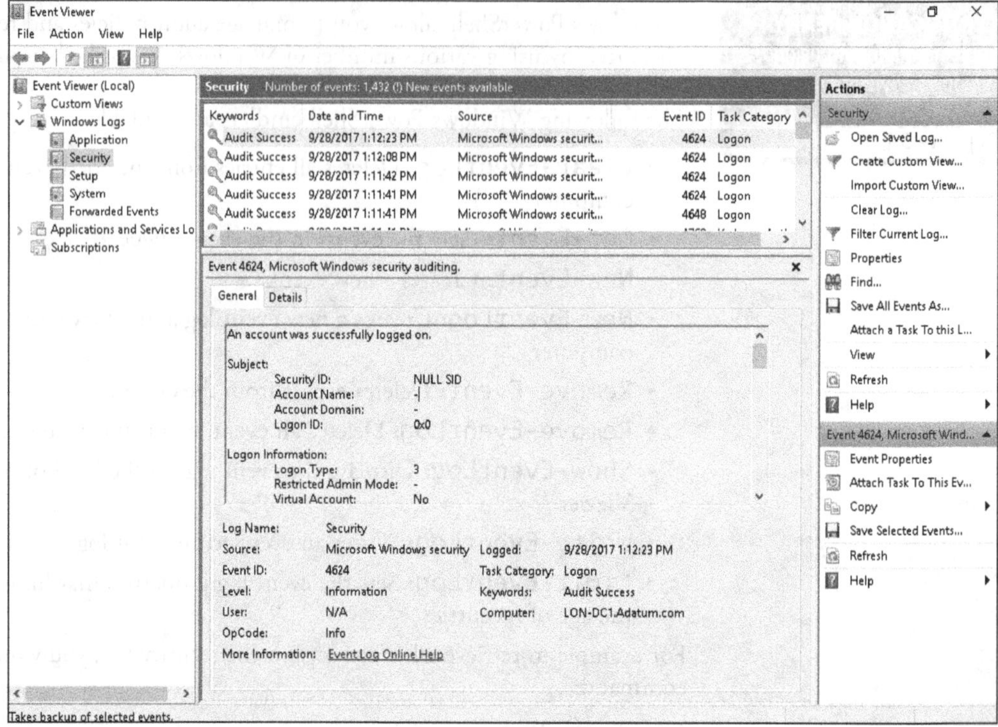

Much like the other logs found in Event Viewer, you usually want to grab certain events. For example, you can use a filter and specify the Event ID range (for example, 4624 shows that an account was successfully logged in and 4663 shows when an something attempted to access an object but was denied.

Creating Expression-Based Audit Policies

CERTIFICATION READY
Create expression-based audit policies
Objective 5.1

Windows Server 2012 introduced new advanced audit policies to implement more detailed and more precise auditing on the file system including configure global based audit policies and expression-based audit. Expression-based audit policies allow you to specify what to audit based on defined properties or attribute for documents (such as a department or country).

Global Object Access Auditing lets you define computer-wide system access control lists for either the file system or registry, rather than manually altering and maintaining SACLs on large sets of shared files or registry entries. In addition, the auditing is implicitly specified, which does not actually modify the files at all.

With ***Dynamic Access Control***, you can define certain attributes that define which department a file belongs to (such as the Finance department) and can be assigned to a larger set of files. You would then specify auditing based on the attribute.

ENABLE DYNAMIC ACCESS CONTROL RESOURCES

GET READY. To enable Dynamic Access Control resources, perform the following steps.

1. Log on to **LON-DC1** as **adatum\administrator** with the password of **Pa$$w0rd.**
2. In Server Manager, click **Tools > Active Directory Administrative Center.**
3. In the Active Directory Administrative Center, navigate to and click the **Dynamic Access Control** node.
4. Expand Dynamic Access Control and then select **Resource Properties**, as shown Figure 11-6.

Figure 11-6

Showing Dynamic Access Control Resource Properties

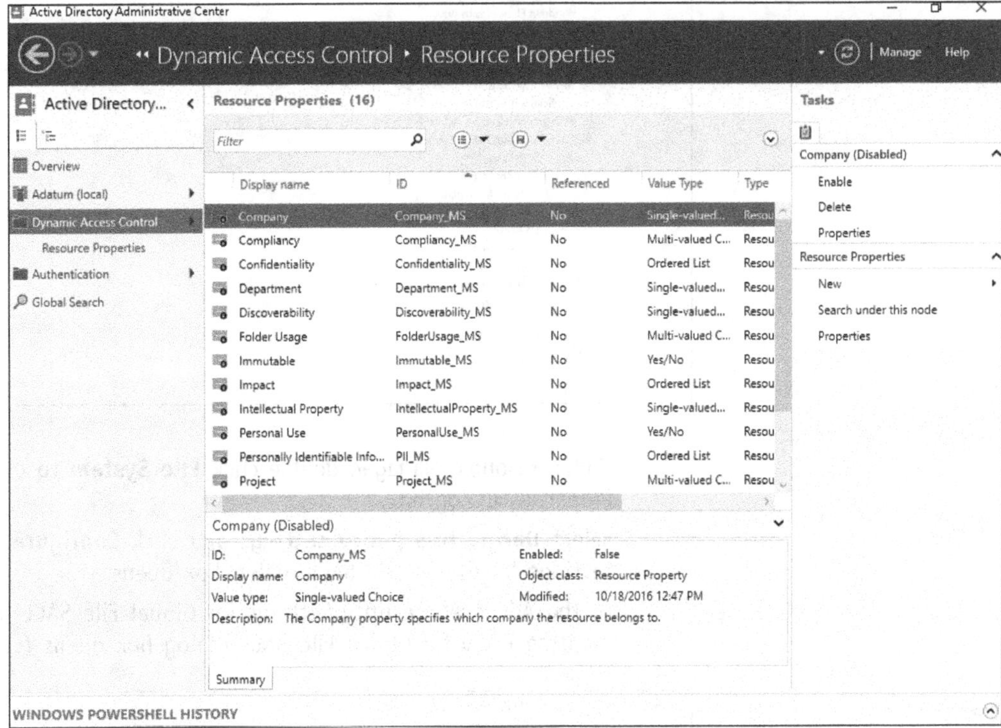

5. Right-click **Department** and choose **Properties.**
6. In the Suggested Values section, click **Add.**
7. In the Add a suggested value dialog box, in the Value and Display name text boxes, type **HR** and then click **OK.**
8. Close the Department dialog box by clicking **OK.**
9. Right-click **Department** and choose **Enable.**

DEFINE GLOBAL OBJECT ACCESS AUDITING

GET READY. To define Global Object Access Auditing, perform the following steps.

1. Log on to **LON-DC1** as **adatum\administrator** with the password of **Pa$$w0rd.** Server Manager automatically opens.
2. Click **Tools > Group Policy Management** to open the Group Policy Management console.
3. Right-click a group policy and choose **Edit.** Group Policy Management Editor opens.
4. Expand **Computer Configuration\Policies\Windows Settings\Security Settings\Advanced Audit policy\Audit Policies** and click **Global Object Access Auditing** to display the Global Object Access Auditing settings (see Figure 11-7).

Figure 11-7

Displaying the Global Object Access Auditing settings

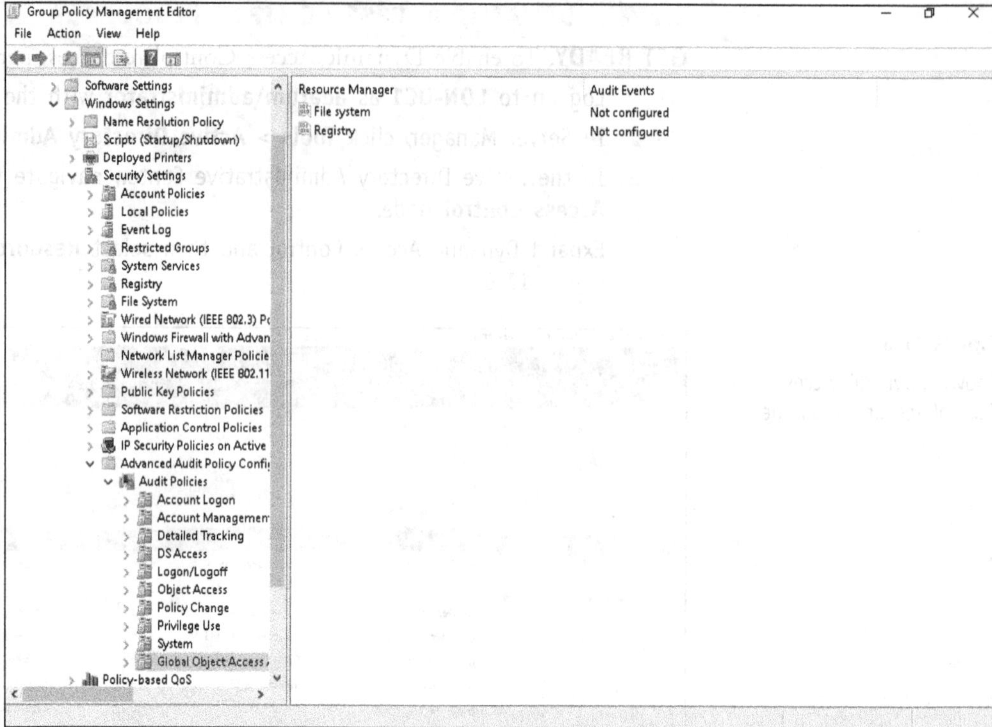

5. Under Resource Manager, double-click **File System** to display the File system Properties dialog box.
6. Select **Define this policy settings** and click **Configure.** The Advanced Security Settings for Global File SACL dialog box opens.
7. In the Advanced Security Settings for Global File SACL dialog box, click **Add.** The Auditing Entry for Global File SACL dialog box opens (see Figure 11-8).

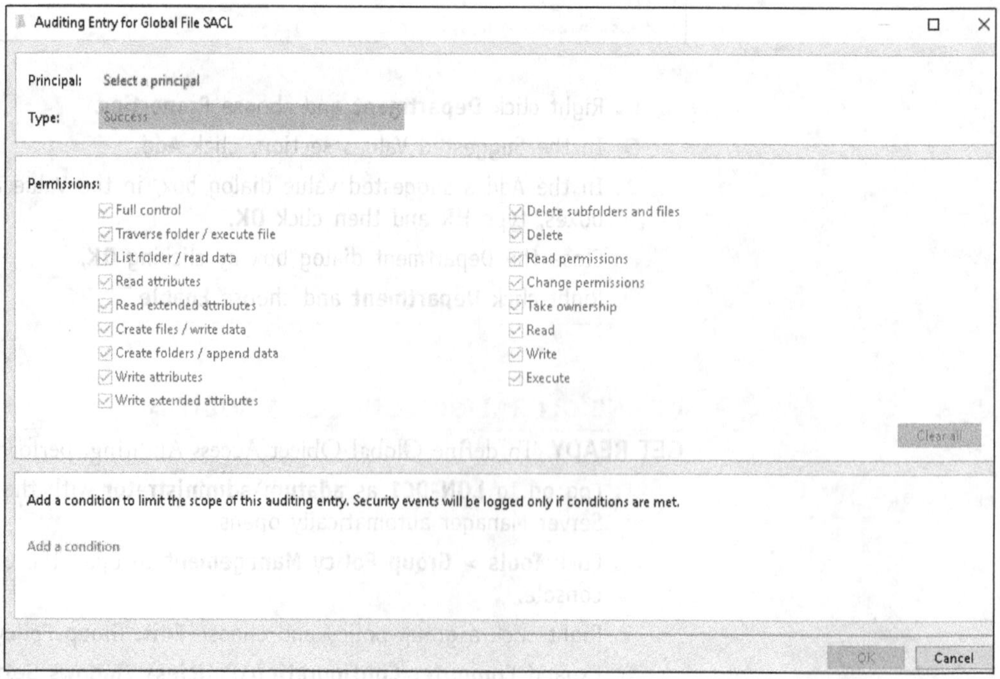

Figure 11-8

Opening the Auditing Entry for Global File SACL dialog box

Auditing Entry for Global File SACL
Principal: Select a principal
Type: Success
Permissions:
Full control
Traverse folder / execute file
List folder / read data
Read attributes
Read extended attributes
Create files / write data
Create folders / append data
Write attributes
Write extended attributes
Delete subfolders and files
Delete
Read permissions
Change permissions
Take ownership
Read
Write
Execute
Clear all
Add a condition to limit the scope of this auditing entry. Security events will be logged only if conditions are met.
Add a condition
OK Cancel

8. Click **Select a principal.** The Select User, Computer, Service Account, or Group dialog box opens. Type a name of a user or group in the Enter the object name to select box and click **OK.**
9. 9For the Type, select **Success**, **Fail**, or **All.**
10. Select the permissions that you want and deselect the permissions that you don't want.
11. Click **Add a condition.** A condition is added (see Figure 11-9).

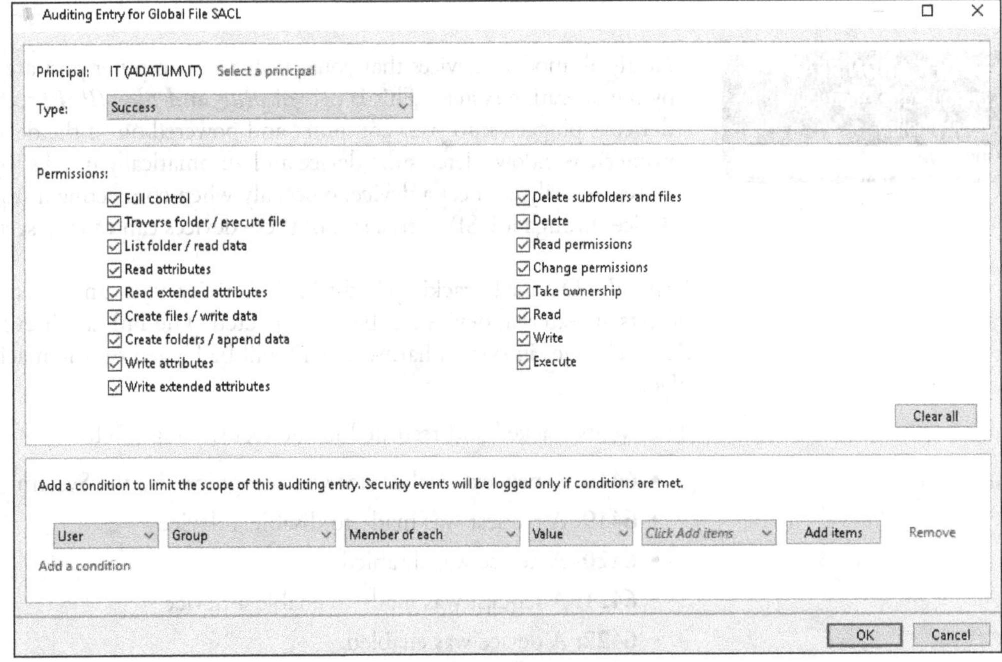

Figure 11-9

Adding a condition

12. Select the following options: **Resource**, **Department**, **Equals**, **Value**, and **HR** (see Figure 11-10).

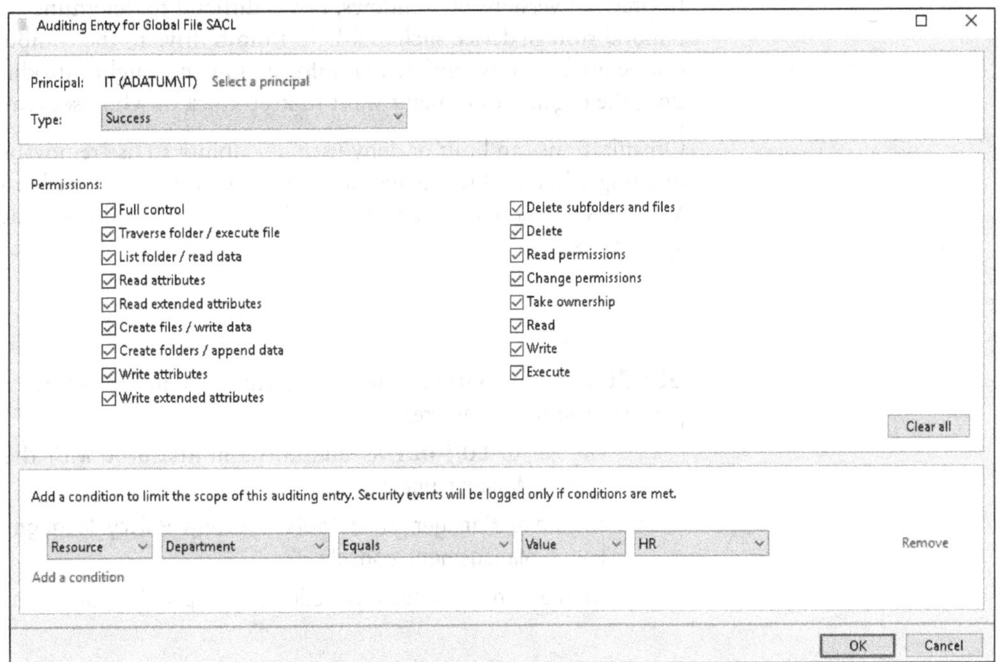

Figure 11-10

Specifying the conditions

13. Click **OK** to close the Auditing Entry for Global File SACL dialog box.
14. Click **OK** to close the Advanced Security Settings for Global File SACL dialog box.
15. Click **OK** to close the File system Properties dialog box.
16. Close the Group Policy Management Editor and Group Policy Management.

Configuring the Audit PNP and Removable Storage Devices Activity Policy

CERTIFICATION READY
Configure the Audit PNP Activity policy
Objective 5.1

Nearly all modern devices that you attach to a computer port are automatically detected by the operating system. This is part of ***plug-and-play (PnP)*** technology. As long as a PnP device is plugged into your computer and powered on (if the device requires power, like a printer), Windows detects the device and automatically installs the drivers. Since PnP allows a user to easily connect a device, especially when connecting a storage or communication device through a USB port, some of these devices can cause a security problem.

Using the Detailed Tracking\Audit PNP Activity, you can determine when Plug and Play detects an external device has been connected. The PnP audit events can be used to track down changes in system hardware and will be logged on the machine where the change took place.

The events tracked and recorded in the security logs include:

- **6416:** A new external device was recognized by the System
- **6419:** A request was made to disable a device
- **6420:** A device was disabled.
- **6421:** A request was made to enable a device.
- **6422:** A device was enabled.
- **6423:** The installation of this device is forbidden by system policy.
- **6424:** The installation of this device was allowed, after having previously been forbidden by policy.

In previous versions of Windows, it was difficult to determine whether a user connects a removal storage device such as a USB thumb drive to the computer. Because the USB devices can be used to copy confidential information and might introduce malware to the organization, the organization might want to keep track of who uses removable storage devices.

Organizations can limit or deny users the ability to use removable storage devices by implementing a Removable Storage Access policy. However, in earlier versions of the Windows and Windows Server operating systems, administrators could not track the use of removable storage devices.

CONFIGURE THE MONITORING OF REMOVABLE STORAGE DEVICES

GET READY. To configure the monitoring of removal storage devices such as USB drives, perform the following steps.

1. Log on to **LON-DC1** as **adatum\administrator** with the password of **Pa$$w0rd.** Server Manager opens.
2. In Server Manager, click **Tools > Group Policy Management** to open the Group Policy Management console.
3. In the console tree, right-click a group policy object and choose **Edit.**

4. Double-click **Computer Configuration**, double-click **Policies**, double-click **Windows Settings**, double-click **Security Settings**, double-click **Advanced Audit Policy Configuration**, double-click **Audit Policies**, and then double-click **Object Access.**
5. Double-click **Audit Removable Storage.** The Audit Removal Storage Properties dialog box opens.
6. Select the **Configure the following audit events** check box, select the **Success** check box, and then click **OK.**
7. Click **OK** to close the Group Policy Management Editor.

If you open the Event Viewer, you should look for event 4663 for successful attempts to access a removal storage device and 4656 for failed attempts.

Configuring the Audit Group Membership Policy

CERTIFICATION READY
Configure the Audit Group Membership policy
Objective 5.1

Since the early days of the Microsoft Server operating system, administrators used groups to manage network permissions. Groups enable you to assign permissions to multiple users simultaneously. A group can be defined as a list of user or computer accounts that functions as a security principal, in much the same way that a user does. Therefore, when someone is added to a group, the user receives rights and permissions that he or she may not have had before. Therefore, you should enable auditing of groups so that you can identify when someone is added to a group.

By enabling the Account Management\Audit Security Group option, you can record the following events:

- **4727:** A security-enabled global group was created.
- **4728:** A member was added to a security-enabled global group.
- **4729:** A member was removed from a security-enabled global group.
- **4730:** A security-enabled global group was deleted.
- **4731:** A security-enabled local group was created.
- **4732:** A member was added to a security-enabled local group.
- **4733:** A member was removed from a security-enabled local group.
- **4734:** A security-enabled local group was deleted.
- **4735:** A security-enabled local group was changed.
- **4737:** A security-enabled global group was changed.
- **4754:** A security-enabled universal group was created.
- **4755:** A security-enabled universal group was changed.
- **4756:** A member was added to a security-enabled universal group.
- **4757:** A member was removed from a security-enabled universal group.
- **4758:** A security-enabled universal group was deleted.
- **4764:** A group's type was changed.

Enabling and Configuring Module, Script Block, and Transcription Logging in Windows PowerShell

CERTIFICATION READY
Enable and configure Module, Script Block, and Transcription logging in Windows PowerShell
Objective 5.1

Module logging allows you to specify the PowerShell modules that you want to log. ***Script block*** stores PowerShell commands that are run without the output, while ***transcription logging*** records the PowerShell commands that are run along with the full result of the command. Since you can do so much with Windows PowerShell, you may consider creating an audit policy of the executed Windows PowerShell commands.

Different from the previous auditing, the auditing of these events is configured through a GPO Computer Configuration\Policies\Administrative Templates\Windows Components\Windows PowerShell. Alternately, you can configure these options using Windows PowerShell.

DEFINE GLOBAL OBJECT ACCESS AUDITING

GET READY. To define Global Object Access Auditing, perform the following steps.

1. On **LON-DC1**, click **Start** and then click **Windows PowerShell.**
2. To see the status of LogPipelineExecutionDetails, execute the following command:

```
Get-Module Microsoft.* |
Select Name, LogPipelineExecutionDetails
```

3. To turn on module logging for a module, type the following and then press **Enter** after each command:

```
Get-Module Microsoft.* | ForEach {
  $_.LogPipelineExecutionDetails = $True
}
Get-Module Microsoft.* |
Select Name, LogPipelineExecutionDetails
```

4. To review the event logs, execute the following two commands:

```
Get-EventLog Security -Newest 100
Get-ChildItem -Path C:\inetpub\wwwroot
```

5. Execute the following command:

```
Get-WinEvent -FilterHashtable @{LogName='Windows
PowerShell';Id ='800'} -MaxEvents 1 |
Select -Expand Message
```

6. In Server Manager, click **Tools > Group Policy Management.**
7. Right-click **Default Domain Policy** and choose **Edit.**
8. Navigate to **Computer Configuration\Policies\Administrative Templates\Windows Components\Windows PowerShell** and view the available options to configure PowerShell settings.
9. Click on each of the five options and read the description of each setting.
10. To configure script logging, you need to configure environment variables. Therefore, navigate to **Computer Configuration\Preferences\Window Settings.**
11. Right-click **Environment**, point to **New**, and then choose **Environment Variable.**
12. In the New Environment Properties dialog box, type the following information:

    Name: **PSLogScriptBlockExecution**

    Value: **0**

13. Click **OK.**
14. Right-click **Environment**, point to **New**, and then choose **Environment Variable**.
15. In the New Environment Properties dialog box, type the following information:

    Name: **PSLogScriptBlockExecutionVerbose**

    Value: **0**
16. Click **OK.**
17. Close the Group Policy Management Editor.
18. In Server Manager, click **Tools > Event Viewer**.
19. Review the Windows logs under System.
20. Navigate to the **Applications and Services/Microsoft/Windows, PowerShell/Operational** node to show you where the PowerShell logs are stored.
21. Close all open windows.

SKILL SUMMARY

IN THIS LESSON YOU LEARNED:

- Auditing provides a record of the users who have logged on, what the users accessed or tried to access, and what action the users performed, such as rebooting, shutting down a computer, or accessing a file.
- To enable auditing, specify which system events to audit using Group Policy or the local security policy (Computer Settings\Policies\Security Settings\Local Policies\Audit Policy).
- Starting with Windows Server 2008 R2, Windows introduced advanced audit policy settings, which enable you to have more control over which events get recorded by using multiple subsettings instead of the traditional nine basic audit settings.
- To manage auditing at the command prompt or by creating scripts, you use the AuditPol.exe command, which displays information about and performs functions to manipulate audit policies.
- Global Object Access Auditing lets you define computer-wide system access control lists for either the file system or registry, rather than manually altering and maintaining SACLs on large sets of shared files or registry entries. In addition, the auditing is implicitly specified, which does not actually modify the files at all.

Knowledge Assessment

Multiple Choice

1. In which of the following locations do you view the security events collected by auditing with group policies?
   a. Log viewer
   b. SysInfo
   c. Event Viewer
   d. Sys Viewer
2. To audit who accessed a file, which of the following must first be enabled?
   a. System auditing
   b. Process tracking
   c. Object access auditing
   d. Directory service access
3. To audit who modified a group policy, which of the following should be changed?
   a. Privilege Use
   b. Policy change
   c. System
   d. Directory service access
4. In which audit group is the Audit Filtering Platform Connection and Audit Filtering Platform Packet Drop located?
   a. System auditing
   b. Process tracking
   c. Object access auditing
   d. Directory service access
5. Which command should be used to show the current audit policies on a machine?
   a. auditpol.exe /get /subcategory:*
   b. auditpol.exe /list /category:*
   c. auditpol.exe /set /subcategory:*
   d. auditpol.exe /backup /file *
6. How many audit policy subsettings are found in the Advanced Audit Policy Settings?
   a. 21
   b. 53
   c. 56
   d. 61

7. Which command clears the audit policy on a computer?
   - **a.** auditpol /clear
   - **b.** auditpol /remove
   - **c.** auditpol /disable
   - **d.** auditpol /undone
8. Which of the following should be used to give you more control over which events to audit?
   - **a.** Granular Control Audit Policy
   - **b.** Pick and Choose Audit Policy
   - **c.** Advanced Audit Policy Settings
   - **d.** User-Defined Audit Policy Settings
9. Which of the following is defined when you configure auditing files and printers?
   - **a.** System Access Control Lists
   - **b.** Global Object Control Lists
   - **c.** Discretionary Access Control Lists
   - **d.** Programmed Access Control Lists
10. Which category is used to audit the registry?
    - **a.** Key auditing
    - **b.** Hive auditing
    - **c.** Object auditing
    - **d.** System auditing
11. Which type of audit policy is used to specify what to audit based on defined properties or attributes for a document?
    - **a.** Attribute detection audit policies
    - **b.** Variable audit policies
    - **c.** Flexible audit policies
    - **d.** Expression-based audit policies
12. Which audit setting is used to record changes to the local users and groups on a computer?
    - **a.** Object access
    - **b.** Logon
    - **c.** Account management
    - **d.** Directory service access

Best Answer

Choose the letter that corresponds to the best answer. More than one answer choice may achieve the goal. Select the BEST answer.

1. Which of the following are reasons *not* to enable auditing for everything? (Choose all that apply.)
   - **a.** Logs quickly fill up
   - **b.** Makes it difficult to find relevant events
   - **c.** Makes it impossible to secure computer
   - **d.** dAffects performance of computer

Matching and Identification

Match the Audit Event category that is used for the following events. Not all items will be used and items can be used more than once.

1. _____ Modify an Active Directory account
2. _____ Operating System logins
3. _____ Changing the time
4. _____ Reboot a server
5. _____ Log on to the computer
6. _____ Auditing a file
7. _____ Auditing a printer
8. _____ Changing user rights
9. _____ Filtering Platform Connection
10. _____ Removable devices

a. Account logon
b. Account management
c. Directory service access
d. Logon
e. Object access
f. Policy change
g. Privilege use
h. Process tracking
i. System

Build List

Specify the correct order of steps necessary to audit a printer. (Not all the steps will be used)

_____ Click Advanced.

_____ Specify what you are auditing such as Success, Fail or both.

_____ Open Printer Properties.

_____ Open Properties.

_____ Select Security.

_____ Select Auditing.

_____ Open View devices and printers.

_____ Open Device Manager.

_____ Click the Add button and add the user or group.

Business Case Scenarios

Scenario 11-1: Establishing an Audit Policy

You just established an audit policy that enables account logon, logon, object access, and account management. However, when you look at the logs, you see a large number of Audit Filtering Platform Connection and Audit Filtering Platform Packet Drop events that consume most of the security logs. Describe how to alleviate this problem.

Scenario 11-2: Monitor the Use of Mobile Storage Devices

Your manager assigns you the task of seeing how many users use mobile storage devices (such as USB thumb drives). Describe your recommended solution.

LESSON 12

Installing and Configuring Microsoft Advanced Threat Analytics (ATA)

70-744 EXAM OBJECTIVE

Objective 5.2 – Install and configure Microsoft Advanced Threat Analytics (ATA). This objective may include but is not limited to the following: Determine usage scenarios for ATA; determine deployment requirements for ATA; install and configure ATA Gateway on a dedicated server; install and configure ATA Lightweight Gateway directly on a domain controller; configure alerts in ATA Center when suspicious activity is detected; review and edit suspicious activities on the attack time line.

Lesson Heading	Exam Objective
Implementing Microsoft Advanced Threat Analytics (ATA)	
• Determining Usage Scenarios for ATA	Determine usage scenarios for ATA
• Determining Deployment Requirements for ATA	Determine deployment requirements for ATA
• Installing ATA	Install and configure ATA Gateway on a dedicated server
	Install and configure ATA Lightweight Gateway directly on a domain controller
• Configuring Alerts in ATA Center when Suspicious Activity is Detected	Configure alerts in ATA Center when suspicious activity is detected
• Reviewing and Editing Suspicious Activities on the Attack Time Line	Review and edit suspicious activities on the attack time line

KEY TERMS

Advanced Threat Analytics (ATA)
Advanced Threat Analytics Center (ATA Center)
ATA Gateway
ATA Lightweight Gateway
honeytoken accounts
intrusion detection systems (IDS)
intrusion prevention systems (IPS)

■ Implementing Microsoft Advanced Threat Analytics (ATA)

THE BOTTOM LINE

A common form of an attack is to compromise user credentials. With the right credentials, a hacker can access just about everything both *within* the network and *on* the network. Besides using malware to capture credentials, hackers can use a wide range of legitimate IT tools that can help them gain access to credentials. Unfortunately, this type of access is usually not discovered for months and can cause significant financial loss, the loss of confidential or sensitive data, or it can affect the reputation of the organization. To help detect intruders, you can use Microsoft Advanced Threat Analytics (ATA).

Intrusion detection systems (IDS) are designed to detect unauthorized user activities, attacks, and network compromises. ***Intrusion prevention systems (IPS)*** are very similar to an IDS, except that in addition to detecting and alerting, an IPS can also take action to prevent a breach from occurring.

There are two main types of IDS/IPS's:

- **Network-based:** A network-based IDS (NIDS) monitors network traffic using sensors that are located at key locations within the network, often in the demilitarized zone (DMZ) or at network borders. These sensors capture all network traffic and analyze the contents of individual packets for malicious traffic. A NIDS gains access to network traffic by connecting to a hub, a network switch configured for port mirroring, or a network Test Access Port (TAP).
- **Host-based:** A host-based system IDS (HIDS) generally has a software agent that acts as the sensor. This agent monitors all activity of the host on which it is installed, including monitoring the file system, logs, and the kernel to identify and alert on suspicious behavior. A HIDS is typically deployed to safeguard the host on which they are installed.

Advanced Threat Analytics (ATA) is an on-premise IDS platform that helps protect your organization from multiple types of advanced targeted cyber attacks and insider threats, including the following:

- Reconnaissance
- Credential compromise
- Lateral movement
- Privilege escalation
- Domain dominance
- Brute force
- Remote execution

It also looks for abnormal behavior, such as anomalous logins, password sharing, modifications of sensitive groups, broken trusts, weak protocols, and known protocol vulnerabilities.

ATA can produce a simple attack timeline showing activity. To reduce false positives, ATA generates alerts only after suspicious activities are contextually aggregated. False positives are alerts that are flagged as a security problem but are not actually a security problem. ATA also provides recommendations for investigation and remediation.

Determining Usage Scenarios for ATA

CERTIFICATION READY
Determine usage scenarios for ATA
Objective 5.2

ATA uses a network parsing engine to capture and parse network traffic to gather authentication, authorization, and information data. To collect the data, you need to determine where and how you will deploy ATA.

For ATA to collect the necessary data, you need to deploy one or both of the following:

- Non-intrusive port mirroring from Domain Controllers and DNS servers to the ATA Gateway
- An ATA Lightweight Gateway (LGW) directly on Domain Controllers

Besides looking at the network packets, ATA can look at the logs and events on the various systems, including your domain controllers.

ATA takes information from multiple data sources, such as logs and events in your network, to learn the behavior of users and other entities in the organization and build a behavioral profile about them. ATA can receive events and logs from:

- Security information and event management (SIEM) integration, where an agent is deployed to the various systems and where the agent will collect the necessary information.
- Windows Event Forwarding (WEF), where Windows can be configured to forward the necessary information to an ATA system.
- Directly from the Windows Event Collector (for the Lightweight Gateway)

Similar to an anti-malware software package, ATA uses signatures, which are stored in a database of known vulnerabilities. The signature contains patterns to look for when looking for signs of intrusion. Therefore, like an anti-malware software package, you need to keep ATA updated so that the database that stores known attack patterns can be updated with newly discovered attack patterns.

ATA also uses anomaly-based detection, where it creates a baseline over a period of time so that it can learn what the normal behavior is. After the baseline is created, it can compare current traffic patterns with the baseline to help detect abnormal activities. Unfortunately, if your network is already compromised when the baseline is created, ATA will determine that the compromised behavior is acceptable.

ATA will monitor Active Directory activity by examining Active Directory Domain Services (AD DS) traffic to understand authentication patterns. Since it is a behavior analytics tool, it can detect when a malicious hacker is hiding behind a valid user account, including when a hacker tries to fool ATA by making changes slowly.

Determining Deployment Requirements for ATA

CERTIFICATION READY
Determine deployment requirements for ATA
Objective 5.2

Every ATA deployment has two primary components: the Advanced Threat Analytics Center and the Advanced Threat Analytics Gateway. The ***Advanced Threat Analytics Center (ATA Center)*** manages the configuration settings for the ATA Gateways and ATA Lightweight Gateways. The ***ATA Gateway*** is installed on a dedicated server that monitors the traffic from your domain controllers using either port mirroring or a network TAP. The ***ATA Lightweight Gateway*** is installed directly on your domain controllers and monitors their traffic directly, without the need for a dedicated server or configuration of port mirroring.

The first component that needs to be installed is the ATA Center. The ATA Center is responsible for receiving data from any of the ATA Gateways, which includes ATA Lightweight Gateways, and stores the data in a database. It detects suspicious activity and abnormal behavior by running the ATA behavioral machine learning algorithms. It also provides a web management interface and it can be configured to send events and emails when abnormal or suspicious activity is detected.

The ATA Center has the following components:

- **Entity Receiver:** Receives batches of entities from all ATA Gateways and ATA Lightweight Gateways.
- **Network Activity Processor:** Processes all the network activities within each received batch.
- **Entity Profiler:** Profiles all the unique entities according to traffic and events.
- **Center Database**: Manages the process of writing network activities and events to the database.
- **Database:** Uses MongoDB for storing all the data in the system, which includes network activities, event activities, unique entities, suspicious activities, and ATA configuration.
- **Detectors:** Use a rules engine and machine learning algorithms to identify abnormal user behavior and suspicious activities on the network.
- **ATA Console:** Used for configuring ATA and monitoring suspicious activities that ATA detects on your network.

Since the ATA Lightweight Gateway resides directly on domain controllers, the ATA Lightweight Gateway monitors a single domain controller. If you manage multiple domain controllers, it is recommended that the ATA Lightweight Gateway is installed on all the domain controllers.

ATA Center requires the following:

- Windows Server 2012 R2 or later.
- The ATA Center and the ATA Gateway must have their time synchronized within five minutes of each other.
- The ATA Center requires a minimum of 30 days of data for user behavior analytics.
- The ATA Center should have at least one network adapter, but if you are using a physical server in a virtual LAN, you should have two adapters.
- When working on a physical server, you must disable non-uniform memory access (NUMA) in the BIOS.

In very large Active Directory deployments, you may need multiple ATA Centers.

The ATA Gateway and ATA Lightweight Gateway monitor network traffic from domain controllers to the ATA Gateway by using port mirroring or deep packet inspection. Port mirroring uses a physical or virtual switch or by using a network Test Access Port (TAP) that forwards all traffic to a designed port. Deep packet inspection (DPI) is a form of filtering used to inspect data packets sent from one computer to another over a network. The ATA Lightweight Gateway is directly installed on a domain controller and accesses the network packets and Windows events directly from the system. You can use a mix of ATA Gateways and ATA Lightweight Gateways.

A single ATA Gateway can monitor traffic from multiple domain controllers. The ATA Gateway requires two network adapters. One for normal communication with the server and another one that is dedicated to listen to the captured traffic via port mirroring. However, while the second network adapter sees all the traffic, only a small percentage of the traffic is analyzed.

The ATA Gateway includes the following components:

- **Network Listener:** Responsible for capturing network traffic and parsing the traffic.
- **Event Listener:** Responsible for capturing and parsing Windows events that are forwarded from a SIEM server on your network.
- **Windows Event Log Reader:** Responsible for reading and parsing Windows events that are forwarded to an ATA Gateway's Windows event log from the domain controllers.
- **Network Activity Translator:** Translates parsed traffic into a logical representation of the traffic that ATA (network activity) uses.
- **Entity Resolver:** Takes parsed data (network traffic and events) and resolves it with AD DS to find account and identity information. It also takes information and matches with the IP addresses that are found in the parsed data.
- **Entity Sender:** Responsible for sending the parsed and matched data to the ATA Center.

Important facts to know about the ATA Gateway include:

- It requires Windows Server 2012 R2 or later.
- You can install an ATA Gateway in either a domain or workgroup.
- You cannot install an ATA Gateway on a domain controller.
- It requires at least two network adapters (management and capture).
- When running ATA components on a virtual machine, ATA Gateway does not support dynamic memory or any other memory ballooning feature.
- The ATA Lightweight Gateway requires dual processor and 6 GB of memory.
- A minimum of 5 GB of space is required; 10 GB is recommended.

Installing ATA

CERTIFICATION READY
Install and configure ATA Gateway on a dedicated server
Objective 5.2

CERTIFICATION READY
Install and configure ATA Lightweight Gateway directly on a domain controller
Objective 5.2

To install ATA, you first need to download the software from the Microsoft website. You also need to perform some pre-work, including creating a domain user account/service account for the ATA, and you need to gather information such as a list of all subnets managed by Dynamic Host Configuration Protocol (DHCP). You also need to ensure that Microsoft Message Analyzer and Wireshark are not installed on any of the servers that are hosting the ATA Gateway or ATA Center because the drivers included within the software will conflict with the ATA Gateway and Lightweight Gateway drivers.

The user account/service account is a user account that needs read access to all the objects in the domain that ATA will be monitoring. It should also have read-only permissions on the Deleted Objects container, so that it can determine of any bulk deletion activities in the domain are occurring.

The high-level steps to install ATA are:

1. Verify that the network between the servers is working properly.
2. Download and install the ATA Center.
3. Configure ATA Gateway domain connectivity settings in the ATA Center.
4. Download the ATA Gateway setup package.
5. Install the ATA Gateway.

INSTALL THE ATA CENTER

GET READY. To install the ATA Center, perform the following steps.

1. Log on to **LON-DC1** as **adatum\administrator** with the password of **Pa$$w0rd.**
2. In Server Manager, click **Tools > Active Directory Users and Computers.**
3. Right-click the **IT** organizational unit (OU) and choose **New > User.**
4. In the New Object – User dialog box, type the following information and then click **Next:**

   First name: **ATA**

   Last name: **Read**

   User logon name: **ataread**
5. In the New Object - User dialog box, in the Password text box and the Confirm password text box, type **Pa$$w0rd.**
6. Clear the check box for **User must change password at next logon.**
7. Click **Next** and then click **Finish.**
8. Close Active Directory Users and Computers.
9. Log on to **LON-SVR1,** as **adatum\administrator** with the password of **Pa$$w0rd.**
10. On **LON-SVR1**, on the desktop taskbar, right-click the Network icon and choose **Open Network and Sharing Center.**
11. On Network and Sharing Center, click **Change adapter settings** and then right-click **Ethernet** and choose **Properties.**
12. Select **Internet Protocol Version 4 (TCP/IPv4)** and then click **Properties.**
13. In the Internet Protocol Version 4 Properties dialog box, click **Advanced.**
14. In the Advanced TCP/IP Settings dialog box, on the IP Settings tab, under IP addresses, click **Add.**
15. In the IP address text box, type **172.16.0.13.** Verify that the Subnet mask defaults to **255.255.0.0.** Click **Add**, click **OK** twice, and then click **Close.**
16. In Server Manager, click **Tools > Internet Information Services (IIS) Manager.**
17. In IIS Manager, expand **LON-SVR1**, expand **Sites**, and then click **Default Web Site.**
18. In the Actions pane, click **Bindings.**
19. Select **https** and then click **Remove.**
20. Click **Yes** and then close all open windows.
21. Open File Explorer, and navigate to the **\\lon-dc1\software** folder.
22. Double-click the **ATA1.8.1.iso.**
23. Double-click the **Microsoft ATA Center Setup.exe.**
24. Select your language on the Microsoft Advanced Threat Analytics form and then click **Next.**
25. Select **I accept the Microsoft Software License Terms** and click **Next.**
26. Since the Windows Update service is disabled for this lab, click **Next.**
27. On the Configure the Center page, select the **Create self-signed certificate** option (as shown in Figure 12-1 and then click **Install.**

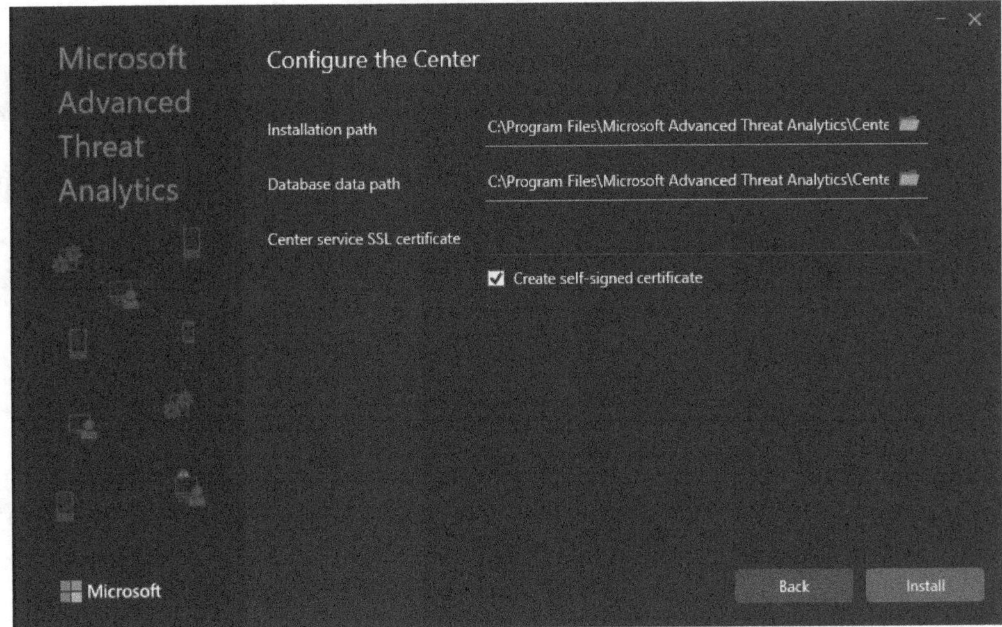

Figure 12-1

Viewing the Configure the Center page

28. After the installation is complete, click the **Launch** button. When you the website's security certificate page appears, click **Configure to this site (not recommended)**.
29. Right-click the **Start** button and choose **Computer Management**.
30. Under System Tools, expand **Local Users and Groups** and then select **Groups**.
31. Right-click **Microsoft Advanced Threat Analytics Administrators** and choose **Add to Group**.
32. Click **Add**, and then in the Enter the object names to select text box, type **Beth**.
33. Click **Check Names** and then click **OK**.
34. Click **Add**, and then in the Enter the object names to select text box, type **ATARead**.
35. Click **Check Names** and then click **OK**.
36. Click **OK** to close the Microsoft Advanced Threat Analytics Administrators Properties dialog box.
37. Close Computer Management.
38. On the Sign-in page, type **Beth** as the username and **Pa55w.rd** as the password. For the Domain, type **adatum.com**. Click **Save**.
39. At the top of the window, click the first button next to Microsoft.
40. In the upper-right corner of the form, click the ellipses (**...**) button (Note that the ellipses are vertical, not horizontal). Then click **Configuration**. The ATA Center appears, as shown in Figure 12-2.

Figure 12-2
Configuring ATA Center

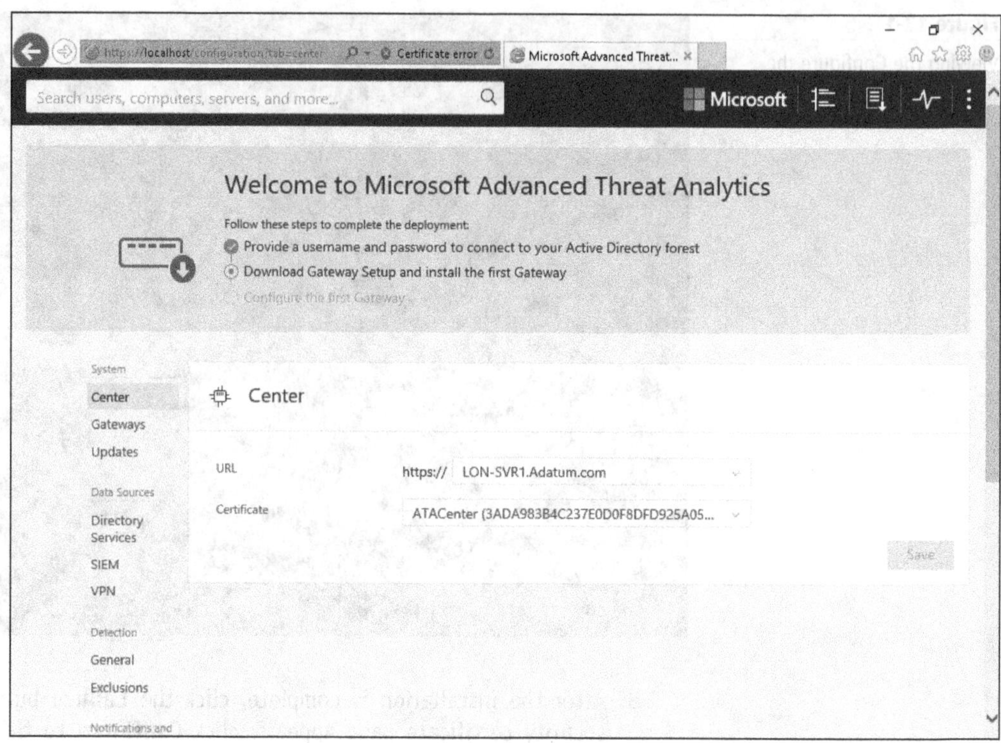

41. For the Certificate, select **LON-SVR1.adatum.com** and then click **Save.**
42. On the left, under Data Sources, click **Directory Services.**
43. On the Directory Services page, type a Username of **ATARead**, a Password of **Pa$$wOrd**, and a Domain of **adatum.com.** Click **Save.**
44. In the blue header, click **Download Gateway setup.**
45. Click **Gateway Setup**, and then save the file at **\\LON-DC1\software.**

INSTALL THE ATA GATEWAY OR ATA LIGHTWEIGHT GATEWAY

GET READY. To install the ATA Center, perform the following steps.

1. On **LON-DC1,** open File Explorer and browse to **\\LON-DC1\software.**
2. Right-click **Microsoft ATA Gateway Setup.zip** and choose **Extract All.**
3. In the Extract Compressed (Zipped) Folders dialog box, click **Extract.**
4. In \\LON-DC1\software\Microsoft ATA Gateway Setup folder, right-click **Microsoft ATA Gateway Setup.exe** and choose **Run as administrator.**
5. The first page prompts you to select your language. By default, English is selected. Click **Next** to accept the default setting.
6. Review the ATA Gateway deployment type. If you are installing on a domain controller, ATA Lightweight Gateway will already selected. If it is not a domain controller, ATA Gateway will be selected. Click **Next.**
7. On the Configure the Gateway page, click **Install.**
8. After the installation is complete, click **Finish.**

When the installation is complete, in the ATA Center, the Lightweight Gateway is running but the Gateway needs to be configured. See Figure 12-3. To configure the gateway, click the gateway name. Then enable the Domain synchronizer candidate, as shown in Figure 12-4. For the ATA Gateway, you need to configure port mirroring.

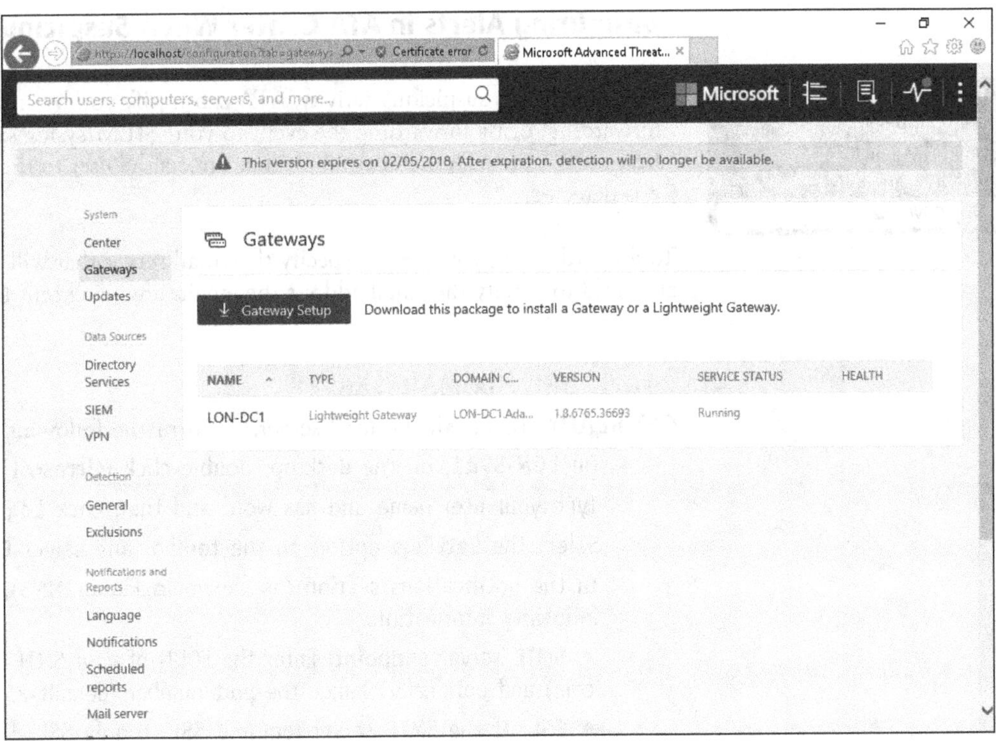

Figure 12-3

Viewing the ATA Gateways

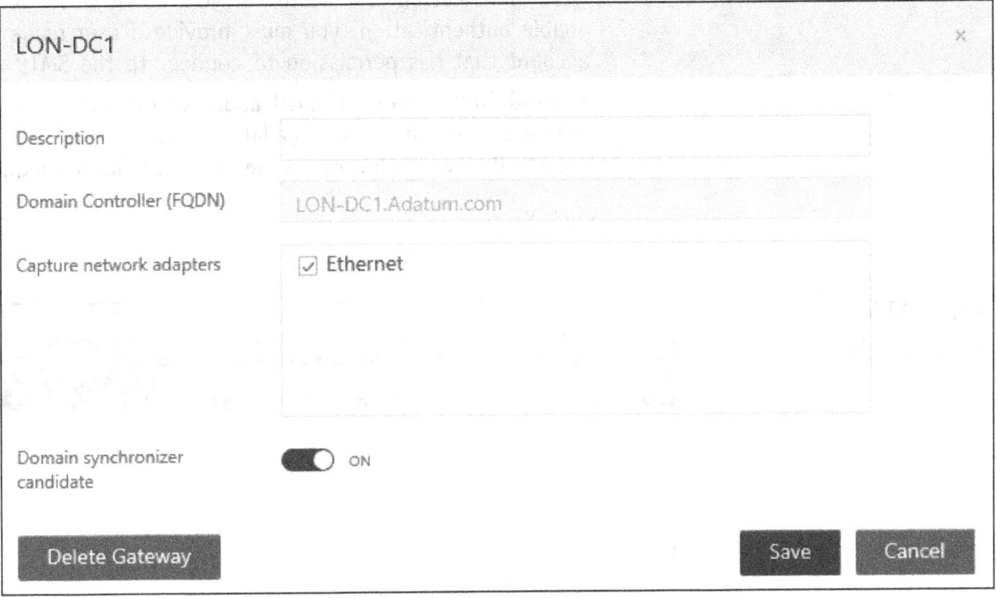

Figure 12-4

Configuring the ATA Gateway

Configuring Alerts in ATA Center When Suspicious Activity is Detected

CERTIFICATION READY
Configure alerts in ATA Center when suspicious activity is detected
Objective 5.2

When it detects suspicious activity, ATA can notify you by email, by using ATA event forwarding, or by forwarding the event to your SIEM/syslog server. When an email notification is sent, ATA includes a link that directs the user to the suspicious activity that was detected.

To forward email, you need to specify the email server that will accept SMTP packets. You also need to specify the email address the emails are being sent from.

CONFIGURE THE MAIL SERVER

GET READY. To install the mail server, perform the following steps.

1. On **LON-SVR1**, on the desktop, double-click **Microsoft ATA Console** icon.
2. Type your user name and password and then click **Log in.**
3. Select the **Settings** option on the toolbar and select **Configuration.**
4. In the notifications section (as shown in Figure 12-5), under Mail server, type the following information:
   - **SMTP server endpoint:** Enter the FQDN of your SMTP server (such as smtp.adatum.com) and optionally change the port number (default 25).
   - **SSL:** If the SMTP server required SSL, toggle SSL. If you enable SSL, you will also need to change the Port number.
   - **Authentication:** Enable this if your SMTP server requires authentication. If you enable authentication, you must provide a user name and password of an email account that has permission to connect to the SMTP server.
   - **Send from:** Enter an email address from whom the email will be sent from. For example, you can use ATA@adatum.com.

   The SMTP server endpoint and Send from fields are required.
5. Click **Save.**

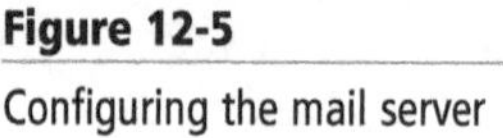

Figure 12-5
Configuring the mail server

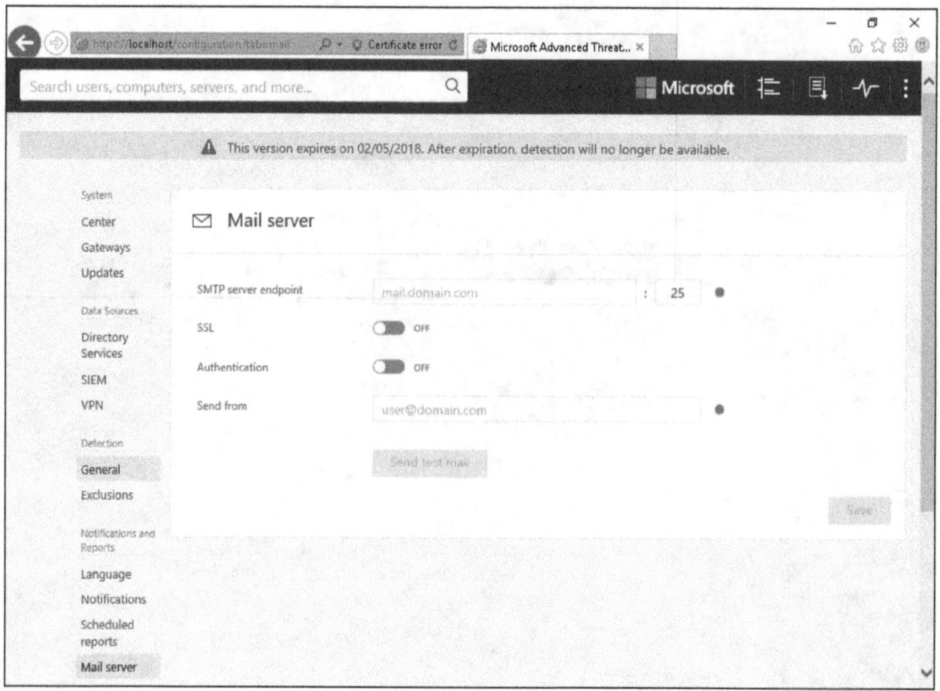

Reviewing and Editing Suspicious Activities on the Attack Time Line

CERTIFICATION READY
Review and edit suspicious activities on the attack time line
Objective 5.2

When you log into the ATA Console, you are automatically taken to the open Suspicious Activities Time Line. Suspicious activities will be listed with the newest suspicious activities on the top of the time line.

Each suspicious activity has the following information:

Entities involved, including users, computers, servers, domain controllers, and resources.

Times and time frame of the suspicious activities.

Severity of the suspicious activity: High, Medium, or Low.

Status: Open, closed, or suppressed.

See Figure 12-6.

Figure 12-6
Viewing suspicious activity

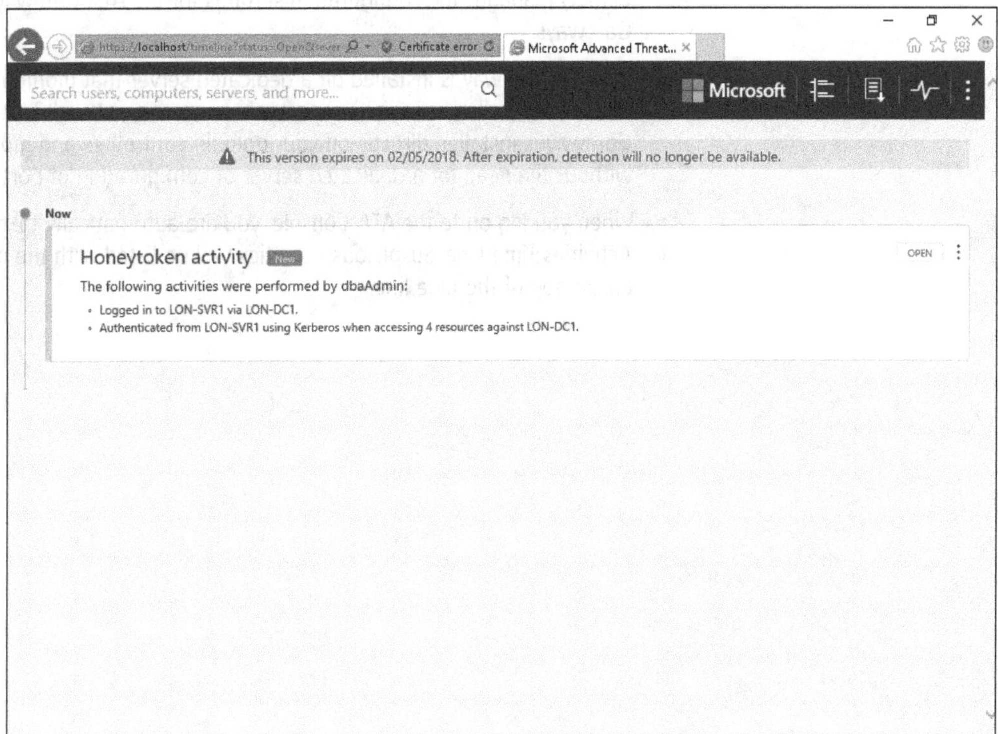

By clicking the ... button, you can perform the following actions:

- Close the alert
- Suppress the alert
- Close the alert and execute the specified system.
- Download details of the alert
- Share the suspicious activity with other people in your organization via email.

It is best practice to rename the domain administrator account to a different non- important looking account. You should then create a non-administrative account named administrator. By switching the accounts, hackers will target the non-administrative account.

ATA allows you define ***honeytoken accounts***, which are accounts that look like administrative accounts but aren't actually administrative accounts. So besides the dummy administrator account, you create other dummy accounts such as dbaAdmin, or EnterpriseAdmin. You can define honeytoken accounts on the General page.

SKILL SUMMARY

IN THIS LESSON YOU LEARNED:

- Intrusion detection systems (IDS) are designed to detect unauthorized user activities, attacks, and network compromises.
- Advanced Threat Analytics (ATA) is an on-premise intrusion detection system (IDS) platform that helps protect your organization from multiple types of advanced targeted cyberattacks and insider threats.
- ATA uses a network parsing engine to capture and parse network traffic to gather authentication, authorization and information data. To collect the data, you need to determine where and how you will deploy ATA.
- Every ATA deployment has two primary components: the Advanced Threat Analytics Center and the Advanced Threat Analytics Gateway. The Advanced Threat Analytics Center (ATA Center) manages the configuration settings for the ATA Gateways and ATA Lightweight Gateways.
- The ATA Gateway is installed on a dedicated server that monitors the traffic from your domain controllers using either port mirroring or a network TAP. The ATA Lightweight Gateway is installed directly on your domain controllers and monitors their traffic directly, without the need for a dedicated server or configuration of port mirroring.
- When you log on to the ATA Console, you are automatically taken to the open Suspicious Activities Time Line. Suspicious activities will be listed with the newest suspicious activities on the top of the time line.

Knowledge Assessment

Multiple Choice

1. Which type of system is Advanced Threat Analytics?
   a. LAPS
   b. EID
   c. IDS
   d. IPS
2. Which type of system is used to detect unauthorized user activities, attacks, and network compromises but is not used to prevent the actual attack?
   a. IDS
   b. IPS
   c. LAPS
   d. EID
3. Which of the following can be detected by ATA? (Choose all that apply)
   a. Brute force attacks
   b. password sharing
   c. Opening of documents
   d. modifications of sensitive groups
4. Which gateway is loaded on a domain controller?
   a. ATA Entity Receiver
   b. ATA Lightweight Gateway
   c. ATA Gateway
   d. ATA Center
5. Which type of Gateway uses port mirroring to capture the necessary traffic?
   a. ATA Entity Receiver
   b. ATA Lightweight Gateway
   c. ATA Gateway
   d. ATA Center
6. How many adapters should be installed on the ATA Gateway?
   a. 1
   b. 2
   c. 3
   d. 4

7. Which of the following is used by ATA to notify you of security problems? (Choose two answers)
   a. Windows popups
   b. Emails
   c. ATA messenger
   d. Events

Best Answer

Choose the letter that corresponds to the best answer. More than one answer choice may achieve the goal. Select the BEST answer.

1. Which of the following is most effective for detecting login security problems on your network?
   a. SCCM
   b. ATA
   c. OMS
   d. SCOM

Build List

1. Specify the correct order to steps necessary to install ATA.

_____ Download and install the ATA Center.

_____ Install the ATA Gateway.

_____ Verify the network between the servers is working properly.

_____ Configure the ATA Gateway domain connectivity settings in the ATA Center.

_____ Download the ATA Gateway setup package.

■ Business Case Scenarios

Scenario 12-1: Installing ATA

You manage a single data center with eight domain controllers and you are deploying ATA. You want to install a single server that will capture all of the necessary packets for security analysis. Describe your recommended solution and describe how to install and configure the ATA.

Scenario 12-2: Installing an IDS

You manage three data centers (each with multiple domain controllers) and 15 sites with a single domain controller. You want to deploy a free Microsoft IDS that will help detect security login problems. Describe your recommended solution and describe how to configure the new solution.

Determining Threat Detection Solutions Using Operations Management Suite (OMS)

LESSON 13

70-744 EXAM OBJECTIVE

Objective 5.3 – Determine threat detection solutions using Operations Management Suite (OMS). This objective may include but is not limited to the following: Determine usage and deployment scenarios for OMS; determine security and auditing functions available for use; determine Log Analytics usage scenarios.

Lesson Heading	Exam Objective
Determining Threat Detection Solutions Using Operations Management Suite (OMS)	
• Determining Usage and Deployment Scenarios for OMS	Determine usage and deployment scenarios for OMS
• Determining Log Analytics Usage Scenarios	Determine Log Analytics usage scenarios
• Determine Security and Auditing Functions Available for Use	Determine security and auditing functions available for use

KEY TERMS

Log Analytics service

Microsoft Operations Management Suite (OMS)

Solutions Gallery

System Center Operations Manager (SCOM)

Determining Threat Detection Solutions Using OMS

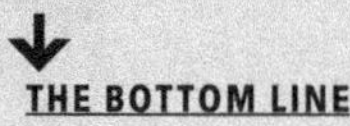

System Center Operations Manager (SCOM) is the part of the System Center suite that is the primary tool for monitoring an on-premise enterprise environment. You can monitor multiple computers, devices, services, and applications using the Operations Manager console. ***Microsoft Operations Management Suite (OMS)*** is a cloud-based collection of management services that helps you manage and protect your cloud and on-premises environments. Microsoft OMS offers log analysis, IT automation, backup and disaster recovery, security, and compliance.

Since OMS is a cloud-based service, it can be quickly implemented with minimal investment. In addition, it can be integrated with System Center 2016 (including Operations Manager) and it can be used to manage and help protect Microsoft Azure or Amazon Web Services (AWS), Windows Server or Linux, and VMware or OpenStack.

OMS provides log analysis, which automatically collect and analyze data and gives you real-time insight about your workloads and servers. Based on what is discovered, the Azure Automation feature can provide configuration management and process automation, including automating administrative processes with runbooks. Runbooks are based on Windows PowerShell and run in Azure.

OMS includes backup and disaster recovery via Microsoft Azure Backup and Microsoft Azure Site Recovery to help protect data and ensure the availability of your servers and applications. It can back up physical and virtual servers running Windows server and it can back up workloads such as Microsoft SQL Server, Microsoft Exchange, and Microsoft SharePoint. You can also replicate virtual machines to a secondary datacenter or extend your datacenter by replicating them to Azure.

OMS can help you identify, access, and mitigate security risks in your infrastructure via the following features:

- The Security and Audit solution collects and analyzes security events on managed systems to identify suspicious activity.
- The Antimalware solution reports on the status of antimalware protection on managed systems.

It can also review security and other updates of managed systems to identify systems that require updates.

DEPLOY AND CONFIGURE OMS

GET READY. To configure and deploy OMS, perform the following steps.

1. Log on to **LON-CL1** as **LON-CL1\Admin** with the password of **Pa$$w0rd.**
2. On **LON-CL1**, open the **Microsoft Edge** browser.

TAKE NOTE* As Microsoft adds new features and fine-tunes existing features, Microsoft often changes their site over time. Therefore, these instructions may not always match the current site.

3. In the Microsoft Edge address bar, type **https://www.microsoft.com/en-us/server-cloud/operations-management-suite** and press **Enter.**
4. Click **Create a free account.**

5. Scroll down and click **Start Free.**
6. On the sign in page, click **Create a new Microsoft account.**
7. On the Create account page, type a name of a Microsoft account (such as John.Smith@msn.com). Then type the related password and then click **Next.**
8. In the Enter code page, type the code that was sent to the email address you specified in the previous step.
9. In the Create New Workspace page, specify the following information:

   Workspace Name: **<FirstName><LastName><Month><Year>**

   Email: **<your email address>**

   Phone Number: **<your cell phone number>**

   Company: **<FirstName><LastName><Month><Year>**
10. For Country, select your country.
11. Select **I agree to the subscription agreement, offer details, and privacy statement** and then click **Create.**
12. On the Link Azure Subscription page, ensure Azure Pass is selected and then click **LINK.**
13. On the Microsoft Operations Management Suite home page (as shown in Figure 13-1), click **Solutions Gallery.**

Figure 13-1

Opening the Microsoft Operations Management Suite

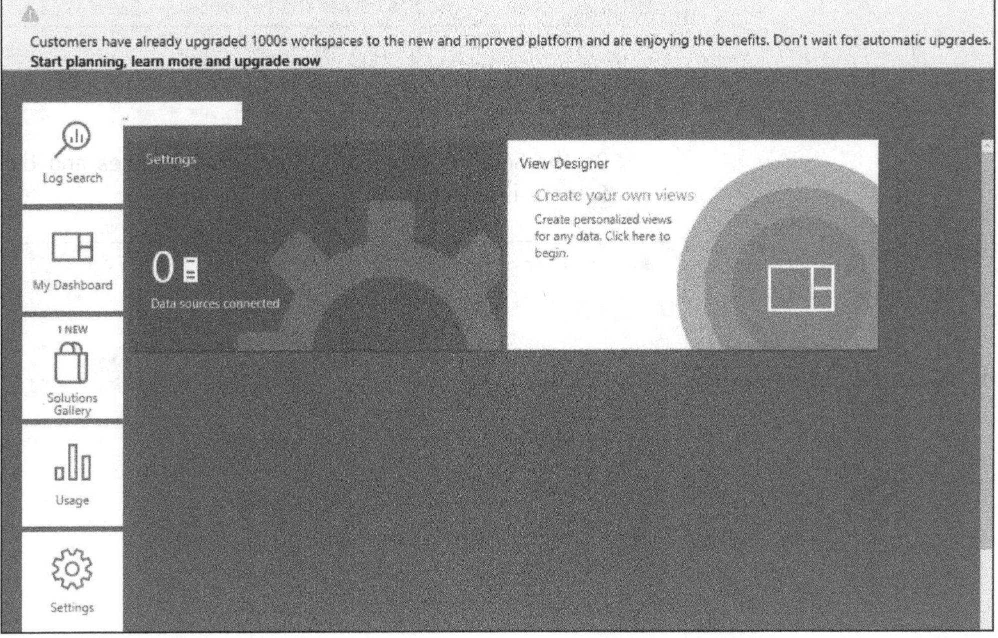

14. On the Solutions Gallery page, review the available solutions (see Figure 13-2) and then click the **home** (house) icon on the left side.

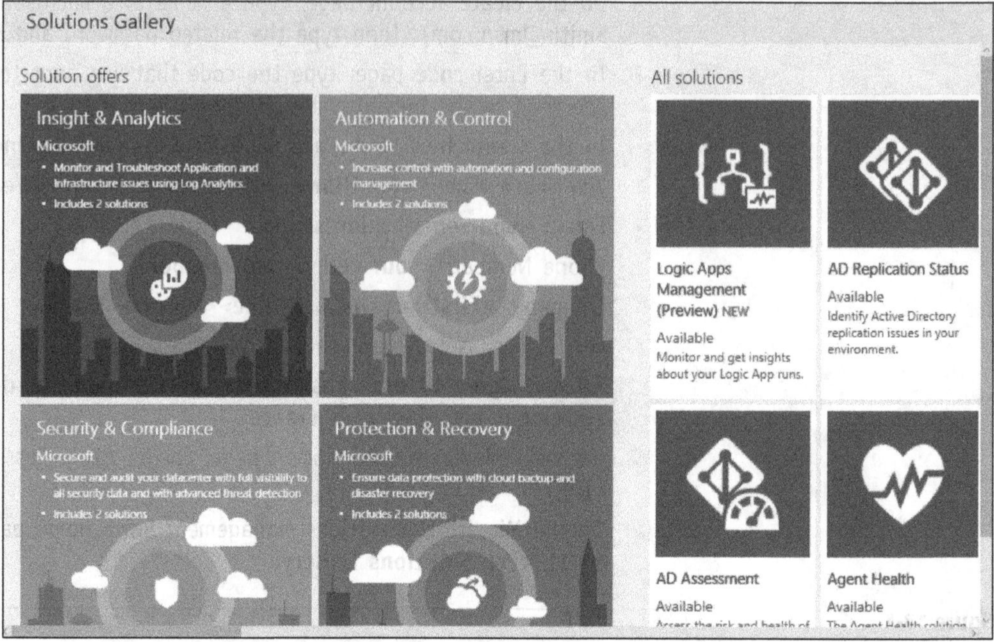

Figure 13-2
Viewing the Solutions Gallery

15. On the Microsoft Operations Management Suite home page, click **Settings** (gear) icon.

16. On the Settings page, click **Connected Sources** and then ensure that **Windows Servers** is selected, as shown in Figure 13-3.

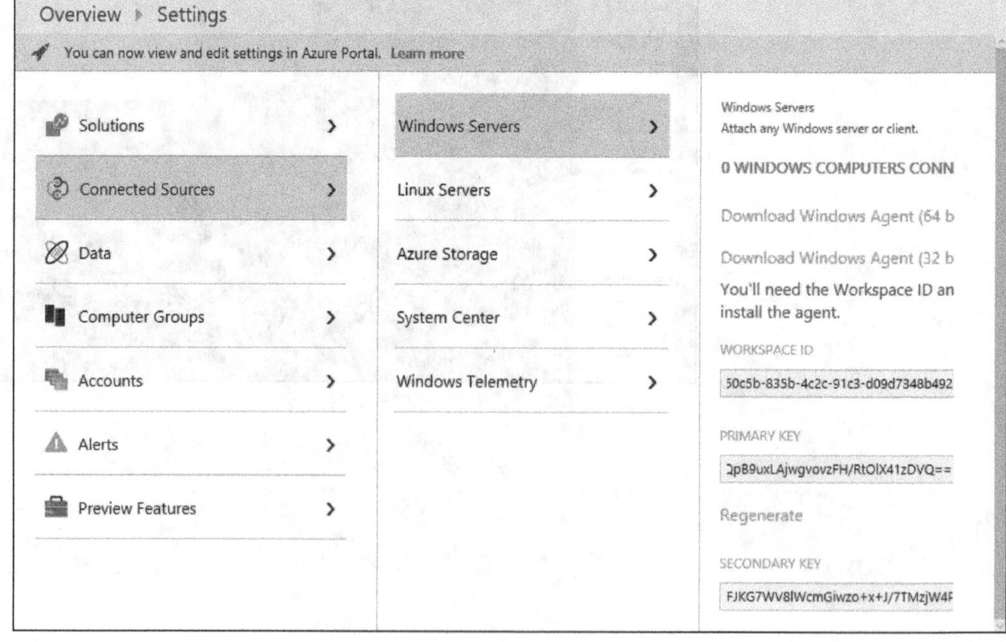

Figure 13-3
Managing connected sources

17. Click the **Start** button, type **Notepad**, and then press **Enter**.

18. Return to Microsoft Edge.

19. In the right pane, copy the WORKSPACE ID and PRIMARY KEY and then paste the IDs in Notepad.
20. Save the Notepad file as **C:\WorkspaceID.txt** (in case you need it later).
21. Return to Microsoft Edge and click **Download Windows Agent (64 bit)**.
22. After **MMASetup-AMD64.exe** downloads, click **Save** and then click **Run.**
23. At the User Account Control prompt, click **Yes.**
24. In the Welcome to the Microsoft Monitoring Agent Setup Wizard, click **Next.**
25. Read the Microsoft Software License Terms and then click **I Agree.**
26. Accept the default destination folder by clicking **Next.**
27. Select **Connect the agent to Azure Log Analytics (OMS)** and then click **Next.**
28. On the Azure Log Analytics page, enter the Workspace ID and Workspace Key and then click **Next.**
29. Click **Install** and then click **Finish.**
30. Right-click the **Start** button and choose **Control Panel.**
31. In Control Panel, click **System and Security** and then click **Microsoft Monitoring Agent.**
32. At the User Account Control prompt, click **Yes.**
33. Click the **Azure Log Analytics (OMS)** tab (as shown in Figure 13-4), select the listed item and then click **Edit.** This allows you to update the Workspace Key. Copy the Workspace Key saved earlier and then click **OK.**

Figure 13-4

Managing the Microsoft Monitoring Agent

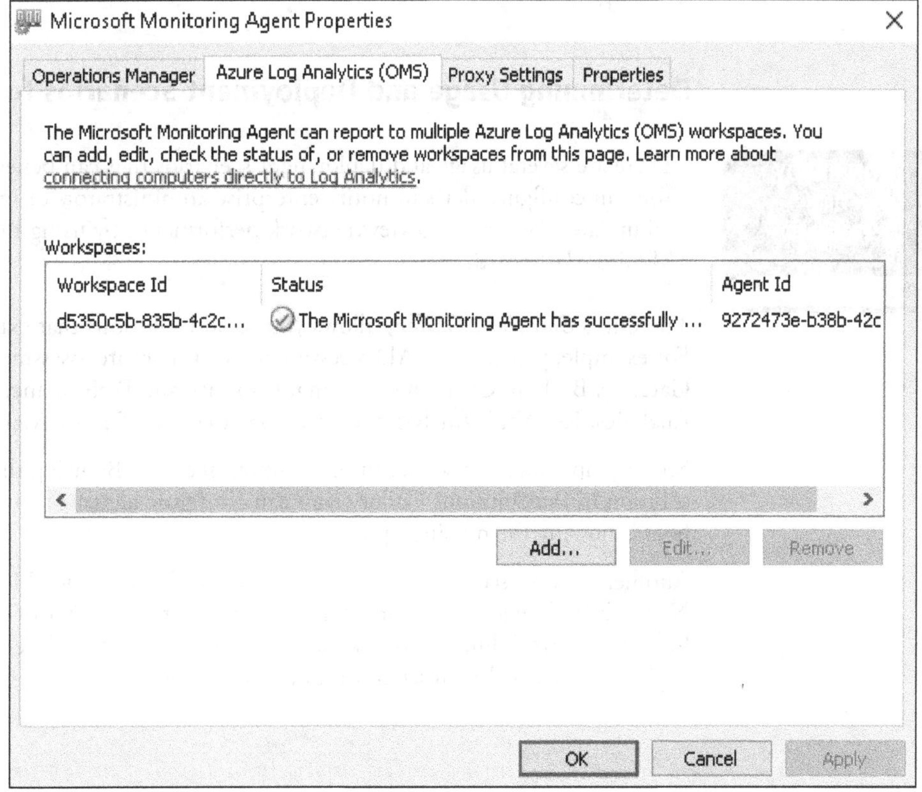

34. Click **Cancel.**
35. Return to the Microsoft Operations Management Suite Overview page and then refresh your browser.

After several minutes, the system information will start populating in OPS, as shown in Figure 13-5. You can click Export to export the found data and you can also click Alert to view alerts and click History to review the history.

Figure 13-5

Reviewing a system in OMS

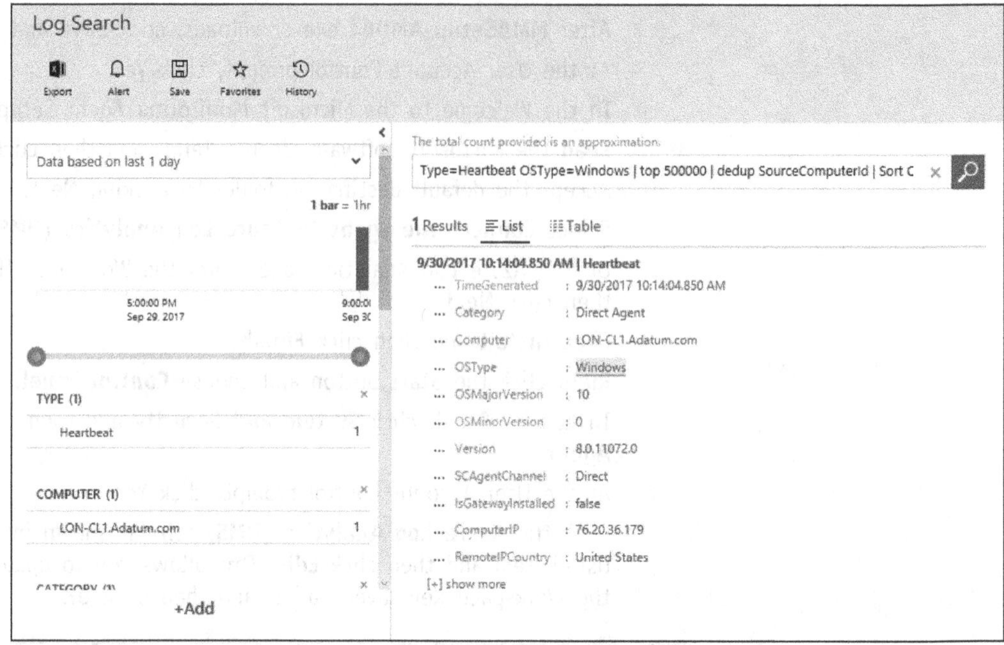

Determining Usage and Deployment Scenarios for OMS

CERTIFICATION READY
Determine usage and deployment scenarios for OMS
Objective 5.3

There are several usage and deployment scenarios that can benefit your organization. You can configure alerts to notify enterprise administrators of missing security and critical updates. You can also view network performance by using the Network Performance Monitor dashboard.

The OMS ***Solutions Gallery*** allows you to add solutions that extend the capability of OMS. For example, you can add AD assessment, Anti-malware assessment, Azure Application Gateway, Backup, Changing Tracking, Capacity and Performance, Upgrade Readiness, DNS Analytics, Key Vault Analytics, Office 365 Analytics, Service Map, and many others.

Security updates are essential in maintaining security. By using the System Update Assessment solution in the Solutions Gallery, you can configure alerts, generate a report, or create a dashboard showing the missing updates.

Another possible scenario is to provide Network Performance Monitor dashboard. The Network Performance Monitor dashboard shows the number of current networks, network links, subnetwork links, network paths, network devices, and network interfaces. Additionally, it gives you a visual representation of areas of concern.

Determining Log Analytics Usage Scenarios

CERTIFICATION READY
Determine Log Analytics usage scenarios
Objective 5.3

The ***Log Analytics service*** collects data from the number of environments and presents the real-time insights in a number of formats. While Log Analytics is part of Azure Cloud services, the data is provided by OMS, agents, and Microsoft Azure Storage. By addition solutions, you add functionality to Log Analytics.

As previously mentioned, you can gather logs from a wide range of sources and services, including Windows and Linux agents, IIS logs, custom text logs, and so on. Configure each data source that you want to collect and the configuration is automatically delivered to each connected source.

You can access Log Analytics through the OMS portal or the Azure portal using any browser. From the portal, you can construct and save queries to analyze collected data, dashboards, and customized views for the data that you find most relevant. Figure 13-6 shows a sample query.

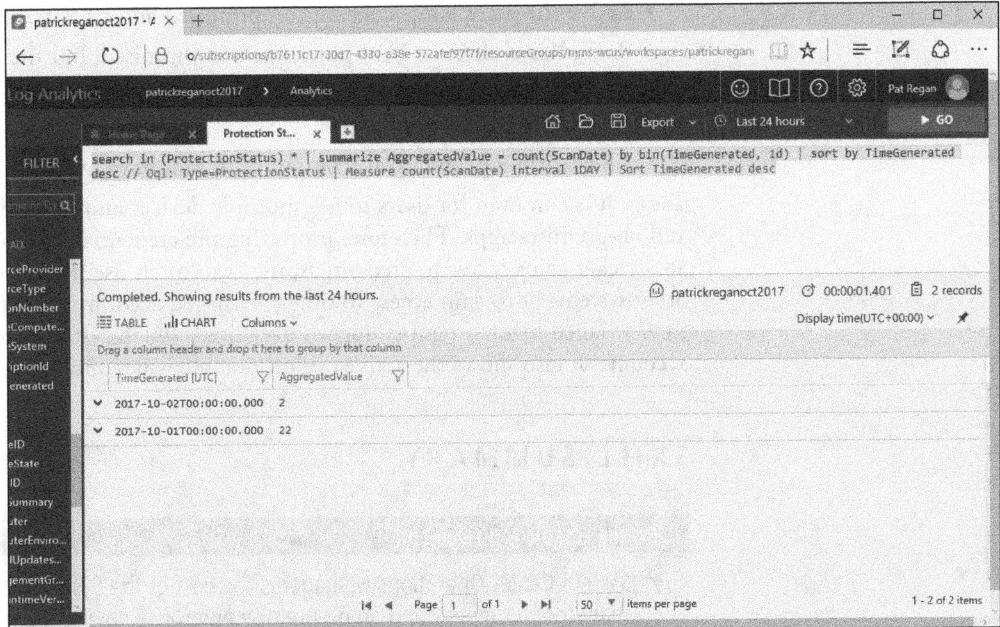

Figure 13-6

Running a query in Log Analytics

To analyze data outside of Log Analytics, you can export the data from the OMS repository into tools such as Microsoft Power Business Intelligence (BI) or Excel. Lastly, you can build custom solutions using the Log Search application programming interface (API).

Determine Security and Auditing Functions Available for Use

CERTIFICATION READY
Determine security and auditing functions available for use
Objective 5.3

The Security and Audit feature in Log Analytics provides a comprehensive view into your organization's IT security. OMS has built-in search queries for notable issues that require your attention.

OMS also has security domains that you can use for monitoring resources, including:

- Update Assessment
- Malware Assessment
- Identity and Access

Updates have already discussed in this lesson. With the Malware assessment, you can view systems that have insufficient protection against malware using the Malware Assessment tile under Security Domains. Use the Malware Assessment dashboard to identify the following security issues:

- **Active threats:** Computers are compromised and have active threats in the system.
- **Remediated threats:** Computers are compromised, but the threats are remediated.
- **Signature out of date:** Computers have malware protection enabled, but the signature is out of date.
- **No real-time protection:** Computers do not have installed antimalware.

Today, it is common for users to use multiple devices and/or access multiple cloud-based and on-premises apps. Therefore, protecting the credentials is more important than ever. As an attacker gains access to credentials, they can often use those credentials to gain access to other systems or to gain access to other privileged accounts. Identity and Access can be used to view failed logon attempts, logons over time, which systems are being accessed, and locked accounts. It also shows the active critical notable issues and active warning notable issues.

SKILL SUMMARY

IN THIS LESSON YOU LEARNED:

- System Center Operations Manager is the part of the System Center suite that is the primary tool for monitoring an on-premise enterprise environment. You can monitor multiple computers, devices, services, and applications using the Operations Manager console.
- Microsoft Operations Management Suite (OMS) is a cloud-based collection of management services that helps you manage and protect your cloud and on-premises environments. OMS offers log analysis, IT automation, backup and disaster recovery, security, and compliance.
- The Log Analytics service collects data from the number of environments and presents the real-time insights in a number of formats. While Log Analytics is part of Azure Cloud services, the data is provided by Microsoft Operations Management Suite, agents, and Microsoft Azure Storage. By adding solutions, you add functionality to Log Analytics.

Knowledge Assessment

Multiple Choice

1. Which Microsoft cloud service helps you manage and protect your cloud and on-premises environments, helps you to analyze logs, performs IT automation based on events, backs up servers, and ensures compliance?
   a. SCCM
   b. SCOM
   c. OMS
   d. ATA
2. Which of the following can be monitored by OMS? (Choose all that apply)
   a. Windows servers
   b. Amazon Web Services
   c. VMWare
   d. Robocopy backups
3. Which of the following is the true power behind OMS that allows you to create a wide range of reports and dashboards?
   a. Azure Backups
   b. Microsoft SharePoint
   c. Log Analytics
   d. Excel
4. Which of the following allows you to extend the capabilities of OMS?
   a. Runbooks
   b. Azure Service Maps
   c. Log Analytics
   d. Solutions Gallery

Best Answer

Choose the letter that corresponds to the best answer. More than one answer choice may achieve the goal. Select the BEST answer.

1. Which of the following should be used to determine which systems do not have the necessary Windows updates, updated antimalware, and change tracking?
   a. SCOM
   b. OMS
   c. SCCM
   d. LAPS

■ Business Case Scenarios

Scenario 13-1: Monitoring Your Data Center and Azure Infrastructure

You need to know when there is a problem with some of your on-premise and Azure servers and services, including when they are not available. In addition, you need to be notified when updates are not deployed in a timely manner. Describe your recommended solution and how to deploy it.

LESSON 14

Securing Application Development and Server Workload Infrastructure

70-744 EXAM OBJECTIVE

Objective 6.1 – Secure application development and server workload infrastructure. This objective may include but is not limited to the following: Determine usage scenarios, supported server workloads, and requirements for deployments; install and configure Nano Server; implement security policies on Nano Servers using Desired State Configuration (DSC); manage local policy on Nano Server; determine usage scenarios and requirements for Windows Server and Hyper-V containers; install and configure containers.

Lesson Heading	Exam Objective
Implementing Windows PowerShell Desired State Configuration (DSC)	(None)
Installing and Configuring Windows Nano Server • Determining Appropriate Usage Scenarios and Requirements for Nano Server • Installing Nano Server • Managing and Configuring Nano Server • Managing Local Policy on Nano Server • Implementing Roles and Features on Nano Server	Determine usage scenarios, supported server workloads, and requirements for deployments Install and configure Nano Server Implement security policies on Nano Servers using Desired State Configuration (DSC) Manage local policy on Nano Server
Installing and Configuring Windows Containers • Determining Appropriate Scenarios for Windows Containers • Determining Windows Container Installation Requirements • Installing and Configuring Windows Server Container Host • Installing and Configuring Docker	Install and configure containers Determine usage scenarios, supported server workloads, and requirements for deployments Determine usage scenarios and requirements for Windows Server and Hyper-V containers

KEY TERMS

container image
ContainerImage
containers
Docker
Docker container
DockerMsftProvider
Hyper-V containers
Local Configuration Manager (LCM)
Nano Recovery Tool
Nano Server
NanoServerPackage
NuGet
OneGet
PacketManagement
PowerShell Desired State Configuration
Windows Server containers

Implementing Windows PowerShell Desired State Configuration (DSC)

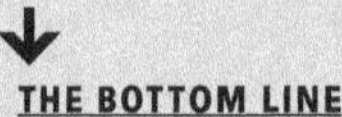

When you manage several servers in a data center, configuring all of them requires a lot of work. The burden of managing them is eased when those servers share a common configuration. To reduce the time necessary to configure all your data center servers, you can use Windows ***PowerShell Desired State Configuration (DSC)*** to manage and maintain systems based on your declared configuration.

Windows PowerShell DSC is an extension of Windows PowerShell and the Windows Management Framework. Instead of creating and executing scripts, you can define the configuration and the configuration will be reapplied based on a specified interval. If a configuration on a system has drifted, it will correct the configuration drift. DSC can be deployed in centralized and decentralized environments, and the systems do not need to belong to an Active Directory domain. It can also be used to manage any operating system with an OMI-compliant Common Information Model (CIM) server, such as CentOS, or other varieties of Linux.

TAKE NOTE*

Although DSC takes some time and effort to establish, its benefits can be seen if you have hundreds of systems (virtual or physical) for which you need to maintain the system configuration.

Some of the configurations that you can apply include:

- Enabling or disabling server roles and features
- Managing registry settings
- Managing files and directories
- Starting, stopping, and managing processes and services
- Managing groups and user accounts
- Deploying new software
- Managing environment variables
- Running Windows PowerShell scripts

The ***Local Configuration Manager (LCM)*** is the DSC engine. It will periodically check whether the configuration is still valid or if drift has occurred. When you configure the LCM, you will either push the configuration to a server, or you will establish an HTTP server, or SMB share, from which the systems will pull the configuration. You will then specify how often it will retrieve the configuration and how often it will check and apply the specified configuration.

The LCM-specific parameters include:

- **RefreshMode:** By default, RefreshMode is set to *Push*, which runs the `Start-DscConfiguration` cmdlet on the system. When the RefreshMode is set to *Pull*, the LCM agent regularly checks a remote HTTP server or Server Message Block (SMB) share for configurations. If the RefreshMode is set to *Disabled*, the LCM does not apply any configurations. Configuring a pull server is not required to use DSC. However, pull servers can be beneficial in large, distributed environments.

- **RefreshFrequencyMins:** This parameter indicates the time intervals, in minutes, at which the LCM polls the remote HTTP server or SMB share for configurations. When configured in Push mode, this value is ignored. The default value is 30 minutes.
- **ConfigurationMode:** This mode indicates the action that the LCM agent takes when applying configurations. By default, the LCM agent is configured to *ApplyAndMonitor*, meaning that the initial configuration is applied. If changes to the configuration occur, they are logged but are not corrected automatically. The *ApplyAndAutoCorrect* configuration mode applies the initial configuration and will automatically apply the deviation during future checks. *ApplyOnly* mode applies the configuration, but does not do anything further after the initial configuration.
- **ConfigurationModeFreqencyMins:** This parameter indicates the time interval, in minutes, at which the LCM checks and, if necessary, reapplies the configurations. By default, this value is every 15 minutes.

To view the available DSC functions and cmdlets available, execute the following command at the Windows PowerShell prompt:

```
Get-Command -Module PSDesiredStateConfiguration
```

USING POWERSHELL

You can manage DSC using Windows PowerShell by using the following cmdlets and functions:

Functions:

- **Configuration:** Names the configuration.
- **Disable-DscDebug:** Stops debugging of DSC resources.
- **Enable-DscDebug:** Starts debugging of all DSC resources, which will be used for troubleshooting.
- **Get-DscConfiguration:** Gets the current configuration of the DSC nodes. If you do not specify a target computer, the cmdlet will get the configuration for the local computer.
- **Get-DscConfigurationStatus:** Retrieves detailed information about completed configuration runs.
- **Get-DscLocalConfigurationManager:** Gets LCM settings and states of LCM for the node.
- **Get-DscResource:** Retrieves the Windows PowerShell Desired State Configuration (DSC) resources present on the computer.
- **New-DscChecksum:** Creates checksum files for DSC documents and DSC resources. This is used when systems are in pull mode to ensure that the correct configuration and resources exist on the target node.
- **Remove-DscConfigurationDocument:** Removes a configuration document (.mof file) from the DSC configuration store.
- **Restore-DscConfiguration:** Reapplies the previous configuration for the node.

Cmdlets:

- **Invoke-DscResource:** Runs a method of a specified DSC resource
- **Publish-DscConfiguration:** Publishes a DSC configuration to a set of computers
- **Set-DscLocalConfigurationManager:** Applies LCM settings to nodes
- **Start-DscConfiguration:** Applies configuration to nodes
- **Test-DscConfiguration:** Tests whether the actual configuration on the nodes matches the desired configuration
- **Update-DscConfiguration:** Checks the pull server for an updated configuration and applies it

To use DSC, you must first create an .mof file using a Windows PowerShell script. The .mof file is a text file that contains the configuration information. The .mof file does not enforce the desired state, but is used to specify what the desired state would be.

To retrieve a list of the DSC managed elements that can be used in configuration files, you can execute the following Windows PowerShell command:

```
Get-DscResource | Select-Object -Property Name, Properties
```

The DSC managed elements include the following:

- **File:** Manages files and folders on a node
- **Archive:** Decompresses an archive in the .zip format
- **Environment:** Manages system environment variables
- **Group:** Allows you to manage local user groups on a node
- **Log:** Writes a message in the DSC event log
- **Package:** Installs or removes a package
- **Registry:** Manages registry key of a node (except HKEY Users)
- **Script:** Executes several PowerShell commands on a node
- **Service:** Manages Windows services (State, Startup Type)
- **User:** Manages local users on a node
- **WindowsFeature:** Adds or removes a role/feature on a node
- **WindowsOptionalFeature:** Adds or removes an optional role/feature
- **WindowsProcess:** Manages a Windows process

You can also use the `Get-DscResource` cmdlet with the `-Syntax` option to get the syntax of the managed elements. For example, to get the syntax for Service, you would execute the following command:

```
Get-DscResource -Name Service -Syntax
```

which responds with:

```
PS C:\Users\PatPC> Get-DscResource -Name Service -Syntax
Service [String] #ResourceName
{
    Name = [string]
[BuiltInAccount = [string]{ LocalService | LocalSystem |
NetworkService }]
    [Credential = [PSCredential]]
    [Dependencies = [string[]]]
    [DependsOn = [string[]]]
    [Description = [string]]
    [DisplayName = [string]]
    [Ensure = [string]{ Absent | Present }]
    [Path = [string]]
    [PsDscRunAsCredential = [PSCredential]]
[StartupType = [string]{ Automatic | Disabled | Manual }]
    [State = [string]{ Running | Stopped }]
}
```

The configuration script that will create the .mof file would be saved with a .ps1 extension. For example, if the following script is saved as Config.ps1 and is executed from a Windows PowerShell prompt as .\config.ps1, a folder called MyFileServerConfig folder will be created with a localhost.mof file. The localhost.mof file will specify to install the Windows features called snmp and DSCServiceFeature, set the service called Spooler to Manual, and stop the Spooler service.

```
configuration MyFirstServerConfig
{
    WindowsFeature snmp
         {
             Name = "SNMP-Service";
          Ensure = "Present"
         }
    WindowsFeature DSCServiceFeature
         {
             Name = "DSCServiceFeature";
          Ensure = "Present"
         }
    Service Spooler
       {
             Name = "Spooler"
             StartupType = "Manual"
             State = "Stopped"
         }
}
MyFirstServerConfig
```

Each configuration can have one or more node blocks and each node block can have one or more resource blocks. You can even use the same resource more than once in the same node block. When typing your configuration script, you have a lot of freedom of how you space the braces. However, because braces are used as pairs (opening and closing braces), it is best to line up opening and closing braces so that you can easily see when a block begins and ends.

The main part of this example has a function called MyFirstServerConfig, which is marked by an opening and closing brace. A function doesn't do anything by itself until the function is called. Therefore, the last line, MyFirstServerConfig, calls up the function MyFirstServerConfig.

To configure the system with the .mof file that was just created, you would execute the following command:

```
Start-DscConfiguration -Wait -Verbose -Path C:\
MyFirstServerConfig
```

The `-Wait` parameter tells Windows that you want to run the command interactively, while the `-Verbose` switch allows you to see a detailed output of what is happening when the configuration is being applied. The path specifies the folder where the .mof file is stored.

CONFIGURE A SYSTEM WITH DSC

GET READY. To configure a system with DSC, perform the following steps.

1. Log on to LON-SVR1 as **adatum\administrator** with the password of **Pa$$w0rd.**
2. If Server Manager does not open, click **Start** and then click **Server Manager.**
3. Click **Tools > Windows PowerShell ISE.**
4. When Windows PowerShell ISE opens, in the top white pane, type the following text, as shown in Figure 14-1.

```
configuration MyFirstServerConfig
{
      WindowsFeature snmp
          {
              Name = "SNMP-Service";
            Ensure = "Present"
          }
      WindowsFeature DSCServiceFeature
          {
              Name = "DSCServiceFeature";
            Ensure = "Present"
          }
      Service Spooler
          {
              Name = "Spooler"
              StartupType = "Manual"
              State = "Stopped"
          }
}
MyFirstServerConfig
```

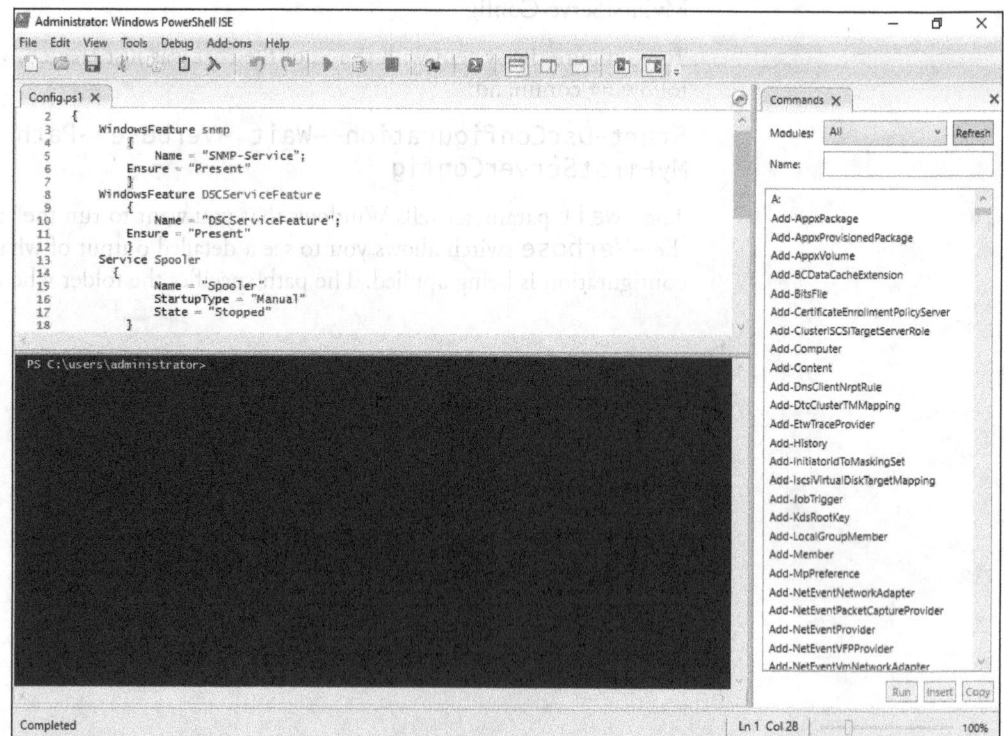

Figure 14-1

Creating a Windows PowerShell script with Windows PowerShell ISE

5. Click **File** > **Save As.** In the Save As dialog box, in the File name text box, type **C:\Config.ps1** and click the **Save** button.
6. Click the blue, bottom pane. Then in the blue, bottom pane, type **CD** and press **Enter.**
7. To create the .mof file, from the Windows PowerShell command prompt, execute the following command:

```
.\config1.ps1
```

8. At the Windows PowerShell command prompt, execute the following command:

```
Start-DscConfiguration -Wait -Verbose -Path C:\
MyFirstServerConfig
```

In order to provision the pull server with configuration files, you need to:

- Run the script that generates node configuration MOFs.
- Use the New-DSCChecksum cmdlet to generate checksum files.
- Copy all MOFs and associated checksum files to the pull server.

Of course, each node must be able to contact the specified pull server. The following script configures the mode to Pull and specifies the pull server.

```
Configuration SimplePullConfiguration
{
LocalConfigurationManager
 {
    ConfigurationMode = 'ApplyOnly'
    ConfigurationID = $guid
    RefreshMode = 'Pull'
    DownloadManagerName = 'WebDownloadManager'
    DownloadManagerCustomData = @
{
ServerUrl = ,http://LON-SVR1.adatum.com:80/PSDSCPullServer.
svc';
     AllowUnsecureConnection = 'true'
    }
  }
}
```

Then, to configure the system for pull mode, you need to configure the LCM by running the Set-DscLocalConfigurationManager cmdlet on each of the pull clients. For example, you may execute the following command:

```
Set-DscLocalConfigurationManager -ComputerName localhost -Path
. -Verbose
```

If you have any problems with DSC, you should open Event Viewer and navigate to the Applications and Services Logs/Microsoft/Windows/Desired State Configuration. You can also use the Test-DscConfiguration and Get-DscConfiguration cmdlets to test your current configuration and to view the current configuration.

Installing and Configuring Windows Nano Server

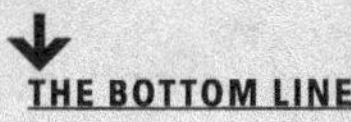

Nano Server is a new installation option for Windows Server 2016. Although it has a small hardware footprint for Server Core, it has no local sign-in capability. It supports only 64-bit applications, tools, and agents.

Different from installing Windows Server Core, you must create a virtual hard disk. You can then use the virtual hard drive on a virtual machine to support a virtualized Nano Server in Hyper-V, or you can configure the Nano Server to start from a .vhd file.

Determining Appropriate Usage Scenarios and Requirements for Nano Server

CERTIFICATION READY
Determine usage scenarios, supported server workloads, and requirements for deployments
Objective 6.1

There are many scenarios where you could take advantage of the Nano Server. For example, if you require higher security, or require a smaller hardware footprint, you should check to see if the Nano Server can run your services and applications.

Some of the scenarios used by Nano Servers include:

- A Hyper-V host computer
- A storage host for a Scale-Out File Server
- A DNS server
- A web server running Internet Information Services (IIS)
- A host computer that runs a container

To install the Nano Server, you need a server running Windows Server 2016 and 800 MB of free disk space. Of course, you might need additional disk space to store data and additional processor and memory for the load that the Nano Server is running.

Installing Nano Server

CERTIFICATION READY
Install and configure Nano Server
Objective 6.1

As previously mentioned, Nano Server cannot be installed directly from the installation media during setup. Instead, you must access the Windows Server 2016 installation media NanoServer folder to generate a Nano Server image.

Nano Server is installed using one of three methods:

- Deploying a VHD image that will be hosted as a virtual machine on a Hyper-V host
- Deploying a VHD as a bootable drive on a physical computer
- Deploying a Nano Server WIM file on a physical computer

To create the Nano Server image, use the `New-NanoServerImage` cmdlets. The options available include the following:

- **Edition:** Lists the Windows Server 2016 edition of the Nano Server. Options are Standard or Datacenter.
- **Deployment type:** Lists the type of deployment. Use *Host* for WIM or bootable VHD and *Guest* for VHDs hosted in Hyper-V.
- **Media path:** Lists the path to the root of the Windows Server 2016 installation media.
- **Base path:** Optionally copies the server binary files to this folder, if you are creating a WIM file.

- **Target path:** Identifies the path and file name, including extension, of the Nano Server image. Options include .vhd, .vhdx, and .wim.
- **Computer name:** Identifies the name of the target Nano Server computer.
- **Computer:** Installs the Hyper-V role.
- **Clustering:** Installs failover clustering.
- **Containers**: Installs host support for Windows Containers.
- **GuestDrivers:** Installs Hyper-V guest drivers for hosting Nano Server as a virtual machine.
- **OEMDrivers:** Installs the same basic drivers for a variety of network adapters and storage controllers that are included in the Server Core installation of Windows Server 2016.
- **Storage:** Installs the File Server role and other storage components.
- **Defender:** Installs Windows Defender anti-malware, including a default signature file.
- **Packages:** Installs certain roles and features. Depending on the packages that are installed, you might need additional package switches.
  - To install Internet Information Server (IIS), use `-Packages Microsoft-NanoServer-IIS-Package`.
  - To install the System Center Virtual Machine Manager agent, use `-Packages Microsoft-Windows-Server-SCVMM-Package`.
  - To install the Network Performance Diagnostics Service (NPDS), use `-Packages Microsoft-NanoServer-NPDS-Package`.
  - To install Data Center Bridging, use `-Packages Microsoft-NanoServer-DCB-Package`.
  - To install the DNS Server role, use `-Packages Microsoft-NanoServer-DNS-Package`.
  - To install Desired State Configuration (DSC), use `-Packages Microsoft-NanoServer-DSC-Package`.
  - To install Secure Startup, use `-Packages Microsoft-NanoServer-SecureStartup-Package`.
  - To install Shielded Virtual Machine, use `-Packages Microsoft-NanoServer-ShieldedVM-Package`.

The steps to create an image include the following:

1. Copy the NanoServerImageGenerator folder from the NanoServer folder on the Windows Server 2016 installation media to a folder on your local machine.
2. Start Windows PowerShell as an administrator and change the directory to the NanoServerImageGenerator folder on your local drive.
3. Import the NanoServerImageGenerator module by using the following Windows PowerShell `Import-Module` cmdlet:

```
Import-Module .\NanoServerImageGenerator -Verbose
```

4. Create the VHD or WIM by using the `New-NanoServerImage` cmdlet with the following syntax:

```
New-NanoServerImage -Edition <edition>

-DeploymentType <deployment type> -MediaPath <media
path> -BasePath <base path> -TargetPath <target path>
-ComputerName <computer name>

-Packages <packages> -<other package switches>
```

DEPLOYING A VHD IMAGE AS A VIRTUAL MACHINE

To create a Nano Server called NANO-SVR1 that will be stored in the nano-svr1.vhdx file, with IIS installed, use the following command:

```
New-NanoServerImage -DeploymentType Guest -Edition Standard
-MediaPath C:\ -BasePath c:\nano -TargetPath c:\nano\nano-svr1.
vhdx -ComputerName NANO-SVR1
-Storage -Package Microsoft-NanoServer-IIS-Package
```

When you are prompted to type a password, type Pa$$w0rd. It will then take a few minutes to generate the nano-svr1.vhdx file.

Once the .vhd or .vhdx file is created, you need to deploy the Nano Server to Hyper-V, by using the following steps:

1. Open Hyper-V Manager.
2. Create a new virtual machine with the new virtual disk file.
3. Boot the virtual machine.
4. Use Hyper-V to connect to the virtual machine.
5. Log on to the Nano Server Recovery Console using the administrator account and password.
6. Obtain the IP address for the virtual machine and connect to the Nano Server by using the remote management tools to manage the server.

CREATE A VIRTUAL MACHINE

GET READY. To create a virtual machine on Hyper-V to run Nano Server, perform the following steps:

1. Log on to a computer running Windows Server 2016 with an administrator account, such as **adatum\administrator** with the password of **Pa$$w0rd.**
2. If Server Manager does not open, click **Start** and then click **Server Manager.**
3. Click **Tools > Hyper-V.**
4. In Hyper-V Manager, right-click the host node and choose **New > Virtual Machine.**
5. In the New Virtual Machine Wizard, on the Before You Begin page, click **Next.**
6. On the Specify Name and Location page, in the Name text box, type **NANO-SVR1** and then click **Next.**
7. On the Specify Generation page, select **Generation 2** and then click **Next.**
8. On the Assign Memory page, select the **Use Dynamic Memory for this virtual machine** option and then click **Next.**
9. On the Configure Networking page, for the Connection option, select a switch, such as **Private Network.** Click **Next.**
10. On the Connect Virtual Hard Disk page, select the **Use an existing virtual hard disk** option.
11. Click the **Browse** button.
12. In the Open dialog box, navigate to and click the **C:\nano\nano-svr1.vhdx** file. Click **Open.**
13. Back on the Connect Virtual Hard Disk page, click **Next.**
14. On the Summary page, click **Finish.**
15. Right-click the NANO-SVR1 and choose **Start.**
16. Right-click the NANO-SVR1 and choose **Connect.**

17. On the logon screen, as shown in Figure 14-2, type **administrator** and then press the **Tab** key. In the Password box, type **Pa$$w0rd** and press **Enter**.

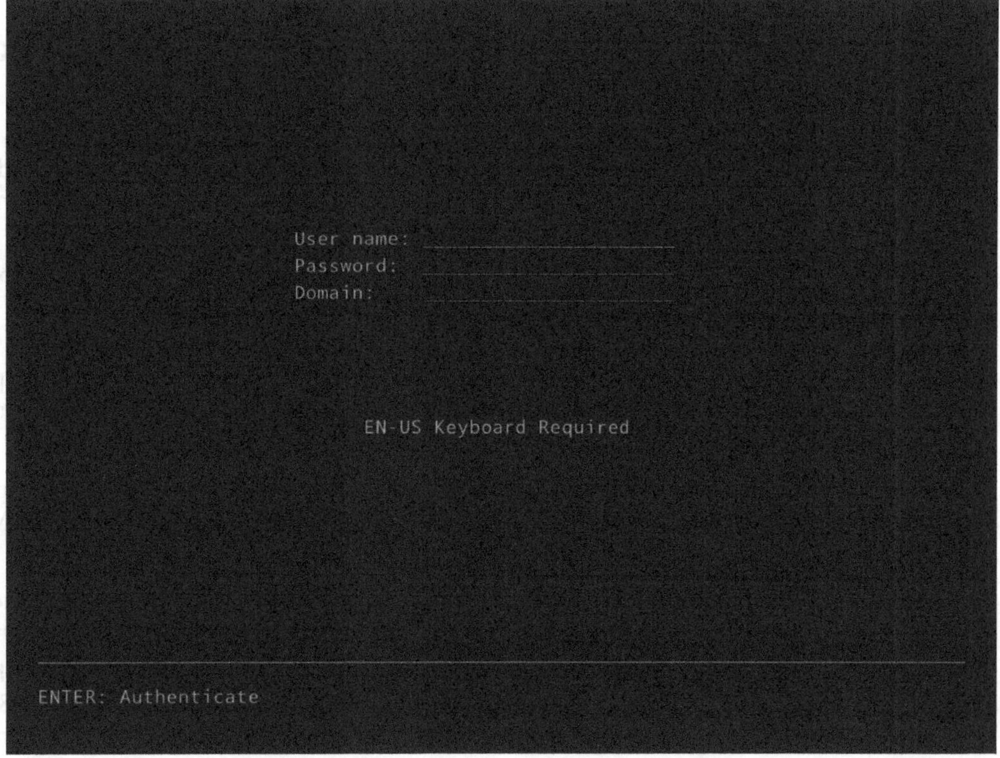

Figure 14-2

Logging on to a Nano Server

18. In the Nano Server Recovery Console (as shown in Figure 14-3), Networking is already selected. Press **Enter**.

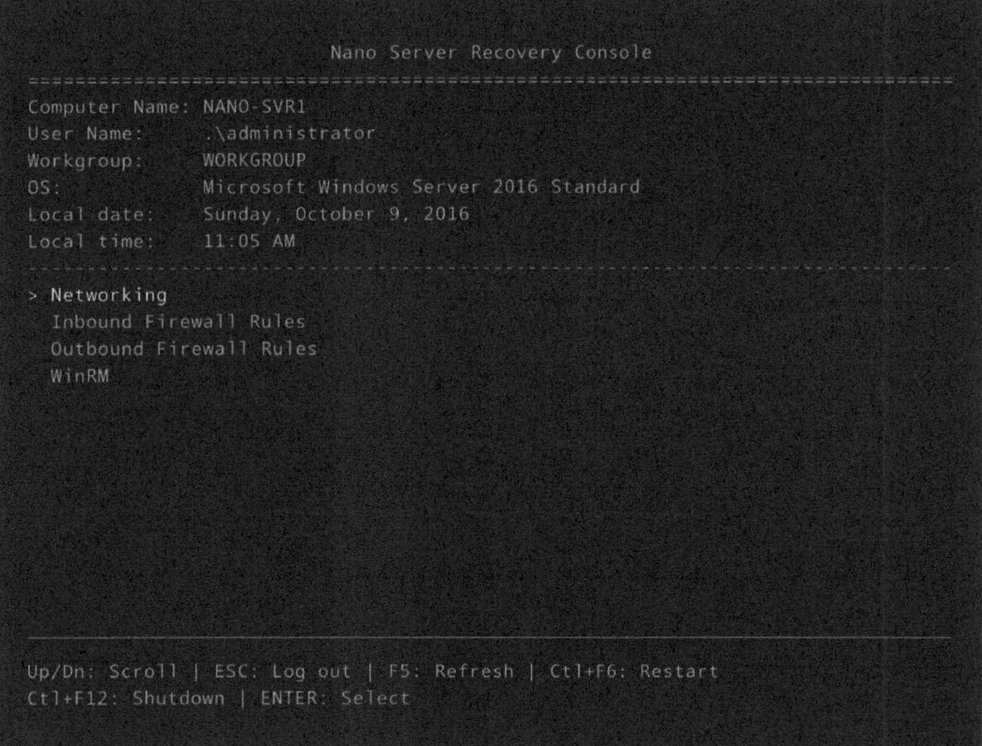

Figure 14-3

Accessing the Nano Server Recovery Console

19. With the Ethernet adapter and MAC address already selected, press **Enter**.
20. Record the IP address and then press **Esc** twice.

DEPLOYING THE NANO SERVER VHD ON A PHYSICAL COMPUTER

To create a Nano Server called NANO-SVR1 that will be stored in the nano-svr1.vhdx file with IIS installed, execute the following command:

```
New-NanoServerImage -DeploymentType Host -Edition Standard
-MediaPath C:\ -BasePath c:\nano -TargetPath c:\nano\nano-svr2.
vhdx -ComputerName NANO-SVR2
-Storage -Package Microsoft-NanoServer-IIS-Package
-OEMDrivers
```

The main difference when running this command is that the DeploymentType is set to Host and you must include the `-OEMDrivers` so that the most common hardware drivers are installed.

After the image is booted, mount the VHD file to the local computer and then use the `bcdboot` command to add a boot entry to the Windows Boot Manager boot menu by opening a command prompt and executing the commands:

1. To create a boot entry called "Nano Server," execute the following command:
   ```
   bcdedit /copy {current} /d "Nano Server"
   When the entry is created, a GUID for the entry is
   displayed, such as {0141898c-3e9e-11e3-8aa8-9b1588913cd5}.
   You need the GUID for the remaining commands.
   ```
2. Then execute the following commands:
   ```
   bcdedit /set {GUID} device vhd=[c:]\Nano\nano-svr2.vhdx
   bcdedit /set {GUID} osdevice vhd=[c:] \Nano\nano-svr2.vhdx
   bcdedit /set {GUID} path \windows\system32\boot\winload.exe
   ```

DEPLOYING A NANO SERVER WIM FILE

To create a Nano Server WIM, execute the following command:

```
New-NanoServerImage -DeploymentType Host -Edition Standard
-MediaPath C:\ -BasePath c:\nano -TargetPath c:\nano\nano-svr3.
wim -ComputerName NANO-SVR3
-Storage -Package Microsoft-NanoServer-IIS-Package
```

Once the WIM file is created, you can deploy it by using WinPE:

1. Ensure the .wim file is accessible from WinPE.
2. Boot into WinPE on the local server.
3. Use diskpart.exe to prepare the local hard drive.
4. Apply the Nano Server image by using dism.exe.
5. Add the WIM file to the boot menu using the bcdboot.exe.
6. Remove the WinPE media if applicable, and reboot the system by using the following command:
   ```
   Wpeutil.exe reboot
   ```

To prepare the local hard drive with Diskpart, execute the following at a command prompt:

```
Diskpart.exe
Select disk 0
Clean
Convert GPT
Create partition efi size=100
Format quick FS=FAT32 label="System"
Assign letter="s"
Create partition msr size=128
Create partition primary
Format quick FS=NTFS label="NanoServer"
Assign letter="n"
List volume
Exit
```

To apply the Nano Server image using the dism.exe command, execute the following command at a command prompt:

```
Dism.exe /apply-image /imagefile:.\Nano\NANO-SVR3.wim /index:1
/applydir:n:\
```

Then, to add to the boot menu, execute the following command:

```
Bcdboot.exe n:\Windows /s s:
```

Managing and Configuring Nano Server

CERTIFICATION READY
Install and configure Nano Server
Objective 6.1

After you install and place the Nano Server, you need to configure the Nano Server, including configuring networking and the firewall, adding the server to the domain, and adding roles and features. You can then manage the server using Server Manager, Windows PowerShell, and other management tools.

Before you make significant changes to a Nano Server running as a virtual machine, you should back up the VM and consider creating a checkpoint of the VM. The disadvantage of the Nano Server is that you can only perform a small set of tasks on the running Nano Server. All other tasks will have to be done remotely.

USING THE NANO RECOVERY TOOL

The main local tool to configure the Nano Server tool is the ***Nano Recovery Tool***. It has all of the tools that will help you establish connectivity to your remote management tools. The front page shows the following:

- Computer name
- User name
- Workgroup or domain name
- The operating system
- Local date and time

You can also configure the following:

- Networking
- Inbound and outbound firewall rules
- WinRM

From the Networking page, perform the following:

- View the MAC address.
- Enable or disable DHCP.
- Configure an IPv4 address and subnet mask.
- Configure an IPv6 address.

When you access the inbound firewall rules or the outbound firewall rules, you can view the various firewall rules. When you select a firewall rule, you can use the F4 key to enable or disable a rule.

The Windows Remote Management (WinRM) protocol allows you to remotely connect to a computer and execute commands remotely using Windows PowerShell or Windows Remote Shell.

To enable Windows Remote Management, select WinRM, and then on the Windows Remote Management page, press Enter twice to confirm.

MANAGING NANO SERVER REMOTELY USING WINDOWS POWERSHELL

To connect to a remote computer, you need to enable WinRS on the remote server. To enable WinRS, use the Nano Server Recovery Console, as shown earlier in this lesson. You can then be on another server or a client that has Windows PowerShell to use the `Enter-PSSession` cmdlet to connect to the Nano Server computer and execute the appropriate Windows PowerShell commands.

To manage Nano Server with Windows PowerShell remoting, you need to add the IP address of the Nano Server to your management computer's list of trusted hosts. To add the Nano Server to the list of trusted hosts, run this command at an elevated Windows PowerShell prompt:

```
Set-Item WSMan:\localhost\Client\TrustedHosts "<IP address of
Nano Server>"
```

MANAGING NANO SERVER REMOTELY USING ADMINISTRATIVE TOOLS

You can redirect an administrative tool based on the Microsoft Management Console (MMC): Open an administrative tool on a remote computer, click and then right-click the snap-in, then choose Connect to another computer.

ADDING NANO SERVER TO DOMAIN

To add a computer to a domain, on a domain controller, use the djoin.exe command to provision the computer and generate an odjblob file and then use the `Set-Item WSMAN:` command to add the Nano Server to a trusted host list. Next, open a remote PowerShell session on the Nano Server to configure the firewall, to copy the odjblob file, and to apply the file to the Nano Server.

ADD A NANO SERVER TO A DOMAIN

GET READY. To add a Nano Server to a domain, perform the following steps.

1. Log on to your domain controller, such as **LON-DC1**, as **adatum\administrator** with the password of **Pa$$w0rd.**
2. Right-click **Start** and choose **Windows PowerShell (Admin).**
3. At the prompt, execute the following command:
   ```
   djoin.exe /provision /domain adatum /machine nano-svr1 /
   savefile .\odjblob
   ```
4. At the command prompt, execute the following cmdlet (where *X* is the IP address of the server). Your IP address will be different.
   ```
   Set-Item WSMan:\localhost\Client\TrustedHosts "172.16.0.X"
   ```
   Type **Y.** When prompted, press **Enter.**
5. At the command prompt, execute the following cmdlet. Your IP address will be different.
   ```
   $ip = "172.16.0.X"
   ```
6. At the command prompt, execute the following cmdlet:
   ```
   Enter-PSSession -ComputerName $ip -Credential $ip\
   Administrator
   ```
7. In the Windows PowerShell credential request dialog box, in the Password box, type **Pa$$w0rd** and then click **OK.**
8. At the command prompt, execute the following cmdlet:
   ```
   netsh advfirewall firewall set rule group="File and
   Printer Sharing" new enable=yes
   ```
9. At the command prompt, execute the following cmdlet:
   ```
   Exit-PSSession
   ```
10. At the command prompt, execute the following cmdlet. Your IP address will be different.
   ```
   net use z: \\172.16.0.X\c$
   ```
11. At the command prompt, type **Z:** and then press **Enter.**
12. At the command prompt, execute the following cmdlet:
   copy c:\odjblob
13. At the command prompt, execute the following cmdlet:
   ```
   Enter-PSSession -ComputerName $ip -Credential $ip\
   Administrator
   ```
14. In the Windows PowerShell credential request dialog box, in the Password box, type **Pa$$w0rd** and then click **OK.**
15. At the command prompt, type **cd** and then press **Enter.**
16. At the command prompt, execute the following cmdlet:
   djoin /requestodj /loadfile c:\odjblob /windowspath c:\windows /localos
17. To reboot the computer, at the command prompt, execute the following cmdlet:
   ```
   shutdown /r /t 5
   ```

Managing Local Policy on Nano Server

CERTIFICATION READY
Implement security policies on Nano Servers using Desired State Configuration (DSC)
Objective 6.1

CERTIFICATION READY
Manage local policy on Nano Server
Objective 6.1

Since Nano Server has a reduced footprint, it does not have Group Policy and the graphical consoles and tools. Therefore, you need to deploy security policy templates and advanced audit setting text files. To deploy these files to multiple Nano Servers, use DSC.

To configure the Nano Server security settings, use the following two files:

- .INF files that contain settings for security-policy templates. .INF files are generated by SecEdit.exe on a server with a Desktop Experience or a Server Core installation or by running the Backup-SecurityPolicy cmdlet in Windows PowerShell.
- .CSV files contain advanced audit settings. You can generate .CSV files by running AuditPol.exe on a server with a Desktop Experience or a Server Core installation, or by running the Backup-AuditPolicy cmdlet in Windows PowerShell.

To invoke the security settings to the Nano Server, import both advanced audit and security-template settings to your Nano Server installation:

```
Import-Module SecurityCmdlets

#replace within these two cmdlets the correct path to your
.INF and .CSV files

$SecInf = "c:\GPO\DomainSysvol\GPO\Machine\microsoft\windowsnt\
SecEdit\GptTmpl.inf"

$AuditCsv = "c:\GPO\DomainSysvol\GPO\Machine\microsoft\win-
dowsnt\Audit\audit.csv"

Restore-SecurityPolicy -Path $secInf

Restore-AuditPolicy -Path $auditCsv
```

After you create and test the security files, you can use DSC to deploy those files.

CONFIGURE A NANO SERVER BY USING DSC

GET READY. To add a Nano Server to a domain, perform the following steps.

1. Log on to your domain controller, such as **LON-DC1**, as **adatum\administrator** with the password of **Pa$$w0rd.**
2. On LON-DC1, click the **Start** button and then click **Windows PowerShell.**
3. To map the drive Z to the your Nano Server, execute the following command (whereby \\172.16.0.x\c$ is the address of your Nano Server):

   ```
   net use z: \\172.16.0.X\c$
   ```

   Execute the following two commands to observe the DSC settings:

   ```
   Get-Command -Module PSDesiredStateConfiguration
   Get-DscResource
   ```

4. Create the following Windows PowerShell variable (whereby \\172.16.0.x\c$ is the address of your Nano Server):

   ```
   $ip = "172.16.0.X"
   ```

   Create another variable by executing the following command:

   ```
   $cred = Get-Credential
   ```

   In the Windows PowerShell Credential Request window, use Adatum\administrator and Pa55w.rd:

5. Open a PSSession to NANO-SVR1 by executing the following command:

   ```
   Enter-PSSession -ComputerName $ip -Credential $Cred
   ```

6. Install the xsmbshare module by executing the following command:

```
Install-Module -Name xsmbshare -Force
```

7. At the NuGet provide prompt message, type **Y** and then press **Enter**.
8. Create an MOF file by executing the following command, which runs the DscNanoConfig.ps1 script:

```
.\DscNanoConfig.ps1 -nodes localhost
```

9. When the Localhost.mof file is created, execute the following command:

```
Start-DscConfiguration -Wait -Force -Verbose -Path .\
FileShare
```

The `Wait` and `Verbose` parameters allow you to see the node elements of the script as they run.

10. Return to File Explorer and then go to **\\NANO-SVR1\NanoShare**.
11. Open the SecuritySettings.txt file in Notepad and observe the message there. Change the word "**Always**" to "**Never**", save the file, and then close Notepad.
12. Return to the Windows PowerShell console and execute the following command:

```
Start-DscConfiguration -Force -Verbose -Path .\FileShare
```

13. Return to File Explorer, refresh the NanoShare location, and open SecuritySettings.txt. The first word in the text should now be "Always".
14. Exit the PSSession, close all open windows, and then sign out of LON-DC1.

Implementing Roles and Features on Nano Server

If you already used the `Set-Item WSMan:\localhost\Client\TrustedHosts` command on a remote computer, you can use the remote computer to get and add Windows server roles and features.

To view a list of current Window Server roles and features, you execute the following command from a remote computer:

```
Get-WindowsFeature -ComputerName nano-svr1
```

To install a Windows feature that is included with the Nano Server, you use the Windows PowerShell `install-windowsfeature` cmdlet. For example, to install the File Server server role (FS-FileServer), execute the following command:

```
Install-WindowsFeature FS-FileServer -ComputerName nano-svr1
```

To install a Windows feature from a package that is not included with the Nano image after you have created the Nano Server image, you need to shut down the Nano Server and mount the disk image of the Nano Server on the Hyper-V server with the Windows PowerShell `Mount-DiskImage` cmdlet. For example, if the Nano Server image was c:\Images\nanoserver.vhd, you would execute the following command:

```
Mount-DiskImage -ImagePath 'C:\Images\nanoserver.vhd'
```

The image will be mounted as a drive letter.

To install a package that is not already included with Nano Server, execute the `Add-WindowsPackage` cmdlet. If the image is mounted to the E drive, to install the DNS Server package, execute the following command:

```
Add-WindowsPackage -Path E:\ -PackagePath C:\NanoServer\
Packages\ Microsoft-NanoServer-DNS-Package.cab
```

When you are done, dismount the disk image using the `Dismount-DiskImage` cmdlet. For example, to dismount the C:\Images\nanoserver.vhd image, execute the following command:

```
Dismount-DiskImage -ImagePath 'C:\Images\nanoserver.vhd'
```

UPDATING A NANO SERVER

To install updates, you need to visit the Microsoft Update Catalog to download cumulative updates for Windows Server 2016. After you download the .msu files and save them to a local directory, such as C:\ServicingPackages, you need to expand the .cab files from the .msu files into separate directories and copy the .cabs into a single folder.

```
mkdir C:\ServicingPackages_expanded

mkdir C:\ServicingPackages_expanded\KB3176936

mkdir C:\ServicingPackages_expanded\KB3192366

Expand C:\ServicingPackages\KB3176936.msu -F:* C:\
ServicingPackages_expanded\KB3176936

Expand C:\ServicingPackages\KB3192366.msu -F:* C:\
ServicingPackages_expanded\KB3192366

mkdir C:\ServicingPackages_cabs

copy C:\ServicingPackages_expanded\KB3176936\Windows10.0-
KB3176936-x64.cab C:\ServicingPackages_cabs

copy C:\ServicingPackages_expanded\KB3192366\Windows10.0-
KB3192366-x64.cab C:\ServicingPackages_cabs
```

When you build the image, execute the following command:

```
New-NanoServerImage -ServicingPackagePath 'C:\
ServicingPackages_cabs\Windows10.0-KB3176936-x64.cab', 'C:\
ServicingPackages_cabs\Windows10.0-KB3192366-x64.cab' -<other
parameters>
```

To apply the cumulative update on a running Nano Server, execute the `Edit-NanoServerImage` cmdlet. For example:

```
Edit-NanoServerImage -ServicingPackagePath 'C:\
ServicingPackages_cabs\Windows10.0-KB3176936-x64.cab', 'C:\
ServicingPackages_cabs\Windows10.0-KB3192366-x64.cab'
-TargetPath .\NanoServer.vhdx
```

■ Installing and Configuring Windows Containers

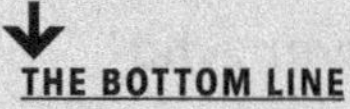

Windows Server 2016 introduced ***containers***, which are lightweight virtual machines that can provide an isolated environment for applications, similar to a virtual machine running on a Hyper-V host. Containers provide a separate operating environment for installed applications that does not affect the rest of the operating system and the operating system does not affect the container. A container is typically used to run a single application.

Containers are also referred to as container-based OS virtualization. A container doesn't have its own copy of the operating system the way a virtual machine does. Instead, the container has a simulated environment that is based on an operating system instance running on the

CERTIFICATION READY
Install and configure containers
Objective 6.1

container host, as shown in Figure 14-4. The container has a virtual namespace with access to files, network ports, and its own list of running processes, which provide the security and reliability of the apps that run within the containers. Because the container is based on another instance, containers can be created quickly.

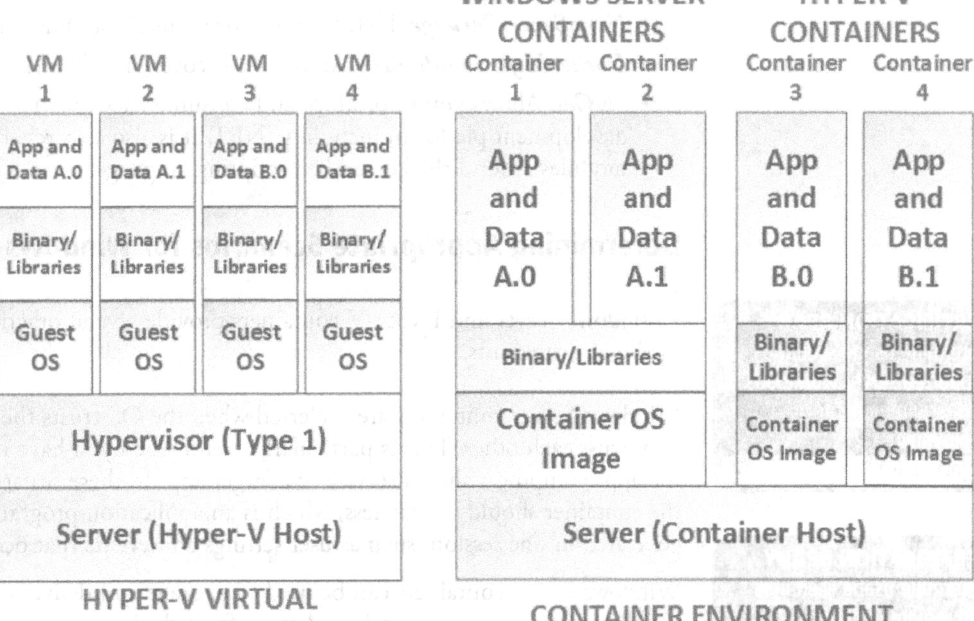

Figure 14-4
Comparing Hyper-V virtual machines and containers

The container host uses namespace isolation to run one or more Windows containers. When the ***container image*** is created, it is derived from the container OS Image (base image, additional binary/libraries, middleware) and applications/data, is stored in a repository, and can be interconnected with other containers to create a larger application. Windows Server 2016 supports two different types of containers, or run times:

- ***Windows Server container***: Shares the OS kernel with the container host and with all other containers that run on the host. Because it shares the OS kernel with the base container, it does not provide complete isolation of the containers. However, it does provide a faster startup.
- ***Hyper-V container:*** Provides a more isolated environment than Windows Server containers as they do not share with other Hyper-V containers.

The containers use the following terms:

- The ***container host*** is a physical or virtual computer that is configured with the Windows container feature.
- The *container OS image* provides the OS environment.
- The **sandbox** provides a layer that consists of all changes made to the container, including file system and registry modifications and software installations. You can keep or discard these changes as needed.
- The **container repository** is the place that the container image and its dependencies (such as libraries) are stored. By using a container repository, you can reuse the image multiple times on a container host.

When you create a container image, you discard the changes to make sure that the container stays pristine or you can save the changes. You can also use the create container that inherits the container changes or converts the changes into a new container image.

PackageManagement (also referred to as ***OneGet***) is used to discover and install software packages over the Internet. PackageManagement is accessed from the https://www.powershellgallery.com. It is a manager of existing package managers/package providers that can be accessed with Windows PowerShell. Some package manager providers include:

- ***ContainerImage:*** Helps you discover, download, and install Windows Container OS images.
- ***NanoServerPackage:*** Helps you discover, install, and download Nano Server Packages.
- ***DockerMsftProvider:*** Allows you to discover, install, and update Docker images.
- ***NuGet:*** Allows you to produce and consume packages. It is used for the Microsoft development platform, including .NET. It is also a searchable repository for scripts and modules around the PowerShell scripting language.

Determining Appropriate Scenarios for Windows Containers

CERTIFICATION READY
Determine usage scenarios, supported server workloads, and requirements for deployments
Objective 6.1

CERTIFICATION READY
Determine usage scenarios and requirements for Windows Server and Hyper-V containers
Objective 6.1

Windows Server and Hyper-V containers provide several practical applications for enterprise environments.

Windows Server containers are preferred when the OS trusts the apps that it hosts and all the apps trust each other. This is particularly useful when you have multiple container apps and the apps compose a shared service of a larger app. In these situations, the apps deployed in the container should be stateless, which is an application program that does not record data generated in one session, such as user settings and events that occur.

Windows Server containers can be used to package and deliver distributed apps quickly. The benefits can be seen when you need to perform deployments on a regular basis or for containers that change often. Containers can be easily adapted to deploy a test environment that matches your production environment and you can deploy this container in Microsoft Azure without changing it.

Hyper-V containers each have their own copy of the Windows OS kernel and have memory assigned directly to them. As a result, the Hyper-V containers provide better isolation, which can allow untrusted apps to run on the same host. In these situations, each Hyper-V container is assigned to a different tenant. If malware or malicious attacks compromised one container host or VM, the other VMs that belong to other customers are not affected.

Determining Windows Container Installation Requirements

Just as you plan a virtual machine deployment, you need to plan for Windows containers. After you determine your needs and determine the appropriate scenario, you need to understand the container host and container requirements.

The Windows container role is only available on:

- Windows Server 2016 and higher, Full and Server Core
- Nano Server
- Windows 10 (build 14352 and newer)

When you want to use Hyper-V containers, you need to install the Hyper-V role. Windows Server container hosts must have the Windows OS installed to C:\, which does not apply when only Hyper-V containers will deploy.

When you deploy a Windows container host on a Hyper-V VM that is hosting Hyper-V containers, you need to enable nested virtualization. Nested virtualization has the following requirements:

- At least 4 gigabytes (GB) of memory available for the virtualized Hyper-V host
- On the host system, you need:
  - Windows Server 2016 and newer
  - Windows 10 (build 10565 and newer)
- On the container host VM, you need:
  - Windows Server 2016 (Full or Server Core)
  - Nano Server
- A processor with Intel VT-x
- The container host VM requires at least two virtual processors

Microsoft restricts which image you can use with each container type, as outlined in Table 14-1.

Table 14-1

Containers That Run on Host Operating Systems

HOST OS	WINDOWS SERVER CONTAINER	HYPER-V CONTAINER
Windows Server with Desktop Experience	Server Core image or Nano Server	Server Core image or Nano Server
Windows Server Core	Server Core image or Nano Server	Server Core image or Nano Server
Windows Server Nano	Nano Server	Server Core image or Nano Server
Windows 10	Not Available	Server Core image or Nano Server

Installing and Configuring Windows Server Container Host

CERTIFICATION READY
Install and configure containers
Objective 6.1

Before you can use containers in Windows Server 2016, you need to deploy a container host, which can be a physical host computer or a VM. You can use Windows Server 2016 with or without Desktop Experience or Nano Server.

When you deploy Windows Server containers on a Nano server, you need to prepare a Nano Server virtual hard disk with the container and Hyper-V capabilities by using the `-Computer` and `-Containers` switches:

```
New-NanoServerImage -MediaPath $WindowsMedia

-BasePath c:\nano -TargetPath C:\nano\NanoContainer.vhdx
-GuestDrivers

-ReverseForwarders -Compute -Containers
```

When you deploy Windows Server host for containers, you perform the following high-level steps:

- Install the container feature using Server Manager or by executing the following command:

  ```
  Install-WindowsFeature Containers
  ```

- Create a virtual switch in Hyper-V Manager or by using the Windows PowerShell `New-VMSwitch` cmdlet.
- When you use a virtual switch configured with Network Address Translation (NAT), you must configure the NAT settings by executing the following command:

  ```
  New-NetNat -Name ContainerNat

  -InternalIPInterfaceAddressPrefix "172.16.0.0/12"
  ```

- Configure media access control (MAC) address spoofing. For example, you can execute the following command:

```
Get-VMNetworkAdapter -VMName Container Host VM | Set-
VMNetworkAdapter -MacAddressSpoofing On
```

To view the available package providers, use the Windows PowerShell **Find-PackageProvider** cmdlet, as shown in Figure 14-5. To display the registered PowerShell galleries, you use the **Get-PSRepository** cmdlet.

Figure 14-5

Displaying available package providers

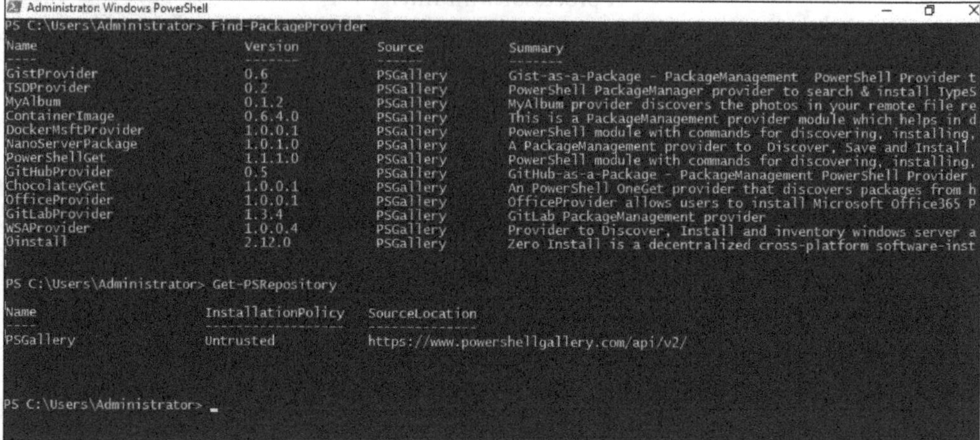

To deploy Windows Server containers, use the following high-level steps:

1. Install the required Windows PowerShell module by executing the following command:
   ```
   Install-PackageProvider ContainerImage -Force
   ```
2. List the available images by name, version number, and description by executing the **Find-ContainerImage** command.
3. Install the named image by executing the following command:
   ```
   Install-ContainerImage -Name ImageName -Version Number
   ```

To run Hyper-V containers, you need to install the Hyper-V role and the container feature. If the host machine is a virtual machine, you need to enable nested virtualization before installing Hyper-V.

Because the Windows Server containers and host share a single kernel, the container's base image must match the host. If the versions are different, the container might start, but functionality might be degraded. Therefore, Windows Server containers are blocked from starting when the build number is different. For example, the Windows Server 2016 RTM version is 10.0.14393.0 (Major.Minor.Build.Revision).

Since the final release of Windows Server 2016, Microsoft has decided to shift more into using Docker to create and manage containers. Containers created with Windows and containers created with Docker are not compatible.

Installing and Configuring Docker

Docker is a collection of open source tools, solutions, and cloud-based services that are used for creating and managing containers. A ***Docker container*** is software wrapped in a complete file system that includes everything it needs to run. Each Docker container runs as an isolated process in the user space on the host OS.

The Open Container Initiative is an open industry standard with Microsoft as one of the founding members, so that developers can create, manage, and deploy both Windows Server and Linux containers by using the similar Docker tool sets. The tool set can be used to manage Windows Server containers and Hyper-V containers. On Windows Server 2016, you can install the Docker daemon for Windows Server hosts, which can be used with Docker containers, tools, and workflows in production Windows environments.

With early versions of Windows 10 and Windows Server 2016, Windows containers run on Windows Server 2016 or Windows 10 and they cannot be used to run Linux containers. However, the Docker tools used to create Windows containers are similar to the Docker tools used on Linux machines to create Linux containers.

TAKE NOTE* In September, 2017, Microsoft announced that future versions of Windows 10 and Windows Server 2016 will support running Docker Linux Containers on Windows with the LinuxKit.

INSTALLING AND CONFIGURING DOCKER ON WINDOWS SERVER 2016 WITH DESKTOP EXPERIENCE

Windows Server 2016 does not include the Docker Engine; you need to install and configure it separately. Before you install Docker, you need to install the Windows container feature. You then need to install the KB3176936 cumulative patch or the latest Windows Server 2016 cumulative patch. You will also need an Internet connection so that you can download the appropriate files.

INSTALL DOCKER ON WINDOWS SERVER 2016

GET READY. To install Docker on Windows Server 2016 and enable the container feature, perform the following steps.

1. Log on to LON-SVR1 as **adatum\administrator** with the password of **Pa$$W0rd.**
2. Click **Start.** When the Start menu appears, type **PowerShell.** From the results, right-click **Windows PowerShell** and choose **Run as Administrator.** The Administrator: Windows PowerShell window opens.
3. To install the OneGet PowerShell module, execute the following command:
   ```
   Install-Module -Name DockerMsftProvider
   -Repository psgallery -Force
   ```
   If you are prompted to install NuGet, type **Y.**
4. To use OneGet to install the latest version of Docker, execute the following command:
   ```
   Install-Package -Name docker -ProviderName
   DockerMsftProvider
   ```
   If a message indicates that the package source is not trusted, prompting you to determine whether you want to install software from DockerDefault, type **Y.**
5. Restart the computer by executing the following command:
   ```
   Restart-Computer -Force
   ```

The Docker service will already be added to the Services console and will already be set to Automatic. Therefore, after the reboot, the Docker service will automatically restart.

INSTALLING AND CONFIGURING DOCKER ON NANO SERVER

Similar to Windows Server 2016, Docker is not included with Nano Server. Therefore, you need to download the software via the Windows PowerShell command prompt.

INSTALL DOCKER ON NANO SERVER

GET READY. To install Docker on Nano Server, perform the following steps.

1. Log on to LON-SVR1 as **adatum\administrator** with the password of **Pa$$W0rd**.
2. Click **Start**. When the Start menu appears, type **PowerShell** and then press **Enter**.
3. Because the Nano Server does not have interactive logon capabilities, you need to add the Nano Server to the trusted hosts of the remote system by executing the following command:

```
Set-Item WSMan:\localhost\Client\TrustedHosts <IP_ADDRESS_
OF_NANOSERVER> -Force
```

4. To create a remote PowerShell session, execute the following command:

```
Enter-PSSession -ComputerName <IP_ADDRESS_OF_NANOSERVER>
-Credential ~\Administrator
```

5. To use the Nano Server, you need to install critical updates by executing the following commands:

```
$sess = New-CimInstance -Namespace root/Microsoft/Windows/
WindowsUpdate -ClassName MSFT_WUOperationsSession
Invoke-CimMethod -InputObject $sess -MethodName
ApplyApplicableUpdates
```

6. Reboot the Nano Server by executing the following command:

```
Restart-Computer
```

7. Then, to create a remote PowerShell session, execute the following command:

```
Enter-PSSession -ComputerName <IP_ADDRESS_OF_NANOSERVER>
-Credential ~\Administrator
```

8. To install the OneGet PowerShell module, execute the following command:

```
Install-Module -Name DockerMsftProvider
-Repository PSGallery -Force
```

9. To use OneGet to install the latest version of Docker, execute the following command:

```
Install-Package -Name docker -ProviderName
DockerMsftProvider
```

10. Reboot the Nano Server by executing the following command:

```
Restart-Computer
```

Because you cannot manage Docker on Nano Server directly, you must prepare the container host by performing the following steps:

1. Create a firewall rule on the container host for the Docker connection (port 2375 for an unsecure connection or port 2376 for a secure connection) by executing the following command:

```
netsh advfirewall firewall add rule name="Docker daemon "
dir=in action=allow protocol=TCP localport=2375
```

2. Configure the Docker Engine to accept incoming connections over TCP by first creating a daemon.json file at c:\ProgramData\docker\config\daemon.json on the Nano Server host using the following command:

   ```
   New-Item -Type File c:\ProgramData\docker\config\daemon.
   json
   ```

3. Execute the following command to add a connection configuration to the daemon.json file:

   ```
   Add-Content 'c:\programdata\docker\config\daemon.json' '{
   "hosts": ["tcp://0.0.0.0:2375", "npipe://"] }'
   ```

4. Use port 2376 if you are using secure connection.
5. Restart the Docker service by executing the following command:

   ```
   Restart-Service docker
   ```

When you plan to use Hyper-V containers, you need to install the Hyper-V role on a Nano Server container host by executing the following two commands:

```
Install-NanoServerPackage Microsoft-NanoServer-Compute-Package
Restart-Computer
```

To manage Docker remotely, you must install the Docker client on a remote system, such as your client workstation. To download and install the Docker client, follow these steps:

To download the Docker client, execute the following command:

```
Invoke-WebRequest "https://download.docker.com/components/
engine/windows-server/cs-1.12/docker.zip" -OutFile "$env:TEMP\
docker.zip" -UseBasicParsing
```

To extract the compressed package, execute the following command:

```
Expand-Archive -Path "$env:TEMP\docker.zip"
-DestinationPath $env:ProgramFiles
```

To add the Docker directory to the system path, execute the following two commands:

```
$env:path += ";c:\program files\docker"
[Environment]::SetEnvironmentVariable("Path", $env:Path + ";C:\
Program Files\Docker", [EnvironmentVariableTarget]::Machine)
```

Once completed, you can access the remote Docker host with the `docker -H parameter:`

```
docker -H tcp://<IPADDRESS>:2375 run -it microsoft/nanoserver
cmd
```

To create an environmental variable DOCKER_HOST, which removes the -H parameter requirement, execute the following command:

```
$env:DOCKER_HOST = "tcp://<ipaddress of server>:2375"
```

With this variable set, the command is reduced to the following:

```
docker run -it microsoft/nanoserver cmd
```

SKILL SUMMARY

IN THIS LESSON YOU LEARNED:

- When you manage several servers in a data center, configuring all of those servers requires a lot of work. The burden of managing several is eased when those servers share a common configuration. To reduce the time necessary to configure all your data center servers, you can use DSC to manage and maintain systems based on your declared configuration.
- Nano Server is a new installation option for Windows Server 2016. Although it has a small hardware footprint for Server Core, it has no local sign-in capability. It supports only 64-bit applications, tools, and agents.
- There are many scenarios where you could take advantage of the Nano Server. For example, if you require higher security or require a smaller hardware footprint, you should check to see whether the Nano Server can run your services and applications.
- After you install and place the Nano Server, you need to configure the Nano Server, including configuring networking and firewalls, adding the server to the domain, and adding roles and features. You can then manage the server using Server Manager, Windows PowerShell, and other management tools.
- Since Nano Server has a reduced footprint, it does not have Group Policy and the graphical consoles, and tools. Therefore, you need to deploy security-policy templates and advanced audit setting text files. To deploy these files to multiple Nano Servers, you would use DSC.
- Windows Server 2016 introduced containers, which are lightweight virtual machines that can provide an isolated environment for applications, similar to a virtual machine running on a Hyper-V host. The containers provide a separate operating environment for installed applications that does not affect the rest of the operating system and the operating system does not affect the container. A container is typically used to run a single application.
- Docker is a collection of open source tools, solutions, and cloud-based services that are used for creating and managing containers. A Docker container is a software wrapped in a complete file system that includes everything it needs to run. Each Docker container runs as an isolated process in the user space on the host OS.

Knowledge Assessment

Multiple Choice

1. Which type of server has a smaller hardware footprint than Server Core and has no local sign-in capability?
   a. Server with Desktop Experience
   b. Nano Server
   c. Reduced Footprint Server
   d. Compressed Server
2. Which of the following is the minimum amount of disk space for a Nano Server?
   a. 400 MB
   b. 800 MB
   c. 1 GB
   d. 1.4 GB
3. Which of the following methods are used to install Nano Server? (Choose three answers.)
   a. Deploy a VHD as a bootable drive on a physical computer.
   b. Deploy a WIM file in Hyper-V.
   c. Deploy a Nano Server WIM file on a physical computer.
   d. Deploy a VHD image that will be hosted as a virtual machine on a Hyper-V host.
4. Which Windows PowerShell cmdlet is used to create a Nano Server?
   a. `Set-NanoServerImage`
   b. `New-NanoServer`
   c. `New-NanoServerImage`
   d. `Create-NanoServer`
5. Which Nano Server tool is used to configure networking, firewall rules, and WinRM?
   a. Nano Recovery Tool
   b. Nano Setup Tool
   c. Nano Configuration Tool
6. Which of the following is a lightweight virtual machine that can provide an isolated environment for applications?
   a. Containers
   b. ESXi node
   c. VDI node
   d. Virtual namespace

7. Microsoft PackageManagement is also known as which of the following?
   a. Sandbox
   b. DockerMsftProvider
   c. NuGet
   d. OneGet
8. Which type of container is used for a more isolated environment?
   a. Windows Server containers
   b. Hyper-V containers
   c. Container repository
   d. OneGet container
9. Which Windows roles or features are required to use Windows or Hyper-V containers? (Choose all that apply.)
   a. Container
   b. Docker
   c. Hyper-V
   d. OneGet
10. Which types of base images can be used with containers? (Choose two answers.)
    a. WindowsDocker
    b. WindowsServerwithDesktop
    c. WindowsserverCore
    d. Nanoserver
11. Which command is used to create a Docker container?
    a. `docker start`
    b. `docker new`
    c. `docker run`
    d. `docker tag`
12. Which of the following is an industry standard for containers?
    a. Docker container
    b. Hyper-V container
    c. Windows container
    d. Resource container

Best Answer

Choose the letter that corresponds to the best answer. More than one answer choice may achieve the goal. Select the BEST answer.

1. Which type of server should be used to create a secure virtual machine that has the smallest security footprint?
   - **a.** Core Server
   - **b.** Nano Server
   - **c.** Server with Desktop Experience
   - **d.** Reduced Server
2. Which type of container provides the best security for an application?
   - **a.** Windows Server containers
   - **b.** Hyper-V containers
   - **c.** Container repository
   - **d.** OneGet container

Matching and Identification

1. Match the term with its definition:

_____ container host

_____ container OS image

_____ container repository

_____ DockerMsftProvider

_____ ContainerImage

a. Used to discover, download, and install Windows container OS images.

b. A physical or virtual computer that is configured with the Windows container feature.

c. The place that a container image and its dependencies are stored.

d. The repository that allows you to discover, install, and update Docker images.

e. Used as a base operating system for the container.

Build List

1. Specify the correct order of the steps necessary for adding a Nano Server to a domain.

_____ On a domain controller, execute the Set-Item WSMan cmdlet that will add the computer to the trusted host list.

_____ Connect to the Nano Server by using the Enter-PSSession cmdlet.

_____ Reboot the Nano Server.

_____ Configure the Windows Firewall on the Nano Server.

_____ On a domain controller, run the `djoin.exe` cmdlet.

_____ Copy the odjblob file to the Nano Server using the `djoin` command.

2. Specify the correct order of steps necessary to installing Docker on Windows Server 2016.

_____ Install the OneGet PowerShell module.

_____ Install the container feature.

_____ Install the docker package from the DockerMsftProvider.

_____ Reboot the computer.

■ Business Case Scenarios

Scenario 14-1: Deploying and Configuring Windows Server 2016

You administer 250 servers running Windows Server 2016 and you need to deploy another 140 servers over the next six months. You want to ensure that each computer has the following configuration performed:

- Certain server roles and features need to be installed.
- A set of default users and groups needs to be created on each server.
- Diagnostic and malware software need to be deployed.
- Several environment variables need to be set.

Describe how to ensure that your current servers and any servers that you install will have this base configuration. Also, describe how to ensure that when these settings are changed, the system is automatically reconfigured.

Scenario 14-2: Adding Features on a Nano Server

You are ready to create the Nano Server. You need to deploy the DNS server role on one server and the web services on two other Nano Servers. On all Nano Servers, you need to make sure Windows Defender and the DSC package is installed. Describe your recommended course of action.

Scenario 14-3: Deploying a Website

Describe how to deploy a website and make it as secure as possible while reducing its resources used.

Scenario 14-4: Running Multiple Containers

You are an administrator of a Hyper-V server that is running 15 containers. You have noticed that one container is using much more memory and processing than the other containers, which is affecting the performance of the other containers. How can you ensure that the container does not use too many resources?

LESSON 15

Implementing a Secure File Services Infrastructure and Dynamic Access Control (DAC)

70-744 EXAM OBJECTIVE

Objective 6.2 – Implement a secure file services infrastructure and Dynamic Access Control (DAC). This objective may include but is not limited to the following: Install the File Server Resource Manager (FSRM) role service; configure quotas; configure file screens; configure storage reports; configure file management tasks; configure File Classification Infrastructure (FCI) using FSRM; implement work folders; configure file access auditing*; configure user and device claim types; implement policy changes and staging; perform access-denied remediation; create and configure Central Access rules and policies; create and configure resource properties and lists.

** This objective is covered in Lesson 11.*

Lesson Heading	Exam Objective
Using File Server Resource Manager Installing File Server Resource Manager Using Quotas Managing Files with File Screening Using Storage Reports Enabling SMTP	Install the File Server Resource Manager (FSRM) role service Configure quotas Configure file screens Configure storage reports
Supporting Work Folders Creating a Work Folder Connecting to a Work Folder	Implement work folders
Using Dynamic Access Control Configuring User and Device Claim Types Creating and Configuring Resource Properties and Lists Implementing a Central Access Policy Implementing Policy Changes and Staging Performing Access-Denied Remediation	Configure user and device claim types Create and configure resource properties and lists Configure File Classification Infrastructure (FCI) using FSRM Create and configure Central Access rules and policies Implement policy changes and staging Perform access-denied remediation
Configuring File Management Tasks	Configure file management tasks

KEY TERMS

active screening
Central Access Policy
Central Access Rules
claim
claims-based access control
classification rules
Dynamic Access Control (DAC)
file group
file screen exception
file screen template
file screening
File Server Resource Manager (FSRM)
hard quota
passive screening
quota template
quotas
Security Token Service (STS)
soft quota
storage reports
token
trusted identity provider
Work Folders

Using File Server Resource Manager

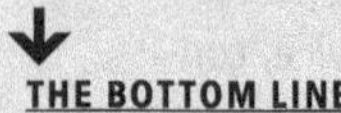

File Server Resource Manager (FSRM) is a suite of tools that enables you to control and manage the quantity and type of data stored on a file server. It enables you to define how much data a person can store, define what type of files that a user can store on a file server, and generate reports about the file server being used.

Using File Server Resource Manager enables you to perform the following tasks:

- Create quotas for a volume or folder tree, including generating e-mails when the quota limits are approached or exceeded.
- Create file screens to control the type of files that users can save
- Send notifications when users try to save a blocked file.
- Schedule periodic storage reports or manually generate a storage report that helps you to identify trends in disk usage.
- Classify files based on defined properties and apply policies based on the classification. You can restrict access to files, encrypt files, and have files expire.

Installing File Server Resource Manager

CERTIFICATION READY
Install the File Server Resource Manager (FSRM) role service
Objective 6.2

Installing FSRM is a simple process because it is a Windows server role.

Like the previous Windows server roles, FSRM is installed with Server Manager as a server role.

INSTALL FILE SERVER RESOURCE MANAGER

GET READY. To install FSRM, perform the following steps.

1. Log on to **LON-SVR2** as **adatum\administrator** with the password **Pa$$w0rd.**
2. In Server Manager, click **Manage > Add Roles and Features** to open the Add Roles and Feature Wizard.
3. On the Before you begin page, click **Next.**

4. Select **Role-based or feature-based installation** and then click **Next.**
5. Click **Select a server from the server pool**, click the name of the server to install FSRM to, and then click **Next.**
6. Scroll down and expand **File and Storage Services** and expand **File and iSCSI Services.** Select **File Server Resource Manager.**
7. When you are prompted to add additional features, click **Add Features.**
8. On the Select server roles page, click **Next.**
9. On the Select features page, click **Next.**
10. On the Confirm installation selections, click **Install.**
11. When the installation is complete, click the **Close** button.

Using Quotas

CERTIFICATION READY
Configure quotas
Objective 6.2

Quotas defined with FSRM limit how much space a folder or volume can use. By using FSRM to create a quota, you limit the amount of disk space allocated to a volume or folder. The quota limit applies to the entire folder's subtree.

When you define the quotas, you can define either a hard quota or a soft quota:

- A ***hard quota*** prevents users from saving files after the space limit is reached and generates notifications when the volume of data reaches the configured threshold.
- A ***soft quota*** does not enforce the quota limit but generates a notification when the configured threshold is met.

NTFS quotas created in FSRM can use e-mail, log an event, run a command or script, or generate a storage report for notification.

CREATING QUOTAS

You can create a quota on a volume or a folder using a quota template or by using custom properties. A ***quota template*** defines quota settings, including space limit, the type of quota (hard or soft), and notification settings when quotas are reached (which can be used to define quotas). It is recommended that you use quota templates because quota templates can be applied to other volumes and folders in the future. In addition, if you modify the template, you have the option to change any quotas that used the quota template in the past.

CREATE A QUOTA TEMPLATE

GET READY. To create a quota template, perform the following steps.

1. Open **Server Manager.**
2. Click **Tools > File Server Resource Manager.** The File Server Resource Manager console opens (see Figure 15-1).

Figure 15-1

Viewing the File Server Resource Manager console

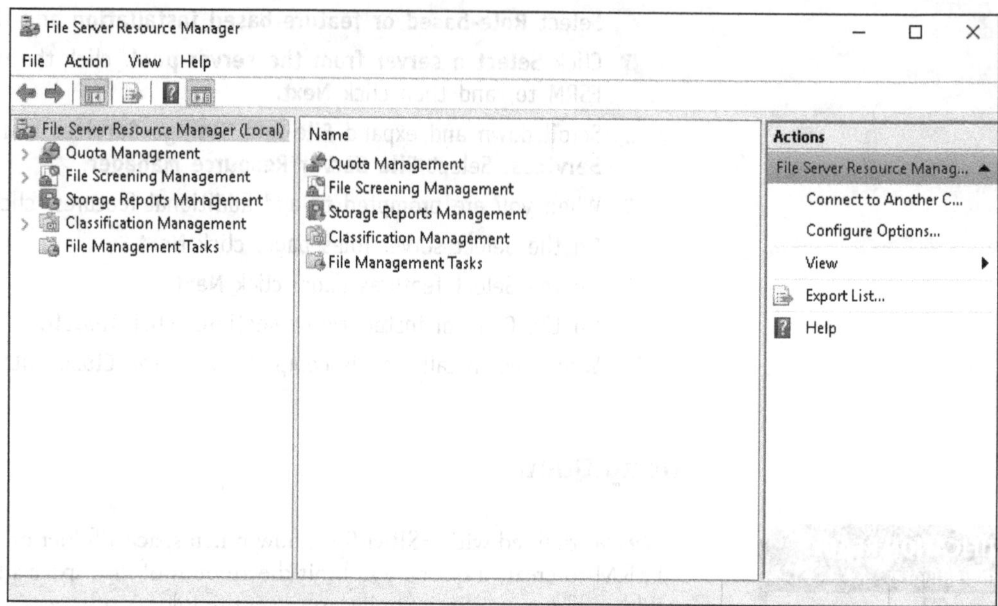

3. Under Quota Management, click, then right-click **Quota Templates** and choose **Create Quota Template**. The Create Quota Template dialog box opens (see Figure 15-2).

Figure 15-2

Opening the Create Quota Template dialog box

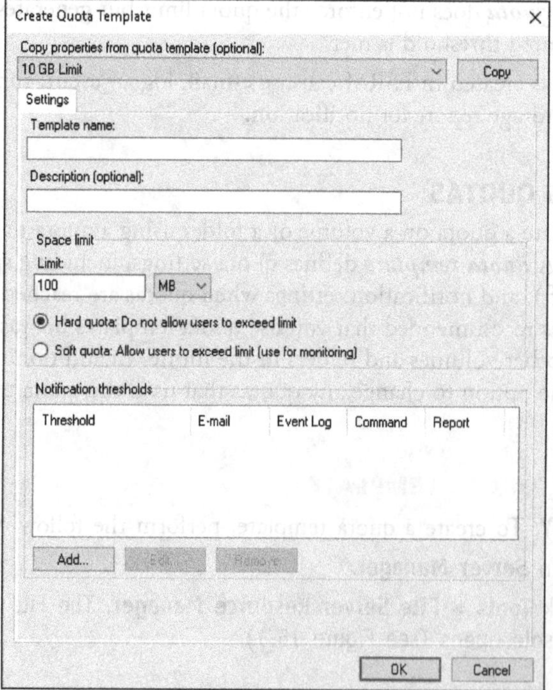

4. If you want to copy the properties of an existing template, you can select a template from the **Copy properties from quota template** drop-down list. Then click **Copy**.
5. In the Template name text box, type a name.
6. In the Description (optional) text box, type a description of the quota.
7. In the Space limit section, in the Limit text box, type a number and specify the unit (KB, MB, GB, or TB).

8. Select **Hard quota** or **Soft quota.**
9. To add a notification, click the **Add** button. The Add Threshold dialog box opens (see Figure 15-3).

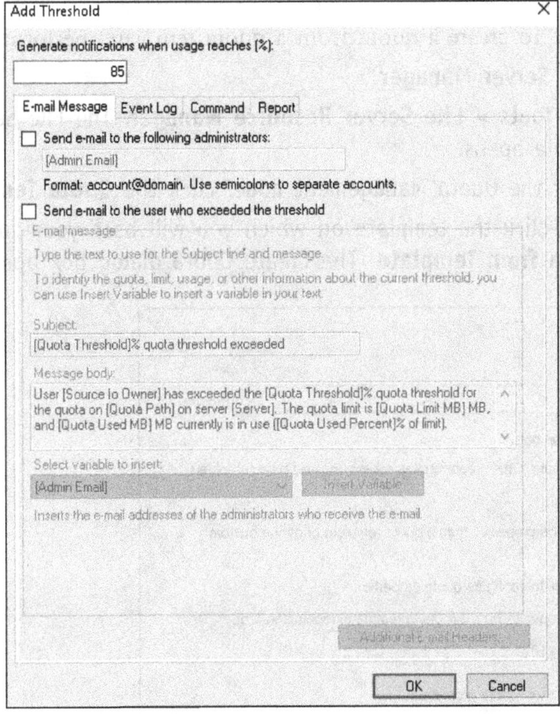

Figure 15-3

Displaying the Add Threshold dialog box

10. To set a quota limit percentage that generates a notification, type a number in the Generate notifications when usage reaches (%) text box. The default is 85%.
11. To configure e-mail notifications, on the E-mail Message tab, set the following options:
    - Select the **Send e-mail to the following administrators** check box, and then enter the names of the administrative accounts that receive the notifications using the account@domain format. Use semicolons to separate multiple accounts.
    - To send e-mail to the person who saved the file that reached the quota threshold, select the **Send e-mail to the user who exceeded the threshold** check box.
    - To configure the message, edit the default Subject line and Message body that are provided. Brackets indicate variable information. For example, [Source Io Owner] variable inserts the name of the user who saved the file that reached the quota threshold.
    - To configure additional headers (including From, Cc, Bcc, and Reply-to), click **Additional E-mail Headers.**
12. To log an event, click the **Event Log** tab. Then select the **Send warning to event log** check box and edit the default log entry.
13. To run a command or script, click the **Command** tab. Then select the **Run this command or script** check box. Type the command. You can also enter command arguments, select a working directory for the command or script, or modify the command security setting.
14. To generate one or more storage reports, click the **Report** tab. Select the **Generate reports** check box and then select which reports to generate. Optionally, you can enter one or more administrative e-mail recipients for the report or e-mail the report to the user who reached the threshold.
15. Click **OK** to save your notification threshold and close the Add Threshold dialog box.

16. Click **OK** to close the Create Quota Template dialog box.

CREATE A QUOTA FROM A QUOTA TEMPLATE

GET READY. To create a quota from a quota template, perform the following steps.

1. Open **Server Manager.**
2. Click **Tools > File Server Resource Manager.** The File Server Resource Manager console opens.
3. Under the Quota Management node, click the **Quota Templates** node.
4. Right-click the template on which you will base your quota and choose **Create Quota from Template.** The Create Quota dialog box opens (see Figure 15-4).

Figure 15-4

Creating a quota using a template

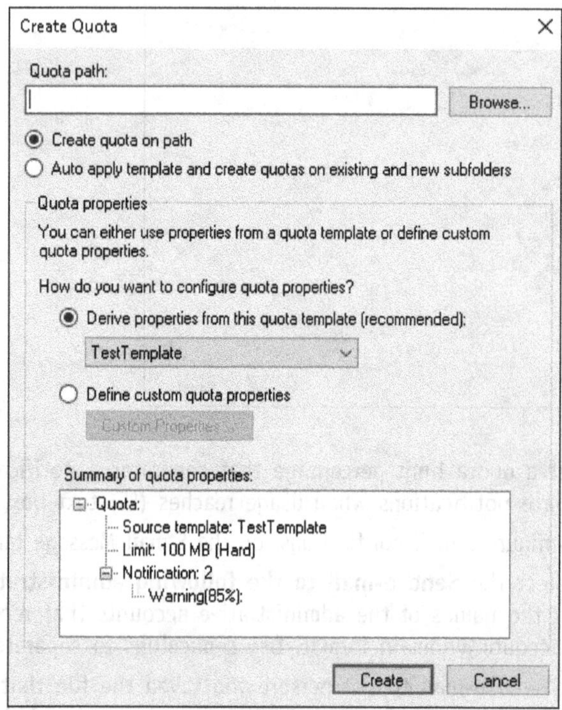

5. In the Quota path text box, type the volume or folder that the quota applies to.
6. Select the **Create quota on path** option.
7. Click **Create.**

If you want to create a quota without using a template, right-click Quotas and choose Create Quota to open the Create Quota dialog box. You can then pull values from a quota template or manually configure the settings.

File Server Resource Manager can also generate quotas automatically by selecting Auto apply template and create quotas on existing and new subfolders. When it is applied to a parent volume or folder, it is applied to each subfolder and each subfolder that is created in the future.

CHANGING QUOTAS TEMPLATES

When you need make changes to a quota template, you can apply those changes to quotas that were created using the original quota template. You can choose to modify only those quotas that still match the original template or all quotas that are derived from the original template, regardless of any changes made to the quotas since they were created.

When you reapply the template, the properties of the quotas are overwritten.

CREATE A QUOTA FROM A QUOTA TEMPLATE

GET READY. To create a quota from a quota template, perform the following steps.

1. Open **Server Manager**.
2. Click **Tools > File Server Resource Manager**. The File Server Resource Manager console opens.
3. Click **Quota Templates** and select the quota template that you want to modify.
4. Right-click the **Quota Template** and choose **Edit Template Properties**. The Quota Template Properties dialog box opens.
5. Modify the quota template properties as needed.
6. Click **OK**. The Update Quotas Derived from Template dialog box opens.
7. Select one of the following options:

   Apply template only to derived quotas that match the original template

   Apply template to all derived quotas

   Do not apply template to derived quotas
8. Click **OK** to close the Update Quotas Derived from Template dialog box.

MONITORING QUOTA USE

In addition to notifications that you set up, you can also view quota usage using one of the following methods with FSRM.

- To view the quota information, click Quota Management and then click Quotas. In the Results pane, you can view the quota limit, the percentage of the limit that is used, the type of quota, and the source template. Figure 15-5 shows the quota usage.
- Running a Quota Usage report is discussed later in this lesson when Storage reports are discussed.

Figure 15-5

Using FSRM to show quota usage

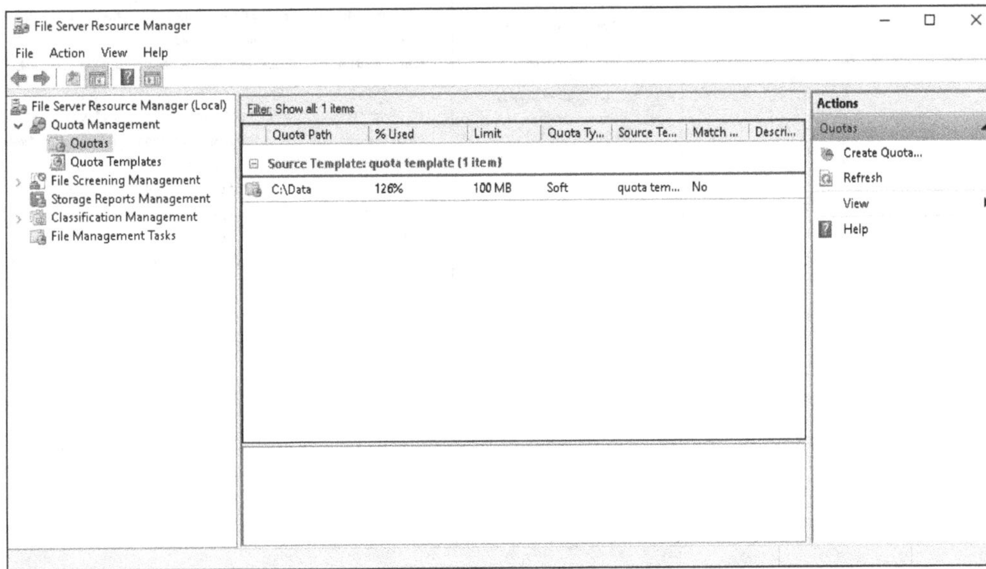

Managing Files with File Screening

CERTIFICATION READY
Configure file screens
Objective 6.2

Often on a corporate network, users try to save files such as movies, music, and games on the corporate server. Unfortunately, although much of this can cause legal problems associated with copyright, it also takes up disk space that can be used for something else, it costs money to provide the storage space, and it makes the backup sets larger. Therefore, Microsoft developed ***file screening***, which allows you to control the type of files that users can save and send notifications when users try to save a blocked file.

In the File Screening Management node of the File Server Resource Manager MMC snap-in, you can perform the following tasks:

- Create and manage file groups, which are used to determine which files are blocked and which are allowed.
- Create file screens to control the types of files that users can save and generate notifications when users attempt to save unauthorized files.
- Create file screen exceptions that override file-screening rules.
- Define file-screening templates to simplify file-screening management.

CREATING FILE GROUPS

A ***file group*** is used to define a namespace for a file screen, file screen exception, or Files by File Group storage report. It consists of a set of file name patterns, which are grouped by the following:

- Files to include
- Files to exclude

FSRM already includes pre-built file groups (see Figure 15-6).

Figure 15-6
Displaying file groups

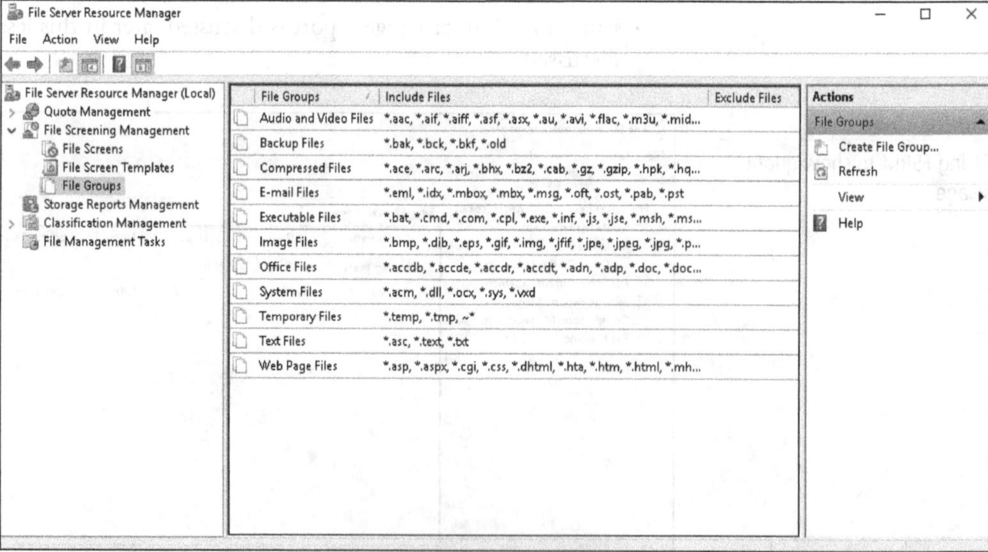

CREATE FILE GROUPS

GET READY. To create a file group, perform the following steps.

1. Open **Server Manager.**
2. Click **Tools > File Server Resource Manager.** The File Server Resource Manager console opens.

3. In File Screening Management, click the **File Groups** node.
4. Right-click **File Groups** and choose **Create File Group.** The Create File Group Properties dialog box opens (see Figure 15-7).

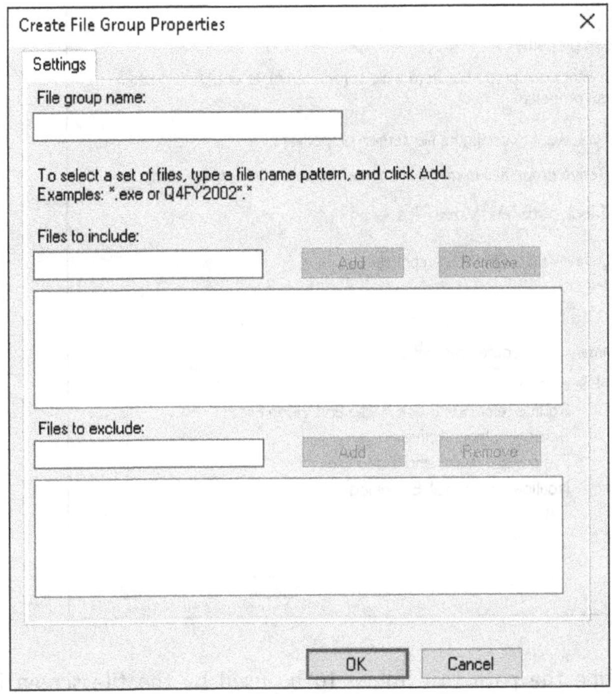

Figure 15-7

Creating a file group with the Create File Group Properties dialog box

5. In the File group name text box, type a name of the file group.
6. To add files to include, type a filename or filename pattern using the * wildcard character in the Files to include text box, and then click **Add.**
7. To add files to exclude, type a filename or filename pattern using the * wildcard character in the **Files to exclude** text box and click **Add.**
8. Click **OK** to close the Create File Group Properties dialog box.

CREATING A FILE SCREEN

When you create a file screen, there are two screening types:

- ***Active screening*:** Prevents users from saving the defined unauthorized files.
- ***Passive screening*:** Allows users to save a file, but allows the monitoring and notification when a user saves an unauthorized file.

CREATE A FILE SCREEN

GET READY. To create a file screen, perform the following steps.

1. Open **Server Manager.**
2. Click **Tools > File Server Resource Manager.** The File Server Resource Manager console opens.
3. Under File Screening Management, click the **File Screens** node.
4. Right-click **File Screens**, and then click **Create File Screen.** The Create File Screen dialog box opens (see Figure 15-8).

Figure 15-8

Creating a file screen with the Create File Screen dialog box

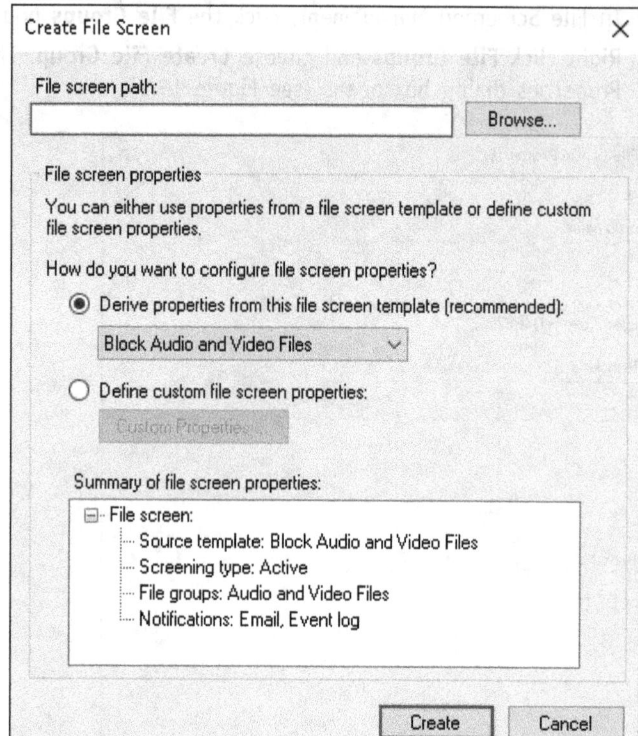

5. Type the path to a folder to be used by the file screen in the File screen path text box. The file screen applies to the selected folder and all of its subfolders.
6. Select **Define custom file screen properties** and then click **Custom Properties**. The File Screen Properties dialog box opens (see Figure 15-9).

Figure 15-9

Opening the File Screen Properties dialog box

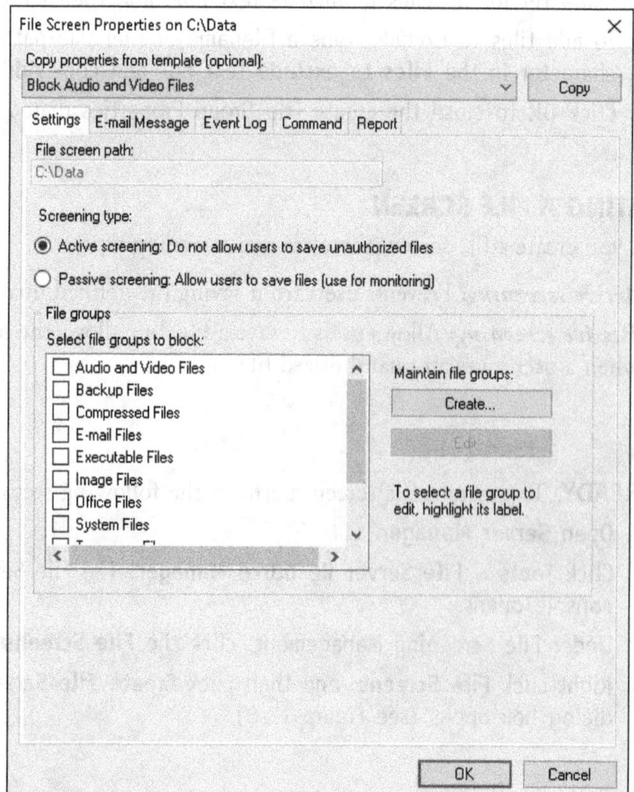

7. If you want to copy the properties of an existing template to use as a base for your file screen, select a template from the Copy properties from template drop-down list. Then click **Copy**.
8. Under Screening type, click the **Active screening** option or the **Passive screening** option.
9. Under File groups, select each file group that you want to include in your file screen.
10. To configure e-mail notifications, click the **E-mail Message** tab, and then set the following options:
    - Select the **Send e-mail to the following administrators** check box, and then enter the names of the administrative accounts that will receive the notifications using the account@domain format. Use semicolons to separate multiple accounts.
    - To send e-mail to the person who saved the file that reached the quota threshold, select the **Send e-mail to the user who exceeded the threshold** check box.
    - To configure the message, edit the default subject line and message body that are provided. Brackets indicate variable information. For example, the [Source Io Owner] variable inserts the name of the user who saved the file that reached the quota threshold.
    - To configure additional headers (including From, Cc, Bcc, and Reply-to), click **Additional E-mail Headers.**
11. To log an event, select the **Event Log** tab. Then select the **Send warning to event log** check box, and edit the default log entry.
12. To run a command or script, select the **Command** tab. Then select the **Run this command or script** check box. Type the command. You can also enter command arguments, select a working directory for the command or script, or modify the command security setting.
13. To generate one or more storage reports, select the **Reports** tab. Then select the **Generate reports** check box, and then select which reports to generate. Optionally, you can enter one or more administrative e-mail recipients for the report or e-mail the report to the user who reached the threshold.
14. Click **OK** to close the File Screen Properties dialog box.
15. In the Create File Screen dialog box, click **Create** to save the file screen. The Save Custom Properties as a Template dialog box opens.
16. To save a template that is based on these customized properties (recommended) and apply the settings, select **Save the custom properties as a template** and enter a name for the template.
17. If you do not want to save a template when you save the file screen, select **Save the custom file screen without creating a template.**
18. Click **OK** to close the Save Custom Properties as a Template dialog box. The new file screen appears under File Screens.

CREATING A FILE SCREEN EXCEPTION

Sometimes, after you have made a file screening, you need to allow exceptions. For example, you might create a file screen that prevents users from saving videos. But now the marketing office needs to save a video of its latest commercial. To allow files that other file screens are blocking, create a ***file screen exception***, which is a special type of file screen that overrides any file screening that would otherwise apply to a folder and all its subfolders in a designated exception path.

CREATE A FILE SCREEN EXCEPTION

GET READY. To create a file screen exception, perform the following steps.

1. Open **Server Manager.**
2. Click **Tools > File Server Resource Manager**. The File Server Resource Manager console opens.
3. Under File Screening Management, click the **File Screens** node.
4. Right-click **File Screens** and choose **Create File Screen Exception.** The Create File Screen Exception dialog box opens.
5. Type the path that the exception applies to in the Exception path text box. The exception applies to the selected folder and all of its subfolders.
6. To specify which files to exclude from file screening, select each file group that you want to exclude from file screening listed under File groups.
7. Click **OK** to close the Create File Screen Exceptions dialog box.

CREATING A FILE SCREEN TEMPLATE

A ***file screen template*** defines a set of file groups to screen, the type of screening to perform (active or passive), and (optionally) a set of notifications that are generated automatically when a user saves, or attempts to save, an unauthorized file. Similar to quota templates, you can simplify the management of file screens by updating the templates, which update all of the file screens that use the template.

CREATE A FILE SCREEN TEMPLATE

GET READY. To create a file screen template, perform the following steps.

1. Open **Server Manager.**
2. Click **Tools > File Server Resource Manager.** The File Server Resource Manager console opens.
3. In File Screening Management, click the **File Screen Templates** node.
4. Right-click **File Screen Templates** and choose **Create File Screen Template.** The Create File Screen Template dialog box opens.
5. If you want to copy the properties of an existing template to use as a base for your new template, select a template from the Copy properties from template drop-down list. Then, click **Copy.**
6. Modify values on the Settings tab including the template name, screening type, and selected file groups to block.
7. Click **OK** to close the Create File Screen Template dialog box.

When you change a file screen template, and click OK to save the changes, you have the following options:

- Apply template only to derived file screens that match the original template
- Apply template to all derived file screens
- Do not apply template to derived file screens

Using Storage Reports

CERTIFICATION READY
Configure storage reports
Objective 6.2

To help you manage storage, you can use FSRM to generate ***storage reports*** that show the state of file server volumes and anyone who exceeds the quota or uses files that aren't allowed.

The reports that FSRM can create are as follows:

- **Duplicate Files:** Shows a list of files that are the same size and have the same last modified date.
- **File Screening Audit:** Creates a list of the audit events generated by file-screening violations for specific users during a specific time period.
- **Files by File Group:** Creates a list of files sorted by selected file groups defined with FSRM.
- **Files by Owner:** Creates a list of files sorted by selected users that own them.
- **Large Files:** Creates a list of files that are larger than a specified size.
- **Least Recently Accessed Files:** Creates a list of files that have not been accessed for a specified number of days.
- **Most Recently Accessed Files:** Creates a list of files that have been accessed within a specified number of days.
- **Quota Usage:** Creates a list of quotas that exceed a specified percentage of the storage limit.

When reports are generated, they are automatically saved in the C:\StorageReports\Scheduled folder. You can also have reports e-mailed to administrators.

SCHEDULE A STORAGE REPORT

GET READY. To schedule a storage report, perform the following steps.

1. Open **Server Manager**.
2. Click **Tools > File Server Resource Manager**. The File Server Resource Manager console opens.
3. Right-click **Storage Reports Management** and choose **Schedule a New Report Task**. The Storage Reports Task Properties dialog box opens (see Figure 15-10).

Figure 15-10

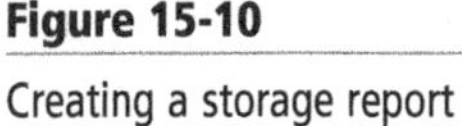

Creating a storage report

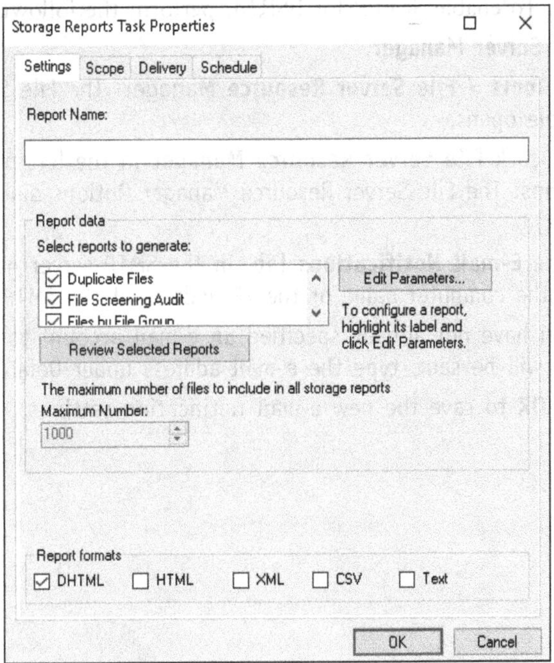

4. In the Report Name text box, type the name of the report.
5. In the Report data section, select the report that you want to generate and deselect the reports that you don't want to generate.
6. Click the **Scope** tab to display it.
7. Select the file groups that you want to include in the report.
8. Click **Add** and browse to the volume or folder that you want to report on and then click **OK.**
9. Click the **Delivery** tab to display it.
10. If you want the reports e-mailed to a user, select the **Send reports to the following administrators** and then type the e-mail address. If you need to send to multiple users, separate the e-mail addresses with semicolons (;).
11. Click the **Schedule** tab to display it.
12. Specify the time and select the days that you want the report to be generated.
13. Click **OK** to close the Storage Reports Task Properties dialog box.

After the reports have been scheduled, you can run a report at any time by right-clicking the storage report and selecting Run Report Task Now. If you need to change a scheduled report, right-click the report and select Edit Report Task Properties.

Enabling SMTP

Various components of the FSRM can send notifications via e-mail. However, to send e-mail, you need to configure FSRM to use Simple Mail Transfer Protocol (SMTP) so that FSRM knows where to forward the e-mail to be delivered.

An SMTP server must be specified as part of the initial FSRM configuration so that quota or file screening e-mail notifications can be sent. However, you must be a member of the Administrators group to enable SMTP.

ENABLE SMTP FOR FSRM

GET READY. To enable SMTP for FSRM, perform the following steps.

1. Open **Server Manager.**
2. Click **Tools > File Server Resource Manager.** The File Server Resource Manager console opens.
3. Right-click **File Server Resource Manager** in the left pane and choose **Configure Options.** The File Server Resource Manager Options dialog box opens (see Figure 15-11).
4. On the **E-mail Notifications** tab, in the SMTP server name or IP address text box, type the computer name or the IP address of the SMTP server.
5. If you have not already specified an e-mail account to which the e-mail notifications will be sent, type the e-mail address under Default administrator recipients.
6. Click **OK** to save the new e-mail notification settings.

Figure 15-11

Specifying the SMTP server

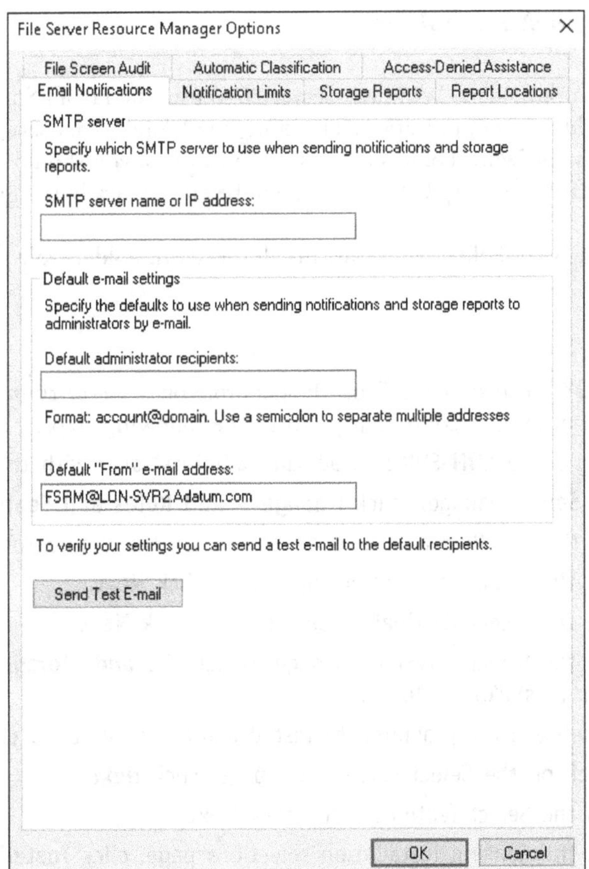

■ Supporting Work Folders

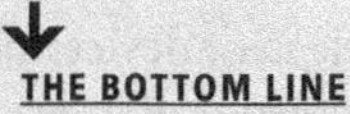

Work Folders allow users to store and access work files on a sync share from multiple devices, including personal computers and devices (including bring-your-own devices). Work Folders are only for individual data and do not support sharing files between users. However, while these files can be accessed from anywhere, the organization maintains control over corporate files by storing the files on centrally managed file servers. To maximize accessibility, you can provide file share-based access to the files stored in a Work Folder or you can use Work Folders with Folder Redirection and Offline Files. In addition, because the files are stored centrally, you can back up the data on a regular basis.

CERTIFICATION READY
Implement work folders
Objective 6.2

Work Folders use the HTTPS protocol to transport data between devices and the Work Folders server. When you configure Work Folders for a user, you configure sync access to a specific sync share. The folder for the user is created in this sync share. When you assign a group with sync access, each user in the group is given a folder on that server. Because a Work Folders client synchronizes only with a single server, you should not assign a user sync access on multiple servers.

When Work Folders is configured on a device, you have the option to wipe the Work Folders data from the device, which removes the Work Folders data only. When the user leaves your organization, it is simple to remove the Work Folders data from all of his devices.

Creating a Work Folder

To use Work Folders, Windows Server 2016 uses the HTTPS protocol for performing Work Folders communication. Therefore, the Work Folder server must have a certificate trusted by the Work Folders devices. In most cases, you should obtain a certificate from an external third-party CA so that it will be automatically trusted.

To create a Work Folder, you must install the Work Folders role and then create a sync share.

INSTALL THE WORK FOLDERS ROLE

GET READY. To install the Work Folders role on a server running Windows Server 2016 that is not a domain controller, perform the following steps.

1. Log on to **LON-SVR2** as **adatum\administrator** with the password of **Pa$$w0rd.**
2. In Server Manager, click **Manage > Add Roles and Features.**
3. In the Add Role and Features Wizard, on the Before You Begin page, click **Next.**
4. On the Select installation type page, click **Next.**
5. On the Select destination server page, click **Next.**
6. On the Select server roles page, select **File and Storage Services\File and iSCSI Services\Work Folders.**
7. When you are prompted to install additional features, click **Add Features.**
8. Back on the Select server roles page, click **Next.**
9. On the Select features page, click **Next.**
10. On the Confirm installation selections page, click **Install.**
11. When the installation completes, click **Close.**

When you create the sync share, two policies become available:

- **Encrypt Work Folders:** The data on the devices is encrypted, but the data on the file server is not encrypted, which will mitigate the risk of data being accessed if the device is lost or stolen.
- **Automatically lock screen, and require a password:** When selected, devices using Work Folders lock the screen after 15 minutes and require a password of at least six characters to unlock. Additionally, if there are 10 unsuccessful sign-in attempts, the device is locked out.

CREATE A SYNC SHARE

GET READY. To create a sync share on a server running Windows Server 2016 and with the Work Folders role installed, perform the following steps.

1. In Server Manager, click **File and Storage Services > Work Folders.** Figure 15-12 shows the Work Folders page.
2. Click the **To create a sync share for Work Folders, start the New Sync Share Wizard** link. Alternatively, you can click **Tasks > New Sync Share.**
3. On the Before You Begin page, click **Next.**

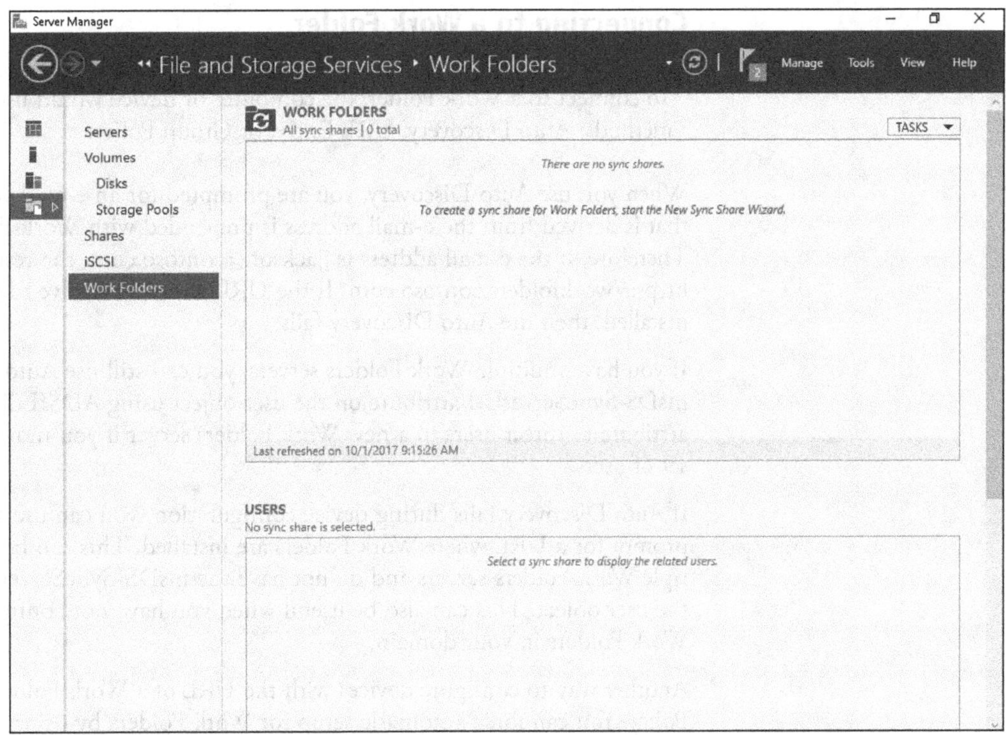

Figure 15-12

Opening the Work Folders page

4. On the Select the server and path page, you can select a folder that is already shared or you can specify a local path (such as **C:\Folder1** or **C:\Data**). Click **Next.**
5. On the Specify the structure for user folders page, select either **User alias (default)** or **User alias@domain.** The user alias is compatible with other technologies, such as folder redirection or home folders. The alias@domain option allows you to use folder names for users across domains. Click **Next.**
6. On the Enter the sync share name page, in the Name and Description text boxes, type a sync share name and description. Click **Next.**
7. On the Grant sync access to groups page, click **Add.** In the Select User or Group dialog box, in the Enter the object name to select text box, type a user name or group name and then click **OK.** Back on the Grant sync access to groups page, click **Next.**
8. On the Specify security policies for PCs page, you can select the following options and click **Next:**
   - **Encrypt Work Folders**
   - **Automatically lock screen, and require a password**
9. On the Confirm selections page, click **Create.**
10. When the sync share is created, click **Close.**

Connecting to a Work Folder

To connect to a Work Folder, the computer or device would use one of the following methods: Auto Discovery, URL Entry, or Group Policy.

When you use Auto Discovery, you are prompted for an e-mail address. The domain name that is derived from the e-mail address is prepended with Work Folders to create a URL. Therefore, if the e-mail address is jjackson@contoso.com, the resulting URL would be https://workfolders.contoso.com. If the URL does not resolve to the server with Work Folders installed, then the Auto Discovery fails.

If you have multiple Work Folders servers, you can still use Auto Discovery by modifying the msDS-SyncServerUrl attribute on the user object using ADSIEdit. You can also modify this attribute to direct users to a new Work Folders server if you move Work Folders for a specific set of users.

If Auto Discovery fails during device configuration, you can use URL Entry, which will prompt for a URL where Work Folders are installed. This can be useful when you have multiple Work Folders servers and do not have the msDS-SyncServerUrl attribute configured on the user object. This can also be useful when you have not configured a DNS host record for Work Folders in your domain.

Another way to configure devices with the URL of a Work Folders server is to use Group Policy. You can force automatic setup for Work Folders by using a computer policy or a user policy. A user policy takes effect for specified users on all devices that they access. A computer policy takes effect for all users on that device.

The user setting is stored in Users\Policies\Administrative Templates\Windows Components\Work Folders\Specify Work Folders. After you enable the GPO setting, you will type the Work Folder URL (such as https://workfolders.contoso.com/sync/1.0). If you then want the policy to automatically configure with the Work Folders client, check the Force automatic setup option. You can use Microsoft Intune to deliver Group Policy Objects (GPOs) for Work Folders to devices that are not domain members.

When you use Group Policy to configure Work Folders, you can force automatic setup. When you force automatic setup, users are not given the option to select where Work Folders data will be stored on the local device. Work Folders data will be stored in the default location of %USERPROFILE%\WorkFolders.

CONNECT TO A WORK FOLDER

GET READY. To connect to a Work Folder, perform the following steps.

1. On a computer running Windows 10, click the **Start** button, type **Control Panel**, and then press **Enter**.
2. Click **System and Security > Work Folders.**
3. On the Manage Work Folders page, click **Set up Work Folders.**
4. On the Enter Your Work Email Address page, in the Work email address text box, type the user's e-mail address. Alternatively, you can click **Enter a Work Folders URL** and, in the Work Folders URL text box, type the Work Folders URL. Click **Next.**
5. On the Introducing Work Folders page, click **Next.**
6. On the Security Policies page, select **I accept these policies on my PC** and then click **Set up Work Folders.**
7. Click **Close.** Figure 15-13 shows the user's Work Folder.

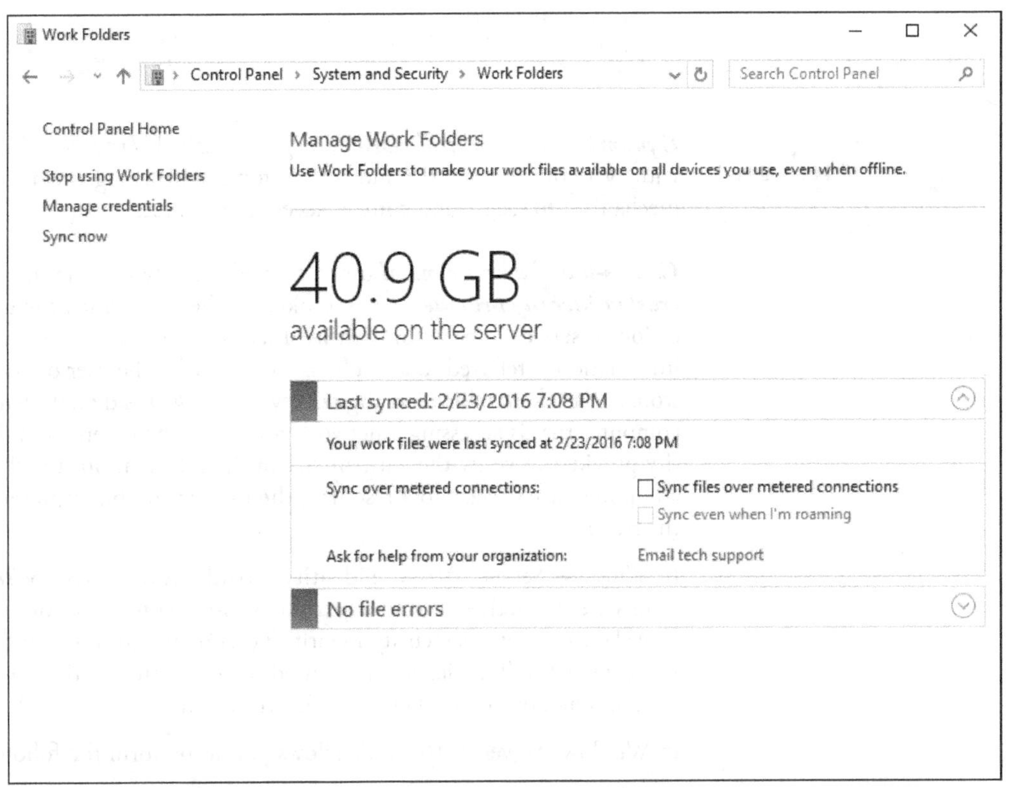

Figure 15-13

Managing your Work Folder

Work Folders use the HTTPS protocol to transport data between devices and the Work Folders server. By using a reverse proxy server, Work Folders can be securely used over the Internet. In addition, you can use Web Application Proxy to enhance the security of Web Folders by integrating Web Folders authentication with AD FS, which allows you to implement multi-factor authentication and restrict connectivity to Work Folders to authorized devices.

If you integrate Microsoft Azure Multi-Factor Authentication with AD FS, you can implement the following methods for additional authentication:

- **Phone calls:** You receive a call on your phone to confirm your authentication and you press the # (pound) symbol to confirm after receiving the call.
- **Text messages:** You receive a text message with a passcode. You respond to the text message and include the passcode.
- **Mobile App:** An authentication prompt appears in the mobile app that you must acknowledge.

When Work Folders are configured on a device, you can wipe the Work Folders data from the device, which removes the Work Folders data only. When the user leaves your organization, it is simple to remove the Work Folders data from all of the user's devices.

Because Work Folders data is stored on a file server, you can perform all of the typical file management functions using File Server Resource Manager and Rights Management Services, including quotas, file screening, classification, and Rights Management.

When you modify a file, the file is replicated very quickly. However, although it is unlikely that a user will change a file on two separate devices before replication occurs, it can happen if one of the devices is offline for an extended period. In addition, if synchronization does not occur, you should ensure the following:

- Work Folders do not synchronize individual files larger than 10 GB.
- There is at least 5 GB of free space on the volume with the Work Folders.
- Quotas are not restricting access to a Work Folder.

■ Using Dynamic Access Control

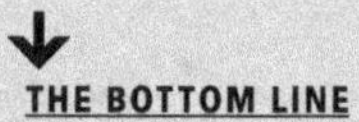

Dynamic Access Control (DAC), originally called *claims-based access control*, was introduced with Windows Sever 2012 and is used for access management. It provides an automatic mechanism to secure and control access to resources.

Claims-based access control uses a trusted identity provider to provide authentication. The ***trusted identity provider*** issues a token to the user, which the user then presents to the application or service as proof of identity. Identity is based on a set of information. Each piece of information is referred to as a ***claim*** (such as who the user or computer claims to be) and stored as a token, which is a digital key. The ***token*** is digital identification for the user or computer that is accessing a network resource. The token has a digital signature of the identity provider to verify the authenticity of the information stored within the token. As users or computers need access to a resource, the user or computer presents the token to get access to the resource.

In Windows Server 2016, the identity provider is the ***Security Token Service (STS)*** and the claims are the Active Directory attributes assigned to a user or device (such as a computer). The claims, the user's security identifier (SID), and group membership are stored inside the Kerberos ticket. The ticket is then used to access protected resources. Of course, claims authorization relies on the Kerberos Key Distribution Center (KDC).

In Windows Server 2016, DAC allows you to perform the following:

- Identify data by using automatic and manual classification or tagging files in an organization.
- Control access to files by applying automatic policies that are controlled by Central Access Policies.
- Audit access by using a Central Audit Policy to ensure compliance and to be used in forensic analysis.
- Use Active Directory Rights Management Service (RMS) to encrypt sensitive documents.
- Offer Access-Denied Assistance, which provides a method for users to request access from the owner of data when he or she is denied access.

Claims-based authorization requires the following:

- Windows Server 2012 or higher must be installed on the file server that hosts the resources that DAC protects.
- At least one Windows Server 2012 or higher domain controller must be accessible by the requesting client.
- If you use claims across a forest, you must have a Windows Server 2012 or higher domain controller in each domain.
- If you use device claims, clients must run Windows 8 or higher.

To enable AD DS for DAC, create a new Group Policy Object (GPO) and then link the GPO to the Domain Controllers organization unit (OU) or edit the Default Domain Controllers Policy GPO . When you enable DAC, you have the option to support claims, compound authentication, and Kerberos armoring. Compound authentication is an extension to Flexible Authentication Secure Tunneling (FAST), which allows Kerberos to create service tickets to devices. The Kerberos armoring fully encrypts Kerberos messages and signs Kerberos errors. Although Kerberos armoring enhances security, it also increases processing time.

ENABLE DAC FOR ACTIVE DIRECTORY DOMAIN SERVICES (AD DS)

GET READY. To enable DAC for AD DS, perform the following steps.

1. Log on to **LON-DC1** as **adatum\administrator** with the password of **Pa$$w0rd.**
2. In **Server Manager**, click **Tools > Group Policy Management.**
3. In the Group Policy Management console, double-click the GPO assigned to the Domain Controllers OU that you want to use to enable DAC.
4. In the Group Policy Management Editor, navigate to **Computer Configuration\Policies\Administrative Templates\System\KDC** and double-click **KDC support for claims, compound authentication and Kerberos armoring.**
5. Click **Enabled** (see Figure 15-14).

Figure 15-14
Configuring KDC Options

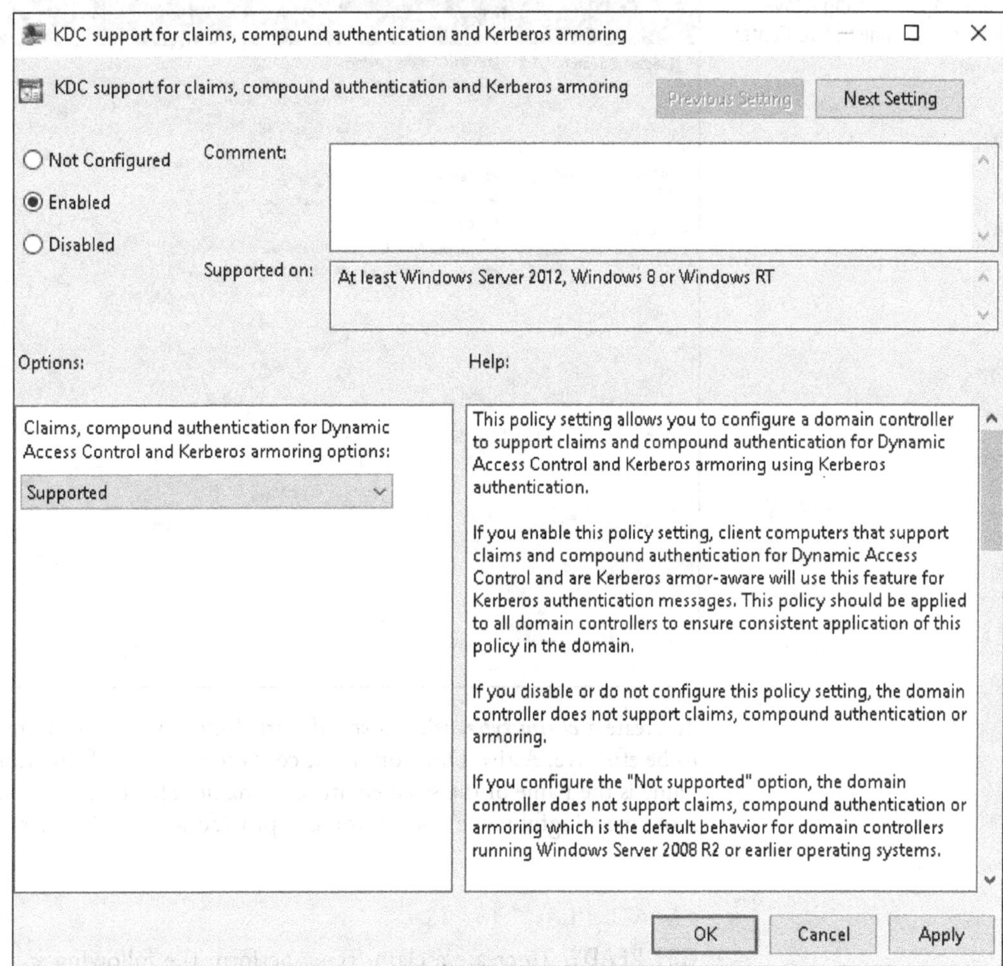

6. Under Options, you can choose one of the following:
   - **Not supported:** Does not provide support for claims, compound authentication, or armoring.
   - **Supported:** Supports claims, compound authentication, and Kerberos armoring for DAC.
   - **Always provide claims:** Provides support for claims.
   - **Fail unarmored authentication requests:** Rejects unarmored Kerberos requests.
7. Click **OK** to close the KDC support for claims, compound authentication and Kerberos armoring dialog box.
8. Close the **Group Policy Management Editor**.

Configuring User and Device Claim Types

CERTIFICATION READY
Configure user and device claim types
Objective 6.2

After you enable support for DAC in AD DS, you must create and configure claims and resource property objects. To create and configure claims, you primarily use the Active Directory Administrative Center.

The most common types of claims are attribute-based claims, which are usually configured with Active Directory Administrative Center, specifically using the Dynamic Access Control node (see Figure 15-15). All claims are stored in the configuration partition in AD DS, which is a forest-wide partition. As a result, all domains in the forest share the claim dictionary.

Figure 15-15

Managing DAC using Active Directory Administrative Center

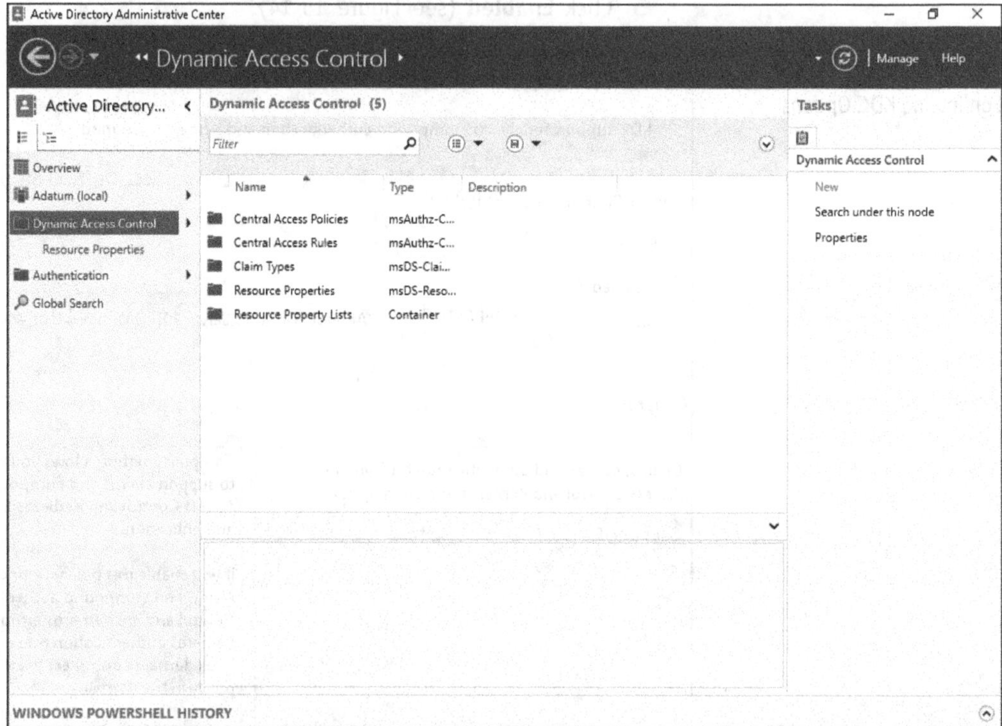

To create a ***claim type***, select a specific attribute from Active Directory. Of course, for DAC to be effective, Active Directory must contain accurate information. By default, the claim name is the name of the selected attribute name. However, you can modify this to give a more meaningful name. Lastly, you can provide suggested values for the claim.

CREATE CLAIM TYPES

GET READY. To create a claim type, perform the following steps.

1. Open **Server Manager.**
2. Click **Tools > Active Directory Administrative Center.** The Active Directory Administrative Center opens.
3. Navigate to the **Dynamic Access Control** node and then click the **Claim Types** container.
4. In the Tasks pane, under Claim Types, click **New** and then click **Claim Type.** The Create Claim Type dialog box opens (see Figure 15-16).
5. With User already selected on the right side of the dialog box, under Source Attribute, scroll down and click **department.**

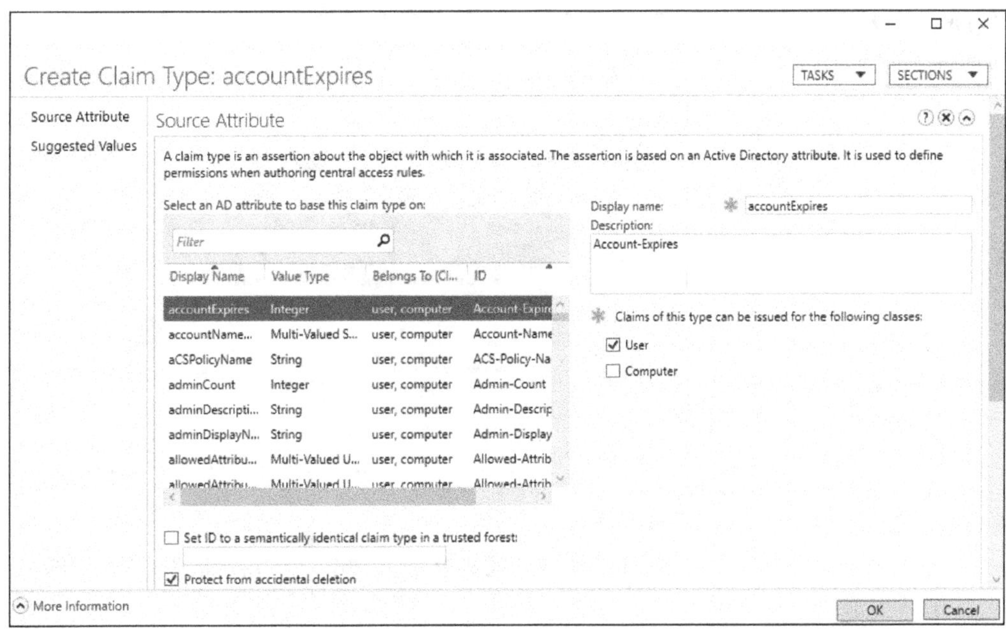

Figure 15-16

Creating a claim type

6. For the display name, to give a more meaningful name, type **Company Department** and then click **OK.** An entry for Company Department is listed under Claim types.
7. In the Tasks pane, under Claim Types, click **New** and then click **Claim Type.**
8. Click to deselect **User** and then click to select **Computer.**
9. Under Source Attribute, scroll down; for Source Attribute, click **description.**
10. Click **OK** to close the Create Claim Type dialog box. The description claim type appears.
11. When the installation is complete, click **Close.**

After you create the claim types, you must configure the resource property objects such as a folder or a file using the Active Directory Administrative Center. You can create your own resource property or you can use preconfigured properties, such as Project, Department, or Folder Usage. Since preconfigured properties are disabled by default, you need to enable the preconfigured property before using them.

Each resource property must be added to at least one resource property list and each resource property list must then be downloaded to the file servers. The Global Resource Property List is downloaded by all servers.

ENABLE RESOURCE PROPERTIES

GET READY. To enable a resource property, perform the following steps.

1. With Active Directory Administrative Center, navigate to and click the **Dynamic Access Control** node. Next, double-click **Resource Properties.**
2. To enable the Department resource property, under Resource Property, right-click **Department** and choose **Enable.**
3. To enable the Confidentiality resource property, under Resource Property, right-click **Confidentiality** and choose **Enable.**
4. To view the Confidentiality settings, double-click **Confidentiality.** The Confidentiality dialog box opens (see Figure 15-17).

Figure 15-17

Viewing the Confidentiality resource property

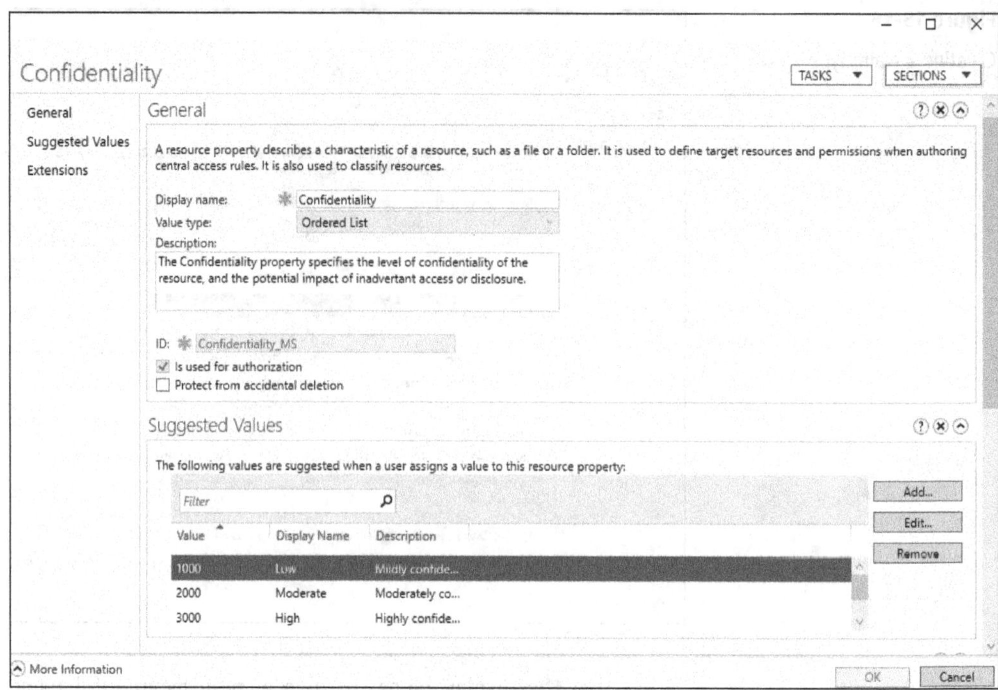

5. Click **Cancel** to close the Confidentiality dialog box.
6. Close Active Directory Administrative Center.

Creating and Configuring Resource Properties and Lists

CERTIFICATION READY
Create and configure resource properties and lists
Objective 6.2

When you configure the properties that are downloaded by files servers and used to classify files or directories, you will use DAC rules to compare user attribute values with resource properties, which are assigned to Resource Properties Lists. You can enable existing properties or create new ones.

CERTIFICATION READY
Configure File Classification Infrastructure (FCI) using FSRM
Objective 6.2

Classification management and file management tasks enable administrators to manage groups of files based on various file and folder attributes. After folders and files are classified, you can automate file and folder maintenance tasks, such as cleaning up stale data or protecting sensitive information. Although classification management can be done manually, you can automate this process with the File Server Resource Manager console.

Classification rules can be created and then scheduled to be applied on a regular basis so that files are automatically scanned and classified based on the content of the file. When you want to perform file classification, you need to determine the following:

- Classifications that you want to apply to documents
- Method that you will use to identify documents for classification
- Schedule for automatic classifications

Of course, to determine the success of the classification, you have to establish periodic reviews.

To manually configure a folder with a classification, you can right-click the folder and choose Properties. In the Properties dialog box, you can then choose the name of the classification and then select the appropriate value. For example, you can choose Department and then select Human Resources. Then all documents within the folder will automatically be classified as the department of Human Resources.

AUTOMATE THE CLASSIFICATION OF FILES

GET READY. To automate the classification of files, perform the following steps.

1. On **LON-SVR2**, log on as **adatum\administrator** with the password of **Pa$$w0rd.**
2. In **Server Manager**, click **Tools > File Server Resource Manager.**
3. Under Classification Management, click **Classification Properties.**
4. To see the new classification property that you created in the previous exercise, right-click **Classification Properties** and choose **Refresh.** The Confidentiality and Department properties appear with a Global scope (see Figure 15-18).

Figure 15-18

Viewing newly created classification properties

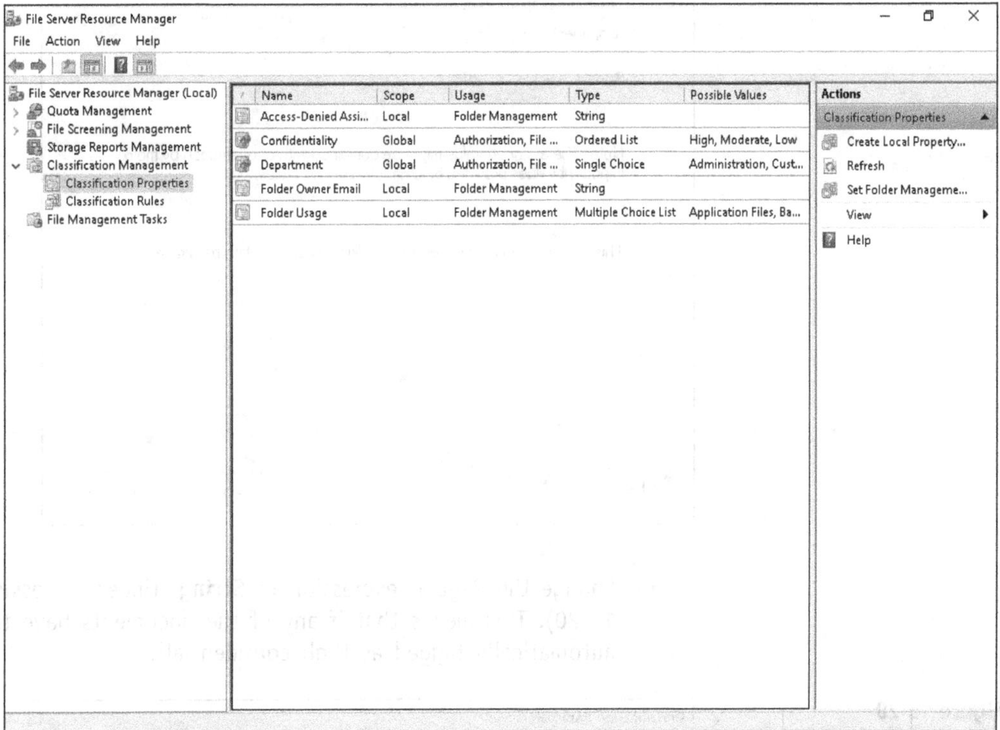

5. Click **Classification Rules.** Next, right-click **Classification Rules** and choose **Create Classification Rule.** The Create Classification Rule dialog box opens.
6. On the General tab, in the Rule name text box, type **Confidentiality.**
7. Click the **Scope** tab.
8. At the bottom of the dialog box, click **Add.** Browse to the **C:\Data** folder and click **OK.** C:\Data is listed under The following folders are included in this scope section.
9. Click the **Classification** tab (see Figure 15-19).
10. The Classification method should already be Content Classifier; the Confidentiality property and High value are set under Property. To configure the Classification parameter, under Parameters, click **Configure.** The Classification Parameters dialog box opens.

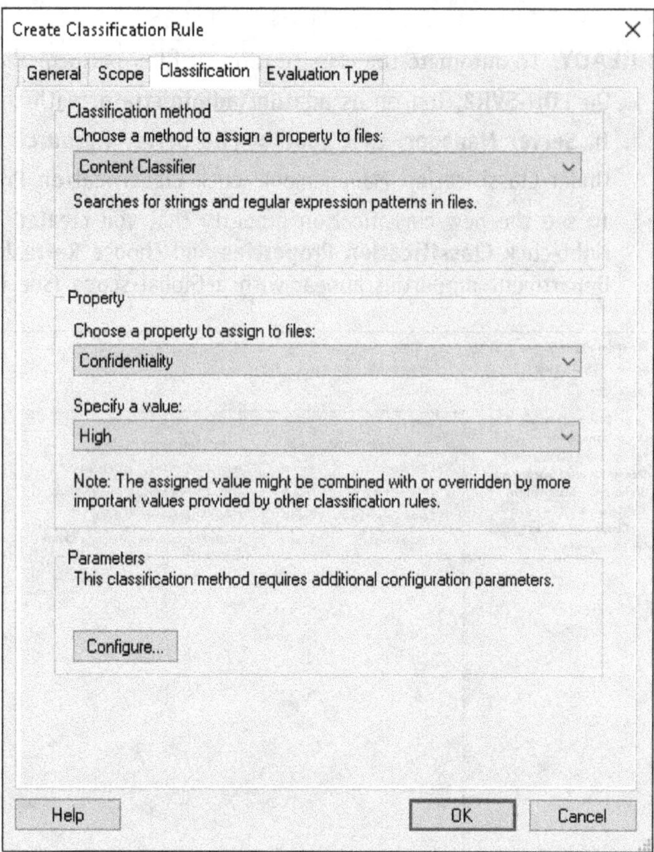

Figure 15-19

Configuring the classification options

11. Change the Regular expression to **String**. Under Expression, type **HR** (see Figure 15-20). This means that if any of the documents have the string HR, they will be automatically tagged as High confidentiality.

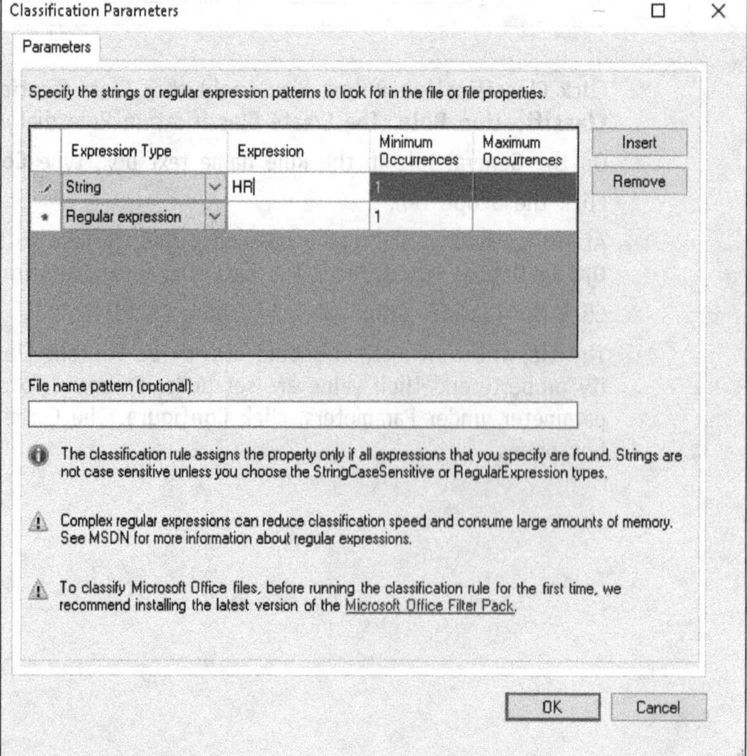

Figure 15-20

Configuring the classification parameters

12. Click **OK** to close the Classification Parameters dialog box.
13. Click the **Evaluation Type** tab.
14. Click to select **Re-evaluate existing property values** and then select **Overwrite the existing value.**
15. Click **OK** to close the Create Classification Rule dialog box.
16. With File Server Resource Manager open, under **Actions** in the right pane, click **Run Classification with All Rules Now.** When you are prompted to choose how you want to run the classification rules, click **Wait for classification to complete** and then click **OK.**
17. In the Automatic Classification Report, review the results and close the report.
18. If a document has the HR string, right-click the document and choose **Properties.**
19. In the Properties dialog box, click the **Classification** tab and then notice that Confidentiality has been set to High (see Figure 15-21).

Figure 15-21

Viewing a document file's classifications

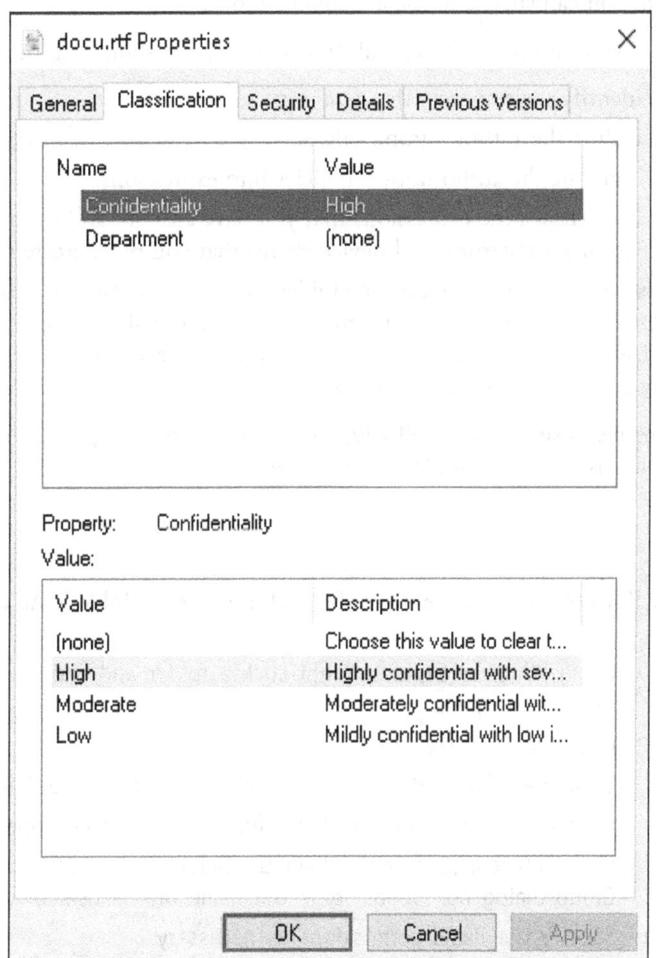

20. Click **OK** to close the Properties dialog box.
21. Close the File Server Resource Manager.

Implementing a Central Access Policy

CERTIFICATION READY
Create and configure Central Access rules and policies
Objective 6.2

To implement classification on a larger scale, you can deploy classification using GPOs to create a Central Access Policy. The Central Access Policy can then be deployed to multiple servers in an organizational unit.

Files stored in shared folders are data files that need to be accessed by multiple users. However, when you apply shared and NTFS permissions, the permissions apply to all files in a specific folder. Unless you constantly monitor the folder and modify the permissions for the folder or the individual files in the folder, the shared and NTFS permissions might not always be a good fit to keep the files secure.

A ***Central Access Policy*** contains ***Central Access Rules*** that grant permissions to objects for a defined group of resources. By default, the rules apply to all resources, but you can limit the resources to which the rule will apply. Once the rule is defined, you can choose to apply it live or you can choose to use a "staging" mode.

Before you implement a Central Access Policy, you should do the following:

1. Identify the resources that you want to protect.
2. Define the authorization policies.
3. Translate the authorization policies into expressions.
4. Break down the expressions that you have created, and determine what claim types, resource properties, and device claims that you must create to deploy the policies.

If you have one file server, or one folder, you don't necessarily need to implement a Central Access Policy. Instead, you can implement conditional access on the folder's Access Control List (ACL). If you have resources across multiple servers or multiple folders, you would most likely benefit from a Central Access Policy.

In the next exercise, you will add conditional access that grants permissions to files in a folder that is classified as Confidentiality – High.

IMPLEMENT CONDITIONAL ACCESS ON A FOLDER'S ACL

GET READY. To implement conditional access on a folder's ACL, perform the following steps.

1. Using Windows Explorer, right-click a folder and choose **Properties.** The Properties dialog box opens.
2. Click the **Security** tab.
3. Click the **Advanced** button. The Advanced Security Settings dialog box opens.
4. Click **Add.** The Permission Entry for Data dialog box opens.
5. Click **Select a principal.** When the Select User, Computer, Service Account, or Group dialog box opens, type the name of the user or group and then click **OK.**
6. Specify the Basic permissions as necessary.
7. At the bottom of the dialog box, click **Add a condition.**
8. For the condition, configure the following:
   Resource > Confidentiality > Equals > Value > High (see Figure 15-22). Click **OK.**

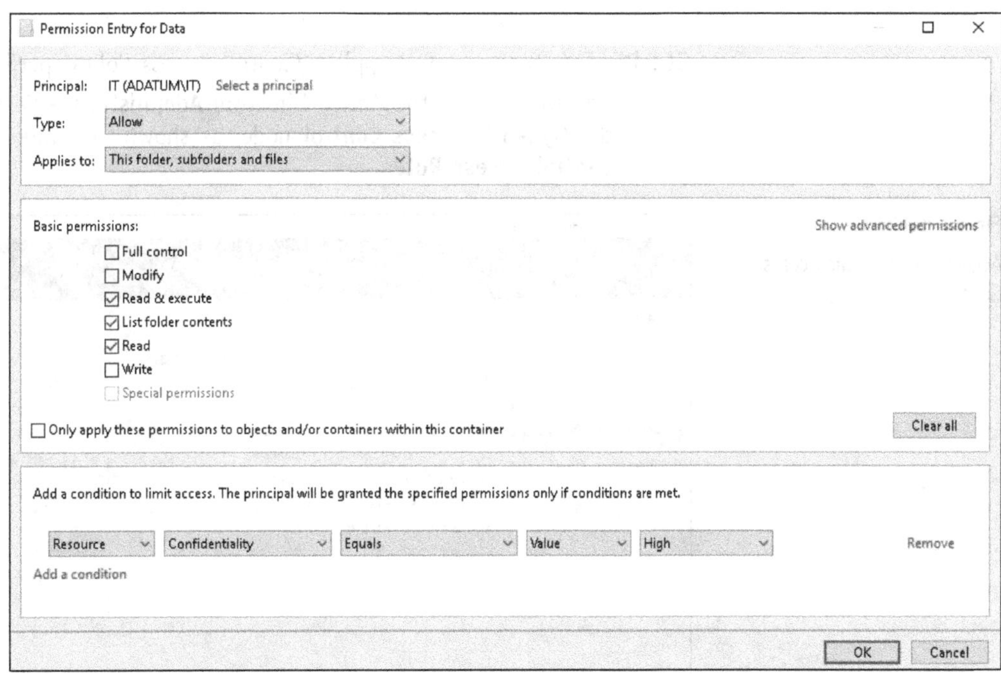

Figure 15-22

Configuring a condition for an ACL

9. Back in the Advanced Security Settings dialog box, you see the condition as shown in Figure 15-23. Click **OK** to close the Advanced Security Settings for Data dialog box.

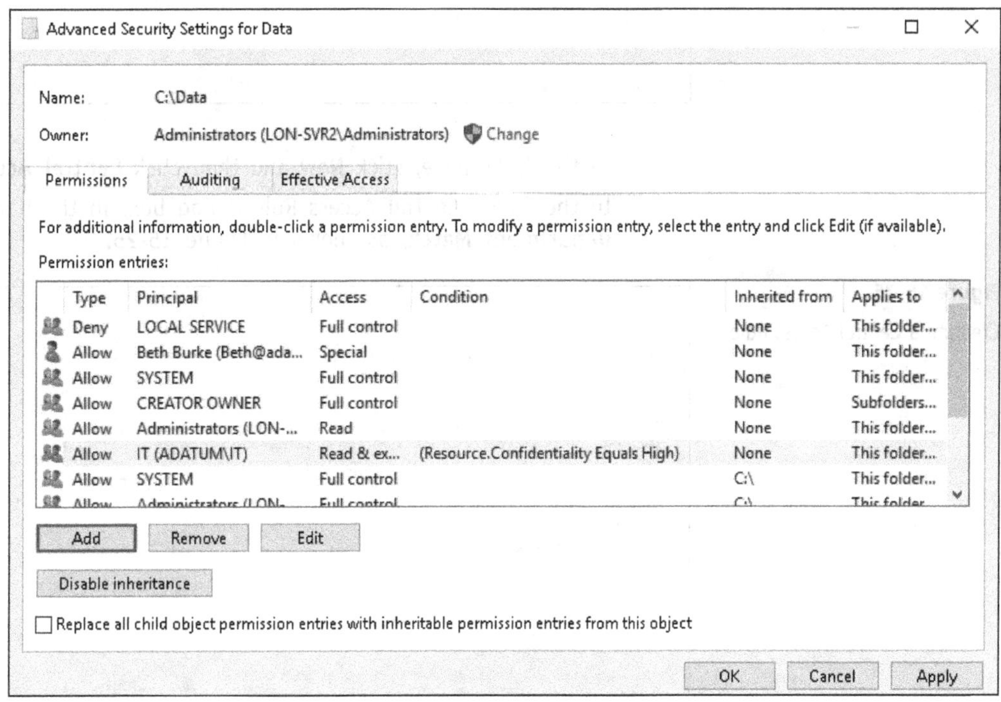

Figure 15-23

Viewing the condition

10. Click **OK** to close the Properties dialog box.

In the next exercise, you will create a Central Access Rule that grants permissions to files in a folder that is classified as Confidentiality – High.

CREATE A CENTRAL ACCESS POLICY

GET READY. To create and apply a Central Access Policy, perform the following steps.

1. On **LON-DC1**, in the Active Directory Administrative Center, navigate to and click the **Dynamic Access Control** node, as shown in Figure 15-24. Next, double-click **Central Access Rules.**

Figure 15-24

Access the Dynamic Access Control node

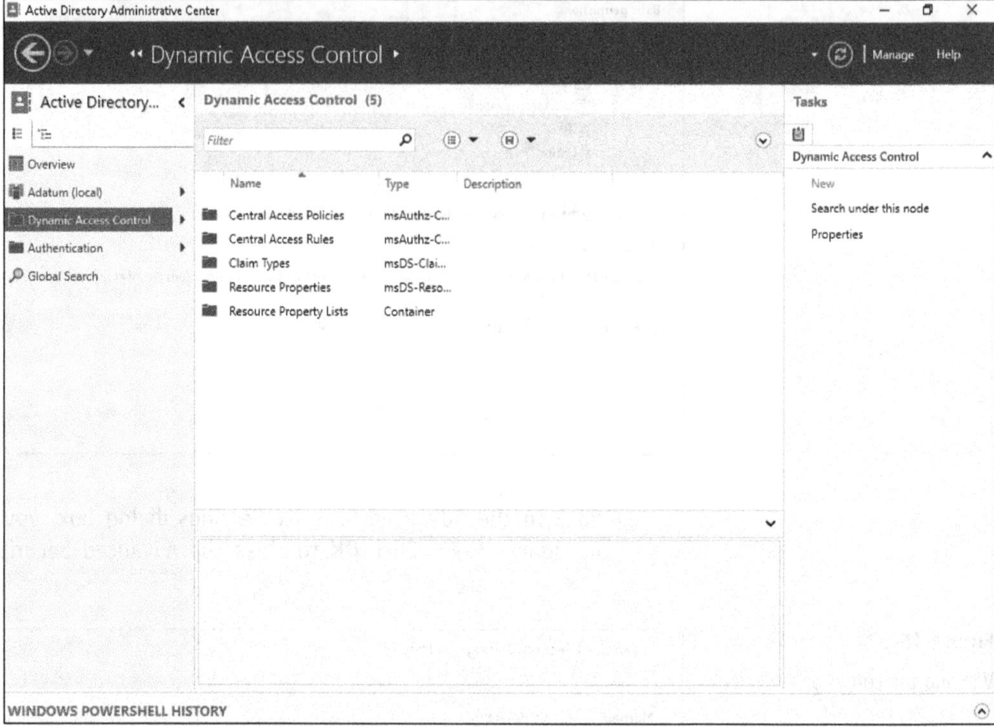

2. In the Tasks pane, click **New** and then click **Central Access Rule**.
3. In the Create Central Access Rule dialog box, in the Name text box, type **Department Match**, as shown in Figure 15-25.

Figure 15-25

Creating a Central Access Rule

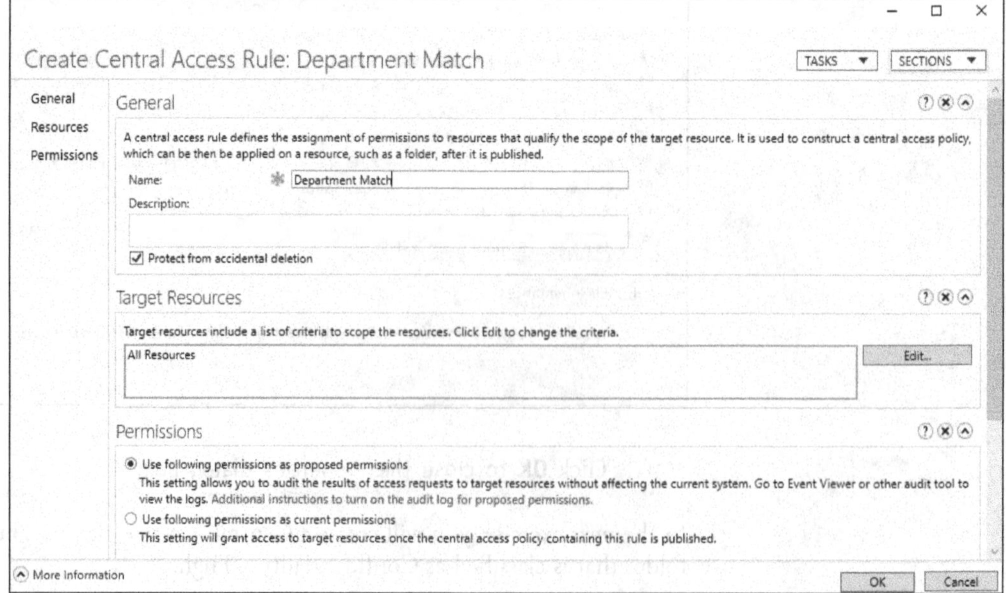

4. In the Target Resources section, click **Edit.**
5. In the Central Access Rule dialog box, click **Add a condition.**
6. Set a condition **Resource-Department-Equals-Value-Research and Development** and then click **OK.**
7. In the Permissions section, select **Use following permissions as current permissions** and then click **Edit.**
8. Select the permission entry for **OWNER RIGHTS** and then click **Remove.** Repeat this step for the Administrators (ADATUM\Administrators) and SYSTEM groups.
9. In the Advanced Security Settings for Permissions dialog box, click **Add.**
10. In the Permission Entry for Permissions dialog box, click **Select a principal.**
11. In the Select User, Computer, Service Account, or Group window, in the Enter the object name to select text box, type **Authenticated Users**, click **Check Names**, and then click **OK.**
12. In the Basic permissions section, select **Modify, Read & Execute, Read**, and **Write.**
13. Click **Add a condition** and then from the Group drop-down list, select **Company Department.** From the Value drop-down list, select **Resource**, and then from the last drop-down list, select **Department.**
14. Verify that you have this expression as a result: User-Company Department-Equals-Resource-Department and then click **OK** three times.
15. In the Tasks pane, click **New** and then click **Central Access Rule.**
16. In the Create Central Access Rule dialog box, in the Name text box, type **Access Confidential Docs.**
17. In the Target Resources section, click **Edit.**
18. In the Central Access Rule window, click **Add a condition.**
19. From the last drop-down list, select **High.**
20. Verify that you have this expression as a result: **Resource-Confidentiality-Equals-Value-High.** Then click **OK.**
21. In the Permissions section, select **Use following permissions as current permissions** and then click **Edit.**
22. Select the permission entry for **OWNER RIGHTS** and then click **Remove.** Repeat this step for the Administrators (ADATUM\Administrators) and SYSTEM groups.
23. In the Advanced Security Settings for Permissions dialog box, click **Add.**
24. In the Permission Entry for Permissions dialog box, click **Select a principal.**
25. In the Select User, Computer, Service Account, or Group window, in the Enter the object name to select text box, type **Authenticated Users**, click **Check Names**, and then click **OK.**
26. In the Basic permissions section, select **Modify, Read and Execute, Read**, and **Write**, and then click **Add a condition.**
27. Set the first condition **User-Company Department-Equals-Value-Managers** and then click **Add a condition.**
28. Set the second condition **Device-Group-Member of each-Value-IT.** If you cannot find IT in the last drop-down list, click **Add items.**
29. In the Select Computer or Group window, type **IT**, click **Check Names**, and then click **OK.**
30. Click **OK** three times.

CONFIGURE A CENTRAL ACCESS POLICY FOR CONFIDENTIAL DOCUMENT IDENTIFICATION

GET READY. To configure a Central Access Policy for confidential document identification, perform the following steps.

1. On **LON-DC1**, in the Active Directory Administrative Center, navigate to and click the **Dynamic Access Control** node. Next, double-click **Central Access Policies.**
2. Under Tasks, click **New** and then click **Central Access Policy.** The Central Access Policy dialog box opens.
3. In the Name text box, type **Protect confidential docs** and then click **Add.**
4. Click the **Access Confidential Docs** rule, click **>>**, and then click **OK** twice.
5. In the Tasks pane, click **New** and then click **Central Access Policy.**
6. In the Name text box, type **Department Match** and then click **Add.**
7. Click the **Department Match** rule, click **>>**, and then click **OK** twice.
8. Close the Active Directory Administrative Center.

APPLY CENTRAL POLICIES TO A FILE SERVER

GET READY. To apply Central Policies to a File Server, perform the following steps.

1. On **LON-DC1**, in Server Manager, click **Tools > Active Directory Users and Computers.**
2. Right-click **Adatum.com** and choose **New > Organizational Unit.**
3. In the New Object – Organizational Unit dialog box, in the Name text box, type **DAC-Protected Servers** and then click **OK.**
4. Close **Active Directory Users and Computers.**
5. In Server Manager, click **Tools > Group Policy Management.**
6. In Group Policy Management Console, right-click **DAC-Protected Servers** and choose **Create a GPO in this domain, and link it here.**
7. In the New GPO dialog box, in the Name text box, type **DAC Policy** and then click **OK.**
8. In the content pane, right-click **DAC Policy** and choose **Edit.**
9. In Group Policy Management Editor window, under Computer Configuration, expand **Policies**, expand **Windows Settings**, expand **Security Settings**, expand **File System**, and then right-click **Central Access Policy** and choose **Manage Central Access Policies.** The Central Access Policies Configuration dialog opens, as shown in Figure 15-26.

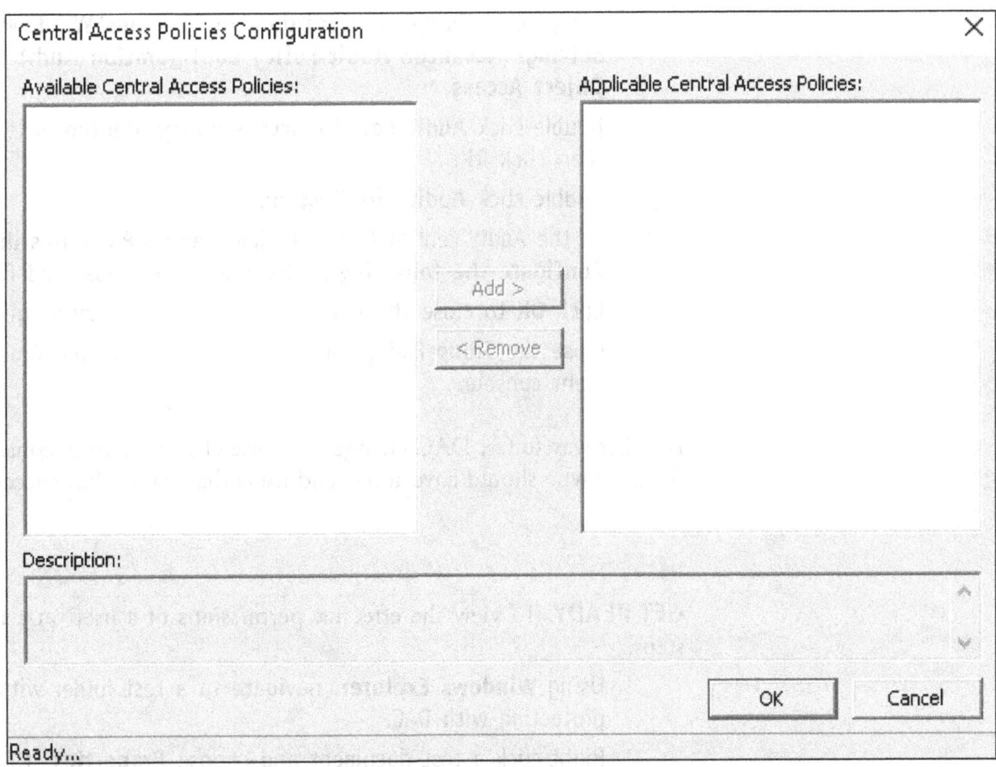

Figure 15-26

Creating a Central Access Rule

10. Press and hold the **Ctrl** key and then click both **Department Match** and **Protect confidential docs.** Click **Add** and then click **OK**.

Implementing Policy Changes and Staging

CERTIFICATION READY
Implement policy changes and staging
Objective 6.2

As you probably already have figured out, DAC can be a powerful tool that helps secure your environment and automates the configuration necessary to secure your resources. However, if you do not properly plan out DAC, when you first implement DAC or when you make changes, you can either grant more access than desired or you can restrict access to the files too much, resulting in an increase of help desk calls.

To help you test implementing DAC or making changes, Windows Server 2016 allows you to perform staging, which allows you to verify the proposed policy updates before enforcing them. To use staging, you deploy the proposed polices along with the enforced policies but you do not actually grant or deny permissions. You then open the Event Viewer on the file server search for Audit Event 4818 in the security logs. The Audit Event 4818 shows the result of the access check that is using the staged policy is different than the access check that is using the enforced policy. However, before the staging appears, you need to first enable Audit Central Access Policy Staging using Group Policies.

CONFIGURE STAGING OF CENTRAL ACCESS POLICY

GET READY. To configure staging of Central Access Policy, perform the following steps.

1. In **Server Manager**, click **Tools** > click **Group Policy Management.**
2. Using the Group Policy Management console, right-click a group policy that you are using to configure DAC and choose **Edit**. The Group Policy Management Editor opens.

3. Navigate to **Computer Configuration\Policies\Windows Settings\Security Settings\Advanced Audit Policy Configuration\Audit Policies** and double-click **Object Access.**
4. Double-click **Audit Central Access Policy Staging**, select all three check boxes, and then click **OK.**
5. Double-click **Audit File System.**
6. In the Audit Central Access Policy Staging Properties dialog box, click to select **Configure the following audit events**, **Success**, and **Failure.**
7. Click **OK** to close the Audit Central Access Policy Staging Properties dialog box.
8. Close the Group Policy Management Editor and the Group Policy Management console.

Another way to test DAC changes is to use effective permissions. Of course, you should test for users who should have access and users that do not have access.

VIEW THE EFFECTIVE PERMISSIONS OF A USER ON A FILE RESOURCE

GET READY. To view the effective permissions of a user on a file, perform the following steps.

1. Using **Windows Explorer**, navigate to a test folder with documents that you are protecting with DAC.
2. Right-click a test document and choose **Properties.** The Properties dialog box opens.
3. Click the **Security** tab and then click the **Advanced** button. The Advanced Security Settings dialog box opens.
4. Click the **Effective Access** tab.
5. Click **Select a user.** (If you need to test computer access, you would instead click **Select a device.**) When the Select User, Computer, Service Account, or Group dialog box opens, type a name of a test user in the Enter the object name to select text box and then click **OK.**
6. Click **Include a user claim.** Select the resource and then type a value as shown in the Figure 15-27.
7. On the Confirm installation selections page, click **Install.**
8. When the installation is complete, click **Close.**

Figure 15-27

Viewing effective permissions

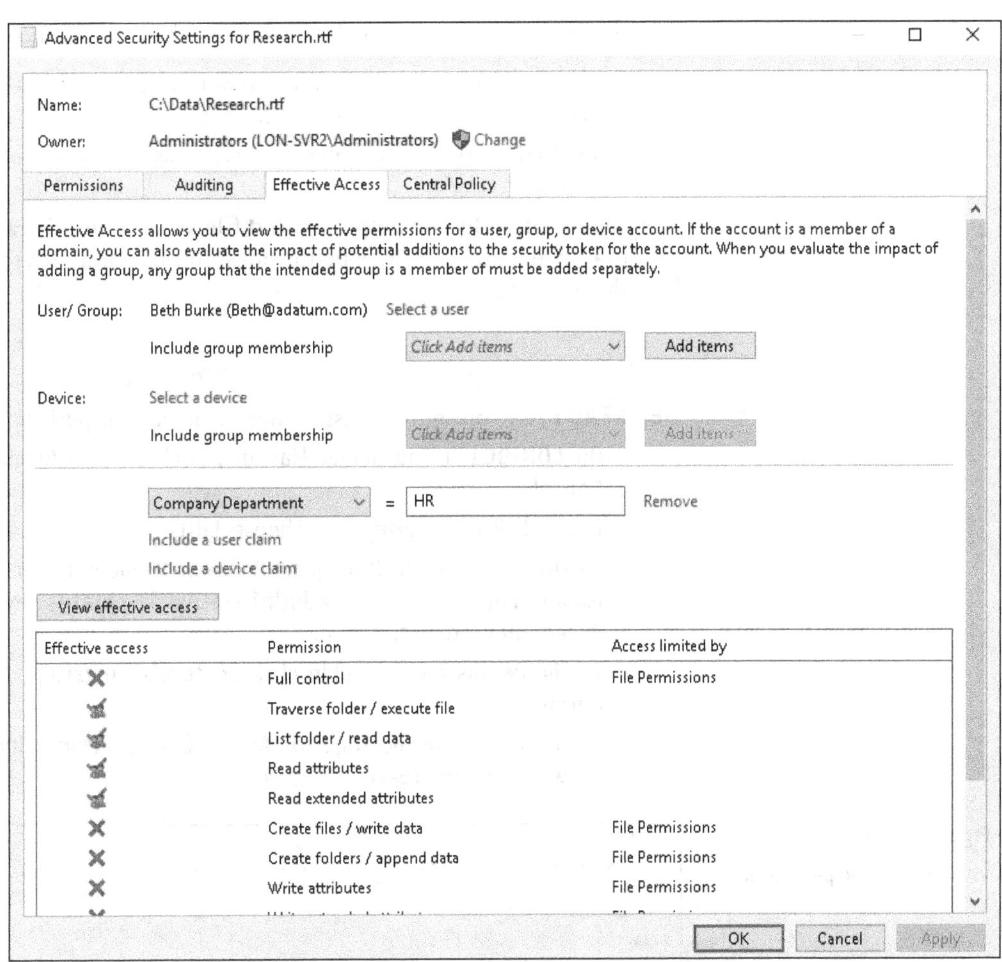

Performing Access-Denied Remediation

CERTIFICATION READY
Perform access-denied remediation
Objective 6.2

When users try to access a remote file and they are denied access, they will typically contact the help desk to get access. Unfortunately, the help desk will usually have to go to the owner of the files to see whether the help desk can be provided with the necessary access or whether the owner of the files must grant the access. Windows Server 2016 includes access-denied assistance feature, which will help users respond to access-denied issues without involving the help desk and redirecting the requester to the owner. Access-denied assistance enables you to customize messages that appear to users when they are denied access to files. Access-denied assistance works only with Windows 8 or higher or Windows Server 2012 or higher. Access-denied assistance is configured using Group Policy or the FSRM Management Properties.

When you plan for access-denied assistance, you should:

- Define messages that users will receive when they attempt to access resources for which they do not have access rights.
- Determine whether users should be able to send a request for access via e-mail.
- Determine recipients for access-request e-mail messages.

You can then determine the method to handle the access-denied errors:

- **Self-remediation:** Specifies customized messages to URLs that direct users to self-remediation websites that your organization provides.
- **Remediation by the data owner:** Enables users to send e-mail messages to data owners to request access.
- **Remediation by the help desk and file-server administrators:** Allows administrators to view the user's effective permissions, so that administrators can determine the cause of the problem.

CONFIGURE ACCESS-DENIED REMEDIATION

GET READY. To configure access-denied remediation, perform the following steps.

1. On **LON-DC1**, using Server Manager, click **Tools > Group Policy Management Console.**
2. Right-click **DAC Policy** and choose **Edit.**
3. In the Group Policy Management Editor window, under Computer Configuration, expand **Policies**, expand **Administrative Templates**, expand **System**, and then click **Access-Denied Assistance.**
4. In the details pane, double-click **Customize message for Access Denied errors** option.
5. In the Customize message for Access Denied errors window, click **Enabled**, as shown in Figure 15-28.

Figure 15-28

Viewing effective permissions

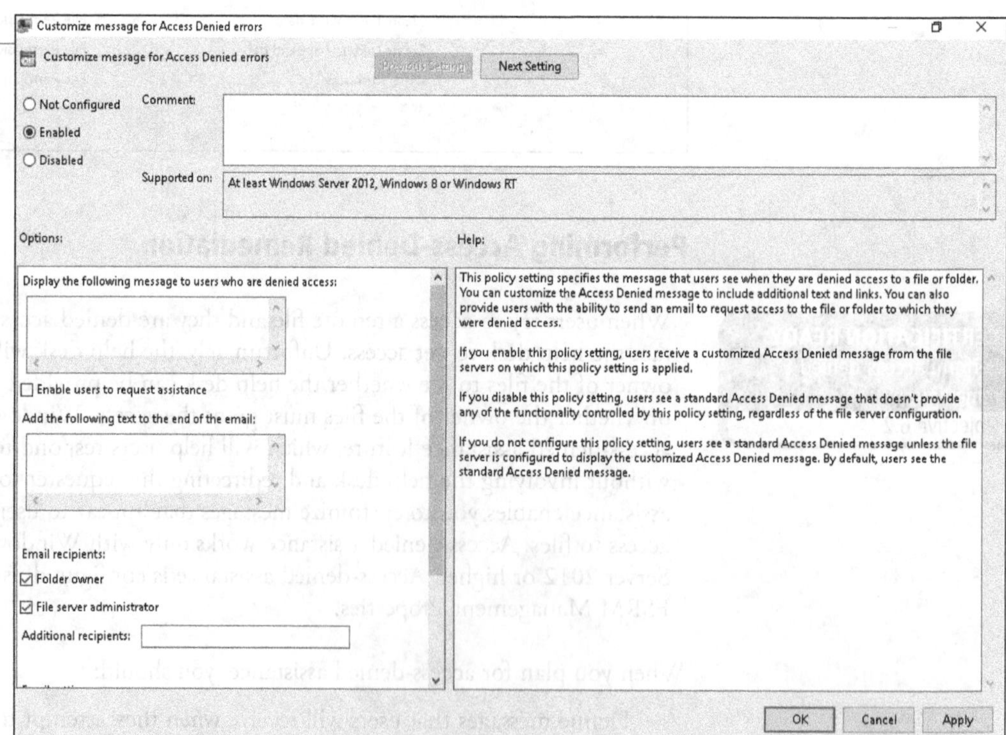

6. In the Display the following message to users who are denied access text box, type **You are denied access because of a permission policy. Please request access.**
7. Select the **Enable users to request assistance** option. Review the other options, but do not make any changes, and then click **OK.**

8. In the details pane of Group Policy Management Editor, double-click the **Enable access-denied assistance on client for all file types** option, click **Enabled**, and then click **OK.**
9. Close Group Policy Management Editor and Group Policy Management Console.

After the server receives the GPO, when you access a file that you do not have permissions to, you will receive the customized message. You can then click Request assistance to review the options for sending a message and then click Close.

Configuring File Management Tasks

FSRM can be used to automate file management tasks such as finding subsets of files and apply simple commands to the files on a regular basis. To identify the files, you can classify the servers via classification rules.

CERTIFICATION READY
Configure file management tasks
Objective 6.2

A common task is to delete or move older files. For example, you can create a custom task that can search for and delete files based on the following properties:

- Location
- Classification properties
- Creation time
- Modification time
- Last accessed time
- Filename

When you run a file expiration task, a new directory is created with the specified expiration directory. The directory will be grouped by the server name on which the task was run and named according to the name of the file management task and the time it was run. When files are moved, the original directory structure will be preserved.

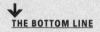

CREATE A FILE EXPIRATION TASKS

GET READY. To create a file expiration task, perform the following steps.

1. Open **Server Manager.**
2. Click **Tools > File Server Resource Manager.** The File Server Resource Manager console opens.
3. Click, then right-click the **File Management Tasks** node and choose **Create File Management Task.**
4. In the Create File Management Task dialog box, on the General tab, in the Name text box, type the name of the task, such as **Delete old files.** If desired, in the Description text box, type a description of what the task is supposed to do and why it is needed.
5. Click the **Scope** tab.
6. Click the Add button. In the Browse For Folder dialog box, in the Folder text box, type **C:\Data** and then click **OK.**
7. Click the **Action** tab.
8. On the Action tab, the Type should already be set to File expiration. In the Expiration directory, specify the folder name as **C:\OldFiles**, as shown in Figure 15-29.

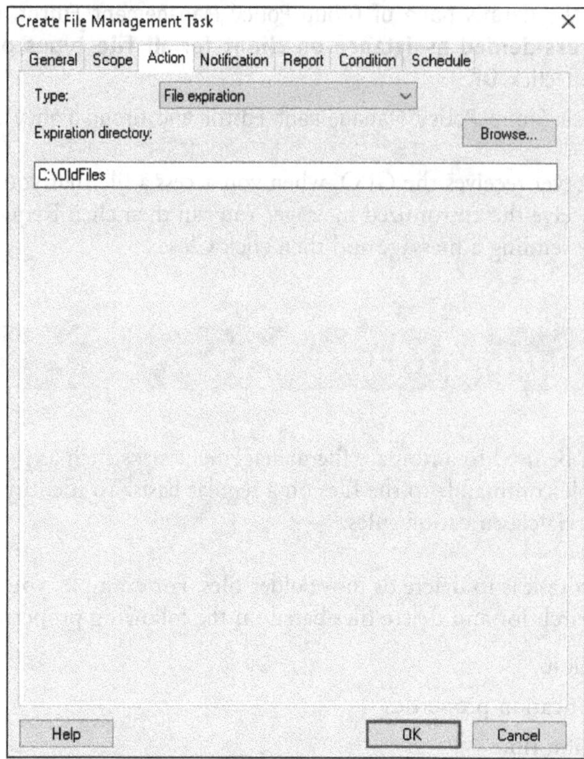

Figure 15-29

Specifying the Expiration directory

9. Click the **Notification** tab. Click **Add** to send e-mail notifications, log an event, or run a command or script a specified minimum number of days before the task performs an action on a file. In the Number of days before task is executed to send notification combo box, type or select a value to specify the minimum number of days prior to a file being expired that a notification will be sent. See Figure 15-30.

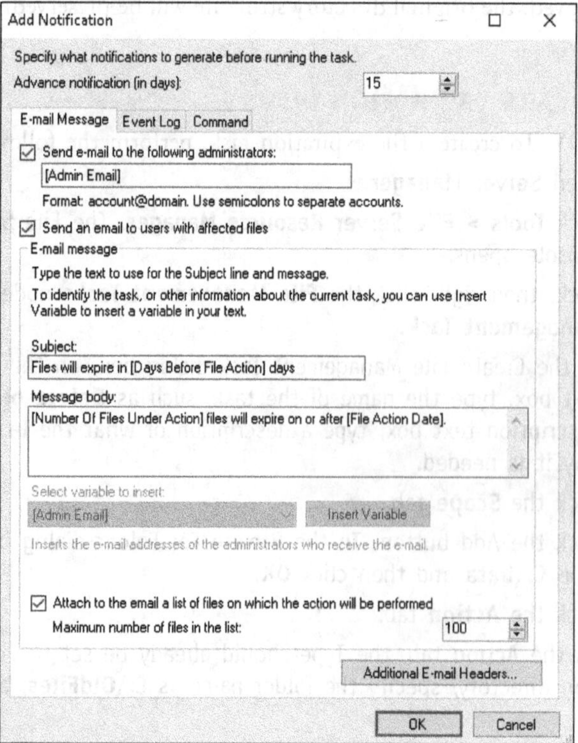

Figure 15-30

Configuring notifications

10. Click **OK** and then click the **Condition** tab (see Figure 15-31).

Figure 15-31

Specifying conditions

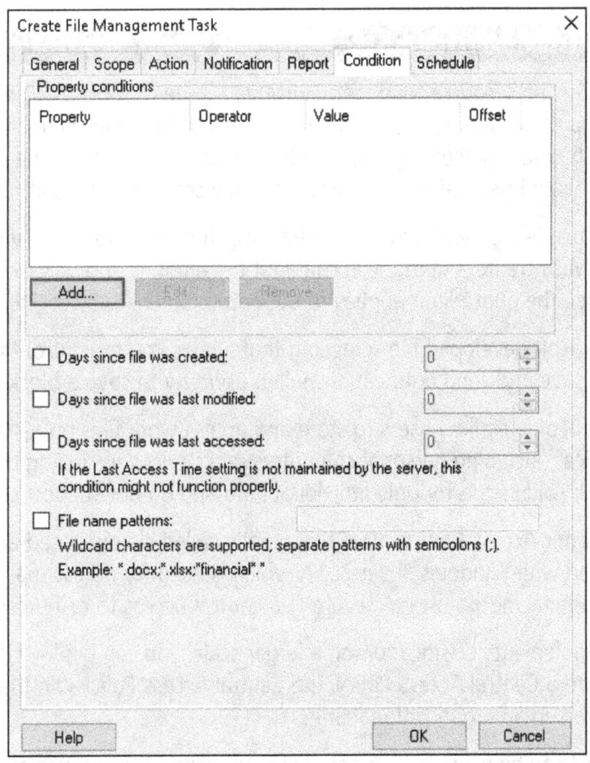

11. When you click the Add button, the Property Condition dialog box opens, where you can specify Property (such as Confidentiality or Department), the Operator (such as Equal, Not equal, Less than, Greater than, Exist, or Not exist), and one of the values of the property chosen.
12. You can also specify one of the following:
    - Days since file was created
    - Days since file was last modified
    - Days since file was last accessed
    - File name patterns
13. Click the **Schedule** tab to specify when you want the task to run. You can specify weekly or monthly, and which days of the week or days of the month to run.
14. Click **OK.**

For the Actions setting, besides expiring/moving files, you can run executable files, scripts, or other custom commands; or you can encrypt the files with Active Directory Rights Management Services (AD RMS).

SKILL SUMMARY

IN THIS LESSON YOU LEARNED:

- File Server Resource Manager (FSRM) is a suite of tools that enables you to control and manage the quantity and type of data stored on a file server. It enables you to define how much data a person can store, define what type of files that a user can store on a file server, and generate reports about the file server being used.
- Quotas defined with FSRM limit how much space a folder or volume can use. By using FSRM to create a quota, you can limit the amount of disk space allocated to a volume or folder. The quota limit applies to the entire folder's subtree.
- Microsoft developed file screening that allows you to control the type of files that users can save and send notifications when users try to save a blocked file.
- Work Folders allow users to store and access work files on a sync share from multiple devices, including personal computers and devices (including bring-your-own devices). Work Folders are for only individual data and do not support sharing files between users.
- Dynamic Access Control (DAC), originally called claims-based access control, was introduced with Windows Sever 2012, which is used for access management. It provides an automatic mechanism to secure and control access to resources.
- To implement classification on a larger scale, you can deploy classification using GPOs to create a Central Access Policy. The Central Access Policy can then be deployed to multiple servers in an organizational unit.
- FSRM can be used to automate file management tasks such as finding subsets of files and apply simple commands to the files on a regular basis. To identify the files, you can classify the servers via classification rules.

Knowledge Assessment

1. Which type of quota used with FSRM prevents users from saving files when the quota is exceeded?
   a. Hard quota
   b. Soft quota
   c. Passive quota
   d. Active quota
2. Which of the following is supported when you define quotas using FSRM? (Choose all that apply.)
   a. Compressing a drive
   b. Placing an event in the Windows logs
   c. Sending an e-mail
   d. Running a command or script
3. Which of the following is performed when you change a quota template? (Choose all that apply.)
   a. Applying template only to derived quotas that match the original template
   b. Resetting all quota templates on the system to the default quota template
   c. Applying template to all derived quotas
   d. Removing all quota templates
4. Which of the following is used to control the type of files that users can save to a file server?
   a. Control Panel
   b. Windows Explorer
   c. EFS
   d. FSRM
5. Which type of screening prevents users from saving the defined unauthorized files?
   a. Hard screening
   b. Soft screening
   c. Passive screening
   d. Active screening
6. Which tool is used to manage file servers, including configuring quotas and blocking certain files?
   a. Quota Management
   b. File Screening
   c. File Server Resource Manager
   d. File Management

7. Which type of quota used by FSRM will send notifications only when the quota is exceeded?
   a. Hard quota
   b. Soft quota
   c. Screen quota
   d. Warning quota
8. Which of the following enables users to use certain files but notifies an administrator via an e-mail when the user saves those types of files?
   a. File scanning
   b. Hard screening
   c. Soft screening
   d. Passive screening
9. Which of the following is set up when you want to allow a file that is blocked with file screening?
   a. Allow rule
   b. Hard exception
   c. Passive exception
   d. Screen exception
10. Which of the following is used to simplify the management of file screens?
    a. Template groups
    b. File screen template
    c. Management groups
    d. File definitions
11. Which of the following is used to grant permissions to those objects on multiple file servers within your domain?
    a. Classification Policy
    b. Central Access Policy
    c. Token Policy
    d. Distributed Access Policy
12. Which of the following best describes how to enable staging of DAC?
    a. Use the `netsh` command.
    b. bUse Active Directory Administrative Center.
    c. Use GPOs.
    d. Use the Dynamic Access Control console.
13. Which log do is viewed when you enable staging when using DAC?
    a. Application
    b. Security
    c. System
    d. Forwarded

14. Which of the following best describes how to test DAC changes before you implement the changes?
    a. Use the DAC emulator.
    b. Use the Dynamic Access Control console.
    c. Use the Computer Management console.
    d. Use staging.
15. Which of the following allows users to store and access work files from a sync share, which can then be accessed from multiple devices (including bring-your-own-devices)?
    a. Offline folders
    b. Folder redirection
    c. Work Folders
    d. Central Placement
16. Which of the following are methods used to connect to a Work Folder? (Choose three answers.)
    a. Group Policy
    b. URL entry
    c. Auto Discovery
    d. ActiveSync Policy

Best Answer

Choose the letter that corresponds to the best answer. More than one answer choice may achieve the goal. Select the BEST answer

1. Which of the following options are used when you want a quota template to be applied to the parent folder, each subfolder, and each subfolder created in the future?
    a. Inherent
    b. Drill-down
    c. Auto apply
    d. Overwrite
2. Which of the following steps can be used to see whether a FSRM quota is exceeded on a folder? (Choose two answers.)
    a. Opening FSRM and select Quotas under Quota Management
    b. Enabling SMTP
    c. Setting up alarms
    d. Running a Quota Usage Report
3. When you configure screening, which of the following is used to apply the screening to a bunch of files?
    a. File group
    b. File list
    c. Screen group
    d. Screen policy

4. Which of the following is used to show a list of duplicate files on a volume?
   - a. Quotas
   - b. File screening
   - c. File comparison
   - d. Storage reports
5. Which of the following best describes how to enable SMTP for FSRM?
   - a. Open the View menu and select Forwarder.
   - b. Select Configure Options.
   - c. Install SMTP server role.
   - d. Install MS Exchange.
6. Which of the following describes the best way to enable Access-Denied Assistant for all of your file servers?
   - a. Using Dynamic Access Control console
   - b. Using File Server Resource Manager
   - c. Using Active Directory Administrative Center
   - d. Using Group Policy Objects
7. Which of the following can be performed when using DAC? (Choose all that apply.)
   - a. Auditing access by using an audit policy.
   - b. Encrypting all files on a server.
   - c. Classifying and tag data.
   - d. Providing Access-Denied Assistance when a user is denied access to a shared file.
   - e. Allowing connections from mobile phones to files protected by DAC.
8. Which of the following are required when using DAC? (Choose two answers.)
   - a. Classification rules
   - b. Resource properties
   - c. Claim types
   - d. Staging
9. Which of the following is used to perform targeted auditing?
   - a. Staging
   - b. Advanced logging
   - c. Dynamic logging
   - d. Global Object Access Auditing

Matching and Identification

1. Identify the tasks you can perform with FSRM.
   a. _____ You can control the type of files that users can save.
   b. _____ You can control the print queue.
   c. _____ You can control who can own a file or folder.
   d. _____ You can create quotas for a volume or folder.
   e. _____ You can restrict access based on defined properties.
   f. _____ You can enforce encryption of a folder.
   g. _____ You can schedule storage reports.
   h. _____ You can limit the depth of a folder.
2. Identify the tasks you can perform with FSRM file screening?
   a. _____ You can specify who can own a file.
   b. _____ You can control the types of files users can save.
   c. _____ You can filter what files can be displayed in a list based on permissions.
   d. _____ You can create file screen exceptions.
   e. _____ You can define file-screening templates.
   f. _____ You can create and manage file groups.

Build List

1. Identify the correct order of steps necessary to create a file screen. Not all steps will be used.

_____ Select Active screening or Passive screening.

_____ Define quotas.

_____ Right-click File Screens and click Create File Screen.

_____ Type the path to a folder.

_____ Define the reports.

_____ Open FSRM.

_____ Select Define custom file screen properties and then click Custom Properties.

_____ Configure notifications, event logging, or commands.

Business Case Scenarios

Scenario 15-1: Blocking Audio and Video Files

You were just hired as an administrator for the Contoso Corporation. You were looking at a file server and you discovered that several users have been using the file server as their personal repositories of audio and videos files that they have downloaded using the corporate network. How should you stop the users from saving these files on the file server?

Scenario 15-2: Managing Disk Space

You manage a file server that is used to store files used by various projects throughout your organization. After a while, you realize that you are quickly running out of disk space. When you looked at the usage, you determined that the reason the system is filling up is that older projects are never removed or archived. Which solution would you propose to deal with this?

Scenario 15-3: Accessing Confidential Data with Personal Devices

Your company just implemented a "bring-your-own-device" policy that allows users to use their own personal smartphones and tablets to access their personal corporate files. Which steps are needed to ensure that the data access is secure, while allowing a syncing of data to the personal devices?

Index

Symbols

A

E

F

O

S

U

V

W

X

Z